THE
GREAT TOWNS
OF
AMERICA

A Guide to the 100 Best Getaways for a Vacation or Lifetime

DAVID VOKAC

WEST PRESS

Library of Congress Cataloging-in-Publication Data

Vokac, David, 1940-
　The great towns of America : a guide to the 100 best
getaways for a vacation or a lifetime / David Vokac.
　　p.　　cm.
　Includes index.
　ISBN 0-930743-06-7　　$18.95
　1. United States—Guidebooks. 2. Cities and towns—United
States—Guidebooks. I. Title.
E158.V65　　　　　1998
917.304'929—dc21　　　　　　　　　　　　　　　98-24830

　　　　　　　　　　　　　　　　　　　　　　　　CIP

West Press
P.O. Box 99717
San Diego, CA 92169

Manufactured in the United States of America
10 9 8 7 6 5 4 3 2 1
First Edition

Preface

Is it possible to leave the city without leaving its amenities behind? To be as close as a stroll to natural grandeur, while enjoying the comforts of civilization like cultural experiences, gourmet cuisine, and gracious lodgings? In the great towns featured in this guidebook, the answer is emphatically *yes!*

Here are the 100 outlands most favored by nature and civilization. All are proud of their unique heritage, and generous in sharing their bounty. Personalities range from deja-vu all-American wholesomeness, to exotic multicultural meccas for fun-seekers. Collectively, they celebrate the diversity and power that is the United States of America.

Whether you're seeking a distinctive vacation, or a new lifestyle, *The Great Towns of America* is intended to serve as the ultimate guide to the 100 foremost recreation and leisure getaways throughout the country. The book takes a comprehensive new look at great towns from Bar Harbor, Maine to Key West, Florida, and from La Conner, Washington to Palm Desert, California, plus everything in between. Features of most interest—including the weather, best restaurants, attractions and lodgings—are systematically described and rated in and around each locality.

I personally visited every great town during more than two years of full-time, independent effort. No payments were accepted. Thus, every listing is described and rated on merit alone. As a result, I believe that this guide is honest and consistent, with detailed information about appealing places across the nation.

For everyone who dreams or plans to pursue adventures in lively playgrounds or peaceful hideaways anywhere in the country, *The Great Towns of America* has the answers. All the information you need to create a visit tailored to your time, finances, and interests is in this guidebook.

"To Joan"

The Great Towns

Port Townsend
La Conner
Langley
Sandpoint ★
★ Whitefish
★ Bigfork
Chelan
Leavenworth
Coeur d'Alene
WASHINGTON
Seaside
Cannon Beach
Newport
Florence
★ Bend
★ McCall
OREGON
MONTANA
NORTH DAKOTA
★ Red Lodge
★ Cody
Bandon
Grants Pass
Gold Beach ★ Ashland
★ Ketchum
IDAHO
★ Jackson
WYOMING
★ Spearfish
SOUTH DAKOTA
Mendocino
Healdsburg
Nevada City
Calistoga
★ St. Helena
Sonoma
★ South Lake Tahoe
NEVADA
★ Park City
NEBRASKA
★ Sonora
Pacific Grove
★★ Monterey
Carmel
CALIFORNIA
UTAH
Steamboat Springs ★
Glenwood Springs ★
★ Estes Park
★ Vail
Aspen ★ ★ Breckenridge
KANSAS
Cambria
★ San Luis Obispo
★ Solvang
★ Ojai
★ St. George
★ Crested Butte
★ Telluride   COLORADO
★ Durango
Palm Desert
Prescott ★
★ Sedona
★ Taos
OKLAHOMA
Pacific Ocean
ARIZONA
NEW MEXICO
TEXAS
Mexico
Fredericksburg ★
San Marcos ★
New Braunfels ★

One inch equals approx. 280 miles

# of America

Canada

MAINE

MINNESOTA

WISCONSIN
Petoskey
Sturgeon Bay
Charlevoix
Traverse City

North Conway
Stowe
Lake Woodstock
Placid
Manchester
Saratoga Springs

Bar Harbor
Camden
Boothbay Harbor
Wolfeboro
Freeport
Kennebunkport
NH

Red Wing
New Ulm
Green Lake
MICHIGAN
Wisconsin Dells
Holland
Galena

NEW YORK
Cooperstown

VT
MA
CT
RI
Chatham

NJ

IOWA

ILLINOIS
INDIANA
OHIO
Marietta
WEST VIRGINIA
PENNSYLVANIA

MD
DE
St. Michaels

MISSOURI

KENTUCKY

Fredericksburg
Charlottesville
VIRGINIA
Williamsburg

Manteo

Branson
Eureka Springs
TENNESSEE
Gatlinburg
Waynesville
Blowing Rock
NORTH CAROLINA

Beaufort

ARKANSAS

SOUTH CAROLINA
Myrtle Beach

MISSISSIPPI
ALABAMA
GEORGIA
Atlantic Ocean

LOUISIANA
Vicksburg
Natchez

St. Simons Island

Covington
Saint Augustine

FLORIDA

Gulf of Mexico
Mount Dora
Vero Beach

Naples

Key West

Contents

Contents

Contents

Introduction

Picture shimmering glaciers on a peak rising just beyond a tranquil lake, or a waterfall tumbling down a red-rock cliff into a deep clear pool. Think of driftwood-strewn beaches; a secret harbor; sand dunes and cactus by a palm-lined oasis; hardwood forests shading gentle mountains and rushing streams; or coconut palms by a warm tropical sea. Now, imagine human-scaled towns, with style and pleasures normally found only in cities, in the midst of these idyllic settings. Welcome to the Great Towns of America.

This is the only detailed guidebook to all of the nation's towns most favored with both urban charms and unforgettable surroundings. It was written to help you discover famous and little-known places that make America remarkable, and enjoy them to the fullest.

A wealth of new information is presented in several ways that set this guidebook apart. (1) All of the best attractions, restaurants, and lodgings (instead of random features) in every locale are identified and described. (2) Attention is focused on recreation and leisure pursuits primarily of interest to adventurous couples and individuals. As a result, isolated hot springs and promising young wineries receive the same careful regard as famed museums and amusement parks. (3) The likelihood of good weather is rated each month in every locale, and supporting data are provided. (4) All material is consistently arranged in a simple, uniform layout that makes it easy to read and to use. (5) Visitors and dreamers inspired to consider migrating to a great town will relish the livability table for the great towns.

The contents and format are designed to quickly provide all of the information you want to get the most from these exciting destinations within your time, finances, and interest.

Great Towns

A "great town" is defined in this guidebook as one of the hundred American localities with the most scenic appeal and memorable leisure-time features—natural and/or cultural attractions, restaurants, and lodgings. Each town and its environs is well worth a visit.

This general concept provided the basis for identifying the great towns of America. Three measures—natural setting; leisure appeal; and distance from major cities—were used in a sequential process of elimination involving all communities under 50,000 in population. Usable water bodies, dramatic landforms, and/or luxuriant vegetation provide the backdrops for all of the most desirable natural settings. Therefore, places lacking impressive surroundings, i.e., more than a few miles from any of these characteristics, were omitted. Places too close to major cities to have an independent identity were also eliminated.

One hundred exceptional locales were found along both coasts, high in the mountains, by clear streams and lakes, and in desert oases. Collectively, they are America's prime sources of getaway excitement. Individually, each has highlights that make it a worthy destination for a delightful weekend or a lengthy vacation. A full chapter devoted to each locality addresses all natural, historic, and leisure-oriented attractions; restaurants; and lodgings. The livability table, comparing key "quality of life" factors, may tempt you to stay even longer.

Weather Profiles—the "Vokac Weather Rating"

Weather plays a crucial role in recreation and leisure, and in successful vacations. Because of this, a great deal of care was taken to obtain and present detailed weather information for great towns throughout the country. The copyrighted weather profiles for each of the hundred locales are the most complete in any travel guidebook.

The "Vokac Weather Rating" © (VWR) measures the probability of "pleasant weather"—i.e., warm, dry conditions suitable for outdoor recreation by anyone dressed in light sportswear. Average high and low temperatures, rainfall, and snowfall for each month (plus the frequency of precipitation) are correlated. Typical weather that can be expected each month is then rated on a scale from "0" to "10." A "0" signifies the most adverse weather with almost no chance that shirt-sleeves and shorts will be comfortable. Every increment of one on the VWR scale represents a 10% greater chance of pleasant weather. For example, a "5" is used where there is a 50% chance that any given day in the month will be pleasant. A "10" pinpoints "great" weather, with warm, dry days almost 100% assured. An easy-to-follow line graph is used to display the month-to-month VWR. Generally, ratings of "7" or above indicate a high probability of desirable conditions for outdoor activity. Ratings of "4" or less suggest increasing likelihood that the weather will restrict comfortable enjoyment of outdoor ventures and/or require special clothing. Great towns with major ski areas within thirty miles have "10" snowflakes (asterisks) displayed for their regular ski season.

As an added convenience, each month of the weather graph has been subdivided into four segments roughly corresponding to weeks. Readers interested in "fine-tuning" the VWR will find the smaller segments helpful. For example, if the ratings for September and October are "10" and "6," the position of the connecting line during the last week (segment) of September indicates an "8" rating. The implication is that weather during that week will normally still be "very good" but no longer "great," as it was earlier in the month.

Attractions

A hallmark of all great towns is that each has a favored natural setting. Every distinctive attraction in and around each locality is described. Included are leisure-time destinations of special interest to adults—like wineries, remote beaches and hot springs—as well as family-oriented places. All kinds of outdoor recreation—bicycling, ballooning, horseback riding, fishing charters, etc.—are also described, and key sources for equipment rentals and guides are named. A call can save time, since many attractions are only open part of the year. As an added convenience, popular categories of attractions are listed alphabetically under general headings such as "boat rentals," "warm water features," or "winter sports," and they are indexed accordingly to help you find similar features anywhere in America.

Restaurants

Sampling various stylings of fresh, flavorful foods is one of the joys of travel. While ubiquitous chains plague most U.S. cities, great towns continue to embrace their celebrated and aspiring chefs who contribute unique talents to the community's cultural milieu.

Introduction

In this book, food and atmosphere (including scenic views where available) are uniformly described for the most noteworthy restaurants from mom-and-pop cafes to temples of haute cuisine. Service is not discussed, because it can vary so much even on a given day.

Emphasis is given to distinctive local specialties. Possibilities range from Wisconsin fish boils or New England steamed lobster to Louisiana Cajun or Rio Grande New Mexican. The price range is summarized. Meals served (B=breakfast, L=lunch, D=dinner) are identified under the restaurant's name. Days closed are not included because they often vary seasonally.

Lodging

Many of the nation's most elegant resorts, signficant historical inns, and gracious bed-and-breakfasts are found in great towns where tourist accommodations often have a long and glorious past. This guidebook's emphasis is placed on unique, significant, or homey accommodations instead of omnipresent chain motels and humdrum lodgings clustered near freeway offramps. As an additional trip planning aid, each locality is also summarized in terms of its: overall number and quality of lodgings; busiest season (prime time); and average percentage by which rates are reduced off-season.

All leisure-oriented amenities available at each lodging are described, whether natural (like a location on a beach or in a forest) or manmade (i.e., outdoor pool, tennis courts, restaurants, etc.). Where available, toll-free phone numbers are provided.

The overall quality of an average bedroom in every lodging is rated according to the author's six-level hierarchy. The following descriptions are consistently used throughout this guidebook: humble (frayed or no-frills); plain (or simply furnished); comfortable (or nicely furnished); attractive (or well-furnished); beautiful; and luxurious. All major room features—fireplace, balcony, etc.—are also identified. The cost of rooms (from the least to the most expensive) is summarized.

Location

Because great towns are inevitably compact, street maps are seldom necessary. To help you locate any listing without a map, all addresses are referenced according to distance (to the nearest mile) and direction from the heart of downtown, plus a street number. The term "downtown" covers all features within roughly one-quarter mile of the busiest portion of each community's main business district.

Ratings

Every feature listed in *The Great Towns of America* is worth a visit. Because of the national scope of this book, many places, including some that were good, are not included due to space constraints and the quantity of better places in the town. Each of the highlights that contribute most to the town's appeal, in the author's opinion, were included in this guidebook. Every feature was personally evaluated by the author. No payments were accepted. As a result, each listing is described on merit alone, and solely reflects the author's judgment. The author's opinion regarding any feature's relative importance is often indicated by the length of its description.

11

Prices

Comparable information is provided about the relative cost of every restaurant and lodging. Because prices change with the economy, it is impossible to know how long specific rates will be in effect. However, relative price levels usually remain constant. For example, a "low-priced" motel (with rooms costing $50 or less in 1998) can be expected to remain a relative bargain in later years when compared to other lodgings—even though the actual price of a room increases—because the other lodgings in that area will typically increase their prices by about the same percentage as the bargain motel. Similarly, a restaurant will usually continue in its relative price category as years go by.

Restaurants: A basic price code was designed to provide a comparable summary of the cost of an average meal at each restaurant. The code is used for all listed restaurants in all locales. Four categories are used to define the cost per person for a "normal" dinner (soup or salad, average-priced entree, and beverage) not including tip, tax, or wine for the meal. The categories and related prices are: *Low:* under $10; *Moderate:* $10 - $16; *Expensive:* $16 - $25; and *Very Expensive:* $25+.

Lodgings: All prevailing rates reflect the "high season" (summer along the coasts and in the mountains, winter in the desert and Florida). Nowadays, travelers should feel free to negotiate the price of a room since most lodgings offer discounts from "regular (rack) rates" to members of auto clubs, business travelers, government employees, military personnel, retirees, and others. The categories of comparable "rack rates" are as follows: *Low:* under $50; *Moderate:* $50-100; *Expensive:* $100-200; and *Very Expensive:* over $200.

Livability of Great Towns

For those who are intrigued by the charms of any of the great towns, the final chapter provides basic data contrasting quality of life indicators of the great towns with each other; with the largest U.S. cities; and with the nation as a whole. A comprehensive table reveals how great towns compare in the following factors: weather, safety, education, health, income, housing costs, and political leanings.

Some Final Comments

All information has been carefully checked, and is believed to be current and accurate. No malice is intended or implied by the judgments expressed, or by the omission of any facility or service from this book.

Because this guidebook celebrates the most memorable great towns and their best features across the nation, it will be challenged about some places that were included and others that were left out. Regardless, the author hopes that *The Great Towns of America* will encourage you to discover and experience their special pleasures.

Mr. Vokac welcomes your comments and questions.

c/o West Press
P.O. Box 99717
San Diego, CA 92169

Prescott, Arizona

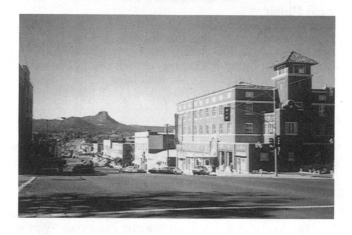

Prescott is a large and lively link to the Old West. Surrounded by a mountain-rimmed ponderosa pine forest, it is the heart of a mile-high "sky island" above the Arizona desert. After gold was discovered in these highlands, Arizona became a territory with Prescott as its first capital and a prosperous trading center.

Most of the symbols of Prescott's rich past are reassuringly maintained, like the classic tree-lined square in the heart of town. Impressive public buildings and monuments, fine museums, shops featuring Southwestern art and culinary treats, plus carefully restored hotels and restaurants are all within an easy stroll. Whiskey Row, one of the most authentic lineups of historic saloons in the West, is as frisky as ever. So is the world's oldest rodeo which has been celebrated here annually since 1888. In the surrounding forests and mountains, hiking, camping, rock climbing, and gold panning are enjoyed, along with boating and fishing in several small scenic reservoirs.

WEATHER PROFILE

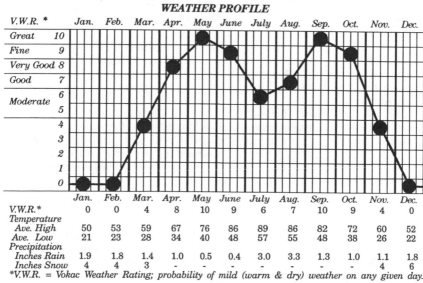

V.W.R.*	Jan.	Feb.	Mar.	Apr.	May	June	July	Aug.	Sep.	Oct.	Nov.	Dec.
V.W.R.*	0	0	4	8	10	9	6	7	10	9	4	0
Temperature												
Ave. High	50	53	59	67	76	86	89	86	82	72	60	52
Ave. Low	21	23	28	34	40	48	57	55	48	38	26	22
Precipitation												
Inches Rain	1.9	1.8	1.4	1.0	0.5	0.4	3.0	3.3	1.3	1.0	1.1	1.8
Inches Snow	4	4	3	-	-	-	-	-	-	-	4	6

*V.W.R. = Vokac Weather Rating; probability of mild (warm & dry) weather on any given day.

ATTRACTIONS

Courthouse Plaza
downtown at Gurley/Montezuma Sts.
The stately three-story Yavapai County Courthouse (1916) is in the center of a square block downtown. The plaza also includes a gazebo, lawns and shady tree-lined walkways reminiscent of Prescott's Yankee heritage. A large equestrian bronze sculpture is a dramatic tribute to Bucky O'Neill, who organized the first United States Volunteer Cavalry—Teddy Roosevelt's "Rough Riders."

Granite Basin
8 mi. NW via Iron Springs Rd.
A picturesque area of granite cliffs and boulders deep in a pine forest provides good hiking and renowned climbing opportunities, plus picnicking and primitive camping next to a fishing pond.

Granite Dells
4 mi. NE on AZ 89
Fanciful granite boulder formations line the highway for about two miles. The area includes a small photogenic reservoir—Watson Lake. Complete campgrounds and picnic facilities are on oak-and-piñon-pine-shaded slopes near the lake.

Phippen Museum of Western Art   *(520)778-1385*
6 mi. N at 4701 AZ 89
The museum honors George Phippen, a founder and first president of Cowboy Artists of America. A ranch-style building houses paintings and sculptures by major Western artists, and a gift shop.

Prescott National Forest   *(520)771-4700*
W & S of town
Luxuriant pines blanket rolling terrain reaching almost 8,000 feet above sea level in this large forest. Several small reservoirs and dramatic granite cliffs are easily accessed. Hiking, rock climbing, camping, jeep touring, fishing, boating and hunting are popular.

Sharlot Hall Museum   *(520)445-3122*
downtown at 415 W. Gurley St.
An outstanding collection of homes and furnishings from Arizona's territorial years has been assembled on several acres that include extensive herb and rose gardens. Major buildings include a two-story log structure that was the first territorial governor's mansion (1864); a replica of the first (1864) schoolhouse; the John C. Fremont House (1875) which he rented while he was territorial governor; the ornate Bashford House (1877); a comprehensive museum complex with both permanent and changing historic exhibits; and a well-stocked gift shop.

Thumb Butte
4 mi. W via Thumb Butte Rd.
This imposing granite outcropping visible west of downtown looks like a closed hand with its thumb extended. There are pine-shaded picnic facilities, running water, and a mile-long hiking trail to the top with fine views of Prescott. Signs along the trail identify vegetation.

Whiskey Row
downtown on W side of plaza on Montezuma St.
For nearly a century, solid brick buildings on the west side of the plaza have housed a concentration of first-rate saloons like the legendary **Palace Bar**. Arts and crafts shops, **Bucky's Bean Bag Gourmet** (fine regional specialties), and good cafes blend so amiably that even teetotalers can comfortably savor the genuine Western spirit of these landmarks.

RESTAURANTS

Dinner Bell Cafe   *(520)445-9888*
downtown at 321 W. Gurley St.
B-L.   *Low*
The hearty Western dishes served here include some of the finest
homemade cinnamon rolls and biscuits for many miles. Don't be put off
by the no-frills facade; this homespun cafe is an Arizona classic.

Gurley Street Grill   *(520)445-3388*
downtown at 230 W. Gurley St.
L-D.   *Moderate*
Superb bread sticks accompany updated American classics like spit-
roasted chicken, gourmet pizzas, and fresh housemade pastas. In a
restored turn-of-the-century brick building, comfortable booths
surround an island bar with a dozen premium tap beers amid a big
dining room that captures the spirit of territorial Prescott.

Hassayampa Inn   *(520)778-9434*
downtown at 122 E. Gurley St.
B-L-D.   *Moderate*
Good contemporary American fare and stylish decor make the hotel's
gracious Peacock Room a popular haven. The friendly adjoining lounge
has also been pleasing thirsty travelers since 1927.

Murphy's Restaurant   *(520)445-4044*
downtown at 201 N. Cortez St.
L-D.   *Moderate*
Murphy's is Prescott's premier source of newfangled Western cuisine.
Seafood and steak are skillfully mesquite-broiled and accompanied by
delicious homebaked bread in a transformed 1890 mercantile on the
National Register. Romantic decor in bustling dining rooms is
enhanced by abundant greenery, antiques, and a nostalgic lounge.

Nolaz Restaurant   *(520)445-3765*
downtown at 216 W. Gurley St.
L-D.   *Moderate*
Creole cookery delights in everything from gumbo, jambalaya, popcorn
shrimp and catfish to praline cheesecake. Personalized artwork and
furnishings in cozy dining rooms contribute to a down-home bayou
feeling in Prescott's zestiest culinary landmark. A live-jazz lounge and
a Louisiana produce shop adjoin.

Pine Cone Inn   *(520)445-2970*
2 mi. S on AZ 89 at 1245 White Spar Rd.
L-D.   *Moderate*
For many years, this big, popular restaurant has featured a classic
American menu emphasizing hearty steaks and housebaked goods.
Old-fashioned comfort prevails for dining and live entertainment.

LODGING
Accommodations are numerous. "Motel Row" (AZ 89 for one mile east
of downtown) has a dozen low and moderately priced lodgings. "High
season" is April through October and weekends year-round. At other
times, prices are usually reduced at least 20%.

Forest Villas Hotel   *(520)717-1200*
3 mi. E on AZ 69 at 3645 Lee Circle - 86301
62 units   *(800)223-3449*   *Expensive*
This handsome motel in the hills opened in 1995 with a view pool.
Each well-furnished room has a private balcony. Executive rooms and
suites also have gas fireplaces and in-room whirlpools.

Hassayampa Inn   *(520)778-9434*
downtown at 122 E. Gurley St. - 86301
68 units   *(800)322-1927*   *Expensive*
Prescott's four-story landmark hotel, built in 1927 and listed on the National Register, is fully restored. The lobby, with its painted ceiling, tiles, and art objects, is a delight. So are the dining room and lounge (see listing), and meeting rooms. Full breakfast and an evening beverage are complimentary. Each cozy guest room is comfortably furnished.

Hotel Vendome/Clarion Carriage House Inn   *(520)776-0900*
just S at 230 S. Cortez St. - 86303
20 units   *(888)468-3583*   *Moderate-Expensive*
A quiet location near the heart of town is a feature of this restored small hotel (circa 1917). Continental breakfast is complimentary, and there is a stylish little bar downstairs. Each updated, well-furnished room features blue-toned decor and all contemporary conveniences, including a private (very modern or nostalgic) bath.

Lynx Creek Farm   *(520)778-9573*
6 mi. E on AZ 69 (Box 4301) - 86302
6 units   *Moderate-Expensive*
Orchards and aviaries distinguish this quiet secluded bed-and-breakfast in the hills. Big, farm-fresh breakfasts are complimentary. Each romantic well-furnished room has a private bath and king bed. "Chaparral Room" and "Country Garden Room" each also has a wood stove and private whirlpool on a view deck.

Prescott Pines Inn Bed & Breakfast   *(520)445-7270*
1 mi. S on AZ 89 at 901 White Spar Rd. - 86303
12 units   *(800)541-5374*   *Moderate*
This country Victorian inn in the pines by the highway offers a full breakfast for an extra charge. Each comfortable unit has a private bath. Several also have gas fireplaces and kitchens.

Prescott Resort Conference Center and Casino   *(520)766-1666*
2 mi. E at 1500 AZ 69 - 86301
161 units   *(800)967-4637*   *Expensive*
Prescott's first resort hotel (1988) is a six-story post-modern tower, perched high atop a hill, with panoramic city views. Amenities include an indoor/outdoor pool, tennis and racquetball courts, fitness center, view restaurant, entertainment lounge, and resort shop. **Bucky's Casino** (Arizona's first in a hotel) features slot machines and poker. Each well-furnished room has a private view balcony.

Prescottonian Motel - Best Western   *(520)445-3096*
1 mi. E on AZ 89 at 1317 E. Gurley St. - 86301
121 units   *(800)528-1234*   *Moderate*
The town's biggest lodging is a contemporary motor inn has a pool and whirlpool (enclosed in winter), restaurant and lounge, and spacious, well-furnished rooms.

BASIC INFORMATION

Elevation: 5,350 feet   Population (1990):   26,592
Location: 96 miles Northwest of Phoenix
Nearest airport with commercial flights: in Prescott
Prescott Chamber of Commerce   (800)266-7534   (520)445-2000
   downtown at 117 W. Goodwin St. (Box 1147) - 86302
   www.prescottt.org

Sedona, Arizona

Sedona is America's most flamboyant townsite. It sprawls amid a luxuriant piñon pine and juniper forest deep in a gigantic natural amphitheater. Multicolored sandstone cliffs, spires, and monuments rise thousands of feet on all sides. The splendid setting also benefits from the region's mildest year-round climate. Sedona was founded in 1902. But, until the 1950s, it remained a tiny village serving isolated ranches and movie crews filming westerns.

Today, the burgeoning town is a major destination resort, artists' colony and showplace of architectural tributes to the inspiring locale. Galleries and studios display beguiling Southwestern arts and crafts in specialty shopping districts that include the renowned Tlaquepaque. Nightlife is relatively scarce, but gourmet dining is plentiful. So are distinctive and diverse lodgings that serve visitors who flock year-round to tour, hike, swim, fish and relax in the scenic wonderland around Oak Creek Canyon.

WEATHER PROFILE

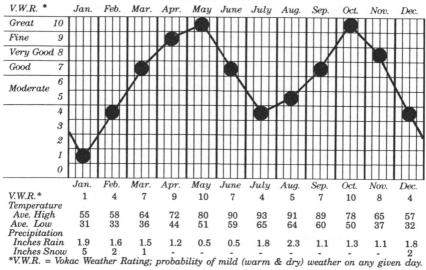

V.W.R.*	Jan.	Feb.	Mar.	Apr.	May	June	July	Aug.	Sep.	Oct.	Nov.	Dec.
V.W.R.*	1	4	7	9	10	7	4	5	7	10	8	4
Temperature												
Ave. High	55	58	64	72	80	90	93	91	89	78	65	57
Ave. Low	31	33	36	44	51	59	65	64	60	50	37	32
Precipitation												
Inches Rain	1.9	1.6	1.5	1.2	0.5	0.5	1.8	2.3	1.1	1.3	1.1	1.8
Inches Snow	5	2	1	-	-	-	-	-	-	-	-	2

*V.W.R. = Vokac Weather Rating; probability of mild (warm & dry) weather on any given day.

17

ATTRACTIONS

Chapel of the Holy Cross   *(520)282-4069*
4 mi. S via AZ 179 & Chapel Rd.
Uniquely perched between two massive red sandstone pinnacles is a remarkable "sculpture church." Completed in 1956 through the inspiration of Marguerite Staude, it is an incomparable synthesis of civilization and nature. The sanctuary is open daily free to visitors.

Coconino National Forest   *(520)282-4119*
surrounds town
The most prominent feature of this huge forest is Mt. Humphreys (12,670 feet), the highest point in Arizona. In winter, its massive slopes support a major skiing complex. Resplendent Oak Creek Canyon is the forest's most popular attraction. High above on the Mogollon Rim, several lakes are hidden in the world's largest ponderosa pine forest.

Grand Canyon National Park   *(520)638-7888*
100 mi. N via AZ 89A & US 180
The Grand Canyon is one of the world's awe-inspiring spectacles. The Colorado River has carved a complex of gorges whose combination of size, color and geological significance is peerless in a canyon over 200 miles long, as much as 18 miles wide and almost one mile deep. South Rim, at an elevation of about 7,000 feet, is open all year. It has (by far) the most popular viewsites, plus Grand Canyon Village. Complete visitor facilities include museums and art galleries. **El Tovar Hotel**, a handcrafted pine-log and fieldstone structure by the rim, has been, since 1905, "the" place to stay and dine with a view into the chasm. From the village, paved roads lead to a series of observation points and trailheads for hiking paths into the canyon.

Oak Creek Canyon
for 16 mi. N along US 89A
Starting in uptown Sedona, the highway parallels a large, clear creek lined by overhanging hardwood trees and colorful towering sandstone formations. Campgrounds, picnic facilities, hiking trails and deep natural pools for swimming and trout fishing abound.

Scenic Trips
To enjoy the Sedona area, a wealth of guided tours are available almost any day year-round. For information and reservations, call:

Balloon Rides	**Red Rock Balloon Adventures**	*(800)258-3754*
Helicopter Flights	**Arizona Helicopter Adventure**	*(800)282-5141*
Horseback Rides	**Kachina Stables**	*(800)723-3538*
Jeep Tours	**Pink Jeep Tours**	*(800)873-3662*
Train Rides	**Verde Canyon Railroad**	*(800)293-7245*

Slide Rock State Park   *(520)282-3034*
8 mi. N on US 89A
Many western movies have featured the famed natural waterslide that ends in a rockbound swimming hole on Oak Creek. Slide Rock and Grasshopper Point (four miles to the south) are extremely popular, but serious hikers can discover more secluded swimming holes.

Tlaquepaque   *(520)282-4838*
just S at 211 AZ 179
Tlaquepaque is a master-planned five-acre showplace of Spanish-Colonial-inspired architecture. It should not be missed. An exemplary collection of unique shops, galleries, and restaurants is surrounded by flower gardens, courtyards, fountains, and sculptures at every turn.

RESTAURANTS

Enchantment Resort   *(520)282-2900*
8 mi. NW via AZ 89A & Dry Cr. Rd. at 525 Boynton Canyon Rd.
B-L-D.   *Very Expensive*
The **Yavapai Dining Room** features Continental and Southwestern cuisine with a light, creative touch in an informally elegant setting. Spectacular window-wall views of colorful cliffs towering nearby are shared with a stylish lounge.

The Heartline Cafe   *(520)282-0785*
2 mi. W at 1610 W. AZ 89A
L-D.   *Expensive*
The Heartline Cafe is one of Arizona's best sources for innovative Southwestern cuisine. Every dish is fresh and flavorful, from entrees like pecan-crusted local trout to fine housemade desserts—the white chocolate mousse with fresh berries is a knockout. Guests have a choice of country-charming dining areas or a heated garden patio.

The Hideaway Restaurant   *(520)282-4204*
just S at 251 AZ 179
L-D.   *Moderate*
Hand-thrown pizzas and other Southern Italian specialties, and pies, are all made fresh from scratch. Dining balconies by Oak Creek are particularly inviting because of an overhanging forest of sycamores.

Judi's Restaurant & Lounge   *(520)282-4449*
2 mi. W by W. AZ 89A at 40 Soldiers Pass Rd.
L-D.   *Expensive*
Barbecued baby back ribs star on a contemporary American menu that also includes several delicious homemade desserts. The popular little hideaway has a cozy firelit dining room and lounge.

L'Auberge de Sedona Resort   *(520)282-1667*
uptown off AZ 89A at 301 L'Auberge Lane
B-L-D.   *Very Expensive*
Sophisticated contemporary French cuisine is served at the inn's lovely creekside dining rooms, outfitted in opulent country French decor. Prix fixe dinners and Sunday brunch are especially memorable in one of the most enchanting locales in the Southwest.

Oaxaca Restaurante & Cantina   *(520)282-4179*
uptown at 321 AZ 89A
B-L-D.   *Moderate*
Distinctive Mexican-style breakfasts and Spanish-Colonial decor have been crowd-pleasers for decades. So are the gracefully arched windows and an alfresco roof deck with expansive red-rock canyon views.

Ranch Kitchen   *(520)282-0057*
just S at Y of AZ 179/AZ 89A
B-L-D.   *Moderate*
Homemade baked goods (pies, breads and large cinnamon rolls) highlight American home cookin' served amid Western bric-a-brac in Sedona's oldest family restaurant.

René at Tlaquepaque   *(520)282-9225*
just S on AZ 179 in Tlaquepaque
L-D.   *Very Expensive*
Rene's has long been one of Arizona's most refined restaurants. Creative Continental and American cuisine is masterfully prepared from seasonally fresh, quality ingredients, and presented amid resplendent neo-Spanish-Colonial decor. An inviting patio is also popular, as is the intimate lounge.

Sedona Airport Restaurant   *(520)282-3576*
3 mi. SW at 1185 Airport Rd.
B-L-D.   *Moderate*
For many years, down-home American dishes like biscuits and gravy
and Southwestern specialties like chile omelets have distinguished this
cheerful coffee shop enhanced by greenery and a picture-window view
of airport runways and rim rock formations.

Sedona Memories Bakery Cafe   *(520)282-0032*
uptown at 321 Jordan Rd.
B-L.   *Moderate*
Delicious Continental-style pastries and breads made here, plus
gourmet sandwiches and salads, have won a loyal following for this
casual little bakery/cafe/takeout with a view deck.

Shugrue's Hillside Grill   *(520)282-5300*
1 mi. S at 671 AZ 179
L-D.   *Expensive*
Seafood is featured in various traditional and updated styles. But, the
real feature of this casual, modish complex of dining rooms, lounge and
alfresco deck is a grand panoramic view of the town and red rocks.

Shugrue's West Restaurant   *(520)282-2943*
3 mi. W at 2250 W. AZ 89A
L-D.   *Moderate*
A full range of contemporary regional specialties has made Shugrue's
one of Sedona's long-time favorites. Armchairs and booths, distinctive
table settings, a fireplace and fine wall art reflect comfortable
Southwestern style. A plush firelit piano bar adjoins.

LODGING

The area has a remarkable selection of fine lodgings of all kinds. Many
are oriented toward the spectacular surroundings. Few are low or
moderate in price during "high season"—March through November
weekends. Rates are often at least 25% lower in winter.

Arroyo Roble Hotel - Best Western   *(520)282-4001*
uptown at 400 N. AZ 89A (Box NN) - 86336
65 units   *(800)773-3662*   *Expensive*
This modern five-story motel overlooks a villa-timeshare complex and
scenic Oak Creek Canyon. Amenities include two (fee) tennis courts
and racquetball courts; plus two large pools (one indoor/outdoor), two
whirlpools, sauna and steam rooms, exercise room, and ping pong.
Most well-furnished rooms have a canyon view from a private deck.
Suites also have a gas fireplace and a large whirlpool bath.

Canyon Villa Bed & Breakfast Inn   *(520)284-1226*
7 mi. S via AZ 179 & Bell Rock Bl. at 125 Canyon Circle Dr. - 86351
11 units   *(800)453-1166*   *Expensive-Very Expensive*
One of Arizona's best bed-and-breakfast inns is a contemporary
showcase of elegant Southwestern style. The pool and posh common
areas have tranquil red rock views. Full gourmet breakfast, afternoon
refreshments, and evening snacks are complimentary. Each luxurious,
individually decorated room has all amenities, plus view patio or
balcony, and a whirlpool bath. Some also have a gas fireplace.

Casa Sedona   *(520)282-2938*
3 mi. W via AZ 89A at 55 Hozoni Dr. - 86336
16 units   *(800)525-3756*   *Expensive*
A handsome adobe was recently built to serve as an elegant bed-and-
breakfast. The well-landscaped, secluded site has a whirlpool, hiking
trails and rim rock views. Full Southwestern style breakfast and

appetizers are complimentary. Each of the beautifully furnished, individually decorated rooms has all amenities plus a gas fireplace and a whirlpool bath. Most also have a private view deck.

Cedars Resort   *(520)282-7010*
  downtown at jct. AZ 179 & AZ 89A (Box 292) - 86339
  39 units   *Low-Moderate*
On a slope by Oak Creek, this modern motel has a pool, whirlpool, and creek access. Recently rehabilitated and newer creekside rooms are large and well furnished. Most offer memorable views and the sound of the creek from big private balconies.

Creekside Inn at Sedona   *(520)282-4992*
  1 mi. S via AZ 179 at 99 Copper Cliffs Dr. (Box 2161) - 86339
  5 units   *(800)390-8621   Expensive-Very Expensive*
A ranch-style home nestled on the banks of Oak Creek became a delightful adult retreat surrounded by gardens and sycamores. Deluxe breakfast and evening refreshments are complimentary. Each beautifully furnished room blends contemporary amenities and the romance of authentic Victorian antiques, and features a large whirlpool bath and private patio with a garden or stream view.

Enchantment Resort   *(520)282-2900*
  8 mi. NW via Dry Creek Rd. at 525 Boynton Canyon Rd. - 86336
  162 units   *(800)826-4180*   *Very Expensive*
Tucked away on the verdant floor of a crimson canyon is an enchanting resort. Contemporary adobe buildings blend perfectly into the dramatic site. Amenities sequestered around lush grounds include five pools and whirlpools; pitch & putt golf; endless jogging and hiking trails; rental bicycles, a complete fitness center; and twelve tennis courts. The main building, a tour de force of Southwestern decor, houses a plush restaurant (see listing), lounge, and a resort shop. Each large, beautifully furnished unit has a private view patio. One- or two-bedroom casitas also have a kitchenette and fireplace.

The Graham Bed & Breakfast Inn   *(520)284-1425*
  7 mi. S via AZ 179 & Bell Rock Bl. at 150 Canyon Creek Dr. - 86351
  10 units   *(800)228-1425   Expensive-Very Expensive*
The Graham is Sedona's premier world-class bed-and-breakfast inn. There are hiking trails into the spectacular red rocks, an outdoor pool and whirlpool in a lovely garden, and bicycles. A deluxe breakfast and afternoon refreshments are complimentary. Each luxurious room is individually decorated and has a private balcony. Most also have a fireplace and a large whirlpool bath. In 1997, the biggest and best suites in Sedona opened. All four have a high-tech kitchen (which even includes a bread maker), a private red rock view deck, gas fireplace, large whirlpool tub, and a delightful waterfall shower.

Inn on Oak Creek   *(520)282-7896*
  1 mi. S at 556 AZ 179 - 86336
  11 units   *(800)499-7896   Expensive-Very Expensive*
One of Arizona's loveliest bed-and-breakfasts opened in mid-1996 in a stylish building so close to Oak Creek that you could fish from your private balcony. Tlaquepaque, across the creek, is within easy walking distance. Peerless gourmet breakfast, afternoon appetizers and refreshments, and evening snacks are complimentary. Each of the cozy, luxuriously furnished rooms is individually themed, and has a gas fireplace and elegant bath with a whirlpool tub. Most also have a private balcony by the picturesque creek.

Junipine Resort   *(520)282-3375*
9 mi. N at 8351 N. AZ 89A - 86336
30 units   *(800)742-7463   Expensive-Very Expensive*
Deep in the heart of Oak Creek Canyon is a delightful condo resort by the creek. It is an ideal base for hiking, swimming, fishing, and relaxing. There is also a canyon-view cafe and lounge. Each contemporary well-furnished two-bedroom unit is oriented toward the creek or red rocks, and has a private deck, kitchen, two baths, and two fireplaces. Some also have a private whirlpool on the view deck.

L'Auberge de Sedona Resort   *(520)282-1661*
uptown off AZ 89A at 301 L'Auberge Lane (Box B) - 86339
100 units   *(800)272-6777*   *Very Expensive*
Nestled among gardens along the sycamore-shaded banks of Oak Creek is one of the Southwest's most renowned inns. The complex includes a delightful country French restaurant (see listing), lounge, and boutique. Guests have use of a large pool and whirlpool on a red rock view patio accessed by a funicular. Each cabin is luxuriously appointed with French antiques and reproductions, and has a fireplace. Some are next to the stream.

Poco Diablo Resort   *(520)282-7333*
2 mi. S on AZ 179 (Box 1709) - 86339
138 units   *(800)528-4275*   *Expensive*
Colorful rock formations surround Sedona's original luxury resort. Contemporary, low-profile buildings share verdant grounds with a (fee) 9-hole golf course, plus two large pools, three whirlpools, a fitness center, four tennis courts, racquetball court, gift shop, view restaurant and lounge. Most of the spacious, well-decorated units have a view patio or balcony. Beautifully decorated rooms added in 1996 also have a gas fireplace and large whirlpool bath.

Sky Ranch Lodge   *(520)282-6400*
3 mi. SW via AZ 89A on Airport Rd. (Box 2579) - 86339
94 units   *(888)708-6400*   *Moderate-Expensive*
This big modern ranch-style motel atop a plateau has a pool and whirlpool, gift shop, and colorful gardens with ponds and fountains. Many units have a gas fireplace and kitchenette, and breathtaking canyon views from the rim of a cliff high above town. Each spacious room is well furnished with Southwestern decor.

BASIC INFORMATION

Elevation: 4,240 feet   *Population (1990): 7,720*
Location: 110 miles North of Phoenix
Nearest airport with commercial flights: Flagstaff - 25 miles
Sedona-Oak Creek Canyon Chamber of Commerce   (800)288-7336
*   uptown at Forest Av. & US 89A (Box 478) - 86339   (520)282-7722*
www.arizonaguide.com / sedona

Eureka Springs, Arkansas

Eureka Springs is a peerless playground of romantic Victoriana. Abundant mineral springs gush from limestone crevices in steep forested hills near the heart of the gentle Ozark Mountains. Reputed healing powers of the water attracted worldwide attention, and by 1880 the village was a boomtown.

The area's 19th century charm is remarkably intact. The entire town is now on the National Register of Historic Places. Substantial stone and brick buildings still cling to steep hillsides along narrow winding streets lined with antique shops, handicraft specialty stores, historic hotels and casual restaurants. Towering trees and gardens sequester nearby Queen Anne mansions and gingerbread cottages that house America's largest collection of bed-and-breakfast inns. Trolleys, horse-drawn carriages, a historic railroad, museums, attractions, and live theaters also reflect the friendly spirit of the Ozarks. Surrounding rivers, lakes, forest and caverns provide recreation year-round.

WEATHER PROFILE

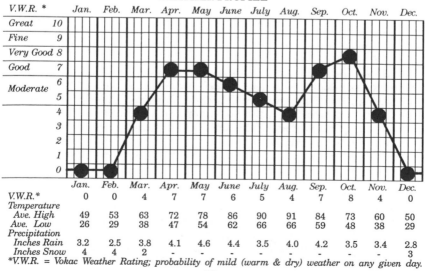

V.W.R. *	Jan.	Feb.	Mar.	Apr.	May	June	July	Aug.	Sep.	Oct.	Nov.	Dec.
V.W.R.*	0	0	4	7	7	6	5	4	7	8	4	0
Temperature												
Ave. High	49	53	63	72	78	86	90	91	84	73	60	50
Ave. Low	26	29	38	47	54	62	66	66	59	48	38	29
Precipitation												
Inches Rain	3.2	2.5	3.8	4.1	4.6	4.4	3.5	4.0	4.2	3.5	3.4	2.8
Inches Snow	4	4	2	-	-	-	-	-	-	-	-	3

*V.W.R. = Vokac Weather Rating; probability of mild (warm & dry) weather on any given day.

ATTRACTIONS

Abundant Memories Heritage Village   *(501)253-6764*
2 mi. N on AR 23
Yesteryear comes alive in twenty-three authentically furnished shops and homes displaying vintage antiques and military memorabilia. Artisans and a live stage program add to the nostalgic look.

Beaver Lake   *(501)789-2380*
10 mi. W via US 62
A large dam on the White River has created a reservoir with more than 400 miles of shoreline, backed by luxuriant Ozark forests and abundant wildlife. Catfish and bass fishing are popular, along with boating, swimming, hiking, picnicking and camping. The **Belle of the Ozarks** features a twelve-mile narrated cruise.

Downtown
downtown is centered N of Main St. along Spring St.
The entire downtown is listed on the National Register of Historic Places. Several blocks of well-preserved Victorian buildings ranging from multistory brick landmarks to cottages house an impressive array of art and crafts galleries, specialty shops, restaurants and lodgings. Stone walkways, architectural flourishes, pocket parks, fountains and sculpture, regularly scheduled trolleys and horsedrawn carriages add to the charm.

Eureka Springs & North Arkansas Railway   *(501)253-9623*
just N at 299 N. Main St.
Vintage steam locomotives and restored passenger cars leave a historic depot for a 45-minute excursion in a scenic Ozark valley. Lunch and dinner rides can also be arranged. An animal conservatory stop includes a petting zoo, and there are historic displays and a gift shop at the depot.

Eureka Springs Gardens   *(501)253-9244*
6 mi. W via US 62
Arkansas' premier botanical gardens feature informal displays in meadow, forest, hillside and rock settings. There is also one of the largest springs in the Ozarks.

Eureka Springs Historical Museum   *(501)253-9417*
downtown at 95 S. Main St.
A 19th century stone building now houses artifacts, memorabilia, photographs and other exhibits that chronicle the unique town's past.

The Great Passion Play   *(501)253-9200*   *(800)882-7529*
2 mi. E via N. Main St. (Box 471)
One of the world's largest-attended outdoor dramas presents the days leading to the death, resurrection and ascension of Jesus Christ. More than 200 authentically costumed actors, plus live animals, perform on a multilevel stage before a 4,000-seat amphitheater. The expansive site also includes **The Christ of the Ozarks**—a seven-story statue; **South Memorial Chapel** where gospel concerts are given before the play; the **Bible Museum; Sacred Arts Center; The New Holy Land/ Tabernacle**; and a section of the **Berlin Wall**.

Kings and White River(s)
6 mi. E (Kings River) and 6 mi. W (White River) on US 62
Two of the South's best rivers for canoeing, whitewater rafting, tubing and swimming are close to town. Trout fishing on the White River below Beaver Lake, and bass fishing on the warmer undammed Kings River, are outstanding. Boat and equipment rentals and guide services are all available.

Onyx Cave   *(501)253-9321*
  7 mi. E via US 62
Unusual onyx formations are the feature of this living cave, along with a blind cave fish display. Half-hour self-guided tours include taped narration. There is also a distinctive gift shop.

Palace Bath House   *(501)253-8400*
  downtown at 135 Spring St.
The Ozarks' only historic operational bathhouse is outfitted with genuine Victorian antiques, including original steam cabinets. Mineral and steam baths, whirlpool, massage and body wraps are available.

Pine Mountain Village and Jamboree   *(501)253-9156*
  1 mi. SE on US 62
A restaurant, shops and two theaters are ensconced behind Victorian-themed buildings, and Ozark craftsmen demonstrate backwoods skills nearby. There is also a 100-foot observation tower. The Jamboree is Eureka Springs' original country music and comedy stage show.

Queen Anne Mansion   *(501)253-8825*
  1 mi. SW on US 62
One of the most impressive among the town's many classic Victorian homes is this three-story mansion full of original stained glass, hand-carved hardwood trim, and period furnishings. Next door, **Wings** is a Victorian home featuring a year-round Christmas theme and exotic birds in aviaries.

Thorncrown Chapel   *(501)253-7401*
  3 mi. W on US 62
An inspired blend of glass and wood resulted in this remarkable modern chapel. Luxuriant woodlands contribute to the serene setting of the delightful sanctuary.

RESTAURANTS

Autumn Breeze Restaurant   *(501)253-7734*
  1 mi. S on Hwy. 23 S
  D only.   *Expensive*
The diverse menu ranges from coconut beer battered shrimp to rack of lamb or prime rib in one of the area's most popular dinner houses. Nearly every table in the secluded, romantic restaurant has a pleasant view of a hollow.

Bavarian Inn Restaurant   *(501)253-7741*
  1 mi. W on Hwy. 62 W
  D only.   *Expensive*
Home-style Czech-German dishes like roast duck are carefully prepared, along with American fare. Try the homemade bratwurst in the casual family dining room or bar.

Bubba's Barbecue   *(501)253-7706*
  1 mi. SW at 60 Kings Hwy.
  L-D.   *Moderate*
A hardwood smoker and natural talent produce lean baby back pork ribs, beans, chili and other Q classics and accompaniments that are some of the region's finest. The warm and friendly down-home decor is just right.

Cafe Luigi Patio Restaurant   *(501)253-6888*
  downtown at 91 S. Main St.
  L-D.   *Moderate*
Robust red sauce works well on the Southern Italian fare. So do the housemade dressings or fresh salads in a casual eatery with a popular outdoor patio.

De Vito's Restaurant   *(501)253-6807*
downtown at 5 Center St.
L-D.   *Moderate*
Trout from their family-owned farm has won critical acclaim. So have skillfully prepared traditional Italian dishes served amid warm, cozy decor in the historic heart of town.

Rogue's Manor at Sweet Spring   *(501)253-4911*
downtown at 124 Spring St.
D only.   *Expensive*
A wide ranging selection of creatively prepared contemporary American fare is offered in a comfortable Victorian home with an intimate lounge with a garden grotto.

Victorian Sampler Restaurant   *(501)253-8374*
1 mi. NW at 33 Prospect St.
L-D.   *Expensive*
Light contemporary fare is featured along with homemade desserts. An enlarged turn-of-the-century home has been transformed to include handsome dining rooms, a full bar, and a gift shop.

LODGING

Eureka Springs may be America's bed-and-breakfast capital. Other kinds of lodgings are similarly abundant, ranging from Victorian hotels to luxury motels or cabins featuring "elegant rusticity." High season is spring through fall. Winter rates are usually reduced 30% or more.

Angel at Rose Hall   *(501)253-5405*
downtown at 56 Hillside Av. (Box 268) - 72632
5 units   *(800)828-4255*   *Expensive*
Landscaped tree-shaded grounds in the historic district surround this luxurious bed-and-breakfast for adults. Full breakfast inside or in the restful courtyard is complimentary. Each beautifully furnished unit includes extras like fresh flowers and gourmet goodies, period antiques, and a whirlpool-for-two. Some also feature a large shower for two.

Arsenic & Old Lace Bed & Breakfast Inn   *(501)253-5454*
1 mi. N at 60 Hillside Av. - 72632
5 units   *(800)243-5223*   *Expensive*
An expansive Victorian home high on a hill in the historic district has become a luxurious bed-and-breakfast inn. Full breakfast and refreshments are complimentary. Each spacious room is beautifully furnished, including antiques and artwork, and a private bath. Some of the units have a whirlpool for two and a fireplace.

Basin Park Hotel   *(501)253-7837*
downtown at 12 Spring St. - 72632
61 units   *(800)643-4972*   *Moderate-Expensive*
Since 1905, this eight-story hotel has been a downtown landmark. The renovated property includes a dining room and bar. Each nicely refurbished room has a private bath. Many have appealing views. Balcony and whirlpool suites are also available.

Bavarian Inn   *(501)253-8128*
1 mi. W on Hwy. 62 W (Route 4, Box 66) - 72632
21 units   *Moderate-Expensive*
This contemporary motel has Old World charm and some romantic touches. Amenities include a pool and a fine Continental restaurant (see listing). Each spacious, beautifully furnished room has a whirlpool tub, gas fireplace, and private balcony.

Cinnamon Valley Resort   *(501)253-5354*

1 mi. SE on US 62 East (Box 717) - 72632

7 units   *(800)424-3344*   *Expensive*

Stylish log cabins are nestled in the woods near two little spring-fed lakes featuring canoeing and fishing. Each modern, well-furnished cabin has a whirlpool for two, (pressed wood) fireplace, full kitchen with microwave oven, a porch with a swing and some antiques and stained glass accents.

Crescent Cottage Inn   *(501)253-6022*

1 mi. N at 211 Spring St. - 72632

4 units   *Moderate-Expensive*

A distinctive Victorian home in the historic residential district has become a gracious bed-and-breakfast. Full breakfast is complimentary. Each beautifully furnished room has a tranquil view, antiques, and a private bath. "Charlotte's Room" and "Miss Adaline's Room" also have a double whirlpool tub, a private entrance, and a veranda.

Crescent Hotel   *(501)253-9766*

1 mi. N at 75 Prospect Av. - 72632

68 units   *(800)342-9766*   *Moderate*

Since 1886, the sprawling five-story landmark has topped a rise with a commanding view of downtown. It's long-past posh, but it has an outdoor pool, (fee) fitness/beauty spa, restaurant, lounge, and gift shop. Each simply furnished room has a private bath and TV.

1876 Inn   *(501)253-7183*

1 mi. S on US 62 East (Route 6, Box 247) - 72632

72 units   *(800)643-3030*   *Moderate*

This modern motor hotel in a forest has a large pool, scenic whirlpool, dining room and gift shop. Each room is well furnished. Three units feature a mirrored whirlpool-for-two.

Grand Central Hotel   *(501)253-6756*

downtown at 37 N. Main St. - 72632

14 units   *(800)344-6050*   *Moderate-Expensive*

The lavishly renovated little 1883 brick hotel is a fine contemporary haven catering to adults. Each spacious, beautifully furnished suite includes some period decor, a refrigerator, and an extra-large whirlpool tub.

Red Bud Valley Resort   *(501)253-9028*

2 mi. SE via US 62 E on Rock House Rd. (Route 1, Box 500) - 72632

17 units   *Expensive*

Deluxe log cabin-style cottages share a peaceful shady hollow with a spring-fed little lake. Swimming, rowboats, fishing, hiking trails and (fee) horseback riding contribute to the allure of this Ozark hideaway. Each attractively furnished log cabin has a complete kitchen and a private porch with a swing and grill. "Country Supreme" and "Grand View" cabins also have a heart-shaped whirlpool-for-two and a wood-burning fireplace.

BASIC INFORMATION

Elevation: 1,300 feet   *Population (1990):   1,900*
Location: 149 miles East of Tulsa, Oklahoma
Nearest airport with commercial flights: Fayetteville, AR - 46 miles
Eureka Springs Chamber of Commerce   (501)253-8737 (800)638-7352
1 mi. SE at 81 Kings Hwy. (Box 551) - 72632
www.eurekasprings.org
Town photo courtesy of Eureka Springs Chamber of Commerce

Calistoga, California

Calistoga is the only town in the country esteemed for both wine and water. Sheltered by oak-covered foothills of Mt. St. Helena at the northern end of the renowned Napa Valley, it is surrounded by vineyards. The village also hosts a remarkable cluster of small hot springs resorts and a bottling plant that ships mineral water worldwide. Calistoga was founded in 1859 by Sam Brannan, California's first millionaire dreamspinner who recognized the potential of the area's warm springs, volcanic mud, and semitropical climate.

Today, the sybaritic relationship between fine wine and warm mineral spas attracts visitors in pursuit of pleasure as well as cures. Skillful renovations have restored a turn-of-the-century feeling to the classic main street. Most major spa and lodging facilities, specialty shops, and a coterie of excellent restaurants and bars are located downtown. Other unusual attractions include a major glider port, a natural geyser, and a petrified forest.

WEATHER PROFILE

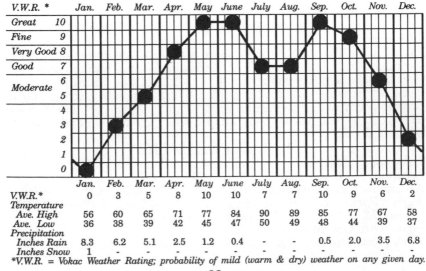

V.W.R.*		Jan.	Feb.	Mar.	Apr.	May	June	July	Aug.	Sep.	Oct.	Nov.	Dec.
Great	10												
Fine	9												
Very Good	8												
Good	7												
Moderate	6												
	5												
	4												
	3												
	2												
	1												
	0												

	Jan.	Feb.	Mar.	Apr.	May	June	July	Aug.	Sep.	Oct.	Nov.	Dec.
V.W.R.*	0	3	5	8	10	10	7	7	10	9	6	2
Temperature												
Ave. High	56	60	65	71	77	84	90	89	85	77	67	58
Ave. Low	36	38	39	42	45	47	50	49	48	44	39	37
Precipitation												
Inches Rain	8.3	6.2	5.1	2.5	1.2	0.4	-	-	0.5	2.0	3.5	6.8
Inches Snow	1	-	-	-	-	-	-	-	-	-	-	-

*V.W.R. = Vokac Weather Rating; probability of mild (warm & dry) weather on any given day.

Ballooning
  Calistoga Adventures   *(707)942-6546*   *(800)333-4359*
  downtown at 1458 Lincoln Av.
The natural beauty of the wine country is unforgettably revealed in an early morning balloon flight followed by champagne and lunch.

Bicycling
Bicycle riding is very popular on scenic byways throughout relatively flat Napa Valley. Bicycles can be rented by the hour or day.
  Getaway Wine Country Bicycle Tours   *(800)499-2453*
  Palisades Mountain Sport   *(707)942-9687*

Flying
  Calistoga Gliders   *(707)942-5000*
  downtown at 1546 Lincoln Av.
You can have the unique thrill of soaring behind a glider pilot on flights that originate and land downtown. Ideal soaring conditions prevail much of the year in one of America's major centers for the sport.

Old Faithful Geyser of California   *(707)942-6463*
  2 mi. N at 1299 Tubbs Lane
One of the few regularly erupting geysers in the world is located in a private park next to Calistoga. Super-heated water erupts to a height of sixty feet or more approximately every forty minutes. There is an exhibit hall, gift shop and picnic area.

Petrified Forest   *(707)942-6667*
  5 mi. W at 4100 Petrified Forest Rd.
This private park contains well-preserved fossil redwood logs. Giant trees were buried eons ago when ash covered a forest uprooted by the concussion of a volcanic eruption of nearby Mt. St. Helena. Walking trails, a museum, gift shop and picnic areas are provided.

Sharpsteen Museum   *(707)942-5911*
  downtown at 1311 Washington St.
Calistoga's offbeat history is depicted in exhibits and a detailed diorama. An attached authentic 1860 cottage from Sam Brannan's original resort was relocated here. Nearby is a peaceful creekside garden.

Warm Water Features
The public can luxuriate year-round in indoor and outdoor warm mineral water pools and whirlpools in genial settings affiliated with in-town lodgings. Steam baths, herbal and blanket wraps, and massages can also be reserved. For a shared sybaritic sensation, try a genuine volcanic ash bath with a close friend.

Wineries
Calistoga, at the northern end of the world famous Napa Valley wine district, is surrounded by outstanding wineries. Delightful tasting and sales facilities and tours attract visitors year-round, especially to:
  Chateau Montelena   *(707)942-5105*
  2 mi. N at 1429 Tubbs Lane
A renowned winery in a castle-like building above a pretty lake. (Fee)
  Cuvaison Winery   *(707)942-6266*
  3 mi. E at 4550 Silverado Trail
Focus is on three premium wines. Oak-shaded picnic grounds. (Fee)
  Sterling Vineyards   *(707)942-3344*
  2 mi. SE via CA 29 at 1111 Dunaweal Lane
Guests take a (fee) aerial tram to a resplendent hilltop winery in one of the nation's most impressive vineyard settings.

RESTAURANTS

All Seasons Cafe   *(707)942-9111*
downtown at 1400 Lincoln Av.
L-D.   *Expensive*
Creative California cuisine is showcased in dishes like grilled rabbit with wild mushrooms or grilled rib-eye steak with cabernet glaze and creamy horseradish sauce, plus homemade pastries, desserts and ice creams. The relaxed and cheerful bistro also features an excellent assortment of regional premium wines.

Bosko's Ristorante   *(707)942-9088*
downtown at 1364 Lincoln Av.
L-D.   *Moderate*
Contemporary California/Italian fare includes creative and traditional pastas and pizzas. The big relaxed trattoria has rock walls with windows overlooking main street, a horseshoe counter and woodburning oven for accents.

Calistoga Inn   *(707)942-4101*
downtown at 1250 Lincoln Av.
L-D.   *Expensive*
Emphasis on fresh ingredients with a light touch results in fine contemporary California specialties. A cozy congestion of tables fills two relaxed dining rooms of a restored inn with a turn-of-the-century feeling. The garden patio is a lovely alternative by a creek next to the wine bar and brewery. An atmospheric lounge adjoins.

Catahoula   *(707)942-2275*
downtown at 1457 Lincoln Av.
L-D.   *Very Expensive*
Catahoula, in the historic Mount View Hotel, is California's best source of Louisiana-inspired cuisine. From file gumbo through grilled quail with eggplant oyster stuffing to decadent desserts like beignet with vanilla ice cream and caramel sauce—here is a fine dining adventure. The simply snazzy dining room has a warm whimsical ambiance highlighted by colorful wall hangings and great wood-burning ovens. Next door is a festive saloon with frequent live entertainment. Out back is a chic cabana bar by the courtyard pool.

Checkers   *(707)942-9300*
downtown at 1414 Lincoln Av.
L-D.   *Moderate*
First-rate designer pizzas and related Italian and California comfort foods are the hallmark of Calistoga's best trattoria. The relaxed interior has an upscale ambiance that is part of the appeal.

Napa Valley Ovens   *(707)942-0777*
downtown at 1353 Lincoln Av.
B-L.   *Expensive*
Sticky buns, cinnamon rolls, croissants and fruit muffins are among morning delights made here. They can be enjoyed with a selection of coffee drinks at several tables overlooking the main street, or to go. Breads are also fine.

Pacifico   *(707)942-4400*
downtown at 1237 Lincoln Av.
L-D.   *Moderate*
Seafood sautes and grilled meats highlight a wide selection of innovative adaptations of Mexican dishes served in a big colorful dining room and cantina with a waterfall.

Wappo Bar & Bistro   *(707)942-4712*
downtown at 1226-B Washington St.
L-D.   *Expensive*
"Regional global cuisine" is promised, and selections from the small, diverse menu are notably flavorful and imaginative. Consider—roast rabbit with mustard, cream and spinach; or lamb with artichoke and dandelion greens. Beyond the simply handsome little dining room is a delightful courtyard with a jasmine bower with an intoxicating fragrance in spring.

LODGING

Relatively limited lodgings downtown all reflect Calistoga's intimate human scale and are oriented around a wide range of hot springs spa facilities. Most are prosaic, but nearby, elaborate bed-and-breakfasts are proliferating. High season is April through October and weekends year-round. Mid-week winter rates are often reduced at least 30%.

Calistoga Spa Hot Springs   *(707)942-6269*
downtown at 1006 Washington St. - 94515
57 units   *Moderate*
Families especially enjoy this contemporary motel, where guests have free use of the big mineral whirlpool, two hot pools, a large warm pool in the courtyard, and exercise equipment. These and complete (fee) spa facilities are also available to the public. Comfortably furnished rooms are spacious and have kitchenettes.

Calistoga Village Inn & Spa   *(707)942-0991*
just NE at 1880 Lincoln Av. - 94515
41 units   *Moderate-Expensive*
This modern single-level motel features a large warm mineral water outdoor pool and a hot indoor whirlpool. A complete (fee) spa facility (highlighting ash/mud baths) is available, and there is a restaurant. Each room is nicely furnished. Some rooms also have a Roman tiled whirlpool tub and kitchenette.

Christopher's Inn   *(707)942-5755*
just W at 1010 Foothill Blvd. - 94515
20 units   *Expensive*
This recently completed bed-and-breakfast has a wealth of upscale touches amid colorful gardens. Breakfast served to your room is complimentary. Each beautifully furnished room includes antiques, and a private bath, plus a woodburning fireplace. Several also have an in-room two-person whirlpool and a garden patio.

Cottage Grove Inn   *(707)942-8400*
downtown at 1711 Lincoln Av. - 94515
16 units   *(800)799-2284*   *Expensive*
The most romantic private cottages in town opened in 1996 amid towering elms. Full breakfast and afternoon wine are complimentary. Each cottage is beautifully furnished with individual decor and state-of-the-art electronics, plus a wood-burning fireplace and an in-bath two-person whirlpool tub.

Golden Haven Spa   *(707)942-6793*
just NE at 1713 Lake St. - 94515
30 units   *Moderate*
A quiet locale is a feature of this modern motel near downtown. Amenities include a warm indoor mineral pool plus a hot whirlpool. Complete (fee) bathhouse/health club facilities are also available. All rooms are comfortably furnished. Some of the recently redecorated rooms have an in-room raised whirlpool.

Indian Springs Resort & Spa   *(707)942-4913*
downtown at 1712 Lincoln Av. - 94515
17 units   *Expensive*
The oldest continuously-operated thermal pool and spa facility in
California includes a restored historic bungalow complex built around
Calistoga's largest outdoor hot springs pool. It is open to the public
(free to guests). On-site thermal geysers and volcanic ash are used in
the complete (fee) bath/health facilities. Each small, simply furnished
unit has a partial kitchen.

Mount View Hotel   *(707)942-6877*
downtown at 1457 Lincoln Av. - 94515
33 units   *(800)816-6877*   *Expensive*
A large pool and whirlpool enhance a garden courtyard with fountain
sculptures behind this small landmark hotel. There is also gourmet
dining (see listing for Catahoula), an entertainment lounge, and a full
service (fee) health and beauty spa. Carefully restored and updated
rooms are individually well furnished. Three cottages also have their
own private patio with a whirlpool.

Roman Spa   *(707)942-4441*
downtown at 1300 Washington St. - 94515
60 units   *(800)820-3822*   *Moderate-Expensive*
Luxuriant semitropical gardens are a delightful complement to tile-
and-stucco motel buildings, an outdoor mineral pool and whirlpool, plus
a hot indoor mineral whirlpool and saunas for guests. Complete (fee)
spa facilities and services for both couples and individuals are located
in an adjoining building. Each room was recently remodeled and
upgraded and is now well furnished. Two rooms also have a large in-
room whirlpool tub.

Silver Rose Inn & Spa   *(707)942-9581*
1 mi. SE at 351 Rosedale Rd. - 94515
20 units   *(800)995-9381 Expensive-Very Expensive*
The Silver Rose Inn is one of the Wine Country's most elegant and
romantic bed-and-breakfasts. Stylish contemporary buildings crown a
well-landscaped knoll and are sequestered in vineyards below.
Amenities include two tennis courts, two pools, whirlpools, and exercise
equipment, plus full (fee) spa facilities and services. Fresh, light
breakfast and afternoon wine and cheese are complimentary. Each
spacious, beautifully furnished room has tranquil mountain or
vineyards views. Many also have a private balcony, gas fireplace and
large in-room whirlpool.

BASIC INFORMATION

Elevation: 365 feet   *Population (1990): 4,468*
Location: 74 miles North of San Francisco
Nearest airport with commercial flights: San Francisco - 85 miles
Calistoga Chamber of Commerce   (707)942-6333
  downtown in the Old Depot Building at 1458 Lincoln Av. #9 - 94515
  www.napavalley.com / calistoga
  www.calistogafun.com

Cambria, California

Cambria is a whimsical village tucked into a pine forest by the sea. It is the southern gateway to the fabled Big Sur coast. Shortly after the Civil War, the first permanent settlement was established along Santa Rosa Creek by farmers and dairymen. Much later, artists and dreamers were attracted by spectacular mountain-backed seascapes and a mild year-round climate.

Today, most businesses are still clustered above the creek along the old main road in two charming town centers, the east village and west village. Numerous sophisticated galleries and specialty shops, romantic restaurants in quaint cottages or in ocean-view dinner houses, and (in lieu of motel chain complexes) distinctive small lodgings complement the serenity and natural beauty of this special place. The ocean is too cold for swimming, but beachcombing, clamming, fishing, hiking, backpacking and camping are popular year-round. So are visits to nearby Hearst Castle.

WEATHER PROFILE

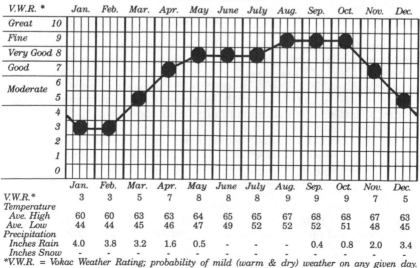

V.W.R. *		Jan.	Feb.	Mar.	Apr.	May	June	July	Aug.	Sep.	Oct.	Nov.	Dec.
Great	10												
Fine	9												
Very Good	8												
Good	7												
Moderate	6												
	5												
	4												
	3												
	2												
	1												
	0												

	Jan.	Feb.	Mar.	Apr.	May	June	July	Aug.	Sep.	Oct.	Nov.	Dec.
V.W.R.*	3	3	5	7	8	8	8	9	9	9	7	5
Temperature												
Ave. High	60	60	63	63	64	65	65	67	68	68	67	63
Ave. Low	44	44	45	46	47	49	52	52	52	51	48	45
Precipitation												
Inches Rain	4.0	3.8	3.2	1.6	0.5	-	-	-	0.4	0.8	2.0	3.4
Inches Snow	-	-	-	-	-	-	-	-	-	-	-	-

*V.W.R. = Vokac Weather Rating; probability of mild (warm & dry) weather on any given day.

Bicycling

Bicycles can be rented by the hour or longer in town to tour scenic highways and byways along the coast and in the hills around Cambria.

Big Sur Coast

N for approximately 80 mi. on CA 1

The bewitching spectacle of a mountain wilderness rising abruptly from an unspoiled sea inevitably thrills those who drive the winding two-lane highway through the fabled Big Sur. Travelers should allow at least a full day to appreciate the remote beaches and lush forested canyons; state parks with well-tended hiking trails, picnic sites and campgrounds; and unconventional galleries and restaurants that complement the area's natural grandeur.

Galleries

in west village on Main St. & East Village on Burton Dr.

More than a dozen galleries and studios feature works by local and regional artists and craftsmen in a variety of specialties. The most famous are **Seekers** (4090 Burton Dr.), a two-story gallery featuring museum-quality works in both functional and artistic glass; and the **Soldier Factory Gallery** (789 Main St.), with polished or painted pewter toy soldiers, chess pieces and whimsical creatures.

Hearst Castle   (805)927-2020   (888)438-4445

8 mi. NW on CA 1 - San Simeon

"La Casa Grande" has a ridge-top position that gives it the appearance of a castle from the distant highway. The imposing 137-foot-high cathedral-like main structure of more than one hundred rooms was William Randolph Hearst's private residence. Construction began in 1919 and continued until Hearst's death in 1951. It is now the focal point of the Hearst San Simeon State Historical Monument that also includes guest residences, terraced gardens, pools, sculptures, unusual plants and many exotic animals. The eclectic collection of extravagant antiques and furnishings was accumulated during Hearst's lifetime of world travel. Visitors may only take conducted tours which take about two hours, and involve much walking and climbing steps. Reservations well in advance are recommended.

Nit Wit Ridge

just above west village via Cornwall at 881 Hillcrest Dr.

On a hillside a short walk above town is a whimsical bric-a-brac mansion. It was built incrementally since 1928 out of found material from bike parts to beer bottles by Art Beal, affectionately known as "Captain Nit Wit." This classic example of folk art construction is listed in the National Register. The private residence can only be viewed from the street, but it is worth finding as another expression, like Hearst's Castle, of what individuality is all about.

San Simeon Beach State Park

2 mi. NW via CA 1 at Moonstone Beach Dr.

Nearly two miles of shoreline with picturesque sandy beaches, tidepools, blufftop trails and vantage points, and ocean-view picnic sites have been set aside for the public.

Shamel County Park

2 mi. W of west village on the coast

A parking area adjoins Cambria's finest sandy beach, an outdoor swimming pool open in summer, and pleasant shady picnic sites.

RESTAURANTS
The Brambles   *(805)927-4716*
in east village at 4005 Burton Dr.
D only.   *Moderate*
An oakwood pit and oven are featured for preparing steaks, prime rib, and fresh seafoods. Homemade baked goods are another specialty of this long-time favorite. Gracious tables and antique decor fill firelit dining rooms in a many-roomed Victorian cottage.

Creekside Gardens   *(805)927-8646*
in east village at 2114 Main St.
B-L.   *Moderate*
An unusual range of homemade breakfast specialties is served in a cheerful little whitewashed cottage, or on a flower-strewn view patio.

The Hamlet Restaurant at Moonstone Gardens   *(805)927-3535*
2 mi. NW of west village on CA 1
L-D.   *Expensive*
Contemporary American fare is served in a casual dining room with a distant ocean view and in an exotic garden/nursery.

Ian's   *(805)927-8649*
in east village at 2150 Center St.
D only.   *Expensive*
New California dishes are skillfully prepared and served amidst post-modern decor in one of Cambria's most sophisticated restaurants. Pastel colors and artistically arranged prints and plants decorate tranquil dining rooms and an expansive lounge.

Linn's Main Bin   *(805)927-0371*
in east village at 2277 Main St.
B-L-D.   *Moderate*
Down-home American classics and Linn's own baked pastries and fruit pies (on display) have been pleasing crowds for years. All can be enjoyed in the comfortable family dining room, or as carryout. A well-stocked gift shop features fresh and preserved producc.

Moonstone Beach Bar & Grill   *(805)927-3859*
1 mi. NW of west village at 6550 Moonstone Beach Dr.
L-D.   *Expensive*
New Orleans-style seafoods are the specialty in this oceanside restaurant. Because the casually elegant dining room has floor-to-ceiling windows on three sides, every guest has an expansive view of the Pacific.

Redwood Cafe   *(805)927-4830*
in east village at 2094 Main St.
B-L.   *Moderate*
Distinctive omelets and baked goods are featured, along with other homemade dishes served in this pleasant little cafe.

Robin's   *(805)927-5007*
in east village at 4095 Burton Dr.
L-D.   *Expensive*
Locally grown produce is featured in ethnic and vegetarian fare served in the peaceful little dining room of a charming old cottage, and on a beautiful vine-covered outdoor terrace when weather permits.

Sea Chest Restaurant & Oyster Bar   *(805)927-4514*
1 mi. NW of west village at 6216 Moonstone Beach Dr.
D only.   *Expensive*
Shellfish and seafood are specialties. When available, the high-rise center cut of halibut is simply outstanding in this popular, intimate

restaurant with quaint nautical decor. There is a fine surf view from the Oyster Bar/dining room. The congenial lounge is set up for cards and board games.

The Sow's Ear   *(805)927-4865*
in east village at 2248 Main St.
D only.   *Moderate*
American country cuisine is skillfully prepared with quality meats, seafood, and local vegetables. Housemade flower-pot bread and desserts are also fine. The deservedly popular woodcrafted dining rooms are firelit, cozy and charming.

LODGING

Accommodations are plentiful and reflect the local serenity and natural beauty. Major chains are thankfully absent. Reservations are often essential in high season (May through October), and on most Saturday nights. At other times, prices may be reduced 20% or more.

Blue Dolphin Inn   *(805)927-3300*
1 mi. NW of west village at 6470 Moonstone Beach Dr. - 93428
18 units   *Expensive*
One of Cambria's most elegant lodgings is near the ocean. Continental breakfast and afternoon tea and refreshments are complimentary. Each individually decorated room is beautifully furnished in an English country mode, and has a fireplace and refrigerator. Some have a whirlpool tub and a garden patio with an ocean view.

Blue Whale Inn Bed & Breakfast   *(805)927-4647*
1 mi. NW at 6736 Moonstone Beach Dr. - 93428
6 units   *Expensive*
The village's finest bed-and-breakfast inn is a contemporary charmer located on a bluff across from the ocean. Full country breakfast and afternoon refreshments are complimentary. Each room offers beautiful European country decor with a refrigerator, canopy bed, soaking tub, and gas fireplace.

Bluebird Motel   *(805)927-4634*
in east village at 1880 Main St. - 93428
37 units   *(800)552-5434*   *Moderate-Expensive*
A creek runs behind this long-established motel in a garden by the heart of town. All of the rooms are comfortable, and the well-furnished creekside suites also have a gas fireplace, refrigerator, and view.

Cambria Landing on Moonstone Beach   *(805)927-1619*
1 mi. NW of west village at 6530 Moonstone Beach Dr. - 93428
26 units   *(800)549-6789*   *Moderate-Expensive*
This stylish motel across from the beach has a whirlpool tub plus complimentary bicycles, wine, and Continental breakfast brought to the room. Each beautifully appointed room has a refrigerator and gas fireplace. Six cottage units also have an in-room whirlpool.

Cambria Pines Lodge   *(805)927-4200*
just S of east village at 2905 Burton Dr. - 93428
125 units   *(800)445-6868*   *Moderate-Expensive*
The 1920s lodge-and-cabin complex above the village in a Monterey pine forest includes the area's largest pool; whirlpool and saunas enclosed in a handsome glass-walled structure; plus a forest-view restaurant and firelit lounge with frequent live entertainment. Breakfast buffet is complimentary. Each small cabin or lodge room is nicely refurbished. Some larger rooms also have a fireplace.

Cambria's Pelican Suites   *(805)927-1500*

1 mi. NW of west village at 6316 Moonstone Beach Dr. - 93428
24 units   *Expensive-Very Expensive*

In 1998, an elegant inn opened across a road from the ocean, and joined Cambria's stellar collection of romantic respites overlooking the coast. There is a small pool and an exercise room. Full breakfast and afternoon refreshments are complimentary. Each spacious room is beautifully decorated, and has a gas fireplace and a private patio or balcony. Some also have a large whirlpool bath and an ocean view.

Fireside Inn - Best Western   *(805)927-8661*

1 mi. NW at 6700 Moonstone Beach Dr. - 93428
46 units   *(800)528-1234*   *Expensive*

This contemporary single-level motel is only fifty yards from Moonstone Beach and has a large pool and whirlpool. Each spacious, attractive room has a refrigerator. Many also have a gas fireplace.

Moonstone Inn   *(805)927-4815*

1 mi. NW of west village at 5860 Moonstone Beach Dr. - 93428
8 units   *(800)821-3764*   *Expensive*

Across the road from Moonstone Beach is an English Tudor-style country inn with a complimentary wine and cheese hour in a glassed-in ocean-view patio with a whirlpool and fireplace. An expanded Continental breakfast is brought to your room. Each well-furnished room has a refrigerator. Some also have a gas fireplace or whirlpool.

San Simeon Pines Seaside Resort   *(805)927-4648*

2 mi. NW at 7200 Moonstone Beach Dr. (Box 117) - San Simeon 93452
60 units   *Moderate*

This redwood ranch-style motel in a pine forest has easy access to the beach, a landscaped outdoor pool, beautiful par-3 9-hole golf course, and an outdoor games area free to guests. Each room is well furnished. Several spacious rooms in an adults-only section also have a wood-burning fireplace and surf view.

Sand Pebbles Inn   *(805)927-5600*

1 mi. NW of west village at 6252 Moonstone Beach Dr. - 93428
23 units   *Expensive*

This romantic little inn overlooks the ocean. Continental breakfast and afternoon tea with refreshments are complimentary. Each spacious room is beautifully furnished in country French decor and has a refrigerator and gas fireplace. Some also have a whirlpool, garden patio, and/or an ocean view.

Sea Otter Inn   *(805)927-5888*

2 mi. NW of west village at 6656 Moonstone Beach Dr. - 93428
25 units   *Moderate*

A heated pool and whirlpool are features of this contemporary motel across from the beach. Each well-furnished room has a refrigerator and gas fireplace. Some also have a whirlpool.

BASIC INFORMATION

Elevation: 60 feet   *Population: 5,382*
Location: 220 miles Northwest of Los Angeles
Nearest airport with commercial flights: San Francisco or LA - 220 mi.
Cambria Chamber of Commerce   (805)927-3624
  in west village at 767 Main St. - 93428
  www.thegrid.net/cambriachamber

Carmel, California

Carmel is one of the world's loveliest collaborations between man and nature. It is a unique seaside village sequestered in a forest of pines and rare Monterey cypress above a slope of fine white sand that extends into the surf of Carmel Bay. Lush vegetation and a wealth of outdoor activities are enjoyed year-round. Father Junipero Serra built a mission here in 1770. Well over a century later, artists and dreamers attracted by the captivating location and mild climate fostered the charm that is still being nurtured.

Fairy tale cottages, fanciful houses, and an astonishing proliferation of cosmopolitan galleries and specialty shops are a highly visible part of the legacy. In spite of its overwhelming popularity, the village still does *not* have: traffic lights, parking meters, neon signs, billboards, or tall buildings. One of America's great concentrations of gourmet restaurants and romantic lodgings serves visitors who flock here to experience Carmel indoors and out year-round.

WEATHER PROFILE

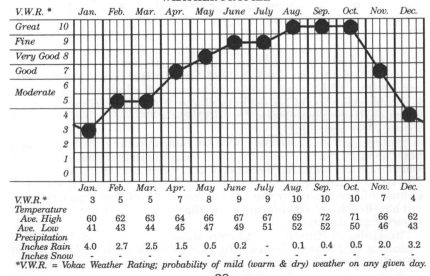

V.W.R. *		Jan.	Feb.	Mar.	Apr.	May	June	July	Aug.	Sep.	Oct.	Nov.	Dec.
Great	10												
Fine	9												
Very Good	8												
Good	7												
Moderate	6 / 5												
	4												
	3												
	2												
	1												
	0												

	Jan.	Feb.	Mar.	Apr.	May	June	July	Aug.	Sep.	Oct.	Nov.	Dec.
V.W.R.*	3	5	5	7	8	9	9	10	10	10	7	4
Temperature												
Ave. High	60	62	63	64	66	67	67	69	72	71	66	62
Ave. Low	41	43	44	45	47	49	51	52	52	50	46	43
Precipitation												
Inches Rain	4.0	2.7	2.5	1.5	0.5	0.2	-	0.1	0.4	0.5	2.0	3.2
Inches Snow	-	-	-	-	-	-	-	-	-	-	-	-

*V.W.R. = Vokac Weather Rating; probability of mild (warm & dry) weather on any given day.

ATTRACTIONS

Bicycling
One of the world's finest auto/bicycle rides—the Seventeen Mile Drive—and other scenic routes provide access to the coastline, mountains and bucolic valleys. Rental bicycles by the hour are available.

Big Sur Coast
S for approximately 80 mi. on CA 1

California Highway 1 is one of the world's most exhilarating scenic drives. A narrow, paved two-lane road winds and dips along the flanks of a mountain wilderness rising precipitously from an unspoiled shoreline. Numerous hiking trails lead from roadside parking areas into groves of the southernmost coast redwoods and fern-shaded canyons, and to remote sandy beaches and coves. Well-located state parks along the route offer memorable camping and picnicking opportunities. Unique galleries, restaurants, and lodgings blend harmoniously into the unforgettable countryside. In the village of Big Sur (25 miles south) the **Big Sur River Inn** (B-L-D—Expensive) offers hearty American fare in a wood-trim dining room and lounge, or on a patio by a stream, plus rustic rooms in the pines, a pool, general store and gallery. Nearby, **Big Sur Lodge** includes **Trails Head Cafe** (B-L-D—Expensive) for tasty American dishes; comfortable cottage-style rooms in the pines; a gift shop and general store. Peerless **Nepenthe** (L-D—Expensive) offers creative American cuisine in a handcrafted dining room/bar and terrace perched high above the ragged coast. The adjoining **Phoenix Shop** has fine local arts, crafts and books. To the south, the **Coast Gallery** (with the **Coast Cafe** dining deck) and **Hawthorne Gallery** are two of America's great showcases for museum-quality regional arts and crafts. Nearby are **Ventana Inn** and the **Post Ranch Inn** (see listings), quintessential examples of affinity between civilization and nature.

Carmel Beach Park
just W at the foot of Ocean Av.

A picturesque beach is backed by a pine-studded slope of fine, dazzlingly white sand. Cold water and undertow preclude swimming, but it is a wonderful place for strolling, picnicking, and sunbathing.

Carmel Mission   *(831)624-1271*
1 mi. S off CA 1 at 3080 Rio Rd.

This key link to early California history was established on a site overlooking the mouth of the Carmel River in 1770 by Father Junipero Serra ("father of the California missions"). It was his residence and headquarters until his death in 1784. He is buried beneath the church floor in front of the altar. The carefully restored mission's museum has a notable collection of his memorabilia and other historic relics.

Carmel River State Park   *(831)624-4906*
1 mi. S on Scenic Rd.

A photogenic ocean beach composed of fine, sparkling white sand is a popular attraction for beachcombers, sunbathers and picnickers. It is unsuitable for swimming because of cold water and currents.

Horseback Riding
Horses can be rented by the hour or longer for guided scenic rides in Pebble Beach, Carmel Valley, or Big Sur. For information and reservations, contact:

The Holman Ranch   *Carmel Valley*   *(831)659-2640*
Molera Horseback Tours *Big Sur* *(800)942-5486* *(831)625-5486*
Pebble Beach Equestrian Center *Pebble Beach* *(831)624-2756*

Point Lobos State Reserve　　*(831)624-4909*
4 mi. S off CA 1
One of the most beautiful reserves on the Pacific coast includes six miles of headlands, secluded sandy coves, tidepools, sea lion rocks, and a natural grove of Monterey cypress. Whale watching is also popular when the awesome animals pass close to shore on their 12,000-mile winter migration to Baja California. Hikers should be wary of poison oak.

Specialty Shops
Barnyard Shops　　*(831)624-8886*　　*(800)833-2276*
2 mi. SE off CA 1 & Carmel Valley Rd.
Here is the premier destination for recreational shopping. Profusions of flowers, music, and intriguing fountains and sculptures lend enchantment to a cluster of rustic barn-style buildings housing more than forty fine specialty shops, galleries, and restaurants, including the peerless **Thunderbird Book Store/Cafe**.
　Crossroads Shopping Village　　*(831)625-4106*
2 mi. SE off CA 1 & Rio Rd.
A prominent Westminster chiming clock/bell tower is the centerpiece for an array of more than one hundred distinctive specialty shops and restaurants amid a colorful mosaic of contemporary California architecture and gardens.

Wineries
Chateau Julien　　*(831)624-2600*
6 mi. E at 8940 Carmel Valley Rd. - Carmel Valley
Tasting and sales of several premium wines are in a handsome chateau-style winery building.
　Galante Vineyards　　*(800)425-2683*
22 mi. E at 18181 Cachagua Rd. - Carmel Valley
This winery opened in 1996 with tastings and sales of premium handcrafted wines in a stylish estate among rose gardens.

RESTAURANTS
Anton & Michel　　*(831)624-2406*
downtown on Mission St. between Ocean & 7th Avs.
L-D.　　　　　　　　　　　　　　　　*Very Expensive*
Fresh seafoods like Pacific salmon or abalone are featured along with an appealing selection of contemporary Continental dishes and luscious desserts in the flagship of a burgeoning local restaurant group. Informally elegant dining rooms give guests a choice of romantic firelight or courtyard fountain views.
Casanova Restaurant　　*(831)625-0501*
downtown on 5th Av. near Mission St.
L-D.　　　　　　　　　　　　　　　　*Very Expensive*
Creative American cuisine showcases fresh regional ingredients and the talent of a classically trained chef in three-course dinners. Homemade desserts are also notable. The recently expanded complex includes a series of cozy, romantic dining rooms around a heated garden patio.
Crème Carmel　　*(831)624-0444*
downtown at San Carlos St. & 7th Av.
L-D.　　　　　　　　　　　　　　　　*Very Expensive*
French cuisine gets a masterful, playful topspin from the European-trained chef in seasonally fresh dishes and luscious desserts made here. Decor is refreshingly understated in the tucked-away, intimate dining room of the acclaimed restaurant.

The French Poodle   *(831)624-8643*
downtown at Junipero & 5th Avs.
D only.   *Expensive*
Classic light French cuisine is given expert attention in the peninsula's
best French restaurant. Consider Dungeness crab legs out of the shell
with champagne sauce, saffron and caviar to begin a meal that might
include provimi veal T-bone for an entree, and a sumptuous dessert
made here. The intimate, informally elegant dining room is the more
romantic for widely spaced tables, a rarity in Carmel.

Katy's Place   *(831)624-0199*
downtown on Mission St. between 5th & 6th Sts.
B-L.   *Expensive*
One of the peninsula's oldest and best breakfast places serves dishes
ranging from several varieties of eggs benedict, or corned beef hash
and eggs to breakfast burritos, waffles, designer pancakes and much
more. The cheerful little cafe has flowers on the tables and a dining
deck shaded by redwood trees.

Michael's at the Barnyard   *(831)622-5200*
2 mi. SE at 3690 The Barnyard
L-D.   *Expensive*
Fine innovative American cuisine ranges from avocado pancakes with
salsa fresca to hickory-smoked pork chop with roasted portabella
mushroom. Luscious desserts are also made here. Stylish neo-
Southwestern firelit dining rooms adjoin an umbrella-shaded alfresco
patio.

PortaBella   *(831)624-4395*
downtown on Ocean Av. between Lincoln and Monte Verde Sts.
L-D.   *Expensive*
One of Carmel's newest gourmet havens offers fresh Mediterranean
country cuisine with assured inventive topspin. Guests can dine in
intimate gracious dining areas or in a charming garden court.

Raffaello Restaurant   *(831)624-1541*
downtown on Mission St. between Ocean & 7th Avs.
D only.   *Expensive*
Northern Italian cuisine with an emphasis on fresh quality ingredients
is still featured in one of the region's oldest gourmet havens. Full linen,
candles, fresh flowers, and firelight contribute to the feeling of intimate
elegance in the tranquil dining room.

Rio Grill   *(831)625-5436*
2 mi. SE at 101 Crossroads Blvd. in the Crossroads
L-D.   *Expensive*
Rio Grill is one of America's premier sources of New California cuisine
with its emphasis on fresh regional ingredients innovatively prepared
in a flavorful array of appetizers through desserts described on a
grazing menu. Avant garde art enlivens a series of cheerful Santa Fe
style alcoves beyond a colorful firelit bar.

Robert Kincaid's Bistro   *(831)624-9626*
2 mi. SE at 227 Crossroads Blvd. in Crossroads
L-D.   *Expensive*
Innovative French and American bistro cuisine is given the careful
attention of one of the Peninsula's most acclaimed chefs. Cozy dining
areas are simply decorated in European country style that keeps
attention on gourmet offerings.

Sans Souci Restaurant   *(831)624-6220*
downtown on Lincoln St. between 5th & 6th Avs.
D only.   *Very Expensive*
For decades, Sans Souci has presented classic French cuisine with an emphasis on fresh seafood. Comfortably elegant decor is accented by a romantic wood-burning fireplace, classical music and well-spaced richly appointed tables.

Tuck Box   *(831)624-6365*
downtown on Dolores St. between Ocean & 7th Avs.
B-L.   *Moderate*
The Tuck Box has been a Carmel tradition for more than half a century. The thatched cottage facade of the tiny English tea room is very photogenic. They feature their own scone mix and preserves in the unpretentious little tea shop.

LODGING

Lodgings in town are abundant, invariably picturesque, and individualistic. Renowned resorts surround the village. High season is May through October, and weekends year-round. Mid-week in winter, rates may be as much as 20% less.

Carmel Valley Ranch   *(831)625-9500*
8 mi. E via Carmel Valley Rd. at 1 Old Ranch Rd. - 93923
100 units   *(800)422-7635*   *Very Expensive*
Noble oak trees shade the grounds of this exclusive hideaway. The contemporary resort offers a (fee) 18-hole championship golf course, putting green and driving range; twelve tennis courts and horseback riding; plus a fitness center, two pools, six whirlpools, sauna, and resort shop. **The Oaks** (B-L-D—Very Expensive) features regional gourmet cuisine with fine valley views. Nearby is an entertainment lounge. Each spacious, luxuriously furnished suite has a fireplace and a private balcony or deck. Several also have a large in-room whirlpool.

Carriage House Inn   *(831)625-2585*
downtown on Junipero Av. between 7th & 8th Avs. (Box 1900) - 93921
13 units   *(800)433-4732*   *Expensive-Very Expensive*
One of the peninsula's best bed-and-breakfasts is a charming adult retreat that captures the spirit of Carmel in quality arts and crafts and thoughtful embellishments. Expanded Continental breakfast served to the room and afternoon wine and appetizers are complimentary. Each spacious, luxuriously furnished room has a fireplace.

Highlands Inn   *(831)624-3801*
4 mi. S on CA 1 (Box 1700) - Carmel Highlands 93921
142 units   *(800)682-4811*   *Very Expensive*
One of the world's great coastal panoramas is the highlight of this delightfully updated resort hotel high above the Big Sur coast. Lush grounds sequester a large pool, three whirlpools, exercise room, bicycles, resort shop, and gourmet market. At the **Pacific's Edge** (L-D—Very Expensive) classic French and California techniques and fresh quality regional ingredients are masterfully combined into some of the best dishes in the state. The sophisticated elegance of the dining room and the panoramic seascape view are, remarkably, as good as the cuisine. Nearby, a plush firelit lounge shares the romantic view. Each spacious unit offers luxurious contemporary furnishings and a private view deck. Most also have a kitchen, spacious whirlpool bath and a fireplace.

La Playa Hotel   *(831)624-6476*
downtown at Camino Real and 8th Av. (Box 900) - 93921
75 units   *(800)582-8900   Expensive-Very Expensive*
The La Playa Hotel is Carmel's most delightful in-town hideaway. On the edge of downtown near the beach, the four-story landmark with its distinctive Mediterranean style is set on impeccably landscaped grounds with a pool, a lounge and the **Terrace Grill** (B-L-D—Expensive), where fresh innovative California cuisine is served in a plush dining room and on a heated open terrace with a spectacular view of the ocean and gardens. Each room is beautifully furnished. Some have an ocean view or a whirlpool tub.

The Lodge at Pebble Beach   *(831)624-3811*
5 mi. S off Seventeen Mile Dr. (Box 567) - Pebble Beach 93953
161 units   *(800)654-9300*   *Very Expensive*
The world famous Lodge at Pebble Beach has an incomparable oceanfront location and a remarkable variety of resort amenities. In addition to the beach, there is a pool, whirlpool and sauna; the legendary 18-hole (fee) golf course; a large state-of-the-art tennis complex; health and fitness center; horseback riding and bicycling; nature trails; plus a promenade of resort shops and fine restaurants, including the renowned **Club XIX** (L-D—Very Expensive) and **The Cypress Room** (B-L-D—Very Expensive), where seafood stars amid glamorous contemporary atmosphere and a superb ocean view. Each room is luxuriously furnished. Most include a private view balcony. Some suites also have a fireplace and whirlpool bath.

Mission Ranch   *(831)624-6436*
1 mi. SE at 26270 Dolores St. - 93923
31 units   *(800)538-8221   Expensive-Very Expensive*
A historic 1850s farmhouse is the heart of a great getaway of charming cottages and lodge buildings on flowery grounds above a meadow that extends to the spectacular coastline at the entrance of Carmel River. Expansive Continental breakfast is complimentary. Amenities include six (fee) tennis courts, plus exercise room, putting green, and piano bar. **The Restaurant** (D only—Expensive) offers fine contemporary American classics amid elegant rusticity and on a patio with splendid views. Each beautifully furnished unit has all contemporary conveniences. The "Meadowview" cottages also have a fireplace, whirlpool bath and private porch with distant ocean view.

Pine Inn   *(831)624-3851*
downtown on Ocean Av. at Lincoln Av. (Box 250) - 93921
47 units   *(800)228-3851   Moderate-Very Expensive*
Carmel's main street landmark is a century-old three-story hotel. Plush Victorian furnishings distinguish common areas, and there is an atrium restaurant and lounge. Rooms and suites are well furnished.

Post Ranch Inn   *(831)667-2200*
29 mi. S on CA 1 (Box 219) - Big Sur 93920
30 units   *(800)527-2200*   *Very Expensive*
Post Ranch Inn is the quintessential Big Sur luxury retreat. The grandeur of a site high above a rugged coast is perfectly matched by tranquil post-modern architecture and artistic decor seamlessly blended into naturally luxuriant grounds. Gourmet Continental breakfast buffet is complimentary. Amenities include two pools, whirlpool, exercise room, hiking trails, (fee) spa treatments, gift shop and **Sierra Mar Restaurant** (L-D—Very Expensive) where gourmet New California cuisine is as sophisticated as the artful dining room and as appealing

as the panoramic coastal view. Each individually decorated room is luxuriously furnished, including a private view deck, fireplace and whirlpool bath.

Quail Lodge Resort & Golf Club   *(831)624-1581*
   4 mi. SE via Carmel Valley Rd. at 8205 Valley Greens Dr. - 93923
   100 units   *(800)538-9516*   *Very Expensive*
Here is the premier resort in Carmel Valley. Manicured grounds provide a serene setting for a championship (fee) 18-hole golf course and four tennis courts, plus hiking trails, putting green, two pools, whirlpool, resort shop and **The Covey** (D only—Very Expensive) where gourmet California cuisine is served in a warmly elegant dining room overlooking a scenic pond. Many of the beautifully furnished units have a gas fireplace and private deck. Four larger suites also have a large whirlpool tub.

Stonepine Resort   *(831)659-2245*
   14 mi. SE at 150 E. Carmel Valley Rd. (Box 1765) - Carmel Valley 93924
   16 units   *Very Expensive*
A Mediterranean manor against oak-covered hills in upper Carmel Valley now serves as an elegant bed-and-breakfast resort. Amenities include a pool, tennis courts, and a complete (fee) equestrian center and gourmet dining room (by reservation). Full breakfast and afternoon repast are complimentary. Each room is individually, luxuriously furnished with antiques and all contemporary conveniences. Several also have a fireplace and whirlpool bath.

Tickle Pink Inn   *(831)624-1244*
   4 mi. S on CA 1 at 155 Highlands Dr. - Carmel Highlands 93923
   35 units   *(800)635-4774   Expensive-Very Expensive*
Spell-binding coastline views distinguish this gracious contemporary motel high above the ocean. Pine-studded grounds shade a whirlpool. Continental breakfast and afternoon wine and cheese are complimentary. Most of the beautifully furnished units have a private view balcony. Some also have a fireplace and large in-room whirlpool tub.

Ventana Inn   *(831)667-2331*
   29 mi. S on CA 1 - Big Sur 93920
   62 units   *(800)628-6500   Expensive-Very Expensive*
Ventana is the progenitor of posh post-modern architecture and decor in California lodgings. The enchanting country inn blends into mountain meadows high above the Big Sur coast with nature trails, two large pools, Japanese-style hot baths, sauna, exercise room, gift shop, and the **Ventana Restaurant** (L-D—Very Expensive) where contemporary California cuisine achieves gourmet status with support from on-site organic herb and vegetable gardens. The dining room is informally elegant, while the expansive garden terrace offers a stunning panoramic seascape. Gourmet Continental breakfast and afternoon wine and cheese are complimentary. Each room is a luxuriously furnished study in elegant rusticity. Many have a private deck, fireplace, and large in-room whirlpool tub.

BASIC INFORMATION

Elevation: 200 feet   *Population (1990):   4,239*
Location: 125 miles South of San Francisco
Nearest airport with commercial flights: Monterey - 8 miles
Carmel Business Association   *(831)624-2522*
   downtown on San Carlos between 5th & 6th Sts. (Box 4444) - 93921
   www.carmelcalifornia.org

Healdsburg, California

Healdsburg is the heart of California's only premium wine producing district in a major river valley. The Russian River flows through town, and is flanked by dozens of vineyards that extend to redwood forests in hills to the west. Settlement began shortly after the Civil War. Growth accelerated once farmers and vintners recognized the potential for premium grapes. Prohibition ended the boom times.

Healdsburg is prospering now. Its peaceful unaffected charm is apparent in the luxuriant palm-shaded plaza that remains the heart of town, and in a riverside park popular for swimming, canoeing, fishing and picnics. Turn-of-the-century buildings near the plaza feature shops full of regional antiques, art, handicrafts, gourmet wines and edibles, plus several fine restaurants. Delightfully individual bed-and-breakfast inns in historic or scenic settings are numerous, and perfectly suited to adult visitors here to enjoy the pleasures of wines and the waterway.

WEATHER PROFILE

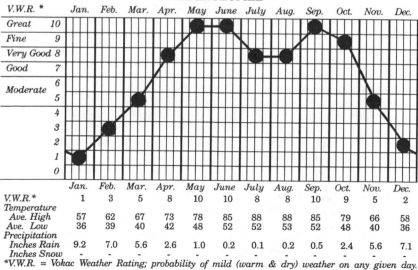

V.W.R.*		Jan.	Feb.	Mar.	Apr.	May	June	July	Aug.	Sep.	Oct.	Nov.	Dec.
Great	10												
Fine	9												
Very Good	8												
Good	7												
Moderate	6												
	5												
	4												
	3												
	2												
	1												
	0												

	Jan.	Feb.	Mar.	Apr.	May	June	July	Aug.	Sep.	Oct.	Nov.	Dec.
V.W.R.*	1	3	5	8	10	10	8	8	10	9	5	2
Temperature												
Ave. High	57	62	67	73	78	85	88	88	85	79	66	58
Ave. Low	36	39	40	42	48	52	52	53	52	48	40	36
Precipitation												
Inches Rain	9.2	7.0	5.6	2.6	1.0	0.2	0.1	0.2	0.5	2.4	5.6	7.1
Inches Snow	-	-	-	-	-	-	-	-	-	-	-	-

*V.W.R. = Vokac Weather Rating; probability of mild (warm & dry) weather on any given day.

ATTRACTIONS
Armstrong Redwoods State Reserve   *(707)869-2015*
18 mi. SW via Westside Rd. & Armstrong Redwood Rd.
Redwoods reaching 300 feet are at the heart of this awe-inspiring
forest in lush coastal foothills. Nature, hiking and riding trails provide
access to the cool, quiet reserve.
Bicycling
Back roads through vineyards, farms and forests along the Russian
River are ideal for bicyclists. Rentals, tours, and all related equipment
are available at:
Healdsburg Spoke Folk Cyclery   *(707)433-7171*
downtown at 249 Center St.
Boating
The Russian River moves slowly through this lush peaceful valley in
summer. That means easy fun for swimming, canoeing or rafting. Half-
day or longer canoe rentals, gear, and shuttles have been available for
many years at:
Trowbridge Canoe Trips   *(707)433-7247 (800)640-1386*
1 mi. SE at 20 Healdsburg Av.
Healdsburg Veterans Memorial Beach Park   *(707)433-1625*
1 mi. SE at 13839 Old Redwood Hwy.
From Memorial Day into September, the town's beach on the Russian
River is the place to be for swimming and fishing. Nearby are shady
picnic sites, a snack bar and canoe rentals.
Lake Sonoma Recreation Area   *(707)433-9483*
12 mi. NW via Dry Creek Rd. at 3333 Skaggs Springs Rd.
An earthfill dam 319 feet high was completed in 1983 to create a lake
that extends nine miles into oak and grass-covered foothills above Dry
Creek. A visitor center and fish hatchery are open year-round. Other
facilities include a marina, store, swimming beaches, campgrounds, and
hiking and riding trails.
Wineries
More than fifty premium wineries surround Healdsburg in the scenic
Russian River, Dry Creek and Anderson Valleys. Many have tasting,
tours, sales, gift shops and picnic facilities. Unlike Napa Valley
wineries, most of these do not charge tasting fees. The best are among
the outstanding wineries of California.
Alderbrook Winery   *(707)433-9154 (800)405-5987*
1 mi. S at 2306 Magnolia Dr.
The Hospitality Center has premium wine tasting and sales, a gourmet
shop, picnic sites and vineyard views from a wrap-around veranda.
Chateau Souverain   *(707)433-8281*
5 mi. N near US 101 at 400 Souverain Rd. - Geyserville
A landmark chateau surrounded by gardens and vineyards has tasting
facilities, a wine shop and restaurant.
Davis Bynum Winery   *(707)433-5852 (800)826-1073*
8 mi. S at 8075 Westside Rd.
A luxuriant hillside above the Russian River is a charming site for
picnics, and for super-premium wine tasting and sales.
Dry Creek Vineyards   *(707)433-1000 (800)864-9463*
4 mi. NW at 3770 Lambert Bridge Rd.
The deservedly popular winery has a vine-covered building for tasting
and sales, plus gardens and shady picnic areas by vineyards.

Ferrari-Carano Vineyards & Winery   *(707)433-6700*
9 mi. NW at 8761 Dry Creek Rd.
One of wine country's most sophisticated destinations is an urbane
young winery with super-premium (fee) wine tasting, sales and a well-
stocked gourmet shop. Surrounding gardens are magnificent.

Korbel Champagne Cellars   *(707)887-2294*
15 mi. SW at 13250 River Rd. - Guerneville
Korbel, founded in the 1870s by natives of Bohemia, has tastes of
premier sparkling wines, sales, tours, a museum, deli and shop in
landmark buildings.

Lambert Bridge Winery   *(707)431-9600 (800)975-0555*
5 mi. NW at 4085 W. Dry Creek Rd.
Premium wine tasting and sales are in a notably romantic tasting
room. Picnic areas are also charming, and there is a gourmet gift shop.

Quivira Vineyards   *(707)431-8333 (800)292-8339*
6 mi. NW at 4900 W. Dry Creek Rd.
A handsome redwood and cedar building houses premium wine tasting,
sales and gifts. Shaded picnic tables overlook vineyards.

Rodney Strong Vineyards   *(707)431-1533 (800)678-4763*
3 mi. S at 11455 Old Redwood Hwy.
A dramatic, post-modern building houses a skylit premium wine
tasting room and well-stocked gift shop artistically encircled by storage
and barrel-aging areas.

Simi Winery   *(707)433-6981*
1 mi. N at 16275 Healdsburg Av.
Founded in 1876, Simi offers excellent tours, tastes of all premium
wines, gift specialties, and picnic facilities on luxuriant grounds.

RESTAURANTS

Bistro Ralph   *(707)433-1380*
downtown at 109 Plaza St.
L-D.   *Expensive*
Healdsburg's best source for contemporary California cuisine is Bistro
Ralph. The emphasis is on fresh quality seasonal ingredients expertly
prepared in presentations that look and taste as good as they sound on
a short appealing menu. The casual avant garde little bistro dining
area and bar are usually deservedly packed.

Costeaux French Bakery   *(707)433-1913*
downtown at 417 Healdsburg Av.
B-L.   *Moderate*
A fine assortment of breakfast pastries, breads, cakes, pies and cookies
is displayed. Light fare and beverages are also served in the upscale
coffee shop or streetside patio, or to go. Sourdough is a specialty.

John Ash & Co.   *(707)527-7687*
11 mi. S on Hwy. 101 at 4330 Barnes Rd. - Santa Rosa
L-D.   *Very Expensive*
John Ash & Co. is one of California's premier sources of fusion cuisine.
International culinary styles are skillfully blended into bold and
beautiful gourmet delights, from exotic appetizers to superb desserts.
The posh firelit dining room is a peaceful backdrop.

Madrona Manor   *(707)433-6831*
1 mi. W at 1001 Westside Rd.
B-D.   *Very Expensive*
Contemporary California cuisine features herbs and produce from their
garden on a prix-fixe dinner menu. The mansion's comfortably elegant
dining rooms capture a serene Victorian spirit.

Mangia Bene *(707)433-2340*
downtown at 241 Healdsburg Av.
D only.   *Expensive*
The comfort cuisine of Northern Italy is given simple careful attention
in Healdsburg's most popular trattoria/pizzeria. There are also several
housemade desserts including a distinctive cannoli using hazelnuts.
Smart relaxed dining areas contribute to the appealing dishes.

Ravenous Cafe *(707)431-1770*
downtown at 117 North St.
L-D.   *Expensive*
Some of the most innovative cuisine in California includes expertly
prepared selections like braised quail in red wine stuffed with sage
leaves and pancetta, or lime and chipotle-marinated skirt steak with
sauteed sweet peppers. Housemade desserts might be an apple tarte
tatin or a strawberry-rhubarb cobbler. The tiny cheerful dining room
is made more attractive by full linen and candles.

Restaurant Charcuterie *(707)431-7213*
downtown at 335 Healdsburg Av.
L-D.   *Moderate*
Creative California cuisine is well-crafted in dishes like house-cured
pork tenderloin with brown sugar and brandy sauce or chicken strips
piccata. Housemade desserts are equally delicious and distinctive. The
young restaurant has a snazzy dining room with a cozy congestion of
wood-toned tables and chairs and avant-garde art objects.

Singletree Inn *(707)433-8263*
just S at 165 Healdsburg Av.
B-L.   *Moderate*
All-American breakfasts made from scratch have been featured since
1980. Biscuits and gravy with omelets, pancakes, french toast, etc. star
at breakfast, as does homemade apple pie later. The coffee shop offers
a choice of padded booths or chairs.

LODGING

Conventional lodgings by the freeway are surprisingly scarce. Happily,
bed-and-breakfast inns emphasizing history or scenery are numerous.
High season is April through October. Apart from weekends, rates are
as much as 30% less at other times.

Belle de Jour Inn *(707)431-9777*
2 mi. N at 16276 Healdsburg Av. - 95448
5 units   *Expensive-Very Expensive*
Bucolic surroundings contribute to the tranquil feeling of this bed-and-
breakfast inn built around a Victorian farmhouse. Full breakfast is
complimentary. Each unit is beautifully furnished. Most include a gas
or wood fireplace and/or a whirlpool tub for two.

Camellia Inn *(707)433-8182*
just NE at 211 North St. - 95448
9 units   *(800)727-8182*   *Moderate-Expensive*
A villa-styled swimming pool is a feature of this bed-and-breakfast in
an impeccably restored Italianate Victorian townhouse surrounded by
lush gardens and camellia bushes. Full buffet breakfast and afternoon
wine and cheese are complimentary. Each individually decorated room
is beautifully furnished with period touches and contemporary
conveniences including a bathroom. Three rooms also have a gas
fireplace and whirlpool bath for two.

Dry Creek Inn - Best Western   *(707)433-0300*
1 mi. N (near Hwy. 101) at 198 Dry Creek Rd. - 95448
102 units   *(800)222-5784*   *Moderate*
Healdsburg's biggest lodging is a contemporary motel with a small pool, whirlpool, and exercise room. A split of wine and Continental breakfast are complimentary. Each room is well furnished.

Grape Leaf Inn   *(707)433-8140*
just N at 539 Johnson St. - 95448
7 units   *Moderate-Expensive*
A Queen Anne Victorian home has been artistically transformed into a gracious bed-and-breakfast. Full country breakfast and afternoon wines and cheeses are complimentary. Period pieces and contemporary decor including private bathrooms and skylights distinguish each beautifully furnished room. Most also have a whirlpool bath for two.

Healdsburg Inn on the Plaza   *(707)433-6991*
downtown at 110 Matheson St. (Box 1196) - 95448
10 units   *(800)431-8663*   *Expensive*
A historic bank building has been transformed to include a gallery on the first floor and a bed-and-breakfast upstairs. Full complimentary breakfast and afternoon refreshments are served in a cheerful solarium and roof garden. Each beautifully furnished room combines period touches and all contemporary conveniences. Most have a gas fireplace and clawfoot tub. "Garden Suite" also has a big whirlpool tub.

Madrona Manor   *(707)433-4231*
1 mi. W at 1001 Westside Rd. (Box 818) - 95448
20 units   *(800)258-4003   Expensive-Very Expensive*
Madrona Manor is a major wine country landmark. The three-story Victorian (1881) is surrounded by lovely gardens, orchards, and a lush forest on a rise above Dry Creek. Amenities include a pool and gourmet restaurant (see listing). Full breakfast buffet is complimentary. Each room is attractively furnished with stately antiques and contemporary decor. All have private baths. Most have a gas or wood fireplace. "Suite 400" also has a large whirlpool bath.

Villa Messina   *(707)433-6655*
3 mi. NW at 316 Burgundy Rd. - 95448
5 units   *Expensive-Very Expensive*
The historic Simi reservoir site is now a hilltop bed-and-breakfast villa amid colorful gardens, plus a pool and whirlpool. Full breakfast and afternoon wine and appetizers are complimentary. Each beautifully furnished room blends antiques, artworks, and all amenities. Most have a whirlpool tub and/or fireplace. All have a view.

Vintners Inn   *(707)575-7350*
11 mi. S on Hwy. 101 at 4350 Barnes Rd. - Santa Rosa 95403
44 units   *(800)421-2584*   *Expensive*
This French-style country hotel is surrounded by luxuriant vineyards. Amenities include a fine restaurant (see John Ash & Co.) and a tranquil whirlpool. Full buffet breakfast is complimentary. Each room is beautifully furnished. Many have a pressed-wood fireplace and private patio or balcony with a vineyard view.

BASIC INFORMATION

Elevation: 104 feet   Population (1990):   9,469
Location: 70 miles North of San Francisco
Nearest airport with commercial flights: Santa Rosa - 12 miles
Healdsburg Chamber of Commerce & Visitors Bureau   (707)433-6935
*   downtown at 217 Healdsburg Av. - 95448   (800)648-9922 (CA)*

Mendocino, California

Mendocino celebrates a romantic appeal out of place and time. Its "place" is an isolated grassy promontory overlooking a wildly beautiful coastline that could be in Maine. The "time" would be Victorian, since the whole village seems to be of whitewashed wooden buildings from the 19th century. Not surprisingly, the town was settled in the 1850s by lumbermen from New England. After the last mill closed during the Depression, its demise was averted by artists and dreamers attracted by the natural beauty and isolation.

Today, Mendocino's legacy of Yankee-Victorian relics and manicured gardens flourishes. Weathered whitewashed structures house unique specialty shops and galleries displaying fine local arts and crafts, and romantic restaurants. A treasury of aesthetic bed-and-breakfast inns sets the romantic mood for capacity crowds here to browse the village; explore secluded coves, headlands, and redwood forests; or seek tranquility.

WEATHER PROFILE

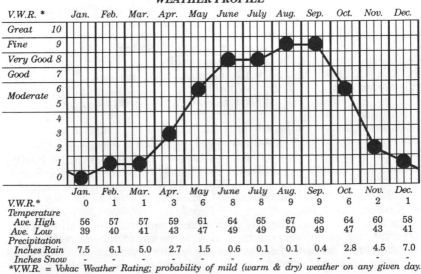

V.W.R. *		Jan.	Feb.	Mar.	Apr.	May	June	July	Aug.	Sep.	Oct.	Nov.	Dec.
Great	10												
Fine	9												
Very Good	8												
Good	7												
Moderate	6 5												
	4 3 2 1 0												

	Jan.	Feb.	Mar.	Apr.	May	June	July	Aug.	Sep.	Oct.	Nov.	Dec.
V.W.R.*	0	1	1	3	6	8	8	9	9	6	2	1
Temperature												
Ave. High	56	57	57	59	61	64	65	67	68	64	60	58
Ave. Low	39	40	41	43	47	49	49	50	49	47	43	41
Precipitation												
Inches Rain	7.5	6.1	5.0	2.7	1.5	0.6	0.1	0.1	0.4	2.8	4.5	7.0
Inches Snow	-	-	-	-	-	-	-	-	-	-	-	-

*V.W.R. = Vokac Weather Rating; probability of mild (warm & dry) weather on any given day.

50

Bicycling
Catch-a-canoe & Bicycles, Too   *(707)937-0273*
1 mi. S off CA 1 at 44850 Comptche-Ukiah Rd.
Bicycles can be rented here by the hour or longer to tour coastal highways and byways that are scenic, but narrow and winding.

Boat Rentals
Catch-a-canoe & Bicycles, Too
1 mi. S off CA 1 at 44850 Comptche-Ukiah Rd.   *(707)937-0273*
Canoe rentals are available from April to October by the hour or day for trips up Big River. It's actually a gentle little river lined by redwood and fir interspersed with sandy beaches and swimming holes. Because the river is tidal for several miles, you can allow the flow of the tides to carry you up and back for a rare experience.

California Western Railroad   *(707)964-6371*   *(800)777-5865*
11 mi. N at foot of Laurel St. - Fort Bragg
The "Skunk" line offers one of America's most scenic train rides. From Fort Bragg on the coast, it twists through forty miles of rugged mountains highlighted by groves of redwoods along the Noyo River to Willits. More than thirty bridges, trestles, and tunnels are along the route—which is inaccessible by car. Diesel and steam trains operate daily year-round. The round trip takes about six hours. Half-day tours in summer months feature open observation cars.

Fishing Charters
9 mi. N on CA 1 - Noyo
Sportfishing is the major year-round attraction in Noyo, a tiny village in a sheltered site near the mouth of the Noyo River. Several oceangoing fishing charters and equipment rentals are especially popular during summer and fall salmon runs.

Jug Handle State Reserve   *(707)937-5804*
5 mi. N on CA 1 - Caspar
At Jug Handle Creek is a remarkable "ecological staircase" phenomenon. Five wave-cut terraces form a staircase with each step holding an ecosystem much older than the one below. On the partially submerged bottom terrace are tidepools with a wealth of marine life. A self-guided nature trail explores all five terraces.

Mendocino Coast Botanical Gardens   *(707)964-4352*
8 mi. N at 18220 CA 1
The **Gardens Grill** (see listing), nursery, and a fine gift shop are at the gardens' entrance. Beyond, miles of self-guided hiking trails wind through natural woods and meadows interspersed with a profusion of rhododendrons, wild lilac, fuchsias, and other seasonal blooms. A fern canyon and rustic bridges extend to a seaside cliff house.

Mendocino Headlands State Park   *(707)937-5397*
surrounding town on S, W, N sides
This park was created to protect natural meadows, wave-carved bluffs, coves, and natural bridges of a promontory that juts into the Pacific around town, and a picturesque sandy beach at the mouth of Big River. Hiking trails, overlooks, picnic sites, and restrooms are well located.

Old Masonic Hall Sculpture
downtown on Lansing St.
Atop a historic building, the whimsical sculpture of Father Time braiding a maiden's hair captures both the artistic and romantic spirit of Mendocino in a century-old piece of whitewashed redwood.

Russian Gulch State Park   *(707)937-5804*
2 mi. N off CA 1

One of the West's great coastal parks includes an idyllic sandy beach where a shallow creek empties into the ocean. Beyond, wave-sculpted headlands reveal coves and tidepools to hikers and beachcombers. In the nearby canyon are shady campsites. A waterfall in a fern-edged grotto highlights an easy five-mile trail.

Van Damme State Park   *(707)937-5804*
2 mi. S off CA 1

Inland from the highway along Little River is a large campground sequestered in a luxuriant pine forest. Nearby is a splendid sandy beach by the stream's outlet. The ocean is inevitably cold for swimming, but ocean kayaking, sport diving and shore fishing are popular. Miles of trails access ocean views, a sword fern canyon, and an ancient pygmy forest of stunted conifers.

Wineries

Vineyards and premium wineries are the major attraction in pretty little Anderson Valley inland from the Mendocino coast. The best produce world-class still or sparkling wines, and are sprinkled along CA 128 near Philo.

Husch Vineyards   *(707)895-3216*
29 mi. SE at 4400 CA 128 - Philo

A wooden cabin houses a pleasant tasting and sales room where their premium wines may be sampled. Tree-shaded picnic tables are nearby.

Navarro Vineyards   *(707)895-3686*   *(800)537-9463*
30 mi. SE at 5601 CA 128 - Philo

A handsome woodcrafted building with vineyard views is used for tasting and sales of the full line of acclaimed super-premium wines—among the author's favorites in the nation. An outdoor deck has picnic tables overlooking gardens and vineyards.

Roederer Estate   *(707)895-2288*
29 mi. SE at 4501 CA 128 - Philo

The American extension of the famed French champagne house offers (fee) sparkling wine tasting and sales in a refined hilltop setting.

Scharffenberger Cellars   *(707)895-2957*   *(800)824-7754*
33 mi. SE at 8501 CA 128 - Philo

A gracious house in a lovely garden is the setting for (fee) tasting and sales of super-premium sparkling wines by the valley's premier producer of sparklers made in the classic French method.

RESTAURANTS

Albion River Inn   *(707)937-1919*
7 mi. S on CA 1 at 3790 N. CA 1 - Albion
D only.   *Expensive*

Albion River Inn Restaurant is one of the two best shoreline dining rooms on the West Coast. Creative California cuisine is expertly prepared using the freshest quality regional ingredients. Examples include Oregon blue cheese salad with raspberry vinaigrette, sauteed petrale sole with rock shrimp and fresh dill, and delectable homemade desserts like fresh peach tart or lemon-poppyseed ice cream. The dining room, perched near the rim of a high bluff, has a window-wall view of gardens and a rocky coast far below. Tables set with full linen, flowers and candles; a stone fireplace; and tony bar also contribute to the romantic ambiance.

Bakeries
Mendocino Bakery & Cafe *10483 Lansing*   *(707)937-0836*
Tote Fete Bakery   *10450 Lansing*   *(707)937-3383*
Mendocino has two fine downtown bakeries displaying a variety of distinctive pastries, desserts and breads that can be enjoyed with assorted beverages and light fare for breakfast and lunch—to go, at a few tables, or in colorful garden patios.

Cafe Beaujolais   *(707)937-5614*
downtown at 961 Ukiah St.
D only.   *Expensive*
The area's premier source of distinctive North Coast cuisine continues to please with acclaimed brick-oven breads, dishes like chicken with kumquat sauce, and homemade desserts like blueberry brioche bread pudding with maple whiskey sauce. A congestion of tables with full linen fills cozy wood-trim dining areas in a converted cottage.

Gardens Grill   *(707)964-7474*
8 mi. N at 18220 N. CA 1 - Fort Bragg
L-D.   *Expensive*
Fresh seasonal fare is featured in contemporary California dishes. The cheerful dining room and umbrella-shaded deck overlook luxuriant gardens. A distinctive gift shop and retail nursery adjoin.

Greenwood Pier Cafe   *(707)877-9997*
16 mi. S at 5928 CA 1 - Elk
B-L-D.   *Expensive*
Innovative North Coast cuisine features vegetables and herbs from their garden; dishes like sage and mustard marinated rabbit or oven-roasted dijon-encrusted rack of lamb with blueberry ginger cabernet reduction; plus housemade ice cream like huckleberry or cranberry mint. The warm plant-filled cafe has a picture-window coast view.

Heritage House   *(707)937-5885*
5 mi. S at 5200 N. CA 1 - Little River
B-D.   *Expensive*
Heritage House, one of America's most celebrated and historic inns, puts culinary emphasis on fresh regional products for creative country cuisine, breads, and desserts. Three elegant dining rooms, including a magnificent domed room, share a spectacular ocean view. So does the handsome firelit lounge.

The Ledford House Restaurant   *(707)937-0282*
8 mi. S at 3000 N. CA 1 - Albion
D only.   *Expensive*
Innovative seasonally fresh California cuisine is expertly prepared into dishes like crisp roasted duckling with strawberry rhubarb sauce. All breads and desserts are homemade (try the avocado cream pie when available). Plush widely spaced tables enhance a large dining room and lounge with a grand window-wall view to the ocean.

Little River Inn   *(707)937-5942*
3 mi. S at 7751 N. CA 1 - Little River
B-D.   *Expensive*
The landmark inn has a nice way with Swedish pancakes and other breakfast specialties. Fresh regional seafood, steaks, and housemade desserts are featured each evening. The gracious dining room (the focal point of a pre-Civil War mansion) has an intimate picture-window view of an enchanting garden.

MacCallum House Restaurant   *(707)937-5763*
downtown at 45020 Albion St.
D only.   *Expensive*
A North Coast grazing menu features seasonally fresh flavorful dishes
and luscious homemade desserts like a praline cookie taco with a
sampling of six ice creams, or a lemon curd Napoleon with mint creme.
The inn's firelit dining room is intimate and charming, as is the cozy
bar with an enclosed dining porch.

Moosse Cafe   *(707)937-4323*
downtown at 10390 Kasten St.
L-D.   *Expensive*
Light and lively California cafe cuisine is served with luscious desserts.
The blackout cake is a mighty must for chocoholics. A fireplace lends
cheer to warm wood tones in the popular cafe.

955 Ukiah Street   *(707)937-1955*
downtown at 955 Ukiah St.
D only.   *Expensive*
At 955 Ukiah Street is some of the finest cuisine on the North Coast.
Seasonally fresh quality ingredients from the region are skillfully
transformed into dishes like boneless salmon filets with apple cider
vinaigrette, chicken with wild mushroom sauce, and exotic desserts like
mango sorbet. A lofty wood-trim dining room is enhanced by tables set
with full linen, and pots brimming with healthy greenery.

North Coast Brewing Company   *(707)964-3400*
11 mi. N at 444 N. Main St. - Fort Bragg
L-D.   *Moderate*
Pub grub becomes cuisine through creative use of seasonally fresh
ingredients and fresh seafood. The wood-trim pub and dining room are
separated by a brew kettle display area in a historic building.

LODGING

In town and along the nearby coast is one of America's great
concentrations of romantic inns. The area's only moderately-priced
rooms are in motels in nearby Fort Bragg. High season is May-into-
October weekends. Winter weekdays may be 10% less.

Albion River Inn   *(707)937-1919*
7 mi. S at 3790 N. CA 1 (Box 100) - Albion 95410
20 units   *(800)479-7944*   *Expensive-Very Expensive*
Albion River Inn is one of the West's great getaways. Stylish
contemporary cottages blend gracefully into lush gardens along a bluff
high above a spectacular little harbor. The gourmet restaurant (see
listing) maximizes the enchanting view, and serves breakfast to guests.
A bottle of premium local wine in your room is also complimentary.
Each luxuriously furnished room is a study in tasteful individual decor
that captures the romantic feeling of the historic site, and has both an
ocean view and fireplace. Some also have a large ocean-view whirlpool
and private deck.

Captain's Cove Inn   *(707)937-5150*
downtown at 44781 Main St. (Box 803) - 95460
5 units   *(800)780-7905*   *Expensive*
Captain's Cove Inn is the only oceanfront lodging in town. The bed-
and-breakfast crowns a bluff overlooking Big River and the coast. A
sumptuous country breakfast is complimentary. Each uniquely
designed room is beautifully furnished. All rooms have a private
entrance, private bath, wood stove or fireplace, and an ocean view.
Most have a private deck.

Greenwood Pier Inn   *(707)877-9997*
16 mi. S at 5928 CA 1 (Box 336) - Elk 95432
12 units   *Expensive-Very Expensive*
The coastal view of sea-carved arches from Greenwood Pier Inn is
unsurpassed. The delightful woodcrafted complex atop an ocean bluff
includes a fine cafe (see listing), first-rate country store, garden shop
and cottages in a luxuriant garden-by-the-sea. Complimentary
Continental breakfast is delivered to your room. Each beautifully
furnished room has a private bath (no TV or phone) and artistic
expressions everywhere. Most have an awesome sea view and a
fireplace. Several also have a view bathtub or whirlpool.

Heritage House   *(707)937-5885*
5 mi. S at 5200 N. CA 1 - Little River 95456
66 units   *(800)235-5885   Expensive-Very Expensive*
The most celebrated inn along California's north coast is a luxurious
and romantic complex of New England-style cottages sprinkled among
expansive gardens on a hillside above a picturesque ocean cove.
Amenities include scenic hiking trails, an elegant dining room (see
listing) and lounge, and a fine country store. Spacious units range from
beautifully furnished old-fashioned rooms to luxuriously furnished
suites. All have a private bath—no TV or phone. Most have a fireplace
or wood stove, and a grand ocean view. Some also have a whirlpool tub
and private deck.

Joshua Grindle Inn   *(707)937-4143*
downtown at 44800 Little Lake Rd. (Box 647) - 95460
10 units   *(800)474-6353*   *Expensive*
A landmark 1879 home is now a lovely bed-and-breakfast surrounded
by gardens. Full breakfast is complimentary. Each beautifully
furnished room features American antiques and a private bathroom (no
phone or TV). Many have a fireplace and an ocean/town view.

Little River Inn   *(707)937-5942*
3 mi. S at 7751 N. CA 1 (Drawer B) - Little River 95456
65 units   *(888)466-5683   Expensive-Very Expensive*
The area's only 9-hole golf course (with a driving range, putting green,
pro shop and fine ocean view) and tennis courts are features of this
classic New England-style resort on extensive well-landscaped grounds
near the ocean. There is also a fine restaurant (see listing) and lounge.
Each beautifully furnished unit has a country modern flair, an ocean
view and all contemporary conveniences. Newer spacious rooms also
have a view deck, fireplace and a large whirlpool bath.

MacCallum House Inn   *(707)937-0289*
downtown at 45020 Albion St. (Box 206) - 95460
19 units   *(800)609-0492*   *Expensive*
One of Mendocino's premier inns includes a stately 1882 home that
may be the most photographed building in town. The recently
upgraded complex amid colorful gardens has a fine restaurant (see
listing) and lounge. Each compact, beautifully furnished room has a
private bath (no phone or TV) and artistic period touches. Many also
have a fireplace, whirlpool, or clawfoot tub for two.

Mendocino Hotel & Garden Suites   *(707)937-0511*
downtown at 45080 Main St. (Box 587) - 95460
51 units   *(800)548-0513   Moderate-Very Expensive*
Perhaps the most visible symbol of Mendocino's Yankee heritage is this
three-story hotel built in 1878. The firelit lobby, bar and dining room

decorated with Victorian antiques, reproductions and artifacts have a kind of movie set pizzazz. Rooms range from small and comfortably furnished to large suites with a fireplace and ocean view.

Reed Manor   *(707)937-5446*
just N off Palette Dr. (Box 127) - 95460
5 units   *Expensive-Very Expensive*
The most beguiling landmark built to serve as an elegant bed-and-breakfast inn tops a hill above town. Light breakfast served to the room and evening beverage are complimentary. Each extra-large room is luxuriously furnished with a seamless blend of period pieces and all contemporary conveniences, including a gas fireplace, a large whirlpool bath, and a private deck. Most have a town/ocean view.

Stanford Inn by the Sea   *(707)937-5615*
1 mi. SE at CA 1 & Comptche - Ukiah Rd. (Box 487) - 95460
40 units   *(800)331-8884   Expensive-Very Expensive*
Stanford Inn by the Sea is Mendocino's most complete bed-and-breakfast resort. Contemporary wood trimmed buildings crown a spacious slope above the sea, where organic gardens of herbs, spices, vegetables and edible flowers—and a herd of curious llamas—contribute to the colorful scene. **The Ravens** (B-D) features creative gourmet vegetarian fare in a congenial setting. Hiking trails lead to a tranquil river and rental canoes. Other amenities include bicycles, a lush greenhouse pool, whirlpool, sauna and exercise room. Full gourmet breakfast, afternoon snacks, and evening wine and appetizers are complimentary. Each luxuriously furnished room has artistic touches and all contemporary conveniences. Most have a private ocean view deck and a fireplace or wood stove.

Stevenswood Lodge   *(707)937-2810*
2 mi. S at 8211 N. CA 1 (Box 170) - 95460
10 units   *(800)421-2810*   *Expensive*
Stevenswood Lodge is preeminent among the North Coast's newer bed-and-breakfasts. The urbane wood-trimmed complex is tucked away amid colorful gardens enhanced by sculptures in a luxuriant forest a short hike from the ocean. Full gourmet breakfast and evening wine and appetizers are complimentary. Each spacious, luxuriously furnished room blends handcrafted hardwood furniture; fine contemporary art; picture window views of forests, gardens, and (some) distant ocean; a fireplace; and all contemporary conveniences.

Surf 'n Sand Lodge   *(707)964-9383*
12 mi. N at 1131 N. Main St. - Fort Bragg 95437
30 units   *(800)964-0184   Moderate-Expensive*
Fort Bragg's finest accommodations are at Surf 'n Sand Lodge which opened in 1996. A long sandy beach lies just beyond a broad meadow by this handsome motel. Each room is well furnished. Most have a good ocean view and a private balcony. Six upstairs units also have a gas fireplace and a two-person in-room whirlpool.

BASIC INFORMATION

Elevation: 60 feet   Population (1990):   1,100
Location: 155 miles Northwest of San Francisco
Nearest airport with commercial flights: Santa Rosa - 95 miles
Fort Bragg-Mendocino Coast Chamber of Commerce   (707)961-6300
11 mi. N on CA 1 at 332 N. Main St. (Box 1141) - Fort Bragg 95437
(800)726-2780
www.mendocinocoast.com

Monterey, California

Monterey is a bonanza of superlative history and geography. It covers a gentle plain between pine-forested hills of the Monterey Peninsula and Monterey Bay—a sheltered inlet of the Pacific Ocean. The idyllic site became the first permanent settlement in California when Spain established a presidio here in 1770. Monterey was a regional capital for Spain until 1822, and for Mexico until 1846 when the United States annexed California. For the next hundred years, the town served as a maritime center.

Today, Cannery Row and Fisherman's Wharf are ingenious, playful transformations from an earlier hard-working era. Downtown, a treasury of historic landmarks blends with urbane shops and galleries. Gourmet and view restaurants are plentiful, and nightlife is diverse and exuberant. Accommodations of all kinds are abundant. So are year-round crowds, due to an unusually mild climate and seemingly endless opportunities for offshore and onshore recreation.

WEATHER PROFILE

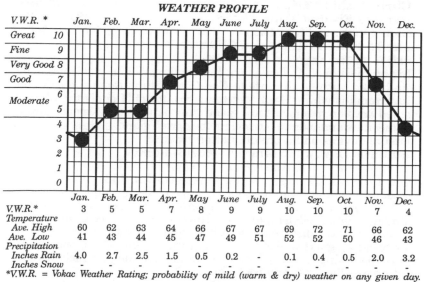

V.W.R.*		Jan.	Feb.	Mar.	Apr.	May	June	July	Aug.	Sep.	Oct.	Nov.	Dec.
Great	10												
Fine	9												
Very Good	8												
Good	7												
Moderate	6												
	5												
	4												
	3												
	2												
	1												
	0												

	Jan.	Feb.	Mar.	Apr.	May	June	July	Aug.	Sep.	Oct.	Nov.	Dec.
V.W.R.*	3	5	5	7	8	9	9	10	10	10	7	4
Temperature												
Ave. High	60	62	63	64	66	67	67	69	72	71	66	62
Ave. Low	41	43	44	45	47	49	51	52	52	50	46	43
Precipitation												
Inches Rain	4.0	2.7	2.5	1.5	0.5	0.2	-	0.1	0.4	0.5	2.0	3.2
Inches Snow	-	-	-	-	-	-	-	-	-	-	-	-

*V.W.R. = Vokac Weather Rating; probability of mild (warm & dry) weather on any given day.

Bicycling

There are exclusive bike paths like the bayside Monterey Peninsula Recreational Trail and scenic routes like the renowned Seventeen Mile Drive. Rentals and information are offered at:

Adventures By the Sea *1 mi. NW at 299 Cannery Row* *(831)372-1807*
Bay Bikes *1 mi. NW at 640 Wave St.* *(831)646-9090*
Cannery Row *(831)649-6690*
starts just NW along Cannery Row

A few hulking cannery buildings and overpasses across Cannery Row still capture some of the flavor of the times before sardines vanished from Monterey Bay around 1950. The noise and smell described in John Steinbeck's *Cannery Row* are gone—replaced by imaginative shops, restaurants and night spots that have brought bright lights, the sound of music, and the smell of good food to ingeniously renovated old buildings and elaborate new structures. The Row is also a staging area for one of America's best beach dives. A unique underwater canyon, kelp forest and abundant sea life in the Monterey Bay National Marine Sanctuary are accessible from shore at San Carlos Beach.

Fisherman's Wharf *(831)373-0600*
downtown at the N end of Olivier St.

Original commercial fishing activities that operated here are long gone. The wharf remains and the over-water buildings have evolved into a colorful potpourri of shops, restaurants, and open-air fish markets. Swarms of visitors are drawn by the bracing nautical atmosphere, marine views, close-up glimpses of harbor seals and sea otters, and the peninsula's major terminus for sportfishing and sightseeing boats.

Fishing Charters

downtown on Fisherman's Wharf

Several sportfishing boats leave daily year-round for deep sea fishing, and salmon fishing in season. Memorable winter whale watching excursions and narrated sightseeing cruises are also featured. The following operators, located on Fisherman's Wharf, offer these services and all necessary equipment:

Chris' Fishing Trips *(831)375-5951*
Randy's Fishing Trips *(831)372-7440*
Sam's Fishing Fleet Inc. *(831)372-0577*
Lake El Estero Park *(831)646-3866*
just E on 3rd St.

This big park next to downtown has walkways and picnic areas by a small lake with boat rentals. For family fun, Dennis the Menace Playground is where Hank Ketcham, creator of "Dennis the Menace," helped develop free-form "hands-on" play equipment. Narrow tunnels, balanced roundabouts, swinging bridges, giant slides, and other unusual devices entice children of all ages.

Monterey Bay Aquarium *(831)648-4888*
1 mi. NW at 886 Cannery Row

One of the world's largest aquariums opened in 1984 in a completely remodeled cannery complex. Visitors are given a unique and exciting view of the native inhabitants of Monterey Bay—sea otters, octopus, salmon, sharks, jellyfish, and five hundred other species of flora and fauna in a naturalistic setting. A highlight is a three-story kelp forest in a towering glass-walled tank. In addition to more than one hundred close-up viewing tanks and six giant tanks, the complex includes a cafe and an excellent gift-and-book shop.

Monterey State Historic Park   *(831)649-7118*
downtown at #20 Custom House Plaza
More than two centuries of impressive history and architectural heritage in California's oldest town is carefully preserved on a seven acre site near Fisherman's Wharf, and in numerous downtown buildings that have been restored and furnished in period antiques. The **Maritime Museum of Monterey** showcases the area's nautical heritage. The **Custom House** (1821) is the oldest government building in California. The **First Theater** (1846) was a sailors' lodging house and the first place in California to charge admission for theatrical performances. Today, Victorian melodramas are performed year-round. **Larkin House** (1834), combining Spanish-Colonial and New England architectural features, became a prototype copied throughout California. Robert Lewis Stevenson boarded and wrote in the **Stevenson House** in 1879. **Colton Hall** (1848), the first American public building in California, was where the state's first constitution was written in 1849. **Royal Presidio Chapel**, the only one of California's four Spanish presidio chapels still standing, has been in continuous use since 1795.

Moped Rentals
Motorized bicycles provide an exhilarating and relatively effortless way to tour the scenic peninsula. For hourly and longer rentals, call:
   Monterey Moped Co.   *1 mi. E at 1250 Del Monte Av. (831)373-2696*

Wineries
Many good wineries are within an hour's drive of Monterey. Two have tasting facilities in town.
   Bargetto Winery   *(831)373-4053*
   1 mi. NW at 700-L Cannery Row
Natural fruit wines, as well as premium varietals, are offered for tastes and sales daily in a pleasant facility with a notable gift shop.
   Ventana   *(831)372-7415*
   5 mi. SE on CA 68 at 2999 Monterey/Salinas Hwy.
A wide range of premium wines is available for tasting and sales in an old limestone building.

RESTAURANTS
Cafe Fina   *(831)372-5200*
downtown at 47 Fisherman's Wharf
L-D.   *Expensive*
Fine New California cuisine is showcased in delicious mesquite barbecued fish, homemade pastas and raviolis, and wood-fired pizzas. Daily fresh seafood dishes are especially appealing in this trim, stylish restaurant overlooking the inner harbor.
Cibo Ristorante   *(831)649-8151*
downtown at 301 Alvarado St.
D only.   *Expensive*
Pasta, pizza and grill dishes with a Sicilian emphasis are well regarded on a grazing menu offered in a large modish dining room.
The Clock Garden   *(831)375-6100*
downtown at 565 Abrego St.
L-D.   *Moderate*
Contemporary American comfort foods include some regional treats like cold poached artichoke and nifty housemade desserts in this local landmark. A warm wood-toned dining room and bar overlook a whimsical clock in a garden pond. A picturesque patio adjoins.

Domenico's   *(831)372-3655*
downtown at 50 Fisherman's Wharf
L-D.   *Expensive*
Fresh fish and prime steaks grilled on an open hearth over mesquite wood, plus homemade pasta, distinguish this long-time favorite. Windows in the plush contemporary dining room overlook the inner harbor.

Fresh Cream Restaurant   *(831)375-9798*
downtown at 99 Pacific St.
D only.   *Very Expensive*
Fresh Cream is one of California's premier dining landmarks. Splendid traditional French cuisine like roast rack of lamb or poached salmon with champagne cream sauce share billing with creative California delights like wild abalone sauteed with lemon sauce. Housemade desserts like hazelnut chip/vanilla ice cream are similarly memorable. Many widely spaced tables in the elegant dining rooms provide an intimate, romantic view of Fisherman's Wharf and the bay.

Montrio   *(831)648-8880*
downtown at 414 Calle Principal
L-D.   *Expensive*
A well-thought-out grazing menu of European-inspired contemporary American dishes has made this young restaurant an early winner. Stylish dining rooms have been fashioned within a historic Monterey firehouse along with an expo kitchen, rotisserie and whimsical bar.

Sardine Factory   *(831)373-3775*
1 mi. N at 701 Wave St.
D only.   *Very Expensive*
Fresh local seafood has distinguished the peninsula's longest-established gourmet dinner house for more than three decades. Traditional dishes include peerless abalone bisque, and there is a long list of luscious desserts. The capacious restaurant offers a variety of elegant dining settings, including a gilt and rococo firelit Victorian room and a grand glass-domed conservatory.

Stokes Adobe   *(831)373-1110*
downtown at 500 Hartnell St.
L-D.   *Expensive*
Southern Mediterranean classics are skillfully translated into a flavorful selection of cutting edge California cuisine with meticulous emphasis on freshness, quality, and regional sources. The culinary appeal of this restaurant that opened in 1996 is coupled with charmingly unpretentious dining rooms in a historic adobe.

Tarpy's Roadhouse   *(831)625-2999*
5 mi. SE at 2999 Monterey-Salinas Hwy. (Hwy. 68)
L-D.   *Expensive*
Zesty New California cuisine ranging from smoky barbeque baby back ribs to honey-mustard rabbit is served on a grazing menu that also describes a variety of luscious housemade desserts. A historic rock-sided roadhouse now includes several whimsically romantic firelit dining areas and an alfresco garden patio.

Triples   *(831)372-4744*
downtown at 220 Olivier St.
D only.   *Very Expensive*
Creative California dishes including homemade desserts are served in posh, intimate dining areas of a historic building and in a romantic outdoor garden patio.

Whaling Station   *(831)373-3778*
1 mi. N at 763 Wave St.
D only.   *Expensive*
Oak-grilled specialties like 22-ounce Porterhouse steak and fresh
seafoods highlight a grazing menu of contemporary and traditional
California cuisine. The large, recently remodeled restaurant remains
one of the peninsula's long-time favorite dinner houses.

LODGING

Lodgings are abundant and diverse including resorts, beachfront motor
inns, and gracious bed-and-breakfasts. Fremont Street is the place to
find the peninsula's less expensive motels. June-to-October is high
season. Non-weekend winter rates may be 30% less.

Doubletree Hotel   *(831)649-4511*
downtown at 2 Portola Plaza - 93940
380 units   *(800)222-8733   Expensive-Very Expensive*
This modern convention-oriented hotel is a six-story landmark between
downtown and Fisherman's Wharf. Amenities include a pool, whirlpool,
(fee) parking, restaurant, bay-view entertainment lounge, and shops.
Each room is well furnished. Some have a fine bay view.

Hotel Pacific   *(831)373-5700*
downtown at 300 Pacific St. - 93940
105 units   *(800)554-5542   Expensive-Very Expensive*
Downtown Monterey's best lodging is a four-story all-suites hotel with
intimate garden courtyards with whirlpools. An expanded Continental
breakfast buffet and afternoon refreshments are complimentary. Each
beautifully furnished suite has a gas fireplace and private deck.

Hyatt Regency Monterey   *(831)372-1234*
1 mi. SE at 1 Old Golf Course Rd. - 93940
575 units   *(800)233-1234   Expensive-Very Expensive*
A scenic 18-hole golf course adjoins this well-landscaped four-story
resort. Amenities include (fee) golf, six tennis courts, and rental
bicycles, plus two pools, two whirlpools, exercise room, health club,
restaurant, and entertainment lounge. Many well-furnished rooms and
suites were recently redecorated and have golf course views.

The Mariposa Inn   *(831)649-1414*
1 mi. S at 1386 Munras Av. - 93940
50 units   *(800)824-2295   Moderate-Expensive*
The best of "motel row" is the Mariposa, a contemporary motel with a
garden court pool and whirlpool. Many of the well-furnished units have
a raised gas fireplace. Spacious, beautifully furnished "Honeymoon
Suites" also have a large in-room whirlpool.

Monterey Bay Inn   *(831)373-6242*
1 mi. N at 242 Cannery Row - 93940
47 units   *(800)424-6242   Expensive-Very Expensive*
Monterey's finest motel has a spectacular site by a sandy cove and
marine sanctuary on the bay at the quiet end of Cannery Row. The
posh, post-modern complex also features a rooftop bay-view whirlpool,
sauna, fitness room, and garage. Most of the beautifully furnished
rooms have a window wall and large private balcony with an ocean
view. Waves lap under the enchanting rooms on the bay side.

Monterey Beach Hotel - Best Western   *(831)394-3321*
2 mi. E at 2600 Sand Dunes Dr. - 93940
196 units   *(800)242-8627   Moderate-Expensive*
A fine sandy beach adjoins this modern four-story hotel that also has

a pool, whirlpool, exercise room, restaurant and lounge. Many of the well-furnished rooms have a dramatic view of the beach and bay, and downtown in the distance.

Monterey Marriott   *(831)649-4234*
downtown at 350 Calle Principal - 93940
341 units   *(800)228-9290   Expensive-Very Expensive*
Monterey's tallest landmark is a plain, modern ten-story convention-oriented hotel near the heart of downtown and the waterfront. Amenities include a pool, whirlpool, exercise room, (fee) parking, rooftop restaurant with a window-wall panorama, sports bar and gift shop. Many of the well-furnished rooms have a bay view.

Monterey Plaza Hotel   *(831)646-1700   (800)334-3999 (CA)*
1 mi. N at 400 Cannery Row - 93940
285 units   *(800)631-1339   Expensive-Very Expensive*
Monterey's most sumptuous full-service hotel opened in 1985 on a choice bayfront location on Cannery Row. The five-story complex is a classic of urbane renewal. There is beach access, an exercise room, (fee) valet parking, gift shop, and view lounge, plus **The Duck Club** (B-L-D —Expensive) where New California cuisine features wood-roasted meats from an expo kitchen served in a casually elegant setting with a superb bay view. Each room is beautifully furnished. Many have a private balcony by the bay.

Old Monterey Inn   *(831)375-8284*
just SW at 500 Martin St. - 93940
10 units   *(800)350-2344   Expensive-Very Expensive*
The most delightful bed-and-breakfast in town is in a historic mansion sequestered amid English gardens a stroll from downtown. Bountiful gourmet breakfast and evening repasts are complimentary. Each spacious, individually decorated room is beautifully furnished with antiques and contemporary touches including a private bath. Many rooms also have a fireplace, and one has a whirlpool bath.

Spindrift Inn   *(831)646-8900*
1 mi. N at 652 Cannery Row - 93940
42 units   *(800)841-1879   Expensive-Very Expensive*
The Spindrift Inn is a gracious getaway above a picturesque beach in the midst of Cannery Row. Valet (fee) parking and waterfront dining are available. Extended Continental breakfast is delivered to your room, and afternoon refreshments and appetizers are complimentary. Each individually decorated, beautifully furnished room has a fireplace and window seat or balcony. Many have a bayfront view.

BASIC INFORMATION

Elevation: 40 feet   Population (1990):   31,954
Location: 120 miles South of San Francisco
Nearest airport with commercial flights: in town
Monterey Peninsula Visitors & Convention Bureau   (831)649-1770
   downtown at 380 Alvarado St. (Box 1770) - 93942
   Info Center just E at Franklin St. & Camino El Estero
   www.monterey.com

Nevada City, California

Nevada City is the picturesque essence of the Mother Lode country. Handsome Victorian homes and businesses line narrow streets that wind through steep forested foothills of the Sierra Nevada. Placer gold was abundant in 1849 when miners founded the town. By 1856 it was California's third largest city with nearly ten thousand residents. After a disastrous fire that year, more substantial businesses were constructed of brick—with iron doors and shutters.

Gold mines and foundries have long since played out. Today, one of the West's most unspoiled Victorian business districts, still illuminated by gas lamps, is the priceless legacy of Nevada City's brief boom era. Downtown is a treasury of historic public buildings; theater and churches; specialty shops featuring Mother Lode artifacts; and blocks of good restaurants, atmospheric bars and saloons; plus the oldest operating hotel west of the Rockies. Nearby forests, lakes, rivers and mountains support all kinds of recreation—even gold panning.

WEATHER PROFILE

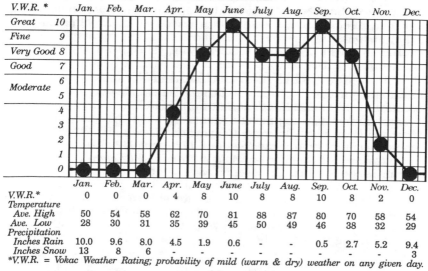

		Jan.	Feb.	Mar.	Apr.	May	June	July	Aug.	Sep.	Oct.	Nov.	Dec.
V.W.R.*		0	0	0	4	8	10	8	8	10	8	2	0
Temperature													
Ave. High		50	54	58	62	70	81	88	87	80	70	58	54
Ave. Low		28	30	31	35	39	45	50	49	46	38	32	29
Precipitation													
Inches Rain		10.0	9.6	8.0	4.5	1.9	0.6	-	-	0.5	2.7	5.2	9.4
Inches Snow		13	8	6	-	-	-	-	-	-	-	-	3

*V.W.R. = Vokac Weather Rating; probability of mild (warm & dry) weather on any given day.

63

Covered Bridge
14 mi. W in Bridgeport
Built in 1862, the longest single-span wood-covered bridge in America extends 225 feet across the South Yuba River at Bridgeport. Scenic hiking trails continue along the canyon to secluded picnic sites and swimming holes.

Empire Mine State Historic Park   *(530)273-8522*
5 mi. S at 10791 E. Empire St. - Grass Valley
California's oldest and richest gold mine is also one of the deepest (9,000 feet) in the world. The grounds include a visitor center, mining exhibits, and the baronial Bourn Mansion. This former residence of the mine owner has been carefully restored and refurbished, as have the formal gardens surrounding the mansion. Guided tours are offered daily, except in winter.

Malakoff Diggins State Historic Park   *(530)265-2740*
15 mi. NE off CA 49
Here from the 1850s to the 1880s was the world's largest hydraulic gold mine. The Malakoff Pit is an awesome testament to the destructive power of water under high pressure. It is a vast hole nearly 600 feet deep, and more than a mile long. A former dance hall is now a Park Museum with hydraulic mining exhibits. Nearby is the giant monitor nozzle that controlled the flow of water against the slopes.

Miners Foundry Cultural Center   *(530)265-5040*
downtown at 325 Spring St.
The historic Miners Foundry (1856) is a group of stone, brick and frame buildings in which the Pelton Wheel (a key link between the water wheel and modern power generation) was first manufactured in 1879. Historic artifacts are exhibited throughout. Great stone walls provide a unique backdrop for performing arts that are staged here year-round.

North Star Mining Museum   *(530)273-4255*
4.5 mi. SW at the south end of Mill St. - Grass Valley
A giant thirty-foot Pelton waterwheel displayed here was the largest of its type in the world when it was installed in 1895. The massive old powerhouse has been transformed into a museum housing a substantial collection of artifacts depicting the history and methods of California gold mining.

Tahoe National Forest   *(530)265-4531*
N and E of town
All of the Sierra Nevada mountains between Nevada City and Lake Tahoe are included in this spectacular forest. Features near town include numerous campgrounds, and miles of well-maintained trails for hiking and backpacking along scenic canyons of the many-branched Yuba and Bear River drainages. Idyllic clear pools attract swimmers, and miles of whitewater rapids appeal to rafters, kayakers, and latter-day Argonauts. In winter, an hour's drive east of town accesses the **Royal Gorge Nordic Ski Resort**, with perhaps the largest system of constantly maintained cross-country ski trails anywhere. Nearby, the historic **Donner Pass** area is the site of several fully developed downhill skiing complexes. An hour beyond lies **Squaw Valley Ski Area** (legacy of the 1960 winter Olympics) and the northwestern shore of Lake Tahoe with facilities for every imaginable water and alpine sport.

Wineries

Indian Springs Vineyards   *(530)478-1068*
downtown at 303 Broad St.
The downtown tasting room and store showcase several award-winning varietals from their Gold Country vineyards.

Nevada City Winery   *(530)265-9463*
downtown at 321 Spring St.
Nevada County's premier premium winery is in the historic foundry complex. A tasting room and shop are dramatically and aromatically perched at the top of wine storage and aging areas.

RESTAURANTS

Cafe Mekka   *(530)478-1517*
downtown at 237 Commercial St.
B-L-D.   *Moderate*
International dishes and spectacular desserts can be enjoyed with coffees, teas and other beverages in this fancifully funky coffeehouse with a wealth of art objects scattered among overstuffed furniture.

Cirino's Italian Restaurant   *(530)265-2246*
downtown at 309 Broad St.
L-D.   *Moderate*
Traditional Italian veal, lamb, seafood and pastas are served in an atmospheric dining room and bar that is a local favorite.

The Country Rose Cafe   *(530)265-6252*
downtown at 300 Commercial St.
L-D.   *Expensive*
Seasonal fresh seafood is featured among first-rate country French cuisine with an innovative flair served in a historic brick building. Warm intimate dining areas complement deservedly popular dishes. So does outdoor seating amid lush greenery.

Friar Tuck's Restaurant   *(530)265-9093*
downtown at 111 N. Pine St.
D only.   *Expensive*
The Gold Camp's finest fondues star, along with steaks, seafood and fowl, in a historic building refitted in brick-and-wood wine cellar decor. The charming little front room bar has a good street view and live entertainment, plus several tap beers and premium wine by the glass.

Happy Apple Kitchen   *(530)273-2822*
11 mi. S via CA 49 at 18532 Colfax Hwy. (CA 174) - Chicago Park
L only.   *Moderate*
Apples are showcased year-round in delectable homemade foods like apple/cream cheese muffins, apple milkshakes, and French apple pie. They're served with lunch fare in a cheerful dining room, on an orchard-view porch, to go, and at a (seasonal) produce stand.

Hollywood Sweets   *(530)272-4470*
2 mi. SE via CA 20 at 12041 Sutton Way - Grass Valley 95945
B-L.   *Moderate*
Hollywood Sweets has one of the West's great bonanzas of baked goods. Delicious pastries, pies, cakes, cookies and luscious exotic items like peppermint kiss, cinnamon sticks, or cocoa puffs, plus breads, rolls and bagels, are displayed in capacious cases by the posh coffee shop.

Kirby's Creekside Restaurant & Bar   *(530)265-3445*
downtown at 101 Broad St.
L-D.   *Moderate*
Kirby's has some of the area's best creative California cuisine in dishes like seafood ravioli with chardonnay cream sauce or smoked stuffed

pork chop with orange port sauce. A stylish dining room and an upstairs bar adjoin Nevada City's only creekside dining deck.

Old Nevada Brewery & Restaurant   *(530)265-3960*
downtown at 107 Sacramento St.
L-D.   *Moderate*
Traditional and innovative California pub grub is taken seriously as an accompaniment to premium brews produced here. The Brewery reopened in 1997 after being closed for nearly a century. The fieldstone landmark includes a plush firelit bar, a kettle-view dining room, beer garden, and historic storage caves (highlight of the tour).

Posh Nosh   *(530)265-6064*
downtown at 318 Broad St.
L-D.   *Moderate*
Designer burgers, sandwiches and pastas highlight lively, hearty fare served in a cozy cellar dining room or alfresco in season.

Sweet Home Bakery   *(530)265-0572*
1 mi. S at 104 Argall Way
B-L.   *Moderate*
The Sweet Home Bakery is one of the Gold Camp's best. Many of the flavorful muffins, croissants, cinnamon rolls, scones and bagels, plus assorted breads, pies, cakes and cookies, feature whole wheat flour—all are delicious served at a few tables or to go.

LODGING

Accommodations are scarce, but distinctive. Many are in historic buildings. High season is weekends from spring through fall. Winter weekday prices may be reduced at least 15%.

Downey House   *(530)265-2815*
downtown at 517 W. Broad St. - 95959
6 units   *(800)258-2815*   *Moderate*
One of the prettiest Victorian homes is an outstanding bed-and-breakfast surrounded by colorful gardens. Full buffet breakfast and afternoon refreshments are complimentary. Each room is beautifully furnished with a contemporary Southwestern motif.

The Emma Nevada House   *(530)265-4415*
just N at 528 E. Broad St. - 95959
6 units   *(800)916-3662*   *Expensive*
An 1856 Victorian home has been impeccably transformed into a gracious bed-and-breakfast. A full gourmet breakfast and afternoon tea and cookies are complimentary. Each of the beautifully furnished rooms has a private bath (two have a whirlpool) and some stylish antiques.

Flume's End   *(530)265-9665*
downtown at 317 S. Pine St. - 95959
6 units   *(800)991-8118*   *Moderate-Expensive*
A charming creek, little waterfalls and lush woods distinguish this restored Victorian bed-and-breakfast. Full breakfast is complimentary. Each room is individually well furnished. Some have a private deck and a peaceful waterfall view. Two also have a whirlpool bath.

Grandmère's Bed & Breakfast   *(530)265-4660*
downtown at 449 Broad St. - 95959
7 units   *Expensive*
A stately whitewashed pre-Civil War inn amid a lovely garden is now a picturesque bed-and-breakfast. Full breakfast and evening cookies and drinks are complimentary. Each beautifully furnished unit features period decor, whimsical touches and a private tub.

Kendall House   *(530)265-0405*
just NW at 534 Spring St. - 95959
5 units   *Expensive*
Contemporary furnishings blend with whitewashed Victorian architecture in this bed-and-breakfast. A picket fence surrounds lawns and gardens with a pool as a centerpiece. Full breakfast is complimentary. Each room is beautifully furnished.

M. L. Marsh House   *(530)265-5709*
just NE at 254 Boulder St. - 95959
6 units   *(800)874-7458*   *Expensive*
One of Nevada City's most gracious homes, built in 1873, is a bed-and-breakfast surrounded by lovely gardens. Full gourmet breakfast and afternoon refreshments are complimentary. Each room is beautifully furnished, including many museum-quality period pieces. The "Parlor Suite" has its original tiled fireplace.

The National Hotel   *(530)265-4551*
downtown at 211 Broad St. - 95959
42 units   *Moderate-Expensive*
Nevada City's biggest landmark is the three-story National Hotel. It is also California's oldest—in continuous operation since 1856. On the National Register, it has a pool, Victorian-style dining room and a genuinely Victorian saloon. Each room is simply furnished with mixed period and modern decor. Some small rooms share baths.

Northern Queen Inn   *(530)265-5824*
just S by CA 20 at 400 Railroad Av. - 95959
86 units   *Moderate*
The area's best motel is a modern complex built along a rushing woodland stream. A big cheerful coffee shop has dramatic waterfall views, and there is a pool, whirlpool, and historic train engine. Each room is well furnished. Spacious loft chalets and cottages have a kitchen and wood-stove fireplace.

The Parsonage   *(530)265-9478*
downtown at 427 Broad St. - 95959
6 units   *Moderate-Expensive*
A handsome Victorian parsonage is now a gracious bed-and-breakfast. Continental breakfast (weekdays) and full breakfast (weekends) and afternoon refreshments are complimentary. Each compact room is beautifully furnished, including museum-quality Victorian pieces and art objects. All have a private bath.

The Red Castle Inn   *(530)265-5135*
just E at 109 Prospect St. - 95959
7 units   *(800)761-4766*   *Expensive*
The premier bed-and-breakfast inn in Nevada City is a four-story pre-Civil War brick Gothic Revival landmark overlooking downtown. Breakfast buffet and afternoon tea and desserts are complimentary. Most of the beautifully furnished rooms have a private bath, period heirlooms, and a private veranda with a view of downtown.

BASIC INFORMATION

Elevation: 2,535 feet   *Population (1990): 2,855*
Location: 150 miles Northeast of San Francisco
Nearest airport with commercial flights: Sacramento - 70 miles
Nevada City Chamber of Commerce   (530)265-2692   (800)655-6569
downtown at 132 Main St. - 95959
www.ncgold.com

Ojai, California

Ojai is the West's Eden. When *Lost Horizons* was made into a movie, overview scenes of "Shangri-La" were filmed of this luxuriant little valley sheltered by towering Coast Range mountains. At the heart of the canyon lies Ojai, secluded among noble oaks and gardens surrounded by fruit and nut orchards. Since early in this century, the town has evolved as an artists' colony and a serene resort.

The compact downtown is a charming combination of inspired Spanish-Colonial architecture, smart shops, and bountiful vegetation that lends itself to relaxing strolls and shopping. Sophisticated studios and galleries display local arts and crafts. Restaurants and lodgings are relatively scarce, but notable. Scenic golf courses, tennis complexes, and riding and hiking trails are enjoyed year-round. An innovative dual trail (horses in one lane/bicycles in another) that parallels the scenic main road into town for nine miles is especially popular. So are Pacific Ocean beaches, only fourteen miles west.

WEATHER PROFILE

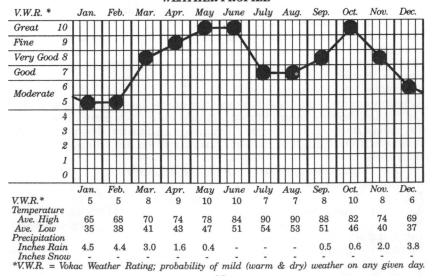

		Jan.	Feb.	Mar.	Apr.	May	June	July	Aug.	Sep.	Oct.	Nov.	Dec.
V.W.R.*		5	5	8	9	10	10	7	7	8	10	8	6
Temperature													
Ave. High		65	68	70	74	78	84	90	90	88	82	74	69
Ave. Low		35	38	41	43	47	51	54	53	51	46	40	37
Precipitation													
Inches Rain		4.5	4.4	3.0	1.6	0.4	-	-	-	0.5	0.6	2.0	3.8
Inches Snow		-	-	-	-	-	-	-	-	-	-	-	-

*V.W.R. = Vokac Weather Rating; probability of mild (warm & dry) weather on any given day.

68

Bart's Books   *(805)646-3755*
just W at 302 W. Matilija St.
Bart's Books is the West's most remarkable outdoor bookstore. More than one hundred thousand used books are shelved in a labyrinth of rooms and courtyards under a giant oak tree that shades customers as they browse or read. After hours, visitors may select books from shelves that line the sidewalk. There is a pay slot in the gate.

Bicycling
A paved separated bikeway extends through Ojai and beyond to miles of flower-bordered paved byways throughout the relatively flat little Shangri-La valley. At every turn are citrus and avocado groves, lush gardens, and grand old California live oaks. Bicycles can be rented at:
Bicycles of Ojai   *just W at 108 Canada St.*   *(805)646-7736*
Friend's Ranch   *(805)646-2871*
5 mi. NW on CA 33 at 15150 Maricopa Hwy.
Fine local citrus, avocados, and nuts are sold at this roadside plant.
Lake Casitas Recreation Area   *(805)649-2233*
6 mi. SW on CA 150
The site of 1984 Olympic events (and record bass and catfish) is a many-armed reservoir surrounded by grass-and-oak-covered hills. Scenic picnic and camp sites overlook the lake. Swimming, waterskiing, and most boats are not allowed (this is a domestic water supply). Certain watercrafts can be launched or rented for fishing or sightseeing only.

Libbey Park
downtown at Ojai Av. & Signal St.
Noble oaks and giant old sycamores preside over lawns and gardens, a fountain court, picnic and play areas, eight tennis courts, and a famed music bowl in a lovely little park in the heart of town.
Los Padres National Forest   *(805)646-8126*
starts 1 mi. N of town
A vast forest extending almost to the coast cloaks towering mountains north of town. Peaks reach pine-covered elevations nearly 9,000 feet above sea level. Giant California condors were recently reintroduced back into the Sespe Condor Sanctuary. The rugged San Rafael Wilderness, Southern California's largest, is northwest of town. Horseback riding, hunting, backpacking, fishing, and camping are popular. Hikers enjoy picturesque trails and natural swimming holes along year-round creeks that are only a few miles from town.

Scenic Drive
for 10 mi. E of downtown
A ten-mile paved loop road (suitable for car or bicycle) showcases the lush valley. It is an especially memorable tour when citrus groves fill the valley with an intoxicating fragrance in spring. Miles of rough stone walls built by Chinese labor a century ago line the road.

Shopping
Rains Department Store   *(805)646-1441*
downtown at 218 Ojai Av.
The centerpiece for the captivating "shopping arcade" downtown is Rains. Ojai's renowned department store is a delightfully fashionable link to a kinder, gentler past. Traditional and contemporary merchandise, and a wealth of one-of-a-kind specialty items, are displayed with a genuine flair.

Valley of "Shangri-La"
3.5 mi. E on CA 150
The panorama representing Shangri-La as seen by Ronald Coleman years ago in the movie *Lost Horizons* is still grand from this hilltop.

RESTAURANTS

Gaslight Restaurant   *(805)646-5990*
4 mi. SW on CA 33 at 11432 N. Ventura Av.
D only.   *Moderate*
A selection of tasty veal dishes, Old World specialties, and al dente vegetables are highlights of a dinner house that has operated here since 1971. The genial dining room adjoins a garden patio and entertainment lounge.

L'Auberge   *(805)646-2288*
just W at 314 El Paseo Rd.
D only.   *Expensive*
French classics including sweetbreads and frog legs have won critical acclaim for this long-established Gallic hideaway in an artistically converted older home on a side street.   There is a casually elegant dining room with a cozy fireplace. Best of all, though, is the wonderfully tranquil garden porch.

Ojai Cafe Emporium   *(805)646-2723*
downtown at 108 S. Montgomery St.
B-L-D.   *Moderate*
The Ojai Cafe Emporium is the village's long-time favorite coffee house/bakery/cafe. Out front is the bakery displaying delights like apple streusel. Beyond, light and lovely New California cuisine is served in cheerful indoor and outdoor dining rooms enlivened by luxuriant greenery.

Ojai Ice Cream & Candy Shoppe   *(805)646-6075*
downtown at 210 E. Ojai Av.   *Moderate*
A variety of flavors of outstanding ice cream and sherbets are made here. So are rich homemade fudges on display in this tempting little takeout shop.

Ojai Valley Inn & Spa   *(805)646-5511*
1 mi. W via CA 150 on Country Club Rd.
B-L-D.   *Expensive-Very Expensive*
The landmark resort's dining facilities were completely renovated in 1998. The **Mar Villa** (D only—Very Expensive) now offers skillfully prepared fresh regional fare in a plush setting overlooking the mountains. The **Oak Cafe** (B-L-D—Expensive) features seasonal New California cuisine in a cheerful wood-trimmed dining room and on a serene oak-shaded terrace above the golf course.

The Ranch House Restaurant   *(805)646-2360*
3 mi. W via CA 33 on S. Lomita Av.
D only.   *Very Expensive*
The Ranch House is the valley's most illustrious restaurant. It is a progenitor of New California cuisine. Long before the regional style was widely known, unusual gourmet dishes were being created here with a light touch enhanced by herbs and vegetables from their garden, and distinctive homemade breads and desserts. The tradition of excellence is wonderfully intact. Picture windows in a refined dining room overlook luxuriant flower and herb gardens. Outside, tables shaded by noble oaks are set amid romantic landscapes, pools, and fountains.

Suzanne's Cuisine   *(805)640-1961*
just W at 502 W. Ojai Av.
L-D.   *Expensive*
Suzanne's is a stellar Southern California dining destination. Fresh regional produce and herbs and spices grown in their own garden have assured inspired New California cuisine since 1992. Epicurean appetizers, soups and salads are complemented by entrees like fresh grilled fish with curry ginger sauce, and desserts like ambrosial apricot and other homemade sorbets. A sophisticated dining room is enhanced by stylish wall hangings. But, the decor tour-de-force is a heated, covered flagstone patio opening onto a lovely garden with a fountain and paths amidst herbs, spices and flowers used in the kitchen.

LODGING

Lodgings in Ojai are scarce. High season is May to October, and weekends all year. Prices are often reduced at least 15% midweek.

Capri Motel   *(805)646-4305*
1 mi. E at 1180 E. Ojai Av. - 93023
29 units   *Moderate*
A large outdoor pool and whirlpool in a tranquil mountain-view setting are features of this modern motel. Each comfortably furnished, spacious room has a private patio or balcony.

The Oaks at Ojai   *(805)646-5573*
downtown at 122 E. Ojai Av. - 93023
46 units   *(800)753-6257*   *Very Expensive*
A historic hotel has become a popular health spa on luxuriant grounds. Prices include three flavorful low-calorie meals daily; plus use of a large swimming pool, whirlpools, saunas and a gym. More than a dozen fitness and self-awareness programs are provided, plus (for a fee) massage, facials and other health and beauty services. There is a gift shop. Each room (two-night minimum) is simply comfortable.

Ojai Valley Inn & Spa   *(805)646-5511*
1 mi. SW via CA 150 on Country Club Dr. - 93023
207 units   *(800)422-6524*   *Expensive-Very Expensive*
The Shangri-La Valley's premier resort was expanded and upgraded for the 1990s. Oak-shaded grounds of the renowned hideaway include two extra-large outdoor pools; a whirlpool; steam rooms and saunas; ping pong; bicycles, plus (for a fee) a world-class 18-hole golf course, putting green, eight tennis courts, horseback riding, and the new spa opened in 1998 with complete fitness and beauty facilities. There are also plush dining rooms (see listing), a lounge, and resort shops. Most of the spacious, beautifully decorated rooms have a private deck. Most suites also have a fireplace.

The Theodore Woolsey House   *(805)646-9779*
1 mi. E at 1484 E. Ojai Av. - 93023
6 units   *Moderate-Expensive*
A century-old landmark is now the area's best bed-and-breakfast inn. Mature trees shade a large outdoor pool and whirlpool. A Continental buffet breakfast, and finger foods each evening, are complimentary. Some period furnishings are used in each well-furnished room.

BASIC INFORMATION

Elevation: 748 feet   *Population (1990): 7,613*
Location: 90 miles Northwest of Los Angeles
Nearest airport with commercial flights: Santa Barbara - 41 miles
Ojai Valley Chamber of Commerce & Visitors Bureau   (805)646-8126
downtown at 150 W. Ojai Av. (Box 1134) - 93024   www.the-ojai.org

Pacific Grove, California

Pacific Grove is a seaside haven of tranquility. Situated along a strikingly beautiful coastline where the waters of the Pacific Ocean and Monterey Bay converge, the town has been evolving as a refined refuge for over a century. Drawn by the setting and a temperate year-round climate, Methodists founded the town in 1875 as a summer retreat. The legacy of the austere settlers was the creation of a genteel haven amidst extravagant surroundings.

Today, shoreline parks with gardens, sandy beaches, coves and winding paths frame the entire ocean and bayside perimeters of town. Inland, trim Victorian houses amid gardens line quiet tree-shaded streets. The tidy feeling of a Northeastern village center at the turn of the century has been meticulously retained in a downtown featuring sophisticated galleries, specialty shops and restaurants. Accommodations range from enchanting Victorian inns to refined motels near the forest home of millions of monarch butterflies.

WEATHER PROFILE

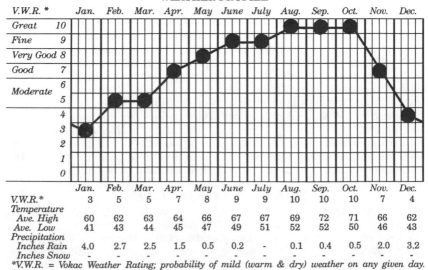

V.W.R. *		Jan.	Feb.	Mar.	Apr.	May	June	July	Aug.	Sep.	Oct.	Nov.	Dec.
Great	10												
Fine	9												
Very Good	8												
Good	7												
Moderate	6												
	5												
	4												
	3												
	2												
	1												
	0												

	Jan.	Feb.	Mar.	Apr.	May	June	July	Aug.	Sep.	Oct.	Nov.	Dec.
V.W.R.*	3	5	5	7	8	9	9	10	10	10	7	4
Temperature												
Ave. High	60	62	63	64	66	67	67	69	72	71	66	62
Ave. Low	41	43	44	45	47	49	51	52	52	50	46	43
Precipitation												
Inches Rain	4.0	2.7	2.5	1.5	0.5	0.2	-	0.1	0.4	0.5	2.0	3.2
Inches Snow	-	-	-	-	-	-	-	-	-	-	-	-

*V.W.R. = Vokac Weather Rating; probability of mild (warm & dry) weather on any given day.

Bicycling
Pacific Rim Cycling *downtown at 214 Forest Av.* *(831)372-2552*
A separated bikeway extends the length of the spectacular bayfront park. Nearby are many additional scenic miles of designated bike routes, including the incomparable Seventeen-Mile Drive.

Butterfly Trees
just W around Lighthouse Av. & Seventeen-Mile Dr.
Pacific Grove is known as "Butterfly Town, U.S.A." because of the annual migration of hundreds of thousands of monarch butterflies to selected groves of trees west of downtown between October and March.

Lovers Point
just N at the bay end of 17th St.
A small bayside park combines sandy coves, dramatic rock formations, Monterey cypress, and green lawns into one of the peninsula's most romantic and photogenic highlights. Normally clear and safe, the water off Bathhouse Beach is a favorite of hearty swimmers in summer.

The Magic Carpet of "Mesembryanthemum"
just N along the bay
This fanciful tongue-twister is the name for masses of ice plants that drape a stretch of Monterey Bay shoreline northwest of Lovers Point. From April through August, a solid lavender pink carpet of tiny flowers provides a brilliant mantle above the rockbound bay.

Pacific Grove Museum of Natural History   *(831)648-3116*
downtown at 165 Forest Av.
This well-regarded museum has a notable exhibit dealing with butterflies. Also, a relief map of the peninsula and bay graphically depicts the great chasm of Monterey Bay, which plummets within a few miles from shore to 8,400 feet below sea level—far deeper than the Grand Canyon. There is also a native plant garden and a well-stocked museum shop.

Point Piños Lighthouse   *(831)648-3116*
1 mi. W at west end of Lighthouse Av.
The oldest continuously operating lighthouse on the Pacific Coast has stood at the entrance to Monterey Bay since 1855. It is open to the public only on Saturdays and Sundays between 1 and 4 p.m.

Seventeen-Mile Drive
starts just W via Lighthouse Av. to Seventeen-Mile Dr.
One of the world's great scenic drives meanders through Pebble Beach and along the splendid coastline between Pacific Grove and Carmel. It is a toll road except to bicyclists and residents. In addition to unforgettable seascapes, highlights include stately homes, legendary golf courses, the Lodge at Pebble Beach, and the Inn at Spanish Bay. Gnarled trees clinging to rocky headlands at The Lone Cypress are among the West's most photographed landmarks.

Shoreline Parks
N & W along Ocean View Blvd. & Sunset Dr.
Among picturesque coastline drives, none is more beguiling than Pacific Grove's, which winds for four miles along a variously flower-bordered, rockbound, and sandy shoreline. The road is a boundary between residential portions of town and a continuous series of seaside parks. Along Monterey Bay, beautifully landscaped parks provide access to numerous sandy beaches tucked into coves along rocky

headlands. Sunbathing, strolling, picnicking, and bicycling are popular, and scuba diving is ideal when the bay is calm and clear. During the summer, glass-bottom boats take visitors out to marine gardens just offshore. On the ocean side, the rugged, rocky shoreline is flanked by low grassy sand dunes stopped short by a pine forest that never quite reaches the sea.

RESTAURANTS

Crocodile Grill   *(831)655-3311*
downtown at 701 Lighthouse Av.
D only.   *Moderate*
Central American fare is skillfully presented in dishes ranging from shrimp cakes with habanero cream sauce to seafood empanada with lobster sauce, plus flavorful desserts. The tropical American theme is nicely carried out in several comfortable dining areas.

Fandango   *(831)372-3456*
downtown at 223 17th St.
L-D.   *Expensive*
One of the region's best sources of European country-style cuisine highlights dishes like braised lamb shank, osso buco, big Porterhouse steaks and paella. Full linen and fresh flowers enliven a series of romantic little dining rooms and a firelit conservatory.

First Awakenings   *(831)372-1125*
1 mi. E at 125 Oceanview Blvd.
B-L.   *Moderate*
Gourmet pancakes from scratch, designer omelets, and thick French toast highlight morning delights served in a light, plant-filled coffee shop and patio in the American Tin Cannery.

The Fishwife at Asilomar   *(831)375-7107*
1 mi. SW at 1996½ Sunset Dr. at Asilomar Beach
L-D.   *Moderate*
Fresh seasonal fish are given a Caribbean accent on a contemporary American menu. Desserts are homemade. Casual little dining areas surround a wood-trimmed bar in this friendly roadside restaurant.

Gernot's Victoria House Restaurant   *(831)646-1477*
downtown at 649 Lighthouse Av.
D only.   *Expensive*
Traditional Continental classics like veal medallion, filet mignon and wild boar can be enjoyed along with selected Old World desserts in plush romantic dining areas in a landmark Victorian mansion.

Melac's   *(831)375-1743*
downtown at 663 Lighthouse Av.
L-D.   *Very Expensive*
Traditional and innovative French cuisine is featured in skillfully prepared dishes that emphasize seasonal freshness. The dining room conveys the charm of a refined country inn.

Old Bath House   *(831)375-5195*
just N at 620 Ocean View Blvd.
D only.   *Very Expensive*
Pacific Grove's most renowned dinner house has a winning way with creative American cuisine that changes seasonally, and luscious desserts. But it is the magnificent view of Monterey Bay and Lovers Point, complemented by elegant decor in an ingeniously converted Victorian bathhouse, that assures continuing status as one of California's most romantic restaurants.

Peppers Mexicali Cafe   *(831)373-6892*
downtown at 170 Forest Av.
L-D.   *Moderate*
Innovative Mexican/American dishes like Yucatan snapper with chiles, citrus and cilantro, or chicken caribe with citrus habanero marinade and tropical salsa fresca are among a host of grazing goodies served in the cozy congestion of a wood-trimmed dining room and bar.

The Tinnery   *(831)646-1040*
just N at 631 Ocean View Blvd.
B-L-D.   *Moderate*
American and international favorites are offered on a well-rounded menu. But the highlight of this handsome restaurant is an expansive window-wall view of Lovers Point Park and Monterey Bay.

Toasties Cafe   *(831)373-7543*
downtown at 702 Lighthouse Av.
B-L.   *Moderate*
Traditional and innovative breakfast specialties ranging from homemade hash to breakfast burrito or designer omelets are the reason for continuing popularity of this country-comfortable cafe.

LODGING

Accommodations are numerous. Most are independent, including several delightful bed-and-breakfast inns and two great resorts in adjacent Pebble Beach. Summer and early fall are prime time. Rates are often reduced 20% or more apart from weekends in winter.

The Centrella   *(831)372-3372*
downtown at 612 Central Av. - 93950
28 units   *(800)233-3372*   *Moderate-Expensive*
An 1889 building is now a large, well-landscaped bed-and-breakfast. An extended Continental buffet breakfast and light evening repast are complimentary. Each well-furnished room, suite and cottage combines old with new. Most have a private bath.

Gatehouse Inn   *(831)649-1881*
downtown at 225 Central Av. - 93950
9 units   *(800)753-1881*   *Expensive*
A stately 1884 home has been fully renovated and upgraded into an appealing bed-and-breakfast. An expanded Continental breakfast and afternoon treats are complimentary. Each well-furnished room blends period and all contemporary conveniences, including a private bath. Some rooms have a clawfoot tub, a fireplace and an ocean view.

Grand View Inn   *(831)372-4341*
just N at 557 Ocean View Blvd. - 93950
10 units   *Expensive*
A landmark Edwardian home across a street from Lover's Point beach was transformed into a gracious bed-and-breakfast in 1994. Full breakfast and afternoon "high tea" are complimentary. Each room is beautifully furnished with a blend of period and contemporary decor.

Green Gables Inn   *(831)375-2095*
just E at 104 5th St. - 93950
11 units   *(800)722-1774*   *Expensive*
One of California's most beguiling Queen Anne-style mansions now serves as a romantic bed-and-breakfast. Full breakfast and evening refreshments are complimentary. The main house and carriage house are on lovely grounds overlooking the bay. While rooms vary in size, and some share bathrooms, all are beautifully furnished, including fine period decor. Some have a fireplace and/or a bay view.

The Inn at Spanish Bay   *(831)647-7500*

2 mi. SW at 2700 Seventeen-Mile Dr. - Pebble Beach 93953

270 units   *(800)654-9300*   *Very Expensive*

One of America's best newer resorts is the Inn at Spanish Bay, perched amid cypress on a bluff above the ocean. The five-story complex includes a (fee) championship 18-hole golf course, eight tennis courts, horseback riding and rental bicycles, a fitness club, plus the beach, a large pool, whirlpool, saunas, and miles of scenic trails. Restaurants include the acclaimed **Bay Club** (D only—Very Expensive) for gourmet Italian cuisine with a golf course and ocean view. **Roy's** (B-L-D—Expensive) offers European/Asian cuisine and the same great view. Each spacious room is luxuriously furnished. All have a gas fireplace. Most have a private patio or balcony with a coast or forest view. Some suites also have a whirlpool bath.

Lighthouse Lodge Suites   *(831)655-2111*

1 mi. NW at 1249 Lighthouse Av. - 93950

32 units   *(800)858-1249*   *Expensive-Very Expensive*

The ocean and (in season) Monarch butterflies are a stroll from this contemporary Cape Cod-style all-suites complex in a natural setting with access to a pool and whirlpool in the lodge across the street. Full breakfast and evening wine and appetizers are complimentary. Each well-furnished suite has a microwave and refrigerator, honor bar, a gas fireplace and a large whirlpool bath.

Martine Inn   *(831)373-3388*

just E at 255 Ocean View Blvd. - 93950

19 units   *(800)852-5588*   *Expensive-Very Expensive*

A classic Mediterranean-style villa built at the turn of the century on a rise above the bay is now a large, luxurious bed-and-breakfast inn. Full breakfast and afternoon appetizers and refreshments are complimentary. Authentic, quality period pieces are used throughout. Each beautifully furnished room has a private bath. Most have a clawfoot tub and sea view. Some also have a wood-burning fireplace.

Rosedale Inn   *(831)655-1000*

1 mi. W at 775 Asilomar Av. - 93950

19 units   *(800)822-5606*   *Expensive*

Asilomar Conference Center is across a street from this redwood motel in the woods. Rustic appearance belies a wealth of contemporary conveniences in each well-furnished room, including a mini-kitchen, gas fireplace and oversized whirlpool bathtub.

Seven Gables Inn   *(831)372-4341*

just N at 555 Ocean View Blvd. - 93950

14 units   *Expensive-Very Expensive*

Monterey Bay is across the street from this luxuriously restored Victorian mansion surrounded by colorful gardens. Full breakfast and English-style "high tea" are complimentary. A wealth of authentic antiques blend comfortably with modern decor and amenities including a private bath. Each beautifully furnished room has an ocean view.

BASIC INFORMATION

Elevation: 50 feet   Population (1990):   16,117
Location: 122 miles South of San Francisco
Nearest airport with commercial flights: Monterey - 5 miles
Pacific Grove Chamber of Commerce   (831)373-3304   (800)656-6650
  downtown at Forest & Central Avs. (Box 167) - 93950

Palm Desert, California

Palm Desert is now California's ultimate desert showplace. Modish low-profile buildings amid luxuriant landscapes fill a once-sandy plain near the base of the towering San Jacinto Mountains. In spite of the choice location and warm, sunny climate, the town was content to live in the shadow of Palm Springs—until the 1970s.

Today, sand dunes have been replaced by emerald-green golf courses (more than in any desert town) and the oases-of-choice are opulent resorts amid palm-shaded pools and lush gardens. The area's unique natural grandeur is now accessible to all in the Living Desert, a dramatic showcase for birds, animals, and plants indigenous to arid lands. The city boasts the region's largest shopping Mecca. The burgeoning collection of sophisticated shops, galleries, and restaurants along El Paseo (a flowery, palm-lined boulevard in the heart of town) is now the desert's toniest. Nearby, an outstanding live theater distinguishes Palm Desert's expansive cultural center.

WEATHER PROFILE

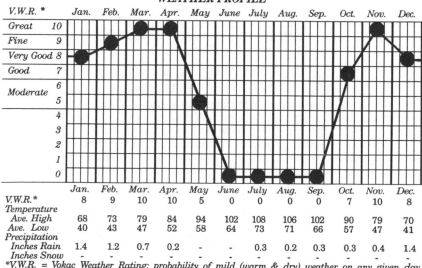

	Jan.	Feb.	Mar.	Apr.	May	June	July	Aug.	Sep.	Oct.	Nov.	Dec.
V.W.R.*	8	9	10	10	5	0	0	0	0	7	10	8
Temperature												
Ave. High	68	73	79	84	94	102	108	106	102	90	79	70
Ave. Low	40	43	47	52	58	64	73	71	66	57	47	41
Precipitation												
Inches Rain	1.4	1.2	0.7	0.2	-	-	0.3	0.2	0.3	0.3	0.4	1.4
Inches Snow	-	-	-	-	-	-	-	-	-	-	-	-

*V.W.R. = Vokac Weather Rating; probability of mild (warm & dry) weather on any given day.

ATTRACTIONS
Aerial Tramway   *(760)325-1449*
18 mi. NW via CA 111 & Tramway Rd.
One of the world's great aerial rides transports passengers from the desert at 2,643 feet to 8,516 feet above sea level on Mount San Jacinto. Two gondolas make the 2½-mile trip in about fifteen minutes several times daily. Both stations have observation decks, picnic areas, a snack shop and lounge. The alpine restaurant features family-style fare with a grand view through the pines to the desert and oases far below. In the state park at the top, hiking, backpacking, and wilderness camping are popular. In winter, cross-country skiing and sledding can be enjoyed in deep snow on the mountain for a startling contrast to warm, dry weather in the desert below.

Balloon Flights
Scenic balloon flights offer a lofty perspective on manmade oases, sand dunes, and pine-forested mountains. For nearly twenty years, passenger flights of about one hour have been arranged from October through May at:
Desert Balloon Charters   *(760)346-8575*
Fantasy Balloon Flights   *(760)568-0997   (800)462-2683*

Bicycling
Bicycle trails are scenic, flat, and easy (and occasionally separated) on many miles of streets in the area. Rental bikes and information are available at several places.

Date Gardens
Jensen's Date & Citrus Garden   *(760)347-3897*
8 mi. E at 80653 Hwy. 111 - Indio
This long-established roadside shop offers free samples, and delicious date shakes. Fresh-squeezed orange, tangerine, and grapefruit juices are also featured in season. The desert's best free showcase garden of subtropical citrus and dates, all carefully labeled, is out back.

Shields Date Gardens   *(760)347-0996   (800)414-2555*
7 mi. E at 80225 Hwy. 111 - Indio
For decades this has been a landmark oasis for travelers interested in enjoying dates in all kinds of configurations (don't miss the shakes), and learning about "the sex life of the date" in their free theater. Seasonal local grapefruit, oranges, etc. are also displayed for sale.

Valerie Jean Date Garden   *(760)397-4357*
20 mi. SE at 66021 Hwy. 86 - Thermal
Since 1928, the nation's oldest commercial date oasis has featured date shakes (reputedly invented here). For another refreshing treat, try the cactus shake. Date samples are generously offered and assorted dates and citrus are available in gift packs or to go.

El Paseo
downtown on El Paseo between Palms-to-Pines Hwy. & Portola Av.
This mile-long boulevard rivals Rodeo Drive in Beverly Hills as the best shopping street in Southern California. Chic boutiques and fine art galleries, interspersed with the greatest conflux of gourmet restaurants in the desert, are enhanced by whimsical sculptures and gardenscapes. Among the tasteful shops, a personal favorite is **The Upper Crust** (73540 El Paseo). This big culinary landmark offers generous samples of preserves, cheese spreads and more from a wealth of well-selected gourmet goodies showcased with premium kitchen wares.

Fabulous Palm Springs Follies   *(960)327-0225*   *(800)967-9997*
downtown at 128 S. Palm Canyon Dr. - Palm Springs
The historic (1936) Plaza Theatre has been skillfully restored to serve as a professional showcase for delightfully lively performances filled with nostalgic song, dance and comedy. Remarkably, every member of the talented cast is more than fifty years old! Adjoining are a museum of Hollywood memorabilia and Walk of Fame.

Golf
The Palm Desert/Palm Springs area is the "Winter Golfing Capital of the World." Nearly one hundred courses include many of championship quality. Many are open to the public, and others offer outside guest privileges. Collectively, they provide a remarkable variety of conditions and beguiling oases. Below are two championship courses giving duffers a choice of naturalistic or oasis scenery.

Desert Willow Golf Resort   *(760)346-0015*
Palm Desert Country Club   *(760)345-2525*
Jeep Tours
Desert Adventures   *(760)324-5337*   *(888)440-5337*
7 mi. NW at 67555 E. Palm Canyon Dr. #A104 - Cathedral City
Jeep trips of two or four hours take visitors into primitive desert mountains south of town to see and hear about animal and plant life, distinctive geological formations, and archaeological sites.

The Living Desert   *(760)346-5694*
2 mi. SE at 47900 Portola Av.
Almost two square miles have been set aside to depict deserts near and far. Botanical gardens contain shady oases with tranquil pools, and a myriad of unusual plants, many with vivid blossoms in spring. Exhibits portray local geology, history and Indian culture. Eagle Canyon, a state-of-the-art habitat for animals of the American desert, highlights geological exhibits reached by self-guided trails. There are also picnic facilities and a gift shop. Closed in summer.

Moorten Botanical Gardens   *(760)327-6555*
11 mi. NW at 1701 S. Palm Canyon Dr. - Palm Springs
Since 1938, this four acre landmark arboretum has displayed thousands of varieties of desert plants from throughout the world.

Palm Canyon   *(760)325-5673*
15 mi. W on Palm Canyon Dr.
America's largest stand of native Washingtonia palms lines a steep, narrow canyon for several miles. Hiking trails lead down to the canyon floor, where a stream meanders among hundreds of palms up to 2,000 years old. Nearby canyons also have lush palm groves, spectacular rock formations, and streams with pools and waterfalls. All (fee) canyons are in somewhat natural condition as part of an Indian reservation.

Palm Springs Desert Museum   *(760)837-0777*
13 mi. NW at 101 Museum Dr. - Palm Springs
This handsome cultural arts center skillfully combines fine art, natural science, and performing arts. Fountains and sculpture gardens embellish landscaped grounds, and there is a museum shop.

Warm Water Feature
Oasis Waterpark   *(760)327-0499*   *(800)247-4664*
10 mi. NW at 1500 Gene Autry Trail
The desert's best waterpark, opened in 1986, has hydro-tubes and speed slides, a lagoon with programmed waves, and hot spa. There is also an elaborate health club, plus food, drinks, and a gift shop open daily mid-March thru Labor Day, and weekends through October.

Cuistot   *(760)340-1000*
downtown at 73-111 El Paseo
L-D.   *Very Expensive*
Cuistot is the desert's quintessential culinary oasis. The peerless chef/owner, Bernard Dervieux, consistently transforms top quality seasonal ingredients into unusual and flavorful dishes that look as good as they taste. Luscious desserts also reflect the chef's classic French background and current orientation toward creative New California cuisine. The modish dining areas and lounge accented with fresh flowers provide an informal backdrop for stellar dining.

Doug Arango's Restaurant & Catering   *(760)341-4120*
downtown at 73-520 El Paseo
L-D.   *Expensive*
Mile-high lemon meringue pie and other decadent delights are on display near the entrance. These and a wide range of lively contemporary California dishes with an Italian accent account for the great popularity of this tony trattoria.

Flower Drum   *(760)323-3020*
13 mi. NW at 424 S. Indian Canyon Dr. - Palm Springs
L-D.   *Moderate*
Flower Drum, a long-established Chinese restaurant in the desert, offers creative and authentic delicacies in a large comfortable dining room with a koi pond, a little stream with an arched bridge, and a mirrored stage with traditional entertainment most evenings.

Jillian's   *(760)776-8242*
1 mi. E at 74-155 El Paseo
D only.   *Very Expensive*
Opened in 1994, this dinner house quickly became a darling of dining cognoscenti for the chef/owner's disciplined, creative approach to New California cuisine. Pastas, breads and fine desserts are made here. Whitewashed adobe rooms and a courtyard provide the look and feel of a posh hacienda.

Kaiser Grille   *(760)779-1988*
1 mi. E at 74-225 Hwy. 111
D only.   *Expensive*
Fans come back for extras and specialties like frozen prickly pear margaritas. Innovative, flavorful grazing fare is served in snazzy, post-modern dining areas backed by an exhibition kitchen with a mesquite grill, wood-burning oven and French rotisserie. There is also a dining patio.

Keedy's Fountain & Grill   *(760)346-6492*
just E at 73-633 Hwy. 111
B-L.   *Low*
Big, frosty lime or orange freezes star along with thirst-quenching real malts or shakes from the fountain, while the grill continues to produce hearty American short order standards as it has for over forty years. This plain popular coffee shop is a true "Blast from the Past."

Le Paon Restaurant   *(760)568-3651*
just S at 45-640 CA 74
D only.   *Very Expensive*
Traditional and innovative French cuisine including dramatic flambés and souffles are served amid candlelit elegance with grand piano stylings and on a garden patio in this venerable dinner house.

Palm Desert, California

Le Vallauris   *(760)325-5059*
13 mi. NW at 385 W. Taquitz Canyon Way - Palm Springs
L-D.   *Very Expensive*
Le Vallauris is Palm Springs' most celebrated culinary haven. Under
the canny guidance of the genial host/owner, traditional and creative
French cuisine is served. Gracious dining rooms in a landmark
bungalow, a romantic tree-shaded garden patio, and a posh piano
lounge display the bonhomie. French cuisine also stars in the related
Le St. Germain (773-6511), recently opened in Indian Wells.

Otani - A Garden Restaurant   *(760)327-6700*
14 mi. NW at 266 Avenida Caballeros - Palm Springs
L-D.   *Expensive*
Otani has the best Japanese food in the desert. All classic styles are
prepared by uniformly skilled chefs in a cookhouse and exposition
kitchens that surround simply comfortable dining areas in a veritable
Shogun's palace with a Japanese garden beyond picture windows.

Palomino Euro Bistro   *(760)773-9091*
downtown at 73-101 Hwy. 111
D only.   *Expensive*
Palomino features a seamless blend of Pacific Northwest and New
California cuisines. Fresh oak-grilled salmon with wild greens and
artichoke tartar and housemade desserts like roasted apple tart in puff
pastry a la mode typify stellar possibilities. The fine fare is favored by
upscale avant-garde dining and bistro areas.

Ristorante Mamma Gina   *(760)568-9898*
downtown at 73-705 El Paseo
L-D.   *Very Expensive*
Mamma Gina is the desert's premier source of Florentine cuisine.
Meals begin with the arrival of three kinds of housemade bread—the
multi-grain is outstanding. Desserts made here are also fine, including
a peerless Italian Napoleon. Gracious service with a flair further
distinguishes the classy congested dining room and lounge.

Wally's Desert Turtle   *(760)568-9321*
2 mi. NW at 71-775 Hwy. 111 - Rancho Mirage
D only.   *Very Expensive*
Contemporary California-Continental cuisine receives nonpareil
treatment in culinary delights like wild mushroom soup, roast duck
with Medjool date sauce, and etherial Grand Marnier dessert souffles.
The desert's most opulent dinner house, opened in 1979, is a split-level
extravaganza of exotic floral sprays, lush greenery, fine art and
artifacts, grand piano stylings, and formally elegant tables.

LODGING

Area lodgings are among America's most abundant and varied. High
season is February to May. Rates are often at least 40% less in
summer.

Desert Hot Springs Spa Hotel   *(760)329-6000*
30 mi. N at 10805 Palm Dr. - Desert Hot Springs 92240
50 units   *Moderate*
The best hot springs hideaway in the desert is in laid-back "Spa Town."
This modern motor hotel encloses eight hot mineral pools (one extra-
large) and whirlpools on a palm-studded courtyard. There are also
saunas, ping pong, and (for a fee) massage; a coffee shop/entertainment
lounge; and a gift shop. Each comfortable room has a big private view
patio or balcony.

81

Palm Desert, California
Givenchy Hotel & Spa *(760)770-5000*
9 mi. NW at 4200 E. Palm Canyon Dr. - 92264
98 units *(800)276-5000* *Very Expensive*
The Givenchy is a new desert gem of understated opulence. Towering mountains frame lush colorful gardens surrounding two outdoor pools, two indoor pools, whirlpools, and a fitness center. Amenities (for a fee) include six tennis courts and a full-service beauty and revitalizing spa with saunas and steam rooms; plus posh gourmet California-French dining, an informal cafe, and an entertainment lounge. Each spacious, luxuriously furnished room is uniquely decorated. Villas have private mountain-view patios.

Hyatt Grand Champions Resort *(760)341-1000*
3 mi. E at 44-600 Indian Wells Lane - Indian Wells 92210
336 units *(800)233-1234* *Very Expensive*
This post-modern pleasure palace opened in 1986 with a neo-Moorish motif worthy of a sultan. Two championship 18-hole golf courses encircle the five-level complex. A palm-shaded courtyard is cooled by four pools and whirlpools, and there are saunas, steam rooms and an exercise room. Fee amenities include golf, twelve tennis courts, a complete beauty/fitness center; and bicycles. Other amenities include a gourmet Southwestern grill, trattoria, deli/cafe, entertainment lounge, and resort shops. Each spacious, luxuriously furnished room has a large private view balcony. Twenty one- or two-bedroom garden villas have a kitchen and a garden whirlpool.

Hyatt Regency Suites Palm Springs *(760)322-9000*
14 mi. NW at 285 N. Palm Canyon Dr. - Palm Springs 92262
192 units *(800)233-1234* *Very Expensive*
Palm Springs' most architecturally significant hotel opened in 1986 in the heart of town. The wedge-shaped complex rises six stories above a marble-clad atrium lobby. Nearby are a long pool, whirlpool, exercise room, gift shop, restaurant and entertainment lounge. Each spacious, beautifully furnished one- or two-bedroom suite has a private balcony with a town or mountain view. Some also have a large whirlpool bath.

Ingleside Inn *(760)325-0046*
13 mi. NW at 200 W. Ramon Rd. - Palm Springs 92264
30 units *(800)772-6655 Expensive-Very Expensive*
Palm Springs' most venerable small hotel is sequestered amid flowering trees. There is a small pool and whirlpool in a garden, plus **Melvyn's** (Continental cuisine in a posh estate-like setting) and a romantic piano lounge. Each room is individually well furnished, including some antiques, plus in-bath steam bath and whirlpool, and a refrigerator stocked with complimentary snacks and beverages. Some spacious suites and villas also have a fireplace and private patios.

Ken Irwin's La Mancha Resort Village *(760)323-1773*
14 mi. NW at 444 Avenida Caballeros (Box 1606) - Palm Springs 92262
66 units *(800)255-1773 Expensive-Very Expensive*
La Mancha is the desert's ultimate resort for playful adults. The Spanish-Colonial complex of condo-style villas has a tropically landscaped pool, cold plunge, and whirlpool; saunas, gym, seven tennis courts, paddle tennis courts, table tennis; plus bicycles and a dining room. Each spacious, luxuriously furnished one- to three-bedroom suite has a kitchen and a garden patio. Most also have a gas fireplace, and a private outdoor pool or whirlpool or both.

Palm Desert, California

La Quinta Resort & Club   *(760)564-4111*
8 mi. SE at 49-499 Eisenhower Dr. (Box 69) - La Quinta 92253
640 units   *(800)598-3828*   *Very Expensive*
La Quinta is the most justifiably celebrated resort in the desert. Built
in 1926, it retains all of its timeless charm. Rugged desert peaks
surround a luxuriant oasis that now includes 25 outdoor pools and 38
whirlpools surrounded by adobe-and-tile casitas and myriad flower
gardens, citrus trees and date palms, a putting green, and exercise
room. Fee amenities include bicycles, 30 tennis courts, four 18-hole
championship golf courses, and a lavish new wellness and fitness spa.
Montanas offers elegant innovative Mediterranean cuisine; **Morgan's**
has contemporary American fare; and the **Adobe Grill** features
regional/Mexican dishes. A flower-filled plaza offers specialty shops
surrounding fountains and waterfalls. Each spacious room is
luxuriously furnished. Many have a fireplace and private garden patio
with a pool and/or whirlpool.

Marriott's Desert Springs Resort & Spa   *(760)341-2211*
4 mi. NE at 74-855 Country Club Dr. - 92260
884 units   *(800)331-3112*   *Very Expensive*
One of America's most spectacular resorts lies amid two 18-hole
championship golf courses, palm-shaded gardens, and ingenious
"waterscaping." An awesome eight-story atrium lobby encloses
waterfalls and part of a lake with a dock for free boat rides. Water
features are everywhere, including five pools and whirlpools, and a
sandy beach. (Fee) amenities include two lush 18-hole golf courses; an
18-hole putting course; 20 tennis courts; bicycle rentals; and a
nonpareil fitness and beauty center with lap, hot and cold pools;
saunas, steam rooms, inhalation room, rock climbing wall, and a
wealth of treatments. There are five fine restaurants, as well as several
options for casual dining, drinks and nightlife, plus stylish resort
shops. Each beautifully furnished room has a large private view deck.

Marriott's Rancho Las Palmas Resort   *(760)568-2727*
3 mi. NW at 41-000 Bob Hope Dr. - Rancho Mirage 92270
450 units   *(800)458-8786*   *Very Expensive*
Marriott's sprawling early-California-style resort was completely
renovated and enhanced in 1998. There are now two pools (one with
a 100-foot waterslide and other water features) and whirlpools in palm-
shaded gardens, and (for a fee) a state-of-the-art European health spa,
27 holes of golf, 25 tennis courts and rental bicycles. There are also
resort shops. Diners can opt for elegant or casual rooms or a lake-view
patio. The lounge has live entertainment and dancing. Each beautifully
furnished room has a private view patio or balcony.

Renaissance Esmeralda Resort   *(760)773-4444*
3 mi. E at 44-400 Indian Wells Lane - Indian Wells 92210
560 units   *(800)552-4386*   *Very Expensive*
Two manicured 18-hole golf courses surround this post-modern eight-
story resort. Date palms shade an oasis courtyard with three giant
pools, two whirlpools, waterfalls and a sandy beach. Fee amenities
include two golf courses; seven tennis courts; a complete fitness center
with a gym, steam rooms, saunas and massage, and bicycles. There are
also gourmet restaurants offering California or Mediterranean cuisine,
a stylish entertainment lounge, and resort shops. Each spacious,
luxuriously furnished room has a small private view balcony. "Spa
Suites" have a large in-room whirlpool.

The Ritz-Carlton Rancho Mirage   *(760)321-8282*
5 mi. NW at 69-900 Frank Sinatra Dr. - Rancho Mirage 92270
240 units   *(800)241-3333*   *Very Expensive*
The desert's most lustrous conference resort crowns a spectacularly landscaped hill with a large pool and whirlpool in a garden court overlooking the desert, a putting green, exercise room, game courts, and (for a fee) ten tennis courts. Restaurants feature sophisticated Continental or Southwestern offerings in gracious settings, while afternoon tea is served in the lounge. Each spacious, elegant room has a private desert-view terrace.

Shadow Mountain Resort   *(760)346-6123*
just SE at 45-750 San Luis Rey Av. - 92260
102 units   *(800)472-3713*   *Expensive-Very Expensive*
Shadow Mountain is the nearest resort to El Paseo. Condos share lush vegetation with four pools (one huge), five whirlpools, saunas, exercise room, seasonal cafe/bar, and (fee) sixteen tennis courts. Each spacious, well-furnished apartment has a kitchenette and private deck.

Villa Royale Inn   *(760)327-2314*
11 mi. NW at 1620 Indian Trail - Palm Springs 92264
31 units   *(800)245-2314*   *Moderate-Very Expensive*
Villa Royale is one of Southern California's most romantic lodgings. The single-level bed-and-breakfast inn has lush tropical gardens and bubbling fountains, two courtyard pools and a whirlpool linked by meandering paths. Light breakfast is complimentary. **Europa** offers guests and the public fine New California cuisine in a posh, peaceful dining room. Each beautifully furnished room is individually decorated with handsome international touches. Many rooms have a fireplace and/or a private patio with a large whirlpool.

The Westin Mission Hills Resort   *(760)328-5955*
7 mi. N at 71-333 Dinah Shore Dr. - Rancho Mirage 92270
512 units   *(800)228-3000*   *Very Expensive*
Gardens and two championship golf courses surround this dramatic neo-Moorish resort. The low-rise complex includes three landscaped pools (one with a sixty-foot waterslide), whirlpools, outdoor game courts, exercise room, steam rooms, (fee) golf, seven tennis courts and rental bicycles, plus fine dining and drinking places and resort shops. Each spacious, well-furnished room has a private view deck.

The Willows Historic Palm Springs Inn   *(760)320-0771*
13 mi. NW at 412 W. Tahquitz Canyon Way - Palm Springs 92262
8 units   *Very Expensive*
A glamorous Mediterranean villa (circa 1927) is now a bed-and-breakfast inn that captures the spirit and elegance of Palm Springs' fabled past. A garden pool, whirlpool, full gourmet breakfast, and afternoon appetizers and wine are complimentary. Each luxuriously furnished room combines quality nostalgia with all contemporary conveniences. Several rooms also have a fireplace, private deck and big clawfoot tub.

BASIC INFORMATION

Elevation: 183 feet   Population (1990):   23,252
Location: 120 miles East of Los Angeles
Nearest airport with commercial flights: Palm Springs - 10 miles
Palm Springs Desert Resorts Convention & Visitors Bureau (760)770-9000
5 mi. NW at 69930 Hwy. 111, Suite 201 - Rancho Mirage 92270
(800)967-3767
www.desert.resorts.com

St. Helena, California

St. Helena is the heart of America's most illustrious wine-producing valley. All around the compact town, a sea of vineyards splashes against oak-covered mountains that frame the flat little valley's floor. The town, founded in 1853, was flourishing as a farming center when grape growing began after the Civil War. Talented wine makers and ideal conditions soon established Napa Valley as the center of California's premium wine production.

Today, St. Helena retains much of the charm of a Victorian farming village in spite of visiting hordes every weekend. The orderly business district features romantic little parks for picnics beneath noble shade trees. Many carefully restored historic buildings house regional specialty and gourmet shops, and a delightful array of sophisticated restaurants. Plush bed-and-breakfast inns provide a romantic base for enjoying hiking, bicycling, ballooning and a wonderful diversity of landmark wineries.

WEATHER PROFILE

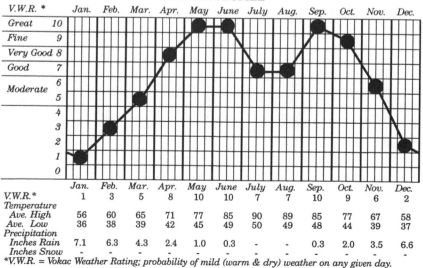

		Jan.	Feb.	Mar.	Apr.	May	June	July	Aug.	Sep.	Oct.	Nov.	Dec.
V.W.R.*		1	3	5	8	10	10	7	7	10	9	6	2
Temperature													
Ave. High		56	60	65	71	77	85	90	89	85	77	67	58
Ave. Low		36	38	39	42	45	49	50	49	48	44	39	37
Precipitation													
Inches Rain		7.1	6.3	4.3	2.4	1.0	0.3	-	-	0.3	2.0	3.5	6.6
Inches Snow		-	-	-	-	-	-	-	-	-	-	-	-

*V.W.R. = Vokac Weather Rating; probability of mild (warm & dry) weather on any given day.

ATTRACTIONS

Bale Grist Mill State Historical Park   *(707)963-2236*
3 mi. N on CA 29
A 36-foot-tall wooden waterwheel has been meticulously reconstructed and once again grinds flour and cornmeal at this picturesque 1846 mill. Nearby, shady picnic sites overlook a creek.

Ballooning
Napa Valley Balloons, Inc.   *(800)253-2224*
Fine weather and lovely countryside make the Napa Valley a natural for hot-air balloon flights. Several companies offer guests champagne flights with a unique vantage to area sights and sounds.

Bicycling
St. Helena Cyclery   *(707)963-7736*
downtown at 1156 Main St.
Relatively flat terrain, fine wine country scenery and attractions, and good weather are all reasons for the enormous popularity of bicycle touring in Napa Valley. Rentals are by the hour and longer.

Bothe-Napa Valley State Park   *(707)942-4575*
4 mi. N on CA 29
Marked hiking trails pass through some of the most easterly stands of Coast redwoods as well as a luxuriant forest of oak and madrone. A pool, picnic tables and creekside campsites are available.

Lake Berryessa Recreation Area   *(707)966-2111*
20 mi. E via CA 128
Swimming, boating, fishing, picnicking and camping are enjoyed on this fifteen-mile-long reservoir in grass-covered hills.

Silverado Museum   *(707)963-3757*
downtown at 1490 Library Lane
One of the world's largest collections of Robert Louis Stevenson memorabilia is displayed in a handsome extension of the St. Helena Public Library Center. The Napa Valley Wine Library is next door.

Wineries
St. Helena is the heart of the world famous Napa Valley wine district. It is now surrounded by thousands of acres of premium vineyards and more than two hundred wineries. Some require an appointment. Many now charge tasting fees. The Chamber of Commerce has detailed guides and maps. Following are among the best premium wineries that still offer free tastes, tours without appointments, attractive picnic facilities and/or gift shops. **Beringer Vineyards** has a must-do "Rhine House" mansion and wine-aging caves tour. At **Louis M. Martini**, the third generation oversees a winery from 1933. **Robert Mondavi Winery** offers renowned wine, tours, and facility, plus summer concerts. **V. Sattui Winery** is a dramatic complex amid gardens and shady picnic areas with the valley's best deli and gift shop. **Silverado Vineyards** has a grand-view tasting room and fine wine. **Sutter Home Winery** features zinfandel, and has a big gift shop and lovely garden. **Domaine Chandon** and **Mumm Napa Valley** both have a tasting fee for their fine sparkling wine and offer notable tours of their showplace méthode champenoise facilities.

Yountville   *(707)944-0904   (800)959-3604*
9 mi. SE off CA 29
A bustling village by 1855, Yountville is now the site of some of the region's finest shops and restaurants. The town park has pleasant, tree-shaded picnic spots. **Vintage 1870** is a dramatically converted brick winery complex housing dozens of specialty shops.

RESTAURANTS

Auberge du Soleil   *(707)963-1211*
5 mi. SE at 180 Rutherford Hill Rd. - Rutherford
L-D.   *Very Expensive*
Fresh flavorful wine country cuisine is prepared using seasonal ingredients from the region. The informally elegant dining room is in a spectacular chateau-style structure high on a hill with panoramic views of the vineyards. Cocktails or wine are unforgettable when savored on the deck by the plush lounge.

Brava Terrace   *(707)963-9300*
2 mi. N at 3010 St. Helena Hwy. North (CA 29)
L-D.   *Expensive*
Creative California cuisine with a Mediterranean slant is skillfully presented in dishes like osso bucco or wild mushroom ravioli, plus unusual treats like homemade potato chips with melted Danish blue cheese, and luscious housemade ice creams and desserts. The robust fare is served in two contemporary dining rooms with modern art and a great stone fireplace, and on a garden terrace.

Brix Restaurant   *(707)944-2749*
7 mi. S at 7377 St. Helena Hwy. (CA 29) - Yountville
L-D.   *Expensive*
Brix is the most delightful addition to gourmet dining in the Wine Country in years. A renowned chef has taken California fusion cuisine to a new level. The mix of bold Oriental flavors and classic European cuisines showcases herbs and vegetables from scenic organic gardens visible (as is the exhibition kitchen) from throughout the comfortably elegant dining room. Here is quintessential dining-as-theater with stellar cuisine, talented service, a dramatic room, and a scene-stealing backdrop of vineyards and mountains.

The Diner   *(707)944-2626*
9 mi. SE off CA 29 at 6476 Washington St. - Yountville
B-L-D.   *Expensive*
Since 1976, fresh ingredients and homestyle cooking have distinguished this simply furnished, old-fashioned diner where breakfasts can be especially good. Moderately-priced Mexican dinners are also part of a longstanding tradition.

Domaine Chandon   *(707)944-2892*
10 mi. SE off CA 29 at 1 California Dr. - Yountville
L-D.   *Very Expensive*
The French have produced a gastronomic showplace for their California sparkling wines made here. Disciplined French haute cuisine, from seasonal appetizers to grand desserts, is enlivened by California creativity and fresh local ingredients. Soaring arched ceiling, glass window walls and warm woods distinguish the plush multilevel dining room as a modern architectural tour de force surrounded by bucolic beauty. Gourmet lunches are served on a flower-strewn outdoor patio during warm months.

The French Laundry   *(707)944-2380*
9 mi. SE off CA 29 at 6640 Washington St. - Yountville
D only.   *Very Expensive*
The French Laundry is one of America's quintessential gourmet hideaways. New California cuisine reflects the acclaimed chef/owner's classic French background and creative talent with the freshest seasonal ingredients. Prix fixe meals are served in several romantic country-elegant rooms with a fireplace or vineyard view in a stone and

redwood building that was a French laundry at the turn of the century. There is also a luxuriant garden patio.

Meadowwood Resort *(707)963-3646*
2 mi. E at 900 Meadowwood Lane
B-L-D. *Very Expensive*
In the **Restaurant at Meadowwood** (D only), dinners are masterfully prepared from fresh and unusual ingredients in California cuisine. Quiet country grace distinguishes a beautiful octagonal dining room complemented by picture window views (shared by a redwood dining deck) to a golf course and forested hills. Downstairs, the **Meadowwood Grill** serves all meals in a more casual setting.

The Model Bakery *(707)963-8192*
downtown at 1357 Main St.
B-L. *Expensive*
A long-established St. Helena institution is still a deservedly popular source for all sorts of first-rate pastries, muffins, desserts and breads. Several tables overlook the displays, and there are a wealth of drinks and light fare for lunch that can also be enjoyed here or to go.

Mustards Grill *(707)944-2424*
7 mi. S at 7399 St. Helena Hwy. (CA 29) - Yountville
L-D. *Expensive*
Mustards is a premier source of New California cuisine. Mesquite-broiled and brick oven-smoked meats are flavorful hallmarks, while fresh, bold support dishes are given a deft light touch. Guests are served in a simply au courant dining room, or amid the whitewashed openness of a cool, screened porch.

Showley's at Miramonte *(707)963-1200*
downtown at 1327 Railroad Av.
L-D. *Expensive*
Creative wine country cuisine is typified by salmon fillet in filo pastry with an orange butter sauce. Assorted luscious desserts like chocolate hoo hoo (chocolate pastry layered with Belgian chocolate cream and cappuccino ice cream) can also be enjoyed at widely spaced, casually elegant tables in dining rooms and a wine bar of a historic building or in a lovely hideaway garden.

Terra *(707)963-8931*
downtown at 1345 Railroad Av.
D only. *Very Expensive*
Pacific Rim fusion cuisine is typified by dishes like broiled sake-marinated sea bass with shrimp dumplings or veal medallions with wild mushroom sauce. Housemade desserts are similarly tempting, and usually delicious. Crisp white linens and blondewood chairs distinguish two large dining rooms in a historic brick building.

Tra Vigne *(707)963-4444*
just S on CA 29 at 1050 Charter Oak Av.
L-D. *Expensive*
Seasonally fresh Italian classics and California updates are all made here from scratch, including grand desserts. Decor in the very popular restaurant is similarly sophisticated. Adjoining the cavernous dining room with walls graced with Italian poster art is a Tuscan-inspired partially-open kitchen and a grandiose polished mahogany bar. The garden patio is similarly appealing on a warm day. There is also a stylish little **Cantinetta** (Italian market/wine bar/deli).

LODGING

St. Helena has become one of the country-inn capitals of the West. The town carefully protects its distinction of having no large-scale or chain accommodations. High season rates (April through October and all weekends) are often reduced by 20% or more in winter.

Auberge du Soleil   *(707)963-1211*
  5 mi. SE at 180 Rutherford Hill Rd. - Rutherford 94573
  52 units   *(800)348-5406*   *Very Expensive*
One of the nation's most lavish hideaways is nestled in an olive grove on a hillside overlooking Napa Valley. Three tennis courts, a large pool, fitness and beauty center, and a renowned restaurant (see listing) are features. Each luxuriously furnished room has a fireplace and a private patio or deck overlooking wine country. Fourteen spacious rooms also have a large whirlpool bath.

Crossroads Inn   *(707)944-0646*
  10 mi. SE at 6380 Silverado Trail - Napa 94558
  4 units   *Very Expensive*
The panoramic vineyard view is outstanding from this bucolic bed-and-breakfast inn's lofty perch. Breakfast served in your suite and afternoon tea is complimentary. Each beautifully furnished room has an in-room whirlpool and overlooks vineyards and the valley.

El Bonita Motel   *(707)963-3216*
  1 mi. S at 195 Main St. - 94574
  41 units   *(800)541-3284*   *Moderate-Expensive*
A landscaped pool, whirlpool, and sauna are attractions of this single-level motel surrounded by gardens. Some comfortably furnished rooms have a whirlpool bath and kitchenette.

Harvest Inn   *(707)963-9463*
  1 mi. S at 1 Main St. (CA 29) - 94574
  54 units   *(800)950-8466*   *Expensive-Very Expensive*
Situated in a working vineyard is a fantasy motor inn for adults. Amid carefully tended gardens with two large pools and whirlpools are imposing, brick Tudor-style buildings lavishly furnished with antiques and quality reproductions. Each spacious room is beautifully appointed. Some suites have a large in-room whirlpool, two fireplaces and a balcony with a private vineyard view.

Meadowwood Resort   *(707)963-3646*
  2 mi. E at 900 Meadowwood Lane - 95474
  99 units   *(800)458-8080*   *Very Expensive*
Two large pools, a whirlpool, a Parcours circuit, and (for a fee) seven championship tennis courts, a 9-hole golf course and a professional croquet court, plus a gift boutique are all available in this magnificent retreat. A world-class restaurant (see listing) overlooks the golf course and majestic oaks in a secluded canyon. Each room is spacious and elegant, and has every contemporary convenience. Many have a fireplace and a private view deck.

Napa Valley Lodge   *(707)944-2468*
  9 mi. SE off CA 29 at 2230 Madison St. - Yountville 94599
  55 units   *(800)368-2468*   *Expensive-Very Expensive*
The valley's premier motel has a large pool and whirlpool by vineyards, and a sauna and exercise room. A champagne buffet breakfast is complimentary. Each room is beautifully furnished and has a private balcony or patio. Some also have fireplace and vineyard view.

Sutter Home Inn   *(707)963-4130*
just S at 277 St. Helena Hwy. South (Box 248) - 94574
3 units   *Expensive*
A picturesque 1884 landmark home is now a plush bed-and-breakfast inn. Colorful gardens extend to the winery's friendly and popular visitor center. Full breakfast is complimentary. Each beautifully furnished room blends Victorian charm with today's conveniences, including a private bath.

Villagio Inn & Spa   *(707)944-2930*
9 mi. SE on Washington St. - Yountville 94599
112 units   *(800)351-1133   Expensive-Very Expensive*
In 1998, a luxurious state-of-the-art motor inn opened next to the Vintage 1870 specialty shopping complex. Vineyards and gardens surround fashionable low-rise building clusters. Amenities include two tennis courts, a lap pool, whirlpools, bicycle rental, a wine bar and (fee) full-service beauty and fitness spa. Continental champagne breakfast buffet, welcome wine and afternoon tea are complimentary. Each spacious, beautifully furnished unit (up to two bedrooms) has a gas fireplace, an oversized bath tub, and a private balcony or veranda.

Vineyard Country Inn   *(707)963-1000*
just S at 201 Main St. - 94574
21 units   *Expensive*
French country decor, plus a pool and whirlpool, enhance this all-suites bed-and-breakfast inn. Full breakfast is complimentary. Each beautifully furnished room has a fireplace. Most have a private deck.

Vintage Inn   *(707)944-1112*
9 mi. SE at 6541 Washington St. - Yountville 94599
80 units   *(800)351-1133   Expensive-Very Expensive*
This deluxe motor inn is a short stroll from the Vintage 1870 shopping complex. A landscaped courtyard includes a pool and whirlpool. Two tennis courts for guests are nearby, and there are rental bicycles. Champagne buffet breakfast and afternoon tea are complimentary. Each beautifully furnished unit has a fireplace and an individual balcony or veranda.

The Wine Country Inn   *(707)963-7077*
2 mi. N off CA 29 at 1152 Lodi Lane - 94574
24 units   *Expensive-Very Expensive*
Hidden away on a slope above a vineyard is a charming bed-and-breakfast motor inn with a pool and whirlpool. Full buffet breakfast and afternoon wine and appetizers are complimentary. Individually decorated rooms have antique furnishings, good vineyard views, and all contemporary amenities including a private bath. Many of the spacious, well-furnished units have a fireplace. Several have a whirlpool (two are on a private deck).

BASIC INFORMATION

Elevation: 256 feet   *Population: 4,990*
Location: 65 miles North of San Francisco
Nearest airport with commercial flights: San Francisco - 76 miles
St. Helena Chamber of Commerce   (707)963-4456   (800)799-6456
downtown at 1080 Main St. (Box 124) - 94374

San Luis Obispo, California

San Luis Obispo is a classic California town. Its location, in a picturesque valley bordered by Coast Range mountains a few miles from the ocean, also benefits from one of the nation's mildest year-round climates. The town is an architectural showcase for a heritage that began when Father Juniper Serra established a mission here in 1772. Over the years, Spaniards and American Indians were joined by settlers from all over the world.

The town's diversity and economic vitality are apparent in one of the state's most handsome business districts. Its centerpiece is still the adobe mission above a sunny plaza, and the adjoining creek is now in a delightful park backed by inviting restaurants and specialty shops. Nearby are two of California's best motor hotels, plus numerous distinctive lodgings that serve visitors here to explore miles of hard sand beaches, vast sand dunes, secluded ocean coves, large scenic reservoirs, picturesque hot springs, and a mountain wilderness.

WEATHER PROFILE

V.W.R. *		Jan.	Feb.	Mar.	Apr.	May	June	July	Aug.	Sep.	Oct.	Nov.	Dec.
Great	10												
Fine	9												
Very Good	8												
Good	7												
Moderate	6												
	5												
	4												
	3												
	2												
	1												
	0												

	Jan.	Feb.	Mar.	Apr.	May	June	July	Aug.	Sep.	Oct.	Nov.	Dec.
V.W.R.*	3	4	6	8	9	10	10	10	10	10	8	4
Temperature												
Ave. High	62	64	65	68	70	74	77	77	78	75	69	64
Ave. Low	42	44	45	46	48	50	52	53	52	50	46	43
Precipitation												
Inches Rain	4.5	4.3	3.1	1.6	0.5	0.1	-	-	0.4	1.0	2.2	4.5
Inches Snow	-	-	-	-	-	-	-	-	-	-	-	-

*V.W.R. = Vokac Weather Rating; probability of mild (warm & dry) weather on any given day.

ATTRACTIONS

Avila Beach
10 mi. SW via US 101 on Avila Rd.
This raffish little town is unique along the central coast for its combination of a south-facing shoreline and a sheltered harbor. In an ongoing major clean-up, soil and sand tainted by underground oil pipes will be replaced, along with many buildings. Facilities include a plain park; fishing pier; charter boats and gear rental concessions. Nearby is a remote, popular nude beach.

Cal Poly   *(805)756-5734*
1 mi. N on California Blvd.
California State Polytechnic University, the fifth oldest unit (1901) of the California university system, is just north of town. About 15,000 full-time students use the subtropically landscaped campus. Impressive buildings include a new world-class performing arts center.

Fishing Charters
Full day or twilight fishing trips with rental equipment can be chartered any time. Fall albacore fishing, and winter whale watching trips, can also be reserved at:
  Avila Beach Sportfishing   *(805)595-7200*
  11 mi. SW via US 101 at W end of Avila Rd.

Food Specialties
  San Luis Sourdough   *(805)543-6142*
  1 mi. S at 3580 Sueldo at Granada
Cognoscenti have sought this tucked-away culinary landmark for years to enjoy some of the best sourdough in the West.

Lopez Lake Recreation Area   *(805)489-1122*
18 mi. SE via CA 227 & Lopez Canyon Rd.
Open year-round, this picturesque reservoir with twenty-two miles of shoreline offers swimming areas, good trout and bass fishing, sailing and windsurfing, a marina with a paved boat launch, and boat rentals. Campsites line oak-studded, grassy slopes near the lake. A food and supplies store, picnic areas, barbecue facilities, restrooms, playgrounds, and a museum are also available. For offbeat excitement, the Mustang Water Slide (see listing) is the area's best onshore feature.

Mission San Luis Obispo de Tolusa   *(805)543-6850*
downtown at Chorro/Monterey Sts.
The "Prince of Missions" is the fifth of the California missions, founded in 1772 by Father Junipero Serra. Built of adobe brick by Chumash Indians with walls up to five feet thick, it was the first in California to have a tiled roof. The restored building still serves as a parish church and also includes a major museum, gift shop, and gardens.

Montana de Oro State Beach   *(805)528-0513*
17 mi. W via Los Osos Valley Rd.
Hiking in rugged hills and headlands above unspoiled sandy beaches and secluded coves is the major attraction in this largely undeveloped park where wildlife and spring wildflowers abound. Beachcombing, clamming, skin diving, shore fishing, and camping are also popular.

Morro Bay Embarcadero
12 mi. NW via CA 1 - Morro Bay
A tourist attraction with a lively nautical atmosphere has developed along the little bay, with many family-oriented gift shops and restaurants. Numerous charter boats are readily available for ocean fishing year-round, and for whale watching tours during the annual winter migration of the great grey whales.

Morro Bay State Park   *(805)772-2560*
11 mi. W via CA 1 & State Park Rd. - Morro Bay
Facilities in this outstanding marine area include a large campground, shady picnic sites, a scenic golf course, nature walks and hiking trails, a museum, plus boat and bicycle rentals. Pismo clamming and fishing, good surfing, skin diving, and cold water swimming are also enjoyed. Remote sand dunes and beaches on the peninsula between the ocean and bay are well worth the walk or boat trip.
Morro Rock
12 mi. W via CA 1 - Morro Bay
A solid rock monolith, Morro Rock, juts 576 feet above Morro Bay. Unfortunately, the natural grandeur of the geological phenomenon is marred by the adjacent giant Morro Bay Power Plant and its three towering 450-foot stacks. Several larger but less precipitous morros create a dramatic "backbone" down the middle of the Los Osos Valley that extends back to San Luis Obispo and beyond.

Warm Water Features
Avila Hot Springs Spa   *(805)595-2359*
8 mi. S at US 101 at 250 Avila Beach Dr. - Avila Beach
This venerable family-oriented hot springs spa has a large warm swimming pool and a small, hotter pool outdoors. These and indoor private hot mineral baths and massage facilities are open year-round.
Mustang Water Slide   *(805)489-8898*
18 mi. SE via CA 227 & Lopez Canyon Rd.
In Lopez Lake Recreation Area, visitors can enjoy two 600-foot curving warm waterslides and four hot mineral whirlpools on an oak-studded hillside above the lake. Open daily June thru Sept.
Sycamore Mineral Springs   *(805)595-7302*
9 mi. SW via US 101 at 1215 Avila Beach Rd. - Avila Beach
Open 24 hours every day, this unique facility rents redwood hot tubs by the hour in seductive natural settings on a steep oak-covered hillside. Among more than two dozen tubs, the ones named "Shangri-La" and "Rendezvous" are especially remote and serene.

Wineries
A major recently-recognized wine-growing district is burgeoning a few miles southeast of town in Edna Valley. Several have free tastes, tours, and gift shops. Many good wineries have also been developed within an hour's drive to the north around Paso Robles and to the south near Solvang. Complete information and a map of all Central Coast wineries can be obtained at the Chamber of Commerce or local bookstores. Currently, the most impressive nearby are:
Cottonwood Canyon Winery   *(805)549-9463*
S via CA 227 at 4330 Santa Fe Rd.
Young winery featuring estate-grown chardonnay and pinot noir.
Edna Valley Vineyard   *(805)544-9594*
S via CA 227 at 2585 Biddle Ranch Rd.
Classic estate-grown and produced chardonnay and pinot noir, plus the valley's most impressive tasting room and winery shop.
Talley Vineyards   *(805)489-0446*
S via CA 227 and Orcut Rd. at 3031 Lopez Dr. - Arroyo Grande
Estate-grown chardonnay and pinot noir, in 1860s adobe tasting room.
Windemere   *(805)542-0133*
S via CA 227 at 3482 Sacramento Dr., Suite E
Award-winning handcrafted wines from famed family-owned vineyards.

RESTAURANTS

Apple Farm Restaurant *(805)544-6100*
1 mi. E at 2015 Monterey St.
B-L-D. Moderate
Their own fine baked goods (appropriately emphasizing apples in traditional and streusel-topped pies, dumplings, baked, raw, and in cider) are featured with all-American homestyle fare in big, country-charming dining rooms that are extremely popular. A fascinating water-powered grist mill and well-stocked gift shop adjoin.

Boston Bagel Co. *(805)541-5134*
downtown at 1127 Broad St. #B
B-L. Low
Boston Bagel Co. displays a delightful selection of some of California's best bagels. All are made from scratch daily with no preservatives in the traditional method—kettled, then baked. They are served with light fare in the little shop, or to go.

Buona Tavola *(805)545-8000*
downtown at 1037 Monterey St.
L-D. Expensive
This delightfully sophisticated Italian restaurant does fine work with traditional and California updates of Northern Italian classics, including luscious housemade desserts. The little dining room is awash in linen and attractive local art, plus a view of the expo kitchen. Out back is a romantic fountain courtyard for alfresco dining.

Caffe Brio *(805)541-5282*
downtown at 1203 Marsh St.
B-L-D. Moderate
Delicious breads, pastries and desserts, plus pastas and raviolis, calzones—even sauces and roasted coffee—are made here from fresh natural ingredients. The traditional and creative Italian dishes are served as takeout, or at casual seating by savory display cases.

F. McLintock's Saloon *(805)773-1892*
9 mi. S via US 101 at 750 Mattie Rd. - Pismo Beach
D only. Expensive
The region's most famous restaurant is the best place to go for very complete meals highlighting Central California's gourmet specialty, oak-pit barbecued steak and ribs. The Western outfits of the staff match the rustic decor of big dining rooms in a historic roadhouse that has expanded with the times. There is also a saloon with live entertainment, plus a "general store," butcher shop, and a large gift shop.

The Gardens of Avila Restaurant *(805)595-7365*
9 mi. SW at 1215 Avila Beach Dr. - Avila Beach
B-L-D. Expensive
Here, innovative California cuisine melds flavors from around the world into memorable dishes. Housemade baked goods and desserts are also delightful. The contemporary comfortable dining room and lounge capture the lush tranquility of the salubrious hideaway.

Giuseppe's *(805)773-2870*
11 mi. S via US 101 at 891 Price St. - Pismo Beach
L-D. Expensive
Seafood casserole baked on a shell is a terrific update of a dish served in this historic building for decades. Other creative California and Italian fare ranges from wood-fired pizzas or saddle of rabbit with sauteed peppers to a silky smooth tiramisu for dessert. The stylish dining room and bar are a friendly pleasant backdrop.

Linn's   *(805)546-8444*
downtown at 1141 Chorro
B-L-D.   *Moderate*
Linn's is San Luis Obispo's best bakery/restaurant. Delectable muffins, cinnamon rolls, and other morning delights are displayed and served along with California fare ranging from breakfast burritos to tri-tip steak and eggs. Traditional and innovative dinners from meat pies to stir fries are served with desserts made here. Clerestory windows by padded booths provide tree views. A gourmet gift shop adjoins.

Madonna Inn   *(805)543-3000*
1 mi. W by US 101 at 100 Madonna Rd.
B-L-D.   *Expensive*
At the Madonna Inn, spectacular homemade pastries and prodigious cakes might go unnoticed by first-timers because of the one-of-a-kind decor. Both the paean-to-pink coffee shop (with its copper-topped tables and elaborate wood carvings) and dining room (aglow in heart-shaped pink leather booths and glittering cupid chandelier) are authentically flamboyant fantasies. Even the restrooms are so unique that women occasionally sneak into the downstairs men's room when the coast is clear just to see the incomparable fixtures.

Old Country Deli   *(805)541-2968*
downtown at 600 Marsh St.
B-L.   *Moderate*
Showcases in this deli are packed with premium-quality home-cured ham, sausage, jerky, cheeses, gourmet foods, and wines of the region. Superb ribs are barbecued over oak wood in front of the store on Saturdays.

Woodstock's Pizza   *(805)541-4420*
downtown at 1000 Higuera St.
L-D.   *Moderate*
The best pizza parlor south of San Francisco may be the original Woodstock's. Guys in the expo kitchen flip white and whole wheat dough for designer pizzas and an infinite number of build-your-own with all kinds of ingredients. Wash it down with several tap beers and other beverages in a big boisterous parlor with electronic games, TVs, and loud music to ward off serious conversations.

LODGING

San Luis Obispo gave the world the word "motel" more than half a century ago. Today, most of the major motel chains and two unique motels have superceded the original Motel Inn in town. Most lodgings are concentrated on Monterey Street east of downtown. High season is summer and most weekends. Rates are usually reduced at least 20% at other times.

Apple Farm Inn   *(805)544-2040*
1 mi. E at 2015 Monterey St. - 93401
69 units   *(800)255-2040   Expensive-Very Expensive*
The Apple Farm is one of Central California's most charming lodgings. The contemporary complex includes a handsome Victorian-style luxury inn; a posh motel with country decor; a famous family restaurant (see listing) and bakery; collectibles and gift shop; and an old mill with a water wheel used to grind wheat, churn homemade ice cream and press cider. Luxuriant gardens surround these buildings, a pool and a whirlpool. Each beautifully furnished inn room blends a country theme and all contemporary conveniences, including a gas fireplace.

The Cliffs at Shell Beach   *(805)773-5000*

9 mi. S via US 101 at 2757 Shell Beach Rd. - Shell Beach 93449

165 units   *(800)826-5838   Expensive-Very Expensive*

Aptly named, the Cliffs is perched on a bluff high above the ocean. The contemporary five-story complex with palm accents has a view pool, whirlpool, sauna, exercise room, a plush dining room with a grand ocean view, and an entertainment lounge. Each spacious room is beautifully furnished. Many have a sea view. "Ocean View Suites" have a large in-room whirlpool and a private ocean-view balcony.

Embassy Suites   *(805)549-0800*

1 mi. W by US 101 at 333 Madonna Rd. - 93405

195 units   *(800)864-6000*   *Expensive*

The area's largest lodging is a modern four-story building with a garden atrium, an indoor pool, four whirlpools, exercise rooms, restaurant and lounge. Full breakfast and evening beverages are complimentary. Each spacious two-room suite is well furnished and has a kitchenette.

Garden Street Inn Bed & Breakfast   *(805)545-9802*

downtown at 1212 Garden St. - 93401

13 units   *Expensive*

A Victorian home near the heart of town has been tastefully restored as a bed-and-breakfast. Full breakfast is complimentary. Each well-furnished room includes original antiques and a private bath (no phone or TV). Most have a clawfoot tub or whirlpool bath. Two also have a gas fireplace.

Kon Tiki Inn   *(805)773-4833*

11 mi. S via US 101 at 1621 Price St. - Pismo Beach 93449

86 units   *Moderate*

This modern four-story motel curves along a well-landscaped blufftop with a private stairway to the beach, a large pool and whirlpool, two tennis courts, racquetball courts, and a fitness center. Each of the well-furnished rooms has an ocean-view patio or balcony. Four also have a gas fireplace.

Madonna Inn   *(805)543-3000*

1 mi. W by US 101 at 100 Madonna Rd. - 93405

109 units   *(800)543-9666   Expensive-Very Expensive*

The Madonna Inn is the West's premier fantasy lodging. For more than forty years, the motor inn by the morro has been delighting travelers with its inimitable flamboyance. The complex includes a restaurant (see listing), coffee shop, bakery, lounge, ladies boutique, men's store, and gourmet gift shop. No two beautifully furnished rooms are alike. Suites with a gas fireplace and especially the unique "rock rooms" (with rock walls, floors, ceilings and waterfall showers!) are now so popular they must be reserved well in advance.

San Luis Bay Inn   *(805)595-2333*

10 mi. SW via US 101 at 3254 Avila Beach Dr. - Avila Beach 93424

51 units   *(800)438-6493*   *Expensive*

This self-contained resort is on a promontory across a highway from a sandy beach and the village of Avila Beach (see listing). Amenities include a (fee) 18-hole golf course, plus four tennis courts, a large outdoor pool, whirlpool, dining room and lounge. Each spacious room is well furnished and has a private patio or balcony—many with an ocean view.

Sea Crest Resort Motel   *(805)773-4608*
10 mi. S via US 101 at 2241 Price St. - Pismo Beach 93449
160 units   *(800)782-8400*   Moderate-Expensive
This large modern motel curves around a big palm-backed pool and whirlpool at the crest of a bluff above the sea. A private stairway extends to the beach. Most of the well-furnished rooms have a private ocean-view balcony or patio. Some also have a large in-room whirlpool.

Sea Venture Resort   *(805)773-4994*
11 mi. S via US 101 at 100 Ocean View Av. - Pismo Beach 93449
50 units   *(800)662-5545*   Expensive-Very Expensive
The Central Coast's most luxurious motor inn is on a broad ocean beach that extends for miles. The post-modern three-story complex (completely renovated in 1995) has a pool, (fee) massage salon, and a tony restaurant and bar with a panoramic ocean view. A Continental breakfast delivered to your room is complimentary. Each beautifully furnished room has a gas fireplace and a private balcony—most with a private two-person whirlpool and an ocean view.

Shelter Cove Lodge - Best Western   *(805)773-3511*
10 mi. S at 2651 Price St. - Pismo Beach 93449
52 units   *(800)528-1234*   Expensive
Sprinkled along a blufftop high above the ocean is a plush motel with palm-accented gardens, sea-view pool and whirlpool, and a picturesque gazebo by a path extending to a secluded cove. Expanded Continental breakfast is complimentary. Each spacious, beautifully furnished room has a private patio or balcony with an ocean view. Four also have a fireplace.

Shore Cliff Lodge - Best Western   *(805)773-4671*
10 mi. S via US 101 at 2555 Price St. - Pismo Beach 93449
99 units   *(800)441-8885*   Expensive
This contemporary three-story motor hotel is aptly named with some buildings seemingly draped over the rim of a high sea cliff. Nicely landscaped grounds include a large pool and whirlpool, sauna, plus a stairway to a sandy cove and a popular ocean-view dining room and entertainment lounge. Each spacious well-furnished room has a private patio or balcony with an ocean view.

Sycamore Mineral Springs Resort   *(805)595-7302*
9 mi. SW via US 101 at 1215 Avila Beach Dr. - 93405
51 units   *(800)234-5831*   Expensive-Very Expensive
One of California's most romantic hideaway resorts was thoroughly upgraded for the millennium. It is tucked away by a luxuriant wooded hillside next to a series of (fee) redwood hot tubs filled with warm mineral waters. Colorful gardens surround the pool and (fee) mineral springs spa complex, a gourmet gift shop, and the delightful **Gardens of Avila Restaurant** (see listing) and lounge. Each beautifully furnished room has a private deck with a warm mineral springs whirlpool.

BASIC INFORMATION
Elevation: 230 feet   *Population: 41,958*
Location: 195 mi. Northwest of Los Angeles
Nearest airport with commercial flights: in town
San Luis Obispo Chamber of Commerce (805)781-2777
   downtown at 1039 Chorro St. - 93401
   www.slonet.org / ~ipslococ

Solvang, California

Solvang is the Danish capital of America. The sights, sounds, and aromas of an authentic Danish village are present here in the heart of the lovely Santa Ynez Valley. All around, lush pasturelands are accented by noble oak trees. Coast Range mountains to the south, and the nearby ocean endow the valley with one of America's mildest climates. Early in this century, a group of Danes established a school and village next to the Spanish Mission Santa Ines. After World War II, visitors began to flock to this unique cultural enclave to savor increasingly Danish specialties and architecture.

Today, their descendants still preside over Scandinavian import shops, gourmet food stores, bakeries, restaurants and inns that reflect the Danish heritage. Shopping and strolling in town, bicycling and wine touring in the valley, hiking and camping in the Coast Range, plus sailing and fishing in Southern California's largest lake and the nearby ocean can be enjoyed year-round.

WEATHER PROFILE

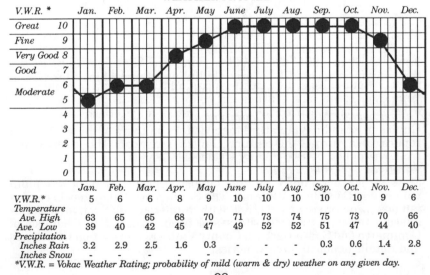

	Jan.	Feb.	Mar.	Apr.	May	June	July	Aug.	Sep.	Oct.	Nov.	Dec.
V.W.R.*	5	6	6	8	9	10	10	10	10	10	9	6
Temperature												
Ave. High	63	65	65	68	70	71	73	74	75	73	70	66
Ave. Low	39	40	42	45	47	49	52	52	51	47	44	40
Precipitation												
Inches Rain	3.2	2.9	2.5	1.6	0.3	-	-	-	0.3	0.6	1.4	2.8
Inches Snow	-	-	-	-	-	-	-	-	-	-	-	-

*V.W.R. = Vokac Weather Rating; probability of mild (warm & dry) weather on any given day.

98

Solvang, California
ATTRACTIONS

Bethania Lutheran Church   *(805)688-4637*
downtown at 603 Atterdag Rd.
This church typifies Danish provincial architecture. It's worth a quiet visit to see the model of a full-rigged ship hanging from the ceiling in accordance with Scandinavian seafaring tradition.

Bicycling
Dr. J's Bicychiatry   *(805)688-6263*
downtown at 1661-B Fir Av.
The less-traveled highways and byways throughout the pastoral Santa Ynez Valley provide unlimited opportunities for leisurely bicycling. Bicycles can be rented here by the hour or longer.

Downtown
around Mission Dr. & Alisal Rd.
All of downtown Solvang's attractions are within comfortable walking distance of numerous large free parking lots that even include public restrooms. The entire area has a Danish motif brimming with architectural surprises. Cobblestone sidewalks beneath old-fashioned gas lamps, fanciful gables, wood-shingled and copper-tiled rooftops, creaking windmills, hand-carved benches, fountains, and statues abound. So do ersatz thatched rooftops, stork nests and birds, and colorful royal guard boxes. Collectively, these embellishments provide a unique pedestrian-oriented showcase for the nation's biggest collection of Scandinavian imports, restaurants, gourmet food and wine shops, and bakeries.

El Capitan, Gaviota, and Refugio Beach State Parks
26, 15 and 24 mi. S on US 101
Warm ocean surfing, scuba diving, and swimming (in summer only); pier fishing (no license required); boating and sailing; picnicking and camping are enjoyed in these well-furnished parks. Sunbathing and people-watching are also popular on fine sandy beaches.

Lake Cachuma Recreation Area   *(805)686-5054*
11 mi. SE via CA 246 & CA 154
The largest reservoir in Southern California provides excellent fishing, boating, and sailing opportunities. Swimming is not permitted in the lake, but there is an outdoor pool, plus a roller skating rink, miniature golf, and a large campground.

Mission Santa Ines   *(805)688-4815*
just E of downtown at 1760 Mission Dr.
Established in 1804, this "hidden gem" was the nineteenth in the Spanish mission chain. The large skillfully restored adobe church is on grounds that include an arched colonnade and garden.

Sightseeing Tour
downtown at Alisal Rd./Copenhagen Dr.
Guides in Scandinavian attire take visitors on tours of the village in a replica of a turn-of-the-century Danish streetcar. The colorful red trolley is pulled by two mighty Clydesdale horses.

Wineries   *(800)218-0881*
Solvang is surrounded by the largest concentration of premium wineries in Southern California. The Santa Ynez Valley has become a famous wine-producing district with numerous distinctive wineries offering tastes, tours, gift shops and picnic areas. The Chamber of Commerce and Santa Barbara County Vintners Association have maps and details about all area wineries.

RESTAURANTS

Ballard Store   *(805)688-5319*
4 mi. NE at 2449 Baseline Av. - Ballard
D only.   *Expensive*
The Ballard Store is the premier restaurant of the Santa Ynez Valley. Contemporary Continental cuisine is consistently well prepared with the freshest quality ingredients, accompanied by homemade breads and desserts. Casually posh dining rooms and a wine bar convey the warm Yankee charm of what was once a country general store.

Brothers   *(805)688-9934*
downtown at 409 First St.
D only.   *Expensive*
In 1996, Solvang got a major boost from the opening of a gourmet restaurant featuring creative California cuisine prepared by talented chef/owner brothers. Seasonally fresh dishes are enhanced by breads and desserts made here. A warm, cozy dining room adjoins a pleasant cobblestone patio.

Cold Spring Tavern   *(805)967-0066*
21 mi. S via CA 154 at 5995 Stagecoach Rd.
L-D.   *Expensive*
Hearty Western fare, including wild game, is accompanied by delicious homemade bread. All of the charm of a bygone era is present in this historic stagecoach stop where the buildings have a ramshackle authenticity unmatched in Southern California. The tiny firelit bar is particularly romantic. An adjacent rowdy log cabin bar has live music.

The Hitching Post II   *(805)688-0676*
2 mi. W at 406 E. CA 246 - Buellton
D only.   *Expensive*
"World's Best Barbeque Steaks" is the immodest claim on their sign. Oakwood Santa Maria-style barbeque for flavorful grilled steaks has earned a lot of fans for this dinnerhouse. Relaxed Western decor complements hearty helpings of good grub, including some unusual surprises like ostrich appetizers.

Little Mermaid   *(805)688-6141*
downtown at 1546 Mission Dr.
B-L-D.   *Low*
The best dishes here are authentic aebleskivers made in an exhibition kitchen and served all day with homemade raspberry jam and Danish sausage in casual, colorful dining rooms. The pleasant little restaurant also has Danish tap beer.

Mattei's Tavern   *(805)688-4820*
6 mi. N on CA 154 - Los Olivos
L-D.   *Moderate*
In continuous operation since 1886, this valley landmark offers prime rib and steaks, plus seafood and a salad bar, in carefully restored Old West dining rooms and on a lovely garden porch. An authentic saloon and parlor with working fireplaces contribute to the nostalgia.

Mollekroen   *(805)688-4555*
downtown at 435 Alisal Rd.
L-D.   *Low*
Well-prepared Danish specialties in Solvang's best and most bountiful smorgaasbord attract enthusiastic crowds to this casual and congested upstairs restaurant. Downstairs, a congenial lounge with a Danish motif provides live entertainment on weekends.

Solvang Restaurant   *(805)688-4645*
downtown at 1672 Copenhagen Dr.
B-L.   *Low*
Tasty aebleskivers are made by a pass-through window up front all
day, and featured along with Danish pancakes and sausages, plus
omelets. All contribute to the popularity of this colorful coffee shop.

LODGING

Motor lodges offering more-or-less Danish architecture and decor have
proliferated downtown. High season is summer, and on weekends year-
round. Nearby Buellton has a little motel row that serves as a backup,
and offers relative bargains midweek. Rates are usually reduced at
least 10% in winter and on non-summer weekdays.

Alisal Guest Ranch   *(805)688-6411*
3 mi. S at 1054 Alisal Rd. - 93463
73 units   *(800)425-4725*   *Very Expensive*
One of the most luxurious guest ranches in America is in a pretty little
canyon near town. Refined single-story bungalows are set amidst
flowers, oaks, and sycamores in 10,000 acres of rolling green foothills.
Facilities include (for a fee) two championship 18-hole golf courses;
seven tennis courts and pro shop; stables for guided horseback rides;
the resort's own small lake for sailing and fishing; and bicycles. Other
amenities include a large landscaped pool and whirlpool; ping pong and
other games; plus a refined dining room and entertainment lounge. At
the newer golf course, the **River Grill** (B-L-D—Expensive), both the
cuisine and decor are innovative and contemporary. Each spacious,
beautifully decorated room has a fireplace and view porch. Rates are
for two people on a modified American plan, breakfast and dinner
included.

The Ballard Inn   *(805)688-7770*
4 mi. NE at 2436 Baseline Av. - Ballard 93463
15 units   *(800)638-2466*   *Expensive*
The most meticulous decor in the valley contributes to the charm of
this elegant young bed-and-breakfast inn. Full breakfast and afternoon
wine and refreshments are complimentary. **Cafe Chardonnay** (D
only— Expensive) has creative wine country cuisine in a warm country
setting. Each room has a full bath, and celebrates an aspect of the
area's past with beautiful furnishings and decorations. Seven rooms
also have a fireplace.

Chimney Sweep Inn   *(805)688-2111*
downtown at 1554 Copenhagen Dr. - 93463
56 units   *(800)824-6444*   *Moderate-Very Expensive*
This Danish contemporary motor inn is backed by an intimate flower-
filled garden with a secluded whirlpool. It was recently doubled in size
to include the Old World-style inn next door. A Danish bakery
breakfast is complimentary. Most rooms are spacious and beautifully
furnished. Six delightful fantasy cottages also have a living room with
a pressed-wood fireplace, kitchen, private patio and a large whirlpool.

Danish Country Inn   *(805)688-2018*
downtown at 1455 Mission Dr. - 93463
82 units   *(800)447-3529*   *Expensive*
A whirlpool overlooking an oak grove and a small pool are features of
this large motor inn, along with a charming oak-view room used for
complimentary full breakfast and cocktail hour for guests. Many of the
spacious, well-furnished rooms have a large private oak-view balcony.

Los Olivos Grand Hotel   *(805)688-7788*
6 mi. N at 2860 Grand Av. - Los Olivos 93441
21 units   *(800)446-2455*   *Very Expensive*
The valley's first small hotel in the European tradition of intimate elegance opened in 1985 in the heart of tiny Los Olivos. Nicely landscaped grounds include a pool and whirlpool. **Remington's** (L-D—Expensive) features gourmet cuisine in a refined dining room. Bicycles, plus wine and appetizers, are complimentary. Each beautifully appointed room has a gas fireplace and a refrigerator. Spacious suites also have an in-bath whirlpool.

The Petersen Village Inn   *(805)688-3121*
downtown at 1576 Mission Dr. - 93463
39 units   *(800)321-8985*   *Expensive*
One of Solvang's best Danish-style motor inns is built around a charming fountain courtyard lined with shops, a bakery, restaurants and a piano bar. European buffet breakfast and wine hour are complimentary. Each well-furnished room is individually decorated with Scandinavian touches. Most have a patio or balcony. "Tower Suite" features an in-bath whirlpool and gas fireplace.

Quality Inn of Solvang   *(805)688-3210*
downtown at 1450 Mission Dr. - 93463
75 units   *(800)457-5373*   *Moderate-Expensive*
The area's only indoor pool, plus a whirlpool and recreation room, enhance this contemporary motel. All rooms are well furnished. Suites have a large whirlpool in a separate room, and a kitchenette.

Solvang Royal Scandinavian Inn   *(805)688-8000*
downtown at 400 Alisal Rd. (Box 30) - 93464
133 units   *(800)624-5572*   *Expensive*
Solvang's largest lodging is a modern three-story hotel with a Danish facade. The convention-oriented facility includes a pool and whirlpool, game room, plus an Old-World-style restaurant and entertainment lounge. Each room is spacious and well furnished. Some have a semi-private view balcony.

Storybook Inn Bed & Breakfast   *(805)688-1703*
downtown at 409 First St. - 93463
9 units   *(800)786-7925*   *Expensive*
Each room in this appealing young bed-and-breakfast inn is named after a famous Hans Christian Andersen story. Continental breakfast (gourmet on weekends) and evening wine and cheese are complimentary. **Brothers** (see listing) is on the first floor. Each beautifully furnished room has antiques, a private bath and a gas fireplace (no TV). Two suites have a large whirlpool bath.

BASIC INFORMATION

Elevation: *490 feet*   *Population (1990):*   *4,741*
Location: *130 miles Northwest of Los Angeles*
Nearest airport with commercial flights: Santa Barbara - 40 miles
Solvang Conference & Visitors Bureau (805)688-6144 (800)468-6765
   downtown at 1511-A Mission Dr. (Box 70) - 93464
Information Center at 1639 Copenhagen Dr.

Sonoma, California

Sonoma is the treasury of Northern California history. For more than 170 years, the heart of town has been a large plaza surrounded by distinctive 19th century buildings. Beyond, its lush pastoral setting in "The Valley of the Moon" extends to gentle grass-and-oak-covered hills north of San Francisco Bay. Sonoma was founded in 1823 by Spanish Franciscan fathers. It became "the birthplace of California viticulture" a decade later with the first major production of non-mission grapes.

The wine industry remains the key to Sonoma's prosperity, with more than thirty premium wineries in the valley. Downtown, the plaza delights strollers and picnickers, and is still the site of California's oldest wine celebration. Historic structures on all sides house distinctive specialty shops, gourmet food stores and restaurants, and atmospheric bars and lounges. Several romantic small hotels and inns in skillfully restored historic structures are on or near the plaza.

WEATHER PROFILE

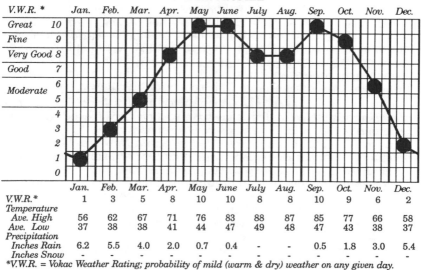

V.W.R. *		Jan.	Feb.	Mar.	Apr.	May	June	July	Aug.	Sep.	Oct.	Nov.	Dec.
V.W.R.*		1	3	5	8	10	10	8	8	10	9	6	2
Temperature													
Ave. High		56	62	67	71	76	83	88	87	85	77	66	58
Ave. Low		37	38	38	41	44	47	49	48	47	43	38	37
Precipitation													
Inches Rain		6.2	5.5	4.0	2.0	0.7	0.4	-	-	0.5	1.8	3.0	5.4
Inches Snow		-	-	-	-	-	-	-	-	-	-	-	-

V.W.R. = Vokac Weather Rating; probability of mild (warm & dry) weather on any given day.

103

Ballooning
Air Flambuoyant   *(800)456-4711*
A champagne flight in a hot-air balloon provides a serene perspective
on the sights and sounds of the "Valley of the Moon."
Bicycling
Good Time Bicycle Co. *18503 Sonoma Hwy.* *(707)938-0453*
Sonoma Valley Cyclery   *20093 Broadway*   *(707)935-3377*
A separated bikeway supplements well-marked highways and byways
in the gentle Valley of the Moon. Bicycles may be rented by the hour
or day to tour the pastoral countryside.
Food Specialties
Sonoma Cheese Factory *on Plaza at 2 Spain St. 996-1931 (800)535-2855*
Vella Cheese Co.   *just E at 315 2nd St. E*   *(707)938-3232*
Acclaimed Sonoma jack cheese and a wealth of others are made and
sold in these long-established factories. Tastes are offered.
Jack London State Historic Park   *(707)938-5216*
9 mi. NW via CA 12 at 2400 London Ranch Rd. - Glen Ellen
The park is part of the famed author's "Beauty Ranch" where he
resided from 1905 until his death in 1916. The "House of Happy
Walls," a large fieldstone structure built in 1919 by his widow, has an
excellent collection of his memorabilia, and is the park interpretive
center. A half-mile trail leads through woods to the grim ruins of "Wolf
House," destroyed by fire shortly before the Londons could move in.
Sonoma State Historic Park   *(707)938-1519*
N side of plaza
A number of major historic structures have been restored downtown.
The Mission San Francisco de Solano, the last (1823) of twenty-one
built by Father Junipero Serra, is a long adobe structure housing many
historic relics. The restored Sonoma Barracks (1836) housed General
Vallejo's troops when he was California's last Mexican governor.
Nearby, his stately Carpenter Gothic home, built in 1851, houses his
mementoes. Lush grounds reflect Vallejo's fascination with horticulture
like the giant old pommelo tree in front of the house.
Spring Lake Regional Park   *(707)539-8092*
17 mi. NW via CA 12 & Montgomery St.
A small reservoir in a lovely rural setting has become a superb water
recreation facility. Tree-shaded grounds include a warm spring-fed
swimming lagoon with a sandy beach. The lake has boating, rentals,
fishing, hiking, bicycle paths, and a campground.
Warm Water Feature
Morton's Warm Springs   *(11 mi. NW) (707)833-5511*
Mineral springs pools are the centerpiece of a historic facility that
includes picnic tables under shade trees in a picturesque location open
to the public.
Wineries
Sonoma is the birthplace of America's premium wine industry. Grapes
for sacramental purposes were first grown here in 1823. Soon, secular
wines were also being produced. After the Civil War, Sonoma became
the state's largest wine producer. It is still one of America's most
illustrious producers of premium wine. For detailed information and a
map of all wineries, contact the Visitors Bureau. Most of the
delightfully individualized facilities have tours, a gift shop, and
attractive picnic areas. Best of all (unlike Napa Valley), almost all still
feature free tasting!

Babette's Wine Bar/Cafe   *(707)939-8921*
on E side of plaza at 464 First St. East
L-D.   *Moderate*
Innovative California cuisine reflecting classic European training is served in a wine bar with several overstuffed sofas, and on an umbrella-shaded courtyard. The adjoining Babette's Dining Room (D only—Very Expensive) features five-course feasts in relaxed plush surroundings.

Bakeries
  Basque Boulangerie Cafe   *(707)935-7687*
  Sonoma French Bakery   *(707)996-2691*
on E side of plaza
B-L.   *Moderate*
These two bakeries share lineage to the original sourdough French bread that has been a famous Sonoma tradition for decades. Both also have a tempting assortment of pastries and desserts primarily to go.

Della Santina's   *(707)935-0576*
just E of plaza at 133 E. Napa St.
L-D.   *Expensive*
Traditional and contemporary Italian cuisine includes a first-rate selection of handmade pasta dishes and sauces and rotisserie meats. A well-thought-out menu also features desserts made here. The spiffy little trattoria adjoins an umbrella-shaded garden court.

Depot Hotel Restaurant & Garden   *(707)938-2980*
just N of plaza at 241 First St. West
L-D.   *Expensive*
Innovative Northern Italian cuisine is prepared from scratch with quality regional ingredients. So are the luscious desserts. A historic (1870) stone building provides intimate dining rooms. Better yet, get a romantic candlelit table by the outdoor pool in a lovely garden court.

Freestyle!   *(707)996-9916*
just S of plaza at 522 Broadway
L-D.   *Expensive*
"American melting pot" characterizes the cuisine served in this major 1998 addition to Wine Country gastronomy. Seasonally fresh, regional ingredients are featured in bold and beautiful dishes that display the chef's free-style talent in a comfortably cosmopolitan setting.

Garden Court Cafe & Bakery   *(707)935-1565*
6 mi. N at 13875 Sonoma Hwy. (CA 12) - Glen Ellen
B-L.   *Moderate*
The best breakfasts in the valley highlight American classics carefully prepared from scratch. The coffee cake and sticky buns are delicious. So are other homemade specialties ranging from sausages to fruit preserves. The cheerful little roadside cafe/bakery is deservedly popular.

The General's Daughter   *(707)938-4004*
just W of plaza at 400 W. Spain St.
L-D.   *Expensive*
Seasonally fresh local produce is featured in gourmet California cuisine. Consider crisp buttermilk and cornmeal onion rings with lemon-pepper aioli or grilled salmon with lobster sauce. Several casually elegant little dining rooms fill a large, refined Victorian home. A garden-view dining porch adjoins.

Sonoma, California
Glen Ellen Inn Restaurant   *(707)996-6409*
8 mi. NW at 13670 Arnold Dr. - Glen Ellen
D only.   *Expensive*
Innovative California cuisine is presented in some delightfully adventurous dishes like a wild mushroom and sausage pastry purse with a brandy mushroom cream sauce, and decadent housemade desserts like frozen lemon bavarian in a cage of chocolate. The cottage's recently expanded little dining room and covered porch nicely balance the sophisticated cuisine.

La Casa Restaurant & Bar   *(707)996-3406*
just E of plaza at 121 E. Spain St.
L-D.   *Moderate*
La Casa has been Sonoma's best Mexican restaurant for more than thirty years. Seafood dishes are a highlight, along with traditional and updated Mexican/California specialties. Several colorful dining rooms and a fountain court adjoin a popular cantina.

Sonoma Mission Inn & Spa   *(707)938-9000*
3 mi. NW at 18140 Sonoma Hwy. (CA 12)
B-L-D.   *Expensive-Very Expensive*
The resort's main dining room is **The Grille** (B-D—Very Expensive) where the region's quality seasonal ingredients are creatively prepared in New California cuisine served amid informal elegance and on a poolside terrace. **The Cafe** (B-L-D—Expensive) offers healthy, hearty country breakfasts and, later, designer pizzas and smoked meats in a cheerful room next to the resort's specialty boutique.

Vineyards Inn   *(707)833-4500*
12 mi. N at 8445 CA 12 - Kenwood
L-D.   *Moderate*
Notable Mexican specialties like shrimp enchiladas and chile verde with marinated pork are served in a lively little roadside cantina, and in a grapevine-covered heated patio. A large stone fireplace lends warmth in winter to the cozy bar and dining room.

LODGING

Accommodations in and around Sonoma are relatively scarce, expensive, and distinctive, ranging from a famed resort to romantic inns. April through October is high season. Rates are often reduced by at least 20% during the winter, except on weekends.

El Dorado Hotel   *(707)996-3030*
on NW corner of plaza at 405 First St. West - 95476
26 units   *(800)289-3031*   *Expensive*
A pre-Civil War landmark has been artistically reconstructed into a small hotel with a lovely garden court, pool, and an upscale Italian restaurant and saloon. A Continental breakfast and split of wine are complimentary. Upstairs, each room has been beautifully furnished, and features a small balcony above the plaza or lush courtyard.

Gaige House Inn   *(707)935-0237*
8 mi. NW at 13540 Arnold Dr. - Glen Ellen 95442
13 units   *(800)935-0237 Expensive-Very Expensive*
A large Victorian mansion next to tiny downtown Glen Ellen is now a peaceful bed-and-breakfast with a big pool in a garden by a stream. A full gourmet breakfast and afternoon refreshments are complimentary. Each spacious room is beautifully furnished with a blend of period pieces and contemporary conveniences including a private bath. Some have both a fireplace and large whirlpool bath.

Kenwood Inn & Spa   *(707)833-1293*
10 mi. N at 10400 Sonoma Hwy. - Kenwood 95452
12 units   *(800)353-6966*   *Very Expensive*
Kenwood Inn & Spa is one of the wine country's most romantic bed-and-breakfasts. Reminiscent of an intimate Italian country villa, the secluded ivy-shrouded inn has a courtyard pool, whirlpool and (fee) full service health and beauty spa. Gourmet breakfast is complimentary. Each beautifully furnished room has a featherbed, pressed-wood fireplace, and sitting area. Two also have a large in-room whirlpool.

Sonoma Chalet   *(707)938-3129*
1 mi. NW at 18935 5th St. West - 95476
7 units   *Moderate-Expensive*
This quaint old chalet has served for years as a bucolic bed-and-breakfast with a sybaritic hot tub and lush grounds. Light breakfast is complimentary. All well-furnished rooms have antiques and a deck. Two share a bath. Cottages also have a kitchen and fireplace.

Sonoma Hotel   *(707)996-2996*
on NW corner of plaza at 110 W. Spain St. - 95476
17 units   *(800)468-6016*   *Moderate-Expensive*
The valley's oldest lodging is a three-story Victorian landmark. A popular restaurant and saloon are downstairs. Continental breakfast and afternoon wine are complimentary. Each small, tidy room has antiques and a washbasin. (The bathroom is down the hall.)

Sonoma Mission Inn & Spa   *(707)938-9000*
3 mi. NW at 18140 CA 12 (Box 1447) - 95476
198 units   *(800)862-4945*   *Expensive-Very Expensive*
A large 1927 Spanish-Colonial style landmark is the valley's exclusive resort hotel. Two lighted tennis courts, two hot mineral water pools, sauna and whirlpools, and (fee) a complete European-style health and beauty spa, plus notable restaurants (see listing) and a lounge, are housed on expansive landscaped grounds. All rooms ranging from cozy to spacious fireplace suites are beautifully furnished. Three big new luxury suites each have a fireplace, whirlpool bath, and private deck.

Sonoma Valley Inn - Best Western   *(707)938-9200*
by the plaza at 550 Second St. West - 95476
82 units   *(800)334-5784*   *Expensive-Very Expensive*
The Valley's best motel has a garden-court pool and whirlpool and fitness center. Light breakfast and bottle of wine are complimentary. Each well-furnished room has a private deck. Many have fireplaces and/or large whirlpool baths. Beautifully furnished "mission-style" suites, opened in 1998, have a fireplace, large in-bath whirlpool bath, and private balcony.

Victorian Garden Inn   *(707)996-5339*
just SE of plaza at 316 E. Napa St. - 95476
4 units   *(800)543-5339*   *Moderate-Expensive*
A secluded bed-and-breakfast inn occupies an 1860s farmhouse and water tower surrounded by lush, authentic Victorian gardens, a small stream, and a large outdoor pool. Expanded Continental breakfast and evening refreshments are complimentary. Each room is beautifully furnished. The spacious "Woodcutters Cottage" also has a fireplace.

BASIC INFORMATION

Elevation: *81 feet*   *Population (1990):*   *8,168*
Location: *50 miles Northeast of San Francisco*
Nearest airport with commercial flights: San Francisco - 60 miles
Sonoma Valley Visitors Bureau   *(707)996-1090*   *(800)576-6662*
on the plaza at 10 E. Spain St. - 95476   *www.sonomavalley.com*

Sonora, California

Sonora is the robust "Queen of the Mother Lode." One of the state's best collections of well-tended Victorian homes and businesses still lends a Gold-Camp flavor to this thriving hub in the Sierra foothills. Gold was discovered here in 1849. When California became a state in 1850, Sonora was already a boom town with perhaps the richest pocket mine in the Mother Lode. The mines played out decades ago, but gold is still being found nearby, including the world's largest pure nugget.

Today, the rich heritage is showcased downtown, where many notable Victorian buildings still serve their original purposes as churches, saloons, or stores, while others now house specialty shops, restaurants and Western-style entertainment spots. Lodgings are not abundant, but include historic hotels downtown and in the vicinity. All around, a remarkable assortment of lakes and rivers in the oak-and-grass-covered foothills and pine-forested mountains provide a bonanza of water-oriented recreation opportunities—including gold panning.

WEATHER PROFILE

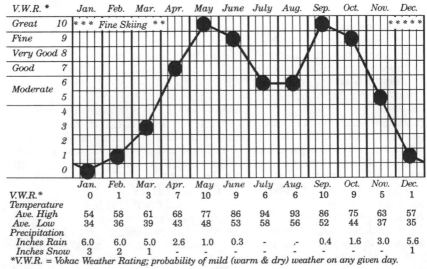

V.W.R.*		Jan.	Feb.	Mar.	Apr.	May	June	July	Aug.	Sep.	Oct.	Nov.	Dec.
Great	10												
Fine	9												
Very Good	8												
Good	7												
Moderate	6 5												
	4 3 2 1 0												

	Jan.	Feb.	Mar.	Apr.	May	June	July	Aug.	Sep.	Oct.	Nov.	Dec.
V.W.R.*	0	1	3	7	10	9	6	6	10	9	5	1
Temperature												
Ave. High	54	58	61	68	77	86	94	93	86	75	63	57
Ave. Low	34	36	39	43	48	53	58	56	52	44	37	35
Precipitation												
Inches Rain	6.0	6.0	5.0	2.6	1.0	0.3	-	.-	0.4	1.6	3.0	5.6
Inches Snow	3	2	1	-	-	-	-	-	-	-	-	1

*V.W.R. = Vokac Weather Rating; probability of mild (warm & dry) weather on any given day.

ATTRACTIONS

Columbia State Historic Park   *(209)532-4301*
4 mi. N off CA 49 on Parrotts Ferry Rd.
For a few years during the 1850s, thousands of people lived here and worked fabulously rich placer mines. The State has restored part of the old business district that may be viewed on a self-guided walking tour. A tour of a gold mine, stagecoach or horseback rides, and gold panning are other options.

Jamestown
3 mi. SW via CA 49 - Jamestown
A narrow main street lined with two-story balconied buildings is the highlight of this Mother Lode relic. The picturesque town has been used as the setting for several classic Hollywood westerns. Specialty shops, several restaurants, plus historic bars and hotels are worth visiting.

Moaning Cavern   *(209)736-2708*
14 mi. NW at 5150 Moaning Cave Rd. - Vallecito
Discovered around 1850, this is California's largest public cavern. A guided tour includes a descent on a 100-foot spiral staircase into a gigantic chamber with impressive formations.

Murphys
18 mi. N via CA 49 & CA 4 - Murphys
California's most delightful little Gold Country hideaway has a picturesque main street with authentic Victorian buildings housing specialty shops, galleries, and cafes. The restored **Murphys Hotel** ((209)728-3444 or (800)532-7684) has been a travelers' landmark since 1856. It still offers nostalgic bedrooms, dining rooms, and an unspoiled saloon with a pot-bellied stove. A recently-added Victorian-style complex has **Grounds** (B-L-D—Moderate) where light and lively California cuisine is served in a cheerful dining room past a fine display of pastries and breads. Nearby, the **Redbud Inn** ((209)728-8533 or (800)827-8533) is Murphys' newest and nicest lodging, with a lovely blend of nostalgia and contemporary amenities like large whirlpools. The area's best wineries (see listing) are near town.

Railtown 1897 State Historic Park   *(209)984-3953*
3.5 mi. SW off CA 49 - Jamestown
Since 1982, the State has operated steam-powered passenger trains over a historic five-mile route through the oak-studded hill country each weekend in summer. The complex includes the old roundhouse, trains and railyard facilities, and depot store.

River Running   *(209)533-4420*   *(800)446-1333*
Sonora is between two of the most famous whitewater streams in the West—the Stanislaus and Tuolumne Rivers. Some of the best rapids are now submerged beneath waters of huge downstream reservoirs. However, exciting one- or two-day raft trips can still be enjoyed further upstream on the remaining portions of the rivers where the scenery and rapids remain unspoiled. Several guide services operate between April and November.

St. James Episcopal Church   *(209)532-7644*
downtown at Washington & Snell Sts.
The photogenic Episcopal church, built in 1859 on a rise at the north end of downtown, may be California's oldest. Many consider it the most beautiful frame building in the Mother Lode. A Victorian mansion across the street is also notable.

Stanislaus National Forest

Sonora, California

Stanislaus National Forest   *(209)532-3671*

starts 5 mi. E of town

All of the Sierra Nevada mountains between Sonora and Yosemite National Park are included in this extraordinary forest. Features near town include dozens of campgrounds and many miles of hiking, backpacking, and horseback riding trails along the splendid canyons of the Tuolumne and Stanislaus river drainages. Upper reaches of these rivers include some of the West's great whitewater rafting opportunities. In calmer stretches, swimmers are attracted to crystal-clear natural pools with sandy beaches. A magnificent stand of sequoia gigantea, the Calaveras Big Trees, has been famous since its discovery in 1852. It is less than an hour by car north of town. A similar distance to the east are trailheads for the Emigrant Wilderness bordered by Yosemite to the south and the crest of the Sierra to the east. This forest of pine and aspen, interspersed with broad meadows and numerous small lakes and streams, is a favorite with fishermen, hunters, and backpackers. In winter, Sonora is an easy drive from Dodge Ridge Ski Area, which was expanded into a major winter sports center. Mt. Reba and Bear Valley Ski Areas are somewhat farther to the northeast.

Water Features   *(209)533-4420*   *(800)446-1333*

A remarkable number of lakes, streams, and reservoirs are within an hour's drive of town. During uniformly hot summers, Sierra waters are a compelling attraction for swimmers, as well as fishermen, water-skiers, sailors, river runners, and all others who enjoy cool, clear water recreation. Public parks with sandy beaches and private coves abound on Don Pedro, New Melones, McClure, Woodward, Modesto, Turlock and other nearby manmade lakes. There are also excellent swimming holes and sandy beaches on the Stanislaus, Tuolumne and other nearby rivers.

Wineries

Several Gold Country wineries are in the area. Two are really special.

Kautz Ironstone Vineyards   *(209)728-1251*

17 mi. N at 1894 Six Mile Rd. - 1 mi. S of Murphys

One of America's most extraordinary young wineries has a Gold Country museum showcasing the world's largest pure gold leaf nugget (found nearby recently!). Other features include a handsome tasting room, a memorable tour of the premium winery (including limestone cellars and luxuriant grounds with elaborate gardens, ponds and a celebrity-event amphitheater) plus an art and jewelry gallery, gourmet deli and bakery, and an expansive gift and wine store.

Stevenot Winery   *(209)728-3436*

21 mi. N at 2690 San Domingo Rd. - 3 mi. N of Murphys

An award-winning picturesque winery and vineyards are tucked at the bottom of a deep gorge. Zinfandel, the Mother Lode's most famous contribution to wine, and other premium varietals are poured in a historic tasting room, and there are tours, sales, gifts and picnic areas.

Winter Sports

Dodge Ridge Ski Area   *(209)965-3474*

33 mi. NE off CA 108 on Dodge Ridge Rd. - Pinecrest

With a vertical drop of 1,600 feet, the longest run is 2+ miles. Seven chairlifts serve the area. Concessions at the base include ski rentals and related facilities and services, plus food and drinks. The skiing season is late November into April.

Yosemite National Park   *(209)372-0200*
52 mi. SE via CA 49 & CA 120
About four million people visit this world famous national park each
year. Its magnificent waterfalls (the highest on the continent) and
sheer granite domes are unsurpassed. Giant sequoia groves, vast high
country wilderness areas, snowfields, and crystal-clear lakes and
streams with sandy beaches are some of the attractions that have won
the acclaim of increasing hordes of recreation enthusiasts since before
the turn of the century. Crowds are smaller and the weather is milder
in spring and fall.

RESTAURANTS

Alfredo's   *(209)532-8332*
downtown at 123 S. Washington St.
L-D.   *Moderate*
Traditional and California-style Mexican dishes include some unusual
specialties like shrimp prepared several ways and desserts like apple
chimichanga. The dining room shares an attractive rock-walled skylit
space with a cozy cantina.

Bella Union Dining Saloon   *(209)984-2421*
3 mi. SW off CA 49 at 18242 Main St. - Jamestown
D only.   *Expensive*
Wild game stars in dishes like grilled elk or quail, or venison
medallions, on a contemporary American menu. Fresh housemade
bread and desserts are other features served in a posh wood-and-brick
dining room and bar with turn-of-the-century charm.

City Hotel   *(209)532-1479*
4 mi. N via Parrotts Ferry Rd. on Main St. - Columbia
D only.   *Expensive*
The City Hotel Dining Room is the Mother Lode of gourmet havens in
the southern Gold Camps. A short tempting selection of contemporary
California cuisine is skillfully prepared from seasonally fresh
ingredients. Costumed staff serve amid restored Gold Rush elegance.
A classic old-time saloon adjoins.

Hemingway's   *(209)532-4900*
downtown at 362 S. Stewart St.
D only.   *Expensive*
Contemporary California dishes are given careful attention, and there
is occasional live entertainment nightly. A large wood-trimmed cottage
was transformed into casually elegant dining rooms adjoining a tiny
shaded dining deck.

Josephine's   *(209)533-4111*
downtown at 286 S. Washington St.
D only.   *Expensive*
Innovative Italian and California cuisine with an emphasis on seasonal
regional produce is prepared with a mesquite grill, rotisserie or wood-
burning oven. An exhibition kitchen is part of the warm Tuscan
ambiance of the dining room behind the Gunn House. A cozy and
charming saloon adjoins.

La Torres' North Beach Cafe   *(209)536-1852*
3 mi. SE at 14317 Mono Way
L-D.   *Moderate*
One of Sonora's best restaurants opened in 1996. Contemporary Italian
cuisine is prepared in an expo kitchen and served in a casual, cheerful
trattoria that has earned increasing popularity.

National Hotel Restaurant   *(209)984-3446*
3 mi. SW off CA 49 at 77 Main St. - Jamestown
L-D.   *Moderate*
Traditional American dishes are served at tables set with full linen
amid mining camp decor in a nostalgic dining room of a restored pre-
Civil War hotel, or on a tranquil vine-covered courtyard. An authentic
little Gold Camp saloon is next door.
Pie Tin   *(209)536-1216*
downtown at 51 S. Washington St.
B-L.   *Moderate*
Homemade cinnamon rolls, muffins, scones and pies can be enjoyed
with light fare in a pleasant old-fashioned coffee shop.
The Smoke Cafe   *(209)984-3733*
3 mi. SW off CA 49 at 18191 Main St. - Jamestown
D only.   *Moderate*
Specialties from all regions of Mexico are the basis for the creative
Mexican and New California cuisine in one of the region's best dining
experiences. Padded booths lend comfort to the boisterous and colorful
dining rooms and cantina, and there is a small streetside patio.
Wilma's   *(209)532-9957*
downtown at 275 S. Washington St.
B-L-D.   *Low*
Country cooking ranges from pecan rolls or biscuits (early) to
traditional fare later like hickory-smoked barbecued meats, soda
fountain treats, and assorted homemade pies. Padded booths and
counter stools overlook whimsical pig art.

LODGING

Lodgings are relatively scarce. But, visitors can choose between
authentically furnished historic hotels and inns or modern motels with
contemporary amenities. High season is summer. Non-weekend rates
at other times are usually reduced 15% or more.
Barretta Gardens Inn   *(209)532-6039*
just S at 700 Barretta St. - 95370
5 units   *(800)206-3333*   *Moderate*
A century-old home on a hillside overlooking Sonora is now a stylish
bed-and-breakfast amid lovely terraced gardens. Full breakfast is
complimentary. Each well-furnished room combines period and
contemporary decor, including a private bath. One room also has a
whirlpool tub for two.
City Hotel   *(209)532-1479*
4 mi. N on Main St. (Box 1870) - Columbia 95310
10 units   *(800)532-1479*   *Moderate*
Built in the midst of the Gold Rush before the Civil War, this small
two-story brick hotel remains a landmark of that era. The fully
restored building exudes Victorian charm, especially in the gourmet
dining room (see listing) and saloon. Expanded Continental breakfast
is complimentary. Each compact room is comfortably furnished with
antiques and has a toilet and marble sink as concessions to modern
times. A shower room is down the hall.
Gunn House   *(209)532-3421*
downtown at 286 S. Washington St. - 95370
19 units   *Moderate*
Many changes since 1851 have added a landscaped pool, Josephine's
restaurant (see listing) and an atmospheric bar. Each simply furnished
room has some period pieces and a private bath.

Jamestown Hotel *(209)984-3902*

3 mi. SW off CA 49 at 18153 Main St. (Box 539) - Jamestown 95327
10 units *(800)205-4901* *Moderate*
The photogenic little brick hotel is a Gold Camp landmark with a nostalgic dining room and firelit pub. All rooms are nicely furnished with antiques and a private bath.

Jamestown Railtown Motel *(209)984-3332*

3 mi. SW off CA 49 on Main St. at Willow (Box 1129) - Jamestown 95327
20 units *Moderate*
A pool and spa are amenities in Jamestown's alternative to period lodging. Each motel room is simply furnished. Some have an in-room two-person whirlpool tub.

National Hotel *(209)984-3446*

3 mi. SW off CA 49 at 77 Main St. (Box 502) - Jamestown 95327
9 units *(800)894-3446* *Moderate*
One of the Mother Lode's oldest continuously operated hotels (1859) has been fully restored. Downstairs is a popular restaurant (see listing) and Gold Rush saloon. An expanded Continental breakfast is complimentary. Each compact room is individually, nicely furnished with antiques and has a sink. All have private baths.

Ryan House *(209)533-3445*

downtown at 153 S. Shepherd St. - 95370
4 units *(800)831-4897* *Moderate-Expensive*
A classic 1855 frame home is now a fully restored bed-and-breakfast amid colorful gardens in the heart of town. Breakfast and afternoon refreshments are complimentary. Each room is well furnished with antiques and reproductions, and has a private bath. The spacious Garden View Suite has a gas log stove and a soaking tub for two.

Sonora Days Inn *(209)532-2400*

downtown at 160 S. Washington St. - 95370
64 units *(800)580-4667* *Moderate-Expensive*
Sonora's historic three-story landmark has been refurbished to continue to serve as the county's only full-service hotel. Amenities include an outdoor pool, restaurant and lounge. Nicely furnished hotel rooms have all contemporary conveniences, and are being upgraded. There are also comfortably furnished motel units out back by a creek.

Sonora Townhouse Motel *(209)532-3633*

downtown at 350 S. Washington St. - 95370
112 units *(800)251-1538* *Moderate-Expensive*
Sonora's largest lodging is a modern motel complex next to downtown with a pool and a whirlpool. Each room is well furnished. There are also three in-room two-person whirlpool tubs and mini-kitchens.

BASIC INFORMATION

Elevation: 1,825 feet *Population (1990): 4,153*
Location: 132 miles East of San Francisco
Nearest airport with commercial flights: Modesto - 50 miles
Tuolumne County Visitors Bureau *(209)533-4420* *(800)446-1333*
downtown at 55 W. Stockton Rd. (Box 4020) - 95370
www.mlode.com / ~nsierra / visitor /

South Lake Tahoe, California

South Lake Tahoe is a matchless recreation bonanza. It is ideally situated in a lush pine forest along the southern shore of one of nature's most sublime high mountain lakes. Growth was slow until the 1950s, when construction of major casinos just across the Nevada state line and an enormous skiing complex established the town as both a year-round action center and a winter sports capital.

Today, a tight cluster of high-rise casinos offers 24-hour gambling and big-name entertainment. The adjoining proliferation of visitor-related facilities in pine-shaded South Lake Tahoe will include a town center for the millennium, and a gondola connecting downtown with the mountains. Sophisticated lodgings are abundant. So are restaurants, including some offering gourmet cuisine or spectacular views. Shops are surprisingly ordinary and scattered, but there are many good sources of outdoor recreation equipment, in keeping with unlimited opportunities to enjoy the area's natural grandeur.

WEATHER PROFILE

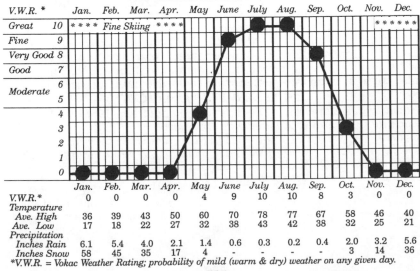

V.W.R.*		Jan.	Feb.	Mar.	Apr.	May	June	July	Aug.	Sep.	Oct.	Nov.	Dec.
V.W.R.*		0	0	0	0	4	9	10	10	8	3	0	0
Temperature													
Ave. High		36	39	43	50	60	70	78	77	67	58	46	40
Ave. Low		17	18	22	27	32	38	43	42	38	32	25	21
Precipitation													
Inches Rain		6.1	5.4	4.0	2.1	1.4	0.6	0.3	0.2	0.4	2.0	3.2	5.6
Inches Snow		58	45	35	17	4	-	-	-	-	3	14	36

*V.W.R. = Vokac Weather Rating; probability of mild (warm & dry) weather on any given day.

114

ATTRACTIONS

Aerial Tramway
Heavenly Aerial Tram   *(530)541-7544*
2 mi. S via Ski Run Blvd. on Saddle Rd.
An enclosed gondola lifts passengers more than 2,000 feet above the lake via an aerial tramway. Views from overlooks and hiking trails at the top to Lake Tahoe and the surrounding mountains are magnificent.

Bicycling   *(530)541-5255*
Miles of exclusive bike paths are on relatively flat, scenic terrain near south shore beaches and around town, and there are a wealth of back-country trails and roads beyond. Numerous shops offer hourly and longer rentals of touring and mountain bikes, and mopeds.

Boat Rentals
Every kind of boating imaginable can be enjoyed on about two hundred square miles of deep, clear water. Visitors can rent an extraordinary assortment of craft—fishing boats, ski or cruising boats, jet skis, sailboats, catamarans, canoes, windsurf boards or inner tubes, by the hour or longer at several marina facilities in town.

Boat Rides
Large modern sightseeing boats cruise several times daily, including a sunset dinner-dance cruise to picturesque Emerald Bay. All feature glass-bottom windows to give passengers an opportunity to scan the crystal-clear depths. Some of the vessels (ranging from a large trimaran to multi-deck paddlewheelers) operate year-round.

M.S. Dixie *(paddlewheeler)*   (530)588-3508
Tahoe Queen *(paddlewheeler)*   *(800)238-2463*   (530)541-3365
Woodwind *(trimaran)*   (702)588-3000

D.L. Bliss and Emerald Bay State Parks   *(530)525-7277*
11 mi. NW on CA 89
The most famous landmark of Lake Tahoe is Emerald Bay, which includes the lake's only island—Fannette. Cut into mountain slopes high above the water, the highway around the bay provides panoramic views that are unforgettable. At the head of the bay is a half-mile trail up to scenic Eagle Falls. A mile-long footpath from Inspiration Point leads steeply down to the shore, where Vikingsholm, a thirty-eight-room mansion, can be toured during the summer. It was built in 1929 as a summer residence patterned after a Viking's castle. On the bay's east side is a large sylvan campground, with fishing, boating, and a swimming beach nearby. Just north, D.L. Bliss offers excellent hiking trails and swimming off one of the lake's finest beaches and a large forested campground.

Fishing Charters
Several sportfishing boats are available daily (year-round) for guided excursions in search of Mackinaw and other big trout and kokanee salmon. These long-time operators offer all necessary services and equipment for trips of various lengths:

Dennis's Fishing Charters   (530)577-6834
Tahoe Sportfishing   *(800)696-7797 (CA)*   (530)541-5448

Horseback Riding
Quiet, wooded trails are found throughout the Tahoe basin. Several riding stables are located near town. The three long-established stables listed offer horse rentals by the hour, half day, or day. They also can provide guides for riders on breakfast, dinner, or moonlight rides, for

fishing or pack trips, and (in winter) sleigh rides.

Camp Richardson's Corral	*8 mi. W on CA 89*	*(530)541-3113*
Sunset Ranch	*7 mi. SW on US 50*	*(530)541-9001*
Zephyr Cove Stables	*4 mi. N*	*(702)588-6136*

Lake Tahoe
the northern border of town
Straddling the California/Nevada state line in a luxuriant pine forest 6,229 feet above sea level is a mountain-rimmed lake that is one of nature's grandest achievements. The water is so clear that a white dinner plate can be seen at a depth of more than sixty feet. Lake Tahoe is the largest deep alpine lake on the continent. In fact, with its twenty-two-mile length, twelve-mile width, and maximum depth of 1,645 feet, the lake's volume would cover the entire State of California with more than a foot of pure water. But statistics can't do justice to this serious contender for the world's most beautiful water body. It's also one of the most usable, with a remarkable assortment of watercraft available for rent, charter, or tours. Onshore recreation facilities are plentiful, yet concentrated to better enjoy the forest, sandy beaches, dramatic bouldered coves, streams and mountains that surround the lake. A seventy-one-mile highway loop around the lake is immodestly described by the South Lake Tahoe Visitor's Bureau as "The Most Beautiful Drive in America" on their map and guide describing points of interest along the route.

Lake Tahoe State Park   *(530)782-2590*
starts 13 mi. NE via US 50 on NV 28
Several miles of the lake's northeastern shoreline are included in this large Nevada park. Pine-shaded picnic grounds near picturesque granite boulders and sandy beaches are especially popular.

Lake Tahoe Visitor Center   *(530)573-2674*
8 mi. W via CA 89 at 870 Emerald Bay Rd.
The U.S. Forest Service provides an ingeniously-designed underground stream profile chamber where you look through glass windows into a large pool on Taylor Creek to watch trout pass. Self-guided trails and guided nature walks also originate from here. This is the best place to get information and maps about the surrounding Eldorado National Forest, and permits for the Desolation Wilderness Area.

South Lake Tahoe Recreation Area   *(530)542-6056*
2 mi. SW at Hwy. 50 & Rufus Allen Blvd.
An impressive contemporary recreation center, museum, and campground are in a pine forest by a long sandy beach that is the local favorite for swimming and sunbathing with splendid views of the mountain-rimmed lake.

Winter Sports
Lake Tahoe has the largest concentration of skiing facilities in the world. There are three downhill ski areas surrounding town, and fifteen near the lake, including Squaw Valley, the site of the 1960 Winter Olympics. Several cross-country skiing centers are located near the south shore. The number and quality of facilities are closely correlated to the spectacular and endlessly varied terrain. Ski rental equipment and lessons for both downhill and cross-country skiing are available at most of the major ski areas, and in town. Non-skiers can rent a snowmobile by the hour or tour with a guide; go for a sleigh ride; or take a toboggan down the hill at Hansen's Resort.

Heavenly Ski Resort   *(702)586-7000*   *(800)243-2836*
2 mi. S via Ski Run Blvd. on Saddle Rd.

One of America's largest ski areas sprawls into two states with spellbinding views of both Lake Tahoe and the Carson Valley. The vertical rise is 3,500 feet with runs up to 5.5 miles long. The summit is 10,040 feet. There are twenty chairlifts (including a gondola). Both day and night skiing are available on well-groomed slopes designed for every ability. All facilities and rentals are at the base for downhill and cross-country skiing. Restaurants, bars and lodgings are at the base, with many more nearby. The season is mid-November through April.

RESTAURANTS

The Beacon Bar & Grill   *(530)541-0630*
8 mi. W at 1900 Jamison Rd.
L-D.   *Expensive*
At Camp Richardson Resort, contemporary comfort foods are enhanced by fine lake and mountain views amid family-oriented surroundings and a lively bar next to the lake.

Cafe Fiore   *(530)541-2908*
1 mi. SW at 1169 Ski Run Blvd.
D only.   *Expensive*
Classic and creative Italian cuisine is carefully prepared, and served in generous portions in an intimate urbane dining room and on a patio when weather permits.

Chart House   *(702)588-6276*
2 mi. NE at 392 Kingsbury Grande - Stateline, NV
D only.   *Expensive*
Contemporary American fare (prime rib, steaks, seafood) is offered at this first-rate representative of a restaurant chain. But, the main attraction is an awe-inspiring panorama of Lake Tahoe from picture windows in the big stylish dining room and lounge high on a hill east of town.

Christiania Inn   *(530)544-7337*
2 mi. S via Ski Run Blvd. at 3819 Saddle Rd.
D only.   *Expensive*
The Christiania Inn features one of the region's premier gourmet havens. Skillfully prepared Continental classics are complemented by romantic contemporary furnishings including a picture window view of a wine cellar and a great stone fireplace. There is also an outstanding handcrafted lounge.

The Driftwood Cafe   *(530)544-6545*
downtown at 4115 Laurel Av.
B-L.   *Moderate*
Distinctive omelets and some unusual specialties like cashew banana nut pancakes or waffles highlight light fare in a pleasant little cafe where breakfast is featured all day.

Evans American Gourmet Cafe   *(530)542-1990*
6 mi. SW at 536 Emerald Bay Rd.
D only.   *Expensive*
Evan's is the best restaurant in South Lake Tahoe. New American cuisine reflects the chef/owner's classic training and creative confidence with choice seasonal ingredients. Gourmet appetizers, pasta, pizza, salads and entrees can be topped off with lavish and luscious housemade desserts. The romantic contemporary decor of a vintage Tahoe cottage is the right setting for fine dining.

The Fresh Ketch   *(530)541-5683*
6 mi. SW via Tahoe Keys Blvd. at 2433 Venice Dr. E
L-D.   *Expensive*
Seafood is emphasized in a large handsome restaurant with upscale contemporary rooms overlooking Tahoe Keys Marina and the lake. The marina-view lounge has plush seating and a wood-burning fireplace.
Harrah's Lake Tahoe   *(702)588-6611*
downtown on US 50 at Stateline, NV   *Moderate-Very Expensive*
Lake Tahoe's most distinguished hotel/casino has two outstanding restaurants. The **Summit** (D only—Very Expensive) presents gourmet Continental cuisine in a formal, opulent setting with a magnificent 16th floor view of Lake Tahoe. The **Forest** (B-L-D—Moderate) features the region's finest buffet amidst unusual gilded forest decor in an 18th floor setting with panoramic mountain and lake views.
Harvey's Resort Hotel   *(702)588-2411*
downtown on US 50 at Stateline, NV   *Expensive*
The area's oldest major hotel/casino now has eight restaurants. **Llewellyn's** (B-L-D—Expensive) presents creative California cuisine in an elegant setting with a panoramic lake view. The **Sage Room Steak House** (D only—Expensive) has featured great beef in an atmosphere of Western elegance for more than half a century.
Nephele's   *(530)544-8130*
1 mi. SW at 1169 Ski Run Blvd.
D only.   *Expensive*
Creative California cuisine is the highlight as it has been since 1977. Fresh seasonal dishes like pecan-encrusted chicken breast with cranberry cucumber relish and nightly specials like wild elk or sauteed venison are presented in an intimate contemporary dining room that is a delightful blend of wood tones and stained glass.
Swiss Chalet Restaurant   *(530)544-3304*
4 mi. SW on US 50 at 2544 Lake Tahoe Blvd.
D only.   *Expensive*
Old-fashioned European and American dishes including house-baked pastries accompany Swiss-themed decor in a large, comfortable dinner house that has been a local landmark for more than forty years.

LODGING

One of the West's greatest concentrations of lodgings extends from the hotel/casinos at stateline for four miles near the south shore. High season is mid-June to mid-September. At other times apart from weekends, rates may be reduced 30% or more.
Caesars Tahoe   *(702)588-3515*
downtown at 55 Hwy. 50 (Box 5800) - Stateline, NV 89449
440 units   *(800)648-3353*   *Expensive*
Caesars' contemporary fourteen-story resort has a lagoon-style indoor pool, whirlpool, saunas, plus (fee) tennis courts and health club. There are also six restaurants; a top-name showroom and nightclub; a vast 24-hour casino; and shops. Most of the well-furnished rooms have a Roman tub and a distant lake or mountain view.
Christiania Inn   *(530)544-7337*
2 mi. S at 3819 Saddle Rd. (Box 18298) - 96151
6 units   *Very Expensive*
Overlooking the base of Heavenly Ski Resort is a classic little bed-and-breakfast inn. A Continental breakfast and decanter of brandy are complimentary. Each spacious, beautifully furnished unit has dramatic ski slope views. Suites also have a fireplace.

Embassy Suites Resort   *(530)544-5400*
downtown at 4130 Lake Tahoe Blvd. - 96150
400 units   *(800)362-2779   Expensive-Very Expensive*
The casinos are only steps from this eight-story all-suites resort for the millennium. Amenities include an indoor pool, whirlpool, sauna, fitness center, stylish restaurant, lounge, and gift shop. Full breakfast and manager's afternoon reception with beverages are complimentary in the tranquil garden atrium with a historic flume and waterwheel. Each spacious, beautifully furnished suite has a kitchenette and stocked mini-bar. Some also have a private balcony with a town/lake view.

Fantasy Inn   *(530)541-6666*
1 mi. SW at 3696 Lake Tahoe Blvd. - 96150
53 units   *(800)288-2463   Expensive-Very Expensive*
The region's most sophisticated paean to passion opened in 1994. Behind a contemporary motel facade are a tantalizing variety of well-furnished adult "theme rooms." Each is spacious and has a large in-room whirlpool, European showers for two, and mood lighting and mirrors. The "Deluxe Theme Suites" are beautifully furnished with elaborate fantasy decor ranging from "Arabian Nights" to "Rain Forest," and extra-large in-room whirlpools and gas fireplaces.

Harrah's Lake Tahoe   *(702)588-6606*
downtown at Hwy. 50 at state line (Box 8) - Stateline, NV 89449
532 units   *(800)427-7247*   *Expensive*
The Lake Tahoe area's preeminent hotel/casino is Harrah's. The contemporary eighteen-story resort has an indoor pool, whirlpools, fitness center, game room and shopping arcade. There are also six restaurants (see listing), a top-name showroom and nightclub, and an expansive 24-hour casino. All of the beautifully furnished rooms have two complete bathrooms. Many also have a grand lake/mountains view.

Harvey's Resort Hotel/Casino   *(702)588-2411*
downtown on US 50 at state line (Box 128) - Stateline, NV 89449
740 units   *(800)427-8397*   *Expensive*
Tahoe's first gaming establishment is now the largest hotel/casino on the lake. The nineteen-story complex has a large pool, whirlpool, health club, game rooms, and a shopping arcade. There are eight restaurants (see listing), entertainment lounges, and a large 24-hour casino. Many beautifully furnished rooms have a superb lake view. Some suites also have a whirlpool and a private view balcony.

Inn by the Lake   *(530)542-0330*
2 mi. SW on US 50 at 3300 Lake Tahoe Blvd. - 96150
100 units   *(800)877-1466*   *Expensive*
The lake and a fine public beach are across the highway from this contemporary motel with a large pool, whirlpool, sauna, and bicycles. Many of the well-furnished rooms have a small private balcony with a lake view.

Lakeland Village   *(530)544-1685*
1 mi. SW at 3535 Lake Tahoe Blvd. - 96150
212 units   *(800)822-5969   Expensive-Very Expensive*
Nestled among pines by Lake Tahoe is a large condo complex with a thousand feet of private sandy beach that is ideal for swimming and sunning. Rental boats, two landscaped pools, a whirlpool, saunas, and (fee) two tennis courts are also available to guests. Each (studio to four-bedroom) unit is well furnished and has a kitchen, fireplace, and private balcony. Unfortunately, only units with three or more bedrooms have lakefront views.

Royal Valhalla Motor Lodge   *(530)544-2233*
just W at 4104 Lake Shore Dr. (Drawer GG) - 96157
80 units   *(800)999-4104*   *Moderate*
This contemporary motel has guest privileges at a splendid private beach across the street. There are also a large outdoor pool and whirlpool. Most of the spacious, well-furnished rooms have a private balcony overlooking the lake.

Tahoe Marina Inn   *(530)541-2180*
2 mi. SW at US 50 & 930 Bal Bijou Rd. (Box 871) - 96150
75 units   *(800)288-2463*   *Moderate-Expensive*
This contemporary condominium resort includes five hundred feet of private sandy beach, a large pool with a fabulous lakeside view, and a sauna. Each spacious, well-furnished unit in the motor inn has a private lakeside balcony or deck. Each of the adjacent condominium units also has a kitchen and fireplace.

Tahoe Seasons Resort   *(530)541-6700*
2 mi. SW at 3901 Saddle Rd. (Box 5656) - 96157
180 units   *(800)540-4874*   *Expensive-Very Expensive*
Near the aerial tramway at Heavenly Ski Resort, this large modern resort in the pines has a pool, whirlpool, two tennis courts, paddleball court, exercise room, restaurant and lounge. Each nicely decorated unit has a living area, bedroom, and a partial kitchenette. Most also have a gas fireplace and large in-bath whirlpool. Some have a slope view.

Timber Cove Lodge - Best Western   *(530)541-6722*
2 mi. SW on US 50 at 3411 Lake Tahoe Blvd. - 96150
262 units   *(800)528-1234*   *Expensive*
This large contemporary motor hotel is on attractively landscaped lakefront grounds including six hundred feet of private sandy beach next to one of the best public beaches on the lake. In addition to fine lake swimming, there is a fishing pier, marina with boat rentals, large pool and two whirlpools, plus a handsome fireplace lobby/lounge and dining room. Each spacious room is well furnished.

BASIC INFORMATION
Elevation: 6,260 feet   *Population: 21,586*
Location: 190 miles Northeast of San Francisco
Nearest airport with regular flights: in town
Lake Tahoe Visitors Authority   (530)544-5050 (800)288-2463
  1 mi. SW at 1156 Ski Run Blvd. - 96150
  www.virtualtahoe.com
South Lake Tahoe Chamber of Commerce   (530)541-5255
  2 mi. SW on US 50 at 3066 Lake Tahoe Blvd. - 96150

Aspen, Colorado

Aspen is the heart of the Colorado Rockies. Romantic, festive, and historic, it is a year-round celebration of urbane and earthly pleasures. In a high valley flanked by several mountains covered with a phenomenal assortment of ski slopes, including one that ends abruptly downtown, Aspen is America's preeminent ski town. In 1879, prospectors found silver on these slopes. A short boom was followed by a half-century decline. In the 1940s, the Aspen Institute and the first ski lifts provided the basis for the town's current role.

Today, the town is alive with the sound of music all summer, and ski slopes have replaced mine tailings. Downtown, landmarks from the Victorian era have been carefully recycled as upscale shops and galleries, gourmet restaurants, plush nightlife, and luxurious lodgings amid pedestrian malls and flowery landscaping. All around, well-tended parks, golf courses, tennis and recreation complexes and bicycle paths lead to pine-forested mountains and streams.

WEATHER PROFILE

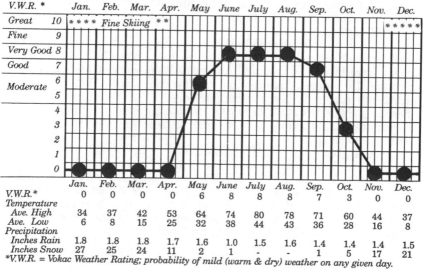

V.W.R.*	Jan.	Feb.	Mar.	Apr.	May	June	July	Aug.	Sep.	Oct.	Nov.	Dec.
V.W.R.*	0	0	0	0	6	8	8	8	7	3	0	0
Temperature												
Ave. High	34	37	42	53	64	74	80	78	71	60	44	37
Ave. Low	6	8	15	25	32	38	44	43	36	28	16	8
Precipitation												
Inches Rain	1.8	1.8	1.8	1.7	1.6	1.0	1.5	1.6	1.4	1.4	1.4	1.5
Inches Snow	27	25	24	11	2	1	-	-	1	5	17	21

*V.W.R. = Vokac Weather Rating; probability of mild (warm & dry) weather on any given day.

ATTRACTIONS

Aerial Tramway
The Silver Queen Gondola   *(970)925-1220   (800)525-6200*
A gondola travels 2.5 miles to the top of Aspen Mountain in 18 minutes for magnificent high country panoramas all summer. There are hiking trails and a restaurant at the summit.

Bicycling
Miles of paved separated bikeways, secondary roads in and around town, and high country trails offer rewarding scenic jaunts. Several places downtown rent bicycles, including:
Aspen Sports   *408 E. Cooper Av. (970)925-6331 (800)544-6648*
Hub of Aspen   *315 E. Hyman Av. (970)925-7970*

The Fountain
downtown at Hyman Av./Mill St.
It looks just like an iron grate sunk into a street when it's not operating. But when it is, the row of dancing water spouts of this computer-programmed fountain delight everyone. Many first-timers (and others) feel compelled to dash through. Only the spry stay dry.

Horseback Riding
T-Lazy-7 Ranch *5 mi. SW at 3129 Maroon Creek Rd. (970)925-4614*
This is the nearest and oldest of several stables surrounded by miles of alpine trails that rent horses by the hour or longer. They will also arrange extended pack trips like the fabulous two-day trip to Crested Butte at the height of fall color, breakfast or dinner rides, and hayrides with entertainment.

Independence Pass
20 mi. SE on CO 82
The scenic eastern route into town taken by early silver prospectors is now a paved, frighteningly narrow highway that crosses the Continental Divide at 12,095 feet. Literally breathtaking panoramas abound. The road is only open from June through the first snowstorm.

Maroon Bells
10 mi. S off CO 82
These two deep purple bell-shaped peaks (both over 14,000 feet high) are probably the most photographed mountains in Colorado. There are picnic sites, scenic hiking trails and fishing around a small foreground lake. The road is closed in summer to private vehicles.

River Running
Several services specialize in half day and longer rafting trips down the Roaring Fork River near town, and on the Colorado and Arkansas Rivers from late May through August. All equipment and meals are provided for scenic, fishing, or whitewater trips. Two downtown outfitters with many years experience are:
Blazing Paddles Raft Trips   *(970)923-4544*   *(800)282-7238*
Colorado Riff Raft   *(970)925-5405*   *(800)759-3939*

Winter Sports
Aspen Highlands   *(800)525-6200*
3 mi. W via CO 82 & Maroon Creek Rd.
The vertical rise is 3,635 feet and the longest run is 3.5 miles. Elevation at the top is 11,700 feet. There are seven chairlifts. All facilities, services and rentals are available at the base for downhill skiing. There are a few restaurants and bars at the base. The ski season is from mid-December to early April.

Aspen Mountain   *(800)525-6200*
downtown at S end of Monarch St.

The premier superstar of Colorado ski areas has a vertical rise of 3,267 feet and the longest run is more than three miles. Elevation at the top is 11,212 feet. There are eight lifts, including a gondola. All facilities, services and rentals are available at the base in town for downhill and cross-country skiing along with an ice skating rink and sleigh rides. More bars, restaurants and lodging facilities are within walking distance of these lifts than any ski area in America. The ski season is late November to mid-April.

Buttermilk Mountain   *(970)925-1220*
2 mi. W via CO 82 & Buttermilk West Rd.

Buttermilk is one of the nation's finest learning mountains. The vertical rise is 2,030 feet and the longest run is three miles. Elevation at the top is 9,900 feet. There are six chairlifts. All essential services, facilities and rentals are available at the base for downhill skiing. A restaurant, bar and a motor hotel are within walking distance at the base. The ski season is early December to early April.

Krabloonik Husky Kennels   *(970)923-4342*
14 mi. SW via CO 82

Thrilling half-day dog sled trips along spectacular mountain trails can be reserved (with lunch) from December through April.

Snowmass Ski Area   *(800)598-2004*
12 mi. W via CO 82 & Brush Creek Rd.

The longest lift-served vertical in the United States now offers 4,406 feet of vertical rise. The longest run is more than four miles. Elevation at the top is 11,835 feet. There are fifteen chairlifts. All services, facilities and rentals are available at the base for both downhill and cross-country skiing. You can ski-in/ski-out to many restaurants, bars, and lodgings. Ski season is late November to mid-April.

RESTAURANTS

Ajax Tavern   *(970)920-9333*
downtown at 685 E. Durant Av.
L-D.   *Very Expensive*

Creative American cuisine features top quality seasonal ingredients in dishes ranging from grilled venison medallions to warm strawberry rhubarb crisp with housemade ice cream. Aspen's most popular dining tavern has umbrella-shaded tables at the base of the gondolas and a stylish wood-trim dining room/bar with crisp full linen.

Campo de Fiori   *(970)920-7717*
downtown at 205 S. Mill St., (downstairs) Mill St. Plaza
D only.   *Very Expensive*

Some of Aspen's finest Italian cuisine includes Tuscan and Venetian specialties and American innovations served in a cozy congested trattoria matching the warmth and flair of the culinary offerings.

The Crystal Palace   *(970)925-1455*
downtown at 300 E. Hyman Av.
D only.   *Very Expensive*

One of America's finest theater/restaurants has been wowing Aspen audiences since 1957. An outstanding original revue of political satire and social humor is performed by multi-talented waiters and waitresses following a gourmet dinner. A resplendent collection of stained glass enhances the intimate, elegant dining-and-entertainment showplace in a historic building.

Hotel Jerome   *(970)920-1000*
downtown at 330 E. Main St.
B-L-D.   *Very Expensive*
Innovative American dinners like rack of lamb with braised lamb ravioli are presented along with housemade desserts in the nostalgic firelit **Century Room**, the hotel's elegant culinary centerpiece. Don't miss the **Jerome Bar**—an Aspen favorite since 1889.

Krabloonik Restaurant   *(970)923-4342*
10 mi. SW off CO 82 at 4250 Divide Rd. - Snowmass Village
D only. (Plus L in winter.)   *Very Expensive*
Innovative cuisine includes wild game like grilled caribou or roasted elk loin when available on a changing menu. The unique restaurant is in a rustic log cabin high in the mountains by the kennel where renowned dog sled tours originate.

La Cocina   *(970)925-9714*
downtown at 308 E. Hopkins Av.
D only.   *Moderate*
Aspen's best New Mexican and Mexican dishes are well represented, and there are housemade desserts like bread pudding laced with a warm whiskey sauce or lemon pie. The charming contemporary dining rooms have been a popular local gathering place for many years.

The Little Nell   *(970)920-6330*
downtown at 675 E. Durant Av.
B-L-D.   *Very Expensive*
Aspen's quintessential dining experience is the Restaurant at Little Nell. The resort's dining room showcases some of the nation's best innovative American cuisine on menus that change seasonally to reflect the chef's artistry with the freshest top quality ingredients. A warm and opulent split-level room has widely spaced tables set with fresh flowers, candle, crystal, china and crisp linen. Picture windows provide an intimate view of a terrace used for warm-weather dining with a dramatic mountain backdrop.

Main Street Bakery & Cafe   *(970)925-6446*
downtown at 201 E. Main St.
B-L-D.   *Expensive*
The finest display in town of delicious pastries, cakes, cookies, bagels and breads is in this amiable coffee shop. All are available to go or with American light fare at inside or (in summer) patio tables.

Piñons   *(970)920-2021*
downtown at 105 S. Mill St.
D only.   *Very Expensive*
One of Aspen's favorite gourmet havens offers innovative American cuisine like pheasant quesadillas with herbed goat cheese and luscious housemade desserts in an upscale post-modern ranch setting.

Poppies Bistro Cafe   *(970)925-2333*
just W at 834 W. Hallam St.
D only.   *Very Expensive*
Contemporary Continental cuisine is showcased in a Victorian house comfortably appointed with authentic antiques and period decor.

Renaissance   *(970)925-2402*
downtown at 304 E. Hopkins Av.
D only.   *Very Expensive*
In the dining room and upstairs bar, an acclaimed chef presents his updated French cuisine. A changing selection of fresh, artistic entrees and desserts is served amid refined Southwestern decor.

Sardy House Hotel and Restaurant   *(970)920-2525*
downtown at 128 E. Main St.
B-D.   *Very Expensive*
Jack's Restaurant in the Victorian landmark features creative American cuisine presented in dishes like pine nut crusted rainbow trout with lemon champagne sauce. The elegant, intimate dining room overlooks lush trees and a distant ski slope view.

LODGING

Lodgings of all kinds are abundant downtown and near the ski slopes. Winter is high season. Rates are often reduced at least 50% in summer, and even more in late spring and early fall.

Aspen Bed and Breakfast Lodge   *(970)925-7650*
just W at 311 W. Main St. - 81611
38 units   *(800)362-7736*   *Expensive*
This modern three-story inn by the main highway has a pool and whirlpool. Expanded Continental breakfast and (during ski season) afternoon beverages and appetizers are complimentary. Each unit is well furnished. Some have a big private balcony and in-bath whirlpool.

Aspen Club Lodge   *(970)925-6760*
downtown at 709 E. Durant Av. - 81611
90 units   *(800)882-2582*   *Very Expensive*
Ski slopes and the gondola are only steps from this contemporary inn with a pool and whirlpool. Breakfast buffet and a pass to the health and racquet facility are complimentary. Each room is beautifully furnished. Suites have a private view balcony, gas fireplace and a large in-bath whirlpool.

Aspen Square   *(970)925-1000*
downtown at 617 E. Cooper Av. - 81611
105 units   *(800)862-7736*   *Very Expensive*
Ski runs are near this modern four-story apartment hotel with a pool and whirlpool. Each well-furnished studio to two-bedroom unit has a kitchen, private balcony (some with slope view) and woodburning fireplace.

The Boomerang Lodge   *(970)925-3416*
just W at 500 W. Hopkins Av. - 81611
34 units   *(800)992-8852*   *Expensive-Very Expensive*
A Frank Lloyd Wright influence is apparent in this venerable, upgraded lodge with a pool and whirlpool in a quiet area. Each well-furnished room has a private terrace or balcony. Most have a gas fireplace. Top floor "luxury rooms" are beautifully furnished and have intimate pine views, while larger units also have a kitchen.

The Gant   *(970)925-5000*
just E at 610 West End St. - 81611
120 units   *(800)345-1471*   *Very Expensive*
One of Aspen's finest condo complexes is a short stroll from ski runs in a quiet area. Amenities include two pools and saunas, three whirlpools, and five (summer) tennis courts. Each well-furnished one- to four-bedroom condo has a kitchen, private balcony and fireplace.

Hotel Aspen   *(970)925-3441*
just W at 110 W. Main St. - 81611
45 units   *(800)527-7369*   *Expensive-Very Expensive*
This tony motel by the main highway has a pool and two whirlpools. Extended Continental breakfast and apres ski buffet are complimentary. Each beautifully furnished room has a private patio or balcony. Four have a whirlpool tub on the balcony with a view.

Hotel Jerome   *(970)920-1000*
downtown at 330 E. Main St. - 81611
93 units   *(800)331-7213*   *Very Expensive*
Aspen's first grand hotel opened in 1889. Impeccably restored to its original Victorian splendor, the four-story National Register landmark has a tranquil courtyard, pool and two whirlpools, exercise room, gift shop, gourmet dining room (see listing), and fabled bar, plus (fee) valet parking. Each spacious room is luxuriously furnished with nostalgic touches and upscale amenities including marble bathrooms with oversized tubs. Many also have an in-bath whirlpool.

The Inn at Aspen   *(970)925-1500*
2 mi. W at 38750 Highway 82 - 81611
120 units   *(800)952-1515   Expensive-Very Expensive*
The only ski-in/ski-out lodging at Buttermilk Mountain is a motor hotel with a view pool, whirlpool, saunas, health and exercise facilities, restaurant and lounge. Each spacious, well-furnished studio has a kitchenette and a private deck—many with a ski slope view.

The Little Nell   *(970)920-4600*
downtown at 675 E. Durant Av. - 81611
92 units   *(800)525-6200*   *Very Expensive*
One of America's best small hotels is perfectly situated where ski slopes end by the gondola in downtown Aspen. The four-story complex is a paradigm of contemporary Western style, with a garden-court pool and whirlpool, gourmet dining room (see listing) and bar, exercise facilities, (fee) parking, and fine shops. Each spacious guest room is individually decorated with elegant furnishings, and includes a fine town/mountain view, and a gas fireplace. Suites also have a whirlpool tub and steam shower. Some have a private deck overlooking slopes.

Molly Gibson Lodge   *(970)925-3434*
just W at 101 W. Main St. - 81611
50 units   *(800)356-6559   Expensive-Very Expensive*
Aspen's most sybaritic motel is a sleek, wood-trimmed complex with two pools, whirlpools and bicycles (in summer). Expanded Continental breakfast is complimentary. Some of the beautifully furnished rooms have an in-room whirlpool, fireplace, and private view deck.

St. Regis Aspen   *(970)920-3300*
downtown at 315 E. Dean St. - 81611
257 units   *(800)325-3535*   *Very Expensive*
This six-story brick hotel, opened in 1993, has a pool, whirlpools, saunas, steam rooms, health and exercise facilities, (fee) bicycles and valet parking, fine dining room and plush lounge, plus resort shops. Each room is spacious and beautifully furnished.

Sardy House Hotel and Restaurant   *(970)920-2525*
downtown at 128 E. Main St. - 81611
20 units   *(800)321-3457*   *Very Expensive*
An 1892 mansion is now a delightful bed-and-breakfast inn with a pool, whirlpool, and sauna. An elegant full breakfast is complimentary in the dining room (see listing). Beautifully furnished rooms have Victorian and contemporary amenities including whirlpool baths.

BASIC INFORMATION

Elevation: 7,910 feet   Population (1990): 5,049
Location: 162 miles Southwest of Denver
Nearest airport with commercial flights: in town
Aspen Chamber Resort Association   (970)925-1940   (800)262-7736
downtown at 425 Rio Grande Place - 81611   www.aspen.com

Breckenridge, Colorado

Breckenridge is a born-again Old Western boom town. In 1859, gold was discovered in a stream almost 9,600 feet above sea level in a broad valley surrounded by some of the highest peaks of the Colorado Rockies. The town flourished briefly, then faded. A century later, a ski area opened the way for a second boom, which is still in progress.

Today, a delightful series of ponds, waterfalls, and rapids bordered by paths and parks adjoin downtown. A colorful mixture of restored 19th century landmarks and new Victorian-style structures house a bonanza of art galleries, specialty shops, excellent restaurants, and saloons. At the base of chairlifts near the heart of town, condo hotels offer luxurious amenities. Plush bed-and-breakfast inns also serve skiers and summer visitors attracted by spectacular peaks, rushing streams, and clear cold lakes. One of the nation's best year-round recreation complexes tops in-town facilities that also include new golf courses, tennis complexes, bicycle paths, and an alpine slide.

WEATHER PROFILE

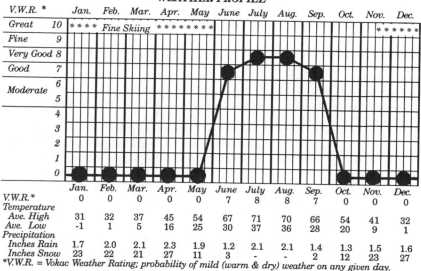

V.W.R.*		Jan.	Feb.	Mar.	Apr.	May	June	July	Aug.	Sep.	Oct.	Nov.	Dec.
Great	10												
Fine	9												
Very Good	8												
Good	7												
Moderate	6												
	5												

V.W.R.*	0	0	0	0	0	7	8	8	7	0	0	0
Temperature												
Ave. High	31	32	37	45	54	67	71	70	66	54	41	32
Ave. Low	-1	1	5	16	25	30	37	36	28	20	9	1
Precipitation												
Inches Rain	1.7	2.0	2.1	2.3	1.9	1.2	2.1	2.1	1.4	1.3	1.5	1.6
Inches Snow	23	22	21	27	11	3	-	-	2	12	23	27

*V.W.R. = Vokac Weather Rating; probability of mild (warm & dry) weather on any given day.

127

ATTRACTIONS

Alpine Slide   *(970)453-5000*
1 mi. W on Ski Hill Rd. at base of Peak 8
A scenic chairlift operates from June to September, taking riders to the top of dual alpine slide tracks and a panoramic view of the Colorado Rockies. Each rider has full control of the speed of the wheeled sled as it travels down the half-mile-long fiberglass track.

Arapahoe National Forest   *(970)468-5434*
around town
This vast forest includes some of the highest peaks in the Rocky Mountains. The continent's highest paved road reaches the summit of 14,260-foot Mount Evans. A good system of dirt roads access numerous ghost towns. There are two wilderness areas, hundreds of miles of hiking trails, Dillon Reservoir, and several major winter sports areas.

Bicycling
There are more than forty miles of separated scenic bikeways in town and on the broad, gently sloping valley floor. Hearty bikers able to pedal at a base elevation nearly two miles high can rent bicycles and gear and get maps and information at several shops in town.

Breckenridge Recreation Center   *(970)453-1734*
1 mi. N at 880 Airport Rd.
One of America's great state-of-the-art recreation centers has both indoor lap and leisure pools, a long waterslide, whirlpools, two climbing walls, track, saunas, gyms, tennis courts and more.

Dillon Reservoir   *(970)668-0376*
6 mi. N on CO 9
Majestic peaks surround a relatively large (five square miles) manmade lake. It is always too cold for swimming at 8,800 feet above sea level, but power and sail boating (rentals are available) and fishing are very popular. The shoreline has numerous pine-shaded picnic and camp sites.

Horseback Riding
Horses are rented by the hour or by the day for rides on forested paths around town. Breakfast rides, steak fries, pack trips and winter sleigh rides can also be arranged at several places around town.

Winter Sports
  Arapahoe Basin   *(888)272-7246*
  19 mi. NE on US 6
The vertical rise is 2,250 feet and the longest run is 1.5 miles. Elevation at the top is 13,050 feet. There are five chairlifts. Limited facilities, rentals and a restaurant are available. Ski season is mid-November to June.

  Breckenridge Ski Resort   *(970)453-5000*   *(800)789-7669*
  downtown via Village Rd.
The vertical rise is 3,398 feet and the longest run is 3.5 miles. Elevation at the top is 12,998 feet. There are thirteen chairlifts. All facilities, services and rentals are available at three base areas in town for both downhill and cross-country skiing. Many bars, restaurants and lodging facilities are within walking distance of the bases. The ski season is November to May.

  Keystone Resort Ski Area   *(970)496-2316*   *(800)222-0188*
  15 mi. N on US 6
The vertical rise is 2,680 feet and the longest run is three miles. Elevation at the top is 12,000 feet. There are fifteen chairlifts,

including two gondolas. All facilities, services and rentals are available at the bases for both downhill and cross-country skiing. Numerous restaurants, bars and lodgings are near the bases. Ski season is November through April.

RESTAURANTS

Blue River Bistro   *(970)453-6974*
downtown at 305 N. Main St.
L-D.   *Moderate*
Generous portions of skillfully presented Southern Italian cuisine including first-rate foccaccio and several housemade desserts are served amid cozy congestion in a colorful Western-style trattoria.

Breckenridge Brewery & Pub   *(970)453-1550*
just S at 600 S. Main St.
L-D.   *Moderate*
All-American comfort foods are served with quality beers and ales produced and bottled here. The impressive stainless steel kettle room is surrounded by relaxed bars, dining areas, and a panoramic peak-view deck.

Briar Rose   *(970)453-9948*
downtown at 109 E. Lincoln St.
D only.   *Expensive*
Sauteed medallions of elk and aged prime rib are specialties among New West cuisine served in one of Colorado's venerable gourmet havens. A cozy array of glass-topped tables and casual decor don't detract from culinary delights. The adjoining saloon has a choice display of trophy game animals and a heraldic nude.

Cafe Alpine   *(970)453-8218*
downtown at 106 E. Adams Av.
L-D.   *Expensive*
One of Colorado's most adventurous grazing menus covers the world of contemporary culinary styles with dishes like Thai chicken salad, or Tandoori roasted game hen, plus fine housemade desserts. Urbane dining rooms, a tapas bar, and lounge fill several levels of a historic building with a splendid stained glass window.

Fatty's Pizzeria   *(970)453-9802*
downtown at 106 S. Ridge St.
L-D.   *Moderate*
Dough is made fresh daily and hand-thrown into the best pizza for miles. Thick or thin crust and all kinds of fresh toppings can be enjoyed in the parlor or on a flowery mountain-view deck.

Hearthstone   *(970)453-1148*
downtown at 130 S. Ridge St.
L-D.   *Expensive*
New West cuisine gets expert attention in dishes like beer-battered jalapeno-wrapped jumbo shrimp, or grilled rack of elk. A historic house now has upstairs and downstairs dining areas with a rustic Western feeling enhanced by barnwood wall trim and a view lounge.

The Lodge at Breckenridge   *(970)453-4813*
2 mi. SE at 112 Overlook Dr.
B-D.   *Expensive*
Even if the New West cuisine wasn't special, and it can be very good, this would be a memorable restaurant. Perched atop a ridge two miles high, a posh Western-style dining room offers an eagle's-eye view of a spectacular mountain range.

Pierre's Riverwalk Cafe   *(970)453-0989*
downtown at 137 S. Main St.
L-D.   *Expensive*
Creative American cuisine includes delightful culinary surprises like
quail salad or cream of lettuce soup. The relaxed upscale dining room
and dining deck share a fine view of town and the mountains.

Poirrier's Cajun Cafe   *(970)453-1877*
downtown at 224 S. Main St.
L-D.   *Expensive*
Authentic Cajun/creole specialties like Cajun popcorn, fried catfish
fingers, po' boys, gumbo, or (seasonally) crawfish etoufee are featured.
Warm cheerful decor in the dining areas and bar also contribute to the
ambiance of this nifty outpost of Louisiana bon temps.

Salt Creek Restaurant & Saloon   *(970)453-4949*
downtown at 110 E. Lincoln Av.
L-D.   *Moderate*
Texas-style barbecue plates, Angus steaks, chili and burgers can be
topped off with pecan pie or pecan brownie a la mode. Above the big
relaxed Western dining room is a mountain-view dining balcony, and
a boot-scootin' dance hall festooned with Old West bric-a-brac.

LODGING

Accommodations in town include a good array of modern condos,
hotels, motels and inns. Most of the area's older and less expensive
motels are in Frisco (9 mi. NW on CO 9). High season is winter. Rates
are usually at least 40% lower from late spring through early fall.

Allaire Timbers Inn   *(970)453-7530*
1 mi. S at 9511 Hwy. 9 (Box 4653) - 80424
10 units   *(800)624-4904   Expensive-Very Expensive*
The region's best bed-and-breakfast opened in 1991 on a ridge
overlooking Breckenridge and the mountains. Massive rough-hewn
logs, great stone fireplaces, a whirlpool with a grand view, and elegant
Western decor complement the site. A hearty gourmet breakfast and
afternoon treats are complimentary. Each room is beautifully furnished
and has a private view deck. Two spacious suites also have a gas
fireplace and large in-room whirlpool.

Beaver Run Resort and Conference Center   *(970)453-6000*
just SW at 620 Village Rd. (Box 2115) - 80424
550 units   *(800)525-2253*   *Very Expensive*
One of Colorado's largest and most complete resorts is Beaver Run.
Amenities of the nine-story complex include a ski-in/ski-out location at
the base of Peak 9, two indoor/outdoor pools, seven whirlpools, sauna,
tennis court, exercise room, indoor mini-golf, restaurant, deli, nightclub,
and shopping arcade. All units ranging from hotel room to four-
bedroom condos are beautifully furnished. Most have fine valley or
mountain views. For romantics, "Colorado Suites" also have a mini-
kitchen, large whirlpool tub, fireplace, and private balcony.

Great Divide Lodge   *(970)453-4500*
just SW at 550 Village Rd. (Box 8059) - 80424
208 units   *(800)321-8444   Expensive-Very Expensive*
You can ski in/ski out of this contemporary wood-trim ten-story
complex. The full-service hotel also has a pool, whirlpools, saunas,
exercise room, restaurant, lounge, and sports shop. Each unit is well
furnished. Some also have a private balcony with ski slope views.

The Hunt Placer Inn   (970)453-7573
just NW at 275 Ski Hill Rd. (Box 4898) - 80424
8 units   (800)472-1430   *Expensive*
This stylish 1994 bed-and-breakfast inn is on the main road to Peak
8 ski area. Full breakfast and afternoon treats are complimentary. All
beautifully furnished rooms are individually themed and include a
private bathroom and deck or balcony with a forest view, but no in-
room phone or TV. Three spacious suites also have a gas fireplace.

Little Mountain Lodge   (970)453-1969
1 mi. SE at 98 Sunbeam Dr. (Box 2479) - 80424
10 units   (800)468-7707   *Expensive*
Massive logs and field stones were used in abundance to create one of
the area's newest and finest bed-and-breakfast inns. Quality Western
art graces common areas, and there is a whirlpool. Gourmet breakfast
and afternoon treats are complimentary. Each individually decorated
room is beautifully furnished with all amenities and a private deck.
Two have a whirlpool bath. Two suites also have a gas fireplace.

The Lodge & Spa at Breckenridge   (970)453-9300
2 mi. SE at 112 Overlook Dr. (Box 391) - 80424
45 units   (800)736-1607   *Expensive*
America's highest full-service motor lodge is perched on a rim two
miles above sea level with breathtaking views of the Rocky Mountains.
Amenities include a complete athletic club and spa with an indoor pool,
two whirlpools, racquetball court, sauna, steam rooms, exercise room,
and a variety of (fee) health and beauty treatments, plus a spectacular
restaurant (see listing) and bar. Each room is well furnished,
combining Western decor and all modern conveniences. Many have
panoramic alpine views.

River Mountain Lodge   (970)453-4711
downtown at 100 S. Park Av. (Box 7188) - 80424
110 units   (800)627-3766   *Expensive-Very Expensive*
This four-story contemporary condominium hotel is at the base of a ski
run near the heart of town (but some distance from the nearest lift).
On-site are a pool, two whirlpools; exercise, sauna and steam rooms;
plus coffee shop, lounge and a sport shop. Each unit (hotel room to
four-bedroom) is well furnished and has a private balcony (many with
river/town view). Larger units also have a gas fireplace.

The Village at Breckenridge - A Wyndham Resort (970)453-2000
downtown at 535 S. Park Av. (Box 8329) - 80424
250 units   (800)800-7829   *Expensive-Very Expensive*
Ski in/ski out access to Peak 9 is the prime feature, along with a lovely
site on Maggie Pond at the south end of downtown. The six-story
complex also has a complete health club with indoor/outdoor pool, eight
whirlpools, steam room, sauna, plus an array of restaurants, bars, and
shops. Each unit (hotel room to three-bedroom) is well furnished. Many
have a kitchen, fireplace, and mountain-view balcony.

BASIC INFORMATION
Elevation: 9,600 feet   *Population (1990): 1,285*
Location: 80 miles West of Denver
Nearest airport with commercial flights: Denver - 90 miles
Breckenridge Resort Chamber   (970)453-6018   (800)221-1091
*   downtown at 311 S. Ridge St. (Box 1909) - 80424*
*   www.gobreck.com*

Crested Butte, Colorado

Crested Butte is a treasure trove of the true Old West. The little cluster of wood-sided buildings lies near the edge of a broad sage-and-grass-covered valley surrounded by majestic peaks of the central Colorado Rockies. Here, almost 9,000 feet above sea level, the town was incorporated in 1880 to supply outlying mining camps. But, discovery of coal in the late 1880s sustained it. The last coal mine closed in 1952, and Crested Butte languished briefly. Development of a major ski area on Mount Crested Butte during the 1960s began the fulfillment of the area's year-round recreation potential. In 1974 the entire town was designated a National Historic District.

Today, the compact historic business district hosts a number of fine restaurants, fascinating bars, art galleries and specialty shops. Visitors are also lured by both winter sports and, in summer, surrounding peaks, forests, streams, and lakes. Accommodations in town are scarce, but charming. Many contemporary lodgings are at the nearby ski area.

WEATHER PROFILE

V.W.R. *		Jan.	Feb.	Mar.	Apr.	May	June	July	Aug.	Sep.	Oct.	Nov.	Dec.
Great	10												
Fine	9												
Very Good	8												
Good	7												
Moderate	6												
	5												
	4												
	3												
	2												
	1												
	0												

	Jan.	Feb.	Mar.	Apr.	May	June	July	Aug.	Sep.	Oct.	Nov.	Dec.
V.W.R.*	0	0	0	0	3	7	8	8	7	1	0	0
Temperature												
Ave. High	29	32	38	47	59	71	77	75	69	57	42	31
Ave. Low	-1	4	7	18	28	34	39	38	30	21	9	3
Precipitation												
Inches Rain	2.7	2.6	2.4	1.7	1.4	1.4	1.8	2.2	1.7	1.4	1.5	2.1
Inches Snow	37	32	30	16	5	1	-	-	1	7	18	29

*V.W.R. = Vokac Weather Rating; probability of mild (warm & dry) weather on any given day.

Bicycling

Bikeways and rugged dirt byways around town go up and down a lot of steep hills. Nevertheless, the scenery is breathtaking—a feeling enhanced by reduced oxygen in this high country. Mountain bikes perfect for touring the demanding countryside can be rented in town. Information, maps, and sightseeing tours are also available.

Curecanti National Recreation Area   (970)641-2337
37 mi. SW via CO 135 on US 50

In a vast sage-and-pine-covered rangeland basin, three manmade lakes on the Gunnison River have been set aside as a major water recreation site. Fishing, boating (and boat rentals), water-skiing, swimming, and camping are popular in summer. Blue Mesa Lake, a twenty-mile-long reservoir, is the area's primary focus of water sports. Scenic two-hour boat trips are the distinctive feature of Morrow Point, a reservoir deep within a canyon of the Gunnison.

Gunnison National Forest   (970)641-0471
around town

There are nearly two dozen peaks over 13,000 feet high in this vast Rocky Mountain highland. Features include a fine winter sports area on the slopes of Crested Butte. Portions of four wilderness areas include the magnificent Maroon Bells-Snowmass wilderness that occupies most of the area between Crested Butte and Aspen. A good system of dirt roads and hundreds of miles of trails provide access to hiking, backpacking, mountain climbing, horseback riding, hunting, boating, fishing and most winter sports.

Historic District   (970)349-6438
downtown on / near Elk Av.

A delightful conglomeration of restored century-old clapboard structures, plus more recent add-ons and similarly-designed newer buildings, are all included in a National Historic District. The main street looks like a studio set for a classic western movie. For whimsy, don't miss Totem Pole Park, created to surround an impressive totem pole made with chain saws in 1974. Or, how about an authentic two-story outhouse? The upper level is offset from the lower level so that it could be used simultaneously by persons on each floor—believe it or not.

Horseback Riding

A horse can provide access to remote wilderness areas in the spectacular Rocky Mountains via hundreds of miles of forest trails. Several area stables offer hourly rentals and guided trail rides.

Lake Irwin   (970)641-0471
10 mi. W via dirt road - near Kebler Pass

Nearly two miles high in the mountains west of town is a clear little lake popular for fishing and small boats (no motors). Hiking trails circle the lake, which features picturesque boulder formations, pine-shaded campgrounds, and picnic facilities.

River Running   (800)545-4505

The Gunnison River offers rafters fairly easy runs and good scenery in summer, especially along The Palisades south of Almont (17 miles south of town). Float fishing is best starting in July—after the heavy spring runoff. More whitewater is available on the Taylor River above Almont. Arrangements can be made for a variety of floats with all equipment provided.

Winter Sports

Crested Butte Mountain Resort   (800)927-8883
3 mi. NE via Gothic Rd. - Mt. Crested Butte

The vertical rise on one of Colorado's most distinctive peaks is 3,062 feet and the longest run is 2.6 miles. Elevation at the top is 12,160 feet. There are nine chairlifts. All facilities, services and rentals are available at the base for both downhill and cross-country skiing. Numerous restaurants, bars and lodgings are at the base. The ski season is mid-November to early April.

RESTAURANTS

Bacchanale   (970)349-5257
downtown at 208 Elk Av.
D only.   *Moderate*
Traditional Italian dishes and homemade desserts have been featured for many years in this small, comfortable restaurant and bar.

The Bakery Cafe   (970)349-7280
downtown at 302 Elk Av.
B-L-D.   *Moderate*
Outstanding croissants, cinnamon rolls, and other baked goods on display are made from scratch daily. They can be taken out or enjoyed with assorted beverages and chili, soups, hearth-baked pizza and other gourmet light fare and desserts in pleasant indoor or patio dining areas. The area's best bakery has been a deserved hit since 1974.

Le Bosquet   (970)349-5808
just SE at 6th & Belleview in Majestic Plaza
L-D.   *Very Expensive*
Classic and creative French gourmet dishes are typified by tenderloin of elk with lingonberry sauce, or salmon and asparagus in puff pastry. Homemade desserts are also delicious. The recently relocated candlelit restaurant and bar has served crowd-pleasing cuisine for more than twenty years.

Paradise Cafe   (970)349-6233
downtown at Elk Av. & Third St.
B-L-D.   *Moderate*
Breakfast specialties include create-your-own omelets and all kinds of pancakes in a relaxed little cafe with a picture-window view of the main street.

Slogar Bar & Restaurant   (970)349-5765
downtown at 517 Second St.
D only.   *Moderate*
Skillet-fried chicken or steak dinners are served family-style in a comfortable restored historic building. There is also a distinctive bar.

Soupçon   (970)349-5448
downtown at 127 Elk Av.
D only.   *Expensive*
Innovative French cuisine including homemade desserts has been featured for many years in a rustic little miner's cabin that is one of the oldest buildings in town.

Wooden Nickel   (970)349-6350
downtown at 222 Elk Av.
D only.   *Moderate*
The town's oldest saloon continues to draw crowds. Steaks and other contemporary Western fare are served at comfortably padded booths near a handsome backbar and fireplace.

LODGING

Lodgings in town are mostly bed-and-breakfast inns. Many condos and two hotels are near the slopes at Mt. Crested Butte. Winter is high season. Rates are reduced as much as 50% at other times.

Crested Butte Club   *(970)349-6655*
 downtown at 512 Second St. (Box 309) - 81224
 7 units   *(800)815-2582   Moderate-Very Expensive*
Crested Butte's most delightful lodging is the Crested Butte Club. Amid Victorian surroundings are an indoor lap pool, two steambaths, three whirlpools, climbing walls and gym, and a pub. Breakfast buffet, happy hour, and health club privileges are complimentary. Each room is beautifully furnished with an artistic Victorian flair blended with all contemporary conveniences, including a private bath and gas fireplace.

Crested Butte Lodge   *(970)349-4747*
 3 mi. NE at 12 Crested Mt. Lane - Mount Crested Butte 81225
 22 units   *(800)950-2133   Moderate-Expensive*
Ski slopes are near this contemporary motor lodge with a large indoor pool, whirlpool, sauna and bar. Each room is well furnished.

Crested Butte Marriott Resort   *(970)349-4000*
 3 mi. NE at 500 Gothic Rd. (Box 81) - Mount Crested Butte 81225
 261 units   *(800)642-4422   Expensive*
Ski slopes and lifts adjoin the area's biggest and most complete hotel. The six-story complex has a small indoor pool, indoor and outdoor whirlpools, saunas, game room, fitness center, two restaurants and bars. All of the beautifully furnished rooms have a private view balcony (many overlooking the ski area) and an in-bath whirlpool.

Gateway   *(970)349-2400*
 3 mi. NE at 18 Snowmass Rd. - Mount Crested Butte 81225
 13 units   *(800)451-5699   Expensive-Very Expensive*
The slope and lifts by the heart of the ski area are adjacent to this four-story contemporary condominium with a whirlpool and sauna. Each of the one- to three-bedroom units is beautifully furnished, and has a kitchen, fireplace, and mountain-view balcony.

The Last Resort Bed & Breakfast   *(970)349-0445*
 downtown at 213 Third St. (Box 722) - 81224
 6 units   *(800)349-0445   Moderate*
Nestled by the banks of Coal Creek near Totem Pole Park is a romantic contemporary bed-and-breakfast with a library, solarium and steam room. Hearty breakfast is complimentary. Each room is attractively furnished and has a private bath. Some also have a whirlpool.

Sheraton Crested Butte Resort   *(970)349-8000*
 3 mi. NE at 6 Emmons Rd. (Box A) - Mount Crested Butte 81225
 252 units   *(888)223-2469   Expensive*
An indoor/outdoor pool and whirlpool, fitness center, deli, restaurant and lounge distinguish Sheraton's five-story modern hotel near ski slopes. Each room is well furnished. Some have fine mountain views.

BASIC INFORMATION
Elevation: 8,900 feet   Population (1990): 1,200
Location: 230 miles Southwest of Denver
Nearest airport with commercial flights: Gunnison - 30 miles
Crested Butte-Mt. Crested Butte Chamber of Commerce (970)349-6438
 downtown at Elk Av./Gothic Rd. (Box 1288) - 81224   (800)545-4505
www.cbinteractive.com

Durango, Colorado

    Durango is the recreation center of the southern Rocky Mountains. It occupies scenic piñon-pine-and-juniper-covered benchlands along the Animas River between the spectacular San Juan Mountains and mesas and plateaus of the vast Southwestern desert. Gold and silver ore discoveries prompted extension of a railroad into this area in 1881. Unlike most Colorado mining towns, Durango never experienced a "bust" because it was always the region's trading crossroads.

    The narrow-gauge railroad that spawned the town is still the area's major attraction. Downtown, the well-landscaped main street is lined with massive brick Victorians and carefully integrated newer structures housing a notable array of art galleries and specialty shops, fine restaurants, and one of the nation's best collections of saloons, live theaters and hotels that perpetuate the spirit of the Old West. Surrounding mountains, rivers, lakes and desert offer unlimited four-season outdoor recreation opportunities.

WEATHER PROFILE

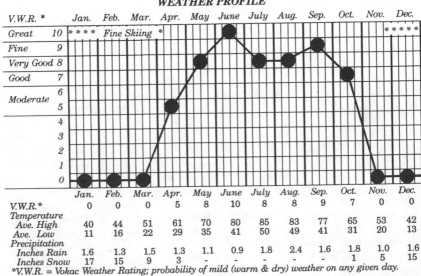

V.W.R.*		Jan.	Feb.	Mar.	Apr.	May	June	July	Aug.	Sep.	Oct.	Nov.	Dec.
Great	10												
Fine	9												
Very Good	8												
Good	7												
Moderate	6												
	5												

	Jan.	Feb.	Mar.	Apr.	May	June	July	Aug.	Sep.	Oct.	Nov.	Dec.
V.W.R.*	0	0	0	5	8	10	8	8	9	7	0	0
Temperature												
Ave. High	40	44	51	61	70	80	85	83	77	65	53	42
Ave. Low	11	16	22	29	35	41	50	49	41	31	20	13
Precipitation												
Inches Rain	1.6	1.3	1.5	1.3	1.1	0.9	1.8	2.4	1.6	1.8	1.0	1.6
Inches Snow	17	15	9	3	-	-	-	-	-	1	5	15

*V.W.R. = Vokac Weather Rating; probability of mild (warm & dry) weather on any given day.

ATTRACTIONS
Alpine Slide   *(970)247-9000*
25 mi. N on US 550
A scenic chairlift operates daily in summer at the Purgatory Ski Area, taking riders to the top of dual alpine slide tracks. The panoramic view of the San Juans is magnificent. So is the ride down a nearly half-mile-long fiberglass course with the rider in control of the sled's speed.

Bicycling
Many miles of scenic, but hilly, highways and byways plus dirt roads and trails surrounding town have made Durango a "mountain bike mecca." Bicycle rentals, tours, and information are available at:

Hassle Free Sports   *1 mi. N at 2615 Main Av.*   *(800)835-3800*
Mountain Bike Specialists   *949 Main Av.*   *(970)247-4066*
Durango & Silverton Narrow Gauge Railroad   *(970)247-2733*
downtown at 479 Main Av.   *(888)872-4607*
America's legendary narrow-gauge passenger train, a National Historic Landmark, has been in continuous service since 1882. Now running a 90-mile round trip between Durango and Silverton, trains depart from the downtown depot each morning and return in the early evening daily from mid-April to late October. There is a shorter trip in winter. Original coal-fired steam engines and passenger coaches are used for the three-plus hour ride through continuously spectacular mountain scenery along the Las Animas River.

Horseback Riding   *(800)525-8855*
Scenic trail rides, breakfast rides, sunset steak rides, plus overnight or longer pack trips and hunting trips can be arranged at more than a dozen stables and outfitters around town

Jeep Tours and Rentals   *(800)525-8855*
Jeeps may be rented by the day or longer during summer. Half or all-day tours can also be reserved at several places to explore fascinating ghost towns, mining relics and scenic attractions surrounding town.

Mesa Verde National Park   *(970)529-4421*   *(800)449-2288*
36 mi. W via US 160 and park road
The only national park dedicated to the works of man features the world's most extensive cliff dwelling ruins. A large plateau, 2,000 feet above surrounding valleys, was the home of Anasazi Indians (the old ones) who mysteriously left about 1300 A.D. Well-preserved evidence of their architectural skills may be viewed from self-guided loop drives, each six miles long. Several ruins are open to the public—mostly via ranger-guided trips. Restaurants, lodgings, and camping facilities are available from late April into October. The park, a visitor center, and museum are open year-round.

Ouray and the Million Dollar Highway   *(970)325-4746*
for approximately 70 mi. N on US 550 to Ouray
One of the world's most memorable mountain highways extends from Durango to Ouray. The all-weather paved highway filled with breathtaking alpine vistas is still not for the faint-hearted. Ouray is a tiny village deep in a lush box canyon surrounded by towering peaks. A waterfall tumbling from a precipitous cliff can be seen all over town. Near its base is a delightful hot spring vapor cave and pool open to the public at **Weisbaden Hot Springs Spa & Lodgings**. The sybaritic grounds have also provided rustic lodgings and health and beauty treatments for more than half a century. Nearby, **Ouray Hot Springs Pool** is a huge oval filled with warm mineral springs water. Hiking, mountain biking, jeep and mine tours are deservedly popular around

town. The compact town center has regional arts and crafts shops, atmospheric saloons, and fine dining at the **Bon Ton Restaurant** in the restored little **St. Elmo Hotel**, or the **Piñon** for dinners like sauteed boneless trout with roasted piñon nuts. Ouray will be a great town again when the recently-purchased landmark Beaumont Hotel is fully restored. Currently, the village's best lodgings are the **China Clipper Inn** and **The Damn Yankee Country Inn**, with beautifully nostalgic rooms with all contemporary conveniences, and extras like a whirlpool. Gourmet breakfasts and afternoon treats are complimentary. Fourteen miles north in Ridgway is **The Adobe Inn**, with superb New Mexican cuisine, atmosphere, and mountain views, plus lodgings. Nearby, the **Chipeta Sun Lodge**, with a unique blend of romantic Southwestern decor and stunning mountain views, is one of Colorado's best bed-and-breakfasts.

River Running
Professional river guides arrange scenic and whitewater river trips in rafts, canoes and kayaks on the Animas River (in town) and others nearby during the summer. Trips of one hour to several days with everything provided can be reserved at nearly a dozen places in town.

San Juan National Forest
starts 5 mi. N of town
Several peaks are more than 14,000 feet high in this huge forest. Features include a major winter sports area and portions of three wilderness areas, including the state's largest. Fiord-like Vallecito Reservoir and others offer a full range of water sports. A good system of roads and trails through lush pine forests provides access to mining relics, waterfalls, streams and lakes. Camping, hiking, backpacking, horseback riding and pack trips, mountain climbing, fishing, hunting (for both big game and upland game birds), water sports, and (in winter) a full range of snow sports are among recreation possibilities.

Silverton
50 mi. N on US 550
Located on the wide floor of the Animas River valley more than 9,000 feet above sea level, the tiny community is surrounded by towering peaks of the San Juan Range. Access to the area is via the dramatic "Million Dollar Highway," jeep roads, or the narrow-gauge railroad from Durango. Numerous well-preserved Victorian buildings house mining memorabilia, restaurants and saloons displaying reminders of the early boom times. The **Wyman Hotel & Inn** is the best lodging, with a delightful blend of nostalgic and contemporary facilities.

Vallecito Lake   *(970)884-9782*
18 mi. NE via Florida Rd.
Colorado's prettiest reservoir (when it is full) offers excellent fishing and boating, plus hiking and horseback riding opportunities in the surrounding mountain wilderness. Sail and motor boats can be rented at several boat docks. Numerous rustic lodges, campgrounds, restaurants, and bars line the twenty-mile shoreline.

Winter Sports
Purgatory Resort   *(970)247-9000   (800)979-9742*
25 mi. N on US 550
The vertical rise is 2,029 feet and the longest run is about two miles. Elevation at the top is 10,822 feet. There are ten chairlifts. All facilities, services and rentals are at the base for both downhill and cross-country skiing. Restaurants, bars, and several lodgings are located near the base. The ski season is late November into April.

Ariano's   *(970)247-8146*
downtown at 150 E. College Dr.
D only.   *Expensive*
Veal skillfully prepared a half dozen different ways leads a diverse menu in Durango's best source of classical Northern Italian cuisine. Intimate upscale dining areas are enhanced by warm wood tones.

Carver's Restaurant & Brew Pub   *(970)259-2545*
downtown at 1022 Main Av.
B-L-D.   *Moderate*
Cinnamon schneck (if you haven't tried it, do) stars among all kinds of morning delights (the best in Durango) on a well-rounded menu of Southwest favorites. Beyond the pastry cases is a warm knotty-pine coffee shop. Pub grub is served later with their outstanding beers and ales in a cozy back room overlooking brew kettles and a biergarten.

Chez Grand-mère   *(970)247-7979*
downtown at 63 Depot Pl.
L-D.   *Very Expensive*
Classic Continental cuisine, meticulously prepared by the chef/owner, is served in sumptuous six-course dinners. To complete the extravaganza, you can try one or all of the spectacular homemade desserts served in warm cozy dining areas with country charm.

937 Main   *(970)259-2616*
downtown at 937 Main St.
L-D.   *Expensive*
In the 937 Main, opened in 1998, New American cuisine is enshrined on an innovative grazing menu that includes brilliant dishes like tomato-basil bisque; pistachio nut crusted sea bass; and chocolate peanut butter lasagne for dessert. The simply stylish dining room, bar and patio provide a pleasant backdrop to sophisticated meals.

Olde Tymer's Cafe   *(970)259-2990*
downtown at 1000 Main Av.
L-D.   *Moderate*
For burgers and other American comfort foods, this is a long-time favorite. The nostalgic corner dining room/bar has a stamped-tin ceiling, worn wood floor, and a greenery-laden courtyard.

Ore House   *(970)247-5707*
downtown at 147 E. College Dr.
D only.   *Expensive*
Traditional Western steaks, trout, and a salad bar have been featured for more than a quarter-century. The nostalgic dining room and saloon are filled with Western bric-a-brac and local art.

Palace Restaurant   *(970)247-2018*
downtown on Main Av. (by train depot)
L-D.   *Expensive*
Contemporary American fare includes trout in four styles. The elegant rusticity of warm wood trim and armchairs, stained glass lamps and a depot view are shared by the dining room, tavern and terrace.

Randy's   *(970)247-9083*
downtown at 152 E. College Dr.
D only.   *Expensive*
New American cuisine ranges from red chile onion rings through piñon trout, plus delicious homemade desserts. Upscale Victorian decor includes a number of candlelit tables at draped booths that capture the romance and intimacy of fine dining long ago.

Red Snapper   *(970)259-3417*
downtown at 144 East 9th St.
D only.   *Expensive*
Durango's premier seafood house features a good selection of fresh fish and shellfish given careful creative attention. Housemade key lime pie stars among desserts. Aquariums contribute to the nautical atmosphere in a cozy wood-toned dining room and bar.

Seasons Rotisserie & Grill   *(970)382-9790*
downtown at 764 Main Av.
D only.   *Expensive*
One of Durango's best restaurants is a newer culinary extravaganza featuring creative American cuisine that is as beautiful as it is flavorful. Imagine a double-cut smoked pork rib chop with a caramelized shallot sage sauce. Housemade desserts are similarly delightful. The urbane dining room/bar is a snazzy congestion of tables where diners overlook Western art and a talented expo kitchen.

Strater Hotel   *(970)247-4431*
downtown at 699 Main Av.
B-L-D.   *Expensive*
In **Henry's**, Old and New West dishes star, along with delicious housemade desserts. Victorian decor in the large dining room is enhanced by an abundance of stained glass and grand piano music at dinner. Next door, the hotel's celebrated **Diamond Belle Saloon** continues its role as one of America's legendary sources for Gay 90s (the last one, not this one) atmosphere including a well-played old-time upright piano.

LODGING

Durango accommodations have long been plentiful. They're now also diverse, from historic hotels to plush inns and resorts, plus a "motel row" on Main Av. (US 550) north of downtown. Summer is high season (except at Purgatory). Rates are usually at least 30% less at other times.

Apple Orchard Inn   *(970)247-0751*
10 mi. N via US 550 at 7758 CR 203 - 81301
10 units   *(800)426-0751*   *Moderate-Expensive*
Trimble Hot Springs is near this delightful bed-and-breakfast in a peaceful mountain valley. Posh contemporary cabins surround a luxuriant garden, and there is a whirlpool. Full gourmet breakfast is complimentary. Each room is beautifully furnished and has all contemporary conveniences including a private bathroom with a radiant heat floor. Several also have a large whirlpool bath and a fireplace.

Doubletree Hotel Durango   *(970)259-6580*
downtown at 501 Camino Del Rio - 81301
159 units   *(800)222-8733*   *Expensive*
Durango's biggest and best contemporary hotel is by the Animas River. The four-story complex has a large indoor river-view pool, whirlpool, sauna and exercise room, handsome dining room by the river, cafe, lounge and gift shop. Many well-furnished rooms have a river view.

General Palmer Hotel   *(970)247-4747*
downtown at 567 Main Av. - 81301
39 units   *(800)523-3358*   *Expensive*
This restored three-story 1890s hotel and annex is near the narrow gauge railroad depot in the heart of town. The lobby, restaurant and lounge are outfitted with charming Victorian relics and replicas. So are well-furnished rooms that have all modern conveniences. Two rooms overlook the trains and have an in-bath whirlpool.

Iron Horse Inn   *(970)259-1010*
5 mi. N at 5800 N. Main Av. (US 550) - 81301
140 units   *(800)748-2990*   *Moderate-Expensive*
Narrow gauge trains run right by this sprawling condo complex with a large indoor view pool, whirlpool and saunas, plus a restaurant and lounge, and general store. Each big, comfortably furnished unit has a fireplace. Most have a loft bedroom and kitchenette.

Lightner Creek Inn   *(970)259-1226*
4 mi. W at 999 C.R. 207 - 81301
10 units   *(800)268-9804*   *Moderate-Expensive*
A stream and pond on attractively landscaped grounds lend charm to one of Durango's two finest bed-and-breakfast inns. A 1903 manor house now serves as an artistic plush hideaway for relaxation or recreation in the foothills. A hearty gourmet breakfast and afternoon treats are complimentary. Each beautifully furnished room includes fine antiques and all modern conveniences.

Rio Grande Inn - Best Western   *(970)385-4980*
downtown at 400 East 2nd Av. - 81301
138 units   *(800)245-4466*   *Expensive*
The train depot is only one block from this contemporary four-story motel with an indoor pool, whirlpool, sauna, exercise room, and gift shop. Expanded Continental breakfast and evening beverages are complimentary. Each room is well furnished. At the adjoining **Hawthorn Suites Ltd.**, spacious two-room suites have a small balcony, kitchenette, and in-bath whirlpool.

Strater Hotel   *(970)247-4431*
downtown at 699 Main Av. (P.O. Drawer E) - 81301
93 units   *(800)247-4431*   *Expensive*
The Strater Hotel is the heart of Durango. The four-story red brick building two blocks from the depot has been the region's premier lodging landmark continuously since 1887. Amenities include a gourmet dining room and entertainment saloon (see listing), the peerless **Diamond Circle Melodrama Theatre** (in summer) plus a large whirlpool. Rooms are beautifully furnished with all modern conveniences and items from one of the world's largest collections of authentic American Victorian walnut antiques.

Tamarron Hilton Resort   *(970)259-2000*
17 mi. N at 40292 US 550 N. (P.O. Drawer 3131) - 81301
300 units   *(800)678-1000   Expensive-Very Expensive*
One of Colorado's great full-service resorts is tucked away in an alpine valley far below majestic surrounding mountains. It is a locale where a wealth of summer and winter recreation opportunities can be reserved. The handsome contemporary lodge and condo complex overlooks a (fee) championship 18-hole golf course and four tennis courts, plus a large indoor/outdoor pool, whirlpools, saunas, elegant view restaurant, coffee shop, lounge and resort shops. Each room is beautifully furnished and has kitchen facilities. Condos also have private mountain-view balconies.

BASIC INFORMATION

Elevation: 6,512 feet   *Population (1990): 12,439*
Location: 335 miles Southwest of Denver
Nearest airport with commercial flights: south of town - 18 miles
Durango Area Chamber Resort Association   *(970)247-0312*
   downtown at 111 S. Camino del Rio (Box 2587) - 81302
   www.durango.org   *(800)463-8726*

Estes Park, Colorado

Estes Park is the West's all-American tourist town. One of the nation's most popular playgrounds lies among hills in a park-like little basin rimmed by snow-capped peaks of the Front Range of the Colorado Rockies. Settlement began after a toll road into the area was opened in 1874 for hunters and sightseers. Completion of the Stanley Hotel in 1909 and creation of Rocky Mountain National Park in 1915 established the village as an international travel destination.

Downtown is now a potpourri of gift shops, homemade candy and other carryout food stores, bars, cafes, and restaurants on flowery, tree-lined streets. It is surrounded by a profusion of family-oriented attractions and motels. Some newer lodgings are clearly intended for romantic couples. All facilities reflect Estes Park's continuing desire to fulfill the needs of vacationers in this ever-popular lofty playground of towering peaks, scenic waterfalls, crystal-clear streams and lakes, and the nation's highest major highway.

WEATHER PROFILE

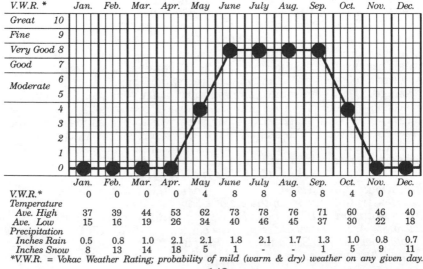

V.W.R.*	Jan.	Feb.	Mar.	Apr.	May	June	July	Aug.	Sep.	Oct.	Nov.	Dec.
V.W.R.*	0	0	0	0	4	8	8	8	8	4	0	0
Temperature												
Ave. High	37	39	44	53	62	73	78	76	71	60	46	40
Ave. Low	15	16	19	26	34	40	46	45	37	30	22	18
Precipitation												
Inches Rain	0.5	0.8	1.0	2.1	2.1	1.8	2.1	1.7	1.3	1.0	0.8	0.7
Inches Snow	8	13	14	18	5	1	-	-	1	5	9	11

*V.W.R. = Vokac Weather Rating; probability of mild (warm & dry) weather on any given day.

Aerial Tramway   *(970)586-3675*
just SE at 420 E. Riverside Dr.
Two enclosed tram cars take visitors to the top of Prospect Mountain daily from mid-May to mid-September. There are fine panoramic views of town and peaks, picnic areas, and hiking trails in the pines.

Amusement Places
Family fun has been provided by several places in town for many years. The two most complete offer attractions like mini-golf courses, bumper cars and boats, miniature train, long rug slide, and arcades.
Fun City   *just SW at 375 Moraine Av.*   *(970)586-2070*
Estes Park Ride-a-Kart *2 mi. E on US 34*   *(970)586-6495*

Boat Rentals
Lake Estes Marina   *(970)586-2011*
2 mi. E on US 34 at 1770 E. Big Thompson Av.
Windsurfing, sailing, boating and fishing equipment can be rented here daily all summer for use on the little reservoir.

Horseback Riding
Scenic trail rides, breakfast or dinner rides, and overnight or longer pack or fishing trips can be arranged at a dozen places, including:
Elkhorn Stables *just W on US 34 at 650 Elkhorn Av.*   *586-5225*
National Park Village Stables *5 mi. W on US 34*   *586-5269*

Museums   *(970)586-4431*
There are several museums in and around town. Collectively, they graphically depict homesteading, ranching and the evolution of handicrafts and tourism in the area.

Rocky Mountain National Park   *(970)586-1206*
3 mi. W on US 34 or US 36
The renowned park contains one of the highest regions in the country along the Continental Divide in the Front Range of the Rocky Mountains. Dominating the spectacular skyline, Longs Peak (14,255 feet) towers above a maze of steep-walled canyons, waterfalls, lakes and cataracts. Dense forests blanket the lower slopes of mountains that reach well above timberline. Hundreds of varieties of wildflowers contribute ephemeral brilliance to upland meadows. Deer, elk, bighorn sheep, beaver and other animals are numerous in this wildlife sanctuary. The awe-inspiring Trail Ridge Road is the only paved highway through the park. At Fall River Pass, the Alpine Visitor Center exhibits and describes the mountain tundra environment. Bear Lake, a photogenic little jewel of glacial origin circled by a self-guided nature trail, is also a very popular trailhead.

Roosevelt National Forest   *(970)498-2775*
N, E and S of town
Numerous tiny glaciers dot the highest peaks of this large forest. These, together with icy lakes, streams, and waterfalls carved into flower-filled upland meadows, provide unlimited summer recreation possibilities accessed by hundreds of miles of trails.

Trail Ridge Road
US 34 for approx. 50 mi. SW to Grand Lake
The highest continuous paved auto road in North America (a four-mile section is over 12,000 feet above sea level) offers breathtaking views of the Rocky Mountains and, far to the east, the Great Plains. For more than eleven miles the road is above timberline. Grand Lake (Colorado's biggest natural water body and the scenic western terminus) is bordered by a popular lakeside resort village.

RESTAURANTS

The Bistro in the Park   *(970)586-1817*
1 mi. SW at 861 Moraine Av.
L-D.   *Expensive*
In this deservedly popular young restaurant, contemporary American bistro cuisine is skillfully prepared in dishes ranging from Dungeness crabcakes to lamb shank provençal on a menu that changes daily. Beyond the warm and cozy dining room is a shaded alfresco deck with mountain views above the highway.

Black Canyon Inn   *(970)586-9344*
1 mi. N at 800 MacGregor Av.
L-D.   *Expensive*
New West dishes like elk loin chop or cherrywood smoked duck are served amid elegant rusticity in an imposing log lodge with a great stone fireplace, solid wood interior and picture-window view of the mountain.

The Dunraven Inn   *(970)586-6409*
3 mi. SW at 2470 CO 66
D only.   *Moderate*
Italian dishes and steaks have been served for many years amid halls and walls festooned with extra dollars left behind.

Estes Park Brewery   *(970)586-5421*
1 mi. SW at 470 Prospect Village Dr.
L-D.   *Moderate*
The village's only microbrewery opened in 1994. An upstairs pub offers good food, games, a big deck and views of both the mountains and brewery/bottling area. Downstairs is a complimentary tasting bar and a big gift shop.

Inn of Glen Haven   *(970)586-3897*
7 mi. N at 7468 County Rd. 43
D only.   *Moderate*
Creative and traditional Continental cuisine is prepared with fresh seasonal ingredients in this charming intimate restaurant that is one of the high country's premier dining favorites.

La Chaumiere   *(303)823-6521*
12 mi. SE on US 36 - Pinewood Springs
D only.   *Expensive*
Expertly prepared innovative American cuisine is offered on a menu that varies daily. Items from the on-premises smokehouse and bakery are noteworthy, as are homemade ice creams. The distinctive dining room has windows overlooking a private deer park and mountains.

Mountaineer Restaurant   *(970)586-9001*
1 mi. SE at 540 S. Saint Vrain Av.
B-L-D.   *Low*
Old-fashioned American breakfasts (biscuits and gravy, corned beef hash, etc.) are good. They make their own cinnamon rolls, pecan rolls, and pies, too, in this gussied-up Western coffee shop.

The Other Side Restaurant   *(970)586-2171*
1 mi. SW at 900 Moraine Av.
B-L-D.   *Moderate*
Traditional American fare which includes really big cinnamon rolls for breakfast is served in a comfortable coffee shop upstairs. Later meals are served in a greenery-filled dining room downstairs with a spectacular view of mountains beyond a beaver pond.

Rock Inn Western Steakhouse   *(970)586-5584*
2 mi. SW on at 1675 CO Hwy. 66
D only.   *Moderate*
The area's best steaks may be the ones you select up front and grill yourself. The steak, or trout, chicken, or buffalo burger come with a salad bar. The big lodge with a rustic-wood interior, mounted trophy animals, and rock fireplace is an authentic yesteryear showcase.

The Stanley Hotel & Conference Center   *(970)586-3371*
1 mi. NE at 333 Wonderview Av.
B-L-D.   *Expensive*
Contemporary American cuisine is served in the hotel's big nostalgic dining room with a raised stage and window-wall mountain view. There is also an entertainment lounge and cafe.

LODGING

Abundant lodgings along US 34 east and west of downtown range from tiny motels to historic hotels and romantic bed-and-breakfast inns. While many close in winter, those that stay open usually discount the summer (high season) rates by 30% or more.

Aspen Winds   *(970)586-6010*
3 mi. W at 1051 Fall River Ct. (Box 5169) - 80517
16 units   *(800)399-6010*   *Expensive*
One of the area's most sybaritic all-suites motels opened in 1994 in a picturesque alpine setting by Fall River. Each of the spacious, well-furnished suites has kitchen facilities, a gas fireplace, and a private view balcony or deck by the river. Six "Spa Suites" also have a large in-room whirlpool with a river view.

Best Western at Lake Estes Resort   *(970)586-3386*
2 mi. E at 1650 Big Thompson Av. (Box 1466) - 80517
57 units   *(800)292-8439*   *Moderate-Expensive*
This low-rise modern motel has two pools, a big whirlpool and sauna on spacious grounds. All of the rooms are well furnished. Six two-room "Chalet Suites" also have kitchenette, big private patio, multi-directional gas fireplace, and a large in-room whirlpool.

Boulder Brook   *(970)586-0910*
2 mi. W at 1900 Fall River Rd. - 80517
16 units   *(800)238-0910*   *Expensive*
Boulder Brook is the Estes Park region's quintessential all-suites lodging. Contemporary wood-trimmed buildings surrounded by pine-shaded lawns and gardens are generously spaced along picturesque Fall River, and there is a tranquil outdoor whirlpool. Each of the large, beautifully furnished suites has kitchen facilities, a private riverfront deck or balcony, a gas fireplace, and a big voluptuous in-room whirlpool with a river view.

Deer Crest   *(970)586-2324*
1 mi. W at 1200 Fall River Rd. (Box 1768) - 80517
26 units   *(800)331-2324*   *Moderate*
This contemporary motel by Fall River has a scenic pool and whirlpool. Each room is well furnished. Mini-suites also have a gas fireplace.

Fawn Valley Inn   *(970)586-2388*
4 mi. W at 2760 Fall River Rd. (Box 4020) - 80517
33 units   *(800)525-2961*   *Expensive*
Fall River adjoins this long-established condo lodge with an outdoor pool, whirlpool, restaurant and lounge. Each one- or two-bedroom unit is comfortably furnished and has a kitchen and gas or woodburning fireplace. Most also have a private mountain-view balcony.

Golden Eagle Resort at the Crags Lodge   *(970)586-6066*
1 mi. S at 300 Riverside Dr. (Box 480) - 80517
40 units   *Moderate-Expensive*
One of Estes Park's most venerable lodgings, opened in 1914, has a pool and whirlpool. A pinewood interior enhances the nostalgic firelit dining room with a window-wall panorama of downtown and the mountains. Many refurbished, nicely furnished suites have a kitchenette and share the grand view.

Ponderosa Lodge   *(970)586-4233*
3 mi. W at 1820 Fall River Rd. - 80517
19 units   *(800)628-0512*   *Moderate-Expensive*
The river and highway border this modern wood-trimmed motel. All of the well-furnished units have patios or balconies overlooking the river, and a (gas or wood) fireplace. Most also have a kitchenette.

Romantic RiverSong   *(970)586-4666*
3 mi. SW via US 36 at 1765 Lower Broadview Rd. (Box 1910) - 80517
9 units   *Expensive-Very Expensive*
Romantic River Song is one of America's great bed-and-breakfast inns. Several small buildings at the end of a dirt road are clustered above a rushing stream and pond in a naturalized garden. Hiking trails lead into adjoining Rocky Mountain National Park. Gourmet breakfast is complimentary. In this peaceful adult fantasy, there are no phones or televisions. But, each room is uniquely and luxuriously furnished with a blend of antique and contemporary decor that captures the romantic spirit of the high country, and has a private bath, woodburning or gas fireplace, and a large soaking tub. Three rooms also have a private view deck and a two-person whirlpool.

The Stanley Hotel & Conference Center   *(970)586-3371*
1 mi. NE at 333 Wonderview Av. (Box 1767) - 80517
92 units   *(800)976-1377*   *Expensive*
The area's most illustrious landmark was built in 1909, by Stanley, of Steamer fame. The stately old four-story whitewashed hotel, on the National Register, continues to serve from a dramatic site high on a hill with a large view pool, fine dining room (see listing) and lounge, and an award-winning theater. Each room is well furnished with a blend of antiques and modern conveniences.

Streamside Cabins   *(970)586-6464*
2 mi. W at 1260 Fall River Rd. (Box 2930) - 80517
19 units   *(800)321-3303*   *Expensive*
Wood-trimmed cabins are clustered in a pine-shaded meadow by Fall River, and there is a distinctive swim/spa that combines features of a swimming pool and whirlpool. Each of the beautifully furnished units has a gas or woodburning fireplace, and kitchen. Some have a private deck by the river.

BASIC INFORMATION

Elevation: 7,522 feet   *Population (1990): 3,184*
Location: 65 miles Northwest of Denver
Nearest airport with commercial flights: Denver - 75 miles
Estes Park Chamber Resort Association (970)586-4431   (800)443-7837
  just E at 500 Big Thompson Av. - 80517
www.estesnet.com

Glenwood Springs, Colorado

Glenwood Springs is a rest-and-recreation capital of the Rockies. Many warm mineral springs punctuate the little valley where the Colorado River leaves spectacular Glenwood Canyon. Pine-forested mountains loom on all sides. Development began in the 1880s with the arrival of a railroad, and miners interested in soaking away their aches and pains. By 1891, the world's largest hot springs pool and a resort hotel were completed.

Today, miners have long since been replaced by visitors here to enjoy the renowned hot springs, run the rivers, and explore the high country. The huge pool, natural vapor caves, and the historic hotel are reassuringly maintained. Across the river, a Victorian depot and other historic downtown buildings are enhanced by flowery parks and landscaped streets. Specialty shops feature regional art plus summer and winter recreation gear. Restaurants and nightlife are also proliferating with Glenwood's resurgence as a four-season destination.

WEATHER PROFILE

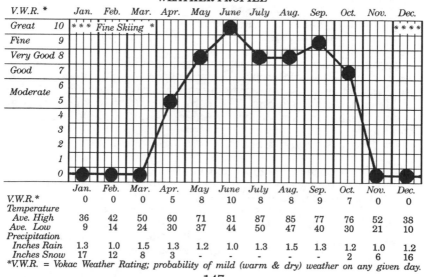

		Jan.	Feb.	Mar.	Apr.	May	June	July	Aug.	Sep.	Oct.	Nov.	Dec.
V.W.R.*		0	0	0	5	8	10	8	8	9	7	0	0
Temperature													
Ave. High		36	42	50	60	71	81	87	85	77	76	52	38
Ave. Low		9	14	24	30	37	44	50	47	40	30	21	10
Precipitation													
Inches Rain		1.3	1.0	1.5	1.3	1.2	1.0	1.3	1.5	1.3	1.2	1.0	1.2
Inches Snow		17	12	8	3	-	-	-	-	-	2	6	16

*V.W.R. = Vokac Weather Rating; probability of mild (warm & dry) weather on any given day.

ATTRACTIONS

Bicycling
A paved bikeway through Glenwood Canyon stars among relatively easy, scenic rides around town. Mountain bikes are also available for getting into the high country. Several places in town have rentals.

Glenwood Canyon
for 18 mi. NE on I-70
One of the Colorado River's most ruggedly beautiful canyons delights sightseers on the meticulously designed and landscaped freeway, and bikers and rollerbladers on the paved parallel recreation trail. The river is a bonanza for white water enthusiasts and fishermen. Side canyon corridors are favored by hikers—especially the short, steep hike to the lush natural alpine gardens at Hanging Lake and Spouting Rock.

Marble Quarry
44 mi. S via CO 82 & CO 133
Marble used in the Lincoln Memorial and the Tomb of the Unknown Soldier in Washington, D.C. was quarried from an awesome pit that is well worth the long steep hike. There is also a museum and a photogenic mill on Crystal River near Marble. The long-closed Colorado Yule Marble Quarry reopened in 1990.

River Running
The Colorado and Roaring Fork Rivers in and near town provide a delightful range of rapids and scenery for white water rafting. Several local companies offer trips of an hour, half day or longer, and provide all necessary equipment and transportation.

Blue Sky Adventures   *(970)945-6605*
Rock Gardens Rafting   *(970)945-6737*
Whitewater Rafting   *(970)945-8477*

Warm Water Features
Hot Springs Lodge & Pool   *(970)945-7131*
downtown at 401 N. River St.
For over a century, visitors have enjoyed the world's largest outdoor hot springs pool. The handsome two-block-long main pool is 90°, while the smaller soaking pool is 104° (complete with mineral water jet chairs). There are also landscaped sunbathing terraces, a looping tubular water slide, poolside restaurant, lounge, sport shop, athletic club, miniature golf and lodge (see listing).

Yampah Spa and Vapor Caves   *(970)945-0667*
just NE at 709 E. 6th St.
A short stroll from the big pool is a stylish adult spa for all sorts of health and beauty treatments. Visitors pass through a stone corridor into the vapor caves—three adjoining rock chambers outfitted with slab marble benches for seating. The eerie tranquility of these natural steam baths has made them one of America's most durable and unique attractions.

White River National Forest   *(970)945-3249*
around town
This giant forest includes much of Central Colorado's finest mountain country. Features include world-renowned winter sports areas at Aspen and Vail. In summer, Glenwood Canyon, seven wilderness areas, and several whitewater streams, accessible via a good system of roads and hundreds of miles of trails, offer limitless opportunities for water sports, hiking, backpacking, horseback riding, pack trips, mountain climbing, hunting, fishing, boating, and camping.

Winter Sports

Sunlight Mountain Resort   *(970)945-7491*   *(800)445-7931*
10 mi. S at 10901 Road 117

The vertical rise is 2,010 feet and the longest run is over two miles. There are three chairlifts. All facilities, services, rentals and food service are available at the base. The ski season is from December through March.

RESTAURANTS

The Bayou   *(970)945-1047*
2 mi. W at 52103 US 6
D only.   *Low*
Catfish, shrimp creole and other Louisiana bayou standards have a local outpost. The roadside dinner house has a relaxed little dining room and bar festooned with bayou bric-a-brac, and a shaded, heated deck with a mountain view beyond the highway.

Calder's Market   *(970)945-2055*
downtown at 730 Grand Av.
B-L.   *Moderate*
Delightfully light scones, beignets and other pastries along with all sorts of premium teas and coffees roasted here are served to go or in one of the prettiest coffee house settings in the state.

Daily Bread Cafe and Bakery   *(970)945-6253*
downtown at 729 Grand Av.
B-L.   *Moderate*
The best breakfast in town includes a fine selection of omelets, humongous skillet dishes and a bodacious breakfast burrito. Baked goods on display are available to go, or are served in a comfortable little coffee shop with regional art and stained glass for sale.

Glenwood Canyon Brewing Company   *(970)945-6565*
downtown at 402 7th St.
L-D.   *Moderate*
This nifty 1996 brew pub became instantly popular not only for well-made beers and ales, but for distinctive pub grub like beer-battered onion rings and beer pretzels. Warm wood tones enliven the bar and two dining areas with padded booths overlooking brew kettles.

Hotel Colorado   *(970)945-6511*
downtown at 526 Pine St.
B-L-D.   *Expensive*
Contemporary American fare like a whole sauteed trout with raspberry almond butter or hickory-smoked chicken is served in a relaxed firelit dining room by the historic hotel's garden court.

Italian Underground   *(970)945-6422*
downtown at 715 Grand Av.
D only.   *Moderate*
The best Italian dining in Glenwood Springs is at the Italian Underground. All kinds of traditional and creative Southern Italian dishes are carefully prepared and generously served amid warm cellar surroundings that are just right for a casual feast.

Redstone Inn   *(970)963-2526*
28 mi. S via CO 133 at 82 Redstone Blvd. - Redstone
B-L-D.   *Expensive*
Wild game like elk steak in filo stars among traditional and contemporary American cuisine. Nostalgic elegance includes fresh flowers and full linen in the large Victorian dining room of this National Historic Landmark hotel.

Sopris Restaurant   *(970)945-7771*
6 mi. S at 7215 CO 82
D only.   *Expensive*
Old-fashioned Continental and American dishes are served amid plush
Victorian rococo atmosphere in a well-established dinner house.

The Village Smithy Restaurant   *(970)963-9990*
13 mi. S on CO 82 at 26 S. 3rd St. - Carbondale
B-L.   *Moderate*
Many omelets and specialty breakfast dishes are prepared with care
from fresh ingredients and served in the relaxed dining room or
colorful patio of an old blacksmith shop.

Wild Rose Bakery   *(970)928-8973*
downtown at 310 7th St.
B-L.   *Moderate*
A splendid display of tasty baked goods includes all kinds of scones,
muffins, cinnamon rolls, cakes, pies and breads to be enjoyed in the
little coffee shop overlooking the goodies, or to go.

LODGING

There are numerous moderately priced modern motels along I-70 west
of downtown. A few historic lodgings reflect the style of the dramatic
locale. Mid-May through September is high season. At other times,
rates are often reduced 20% or more.

Antlers - Best Western   *(970)945-8535*
just W at 171 W. 6th St. - 81601
100 units   *(800)626-0609*   *Moderate-Expensive*
This modern motel has a pool, whirlpool, and a platform tennis court
on attractive grounds. Each room is well furnished.

Hot Springs Lodge Hotel   *(970)945-6571*
downtown at 415 E. 6th St. (Box 308) - 81602
107 units   *Moderate*
The world's largest hot springs pool (more than 400 feet long) adjoins
this contemporary five-story motor lodge. Other amenities include a
whirlpool, plus (fee) water slide, vapor caves and health club, mini-golf,
restaurant and lounge. All rooms are well furnished. Some also have
a private view balcony.

Hotel Colorado   *(970)945-6511*
downtown at 526 Pine St. - 81601
128 units   *(800)544-3998*   *Moderate-Expensive*
Built in 1893 on a rise above the Colorado River, this handsome five-
story hotel on the National Register was known as Teddy Roosevelt's
Western White House. The peach-colored sandstone landmark has a
whirlpool, sauna, steam room, rental bicycles, and a gift shop, plus a
firelit dining room (see listing) and lounge. The world's largest hot
springs pool is only steps away. Rooms have all modern conveniences
and are comfortably furnished.

Hotel Denver   *(970)945-6565*
downtown at 402 7th St. - 81601
60 units   *(800)826-8820*   *Moderate-Expensive*
A historic hotel across from the Depot and river has been restored to
its art deco grace including antique clock, piano and mother-of-pearl
train picture. Each room is comfortably furnished with all
contemporary conveniences. Amenities include an exercise room and
the new Glenwood Canyon Brewing Company (see listing).

The Kaiser House   *(970)928-0101*
just S at 932 Copper Av. - 81601
7 units   *Moderate-Expensive*
The Kaiser House is a photogenic Queen Anne-style (1902) home that now serves as the town's premier bed-and-breakfast. The meticulously restored building and grounds include a whirlpool and workout equipment. Full breakfast is complimentary. Each room is attractively furnished, including antique accents.

Ramada Inn   *(970)945-2500*
just W (by I-70) at 124 W. 6th St. - 81601
123 units   *(800)332-1472*   *Moderate-Expensive*
One of the area's most complete contemporary lodging is a four-story motor hotel with a small indoor pool, whirlpool, exercise room, plus a coffee shop and entertainment lounge. Units are well furnished. Four suites also have a kitchenette, in-bath whirlpool and fireplace.

Redstone Castle   *(970)963-3463*
28 mi. S via CO 133 at 58 Redstone Blvd. - Redstone 81623
16 units   *(800)643-4837*   *Expensive*
A turreted mansion built in 1889 by a coal baron, is now an imposing bed-and-breakfast inn with elaborate stonework and woodwork, plus many original fixtures and furnishings. Expanded Continental breakfast is complimentary. You can experience a brush with the past in comfortably furnished rooms with well-worn antiques, no phones and (in the servants' quarters) shared baths.

Redstone Inn   *(970)963-2526*
28 mi. S via CO 133 at 82 Redstone Blvd. - Redstone 81623
35 units   *(800)748-2524*   *Moderate-Expensive*
A handsome three-story hotel with a clock tower that has been a village landmark for a century has been upgraded to include a pool, whirlpool, exercise equipment, and a posh restaurant (see listing) and lounge. Antiques and fireplaces contribute to yesteryear ambiance. Each room is nicely furnished.

Silver Spruce Motel   *(970)945-5458*
just W (by I-70) at 162 W. 6th St. - 81601
90 units   *(800)523-4742*   *Moderate*
This chalet-style motel has a whirlpool. Some of the comfortably furnished rooms have a gas or wood fireplace and/or an in-bath whirlpool.

Sunlight Mountain Inn   *(970)945-5225*
10 mi. S at 10252 County Rd. 117
20 units   *(800)733-4757*   *Moderate*
The local ski area adjoins this contemporary bed-and-breakfast inn. Winter activities include alpine and cross-country skiing, ice skating and sleigh rides, while horseback riding and hiking are popular in summer. Other amenities include a whirlpool, dining room and bar. Full breakfast is complimentary. Some of the comfortably furnished rooms have ski slope views.

BASIC INFORMATION

Elevation: 5,747 feet   *Population (1990): 6,561*
Location: 157 miles West of Denver
Nearest airport with commercial flights: Eagle - 30 miles
Glenwood Springs Chamber Resort Association (970)945-6589
just S at 1102 Grand Av. - 81601   *(800)221-0098*
www.glensape.com

Steamboat Springs, Colorado

Steamboat Springs is an exciting blend of the Old and New West. Surrounded by lush rangeland, the town lies in a broad upland valley flanked on the east by the northern Colorado Rockies. The agricultural potential of the Yampa River Valley first attracted ranchers and homesteaders to this area in the 1870s. After a century of slow growth, development of a vast skiing complex at nearby Mt. Werner established the town's current role as "Ski Town, U.S.A."

The town's handsome business district remains the vital core for the area. Many new structures complement restored turn-of-the-century buildings. Galleries and specialty shops have joined an outstanding cluster of Western ware stores. Distinctive restaurants and bars are also proliferating, often with plush Western decor appreciated as much by farmers and ranchers as by sportsmen and après-skiers. The area's luxurious lodgings are at the base of Mt. Werner, while motels and inns are downtown and nearby.

WEATHER PROFILE

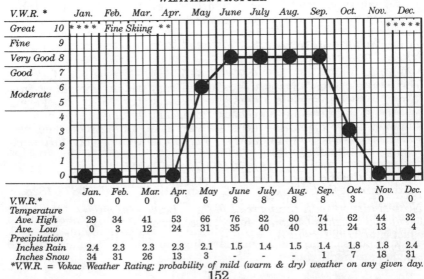

		Jan.	Feb.	Mar.	Apr.	May	June	July	Aug.	Sep.	Oct.	Nov.	Dec.
V.W.R.*		0	0	0	0	6	8	8	8	8	3	0	0
Temperature													
Ave. High		29	34	41	53	66	76	82	80	74	62	44	32
Ave. Low		0	3	12	24	31	35	40	40	31	24	13	4
Precipitation													
Inches Rain		2.4	2.3	2.3	2.3	2.1	1.5	1.4	1.5	1.4	1.8	1.8	2.4
Inches Snow		34	31	26	13	3	-	-	-	1	7	18	31

*V.W.R. = Vokac Weather Rating; probability of mild (warm & dry) weather on any given day.

ATTRACTIONS

Aerial Tramway
Steamboat Ski Area Gondola   *(970)879-6111*
3 mi. SE via US 40 & Mt. Werner Rd.
A six-passenger gondola takes passengers to the top of Mt. Werner for spectacular panoramic views in summer. Dining, picnic sites, and hiking trails are at the top.

Ballooning
Half-hour and longer champagne flights over the scenic Yampa Valley are available. For reservations and information, call:
Balloons Over Steamboat   *(970)879-3298*
Pegasus Balloon Tours   *(800)748-2487*

Bicycling
Sore Saddle Cyclery   *(970)879-1675*
downtown at 1136 Yampa Av.
Relatively easy rides can be enjoyed on highways and byways and scenic separated bikeways in and near town. Rentals, repairs and sales are available at this architecturally unique bike shop, among others.

City Park   *(970)879-4300*
just N at Lincoln Av. & 13th St.
Four distinctive natural hot springs features are identified in a delightful town park by the Yampa River. It is a popular take-out point for rafters and tubers on the gentle river through town.

Horseback Riding
Hourly rentals for scenic rides, breakfast or dinner rides, and pack trips can be arranged at several nearby stables, including:
All Seasons Ranch   *(970)879-0095*
Del's Triangle Three   *(970)879-3495*

River Running
Professional river guides lead half-day and longer scenic whitewater trips in rubber rafts or McKenzie boats. Or, you could rent a tube for a relaxed float through town. The Yampa and nearby rivers are in demand from May to September. For reservations and details, contact:
Bucking Rainbow Outfitters   *(970)879-3060*
Buggywhips Rafting   *(970)879-8033*
Routt National Forest   *(970)879-1722*
N, E and SW of town
This large forest includes numerous remote hot springs, and the Mt. Zirkel Wilderness Area with 200 miles of trails and more than seventy lakes. The Steamboat Ski Area is a renowned winter destination. Camping, hiking, horseback riding and pack trips, fishing, hunting, and winter sports are seasonally popular.

Steamboat Lake State Park
25 mi. N on County Rd. 129
Steamboat Lake is a sprawling 1,100-acre reservoir in an expansive rangeland basin. Shore picnics and camping nearby are popular, as are fishing, boating (rentals are available), water-skiing and swimming (on the warmest days).

Warm Water Feature
Steamboat Springs Health & Recreation   *(970)879-1828*
just SE at 136 Lincoln Av.
The premier attraction in Steamboat Springs is a superb warm mineral springs complex open year-round. An Olympic-sized outdoor pool, soaking pools in gardens, an exhilarating 350-foot hydro-tube slide, and saunas are highlights.

Strawberry Park Hot Springs   *(970)879-0342*
8 mi. N

Steep forested slopes surround four idyllic levels of naturalistic pools of different temperatures combining hot springs and creek waters. There is a tepee changing room. Massage and cabins are available.

Winter Sports

Howelsen Ski Area   *(970)879-8499*
downtown via 5th St. on River Rd.

World records have been set here on a long-established ski jumping facility overlooking downtown. The thrilling 4,800-foot bobsled course is open to the public. Skiing and ice skating are also popular. Tennis courts, sports fields, and rodeo grounds at the base are used in summer.

Steamboat Ski Area   *(970)879-6111*
3 mi. SE via US 40 & Mt. Werner Rd.

The vertical rise is 3,668 feet and the longest run is over three miles. Elevation at the top is 10,568 feet. There are eighteen chairlifts, including a gondola. All facilities, services and rental are available at the base for downhill and cross-country skiing, and for most other winter sports. Many restaurants, bars, and lodgings are within walking distance of the lifts. The ski season is late November to mid-April.

RESTAURANTS.

Antares   *(970)879-9939*
downtown at 57½ 8th St.
D only.   *Very Expensive*

New American cuisine is the style for an eclectic selection of fresh creative dishes and desserts adapted from many regions of the world. Warm wood tones contribute to an upscale ambiance in a historic stone building that is a popular culinary destination.

Cajun Connection   *(970)879-4901*
downtown at 628 Lincoln Av.
L-D   *Moderate*

All sorts of Cajun treats and desserts like bread pudding and beignets are authentic. A split-level dining room features wood-and-plant-trimmed booths and some Cajun wall hangings.

L'Apogee   *(970)879-1919*
downtown at 911 Lincoln Av.
D only.   *Expensive-Very Expensive*

Classic French cuisine and American adaptations like antelope sauteed with wild mushroom sauce can be topped off with a dessert from a spectacular display in the simply elegant, candlelit dining room. Next door, in **Harwig's Grill** (Expensive), a grazing menu of international specialties is offered in a usually crowded bistro setting.

La Montaña   *(970)879-5800*
3 mi. SE at 2500 Village Dr.
D only.   *Expensive*

Creative Southwestern dishes like elk loin medallions with a pecan nut crust and bourbon cream sauce have been featured for years. The colorful, relaxed second floor dining room, cantina, and deck provide some mountain/village views.

Mattie Silks   *(970)879-2441*
3 mi. SE at 1890 Mt. Werner Rd.
D only.   *Moderate-Expensive*

New American cuisine stars in posh Victorian-styled dining rooms. The casual **Cat House Cafe** (Moderate) has an eclectic grazing menu and refreshing desserts. There is also a wood-trimmed saloon.

Old West Steak House   *(970)879-1441*
downtown at 1104 Lincoln Av.
D only.   *Expensive*
The Old West Steak House is the region's best source for Angus beef.
Delicious steaks and prime ribs have been served for many years in a
comfortable dining room showcasing a wealth of Western artifacts and
wall art. An upstairs lounge has the cushiest sofas in town and two
levels of unique barrels-for-two for tête-à-têtes.

The Shack Cafe   *(970)879-9975*
downtown at 740 Lincoln Av.
B-L.   *Moderate*
Hearty American omelets, waffles, hot cakes, french toast, and specials
suggest why the cheerful, wood-trimmed cafe and covered patio is one
of Steamboat's most popular morning places.

Steamboat Brewery & Tavern   *(970)879-2233*
downtown at 435 Lincoln Av.
L-D   *Moderate*
Upscale pub grub of all kinds is treated with care and creativity and
served in a spiffy wood-and-plant-trimmed dining room and pub with
a picture-window view of the brew kettles.

Steamboat Smokehouse   *(970)879-7427*
downtown at 912 Lincoln Av.
L-D.   *Moderate*
Honest-to-goodness Texas-style hickory-smoked pit barbecue shows up
in brisket, ribs, sausages and occasional seasonal game and fish
specialties. Close to a dozen tap beers are another feature, along with
peanut buckets everywhere and all kinds of trophy heads displayed on
walls above warm wood booths and a peanut-shell-strewn floor.

Steamboat Yacht Club   *(970)879-4774*
downtown at 811 Yampa Av.
L-D.   *Expensive*
New West cuisine typified by orange pecan trout is complemented by
a view of both the ski jump hill and the Yampa River. Window walls
frame three sides of a big comfortable dining room with abundant
greenery and a river-rock wall. There is also a posh lounge and an
umbrella-shaded deck in this deservedly popular restaurant.

LODGING

Plentiful accommodations include motels in and near downtown and
hotels and condos at nearby Mt. Werner. Winter is high season. Rates
are generally at least 40% less from spring through fall.

Bear Claw Condominiums   *(970)879-6100*
3 mi. SE at 2420 Ski Trail Lane - 80487
67 units   *(800)232-7252*   *Very Expensive*
Bear Claw is perfectly positioned on the main slope of Mt. Werner by
chairlifts to ski in/ski out. Other amenities of the stylish five-story
condo complex include a large pool, whirlpool, sauna, and a lounge.
Each beautifully furnished one- to four-bedroom condo has a gas
fireplace, kitchen, and a private balcony (many with superb slope views).

Chateau Chamonix   *(970)879-7511*
3 mi. SE at 2340 Apres Ski Way - 80477
27 units   *(800)833-9877*   *Very Expensive*
This luxury condo complex offers ski-in/ski-out access to Mt. Werner,
and there is an indoor/outdoor pool, whirlpool and sauna. Each two- or
three-bedroom condo is beautifully furnished and has a gas fireplace,
kitchen, in-bath whirlpool, and private slope-view balcony.

Ptarmigan Inn - Best Western *(970)879-1730*
3 mi. SE at 2304 Apres Ski Way (Box 3240) - 80477
77 units *(800)538-7519 Expensive-Very Expensive*
Nestled by the slopes and lifts at the base of Mt. Werner is this
modern four-story ski-in/ski-out motor lodge with a pool, whirlpool,
sauna, restaurant, lounge and ski rental shop. Each unit is well
furnished. Many have a fine ski slope view. Some have a private deck.

Rabbit Ears Motel *(970)879-1150*
just SE at 201 Lincoln Av. (Box 770573) - 80477
65 units *(800)828-7702 Moderate-Expensive*
Directly across from the town's outstanding hot springs pool complex
is a modern motel with the area's only units by the Yampa River. All
rooms are well furnished. Some have a private riverfront balcony.

Ramada Vacation Suites Hilltop *(970)879-2900*
1 mi. SE at 1000 High Point Dr. (Box 770388) - 80477
62 units *Expensive*
High on a hill between downtown and Mt. Werner is a modern five-
story motor hotel with two tennis courts, a big indoor pool and
whirlpool, saunas, restaurant, lounge, and gift shop. Each renovated
and expanded suite is well furnished. Many have a fine view.

Sheraton Steamboat Resort *(970)879-2220*
3 mi. SE at 2200 Village Inn Court (Box 774808) - 80477
318 units *(800)848-8878 Very Expensive*
Mt. Werner's foremost full-service resort hotel has a prime ski-in/ski-
out location at the base of the slopes by the gondola. The contemporary
eight-story complex has a large pool, whirlpools, saunas, steamrooms,
exercise room, bakery, restaurant, lounge and resort shops. Nearby are
a (fee) championship 18-hole golf course and tennis courts. Each
recently renovated unit is beautifully furnished and has a slope, village
or valley view from a private balcony.

Sky Valley Lodge *(970)879-7749*
8 mi. SE at 31490 E. Highway 40 (Box 3132) - 80477
24 units *(800)538-7519 Expensive*
High on a forested slope in the mountains near Rabbit Ears Pass is a
massive timber-and-stone bed-and-breakfast lodge with a whirlpool and
saunas. Extended Continental breakfast is complimentary. Each room
is comfortably furnished.

Torian Plum *(970)879-8811*
3 mi. SE at 1855 Ski Time Square Dr. - 80487
44 units *(800)228-2458 Very Expensive*
The elegant eight-story Torian Plum condo complex is in a choice
location in the heart of the village at the base of the slopes and lifts on
Mt. Werner. Other amenities include a pool, two whirlpools (four
whirlpools plus a sauna in ski season) and four tennis courts (in
summer). Each of the one- to three-bedroom condos is beautifully
furnished and has a kitchen, gas fireplace, in-bath whirlpool, and
private balcony, many with fine ski slope views.

BASIC INFORMATION

Elevation: 6,695 feet *Population (1990): 6,695*
Location: 168 miles Northwest of Denver
Nearest airport with commercial flights: Hayden - 20 miles
Steamboat Springs Chamber Resort Association *(970)879-0800*
just S at 1255 S. Lincoln Av. (Box 774408) - 80477 *(800)922-2722*
www.steamboat-chamber.com

Telluride, Colorado

Telluride is a matchless Victorian relic with a silver-lined past and a solid gold future. Some of the nation's highest peaks tower majestically above pine-covered slopes that rise precipitously from the level floor of a narrow little valley almost 9,000 feet above sea level. Within earshot, the state's highest waterfall tumbles into the box canyon and becomes a major stream through town. Telluride was founded as a gold and silver mining boomtown in the 1870s, with sturdy brick buildings and a wild reputation for its gaming and sporting house district. But, only about 500 residents remained by 1972 when the Telluride Ski Area opened, and the "white gold" boom began.

Today, the skiing complex has become one of the most exalted in the West, and the whole town is a National Historic Landmark. The charming business district is lined with galleries and specialty shops, fascinating saloons, distinctive restaurants, and lodgings ranging from converted boarding houses to luxurious condo hotels.

WEATHER PROFILE

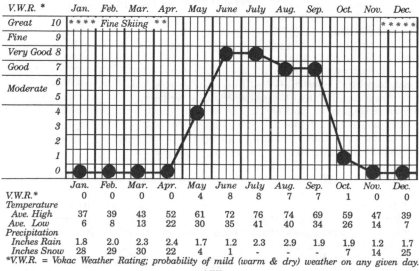

		Jan.	Feb.	Mar.	Apr.	May	June	July	Aug.	Sep.	Oct.	Nov.	Dec.
V.W.R.*		0	0	0	0	4	8	8	7	7	1	0	0
Temperature													
Ave. High		37	39	43	52	61	72	76	74	69	59	47	39
Ave. Low		6	8	13	22	30	35	41	40	34	26	14	7
Precipitation													
Inches Rain		1.8	2.0	2.3	2.4	1.7	1.2	2.3	2.9	1.9	1.9	1.2	1.7
Inches Snow		28	29	30	22	4	1	-	-	-	7	14	25

*V.W.R. = Vokac Weather Rating; probability of mild (warm & dry) weather on any given day.

Aerial Tramway
Gondola   *(970)728-3041*
downtown at S end of Oak St.
In 1996, a unique transportation system connected Telluride with Mountain Village and the rest of the ski area high above town. Each gondola provides a remarkably scenic free ride for eight passengers.

Bicycling
A variety of bicycle rentals or tours can be arranged downtown to explore the relatively flat valley or the breathtaking high country.
Back Country Biking   *(tours)*   *(970)728-0861*
Telluride Sports   *(rentals)*   *(970)728-4477*   *(800)828-7547*

Bridal Veil Falls
2 mi. E via Colorado Av.
Colorado's highest waterfall tumbles down mist-shrouded cliffs at the end of a box canyon visible from downtown. The 1904 hydroelectric plant perched atop the falls is now a National Historic Landmark.

Historic District   *(970)728-3041*
downtown on/near Colorado Av.
Victorian buildings earned a National Historic Landmark designation for the entire town, including the still-used San Miguel County Courthouse, constructed in 1887 of brick. Next door, the "Galloping Goose" is a unique Depression-era railway bus. "The Cribs" on Pacific Street are remnants of a once-bawdy gambling and red-light district. The tiny stone jail on Spruce Street is now a library.

Horseback Riding
Roudy's Telluride Horseback Adventures *(970)728-9611 (800)828-7547*
In addition to guided trail rides of various durations, chuckwagon breakfasts and dinners are offered, and pack trips can be arranged.

Jeep Tours
Telluride Outside   *(970)728-3895*   *(800)831-6230*
Guided jeep tours explore the many fascinating ghost towns, mining ruins and scenic attractions in the mountains surrounding town.

Uncompahgre National Forest   *(970)874-6600*
around town
Several peaks are over 14,000 feet high in this vast forest. Features include the superb winter sports complex at Telluride. One of America's most photographed peaks, Mt. Sneffels, is a few miles north of town. Many miles of hiking trails, paved roads and rugged dirt roads pass ghost towns, old mines, streams, waterfalls and a few small lakes, all backed by a magnificent alpine skyline. Camping, hiking, backpacking, horseback riding, jeep tours, pack trips, mountain climbing, fishing, hunting and snow sports are all seasonally popular.

Winter Sports
Telluride Outside   *(970)728-3895*   *(800)831-6230*
Sleigh rides or snowmobiling can be arranged in winter.
Telluride Ski Resort   *(970)728-3856*
downtown at S end of Oak St.
Magnificent peaks surround ski slopes where the vertical rise is 3,165 feet and the longest run is almost three miles. Elevation at the top is 12,247 feet. There are ten chairlifts, and a free gondola linking Telluride with the Mountain Village. All facilities, services and rentals for downhill and cross-country skiing, plus ice skating, sleigh rides, and snowmobiling, are at the base downtown, along with many bars, restaurants and lodgings. The season is late November into April.

RESTAURANTS

Baked in Telluride   *(970)728-4775*
downtown at 127 S. Fir St.
B-L-D.   *Moderate*
Croissants, bagels, cinnamon rolls, and a wealth of other morning
delights are displayed, along with outstanding pizzas later. It's all
available to go, or in the plain coffee shop or mountain-view deck with
coffees or brews from Telluride's only brew pub.

Cafe San Sophia   *(970)728-3001*
downtown at 330 W. Pacific Av.
D only.   *Expensive*
The Cafe San Sophia is one of the most exciting restaurants in the
Rocky Mountains. The inn's dining room showcases American fusion
cuisine with a peerless Southwestern orientation in dishes like
horseradish-crusted pork tenderloin with raspberry demi-glaze and
charred tomato-mint salsa. The intimate dining room offers modish
elegance enhanced by superb views of the box canyon and mountains.

Cosmopolitan   *(970)728-1292*
downtown at 300 W. San Juan Av.
D only.   *Expensive*
In the Hotel Columbia, fresh and flavorful New American cuisine like
crispy smoked catfish or grilled leg of lamb with sweet and spicy black
bean sauce is served in a stylish dining room beyond a snazzy bar, and
on a deck by the gondola. All have a fine view of the slopes.

Floradora   *(970)728-3888*
downtown at 103 W. Colorado Av.
L-D.   *Moderate*
Southwestern and international dishes include some nifty nods toward
Mexico. As interesting are homemade desserts and libations like a
kahlua milkshake. Telluride's oldest dining/drinking place is a funky,
festooned delight.

La Marmotte   *(970)728-6232*
downtown at 150 W. San Juan Av.
D only.   *Very Expensive*
Contemporary French provincial cuisine is featured on a seasonal
menu and in delicious housemade desserts like crème brûlée. Crusty
sweet french bread precedes each meal served amid cozy congestion in
an urbane dining room backed by a raised exhibition kitchen.

Maggie's Hometown Bakery   *(970)728-3334*
downtown at 217 E. Colorado Av.
B-L.   *Moderate*
The humongous cinnamon nut roll alone would be worth a trip. But,
there are also assorted croissants and breads that can be enjoyed with
coffees and/or hearty meals in the little parlor or to go.

The Peaks Resort & Spa   *(970)728-6800*
8 mi. SW at 136 Country Club Dr. in Mountain Village
B-L-D.   *Very Expensive*
Creative "Colorado ranchlands" cuisine and healthy spa cuisine are
featured in **Sundance** (D only), the resort's culinary showcase. Nearby,
Legends (B-L) features light American cuisine. Both upscale dining
rooms have memorable views of majestic peaks.

The PowderHouse Restaurant   *(970)728-3622*
downtown at 226 W. Colorado Av.
D only.   *Expensive*
Creative American cuisine with a Colorado slant includes wild game

specialties like elk or quail. For more than a decade, the chef/owner has provided made-from-scratch dishes that appeal to natives and visitors in several wood-trim dining areas downstairs.

Rustico Ristorante *(970)728-4046*
downtown at 114 E. Colorado Av.
L-D.   *Expensive*

Since 1996, classic and updated Italian cuisine has been featured here on an extensive grazing menu. The dining room and bar are a smooth blend of Telluride and Tuscan decor in tasteful dining areas and a bar.

Sofio's *(970)728-4882*
downtown at 102 E. Colorado Av.
B-D.   *Moderate*

Breakfasts feature Mexican and contemporary American dishes ranging from huevos rancheros to fruit pancakes or sunshine omelets. It's all very good in this modern Southwestern-style restaurant.

221 S. Oak *(970)728-9507*
downtown at 221 S. Oak
D only.   *Very Expensive*

In one of Telluride's most sophisticated restaurants, international cuisine gets a creative topspin from expertly prepared quality ingredients on a short list of distinctive dishes and desserts. The cozy, simply stylish dining room is built into a historic house.

LODGING

All major kinds of lodgings are numerous in town and in the mountain village. Many offer spectacular alpine views. High season is winter. In spring and fall, rates are often reduced by 40% or more.

Camel's Garden Hotel *(970)728-9300*
downtown at 250 W. San Juan Av. (Box 4145) - 81435
37 units   *(888)772-2635*   *Very Expensive*

In 1997, a four-story luxury hotel opened by the gondola and river. Amenities include a large whirlpool, steam rooms, a shop, and Wildflour (B-L-D—Expensive), an outstanding bakery/cafe with a snazzy dining room and bar and mountain/tram-view deck. Each beautifully furnished room has a gas fireplace and large soaking tub. Condos up to three bedrooms also have a kitchen. Expanded Continental breakfast and afternoon treats are complimentary.

Hotel Columbia Telluride *(970)728-0660*
downtown at 300 W. San Juan Av. (Box 800) - 81435
21 units   *(800)201-9505 Expensive-Very Expensive*

By the little San Miguel River is a handsome four-story hotel, opened in 1996 steps from a chairlift, gondola, and the river. In addition to ski-in/ski-out appeal, amenities include an exercise room, rooftop hot tub, gourmet restaurant (see Cosmopolitan) and bar. An extended housemade Continental breakfast and afternoon wine and appetizers are complimentary. Each beautifully furnished room has a gas fireplace and a long soaking tub. Most also have a steam shower and a private balcony (many with fine mountain views).

The Ice House *(970)728-6300*
downtown at 310 S. Fir St. (Box 2909) - 81435
42 units   *(800)544-3436 Expensive-Very Expensive*

Here is a stylish contemporary four-story motel with an indoor/outdoor pool with a mountain view, whirlpool and steam room. Ski slopes and lifts are within half a block. Extended Continental breakfast and afternoon appetizers are complimentary. Each spacious, beautifully furnished unit has a private view balcony and a six-foot soaking tub.

New Sheridan Hotel   *(970)728-4351*
downtown at 231 W. Colorado Av. (Box 980) - 81435
32 units   *(800)200-1891*   *Expensive*
The New Sheridan Hotel has welcomed guests for more than a century
in the heart of town. The three-story brick landmark has two rooftop
whirlpools and a fitness center. The New Sheridan Chop House (D
only—Expensive) serves favorful steaks, chops and game like elk or
caribou in a handsome setting with a fine view. Full breakfast and
afternoon wine are complimentary. Each room is well furnished with
period decor and modern appliances. Some rooms share a bath. Others
have an in-bath whirlpool.

The Peaks Resort & Spa   *(970)728-6800*
8 mi. SW at 136 Country Club Dr. in Mtn. Village (Box 2702) - 81435
174 units   *(800)789-2220*   *Very Expensive*
The region's premier resort hotel has a choice site in the ski area above
town. The post-modern facade of the eight-story complex belies
luxurious Southwestern decor throughout. Amenities include two
indoor pools (one is indoor/outdoor), a high-tech indoor water slide,
whirlpools, sauna, steam rooms, exercise equipment, rock climbing
wall, and a world-class (fee) athletic and beauty spa, 18-hole golf
course, five tennis courts, racquetball and squash courts, rental
bicycles, plus a gourmet restaurant (see listing), entertainment lounge
and resort shop. Each spacious unit is beautifully furnished. Many
have a private mountain-view balcony. Some have a whirlpool bath.

Pennington's Mountain Village Inn   *(970)728-5337*
6 mi. SW at 100 Pennington Ct. in Mtn. Village (Box 2428) - 81435
12 units   *(800)543-1437*   *Expensive-Very Expensive*
Overlooking a golf course framed by the majestic Rockies is a posh
young bed-and-breakfast. Amenities include a whirlpool and steam
room. Full gourmet breakfast and wine and appetizers are complimentary. Each beautifully furnished room has a private deck. Honeymoon
suites also have a whirlpool tub and superb mountain views.

The San Sophia   *(970)728-3001*
downtown at 330 W. Pacific Av. (Box 1825) - 81435
16 units   *(800)537-4781*   *Expensive-Very Expensive*
Downtown's best bed-and-breakfast inn is in a modern Victorian-style
building with a tower observatory and a whirlpool tub. The gondola is
within a block. Full breakfast and afternoon wine and appetizers are
complimentary in the Cafe San Sophia (see listing). Each room is a
beautifully furnished blend of period and contemporary conveniences,
including a large oval bathtub. Some have scenic mountain views.

The Victorian Inn   *(970)728-6601*
downtown at 401 W. Pacific Av. (Box 217) - 81435
27 units   *Moderate*
This convenient motel is within walking distance of downtown, a
chairlift and a river trail, and it has a sauna and hot tub. Each unit is
comfortably furnished. Some share a bath.

BASIC INFORMATION

Elevation: *8,750 feet*   *Population (1990):*   *1,309*
Location: *340 mi. Southwest of Denver*
Nearest airport with commercial flights: *west of town - 6 miles*
Telluride Visitor Information Center   *(970)728-3041*   *(800)525-3455*
 just W at 666 W. Colorado Av. (Box 653) - 81435 www.telluridemm.com

Vail, Colorado

Vail is America's foremost planned ski town. The illustrious community fills a narrow forested valley deep in the central Colorado Rockies. Youngest of the great towns, it was founded in 1962 when both the townsite and ski runs were completed. Later, opening of the interstate highway from Denver generated exuberant growth.

Today, the original alpine-style architecture has been somewhat subordinated to more monumental, angular structures in newer areas. But, Vail's two master-planned commercial and skiing centers are still built around pedestrian-only cores interconnected by a high-tech tram system. Abundant artistic amenities—fountains, sculptures, flower-strewn walkways, courtyards, and parks by the creek distinguish an impressive collection of chic galleries, boutiques, sidewalk cafes, restaurants, and lounges. Accommodations are abundant. Many are in opulent high-rise condominium hotels an easy stroll from both the slopes and the village centers.

WEATHER PROFILE

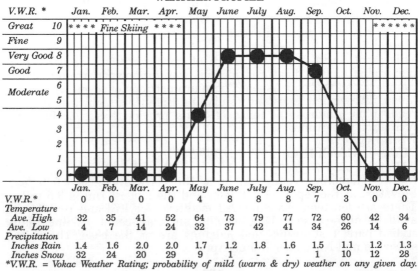

V.W.R. *		Jan.	Feb.	Mar.	Apr.	May	June	July	Aug.	Sep.	Oct.	Nov.	Dec.
Great	10												
Fine	9												
Very Good	8												
Good	7												
Moderate	6												
	5												
	4												
	3												
	2												
	1												
	0												

	Jan.	Feb.	Mar.	Apr.	May	June	July	Aug.	Sep.	Oct.	Nov.	Dec.
V.W.R.*	0	0	0	0	4	8	8	8	7	3	0	0
Temperature												
Ave. High	32	35	41	52	64	73	79	77	72	60	42	34
Ave. Low	4	7	14	24	32	37	42	41	34	26	14	6
Precipitation												
Inches Rain	1.4	1.6	2.0	2.0	1.7	1.2	1.8	1.6	1.5	1.1	1.2	1.3
Inches Snow	32	24	20	29	9	1	-	-	1	10	12	28

*V.W.R. = Vokac Weather Rating; probability of mild (warm & dry) weather on any given day.

ATTRACTIONS

Aerial Tramway
Eagle Bahn Gondola
1 mi. W at Lionshead
An enclosed gondola whisks visitors into the mountains above Vail throughout summer. Hiking trails (including a "Berry Picker's Trail" back into town), picnic sites, and a restaurant are at the top. You can bring your mountain bike along for the descent of your life, or take the gondola back.

Betty Ford Alpine Gardens   *(970)476-0103*
just E on Frontage Rd.
Hundreds of varieties of mountain wildflowers normally found both above and below timberline are beautifully displayed amid ponds and waterfalls in the world's highest public alpine gardens.

Bicycling
An excellent system of separated bikeways in and near town contributes to the popularity of short scenic trips along the relatively flat valley floor, and mountain bikes provide access to the high country. Bicycle rentals and maps are available at several locations, including:
Base Mountain Sports   *(970)476-4515*
Christy Sports   *(970)476-2244*

Colorado Ski Museum & Ski Hall of Fame   *(970)476-1876*
downtown at 231 S. Frontage Rd.
One of the most comprehensive collections of ski artifacts and films documents the history of skiing and honors individuals who have most influenced Colorado skiing. There is a gift shop.

Horseback Riding
Stables rent horses by the hour for guided scenic trail rides and/or chuck wagon cookouts. Wilderness pack trips can also be arranged at several places in the valley.

River Running
Several river guide services feature half day or full day rafting trips on the upper Colorado River—including picturesque Glenwood Canyon—during summer. All equipment and meals are provided for these white-water trips. Contact:
Colorado River Runs   *(800)826-1081*
Timberline Tours   *(970)476-1414*

White River National Forest   *(970)827-5715*
around town
This giant forest comprises much of northcentral Colorado's finest mountain country. Features include world-renowned winter sports complexes at Vail and Aspen. There are portions of seven wilderness areas, many small lakes and reservoirs. Extensive highways and dirt roads plus hundreds of miles of trails provide access to limitless recreation opportunities.

Winter Sports
Beaver Creek Resort   *(970)949-5750*
11 mi. W via I-70
In this glamorous young ski area, the vertical rise is 4,040 feet. Elevation at the top is 11,440 feet, and the longest run is 3.5 miles. There are fourteen chairlifts. All facilities, services and rentals are available at the base for both downhill and cross-country skiing. Many stylish bars, restaurants and lodgings are at the base. The skiing season is mid-November to mid-April.

Vail Ski Resort *(970)476-5601*
downtown at Vail Village & Lionshead

Vail, often ranked the Number One ski resort in America, is the largest single-mountain skiing complex on the continent. The vertical rise is 3,330 feet and the longest run is 4.5 miles. There are twenty chairlifts and one enclosed gondola. All facilities, services and rentals are available at the base in town for both downhill and cross-country skiing. At Eagle's Nest (reached by gondola), the **Adventure Ridge** recreation park offers lift-served sledding, snowboarding, ice skating, snowmobiling, and dining in a new family-oriented complex for non-skiers. Several dozen restaurants, bars, and lodgings are within walking distance of the slopes. The skiing season is mid-November through April.

RESTAURANTS

Blu's *(970)476-3113*
in Vail Village at 193 E. Gore Creek Dr.
B-L-D.   *Moderate*
One of Vail's finest and most popular restaurants offers creative American cuisine ranging from Oriental chicken salad to honey-pepper-glazed pork chop with sauteed spinach. The warm, relaxed dining room and bar overlook a colorful patio by the river.

Gasthof Gramshammer *(970)476-5626*
in Vail Village at 231 E. Gore Creek Dr.
L-D.   *Expensive*
In the ever-popular **Pepi's Restaurant & Bar**, wild game is a highlight of contemporary and traditional German cuisine. Consider smoked pork shank in a light cream sauce with sauerkraut served amid gracious Old World gemutlichkeit.

Golden Eagle Inn *(970)949-1940*
11 mi. W in the Village Hall at Beaver Creek Plaza - Beaver Creek
L-D.   *Expensive*
Game specialties like medallions of pan-seared deer or roast loin of elk star among creative American dishes served at booths in several dining areas and on an umbrella-shaded flowery courtyard.

Poste Montane Lodge *(970)949-5540*
11 mi. W in Beaver Creek Plaza - Beaver Creek
L-D.   *Expensive*
In **Legends Restaurant**, New Western dishes like chile-crusted seared salmon with a raspberry tomatilla salsa are served amid posh mountain lodge decor, and there is an umbrella-shaded courtyard.

The Saloon *(970)827-5954*
7 mi. SW at 146 N. Main St. - Minturn
D only.   *Expensive*
Inventive Mexican dishes include specialties like shrimp enchilada topped with cheese and red chile or char-broiled quail. A turn-of-the-century building now houses a dining room with relaxed Old West atmosphere, and a great raised fireplace in the saloon.

Sitzmark Lodge *(970)476-3696*
in Vail Village at 183 Gore Creek Dr.
D only.   *Expensive*
Classic Continental cuisine has been expertly prepared in this landmark at the **Left Bank Restaurant** for nearly thirty years. The refined dining room with an intimate creek view continues to earn both critical and popular acclaim.

Sonnenalp Golf Club   *(970)926-3528*
11 mi. W via I-70 at 1265 Berry Creek Rd. - Edwards
L-D.   *Expensive*
In the **June Creek Grill**, New American bistro cuisine includes
innovative dishes like grilled double-cut pork chop with buttermilk-
fried shallots, cactus and rhubarb chutney. The tony split-level dining
room has a window wall, massive river-rock fireplace, and a dining
deck that shares the golf-course-and-mountain view.
Sonnenalp Resort of Vail   *(970)476-5656*
in Vail Village at 20 Vail Rd.
D only.   *Expensive*
In the **Swiss Chalet**, several kinds of fondue and raclette are
specialties among classic Swiss dishes. One of the most atmospheric
wood-trim dining rooms in town also has a lovely view past a dining
deck to the stream and mountains.
Sweet Basil   *(970)476-0125*
in Vail Village at 193 E. Gore Creek Dr.
L-D.   *Very Expensive*
Some of Colorado's best creative American cuisine has been featured
in Sweet Basil for years. Almond-crusted pork chop with polenta
mashed potatoes or grilled New York steak with chile rellano and black
bean sauce typify entrees on a menu that changes seasonally to feature
the freshest and best available ingredients. Intimate, polished dining
areas adjoin a lovely deck near a landscaped stream.
The Tyrolean Inn Restaurant   *(970)476-2204*
in Vail Village at 400 E. Meadow Dr.
D only.   *Very Expensive*
Game specialties like sauteed elk medallions or buffalo London broil
are featured along with an appealing array of other meat entrees in
the New American cuisine style. Charming Tyrolean decor is well-
brought-off in a sleigh-frame chandelier and warm wood tones, fresh
flowers, full linen, and a choice of booths or armchair comfort.
Vail Athletic Club Hotel & Spa   *(970)476-6836*
in Vail Village at 352 E. Meadow Dr.
D only.   *Expensive*
In **Terra Bistro**, light and lively American bistro cuisine is skillfully
prepared and served in a handsome dining room/bar with a picture-
window view (shared by a scenic deck) above the creek.
Vail Cascade Hotel & Club   *(970)476-7111*
2 mi. W at 1300 Westhaven Dr.
D only.   *Very Expensive*
In **Alfredo's**, New American cuisine is expertly prepared using fresh
quality seasonal ingredients and local specialties like Colorado buffalo.
The three kinds of housemade rolls that begin each meal are
outstanding, as are the ice cream and sorbets for dessert. Sophisticated
dinners are enhanced by the grand piano stylings of Peter Vavra, a
legendary fixture in the adjoining plush lounge.

LODGING

Accommodations are abundant. Most of the best are in hotels and
condo resorts within walking distance of ski slopes. Winter is "high"
season. Most lodgings reduce their rates by at least 50% in summer
and more in spring and fall. There are almost no conventional motels
in town, and no inexpensive facilities for many miles.

Antlers at Vail   *(970)476-2471*

1 mi. W at 680 W. Lionshead Pl. - 81657

70 units   *(800)843-8245*   *Very Expensive*

You can walk to the gondola and ski runs from this modern seven-story condominium motel by a creek with a pool, whirlpool, and saunas. Well-furnished units, ranging from studios to three bedrooms, have a kitchen, gas fireplace, and a private balcony—many with creek and mountain views.

Christiania at Vail   *(970)476-5641*

in Vail Village at 356 E. Hanson Ranch Rd. - 81657

22 units   *(800)530-3999*   *Very Expensive*

At Christiania, you can ski-in/ski-out from an ideal location in the village by lifts at the base of the mountain. The remodeled ski lodge with European decor also has a pool and sauna. Each room is well furnished. Two units also have a private mountain-view balcony and gas fireplace.

Embassy Suites - Beaver Creek Lodge   *(970)845-9800*

11 mi. W at 26 Avondale Lane (Box 2578) - Beaver Creek 81620

73 units   *(800)362-2779*   *Very Expensive*

The only all-suites lodging in Vail Valley is nestled at the base of ski slopes within walking distance of lifts at Beaver Creek. Amenities of the six-story contemporary hotel include an indoor/outdoor pool, whirlpool, sauna, steam room, exercise room and shops, plus restaurant and lounge. Full breakfast and manager's afternoon cocktail reception are complimentary. Each beautifully furnished two-room suite has a kitchenette, gas fireplace, and standing view balcony.

Hyatt Regency Beaver Creek Resort & Spa   *(970)949-1234*

11 mi. W at 50 W. Thomas Pl. (Box 1595) - Beaver Creek 81620

295 units   *(800)233-1234*   *Very Expensive*

Ski runs and lifts are right outside your door at Hyatt's landmark in the heart of Beaver Creek Resort Village. The cosmopolitan six-story complex has a new (fee) full-service health and beauty spa, plus an indoor/outdoor pool, whirlpools, sauna, steam rooms, exercise room, rental bicycles, shopping arcade, gourmet restaurant, deli, and entertainment lounge. Each room is beautifully furnished. Many have fine ski slope views, and standing-only balconies.

Lion Square Lodge & Conference Center   *(970)476-2281*

just W at 660 W. Lionshead Pl. - 81657

118 units   *(800)525-5788*   *Very Expensive*

Bordering Gore Creek by the gondola is a newly refurbished seven-story condo hotel with a big pool by the river, whirlpool, saunas, restaurant and lounge. Most of the well-furnished rooms (up to three bedrooms) have a gas fireplace and view deck.

The Lodge at Cordillera   *(970)926-2200*

17 mi. W via I-70 at 2205 Cordillera Way (Box 1110) - Edwards 81632

56 units   *(800)877-3529*   *Very Expensive*

The region's most isolated resort is a posh ridgetop motor lodge that doubled in size in 1997. Amenities include two nearby (fee) championship 18-hole golf courses and a 10-hole executive course by the lodge, plus two tennis courts, two pools (one big indoors), whirlpools, saunas, steam rooms, exercise room, rental bicycles, health and beauty spa, and resort shops. A refined gourmet restaurant and lounge share expansive views. Most of the beautifully furnished rooms have a gas or woodburning fireplace and a private deck with a mountain view.

The Lodge at Vail   *(970)476-5011*
in Vail Village at 174 E. Gore Creek Dr. - 81657
119 units   *(800)331-5634*   *Very Expensive*
Ski slopes, chairlifts and the village adjoin this venerable six-story hotel that was recently upgraded. Amenities include a pool, whirlpool, sauna and exercise room, plus a fine dining restaurant, cafes, and **Mickey's Lounge**, where Mickey Poage, a legendary piano virtuoso, has delighted crowds for many years. All of the attractively furnished rooms have a mountain or village view. Beautifully furnished suites (up to three bedrooms) also have a kitchen, fireplace, and private view deck.

Sitzmark Lodge   *(970)476-5001*
in Vail Village at 183 Gore Creek Dr. - 81657
35 units   *Expensive-Very Expensive*
Ski slopes are a short stroll from this stylish motor lodge by a creek in the heart of the village. The four-story complex has a small pool, whirlpool, sauna, gourmet restaurant (see listing) and lounge, and gift shop. Each spacious room is well furnished and has a private balcony.

Sonnenalp Resort of Vail   *(970)476-5856*
in Vail Village at 20 Vail Rd. - 81657
150 units   *(800)654-8312*   *Very Expensive*
Vail's most complete European-style resort includes three complexes (Bavaria, Swiss and Austria Haus) along Gore Creek in the heart of the village. Amenities include two pools (one indoor/outdoor), whirlpool, four restaurants (see listing) and lounge, two boutiques, and (fee) full-service spas, plus 18-hole golf course and four tennis courts eleven miles west. Each unit is beautifully furnished. Spacious suites also have a gas fireplace, large soaking tub, and small view balcony.

Vail Athletic Club Hotel & Spa   *(970)476-0700*
in Vail Village at 352 E. Meadow Dr. - 81657
38 units   *(800)822-4754*   *Very Expensive*
Nestled by Gore Creek a short stroll from the heart of the village, slopes and chairlifts is a modish small hotel with an indoor pool, whirlpools, saunas, steam rooms, exercise room, rock climbing wall, squash court, and (fee) complete fitness and beauty treatments, plus restaurant (see listing) and lounge. Continental breakfast buffet is complimentary. Each beautifully furnished room has a view deck. Studios and suites also have a kitchen, and some have a gas fireplace.

Vail Cascade Hotel & Club   *(970)476-7111*
2 mi. W at 1300 Westhaven Dr. - 81657
289 units   *(800)420-2424*   *Very Expensive*
One of Colorado's great ski-in/ski-out resort hotels is nestled by Gore Creek thirty feet from a high-speed chairlift and groomed slopes. The newly and completely renovated four-story complex includes a pool, whirlpool, saunas, and a (fee) health club with indoor/outdoor tennis, squash, racquetball, exercise equipment, steam room, and complete fitness/beauty spa, plus sports rentals, movie theater, resort shop, gourmet restaurant (see listing), cafe, and entertainment lounge. Some of the beautifully furnished rooms also have a private creek-and-mountain-view deck, a gas fireplace, and whirlpool bath.

BASIC INFORMATION

Elevation: *8,200 feet*   *Population (1990): 3,659*
Location: *100 miles West of Denver*
Nearest airport with commercial flights: Eagle - 35 miles
Vail Valley Tourism & Convention Bureau (970)476-1000 (800)525-3875
in Vail Village at 100 E. Meadow Dr. - 81657   www.vail.net\vvtcb

Key West, Florida

Key West is the most flamboyant fun-loving town in America. Far out in the Atlantic Ocean by the Gulf of Mexico lies an eight-square-mile island that is a treasury of natural and manmade sensual distractions. Just offshore is the longest living coral reef in the western hemisphere. Here is America's only major town accessible by road that has never seen snow or frost. After a century as a naval and maritime island outpost, real growth followed completion in 1938 of the Overseas Highway that extends for more than one hundred miles from the Florida mainland via bridges and islands. Mainlanders in search of a tropical paradise have been flocking here ever since.

Today, coconut palms and fragrant plumeria trees flourish along white sand beaches. Blocks of historic flower-trimmed buildings house a beguiling profusion of galleries and shops, restaurants, open-air bars, theaters, quaint inns and waterfront hotels that all proudly display Key West's cosmopolitan conviviality and sensuality.

WEATHER PROFILE

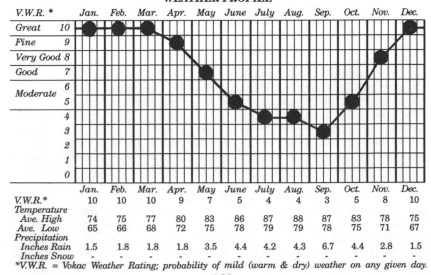

V.W.R.*		Jan.	Feb.	Mar.	Apr.	May	June	July	Aug.	Sep.	Oct.	Nov.	Dec.
Great	10												
Fine	9												
Very Good	8												
Good	7												
Moderate	6												
	5												
	4												
	3												
	2												
	1												
	0												

	Jan.	Feb.	Mar.	Apr.	May	June	July	Aug.	Sep.	Oct.	Nov.	Dec.
V.W.R.*	10	10	10	9	7	5	4	4	3	5	8	10
Temperature												
Ave. High	74	75	77	80	83	86	87	88	87	83	78	75
Ave. Low	65	66	68	72	75	78	79	79	78	75	71	67
Precipitation												
Inches Rain	1.5	1.8	1.8	1.8	3.5	4.4	4.2	4.3	6.7	4.4	2.8	1.5
Inches Snow	-	-	-	-	-	-	-	-	-	-	-	-

*V.W.R. = Vokac Weather Rating; probability of mild (warm & dry) weather on any given day.

ATTRACTIONS
Audubon House & Gardens   *(305)294-2116*
downtown at 205 Whitehead St.
John James Audubon, one of America's most noted wildlife painters, lived in this gracious antebellum house in 1832. Many of his original engravings are displayed along with authentic period antiques. Tropical native and exotic plants are labelled in the garden, and there is a notable museum store.
Beaches   *(305)292-8155*
1 mi. S
Coconut palms provide an authentically tropical backdrop to Key West's white-sand beaches. The four best all face the Atlantic Ocean. A stroll from downtown on Southard St. ends at a big popular beach by Civil-War-era **Fort Zachary Taylor**. **South Beach** at Duval and South Streets is picturesque, and close to the southernmost point in America reachable by highway. **Higgs Beach** on Atlantic Blvd. and **Smothers Beach** on Roosevelt Blvd. also have sailboat or jet ski rentals, and parasailing.
Bicycling
Flat terrain, colorful neighborhoods, tropical vegetation and spectacular waterfronts make Key West a peerless locale for easy bicycling. It may also be the moped and motor scooter capital of America. All kinds of bicycles, plus scooters and mopeds for one or two people, can be rented by the hour or longer at:
   Adventure Scooter & Bicycle Rentals   *(305)293-9933*
   Paradise Rentals   *(305)292-6441*
   Pirate Scooters   *(305)295-0000*
Boat Rentals   *(305)294-2587*
Sailboats, catamarans, windsurfers, powerboats, jet skis, pontoon boats, rafts, kayaks and other watercraft, plus lessons, guide service and equipment can be rented by the hour or longer at many places along the waterfront in town.
Boat Rides
The clear tropical waters of the Atlantic Ocean and the Gulf of Mexico are awash with fascinating islands and the longest living coral reef in the Western Hemisphere. A remarkable variety of two-hour or longer cruises begin at the marinas in town. Most feature diving and snorkeling. Some of the best for fun and romance are:
   Discovery Glass Bottom Boat *underwater reef view room* 293-0099
   Fury Catamarans *65-foot cat—champagne sunset sail*   294-8899
   Schooner Appledore *86-foot windjammer, sunset sail*   296-9992
Conch Train Tours   *(305)294-5161*   *(800)868-7482*
downtown at 303 Front St.
A jaunty little trackless train with open-air cars takes visitors for a fourteen-mile narrated tour of the island. It is a uniquely Key West way to spend 1½ hours being educated and entertained with an overview of places to go and things to see.
Curry Mansion   *(305)294-5349*
downtown at 511 Caroline St.
One of the island's architectural landmarks is this 1899 mansion on the National Historic Register. The romance of Victorian art and architecture is beautifully evoked in period antiques, Tiffany glass, and original Audubon paintings that distinguish 22 rooms, along with porches, verandas and a widow's walk.

Downtown
Old Town, just inland from the Gulf of Mexico, boasts the largest district of 19th century wooden structures on the National Historic Register. Here is also the only major downtown reachable via America's highways that has never seen snow, sleet or freezing temperatures. Amid graceful coconut palms and fragrant plumeria trees twenty feet high, unique Conch-style buildings and related tropical architecture and landscapes have flourished for well over a century. The district's delightfully human scale rewards strollers with a slew of galleries and gourmet treats like conch fritters and Key lime pie. Prodigious numbers of bars and live entertainment saloons and theaters also make this one of America's most wide-awake and uninhibited nightlife capitals. Most of the island's best waterfront hotels and inns are also here.

Ernest Hemingway House   *(305)294-1575*
  just S at 907 Whitehead St.
The novelist penned most of his greatest works in an 1851 mansion he purchased in 1931. Guided tours include his writing studio, tropical gardens including the town's first pool, and dozens of cats descended from Hemingway's felines.

Fishing/Diving/Snorkeling Charters   *(305)294-2587*
Six hundred varieties of fish are reported to swim in the clear warm waters around Key West and the longest living coral reef in the Western Hemisphere. Guided half-day and longer sportfishing trips are abundantly available. Conditions are also ideal for diving, and snorkeling (which doesn't require any previous experience). There are more charter boats per square mile here with all necessary gear to get you in the water than anywhere in the world.

The Florida Keys   *(305)294-2587*
  downtown from Whitehead & Fleming Sts. and NE on US 1
Key West is connected to Florida by a scenic (and engineering) marvel aptly known as the Overseas Highway (US 1). More than forty bridges (some as much as seven miles long) connect dozens of small, flat islands on a two-lane road that extends for 113 miles. Developments are mostly plain. A fabulous exception is **Little Palm Island** ((305)872-2524 or (800)343-8567). At m.m. 28.5, a launch takes guests to a tiny island with a posh mini-resort that is America's most unique tropical paradise. Farther along US 1 are three notable towns. All are casual and oriented toward fishing and diving. **Marathon** (around m.m. 50) has several restaurants and lodgings by the water. Nearby is **Hawk's Cay Resort & Marina** ((305)743-7000) at m.m. 61, a big, modish Caribbean-style resort with a tropical lagoon, sandy beach, and a wealth of recreation options on land and sea. The self-proclaimed "Sport Fishing Capital of the World," **Islamadora** (around m.m. 82), has all sorts of related businesses. **Cheeca Lodge** ((305)664-4651 or (800)327-2888) at m.m. 82 is a plush, complete oceanfront resort where coconut palms shade a saltwater lagoon, beach and pools. **Key Largo** (around m.m. 100) claims to be the "Diving Capital of the World." **John Pennekamp Coral Reef State Park** ((305)451-1202), America's premier underwater park, parallels the island with spectacular marine and plant life. Restaurants include **Frank Keys Cafe** ((305)453-0310) at m.m. 100, one of the Key's finest. Among resorts, **The Westin Beach Resort Key Largo** ((305)852-5553 or (800)826-1006) at m.m. 97 is a big gulf-front beach hotel with many amenities.

Key West Aquarium   *(305)296-2051*
downtown at 1 Whitehead St.
Key West's oldest attraction is small, but notable, with shark and
turtle feedings, and a "touch tank" with live denizens of the ocean and
gulf. Guided narrated tours are available.

Key West Lighthouse Museum   *(305)294-0012*
just S at 938 Whitehead St.
The lighthouse-keeper's quarters is a 19th century clapboard with
exhibits depicting the maritime history of the keys. A spiral staircase
to the top of the pre-electricity tower offers fine views.

Mel Fisher Maritime Heritage Museum   *(305)294-2633*
downtown at 200 Green St.
Solid gold bars and coins, emeralds, gold and silver jewelry and
religious objects, cannons and weapons are among the treasure
recovered from two 17th century Spanish galleons that sank during a
hurricane near town. Dazzling displays are coupled with exhibits
depicting techniques of underwater treasure hunting and archeology.

The Oldest House/Wrecker's Museum   *(305)294-9502*
downtown at 322 Duval St.
The oldest house in the Keys (circa 1829) was built in the island's
unique "conch" style with a "landlubber's tilt" and a ship's hatch in the
roof. It now houses period antiques, displays of Key West's wrecking
industry, maritime memorabilia, a garden, and an antique cookhouse.

The Sunset Celebration
downtown off Duval St. end
Key West's most unique attraction recurs nightly when the natural
grandeur of a tropical sunset is celebrated by zany natives at the docks
of Mallory Square. Dozens of local entertainers, vendors, and artisans
stake out their space to beguile crowds of spectators who begin gathering about an hour before sunset, and linger longer for the "happening."

RESTAURANTS

Bagatelle   *(305)296-6609*
downtown at 115 Duval St.
L-D.   *Expensive*
Caribbean cuisine like sauteed grouper with macadamia nut crust
served with mango passion fruit sauce is skillfully presented in a
stylish Victorian home and on the wraparound veranda.

Blue Heaven   *(305)296-8666*
just S at 729 Thomas St.
B-L-D.   *Moderate*
Eclectic Caribbean cuisine is purely delightful in dishes like warm
banana bread and sauce with banana slices and homemade vanilla ice
cream. Wild tropical courtyard decor complete with strolling roosters,
chickens and a rope swing is a perfect complement to the exciting fare.

Chico's Cantina   *(305)296-4714*
5 mi. NE at 5230 U.S. Highway 1
L-D.   *Moderate*
Acclaimed homemade Mexican specialties (like shrimp and other
fajitas, fish adobado grilled in corn husks, or chicken chipotle) are
served in a comfortable cafe and cantina.

El Siboney Restaurant   *(305)296-4184*
just E at 900 Catherine St.
L-D.   *Low*
Cuban cuisine is featured in skillfully prepared authentic dishes served
in a casual, colorful restaurant with a loyal following.

Half Shell Raw Bar   *(305)294-7496*
downtown at 231 Margaret St.
L-D.   *Moderate*
Conch chowder and other seafood comes direct from their fish market.
A funky fun setting with occasional live entertainment has earned a
solid following for this cafe/bar with a lot of local color on the
waterfront.

Kelly's Caribbean Bar, Grill & Brewery   *(305)293-8484*
downtown at 301 Whitehead St.
L-D.   *Moderate*
Micro-brews made here in America's southernmost brewery are paired
with Caribbean and American fare in a historic building and in a
colorful garden under a canopy of trees.

Key West Key Lime Pie Co.   *(305)294-6567 (800)872-2714*
downtown at 701 Caroline St.   *Moderate*
Smooth, dense and flavorful Key Lime Pie (the island's ubiquitous
culinary contribution) is available to go by the slice or whole pie (which
can also be shipped).

Louie's Backyard   *(305)294-1061*
1 mi. S at 700 Waddell Av.
L-D.   *Very Expensive*
One of the Key's most renowned restaurants specializes in delicious
creations from fresh local seafood. Guests have a choice of casually
elegant dining rooms in a romantic old home or a picturesque lounge
deck by a tropical ocean beach. The deck lounge on a pier is also
deservedly popular.

Mangoes   *(305)292-4606*
downtown at 700 Duval St.
L-D.   *Moderate*
Contemporary Caribbean cuisine stars in dishes that celebrate the
diversity of local culinary roots. Dine casually indoors or in a tropical
garden.

Pepe's Cafe   *(305)294-7192*
downtown at 806 Caroline St.
B-L-D.   *Expensive*
Homemade bread and jams help explain why their all-American
breakfasts are among the best. Other meals also attract crowds to a
casual little storefront dining room, or an appealing tree-shaded patio
or bar in one of the oldest restaurants in town.

Sloppy Joe's Food Company   *(305)294-5717*
downtown at 201 Duval St.
L-D.   *Moderate*
Maybe they did invent the Sloppy Joe here. Anyway, the famed
sandwich and other fun food, and a great bar with lots of live
entertainment, continue to draw crowds as they did when this was one
of Earnest Hemingway's favorite haunts.

Square One Restaurant   *(305)296-4300*
1 mi. S at 1075 Duval St.
D only.   *Expensive*
New American cuisine gets a classy local spin in dishes like sauteed
conch cakes with cilantro corn relish and gingered gazpacho sauce, or
grilled herb-marinated pork tenderloin with Jamaican rum and fresh
banana guava chutney. Guests can opt for an intimate, chic dining
room or a tropical courtyard.

Accommodations are abundant and varied, ranging from romantic bed-and-breakfast inns to oceanfront hotels. Winter is the "high season." Rates are often reduced 40% and more at other times.

The Gardens Hotel *(305)294-2661*
downtown at 526 Angela St. - 33040
17 units *(800)526-2664* *Very Expensive*
Colorful tropical gardens surround one of Florida's most elegant small hotels. Brick-lined pathways meander among exotic plants to fountains and a pool and whirlpool. An extensive Continental breakfast is served in a solarium or on wide porches. Each uniquely decorated unit is luxuriously furnished with all modern conveniences including whirlpool tub, plus stocked (honor) bar and porch seating area. The "Eyebrow Cottage" and "Master Suite" are among the most spectacularly romantic anywhere.

Heron House *(305)294-9227*
downtown at 512 Simonton St. - 33040
23 units *(800)294-1644* *Expensive*
Classic Key West style reflects artistic sensitivity in both the restored historic Conch houses and luxuriant tropical gardens featuring rare handgrown orchids by a tiled, lap-friendly pool. Expanded Continental breakfast and afternoon wine and snacks are complimentary. Each individually decorated room is beautifully furnished, including quality art objects by local artisans. Most have a private deck or balcony, and three suites have an oversized whirlpool bath.

Holiday Inn La Concha Hotel *(305)296-2991*
downtown at 430 Duval St. - 33040
160 units *(800)745-2191* *Expensive-Very Expensive*
A seven-story pink landmark hotel has been the heart of the main street since 1925. After award-winning restoration back to the colorful mystique of the 1920s, the hotel is popular again. Amenities include a pool, (fee) mopeds and bicycles, a sidewalk saloon, casual dining room and a rooftop view lounge. Some rooms are compact, and all are well furnished. Some have view balconies.

Hyatt Key West *(305)296-9900*
downtown at 601 Front St. - 33040
120 units *(800)233-1234* *Very Expensive*
The Gulf of Mexico borders this upscale contemporary five-story complex. Amenities include a beach, pool, whirlpool, exercise room and (fee) bicycles, mopeds, and marina with all kinds of watercraft, scuba, and snorkeling gear rentals, plus restaurants and a lounge with a grand sunset view on the Gulf. Each beautifully furnished unit has a private balcony. Some have a whirlpool tub.

Marriott's Casa Marina Resort *(305)296-3535*
1 mi. S at 1500 Reynolds St. - 33040
314 units *(800)626-0777* *Very Expensive*
Key West's largest resort opened in 1921. After complete renovation, the spectacular four-story complex captures the colorful relaxed lifestyle of the island, the grace of a bygone era, and the utmost in today's conveniences. In addition to more than 1,000 feet of oceanfront beach, coconut-palm-shaded grounds include two pools, whirlpool, sauna, and health club. Fee amenities include three lighted tennis courts, mopeds and bicycles, charter fishing, scuba/snorkeling gear, and all kinds of watercraft. Many of the beautifully furnished units have an ocean view. Some have private balconies.

Key West, Florida
Marriott's Reach Resort   *(305)296-5000*
1 mi. S at 1435 Simonton St. - 33040
150 units   *(800)228-9290*   *Very Expensive*
This contemporary five-story oceanfront resort has a sandy beach and pier, pool and steamroom, plus (for a fee) all kinds of on- and in-water activities and gear. There is also an upscale restaurant and entertainment lounge. Each beautifully furnished unit has a private view patio or balcony.

Ocean Key House   *(305)296-7701*
downtown at 0 Duval St. - 33040
104 units   *(800)328-9815*   *Very Expensive*
One of the island's most elegant contemporary lodgings is an all-suites five-story resort with a palm-shaded pool and an oceanfront marina. Fee opportunities include a dazzling choice of on- or in-water activities. There are also view lounges and a fine restaurant. Each spacious, beautifully furnished one- or two-bedroom suite includes an oversized whirlpool tub, a large private balcony with town or water views, and a full kitchen.

Pier House Resort and Caribbean Spa   *(305)296-4600*
downtown at 1 Duval St. - 33040
142 units   *(800)327-8340*   *Very Expensive*
Island elegance is achieved in this low-profile contemporary resort sprawling among coconut palms on the Gulf. Amenities include a beach, pool, whirlpool, and (fee) health club, mopeds and bicycles, all sorts of on- and in-water sports and gear, plus acclaimed restaurants and entertainment lounges. Paddle fans and wicker furniture are part of the beautiful decor of each unit. Most have private view balconies. Some have a fireplace, whirlpool tub and steamroom.

Pilot House Guest House   *(305)293-6600*
downtown at 414 Simonton St. - 33040
14 units   *(800)648-3780*   *Expensive-Very Expensive*
A classic Victorian mansion was artistically restored and enhanced in 1990. Colorful tropical gardens surround buildings, a courtyard pool, and whirlpool. Antiques and tropical furnishings like paddle fans complement contemporary conveniences. Each beautifully decorated room has a marble bath and kitchenette. Some units also have a spacious whirlpool tub.

Sheraton Suites Key West   *(305)292-9800*
2 mi. SE at 2001 S. Roosevelt Blvd. - 33040
184 units   *(800)325-3535*   *Very Expensive*
Here is an upscale all-suites hotel with an appealing tropical style. The contemporary four-story complex faces an ocean beach, and has a big freeform pool and waterfall, whirlpool, exercise room, and (fee) mopeds. Each one-bedroom suite is beautifully furnished. Some have a whirlpool tub.

BASIC INFORMATION
Elevation: 5 feet   Population (1990): 24,832
Location: 160 miles Southwest of Miami
Nearest airport with commercial flights: in town
Key West Chamber of Commerce   (305)294-2587
* downtown at 402 Wall St. - 33040   (800)527-8539*
Florida Keys & Key West Visitors Bureau   (305)296-1552
* Box 1147 - 33041   (800)352-5397*
* www / fla-keys.com*

Mount Dora, Florida

Mount Dora is the prettiest inland village of Florida. Gentle hills (some of the state's highest) rise above scenic Lake Dora. Numerous other small lakes, plus citrus orchards and forests of hardwoods and pine, fill the surrounding semitropical countryside. From the earliest settlement well over a century ago, the town has grown slowly but steadily thanks to citrus and tourism.

The original symbol of Mount Dora's auspicious beginnings, the Lakeside Inn, is still delighting visitors as a lakeside landmark. Palms and towering hardwoods shade waterfront parks and line streets where tidy, whitewashed homes surrounded by manicured gardens are reminiscent of Victorian New England. The flowery little business district fills historic and contemporary buildings with distinctive specialty and antique shops, galleries, restaurants and quaint inns. Free of fast foods and chains, it is a gracious contrast to the hustle and bustle of nearby Orlando and the mega-amusement parks beyond.

WEATHER PROFILE

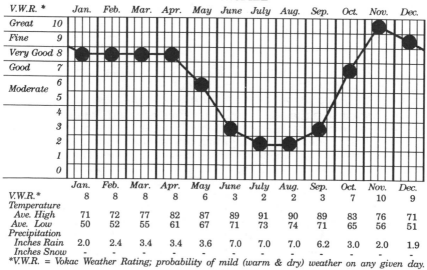

		Jan.	Feb.	Mar.	Apr.	May	June	July	Aug.	Sep.	Oct.	Nov.	Dec.
V.W.R.*		8	8	8	8	6	3	2	2	3	7	10	9
Temperature													
	Ave. High	71	72	77	82	87	89	91	90	89	83	76	71
	Ave. Low	50	52	55	61	67	71	73	74	71	65	56	51
Precipitation													
	Inches Rain	2.0	2.4	3.4	3.4	3.6	7.0	7.0	7.0	6.2	3.0	2.0	1.9
	Inches Snow	-	-	-	-	-	-	-	-	-	-	-	-

*V.W.R. = Vokac Weather Rating; probability of mild (warm & dry) weather on any given day.

175

Boat Rides

The Dora Canal is actually a mile-long river that connects Lakes Dora and Eustis. The beauty of the cypress trees and other native subtropical vegetation has made this a popular recreation site for more than a century. Several companies offer cruises of about two hours.

Captain Charlie's "Miss Dora"   *(352)343-0200*
Captain Dave's Dora Canal Cruises   *(352)343-3889*
Heritage Lake Tours   *(352)343-4337*
Rusty Anchor   *(in-town-lake cruises too)*   *(352)383-3933*

Downtown
around Donnelly St. & 5th Av.

Mount Dora's long, genteel past is proudly preserved on a historic picture-postcard main street that ends in a scenic park near a refined historic inn on Lake Dora. Nearby, a stately city hall tops a hill above a handsome block-square park. Numerous specialty and antique shops and restaurants on tree-lined streets fill out the compact district. Horse-drawn carriages are available for romantic tours of the area.

Ocala National Forest   *(352)625-2520*
10 mi. N on FL 19

America's most southerly national forest is also one of the flattest. Large stands of pine and hardwoods shade an abundance of crystal-clear streams and lakes fed by prodigious springs flowing at a constant 72°F. Salt and Juniper Springs are especially popular for swimming and boating. Hiking trails, picnic areas and campgrounds are plentiful.

Palm Island and Gilbert Parks   *(352)735-7183*
just S at Tremain St. & Liberty Av.

Palm Island Park offers one of the most beautiful nature walks in Florida. Boardwalks extend through semitropical cypress, palms and other lush foliage out onto the lake. Wildlife is abundant—you might even see a bald eagle, raccoon or alligator. Picnicking and fishing are also enjoyed here and in nearby Gilbert Park, distinguished by a photogenic lighthouse on the shoreline.

Silver Springs   *(352)236-2121*
45 mi. NW via US 441 at 5656 E. Silver Springs Blvd. - Ocala

The crystal-clear Silver River begins at what is reputedly the world's largest artesian spring formation. In the landmark nature park, narrated glass-bottom boat tours provide views of underwater life as much as forty feet under the boat. Other features include the jungle cruise and the lost river voyage, plus a jeep safari, petting zoo, and animal shows. Nearby **Wild Waters** is a major water park.

Walt Disney World   *(407)824-4321*
40 mi. S via US 441 and I-4 - Lake Buena Vista

Mount Dora is less than an hour by car from the world's most gigantic amusement complex, but a world away from the bustle. Since opening in 1971, Walt Disney World has grown into a vast vacation destination amid 43 square miles of semitropical forests and lakes. There are now four major theme parks: **Magic Kingdom Park; Epcot; Disney-MGM Studios;** and **Disney's Animal Kingdom Park**. There also are three expansive, imaginatively themed water parks (**Blizzard Beach, River Country** and **Typhoon Lagoon**). The **Disney Institute** offers a new kind of learning-by-doing vacation. **Downtown Disney Pleasure Island** has a glittering nightclub complex, restaurants and shops. There are also several fine golf courses. Among many notable resort hotels, **Disney's Boardwalk**, **Disney's Beach Club and Yacht Club Resorts**, **Disney's Grand Floridian Resort**, **Disney's Wilderness Lodge**, and **Walt Disney World Dolphin and Swan** are the best. All offer a fine combination of convenience to parks, distinctive style, smart rooms, and a wealth of amenities for adults and children.

RESTAURANTS

The Gables Restaurant   *(352)383-8993*
   downtown at 322 N. Alexander St.
   L-D.   *Expensive*
Contemporary American dishes are skillfully prepared in one of Mount Dora's favorite restaurants. Guests are served in a comfortable country setting, in the lounge, or on the front porch.

Lakeside Inn   *(352)383-4101*
   downtown at 100 N. Alexander St.
   B-L-D.   *Expensive*
Fine dining with a view is offered in the landmark hotel's **Beauclair Restaurant**. There is also a stylish lounge with entertainment on weekends.

New York Bagel & Deli   *(352)383-5232*
   downtown at 122 E. Fourth St.
   B-L.   *Moderate*
Several kinds of bagels are very good. They're served with all of the right, light stuff in this casual deli.

Palm Tree Grill   *(352)735-1936*
   downtown at 351 N. Donnelly St.
   L-D.   *Moderate*
Italian cuisine stars in dishes ranging from crab-stuffed scampi to pizza or sausage roll. Tiramisu and cannoli are also well regarded in this popular trattoria.

The Park Bench   *(352)383-7004*
   downtown at 116 E. Fifth Av.
   L-D.   *Expensive*
The contemporary American and international cuisine served here is some of the best in the region, and desserts (like the caramel-pecan pie) can be outstanding. Warm, cheerful dining rooms overlook the handsome town square park across a street.

The Windsor Rose English Tea Room   *(352)735-2551*
   downtown at 144 W. Fourth Av.
   L only.   *Moderate*
Fresh scones served with imported Devonshire double cream, and pastries (like very berry tarts), are authentically British-style, as are entrees like Cornish pasty, teas and other drinks. Cozy decor and a garden shop next door are part of the charm.

LODGING

Accommodations are relatively scarce, but diverse—ranging from a landmark lakeside hotel through bed-and-breakfasts to modern motels. Winter is high season. Summer rates may be reduced 20% or more.

Comfort Inn   *(352)383-3400*
   4 mi. NW at 16630 US 441 West - 32757
   89 units   *(800)228-5150*   *Moderate*
One of the area's newest motels is near Lake Woodward with a pool, whirlpool and exercise room. Comfortable rooms with kitchenettes are available, and there is a whirlpool suite.

Darst Victorian Manor   *(352)383-4050*
downtown at 485 Old Highway 441 - 32757
5 units   *Expensive*
The region's best bed-and-breakfast is an elegant reproduction of an
expansive Victorian home overlooking Lake Dora a pleasant stroll from
the heart of town. A pool and whirlpool were recently added to
manicured grounds. Gourmet country breakfast and afternoon tea and
treats are complimentary. Beautiful furnishings celebrate the ambiance
of a bygone era while offering all modern conveniences. "Queen
Victoria" and "Oak Splendor" both overlook Lake Dora and feature a
remote control gas fireplace.

The Emerald Hill Inn   *(352)383-2777*
5 mi. SW at 27751 Lake Jem Rd. - 32757
4 units   *(800)366-9387*   *Moderate-Expensive*
Amidst rolling hills and luxuriant trees is a handsome bed-and-
breakfast fashioned from a 1941 estate overlooking a small lake. An
expanded Continental breakfast is complimentary. Two of the well-
furnished rooms share a bath, while "The Diamond" and "The Peridot"
both have a lake-view patio and a distinctive bathroom.

Lakeside Inn   *(352)383-4101*
downtown at 100 N. Alexander St. - 32757
88 units   *(800)556-5016*   *Expensive*
Established in 1883, this lakefront landmark is on the National
Register of Historic Places. Amenities include a small sandy beach,
boat dock, outdoor pool, two lighted tennis courts, plus a fine dining
room (see listing) and entertainment lounge. All of the well-furnished
renovated rooms have private baths and combine traditional ambiance
of an earlier era with modern amenities.

Magnolia Inn   *(352)735-3800*
downtown at 347 E. Third Av. - 32757
4 units   *(800)776-2112*   *Expensive*
A classic Roaring 20s estate in a quiet residential area by the heart of
town has become a handsome bed-and-breakfast. Lavish gardens,
sunny terraces and a whirlpool are featured, along with full
complimentary breakfasts flavored with their own herbs. Each
uniquely decorated, well-furnished room has a private bath.

Mission Inn Golf & Tennis Resort   *(352)324-3101*
16 mi. SW via SR 19 at 10400 CR 48 Howey-in-the-Hills - 34737
191 units   *(800)874-9053*   *Expensive*
Lush subtropical grounds surround this contemporary resort with
special appeal to golfing enthusiasts. Amenities include an outdoor
pool, whirlpool, exercise room, jogging trail and (fee) two 18-hole golf
courses (one of championship quality), eight tennis courts, a marina
with a variety of watercraft, and rental bicycles, plus three restaurants
and an entertainment lounge. Each room is beautifully furnished and
has a private balcony or patio.

BASIC INFORMATION

Elevation: 180 feet   *Population (1990): 7,196*
Location: 30 miles Northwest of Orlando
Nearest airport with commercial flights: Orlando - 40 miles
Mount Dora Area Chamber of Commerce   (352)383-2165
  downtown at 341 N. Alexander St. (Box 196) - 32757
  www.mt-dora.com

Naples, Florida

Naples is an urbane enclave in a water wonderland. Miles of bays and canals reflect the Italian namesake. To the east, Big Cypress Swamp extends to the vast unique maze of waterways that is Everglades National Park. Nearby, to the south is the first of ten thousand islands, and the western border of town is miles of sandy beaches along the Gulf of Mexico. Naples was settled as a fishing village. By the 1880s, transformation into a resort community had begun as warm winters and the exotic locale began to attract visitors.

Today, coconut palms and tropical foliage provide a luxuriant frame to beaches, parks and upscale neighborhoods. Downtown, flowers line streets full of tony boutiques and sophisticated restaurants. Along the many surrounding waterfronts, beach-going, all kinds of aquatic sports, and golf (on more than fifty courses) are highlights among pleasurable pursuits. Several luxury resort hotels offer a wealth of contemporary cosmopolitan facilities in choice sites by the Gulf.

WEATHER PROFILE

V.W.R. *		Jan.	Feb.	Mar.	Apr.	May	June	July	Aug.	Sep.	Oct.	Nov.	Dec.
Great	10	●											
Fine	9		●	●	●							●	●
Very Good	8												
Good	7										●		
Moderate	6												
	5					●							
	4												
	3												
	2						●	●	●	●			
	1												
	0												

	Jan.	Feb.	Mar.	Apr.	May	June	July	Aug.	Sep.	Oct.	Nov.	Dec.
V.W.R.*	10	9	9	9	5	2	2	2	2	7	10	10
Temperature												
Ave. High	75	76	80	84	88	90	91	91	90	85	80	77
Ave. Low	52	54	57	61	66	71	73	74	73	67	59	55
Precipitation												
Inches Rain	1.5	2.2	2.6	1.6	3.9	9.0	8.1	7.4	8.5	3.2	1.4	1.4
Inches Snow	-	-	-	-	-	-	-	-	-	-	-	-

*V.W.R. = Vokac Weather Rating; probability of mild (warm & dry) weather on any given day.

ATTRACTIONS
Beaches   *(941)434-4698*
   1 mi. W on 5th Av. S
Coconut palms back ten miles of sandy beaches bordering the Gulf of
Mexico in town. Fishermen enjoy the Naples Pier, while swimmers and
sunbathers flock to Lowdermilk Park off Banyan Blvd.
Bicycling
Flat terrain, manicured neighborhoods, tropical vegetation and many
miles of photogenic waterfronts make Naples superb for touring. All
kinds of bicycles can be rented at several places in town.
Boat Rentals
Sailboats, powerboats, pontoon boats, jet skis and other watercraft can
be rented by the hour or longer at several places in and near town.
Boat Rides
The canals of Naples, nearby Marco Island, and the Gulf of Mexico
offer views of posh waterfront homes, natural mangrove-lined islands,
abundant birdlife and (possibly) manatees. Several companies offer
narrated sightseeing and sunset cruises of 1½ hours or longer. The
Naples Princess also has complete food and beverage service.
   Double Sunshine   *2-deck catamaran*   *(941)263-4949*
   Naples Princess   *80-foot cruising yacht*   *(941)649-2275*
   Sweet Liberty   *53-foot catamaran*   *(941)793-3525*
Everglades City (35 mi. SE) is the gateway to the Everglades. The
most exhilarating and popular way to explore the enormous maze of
scenic wilderness waterways is aboard an airboat. Fast and relatively
quiet tours of an hour or longer are plentiful. The most notable include:
   Eden of the Everglades   *(800)543-3367*
   Florida Boat Tours   *(800)282-9194*
   Jungle Erv's Airboat World   *(800)432-3367*
   Wooten's   *(800)282-2781*
Caribbean Gardens   *(941)262-5409*
   2 mi. NE at 1590 Goodlette Rd.
The Caribbean Gardens are a genuine tropical jungle. Thousands of
species are present along a self-guiding trail in the expansive preserve
begun in 1919. The jungle setting is enhanced by exotic animals. A
highlight is the half-hour narrated boat cruise past free-roaming
primates on a tropical island. Other features include wild animal
shows, a petting farm, snack bar, picnic areas, and a gift shop.
Collier County Museum   *(941)774-8476*
   2 mi. SE at 3301 E. Tamiami Trail (US 41)
A five-acre historical park features a restored 1920s Naples cottage,
native garden and orchid house, an archeological laboratory, and
exhibits that trace the area's natural and cultural history.
Collier-Seminole State Park Boat Tours   *(941)642-8898*
   17 mi. SE at 19800 E. Tamiami Trail (US 41)
Alligators and manatees are often seen on narrated hour-long pontoon-
boat tours into the Everglades, cypress and mangrove swamps. Other
features of the big park include a boardwalk nature trail, interpretive
center, two campgrounds, boat rentals and park store.
The Conservancy   *(941)262-0304*
   1 mi. N at 1450 Merrihue Dr.
Naples Nature Center features hands-on exhibits and programs, a
wildlife rehabilitation center, and a narrated boat ride (or walk)
through a mangrove forest. There are also canoe and kayak rentals
and the **Nature Store. Briggs Nature Center** (9 mi. S off FL 951)

has nature exhibits (including a butterfly garden); guided pontoon boat or canoe trips; boat rentals; and self-guided boardwalk hikes.

Corkscrew Swamp Sanctuary   *(941)348-9151*
23 mi. NE via FL 846

The National Audubon Society owns the world's largest known forest of old-growth bald cypress. They strive to maintain it as part of a major pristine wilderness. A self-guided two-mile Boardwalk Trail winds among towering cypress (said to be more than 500 years old) that is also a haven for nesting Wood Storks and other birds and animals.

Downtown
around 5th Av. S

A few blocks from the Gulf, tropical palms and flowers, fountains and sculpture contribute to the big vibrant business district's delightfully human scale. Many modish stores also display a wealth of quality arts and crafts, while gourmet restaurants feature notable regional specialties. Naples (narrated) Trolley Tours (262-7300) cover more than 100 points of interest and allow free reboarding.

Everglades National Park   *(305)242-7700*
35 mi. SE via US 41 - Everglades City

America's largest subtropical park includes more than 2,000 square miles of wilderness area, and Cape Sable, the southernmost point on the U.S. mainland. It is a labyrinth of (fresh and salt) waterways, mangrove forests, and open prairies, none of it more than a few feet above sea level. Several species of palms are here, too, along with abundant wildlife, including rare and colorful birds, manatee, sea turtles and even crocodiles. Facilities include visitor centers, hiking and canoe trails, boardwalks, campgrounds, food and lodging. Boating and fishing are popular. The most memorable way to experience the wilderness is via airboat. Many leave from Everglades City.

Everglades National Park Boat Tours   *(941)695-2591*
37 mi. SE via US 41 - Everglades City

The official concessionaire for scenic boat tours in the national park leaves the park's ranger office several times daily. A mangrove wilderness trip of nearly two hours goes up Turner River where you might see alligators, bald eagles and water turkeys. The Ten Thousand Island Cruise winds for 2½ hours among islands by the Gulf of Mexico, with a stop for shell hunting. At times, porpoises play by the boat.

Fishing Charters   *(941)262-6141*

A remarkable number of boats in and near town are used for guided offshore and backwater sportfishing trips. The Gulf of Mexico, the 10,000 islands, and the Everglades are all accessible in half-day charters. Longer trips can also be reserved with all equipment.

RESTAURANTS

Bistro 821   *(941)261-5821*
downtown at 821 Fifth Av. S
D only.   *Expensive*

Fresh creative New American cuisine is carefully prepared and served in a classic bistro setting.

Chardonnay   *(941)261-1744*
2 mi. N at 2331 Tamiami Trail N
D only.   *Very Expensive*

French and Continental dishes, including house-baked breads and desserts, are skillfully presented. Semi-formal elegance where jackets are appropriate for men further distinguishes the refined dinner house.

First Watch Restaurant   *(941)434-0005*
2 mi. NW at 1400 Gulf Shore Blvd. N
B-L.   *Expensive*
One of the region's most popular sources of morning delights like oatmeal-apple pancakes offers cheerful dining areas with a picture-window view of an oceanfront park.
Mangrove Cafe   *(941)262-7076*
downtown at 878 Fifth Av. S
L-D.   *Expensive*
Seafood, fruits, and vegetables native to Southwest Florida become creative specialties like alligator and conch chowder and homemade plantain chips with mango chutney in this delightful modish cafe.
Pazzo   *(941)434-8494*
downtown at 853 Fifth Av. S
D only.   *Expensive*
The light and lively Italian cuisine is deservedly popular in this truly classic upscale bistro.
The Registry Resort Naples   *(941)597-3232*
5 mi. NW at 475 Seagate Dr.
B-L-D.   *Very Expensive*
Lafite (D only) is acclaimed for New American cuisine with a Southern accent. (The seared filet mignon with gorgonzola and vidalia onion etouffe is superb.) A harpist contributes to the opulent formality. Two other dining venues in the landmark resort offer excellent casual fare in memorable settings.
The Ritz-Carlton Naples   *(941)598-3300*
7 mi. N at 280 Vanderbilt Beach Rd.
B-L-D.   *Very Expensive*
The Dining Room (D only) is renowned for expertly prepared seasonal fresh fish presented amid elegant surroundings. Two other restaurants in the luxurious resort offer fine casual fare in posh settings.
Terra   *(941)262-5500*
1 mi. S at 1300 Third St. S
L-D.   *Very Expensive*
Downstairs, creative classical cuisine in a casually elegant setting continues to attract a loyal following. The lounge features live entertainment later on weekends. Upstairs, light innovative fare and delightful desserts are served in an informal bistro.
The's Waterfront Cafe   *(941)775-8115*
just E at 1444 Fifth Av. S
L-D.   *Moderate*
Herb-crusted corvina, conch fritters and sizzling shrimp fajitas are appealing seafood possibilities in this jaunty wood-trimmed contempo cafe, bar and patio with a water view.
Tony's Off Third   *(941)262-7999*
1 mi. S at 1300 Third St. S
B-L-D.   *Expensive*
Sticky buns, cinnamon rolls and assorted other pastries, plus breads and desserts, star with light contemporary fare. The bakery shares a location by a popular courtyard with a coffee bar and wine shop.
Villa Pescatore   *(941)597-8119*
7 mi. N at 8920 Tamiami Trail N
L-D.   *Very Expensive*
Seafood with an Italian accent has earned critical acclaim for this casually elegant dinner house.

LODGING
Area accommodations are plentiful. Few are on the beach. Winter is high season. Rates in summer are usually reduced at least 40%.

Edgewater Beach Hotel   *(941)403-2000*
 2 mi. NW at 1901 Gulf Shore Blvd. N - 34102
 126 units   *(800)821-0196*   *Very Expensive*
A white sand beach on the Gulf of Mexico adjoins this modern seven-story all-suites hotel. Other amenities include a pool and exercise room, (fee) wind surfing, bicycles and sailboats, plus an entertainment lounge and gulf-view restaurant. One- and two-bedroom beautifully furnished suites have a living room, patio or view balcony, and kitchenette.

La Playa Beach Resort   *(941)597-3123*
 7 mi. N at 9891 Gulf Shore Dr. - 34108
 195 units   *(800)237-6883*   *Very Expensive*
This contemporary gulf-front resort includes a fifteen-story tower overlooking the beach, two pools, four tennis courts, plus (fee) sailing, waverunners, and a beachfront dining room and lounge. Each spacious, beautifully furnished unit has a private sea-view balcony.

The Naples Beach Hotel & Golf Club   *(941)261-2222*
 2 mi. NW at 851 Gulf Shore Blvd. N - 34102
 316 units   *(800)237-7600*   *Very Expensive*
Here is the only hotel in Southwest Florida with both an 18-hole golf course and a beachfront location. A white sand beach frames an expansive nine-story complex. The fully-renovated half-century-old resort has a pool and (fee) 18-hole golf course, driving range, putting green, four tennis courts, bicycles, and watercraft, plus beach-view restaurants and an entertainment lounge. All units are beautifully furnished. Many have private view balconies and kitchenettes.

The Registry Resort Naples   *(941)597-3232*
 5 mi. NW at 475 Seagate Dr. - 34103
 474 units   *(800)247-9810*   *Very Expensive*
One of Florida's best contemporary resorts, built around a handsome eighteen-story high rise, epitomizes Naples' opulence in a refreshingly unpretentious way. A half-mile walkway leads to the beach across an ancient mangrove lagoon. Luxuriant tropical gardens frame three pools and whirlpools. Fee attractions include fifteen tennis courts, health club, bicycles and all sorts of watercraft, plus gourmet dining (see listing), lounge and night club. Each luxuriously furnished room has a large private gulf-view balcony.

The Ritz-Carlton Naples   *(941)598-3300*
 7 mi. N at 280 Vanderbilt Beach Rd. - 34108
 463 units   *(800)241-3333*   *Very Expensive*
Miles of secluded beach adjoin one of Florida's most prestigious resorts. The contemporary fourteen-story classic is accented by manicured gardens. Amenities include the beach, pool, whirlpool, bicycles and (for a fee) complete fitness center, six lighted tennis courts, and all kinds of watercraft. The Dining Room features gourmet cuisine in an opulent setting, and there are other fine dining and drinking venues. Each luxuriously furnished unit has a private balcony with a gulf view.

BASIC INFORMATION
Elevation: 10 feet   Population (1990): 19,505
Location: 110 miles West of Miami
Nearest airport with commercial flights: in town
Naples Chamber of Commerce   (941)262-6141
 downtown at 895 Fifth Av. - 34102   www.naples-online.com

St. Augustine, Florida

St. Augustine is a unique celebration of an extraordinary past. Tidewaters provide a sheltered harbor two miles from sandy beaches by the Atlantic Ocean. Ponce de Leon landed here in 1513 in search of the legendary Fountain of Youth. He didn't find it. But, as the first European on the North American mainland, he claimed the continent for Spain. The town was established in 1565, making it the oldest permanent European settlement in America. More than three centuries of cultural upheavals passed before Henry Flagler provided a railway link and developed lavish resorts here in the 1880s.

Today, monumental and intimate buildings from various eras are shaded by towering palms and moss-draped hardwoods. Flowers accent narrow streets lined with one-of-a-kind shops, restaurants, bars, museums, and romantic inns. Dramatic statues punctuate the main plaza. Just beyond on the unspoiled bayfront, cruise boats and horse-drawn carriages await sightseers, as they have for over a century.

WEATHER PROFILE

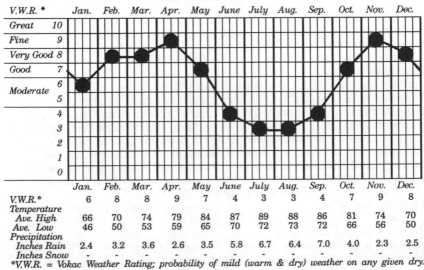

V.W.R.*		Jan.	Feb.	Mar.	Apr.	May	June	July	Aug.	Sep.	Oct.	Nov.	Dec.
V.W.R.*		6	8	8	9	7	4	3	3	4	7	9	8
Temperature													
Ave. High		66	70	74	79	84	87	89	88	86	81	74	70
Ave. Low		46	50	53	59	65	70	72	73	72	66	56	50
Precipitation													
Inches Rain		2.4	3.2	3.6	2.6	3.5	5.8	6.7	6.4	7.0	4.0	2.3	2.5
Inches Snow		-	-	-	-	-	-	-	-	-	-	-	-

*V.W.R. = Vokac Weather Rating; probability of mild (warm & dry) weather on any given dry.

184

Anastasia State Recreation Area   *(904)461-2033*
   3 mi. SE on FL A1A

Coquina quarries used by the Spanish to build America's first masonry fort are here. Nearby is a broad beach flanked by high white dunes along the Atlantic Ocean. Hiking trails, picnic areas and a complete campground are located along a tidal marsh. Swimming and fishing are popular. Sailboards and bicycles can also be rented.

Beaches
   3 mi. SE via FL A1A

Miles of broad sand beaches border the Atlantic Ocean to the north and south of town. Numerous accesses are identified along the main highway (FL A1A) which parallels the coast. Driving on St. Augustine's beaches is permitted. Swimming, surfing, body-boarding and fishing are other popular pastimes.

Boat Rentals

Sailboats, power boats and jet skis can be rented by the hour or longer at several places in and near town.

Boat Rides
   Victory III Scenic Cruise   *(904)824-1806*   *(800)542-8316*
   just S of FL A1A bridge

A 1¼-hour tour of the bay includes a narrated cruise along the picturesque downtown waterfront.

Castillo de San Marcos National Monument   *(904)829-6506*
   downtown on Avenida Menendez at 1 S. Castillo Dr.

The oldest masonry fort in America was completed in 1695. Coquina, a soft local shellrock, was used for massive walls that rise thirty feet above a moat (on three sides) and the bay (on the fourth side). More than sixty cannons once lined the gundeck. Although attacked more than once, the fort was never conquered. From the deck, visitors have a fine view of the bay, downtown, a partially rebuilt city wall, and the Old City Gate. Exhibits trace its remarkable history through 1900 when it was decommissioned.

Colee's Sightseeing Carriages   *(904)829-2818*
   downtown on Avenida Menendez

Horse-drawn carriages are a relaxing way to enjoy a narrated tour of the bayfront and narrow streets of the historic downtown area. Evening tours are especially romantic. This operator has been serving the carriage trade with horse-drawn vehicles since before the advent of cars.

Downtown
   centered around St. George St. & Cathedral Place

Downtown St. Augustine by Matanzas Bay is one of America's most delightfully human-scaled business districts. Over more than 400 years it has become a treasury of architectural landmarks and intimate historic structures amid colorful subtropical gardens. Many regional specialty shops, gourmet food stalls, and sophisticated restaurants tempt pedestrians on St. George Street (closed to vehicles) and narrow palm-lined streets nearby. Several fine inns are within an easy stroll of the picturesque plaza in the heart of town.

Fishing Charters
   Camachee Cove Sportfishing Charters   *(904)825-1971*
   3 mi. NE on FL A1A

Sportfishing trips with everything furnished can be reserved to locales ranging from the Intracoastal Waterway to the Gulf Stream.

Flagler College   *(904)829-6481*
downtown at 74 King St.
In 1888, Henry Flagler opened the Ponce de Leon Hotel, a masterpiece
of Spanish Renaissance architecture. The monumental structure (on
the National Historic Register) became a college in 1967. Lavish
fixtures, including 75 windows by Louis Tiffany (who designed the
interior and later became famous for his glass artistry) and an 80-foot-
high rotunda with distinctive female murals can be viewed during
guided tours in summer. The public can also attend concerts and
performing arts year-round.

Florida Heritage Museum   *(904)829-3800*   *(800)397-4071*
just N at 167 San Marcos Av.
The **Old Jail** (circa 1890s) now houses a large collection of weapons
used in crimes, plus photographs and exhibits related to prison life.
Next door, the **Florida Heritage Museum** traces Florida's growth
from pre-European cultures through the 1800s with extensive displays
of relics and Flagler memorabilia. **Historical Tours** offers a variety
of narrated hour (and longer) tours of areas in and near town aboard
open-air trolleys.

Fountain of Youth Archeological Park *(904)829-3168 (800)356-8222*
just N via FL A1A at 11 Magnolia Av.
Expansive subtropical grounds include Ponce de Leon's reputed landing
place in 1513 when he became the first European to set foot on the
mainland of North America. Nearby is the spring claimed to be the
Fountain of Youth, museum exhibits related to Spanish colonization,
a planetarium, a two-story revolving globe, and a well-stocked gift
shop.

The Lightner Museum   *(904)824-2874*
downtown at 75 King St.
The former Hotel Alcazar (another of Henry Flagler's elaborate hotels
opened in 1888) became a major museum in 1948. Otto Lightner, a
Chicago publisher and editor of *Hobbies Magazine*, converted the
empty hotel into three floors of outstanding artifacts of Victorian daily
life. Extensive collections of Tiffany stained glass, cut crystal, and
costumes are highlights, along with mechanical musical instruments
that are deomonstrated daily. The former indoor pool is a mall with
quality antique shops.

Marineland   *(904)471-1111   (800)824-4218*
18 mi. S on FL A1A at 9507 Ocean Shore Blvd. - Marineland
The world's original oceanarium still features giant salt and freshwater
tanks full of exotic marine life. Subtropically landscaped grounds by an
Atlantic beach also feature performing dolphins and other sea animal
shows, underwater hand-feeding of saltwater fish, a natural habitat for
alligators and birds, penguin park, Aquarius Cinema, and a seashell
museum.

Oldest House   *(904)824-2872*
just S at 14 St. Francis St.
The St. Augustine Historical Society's Gonzalez-Alvarez House is on a
site continuously occupied since the early 1600s. The current building,
with coquina walls and hand-hewn cedar beams, dates from the early
1700s. Room furnishings reflect its use as a Spanish, British and
American home for over 250 years. The complex also includes
museums dedicated to the town's history and Florida's army, a library,
ornamental garden, and museum store.

St. Augustine Alligator Farm   *(904)824-3337*
2 mi. SE on FL A1A at 999 Anastasia Blvd.
The world's original alligator attraction was founded here more than a century ago in 1893. The complex features the only complete collection of all twenty-three species of crocodilians. An elevated walkway winds through a lush lagoon where wild swamp creatures of all kinds can be seen in their natural habitat. Alligators and other wildlife shows are presented hourly.

St. Augustine Lighthouse & Museum   *(904)829-0745*
2 mi. E via FL A1A & Old Beach Rd. at 81 Lighthouse Av.
The restored lightkeeper's house now houses maritime memorabilia, a related video presentation, a gallery of local art, and a gift shop. The adjoining candy-striped lighthouse tower is 165 feet tall. Visitors may climb 219 steps for a fine panorama of the old town and surrounding waterways.

Sightseeing Trains   *(904)829-6545*   *(800)226-6545*
just N at 170 San Marco Av.
A fun, fast way to get acquainted with St. Augustine is aboard one of the open-air cars pulled by a jaunty little rubber-tired engine. A narrated tour with stop-off privileges to attractions covers seven miles in one hour. Trains depart every 15-20 minutes throughout the day.

Spanish Quarter Museum   *(904)825-6830*
downtown at 29 St. George St.
St. Augustine's Restored Spanish Quarter is a living history showcase of many reconstructed and restored homes and buildings from the 18th century Colonial period. Costumed guides demonstrate crafts like weaving, woodworking and cooking amid period artifacts and decor. There is a notable museum store.

RESTAURANTS

Columbia Restaurant   *(904)824-3341 (800)227-1905*
downtown at 98 St. George St.
L-D.   *Expensive*
Florida's famous little chain of restaurants featuring Spanish and Cuban cuisine is well represented. The paella, or red snapper alicante, are fine and the in-house bakery displays delicious guava and cream cheese turnovers and many other enticements. The bustling dining courtyard and atrium are a horticultural delight.

Conch House Restaurant   *(904)829-8646*   *(800)940-6256*
1 mi. E at 57 Comares Av.
B-L-D.   *Expensive*
Conch stars in fritters, steamed and burgers, along with a Florida cracker feast in a marina-view dining room, deck and patio.

Creekside Dinery   *(904)829-6113*
2 mi. SW at 160 Nix Boatyard Rd.
D only.   *Moderate*
Fresh local seafood, chicken, and beef become the right stuff amidst Florida cracker decor distinguished by a jasmine-shrouded wraparound porch under mature magnolia trees.

Gypsy Cab Company   *(904)829-8244*
1 mi. E at 828 Anastasia Blvd.
L-D.   *Expensive*
Hearty helpings of creative regional cuisine, including delicious desserts like key lime pie and Florida peach cake, have made this easy-going Bohemian bistro one of the region's most popular dining destinations.

King's Forge Restaurant & Lounge   *(904)829-1488*
downtown at 12 Avenida Menendez
L-D.   *Expensive*
An appealing selection of contemporary American steaks, seafood, and
chicken dishes complements a spectacular view of the fort from the
second floor dining room and balcony.

La Parisienne Restaurant   *(904)829-0055*
downtown at 60 Hypolita St.
L-D.   *Expensive*
Authentic French and Continental specialties and housemade baked
goods and desserts are served in a casually elegant setting with Old
World touches.

The Monk's Vineyard   *(904)824-5888*
downtown at 56 St. George St.
L only.   *Moderate*
The grilled catch, shrimp casserole, designer sandwiches and salads,
and homemade desserts, plus decor appropriate to the name, have
made this a deservedly popular place for lunch.

The Oasis   *(904)471-3424*
4 mi. SE at 4000 S. A1A & Ocean Trace Rd.
B-L-D.   *Moderate*
American comfort food for the whole family includes jumbo muffins and
homemade biscuits and desserts. The casual beach restaurant also
sports an upper deck and bar with open-air seating.

Old City House Restaurant   *(904)826-0781*
downtown at 115 Cordova St.
D only.   *Expensive*
Creative American cuisine has won critical acclaim for this casually
elegant restaurant in the Old City House Inn.

Saltwater Cowboy's   *(904)471-2332*
5 mi. SE via A1A at 299 Dondanville Rd.
D only.   *Moderate*
Saltwater Cowboy's is one of the region's best restaurants. "Florida
Cracker" dishes (alligator tail, catfish, frog legs, etc.) are delicious, as
are less adventurous broiled and baked seafoods, open-pit barbecue
meats and homemade pies. Dining rooms overlooking a saltwater
marsh capture the charm of a turn-of-the-century fish camp.

LODGING

Modern motels are abundant on the outskirts, while many first-rate
bed-and-breakfast inns enhance the historic heart of town. Weekends
and winter are prime time. Rates are often reduced 15% or more at
other times.

Alexander Homestead   *(904)826-4147*
downtown at 14 Sevilla St. - 32084
4 units   *(800)555-4147*   *Moderate-Expensive*
A Victorian home was transformed into a bed-and-breakfast with many
heirlooms and artifacts. Breakfast is complimentary. Each well-
furnished room has a private bath. The "Alexandria" has a whirlpool
bath and woodburning fireplace.

Anchorage Motor Inn   *(904)829-9041*
other side of bridge from downtown at 1 Dolphin Dr. - 32084
38 units   *Moderate*
A location by the Bridge of Lions is a real feature. The modern bayside
motel also has a pool. Each comfortable room has a private balcony or
patio overlooking the water and downtown.

Casa de la Paz   (904)829-2915
downtown at 22 Avenida Menendez - 32084
6 units   (800)929-2915   *Moderate-Expensive*
A handsome Mediterranean-style home is now a gracious bed-and-breakfast with quality antiques and contemporary conveniences. Full breakfast is complimentary. All rooms are well furnished.

Casa de Suenos Bed & Breakfast   (904)824-0887
downtown at 20 Cordova St. - 32084
6 units   (800)824-0804   *Moderate-Expensive*
A turn-of-the-century Mediterranean-style home now provides Old World style and contemporary comfort. A full breakfast and other treats and bicycles are complimentary. Each well-furnished room has a private bath. One room has an in-room whirlpool and a fireplace.

Casablanca Inn Bed & Breakfast   (904)829-0928
downtown at 24 Avenida Menendez - 32084
12 units   (800)826-2626   *Moderate-Expensive*
Verandas overlook the bay and historic district from this carefully restored 1914 home. Full breakfast and afternoon refreshments are complimentary. Each well-furnished room has some antiques and a private bath, but no phone or TV.

Cedar House Inn   (904)829-0079
downtown at 79 Cedar St. - 32084
6 units   (800)233-2746   *Moderate-Expensive*
A restored 1893 Victorian home now offers period furnishings plus complimentary full breakfast and other treats, bicycles and an outdoor whirlpool. Each well-furnished room has a whirlpool or clawfoot tub, not no phone.

Holiday Inn - Beachside   (904)471-2555
4 mi. SE at 860 A1A Beach Blvd. - 32084
151 units   (800)626-7263   *Moderate-Expensive*
The area's biggest oceanfront lodging is a five-story motor inn by the beach with a pool, coffee shop, and lounge. Each room is well furnished. Many have ocean view balconies.

Radisson Ponce de Leon Golf & Conference Resort (904)824-2821
3 mi. N at 4000 U.S. Highway 1 North - 32095
193 units   (800)333-3333   *Moderate*
St. Augustine's premier golf resort borders marshlands some distance from downtown or the beach. Amenities include an oversized pool, six tennis courts, putting green and (fee) 18-hole golf course, plus a restaurant, entertainment lounge, and gift shop. Each spacious room is newly redecorated and well furnished.

Westcott House   (904)824-4301
downtown at 146 Avenida Menendez - 32084
9 units   *Expensive*
This romantic Victorian overlooking the bay features the elegance of yesteryear with all modern conveniences. Continental breakfast is complimentary. Each room is beautifully furnished with antiques.

BASIC INFORMATION

Elevation: 7 feet   *Population (1990):* 11,692
Location: 38 mi. Southeast of Jacksonville, FL
Nearest airport with commercial flights: Jacksonville - 48 miles
St. Augustine Visitors Info Center   (904)825-1000
 just N at 10 Castillo Dr.
St. Johns County Visitors & Conv. Bureau (904)829-1711 (800)653-2489
 just S at 888 Riberia St., Suite 250 - 32084   *www.oldcity.com*

Vero Beach, Florida

Vero Beach is the refined respite along Florida's teeming east coast. The heart of town is on a subtropical barrier island with miles of soft sand beaches along the Atlantic Ocean. Indian River and the Intracoastal Waterway parallel the strand two miles inland. Settlement began with construction of a coastal railroad about a century ago. Major growth didn't begin until the 1950s, when Indian River citrus won renown, and the local abundance of water recreation sites and warm winters finally caused tourism to surge.

Transformation into a resort community continues today, with most recent development occurring on the island near the beach. A trim little oceanfront business district is replacing the original town center on the mainland with a growing number of specialty shops and most of Vero Beach's finest restaurants. The best lodgings all have choice locations by the beach in or near the "new downtown," and Disney's first oceanfront resort is only a few miles north.

WEATHER PROFILE

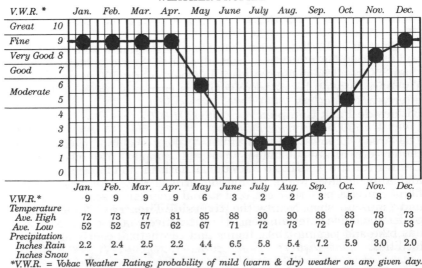

V.W.R. *		Jan.	Feb.	Mar.	Apr.	May	June	July	Aug.	Sep.	Oct.	Nov.	Dec.
Great	10												
Fine	9												
Very Good	8												
Good	7												
Moderate	6												
	5												
	4												
	3												
	2												
	1												
	0												

	Jan.	Feb.	Mar.	Apr.	May	June	July	Aug.	Sep.	Oct.	Nov.	Dec.
V.W.R.*	9	9	9	9	6	3	2	2	3	5	8	9
Temperature												
Ave. High	72	73	77	81	85	88	90	90	88	83	78	73
Ave. Low	52	52	57	62	67	71	72	73	72	67	60	53
Precipitation												
Inches Rain	2.2	2.4	2.5	2.2	4.4	6.5	5.8	5.4	7.2	5.9	3.0	2.0
Inches Snow	-	-	-	-	-	-	-	-	-	-	-	-

*V.W.R. = Vokac Weather Rating; probability of mild (warm & dry) weather on any given day.

ATTRACTIONS

Beaches   *(561)231-5790*
Waters of the nearby Gulf Stream warm the Atlantic Ocean along miles of white sand beaches in town. Swimming, diving and surfing are popular, along with beachcombing and fishing. A pier, and parks with lifeguards, showers, restrooms and picnic facilities are major destinations along the strand in town.

Bicycling
The ocean, Indian River and subtropical landscapes are scenic backdrops to tours along Vero Beach's flat barrier island. All sorts of bicycles can be rented by the hour or longer at shops in the area.

Boat Rentals
Fishing and pontoon boats, jet skis, canoes and kayaks can be rented for adventures on miles of the placid, picturesque Indian River estuary. Rentals can be arranged for a half day or longer at several places in and near town.

Fishing Charters
Both Indian River (the longest estuary on the continent) and deep sea waters offer rich sportfishing rewards. Numerous charters leave from Vero Beach and vicinity. Guides and all equipment are provided for half and full day trips.

Food Specialty
Hale Groves   *(561)562-3653   (800)289-4253*
just S at 580 S. US 1
Hale Groves is America's preeminent provider of citrus products. A local business started in 1947 now has their own groves of famed Indian River citrus, a packing plant in nearby Wabasso, four modern friendly stores and a catalog full of premium citrus, juices and related gourmet gifts. Florida's finest citrus comes from this area, and Hale's still offers a free glass of remarkably sweet fresh juice.

Indian River Citrus Museum   *(561)770-2263*
2 mi. W at 2140 14th Av.
The renowned Indian River fruit industry, centered around Vero Beach, is traced from the Spanish explorers through today. Features include historic photographs, artifacts and memorabilia, video, guided citrus tours and a gift shop.

McKee Botanical Gardens   *(561)234-1949*
4 mi. N at 4871 N. FL A1A
Founded in 1932, the garden features a mixture of native vegetation and tropical plants and trees from all over the world. A stand of more than 300 royal palms and a giant live oak nearly 500 years old star. The once-thriving botanical collection is currently under restoration after years of neglect.

Riverside Park Complex   *(561)231-0707*
just W at 3001 Riverside Park Dr.
The area's foremost park is situated along the Indian River. The centerpiece is an outstanding cultural complex. The neo-classical **Center for the Arts** has a collection of national and international art, and also displays works by Florida artists. Other features include films, concerts, performances, educational programs, a sculpture garden and a museum shop. Nearby, the **Riverside Theatre** (231-6990) offers professional live entertainment. The attractively landscaped park also has bike and jogging trails, tennis and racquetball courts and picnic facilities.

Sebastian Inlet State Recreation Area   *(561)589-9659*

16 mi. N at 9700 S. FL A1A - Melbourne Beach

Indian River and the Atlantic Ocean border what is said to be Florida's most-visited state park. A remarkable diversity of plants and wildlife (including one-third of American manatees) share the choice location by the estuary inlet. This is generally regarded as one of the best surfing sites on the eastern seaboard. In addition, swimming, diving, fishing, clamming and boating are enjoyed, and there are extensive picnic facilities and complete campgrounds.

RESTAURANTS

Beachside Restaurant   *(561)234-4477*

downtown at 3125 Ocean Dr.

B-L-D.   *Moderate*

The most (deservedly) popular breakfast place for miles has featured carefully prepared homestyle American dishes for years. Hanging plants and flowers enliven the cozy congested dining room.

The Black Pearl   *(561)234-4426*

downtown at 2855 Ocean Dr.

L-D.   *Expensive*

Creative American cuisine like onion-crusted grouper with a citrus glaze and homemade desserts have won critical and popular acclaim for a dinner house with similarly eclectic decor.

Cafe Du Soir   *(561)569-4607*

2 mi. W at 21 Royal Palm Blvd.

D only.   *Very Expensive*

Classic French cuisine is skillfully attended in a casually elegant (jackets suggested) upstairs dinner house with an established following.

Mr. Manatee's Casual Grille   *(561)569-9151*

2 mi. W at 30 Royal Palm Blvd.

L-D.   *Moderate*

All sorts of finger foods like popcorn bay scallops or gator-tail bites are featured on a contemporary American menu. The relaxed, riverfront restaurant also has a bar and outside seating.

Ocean Grill   *(561)231-5409*

downtown at 1050 Sexton Plaza

L-D.   *Expensive*

Mediterranean seafood chowder and pompano with apricot butter are fine examples of seafood specialties served in a comfortably rustic dining room and lounge overlooking the beach and surf.

Riverside Cafe   *(561)234-5550*

just W at 1 Beachland Blvd.

L-D.   *Moderate*

All-American pub grub includes some treats like regional fresh seafood and housemade tequila lime pie. Funky dining areas and a bar are on the waterfront and share a fine view of the Intracoastal Waterway and the Barber Bridge.

Tangos   *(561)231-1550*

downtown at 925 Bougainvillea Lane

D only.   *Very Expensive*

The area's best dinner house transforms local seafood and produce into creative American cuisine, complemented by housemade breads and luscious desserts like banana bread pudding with butter rum ice cream. European bistro decor offers a casually chic setting with a view of the open show kitchen, or patio dining.

LODGING

Accommodations are plentiful. Most are surprisingly prosaic. The best are by the beach. Winter is high season. Rates are usually reduced at least 20% in summer.

Aquarious Oceanfront Resort Motel   *(561)231-5218*
1 mi. S at 1526 S. Ocean Dr. - 32963
27 units   *Moderate-Expensive*
This oceanfront apartment motel has a pool. Compact standard motel rooms and larger units with kitchens lack ocean views.

Disney's Vero Beach Resort   *(561)234-2000*
7 mi. N via A1A at 9250 Island Grove Terrace - 32963
172 units   *(800)359-8000   Expensive-Very Expensive*
Disney's first oceanfront resort opened in a remote natural area in 1995. The family-oriented five-story complex has a Victorian seaside resort theme. Amenities include the beach, large pool, whirlpool, sauna, two lighted tennis courts, sports court, exercise room, game room, resort store and two restaurants. Beautifully furnished units have a private balcony or porch and range from garden-view hotel rooms to two-bedroom oceanside suites or cottages with a kitchen and a whirlpool bath.

Doubletree Guest Suites   *(561)231-5666*
downtown at 3500 Ocean Dr. - 32963
55 units   *(800)841-5666*   *Very Expensive*
The beach borders this contempo four-story motor hotel with a palm-shaded pool, whirlpool, coffee shop and lounge. Each spacious one- or two-bedroom suite is beautifully furnished. Many have a private ocean-view balcony.

Holiday Inn Oceanside   *(561)231-2300*
downtown at 3384 Ocean Dr. - 32963
104 units   *(800)465-4329*   *Expensive*
This refurbished motor hotel bordering the beach in the heart of the seaside downtown area has a pool, coffee shop and entertainment lounge. Each unit is well furnished. Many have a private patio or balcony with an ocean view.

Palm Court Resort   *(561)231-2800*
downtown at 3244 Ocean Dr. - 32963
110 units   *(800)245-3297*   *Moderate-Expensive*
A splendid beach adjoins this five-story modern motor hotel in the heart of the action. A pool, restaurant and entertainment lounge are also available. Units are well furnished. Many have a private ocean-view patio or balcony.

Vero Beach Inn   *(561)231-9547*
1 mi. N at 4700 N. FL A1A - 32963
104 units   *(800)227-8615*   *Moderate*
A lovely beach adjoins this four-story modern motor hotel with a large outdoor pool, coffee shop and entertainment lounge. Each unit is comfortably furnished. Many have an ocean view.

BASIC INFORMATION

Elevation: 14 feet   Population (1990): 17,350
Location: 100 miles Southeast of Orlando
Nearest airport with commercial flights: in town
Indian River County Chamber of Commerce (561)567-3491
   downtown at 1216 21st St. (Box 2947) - 32961   (800)338-2678 x 802
www.vero-beach.fl.us/chamber

St. Simons Island, Georgia

St. Simons Island is the heart of Georgia's semitropical barrier islands. The largest of these "Golden Isles" bordering the Atlantic Ocean was settled by the English in 1736. Rich live oak timberlands and cotton plantations sustained development until the Civil War when Sherman's forces destroyed the estates, and the island became a forgotten backwater. The island's destiny as a warm winter getaway began in the 1920s when East Coast millionaires began transforming plantations into resorts.

Today, sandy beaches and coastal water sports can be enjoyed by everyone. The island's pristine marshes are a nature lover's paradise, and a backdrop to championship golf courses. Magnificent live oaks form moss-draped canopies over roads and pathways in and beyond the village. By the waterfront in the heart of town, a choice little array of galleries, shops and restaurants features local art and coastal cuisine. Lodgings are scarce, but include three fine resorts.

WEATHER PROFILE

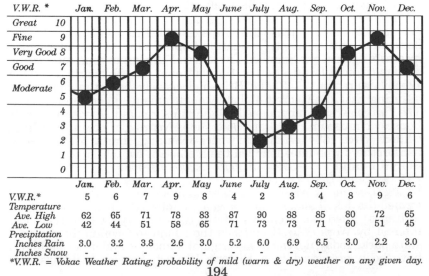

V.W.R. *		Jan.	Feb.	Mar.	Apr.	May	June	July	Aug.	Sep.	Oct.	Nov.	Dec.
Great	10												
Fine	9												
Very Good	8												
Good	7												
Moderate	6 5												
	4												
	3												
	2												
	1												
	0												

	Jan.	Feb.	Mar.	Apr.	May	June	July	Aug.	Sep.	Oct.	Nov.	Dec.
V.W.R.*	5	6	7	9	8	4	2	3	4	8	9	6
Temperature												
Ave. High	62	65	71	78	83	87	90	88	85	80	72	65
Ave. Low	42	44	51	58	65	71	73	73	71	60	51	45
Precipitation												
Inches Rain	3.0	3.2	3.8	2.6	3.0	5.2	6.0	6.9	6.5	3.0	2.2	3.0
Inches Snow	-	-	-	-	-	-	-	-	-	-	-	-

*V.W.R. = Vokac Weather Rating; probability of mild (warm & dry) weather on any given day.

Beaches
1 mi. NE via Ocean Blvd.
Several miles of sandy public beaches face the Atlantic Ocean. Access is easy at Massengale Park, where there are picnic facilities and restrooms, and around the Coast Guard Station on East Beach.

Bicycling
A fine system of bike paths, rural lanes in sylvan tunnels of moss-shrouded oaks, and relatively flat terrain connect peaceful village streets, historic sites, and coastal byways. Half-day and longer rentals, plus maps and accessories, are available at:

Barry's Beach Service, Inc.	*(912)638-8053*
Benjy's Bike Shop	*(912)638-6766*
Island Bike Shop	*(912)638-0705*

Boat Rentals
Barry's Beach Services Inc.   *(912)638-8053*
1 mi. N at 420 Arnold Rd.
Sailboats and sea kayak rentals and lessons are available here. You can also arrange a kayak nature tour.

Boat Rides
Scenic boat trips range from marsh tours on pontoon boats to river and coastal nature cruises featuring alligator or dolphin watching. Sunset, moonlight or dinner cruises can also be reserved at several charters.

Downtown
centered around Mallory St. S of Ocean Blvd.
"The Village" is a picturesque little heart of town with trim historic and contemporary buildings surrounded by flowers and ancient oaks draped with moss. Regional handicrafts and food specialties are featured in numerous shops and restaurants near a palm-studded park and fishing pier by the ocean. Narrated trolley tours begin here.

Fishing Charters
A wealth of saltwater sportfishing and diving adventures can be arranged for in-shore, offshore, deep sea and Gulf Stream locales. Guided half-day and longer trips with all equipment can be reserved on the island with several charter companies.

Fort Frederica National Monument   *(912)638-3639*
7 mi. N on Frederica Rd.
Georgia's founder, James Oglethorpe, established a fort and a walled settlement with a moat on this blufftop in 1736 to defend English interests against the Spanish. The site was the largest and most costly British colonial fortification on the continent. At the nearby Battle of Bloody Marsh in 1742, the British decisively beat the Spaniards, assuring that the Georgia Colony would remain under English rule. The fort was soon abandoned. Only ruins remain. A visitor center houses a museum, film, and gift shop. Nearby is beautiful Christ Church (circa 1884) on the site where John and Charles Wesley (English brothers who later founded the Methodist church) first preached.

Jekyll Island   *(912)635-3636   (800)841-6586*
15 mi. S via US 17 & GA 50
In 1886, some of America's richest families bought the island and formed the Jekyll Island Club. Soon a grandiose clubhouse and elegant "cottages" filled the exclusive winter retreat. Later generations lost interest by World War II and sold the island to Georgia for use as a state park. Today, dozens of the original mansions and other buildings have been preserved in a Historic District. Service buildings now

serve as restaurants and specialty shops, while the original clubhouse is a hotel. Visitors can explore the Historic District on foot, by tram, or in a horse-drawn carriage. Numerous oceanfront lodgings and restaurants are sprinkled for several miles along Beachview Drive. For a contemporary counterpoint, **Summer Waves Water Park** features a wave pool, lazy river and assorted waterslides.

Museum of Coastal History   *(912)638-4666*
   just E at 101 12th St.
A restored 1872 lighthouse keeper's home houses exhibits of local history. The adjacent 104-foot-high brick lighthouse has been in continuous use since 1872. The view from the top is outstanding.

RESTAURANTS

Allegro Garden Room   *(912)638-7097*
   2 mi. N at 2465 Deinere Rd.
   D only.   *Expensive*
Some of the best contemporary American cuisine in the region is featured on an eclectic menu offered in a chic dining room. There is also a sophisticated cafe and courtyard dining.

Bennie's Red Barn   *(912)638-2844*
   5 mi. N at 5514 Frederica Rd.
   D only.   *Moderate*
Steaks and seafood can be fine from the oak wood grill, and toothsome pecan and key lime pies are made here. A big rustic barn has been comfortably outfitted to please hungry guests since 1954.

Blanche's Courtyard   *(912)638-3030*
   downtown at 440 Kings Way
   D only.   *Moderate*
Fresh broiled seafood, steaks, and fowl have been served amid cozy Bayou Victorian atmosphere for more than two decades.

Brogen's   *(912)638-1660*
   downtown at 200 Pier Alley
   L-D.   *Moderate*
Charbroiled burgers and other American comfort foods provide an excuse to relax in the laid-back bar or dining porch with an ocean view.

CJ's Italian Restaurant   *(912)634-1022*
   downtown at 405 Mallory St.
   D only.   *Moderate*
The fresh bread sticks with marinara sauce alone would be worth a trip. But, some of the best handcrafted pizzas and calzones in Georgia are served with tap beers in a classy little parlor.

Delaney's   *(912)638-1330*
   2 mi. N at 3415 Frederica Rd.
   L-D.   *Expensive*
Top-quality provisions are skillfully prepared for well-regarded contemporary American cuisine served in a casually sophisticated bistro.

Dressner's Village Cafe   *(912)634-1217*
   downtown at 223 Mallory St.
   B-L.   *Low*
Breakfast is featured all day (including biscuits made from scratch) in a simply comfortable coffee shop.

Frannie's Place Restaurant   *(912)638-1001*
   downtown at 318 Mallory St.
   L only.   *Moderate*
Award-winning Brunswick stew and other coastal Georgia specialties are complemented by impressive desserts in this intimate cottage.

LODGING

Island lodgings are scarce. While most are prosaic, there are three delightful resorts. Spring and summer are high season. Rates are usually reduced as much as 30% at other times.

The Cloister   *(912)638-3611*
  5 mi. NE on Sea Island Dr. - Sea Island 31561
  262 units   *(800)732-4752*   *Very Expensive*
One of America's most exclusive coastal resorts is tucked away on a little island by the ocean. Facilities include a beach club with a private beach, two pools, whirlpool, steam room, sauna, and exercise equipment. Fee amenities include a golf club with 54 holes, eighteen tennis courts, riding stables, trap and skeet shooting, aquatic gear and lessons, dock fishing, boat cruises, bicycles and fitness/beauty spa. All meals are included in opulent or sea-view dining rooms. Some of their luxuriously furnished units have a private deck and an oceanfront view.

The King and Prince Beach & Golf Resort   *(912)638-3631*
  1 mi. NE at 201 Arnold Rd. (Box 20798) - 31522
  169 units   *(800)342-0212*   *Expensive-Very Expensive*
For more than sixty years, this Mediterranean-style oceanfront resort has sprawled along a white sand beach. Amenities include a large indoor pool and whirlpool, three outdoor pools, four tennis courts, exercise rooms, and (fee) golf nearby, watercraft, and bicycles. There is also a fine beachfront dining room and lounge. Each unit is beautifully furnished. Many have an oceanview deck, including 45 villas with kitchens.

Queen's Court   *(912)638-8459*
  downtown at 437 Kings Way - 31522
  23 units   *Moderate*
The heart of the village and a beach are within walking distance of this motel. Each unit is comfortably furnished.

St. Simons Inn by the Lighthouse   *(912)638-1101*
  downtown at 609 Beachview Dr. - 31522
  34 units   *Moderate*
A beach is a short stroll from this motel with a small pool. Each comfortable unit has a kitchenette. Some have a whirlpool tub.

Sea Gate Inn   *(912)638-8661*
  1 mi. NE at 1014 Ocean Blvd. - 31522
  48 units   *(800)562-8812*   *Moderate-Expensive*
An ocean beach adjoins this motel with a pool. Each unit (up to two bedrooms) is nicely furnished. Some have a private beachfront deck.

Sea Palms Golf and Tennis Resort   *(912)638-3351*
  5 mi. N at 5445 Frederica Rd. - 31522
  140 units   *(800)841-6268*   *Expensive*
This upscale conference resort overlooks marshes and golf courses. In addition to 27 holes of (fee) championship golf, there are two pools, 12 (fee) tennis courts, rental bicycles, a restaurant and lounge. Each spacious, well-furnished unit has a private patio or balcony.

BASIC INFORMATION

Elevation: 10 feet   Population (1990): 12,026
Location: 80 miles North of Jacksonville, FL
Nearest airport with commercial flights: Brunswick - 12 miles
Brunswich & the Golden Isles Visitors Bureau   (912)265-0620
  7 mi. W at 4 Glynn Av. - Brunswick 31520   (800)933-2627
St. Simons Island Visitors Center   (912)638-9014
  downtown at 530 B Beachview Dr. - 31522

Coeur d'Alene, Idaho

Coeur d'Alene is the hub of a Rocky Mountain water wonderland. Surrounded by lakes and rivers, it shares the northern shore of one of the world's most beautiful lakes with a luxuriant pine forest that extends to nearby mountains and beyond. Originally a military outpost after the Indian Wars during the late 19th century, the town prospered with the coming of the transcontinental railroad and the lumber industry, and a brief, colorful steamboating era.

Coeur d'Alene is now a large and lively vacation destination. One of America's best resorts connects a picturesque downtown to a superb lakefront park with colorful gardens, tree-shaded picnic sites, a scenic promenade by a long sandy beach, swimming areas, a handsome museum, and a municipal pier for a variety of lake cruises. An increasing number of distinctive restaurants, specialty shops and lodgings serve visitors here to enjoy the lake and surrounding rivers, forests and mountains.

WEATHER PROFILE

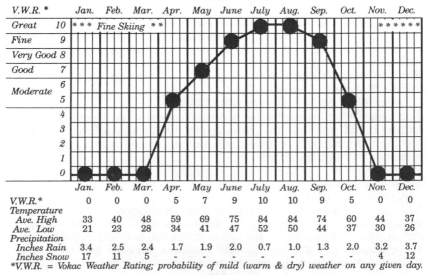

V.W.R. *		Jan.	Feb.	Mar.	Apr.	May	June	July	Aug.	Sep.	Oct.	Nov.	Dec.
V.W.R.*		0	0	0	5	7	9	10	10	9	5	0	0
Temperature													
Ave. High		33	40	48	59	69	75	84	84	74	60	44	37
Ave. Low		21	23	28	34	41	47	52	50	44	37	30	26
Precipitation													
Inches Rain		3.4	2.5	2.4	1.7	1.9	2.0	0.7	1.0	1.3	2.0	3.2	3.7
Inches Snow		17	11	5	-	-	-	-	-	-	-	4	12

*V.W.R. = Vokac Weather Rating; probability of mild (warm & dry) weather on any given day.

198

ATTRACTIONS

City Park and Beach   *(208)769-2252*
just W of downtown
One of the West's most picturesque urban parks has a long sandy south-facing beach on Lake Coeur d'Alene. Lifeguards oversee popular lake swimming in summer. A lakefront promenade extends to the world's longest floating boardwalk downtown. Noble trees shade choice picnic and recreation facilities throughout the park.

Coeur d'Alene National Forest   *(208)765-7223*
begins 3 mi. E
Recreation opportunities abound on mountains, lakes, and rivers in this lush pine forest. Boating, fishing, swimming, camping, hiking, backpacking, and hunting are popular. River running is a special feature of the Coeur d'Alene River. Various winter sports are also enjoyed.

Lake Coeur d'Alene
adjacent to downtown on S side
One of the loveliest lakes in the nation is more than thirty miles long, averages two miles wide, and has 110 miles of shoreline. Surrounded by mountains and lush pine forests, it is a deservedly renowned destination. Scenic lake cruises lasting two hours or all day can be arranged. So can float plane flights, parasailing, fishing charters, and all kinds of watercraft rentals. Lakeside recreation facilities in town and scattered down-lake provide a notable variety of boating, water-skiing, fishing, swimming, and camping opportunities in summer. A scenic loop highway circles the lake and provides access to numerous recreation sites and viewpoints.

Museum of North Idaho   *(208)664-3448*
downtown at 108 Northwest Blvd.
This contemporary museum features a notable exhibit from the days when Lake Coeur d'Alene was the steamboating capital of the West. Other exhibits depict the history of logging and Indians in the area.

Silverwood Theme Park   *(208)683-3400*
15 mi. N on US 95
Part of the region's biggest family fun park looks like a turn-of-the-century mining town with restaurants, saloon, general store, and theaters. Over in Country Carnival is a steam train and whitewater rapids. The largest wooden roller coaster in the Northwest, a looping metal coaster, and a log flume ride, are highlights among many other attractions.

Warm Water Feature
Wild Waters   *(208)667-6491*
1.5 mi. N at 2119 N. Government Way
From late May into September, assorted waterslides race down a sixty-foot-high hill and end in heated pools. Other attractions include a soothing inner tube river ride, a large lawn for picnics and sunbathing, a snack shop and an arcade.

Winter Sports
Silver Mountain   *(208)783-1111*
38 mi. SE off I-90 - Kellogg
The world's longest (3 miles) gondola provides access to Silver Mountain in 19 minutes. The vertical rise is 2,200 feet and the longest run is well over two miles. Elevation at the top is 6,300 feet. There are five chairlifts and the gondola. All facilities, services and rentals are available at the area. The skiing season in mid-November to April.

RESTAURANTS
The Beachouse Restaurant   *(208)664-6464*
2 mi. E at 3204 E. Coeur d'Alene Lake Dr.
L-D.   *Expensive*
Contemporary American fare is topped by a good variety of steaks prepared with a special extra-heat oven. Don't miss their huckleberry cobbler. The popular lakeside roadhouse offers comfortable dining areas, an alfresco deck, and bar that share a lovely lakefront view.

The Cedars Floating Restaurant   *(208)664-2922*
2 mi. W via US 95 on Blackwell Island
D only.   *Expensive*
Savory seafood like crabcakes and (seasonal) Copper River salmon star among fine contemporary American dishes served along with delicious sourdough french bread and a choice of soup or salad bar. The big comfortable semicircular dining room provides a grand panoramic view of the lake, downtown, and mountains from its floating base. A jaunty lounge and alfresco view deck adjoin.

The Coeur d'Alene Resort   *(208)765-4000*
downtown at 115 S. 2nd St.
B-L-D.   *Expensive*
Beverly's (L-D) is one of the great resort dinner houses in the West. Traditional and innovative American cuisine, where the presentation is as artistic as the food is flavorful, is showcased in dishes like ostrich satay appetizers and luscious desserts topped by a huckleberry souffle. A window-wall view of the lake and mountains from the seventh-floor dining areas and lounge is sublime. **Dockside** (B-L-D) serves contemporary American fare in a big handsome tri-level dining room overlooking the lake and marina. A plush entertainment lounge adjoins.

Cricket's Restaurant & Oyster Bar   *(208)765-1990*
downtown at 424 Sherman Av.
L-D.   *Moderate*
A long list of grazing possibilities includes most American comfort foods, and there are more than a dozen tap beers to wash it down. The lounge and dining areas are festooned with a wealth of nifty nostalgic artifacts. Out back, a covered dining deck overlooks the lake.

Hudson's Hamburgers   *(208)664-5444*
downtown at 207 Sherman Av.
L only.   *Low*
The specialty hasn't changed in ninety years—burgers, plain and simple. Their freshness and quality still fill the little cafe with fans.

Jimmy D's   *(208)664-9774*
downtown at 320 Sherman Av.
L-D.   *Expensive*
Fresh Northwestern cuisine is expertly prepared in outstanding dishes like (seasonal) Yukon salmon, clams in citrus saffron cream, and cheese-topped foccacia. The sophisticated fare is complemented by a dining room and bar with the panache of a Continental sidewalk cafe.

Roger's Homemade Ice Cream   *(208)765-5419*
1 mi. E at 1224 Sherman Av.
L-D.   *Low*
A dozen flavors of homemade ice cream star in all kinds of cold treats. There are also burgers and other light fare in this little corner stand with a covered picnic seating area.

3rd Street Cantina   *(208)664-0581*
downtown at 201 N. 3rd St.
L-D.   *Moderate*
Third Street Cantina is deservedly one of the most popular restaurants
in the region. All sorts of traditional and innovative Mexican dishes are
carefully prepared and served amid elaborate tropical decor in four
whimsical dining areas that include a fabric cactus garden.

Wilson Frank's Restaurant & Bakery   *(208)667-9459*
downtown at 501 Sherman Av.
B-L-D.   *Low*
Old-fashioned American fare is served in simple abundance along with
cinnamon rolls and assorted pies displayed up front. Lots of nostalgic
touches and wood-trim bolster the family-friendly decor.

The Wine Cellar   *(208)664-9463*
downtown at 313 Sherman Av.
L-D.   *Moderate*
Deli cases with beautiful displays of salads and specialty bread made
here herald flavorful gourmet lunches. Each evening, candlelit dining
in urbane cellar rooms can be enjoyed with fine wines from their shop,
and live entertainment most nights.

LODGING

A world-class lakefront resort is backed by several fine bed-and-
breakfast inns, and modern motels are plentiful. Summer is high
season. At other times, rates are often at least 30% less.

Ameritel Inn   *(208)665-9000*
3 mi. N (near I-90) at 333 Ironwood Dr. - 83814
118 units   *(800)600-6001*   *Expensive*
The area's finest water park adjoins this spiffy four-story motel that
opened in 1997 with an indoor pool, whirlpool and fitness center.
Expanded Continental breakfast and cookies are complimentary. Each
room is well furnished. Four suites have a large in-room whirlpool.

Baragar House   *(208)664-9125*
just W at 316 Military Dr. - 83814
3 units   *(800)615-8422*   *Moderate-Expensive*
A craftsman-style bungalow a stroll from the shoreline park now serves
as a charming bed-and-breakfast with a whirlpool and sauna. Full
family-style breakfast and afternoon refreshments are complimentary.
Two of the well-furnished rooms share a bath. The spacious
Honeymoon Suite has an antique clawfoot tub and a curved-glass two-
head shower. Each room has a unique "sleep under the stars" feature.

The Blackwell House   *(208)664-0656*
just E at 820 Sherman Av. - 83814
8 units   *(800)899-0656*   *Moderate-Expensive*
A stately turn-of-the-century home has been skillfully restored to serve
as a landmark bed-and-breakfast. Full breakfast is complimentary.
Each room, varying from cozy to spacious, is well furnished with the
look of yesteryear. Two share a bath.

Cavanaugh's Templin's Resort - Best Western *(208)773-1611*
8 mi. W (via I-90) at 414 E. 1st Av. - Post Falls 83854
167 units   *(800)283-6754*   *Moderate-Expensive*
The Spokane River adjoins this modern resort with a riverside beach,
marina, indoor pool, whirlpool, sauna, tennis courts, exercise room, and
a gift shop, plus rental boats and cruises, a restaurant and lounge with
live entertainment. Each room is well furnished. Most have a private
balcony or patio overlooking the river.

Coeur d'Alene Inn   *(208)765-3200*
3 mi. N (near I-90) at 414 W. Appleway - 83814
123 units   *(800)251-7829*   *Expensive*
This newer conference-oriented motor hotel has a large indoor/outdoor
pool, whirlpool, fitness center, restaurant and high-tech entertainment
lounge. Each spacious room is well furnished.

The Coeur d'Alene Resort   *(208)765-4000*
downtown at 115 S. 2nd St. (Box 7200) - 83816
337 units   *(800)688-5253*   *Expensive-Very Expensive*
One of America's great resort hotels opened in 1986 in a perfect site on
the lake shore adjacent to downtown. An excellent public beach and
park are less than a block away. Amenities in the distinctive eighteen-
story complex include a marina with a variety of boat charters, cruises
and rentals, and the world's longest floating boardwalk. There are also
two large pools (one indoors), wading pool, whirlpools, saunas, exercise
room, bicycle rentals, (nearby) a private beach and (fee) picturesque 18-
hole golf course with a unique floating 14th green, plus full-service
fitness and beauty spa; delightful dining, drinking and dancing
facilities (see listing) and a stylish shopping plaza. Each room is
luxuriously outfitted with state-of-the-art conveniences. Spacious
minisuites in the Lake Tower have a private balcony with a panoramic
lake view, and most have an objet d'art gas fireplace.

Comfort Inn   *(208)765-5500*
3 mi. N (near I-90) at 280 W. Appleway - 83814
50 units   *(800)228-5150*   *Moderate*
An indoor pool, whirlpool and sauna are features of this contemporary
motel. All of the rooms are well furnished, and there are efficiencies,
plus several suites featuring a large in-room whirlpool.

Gregory's McFarland House Bed & Breakfast   *(208)667-1232*
just N at 601 Foster Av. - 83814
5 units   *(800)335-1232*   *Expensive*
A handsome turn-of-the-century house is now a refined bed-and-
breakfast inn. Full breakfast is complimentary. Each room is
beautifully furnished with a blend of antiques and modern touches,
and has a private bath with a claw-footed tub and shower.

Rodeway Inn Pines Resort Motel   *(208)664-8244*
1 mi. NW at 1422 Northwest Blvd. - 83814
65 units   *(800)651-2510*   *Moderate*
This modern motel among the pines has indoor and outdoor pools and
a whirlpool, plus a coffee shop. Each room is nicely furnished.

Shilo Inn   *(208)664-2300*
3 mi. NW (near I-90) at 702 W. Appleway - 83814
138 units   *(800)222-2244*   *Moderate-Expensive*
Extra touches distinguish this contemporary four-story motel—an
indoor pool, whirlpool, sauna, steam room and exercise room. Each
attractively furnished room has a mini-kitchen.

BASIC INFORMATION

Elevation: 2,152 feet   *Population (1990): 24,561*
Location: 312 miles East of Seattle
Nearest airport with regular flights: Spokane - 35 miles
Coeur d'Alene Chamber of Commerce   *(208)664-3194*
  1 mi. N at 1621 N. 3rd St. - 83814
  www.coeurdalene.org
Coeur d'Alene Visitor Center   *(208)665-2350*

Ketchum, Idaho

Ketchum is the unheralded gateway to a vast mountain realm. Well over a mile high, this agreeable blend of the Old and New West occupies an attractive little river valley at the base of a towering mountain. To the north, jagged peaks of the Sawtooth Range accent an enormous wilderness with endless pine forests, clear lakes, and rushing streams. Ketchum, founded in 1881 as a supply point for surrounding silver mines, later became the largest sheep shipping station in the nation. In 1936, the Union Pacific Railroad established "Sun Valley" one mile east. The West's first ski resort was soon famous.

Today, the Sun Valley Resort continues as a renowned getaway, and Ketchum has secured its future as a winter and summer vacation destination. The compact town center houses a fine assortment of art galleries, Western ware shops, gourmet food stores, and bars with live entertainment. Excellent restaurants and lodgings downtown and nearby cater to throngs of travelers intent on experiencing the real West.

WEATHER PROFILE

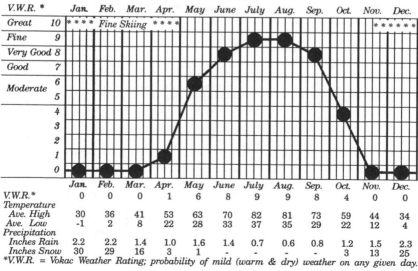

V.W.R.*		Jan.	Feb.	Mar.	Apr.	May	June	July	Aug.	Sep.	Oct.	Nov.	Dec.
V.W.R.*		0	0	0	1	6	8	9	9	8	4	0	0
Temperature													
Ave. High		30	36	41	53	63	70	82	81	73	59	44	34
Ave. Low		-1	2	8	22	28	33	37	35	29	22	12	4
Precipitation													
Inches Rain		2.2	2.2	1.4	1.0	1.6	1.4	0.7	0.6	0.8	1.2	1.5	2.3
Inches Snow		30	29	16	3	1	-	-	-	-	3	13	25

*V.W.R. = Vokac Weather Rating; probability of mild (warm & dry) weather on any given day.

ATTRACTIONS

Aerial Tramway
Bald Mountain Chair Lift   *(208)622-2231*
just S via Main St. on Serenade Dr.
A chairlift operates in summer from the base of River Run to give passengers thrilling views from atop Bald Mountain.

Bicycling   *(800)634-3347*
More than thirty miles of paved trails around town offer spectacularly scenic, relatively easy bicycling. Bicycle rentals, repairs and sales are available daily at several places downtown.

Boat Rentals
River runners can rent inflatable rafts, kayaks, even tubes, and all accessories in Ketchum for private expeditions on the popular Salmon River out of Stanley.

River Running   *(800)634-3347*
60 mi. N on ID 75 - Stanley
A scenic day float trip down the headwaters of the Salmon River is a wonderful way to experience the rugged grandeur of the Sawtooth National Recreation Area. Several river guide services feature this exhilarating run. Lunch, all equipment, and transportation from Ketchum are provided. Other whitewater trips of up to six days can also be arranged.

Sawtooth National Recreation Area   *(800)260-5970*
starts 8 mi. N of town via ID 75
Well-named granite spires of the Sawtooth Range provide an inspiring backdrop to the rugged heart of an enormous system of national forests. The Redfish Lake Visitor Center contains history, geology, plants and wildlife exhibits. Self-guided trails and a variety of programs are offered. Picturesque Redfish Lake has boat rentals and cruises to trailheads at the far end of the lake, fishing, and scenic beaches. Lodging and supplies are available nearby. One-day river runs can be arranged in rustic Stanley, a tiny social center for the wilderness that looks like an Old West movie set. Beyond, hundreds of miles of trails thread among high-country wooded valleys, snow-capped peaks and gemlike lakes. In summer, the area is a bonanza for hiking, mountain climbing, horseback riding, backpacking, camping, fishing, boating and both cold and warm water swimming.

Winter Sports
Ice Skating   *(208)622-2151*
1 mi. NE via Sun Valley Rd.
At Sun Valley Lodge, year-round ice skating is open to the public daily on world-renowned, full-sized indoor and outdoor ice rinks.

Sun Valley Ski Area   *(208)622-2151*
1 mi. S at end of Ski Lift Rd.
Bald Mountain, with Ketchum along its base, is a world-class delight for skiers. The vertical rise is 3,400 feet and the longest run is three miles. Elevation at the top is 9,150 feet. There are thirteen chairlifts. All facilities, services and rentals are plentiful at the area for downhill and cross-country skiing. The ski season is late November through April. The "Queen Mother of Western Skiing," 1.5 miles east near Sun Valley Lodge, is where the world's first chairlift began operation more than sixty years ago. Today, Sun Valley's Dollar Mountain Ski Area has four chairlifts to beginner and intermediate slopes with a vertical rise of 630 feet.

Chandler's Restaurant   *(208)726-1776*
downtown at 200 S. Main St.
D only.   *Expensive*
Traditional American and Continental dishes are appealingly updated
including distinctive specialties like seared elk loin. Ginger ice cream
stands out among luscious homemade desserts. An intimate cabin
includes several warm, informally elegant dining areas and a pine-
shaded courtyard with heat lamps.

Cristina's Restaurant   *(208)726-4499*
downtown at 520 2nd St. E.
B-L.   *Expensive*
Pastries and breads made and displayed here are delicious accompaniments to light, bright meals served in a simply posh dining room and
on a lovely garden court.

Evergreen Bistro   *(208)726-3888*
downtown at 171 1st Av.
D only.   *Very Expensive*
One of Ketchum's oldest gourmet havens features New American
cuisine in dishes ranging from vodka and dill-cured salmon with
vidalia onions to blackened trout filet with a lemon chive sauce.
Housemade desserts are similarly adventurous. Plush table settings
blend smoothly with avant-garde wall hangings in the dramatic rock-
walled main dining room, and there is a covered dining terrace.

Ketchum Grill   *(208)726-4660*
downtown at 520 East Av.
D only.   *Expensive*
One of Ketchum's most deservedly popular purveyors of contemporary
American cuisine offers a wide-ranging grazing menu with skillfully
prepared dishes that include distinctive highlights like braised Idaho
lamb shank. Their housemade rosemary-currant and walnut wheat
breads are superb, as are desserts ranging from sorbets to vanilla bean
creme brule. A historic home now offers a congenial relaxed setting,
and the shaded patio has a fine mountain view.

The Kneadery   *(208)726-9462*
downtown at 260 Leadville Av.
B-L.   *Expensive*
Ketchum's longest-established breakfast place continues to set the
standard for contemporary Western fare served in a handsome wood-
and-greenery-trimmed coffee shop and on a lovely garden patio.

Michel's Christiania   *(208)726-3388*
downtown at 303 Walnut Av.
D only.   *Very Expensive*
Classic French cuisine is served along with homebaked breads and
desserts in a casually elegant dining room and in a fountain courtyard.
The bar offers more casual fare and setting.

Otter's Restaurant   *(208)726-6837*
downtown at 180 W. 6th St.
D only.   *Expensive*
Wild game is a specialty on a grazing menu of creative American
cuisine reflected in dishes as diverse as rock shrimp cakes, fondue,
lamb osso bucco or warm wild mushroom salad. Luscious desserts are
also homemade in this delightful young restaurant with a congenial
wine bar and refined dining room by a deck with a fine mountain view.

Perry's Bakery & Eatery   *(208)726-7703*
downtown at 131 W. 4th St.
B-L.   *Moderate*
All sorts of skillfully prepared baked items and desserts are displayed
and served with light fare for breakfast. Deli-style lunches feature big
creative sandwiches, soups or salads served at warm wood-trimmed
tables set with flowers or on a sunny deck.

Pioneer Saloon   *(208)726-3139*
downtown at 308 N. Main St.
D only.   *Expensive*
There is no question about where to go in this area for prime ribs or
steaks with a classic Western treatment (including support dishes like
giant Idaho potatoes). The Pioneer Saloon has been *the* place for many
years. Happily, the rustic Old-West-saloon decor and generous vittles
remain unchanged.

Sawtooth Club   *(208)726-5233*
downtown at 231 N. Main St.
D only.   *Moderate*
Rack of lamb, steaks, chops, ribs and chicken are especially flavorful
over a natural mesquite wood fire. There is also a fine selection of light
fare. An amiable bar with sofas and a see-through fireplace is below
the large comfortable dining rooms.

Soupçon   *(208)726-5034*
downtown at 231½ Leadville Av.
D only.   *Expensive*
A short but well-thought-out list of creative American cuisine is served
along with delicious homemade desserts in one of the most romantic
little log cabins in the area.

Sun Valley Lodge Dining Room   *(208)622-2135*
1 mi. NE via Sun Valley Rd. - Sun Valley
D only.   *Expensive*
Contemporary international cuisine includes some delightful regional
dishes like broiled lamb chops or medallion of elk, plus delectable
housemade baked goods and desserts. In one of the West's paragons of
updated art deco opulence, jackets are appropriate in the imposing and
resplendent dining room. Downstairs, **Duchin Lounge** features the
delightful grand piano stylings of Joe Fos, the author's favorite lounge
pianist, whose infectious smile is as memorable as his gracious manner
and his musical forte.

Warm Springs Ranch Restaurant   *(208)726-2609*
1 mi. W at 1801 Warm Springs Rd.
D only.   *Expensive*
An Idaho specialty, lamb, is featured here in leg of lamb, chops or
shank, along with a wealth of traditional steaks and other Western
fare. Large wood-trimmed dining rooms and a saloon capture the
ambiance of Ketchum's past, and there is an inviting creekside deck.

LODGING

For more than half a century, the Ketchum area has provided some of
the West's most lavish accommodations—thanks to Sun Valley.
Lodging in town was relatively scarce, plain, and aimed at action-
oriented, budget-conscious recreationists. Recent construction has
added handsome accommodations in prime locations downtown and in
scenic sites nearby. High season is both winter and summer. Spring
and fall rates are normally at least 25% lower.

The Christophe Condo Hotel   (208)726-5601
just S at 351 2nd Av. S (Box 21) - 83340
35 units   (800)521-2515   *Expensive*

A little rushing stream is near this modern condominium complex with a view pool and two whirlpools. As an added attraction, it is within walking distance of both ski lifts and downtown. All rooms are well furnished. The spacious one- or two-bedroom condominiums are the best bets. Each has a kitchen and fireplace. Many also have a large in-room whirlpool.

Elkhorn Resort Sun Valley   (208)622-4511
3 mi. E on Elkhorn Rd. (Box 6009) - Sun Valley 83354
132 units   (800)355-4676   *Expensive*

One of the area's most complete full-service resorts has a large pool and whirlpool, fitness center with sauna, access to miles of paved bike and hiking trails, plus (fee) championship 18-hole golf course, a tennis center, and bicycles in summer. On-site downhill and cross-country skiing are featured in winter. There are also restaurants and an entertainment lounge. Each room is well furnished. Seven suites have a kitchenette, fireplace and whirlpool bath.

Heidelberg Inn   (208)726-5361
1 mi. NW at 1908 Warm Springs Rd. (Box 5704) - 83340
30 units   (800)284-4863   *Moderate-Expensive*

A small pool, whirlpool and sauna distinguish this modern motor lodge between downtown and Bald Mountain. Continental breakfast delivered to the room is complimentary, and there are rental bicycles. Each spacious room is well furnished. Some have a fireplace, kitchenette and a mountain view.

Idaho Country Inn   (208)726-1019
1 mi. N at 134 Latigo Lane - (Box 2355 in Sun Valley 83353)
10 units   (800)250-8341   *Expensive*

Overlooking the mountains from a slope above a quiet neighborhood is one of Idaho's best bed-and-breakfasts. The classic contemporary inn captures the charm of the northern Rocky Mountains in log beams and river rock and panoramic views. A whirlpool and full breakfast are complimentary. Each spacious, beautifully furnished room is individually themed to local history and has a private view deck plus all contemporary conveniences.

Kentwood Lodge - Best Western   (208)726-4114
downtown at 180 S. Main St. (Box 2172) - 83340
55 units   (800)805-1001   *Expensive*

One of the area's newest motor inns has an indoor pool, whirlpool, and exercise room in a handsome Western building. Each well-furnished room includes custom log furniture, microwave and refrigerator. Some have a gas fireplace, private balcony and/or a whirlpool bath.

Knob Hill Inn   (208)726-8010
just N at 960 N. Main St. (Box 800) - 83340
24 units   (800)526-8010   *Expensive-Very Expensive*

One of the region's most luxurious bed-and-breakfast inns has a lap pool, whirlpool, sauna and exercise room. A cafe open to the public (B-L —Moderate) has the best European light fare in Ketchum. Nearby, **Felix** (D only—Expensive) offers creative American and Mediterranean cuisine in a plush room overlooking an alpine garden and mountains. Full breakfast is complimentary to guests. Each spacious room is beautifully furnished. Many have a fireplace.

Ketchum, Idaho

The River Street Inn *(208)726-3611*
downtown at 100 River St. W. (Box 182 in Sun Valley 83353)
  8 units   *(888)746-3611*   *Expensive*
A babbling brook runs next to this classy, contemporary bed-and-breakfast inn. Full breakfast is complimentary. Each spacious, well-furnished room has all modern conveniences, including a deep Japanese soaking tub with a view.

Sun Valley Resort *(208)622-2151*
1 mi. NE via Sun Valley Rd. (Box 10) - Sun Valley 83353
  540 units   *(800)786-8259   Expensive-Very Expensive*
The "Grande Dame of American Ski Resorts" is still the largest single accommodation in the area. It now comprises a well-maintained lodge more than half a century old, a newer inn, and hundreds of clustered condominiums. A remarkable array of amenities includes three pools, whirlpool, sauna, recreation and game rooms, plus (for a fee) an 18-hole golf course, renowned indoor and outdoor ice skating rinks, dozens of tennis courts, bowling, bicycle rentals, horseback riding, and trap and skeet shooting. In winter, downhill and cross-country skiing and sleigh rides are available on-site. Other facilities include a grandiose dining room and posh entertainment lounge (see listing), plus coffee shops, bars, and resort shops. All rooms are beautifully decorated. Some have a private view patio or balcony, and a fireplace.

Tamarack Lodge *(208)726-3344*
downtown at 291 Walnut Av. (Box 2000 in Sun Valley 83353)
  26 units   *(800)521-5379*   *Moderate-Expensive*
This modern motor lodge has an indoor pool and a whirlpool. Each spacious, comfortably furnished room has either a private patio or balcony. A few third-floor rooms also have good mountain views. Suites have a fireplace.

Tyrolean Lodge - Best Western *(208)726-5336*
just S at 260 Cottonwood St. (Box 202 in Sun Valley 83353)
  56 units   *(800)333-7912*   *Moderate-Expensive*
The closest lodging to the River Run Ski lifts at the base of Bald Mountain is this contemporary motel with a Tyrolean motif, a view pool, three whirlpools, and an exercise room, plus rental bicycles. All of the rooms are attractively furnished. Some suites also have a mini-kitchen and a large in-room whirlpool.

BASIC INFORMATION

Elevation: 5,817 feet   *Population (1990): 2,523*
Location: 280 miles Northwest of Salt Lake City
Nearest Airport with commercial flights: Hailey - 12 miles
Sun Valley/Ketchum Chamber of Commerce (208)726-3423 (800)634-3347
  411 N. Main, Ketchum; mail: Box 2420, Sun Valley 83353
  www.visitketchum.com

McCall, Idaho

McCall is a hideaway recreation hub for the northern Rocky Mountains. The village is in a luxuriant pine forest on the southern shore of a picture-postcard lake framed by rugged peaks. It is a gateway to the rugged grandeur of the famed "River-of-No-Return" country. A sawmill and logging railroad were built here around the turn of the century to harvest vast forests in the area. Their eventual demise made it possible, in the 1970s, for the town to begin to fulfill its more distinguished destiny as an outdoor recreation capital.

Today, McCall has a kind of rustic vitality. Both the mill site and the railroad right-of-way are being replaced with residences, shops and trails. Lakefront parks feature scenic pine-shaded picnic sites, swimming areas, and sandy beaches. The village center is still surprisingly tiny with a mix of prosaic shops, restaurants and nightlife scattered along the main road through town. Accommodations are also relatively scarce, but include a handsome resort hotel on the lakefront.

WEATHER PROFILE

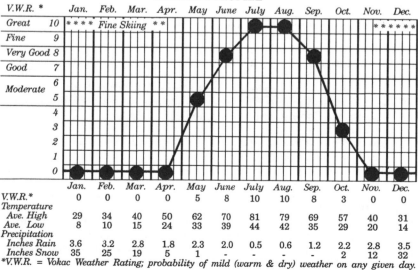

V.W.R.*	Jan.	Feb.	Mar.	Apr.	May	June	July	Aug.	Sep.	Oct.	Nov.	Dec.
V.W.R.*	0	0	0	0	5	8	10	10	8	3	0	0
Temperature												
Ave. High	29	34	40	50	62	70	81	79	69	57	40	31
Ave. Low	8	10	15	24	33	39	44	42	35	29	20	14
Precipitation												
Inches Rain	3.6	3.2	2.8	1.8	2.3	2.0	0.5	0.6	1.2	2.2	2.8	3.5
Inches Snow	35	25	19	5	1	-	-	-	-	2	12	32

*V.W.R. = Vokac Weather Rating; probability of mild (warm & dry) weather on any given day.

ATTRACTIONS

Boat Rentals
Harry's Dry Dock & Sports Marina   *(208)634-8605*
downtown at 1300 E. Lake St.
Fishing boats, ski boats, canoes and pontoons can be rented by the hour or day at this full-service marina.

North Beach State Recreation Area   *(208)634-2164*
9 mi. N via ID 55 on Warren Wagon Rd.
The longest sandy beach in the area separates a dense pine forest from the tranquil north shore of Payette Lake. Nearby, the slow-moving, sandy-bottomed Payette River is well-suited to lazy river floats.

Payette Lake   *(208)634-3006*
adjacent to town on the north
The scenic sylvan gem of the central Idaho mountains is seven miles long. It is surrounded by luxuriant pine forests and an attractive mixture of public parks and residential areas. A loop road (partly gravel) circles the lake and provides numerous overlooks and sandy beach accesses. Boating, water-skiing, swimming and fishing are popular. Three picturesque public beaches are located in McCall on the southern shore. City Park, a tiny downtown grassy slope extending to the lake, is perfect for sunning and sightseeing. Rotary Park, one mile west at the Payette River outlet, features pine-shaded picnic tables and a sandy-bottomed swimming area. Davis Beach, a half mile north, has a long beach and pine-shaded picnic tables.

Payette National Forest   *(208)634-0700*
surrounding town
This huge forest includes roads west of town that access awesome overlooks of the Grand Canyon of the Snake River, the world's deepest gorge. The highlight of the area east of town is a vast wilderness of peaks and canyons, mountain lakes and streams, and forested hills with some of the West's finest hiking, backpacking, pack trips, hunting, and fishing. It also includes a beautiful stretch of the Salmon River—the River of No Return—renowned as one of the world's great river running locations. A major ski area is west of town.

Ponderosa State Park   *(208)634-2164*
2 mi. NE on Payette Lake
One of the West's best state parks is in one of Idaho's largest stands of ponderosa pines along the east shore of Payette Lake. Summer facilities include a visitor center, six miles of nature trails, a picturesque swimming area with a sandy beach, a boat launch, a five-mile scenic overlook drive, fishing sites, pine-shaded picnic facilities, and a full service campground with some delightful lake-view sites. Winter activities include cross-country skiing, snowshoeing, sledding, ice skating, ice fishing, and snowmobiling.

River Running
Salmon River Challenge   *(800)732-8574*
44 mi. NW via ID 55 & US 95 - Riggins
Half-day to six-day raft trips are offered on the legendary Salmon River east of Riggins during the summer. Several other companies also operate out of Riggins with daily and longer whitewater trips.

Warm Water Features
McCall is in the midst of one of the West's greatest concentrations of geothermal springs. Some have been fully developed with swimming pools. Others remain sublime natural attractions of the high country wilderness. The Chamber has information and maps.

Winter Sports
  Brundage Mountain Ski Area   *(208)634-4151 (800)888-7544*
  10 mi. NW via ID 55
The vertical rise is 1,800 feet and the longest run is 1.5 miles. Gorgeous lake views reward skiers from the top (7,600 feet) reached by three chairlifts. Essential facilities, services and rentals are available at the base for downhill skiing. There is a restaurant. The ski season is mid-November to mid-April.

RESTAURANTS

Harvest Moon Market/Delicatessen/Bakery   *(208)634-5578*
  downtown at 1133 E. Lake St.
  B-L.   *Moderate*
The best bakery for a hundred miles has some outstanding treats like raisin-nut or cranberry cinnamon rolls, all kinds of delicious bagels, breads, and desserts made from scratch daily. It's all served with light fare in a cheerful coffee house by a garden. They also stock a fine selection of specialty foods for gourmet picnics or a custom gift basket.

Lardos Grill & Saloon   *(208)634-8191*
  1 mi. W at 600 Lake St.
  L-D.   *Moderate*
Traditional American fare is featured in a long-established family-oriented restaurant with a warm wood-toned interior enhanced by nostalgic furnishings. An atmospheric lounge has a dramatic backbar and pot-bellied stove.

McCall Brewing Company   *(208)634-2333*
  downtown at 807 N. 3rd St.
  L-D.   *Moderate*
All kinds of contemporary pub grub including beer-battered fish and chips or hickory-smoked primo rib can be enjoyed with a selection of fresh handcrafted ales. The warm and friendly wood-trimmed pub overlooks gleaming kettles. An upstairs deck provides a panorama of town, the lake, and mountains.

The Mill   *(208)634-7683*
  just S at 324 N. 3rd St.
  D only.   *Expensive*
Steaks and prime rib are the mainstays on a contemporary American menu. Rustic hunting lodge decor complements the hearty portions in this long-time favorite. There is also a piano bar.

The Pancake House   *(208)634-5849*
  1 mi. S at 209 N. 3rd St.
  B-L.   *Moderate*
For many years, locals and travelers have converged on the area's finest roadside cafe for genuine American homestyle cooking. The cinnamon rolls, breads and even the jams are homemade, and regional specialties like huckleberry pancakes are featured in season. A flower-strewn waiting deck adjoins comfortable, rustic dining rooms.

Shore Lodge   *(208)634-2244*
  1 mi. W at 501 W. Lake St.
  B-L-D.   *Moderate-Expensive*
McCall's finest lakefront lodging offers **The Narrows Restaurant** (D only—Expensive) where contemporary Northwest cuisine includes game and seafood in an expansive atrium-style dining room with an outstanding panoramic view of Payette Lake shared with a stylish entertainment lounge. **The Patio Cafe** (B-L—Moderate) serves contemporary American fare with a spectacular view of the lake.

LODGING

Bear Creek Lodge   *(208)634-3551*
5 mi. NW at 3492 Hwy. 55 (Box 8) - New Meadows 83654
13 units   *(888)634-2327*   *Expensive-Very Expensive*
This contemporary wood-trim lodge borders a meadow in a forest near Brundage Mountain Ski Area. The dining room serves distinctive Northwestern cuisine amid refined rusticity. A lounge shares the peaceful alpine view. There is also a whirlpool. Full breakfast is complimentary. Each room is well furnished and has a mini-kitchen and gas fireplace. Four cabin units also have an in-bath whirlpool.

Best Western McCall   *(208)634-6300*
just S at 415 N. 3rd St.(Box 4297) - 83638
75 units   *(800)528-1234*   *Moderate-Expensive*
One of McCall's newest motels has a large indoor pool, whirlpool, and exercise room. Each spacious room is well furnished. Three maxi-suites have a large in-room whirlpool.

Hotel McCall   *(208)634-8105*
downtown at 1101 N. 3rd St. (Box 1778) - 83638
22 units   *Moderate*
Payette Lake is across a street from this restored 1904 landmark. Once a railroad hotel, it is now a bed-and-breakfast inn with complimentary extended Continental breakfast, plus afternoon wine and treats. A restaurant serves contemporary American lunches and dinners. Each room is nicely furnished and most have a private bathroom. Some have a pleasant lake view.

Riverside Motel   *(208)634-5610*
1 mi. W at 400 W. Lake St. (Box 746) - 83638
28 units   *(800)326-5610*   *Low-Moderate*
McCall's only motel by the scenic Payette River has a whirlpool. It is across a highway from the lake and a town beach. Each room is nicely furnished. The upstairs suite has a fireplace and a river/lake view, and there are condominiums available.

Scandia Inn Motel   *(208)634-7394*
just S at 401 N. 3rd St. (Box 1436) - 83638
17 units   *Low*
This modern single-story motel is in a quiet location a few blocks from the lake, and has a sauna. Each room is comfortably furnished.

Shore Lodge   *(208)634-2244*
1 mi. W at 501 W. Lake St. (Box 1006) - 83638
116 units   *(800)657-6464*   *Moderate-Expensive*
Shore Lodge has a picture-perfect setting by lovely Payette Lake. The three-story resort hotel with the feel of a rustic hunting lodge has a private sandy beach for swimming, a boat dock, two pools, sauna, game room, exercise room, and a tennis court, plus scenic fine dining (see listing) and lounge facilities. Each room is simply comfortable with both newer and rustic furnishings. Most have a superb lake/mountain view from a private patio or balcony.

BASIC INFORMATION
Elevation: *5,030 feet*   *Population (1990):* *2,005*
Location: *450 miles Northwest of Salt Lake City*
Nearest airport with commercial flights: *Boise - 115 miles*
McCall Area Chamber of Commerce   *(208)634-7631*
   downtown off Lake St. (Box D) - 83638
   www.mccall-idchamber.org

Sandpoint, Idaho

Sandpoint is a civilized complement to a naturally inspired setting. It occupies a superlative piece of shoreline along one of the West's finest large sylvan lakes. Sheltered by surrounding pine-forested mountains, the town has a relatively temperate four season climate. Idaho's first permanent structure was built nearby in 1809. But, major settlement in the isolated location was forestalled until the 1880s following the completion of a transcontinental railroad through the townsite coupled with development of a local timber industry.

The railroad and forest products are still important. Today, however, with a splendid lakeside location and a major ski area nearby, Sandpoint is being "discovered" as a year-round vacation destination. Downtown blends a frontier heritage and a contemporary Western outlook in a number of specialty shops, galleries, and appealing restaurants. Most lodgings are near downtown and a large lakefront park with sandy beaches, swimming areas, and an adjoining marina.

WEATHER PROFILE

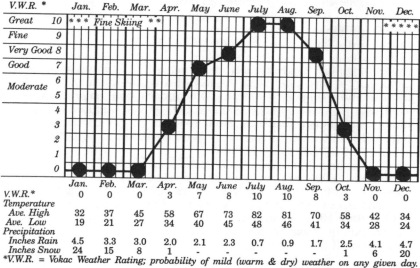

V.W.R.*		Jan.	Feb.	Mar.	Apr.	May	June	July	Aug.	Sep.	Oct.	Nov.	Dec.
Great	10												
Fine	9												
Very Good	8												
Good	7												
Moderate	6												
	5												

	Jan.	Feb.	Mar.	Apr.	May	June	July	Aug.	Sep.	Oct.	Nov.	Dec.
V.W.R.*	0	0	0	3	7	8	10	10	8	3	0	0
Temperature												
Ave. High	32	37	45	58	67	73	82	81	70	58	42	34
Ave. Low	19	21	27	34	40	45	48	46	41	34	28	24
Precipitation												
Inches Rain	4.5	3.3	3.0	2.0	2.1	2.3	0.7	0.9	1.7	2.5	4.1	4.7
Inches Snow	24	15	8	1	-	-	-	-	-	1	6	20

*V.W.R. = Vokac Weather Rating; probability of mild (warm & dry) weather on any given day.

213

ATTRACTIONS

Bicycling
Separated bikeways on gentle terrain through town and across an arm of the lake via the Pedestrian Long Bridge give riders fine views of the waterfront and mountains. Rentals are also available for mountain bikes that can access the surrounding high country.

Boat Rentals
Sailboats, canoes, paddle boats and windsurfer rentals and lessons are available at several places in and near town.

Cedar Street Bridge   *(208)263-2265*
downtown at E end of Cedar St.
The retail outlet for **Coldwater Creek Nature and Clothing Store** (a major mail-order firm) anchors specialty shops, galleries, and food service incorporated onto a dramatic two-level pedestrian bridge over Sand Creek. The 400-foot-long complex has massive glass windows that provide tranquil views of the lake and mountains.

Fishing Charters
Full- or half-day sportfishing trips on Lake Pend Oreille in search of record trout (all gear furnished) can be reserved at several in-town charters.

Kaniksu National Forest   *(208)263-5111*
surrounding town
This huge preserve includes parts of both Lake Pend Oreille and Priest Lake, plus numerous beautiful small lakes in an emerald empire of dense forests and rugged mountains. In addition to excellent boating, fishing, and swimming opportunities, more than 1,000 miles of scenic trails provide access for hikers, backpackers, campers and guided hunting and fishing parties.

Lake Pend Oreille
adjacent to town
Idaho's largest lake was formed by glaciers that carved a trough now filled for more than forty miles by water that reaches a depth of 1,150 feet. Lofty peaks and dense pine forests surround the lake, which is famous for sportfishing. Fourteen varieties of game fish include record-sized kamloops (the world's largest rainbow trout). Recreation facilities lining sandy beaches and sheltered coves along the 111-mile shoreline provide swimming, boating, water-skiing, camping, picnicking hiking and biking opportunities in summer.

Sandpoint City Beach   *(208)263-3158*
downtown at E end of Bridge St.
A quarter-mile sandy beach and splendid lake and mountain panoramas distinguish a well-tended park covering the end of a little peninsula by downtown. Landscaped grounds include a bathhouse, boat launching facilities, public dockage, kiddie pool, playground, tennis courts, and picnic tables with fireplaces.

Schweitzer Mountain Resort   *(208)263-9555   (800)831-8810*
11 mi. NW off US 95
Atop Schweitzer Mountain (6,400 feet above sea level), the panorama of fiord-like lakes and mountains is truly memorable. The vertical drop is over 2,400 feet, and there are six chairlifts. All facilities, services, and rentals are available at the area for skiing. Lodging, restaurants, and bars are open at the base for skiing season and in summer when hiking, biking (mountain bike rentals), and scenic lift rides attract visitors.

Delightful Diversions   *(208)263-8331*
downtown at 330 N. First Av.
L-D.   *Moderate*
Delicious homemade ice creams and sherbets are served in all kinds of
tempting fountain treats. Homemade candies, fudges and huckleberry
specialties can also be enjoyed at a dining bar and creek-view deck.

Eichardt's Pub, Grill and Coffee House   *(208)263-4005*
downtown at 212 Cedar St.
L-D.   *Moderate*
A pleasing selection of pub grub ranges from green chile stew to buffalo
burgers. Nearly a dozen tap beers and live entertainment are also
offered amidst worn brick and wood-trim decor.

The Garden Restaurant   *(208)263-5187*
downtown at 15 E. Lake St.
L-D.   *Moderate*
Contemporary American dishes include specialties like sauteed halibut
cheeks. Homemade bread begins each meal in a lovely greenhouse
setting overlooking a marina. There is also a plush and charming
lounge, as well as alfresco waterfront dining in summer

Hydra Restaurant   *(208)263-7123*
downtown at 115 W. Lake St.
L-D.   *Moderate*
Contemporary American fare (seafood and prime rib with a salad bar)
is served amid several levels of cozy wood-crafted dining rooms. The
long-established family favorite also has a popular lounge.

Jalapeños   *(208)263-2995*
downtown at 116 N. First Av.
L-D.   *Low*
Well-prepared traditional and innovative Mexican dishes ranging from
chile verde to fish tacos can be enjoyed with assorted beverages
including huckleberry margaritas. The colorful, comfortable dining
room cantina and deck share a view of the lake.

Panhandler Pies   *(406)263-2912*
downtown at 120 S. First Av.
B-L-D.   *Moderate*
Old-fashioned American comfort foods are abundant, and housemade
big apple cinnamon rolls and a wealth of pies are displayed in knotty-
pine-trimmed dining rooms bordered by a passel of Western artifacts.

Power House Bar & Grill   *(208)265-2449*
downtown at 120 E. Lake St.
L-D.   *Moderate*
Rotisserie chicken or beef, and pork ribs star in the spiffy transformed
old powerhouse by Sand Creek.

Swan's Landing   *(208)265-2000*
3 mi. S (at S end of bridge) at 1480 Lakeshore Dr. - Sagle
L-D.   *Moderate*
Swan's Landing is the best restaurant in Sandpoint. The talented chef
combines contemporary Northwestern cuisine with a Southwestern
flair in dishes like salmon with raspberry chipotle or crab empanadas.
Results are as colorful as they are fresh and flavorful. The dining room
is in a big, wood-trimmed building with a rock fireplace, regional art
objects and a panoramic view of the lake and mountains. There is also
a plush bar and umbrella-shaded view deck.

LODGING

Most of the area's best lodgings are near both downtown and the beach. Late June into September is high season. Prices are usually at least 25% less in spring and fall.

Coit House Bed & Breakfast   *(208)265-4035*
downtown at 502 N. Fourth Av. - 83864
4 units   *Moderate*
A charming 1907 Victorian manor house is now Sandpoint's finest bed-and-breakfast inn. Full gourmet breakfast is complimentary. All rooms have a private bath and are individually well furnished, tastefully blending period pieces with modern conveniences.

Connie's Motor Inn - Best Western   *(208)263-9581*
downtown at 323 Cedar St. (Box 126) - 83864
53 units   *(800)282-0660*   *Moderate*
This conventional modern hotel has a pool, whirlpool, dining room and lounge. Each room is well furnished. Some have a whirlpool bath.

Edgewater Resort Motor Inn   *(208)263-3194*
downtown at 56 Bridge St. (Box 128) - 83864
55 units   *(800)635-2534*   *Expensive*
Sandpoint's best beachfront rooms are in a modern motor inn by the splendid lakeshore park. Amenities include a private sandy swimming beach, a dock, whirlpool, and saunas. The **Beach House Restaurant and Lounge** (B-L-D—Moderate) feature regional cuisine with a lake view. Each comfortable room has a private deck overlooking the lake and mountains. Two also have a large in-room whirlpool.

Green Gables Lodge   *(208)265-0257*
11 mi. NW via US 95 at 10000 Sweitzer Mountain Rd.(Box 815)-83864
82 units   *(800)831-8810*   *Expensive*
Ski slopes and chairlifts adjoin this contemporary six-story lodge at Schweitzer Mountain Resort. The complex also has a big pool, three whirlpools, a bar and grill. Each spacious well-furnished room has an intimate view of ski slopes or a distant view of the lake. Some also have a large in-room two-person whirlpool.

Lakeside Inn   *(208)263-3717*
downtown at 106 Bridge St. - 83864
60 units   *(800)543-8126*   *Moderate-Expensive*
The marina adjoins this modern motel with a dock, two whirlpools, and a sauna. Many of the comfortable rooms have private patios or balconies with a water view. Two have a gas fireplace and a large in-room whirlpool.

Quality Inn Sandpoint   *(208)263-2111*
just N at 807 N. Fifth Av. (Box 187) - 83864
57 units   *Moderate*
A big indoor garden pool, whirlpool, restaurant and lounge distinguish this contemporary motor inn. Each room is comfortably furnished. Kitchenettes and whirlpool baths are available.

BASIC INFORMATION

Elevation: 2,085 feet   Population (1990): 5,203
Location: 350 miles East of Seattle
Nearest airport with commercial flights: Spokane - 80 miles
Greater Sandpoint Chamber of Commerce   (208)263-2161
*   1 mi. N on U.S. 95 (Box 928) - 83864   (800)800-2106*
*   www.keokee.com / sptonlin.html*

Galena, Illinois

Galena is a timeless treasury of Midwestern heritage and scenery. Rugged forested hills and bucolic landscapes surround the village on slopes above a gentle stream near its junction with the Mississippi River. Settlement began with America's first large mineral rush, as fortune-seekers flocked to the area's rich deposits of lead ore. By the 1850s, Galena was the busiest steamboating port between St. Louis and St. Paul. But, as trains replaced steamboats, and the river silted in, the town dwindled to a quiet backwater by the turn of the century. Thanks to decades of economic stagnation that followed, nearly 1,000 grand old structures were not razed or modernized.

Today, that legacy is preserved on the National Historic Register. Curving streets are lined with unbroken rows of solid brick buildings housing a bonanza of museums, and shops brimming with regional antiques, arts, crafts, and culinary treats. Many romantic hotels and inns also affirm Galena's splendid past.

WEATHER PROFILE

V.W.R. *		Jan.	Feb.	Mar.	Apr.	May	June	July	Aug.	Sep.	Oct.	Nov.	Dec.
Great	10	*	Fine Skiing	*									
Fine	9											* * * * *
Very Good	8												
Good	7												
Moderate	6												
	5												
	4												
	3												
	2												
	1												
	0												

	Jan.	Feb.	Mar.	Apr.	May	June	July	Aug.	Sep.	Oct.	Nov.	Dec.
V.W.R.*	0	0	0	3	7	7	7	8	8	5	0	0
Temperature												
Ave. High	27	31	43	58	70	79	84	82	74	61	45	32
Ave. Low	10	14	26	39	50	59	64	62	54	43	29	18
Precipitation												
Inches Rain	1.3	1.3	2.1	2.3	3.7	4.0	3.3	3.1	3.4	2.6	2.6	1.3
Inches Snow	9	8	7	2	-	-	-	-	-	-	3	7

*V.W.R. = Vokac Weather Rating; probability of mild (warm & dry) weather on any given day.

217

Bicycling
Rolling hills and tree-shaded country roads are delightful reasons for renting a mountain bike to explore the Galena area.
Chestnut Mountain Bike Rental   *(800)397-1320*
Galena Mountain Bike Rental   *(815)777-3409*

Boat Rides
Galena was once the busiest port between St. Louis and St. Paul. Eventually, the river silted up through town. But, a few miles west, the mighty Mississippi rolls on. Several large nostalgic riverboats offer a choice of casinos, sightseeing, brunch, dinner, live entertainment or overnight cruises.

Downtown   *(815)777-0203*
downtown is centered around Main & Hill Sts.
One of America's most picturesque collections of Victorian brick buildings rises from curving terraces above the little Galena River. Hundreds of structures are on the National Historic Register. Many are full of prime collectibles, making Galena a bonanza for antique hunters. Fine regional art, crafts and foods are also abundant, along with a cornucopia of dining and drinking places. For a step back in time, get a Visitor Center map outlining a walking tour, or board the Galena Trolley for a narrated hour-long tour past historic sites.

Galena-Jo Daviess County History Museum   *(815)777-9129*
downtown at 211 S. Bench St.
An 1858 Italianate house features artifacts and pictures from the Civil War period. Don't miss the monumental painting "Peace in the Union" depicting Lee's surrender to Grant in 1865 by Thomas Nast (one of the earliest illustrators of Santa Claus). There is also an audio-visual presentation, plus a gift and book shop.

The Old Market House State Historic Site   *(815)777-3310*
downtown at 123 N. Commerce St.
Built in 1845, the town's original focal point is one of the oldest remaining market houses in the Midwest. The fully restored state historic site contains exhibits of 19th century Galena architecture and commerce. The surrounding square is still used as a farmer's market every Saturday morning from May to October.

Ulysses S. Grant Home State Historic Site   *(815)777-0248*
1 mi. SE at 500 Bouthillier St.
Galena citizens gave this two-story Italianate house to General Grant upon his triumphant return from the Civil War in 1865. The building has been thoroughly restored and decorated with authentic period pieces and Grant family memorabilia. Nearby is a lovely tree-shaded park with a statue of Grant by the river across from downtown.

Vinegar Hill Lead Mine & Museum   *(815)777-0855*
6 mi. N on IL 84 at 8885 N. Three Pines Rd.
By the mid-1850s, Galena was the lead mining capital of the world. This is now the only lead mine in Illinois open for tours, and there is a museum containing area relics.

Winter Sports
Chestnut Mountain Ski Resort   *(815)777-1320*   *(800)397-1320*
8 mi. SE via Blackjack Rd. at 8700 W. Chestnut Rd.
This resort overlooking the Mississippi River features alpine skiing in winter with a vertical rise of 475 feet and half-mile-plus runs. There are four chairlifts. All facilities, services and rentals are available at the base, along with restaurants, lounges, and lodgings (see listing).

Bubba's   *(815)777-8030*
downtown at 300 N. Main St.
L-D.   *Moderate*
Barbecue, pasta and fresh seafood are served amidst cheerful decor in
a transformed Victorian building. Upstairs is more refined. There is a
lounge.

Cafe Italia   *(815)777-0033*
downtown at 301 N. Main St.
L-D.   *Moderate*
The bread sticks are baked to order and the Italian dishes are freshly
prepared daily. So is their seafood casino specialty, and more in this
busy, casual cafe and lounge in a pre-Civil War building.

De Soto House Hotel   *(815)777-0090*
downtown at 230 S. Main St.
B-L-D.   *Moderate*
The restored 1855 hotel serves dinner in the **Generals' Restaurant**.
Creative American cuisine like a thick baked port chop stuffed with
sage dressing, or chicken breast in a basil cream sauce, star in the
comfortable dining room. There is also an atrium coffee shop and a pub.

Eagle Ridge Inn & Resort   *(815)777-2444*
6 mi. E on US 20 at The Galena Territory
B-L-D.   *Moderate-Expensive*
Regional American cuisine is featured in dishes like pheasant pot pie
in the resort's informally elegant **Woodlands Restaurant & Lounge**.
There is also casual dining, an old-time ice cream parlor, and a general
store for gourmet deli and more.

Eldorado Grill   *(815)777-1224*
downtown at 219 N. Main St.
D only.   *Moderate*
Naturally-raised meats and produce are featured, and they make all
of their own sauces. House-smoked chicken enchiladas or grilled turkey
breast mole typify creative Southwestern cuisine that has won critical
acclaim. The real, fresh-squeezed lime margaritas also contribute to the
well-earned popularity of this appealing two-floor restaurant with
relaxed Southwestern decor.

Fried Green Tomatoes   *(815)777-3938*
2 mi. SE at 1301 N. Irish Hollow Rd.
D only.   *Moderate*
Contemporary Italian dishes are offered along with carefully prepared
Black Angus steaks, chops and fresh seafood. A historic brick farm-
stead with wraparound porches now has an upscale country feeling.

Silver Annie's   *(815)777-3131*
downtown at 124 N. Commerce St.
D only.   *Moderate*
American and Italian preparations of thick-cut   chops, steaks, and
seafood are served with homemade desserts plus piano and vocal entertainment amid cozy Victorian decor in a historic limestone building.

Vinny Vanucchi's   *(815)777-8100*
downtown at 201 S. Main St.
L-D.   *Moderate*
Breaded pepper rings and housemade french fries are among the treats
served with traditional Italian fare. The friendly neighborhood-style
restaurant beyond an old-fashioned deli and import store is on three
levels and includes a full bar and outdoor cappuccino garden.

There are few motels, but appealing resorts, hotels and bed-and-breakfast inns in historic buildings are numerous. Spring through fall weekends are prime time. Weekdays, especially in winter, are usually at least 15% less expensive.

Belle Aire Mansion Guest House　　　*(815)777-0893*
2 mi. NW at 11410 US 20 NW - 61036
5 units　　　　　　　　　　　　　　*Moderate-Expensive*
A pre-Civil War Federal-style home on expansive grounds in a peaceful setting now serves as a handsome bed-and-breakfast. Full breakfast is complimentary. While guest rooms have no phone or TV, they are well furnished with antiques and reproductions, and have a private bath. Three rooms also have a gas fireplace, while the Garden Vue Suite also has an in-room double whirlpool.

Captain Gear Guest House　　　*(815)777-0222*
just S at 1000 S. Bench St. - 61036
3 units　　　　　　*(800)794-5656*　　　　　　*Expensive*
One of Illinois' most romantic bed-and-breakfasts is on four secluded acres overlooking the Galena River. The Southern-style 1855 brick home is on the National Register. Formal breakfast is complimentary. Each room is beautifully furnished with quality antiques and has a sitting area, gas fireplace, and private bath. One also has a double whirlpool tub.

Chestnut Mountain Resort　　　*(815)777-1320*
8 mi. SE at 8700 W. Chestnut Rd. (Box 328) - 61036
120 units　　　　　*(800)397-1320*　　*Moderate-Expensive*
Atop a wooded palisade overlooking the Mississippi River is a four-season resort. Amenities of the four-story complex include a (fee) major ski area (see listing), half-mile-long alpine slide, tennis courts, mini-golf, and mountain bike rental, plus an indoor pool, whirlpool, sauna, restaurant, lounge, and gift shop. Many of the rooms in the main lodge have been remodeled and are comfortably furnished.

De Soto House Hotel　　　*(815)777-0090*
downtown at 230 S. Main St. - 61036
55 units　　　　　*(800)343-6562*　　　　　　*Expensive*
Downtown Galena's lodging landmark is this 1855 four-story hotel with a wealth of Victorian touches, restaurants (see listing) and a lounge. Each well-furnished room has all contemporary conveniences, including a private bath. Two suites also have a gas fireplace.

Eagle Ridge Inn & Resort　　　*(815)777-2444*
8 mi. E on US 20 at The Galena Territory
80 units　　　　*(800)892-2269*　*Expensive-Very Expensive*
Eagle Ridge is one of the Midwest's best four-season resorts. Amenities of the contemporary three-story complex overlooking Lake Galena include four (fee) championship golf courses with 63 holes plus all related facilities, horseback riding, four tennis courts, water craft, and rental bicycles, plus a marina, hiking trails, three pools (one indoors), whirlpool, sauna, sports court, exercise room, restaurants (see listing), nightclub and shops. Cross-country ski trails, an ice rink and sledding hill are winter features. Most of the beautifully furnished inn rooms have a private patio or balcony (some with a lake view). Three suites also have a fireplace. There are also many one- to four-bedroom beautifully furnished resort homes with a kitchen and fireplaces. Some suites and homes also have a whirlpool tub.

Early American Settlement   *(815)777-4200*
4 mi. S at 9401 Hart John Rd. (Box 250) - 61036
12 units   *(800)366-5647*   *Expensive*

Nestled in quiet rolling hills near a stream suitable for canoeing is a romantic reproduction of an 1830s log village. Each well-furnished one-room cabin includes authentic hand-hewn pine logs, pine floor and ceiling, and exposed loft beams, plus a wealth of contemporary conveniences—phone, TV, refrigerator, gas fireplace, plus full bathroom including a double whirlpool tub.

Log Cabin Guest House   *(815)777-2845*
1 mi. NW at 11661 W. Chetlain Lane - 61036
5 units   *Expensive*

For a romantic return to Midwestern American roots, this cluster of authentic 160-year-old log cabins amid rolling farmland is hard to beat. But, you won't be roughing it. Each is well furnished with antiques and a woodburning fireplace. Each also has today's amenities including TV, refrigerator, microwave, and a large whirlpool tub.

Park Avenue Guest House   *(815)777-1075*
downtown at 208 Park Av. - 61036
4 units   *(800)359-0743*   *Moderate-Expensive*

An 1897 Queen Anne Victorian with a screened wrap-around porch overlooking gardens has become a bed-and-breakfast. Hearty Continental breakfast is complimentary. Each well-furnished room has some antiques and a private bath, but no phone. Three also have a gas fireplace.

Quiet House Suites - Best Western   *(815)777-2577*
1 mi. E at 9923 US 20 West - 61036
42 units   *(800)528-1234*   *Expensive*

An indoor/outdoor pool, whirlpool, and fitness center are amenities of this contemporary motel. All rooms are well furnished. There are also romantic theme rooms ranging from Mississippi Riverboat to Roman. Some have a whirlpool for two and a private balcony.

Renaissance Suites & Rooms   *(815)777-0123*
just S at 324 Spring St. (US 20) (Box 291) - 61036
10 units   *Moderate-Expensive*

Two red-brick antebellum buildings now serve as a distinctive inn. Each well-furnished room features period antiques and all modern conveniences. The five suites also have a gas fireplace, a two-person whirlpool tub, stained-glass windows, and skylights.

Stillman's Country Inn   *(815)777-0557*
1 mi. SE at 513 Bouthillier St. - 61036
7 units   *Moderate-Expensive*

The imposing red-brick Stillman Mansion, built in 1858, is now a country inn. Continental breakfast is complimentary. Each well-furnished room has some authentic Victorian furnishings and most modern conveniences except phones. Some rooms also have a gas fireplace and a large in-room whirlpool tub.

BASIC INFORMATION
Elevation: 610 feet   Population (1990):   3,647
Location: 170 miles West of Chicago
Nearest airport with commercial flights: Dubuque, Iowa - 22 miles
Galena/Jo Daviess County Conv. & Visitors Bureau (815)777-0203
downtown at 101 Bouthillier St. - 61036   (800)747-9377
www.galena.org

Covington, Louisiana

Covington is an undiscovered bonanza of food and fun—Louisiana-style. Giant oaks shade Victorian neighborhoods nestled along the banks of the quiet Bogue Falaya River. A few miles south is vast Lake Pontchartrain, with New Orleans on the far shore. Dense forests and abundant water led to settlement in 1813, and prosperity as a health and recreation destination until after the Civil War. When railroads supplanted steamboats, the town became a backwater.

The good times roll again in Covington. Increasing numbers escape to the area's quiet charms—exotic bayous, luxuriant piney woods, fresh air, mild winters—and food. Louisiana cuisine, featuring fresh local seafood and produce, and soul-stirring sauces, stars in one of America's foremost concentrations of gourmet restaurants. Restored Victorian buildings house a growing array of culinary showplaces, galleries, specialty and antiques stores. In marked contrast, lodgings are scarce and mostly prosaic.

WEATHER PROFILE

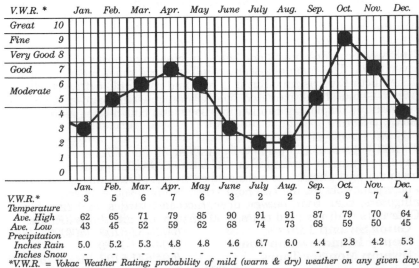

V.W.R. *		Jan.	Feb.	Mar.	Apr.	May	June	July	Aug.	Sep.	Oct.	Nov.	Dec.
Great	10												
Fine	9												
Very Good	8												
Good	7												
Moderate	6												
	5												
	4												
	3												
	2												
	1												
	0												

	Jan.	Feb.	Mar.	Apr.	May	June	July	Aug.	Sep.	Oct.	Nov.	Dec.
V.W.R.*	3	5	6	7	6	3	2	2	5	9	7	4
Temperature												
Ave. High	62	65	71	79	85	90	91	91	87	79	70	64
Ave. Low	43	45	52	59	62	68	74	73	68	59	50	45
Precipitation												
Inches Rain	5.0	5.2	5.3	4.8	4.8	4.6	6.7	6.0	4.4	2.8	4.2	5.3
Inches Snow	-	-	-	-	-	-	-	-	-	-	-	-

*V.W.R. = Vokac Weather Rating; probability of mild (warm & dry) weather on any given day.

Bicycling
Flat terrain, rivers and bayous and abundant byways shaded by moss-draped cypress, oak, and pine attract riders. The Tammany Trace, a 31-mile scenic rails-to-trails conversion, is especially popular. Bicycles can be rented by the hour or longer in and around town.

Boat Rentals
Power boats, canoes and (on the Bogue Chitto River) tubes can be rented for exploring the gentle waterways around town.

Downtown
centered around Boston & Columbia

Long ago, steamboats docked by the heart of town and a hotel provided stylish lodgings. The docks and the hotel are gone, but the historic downtown is making a comeback. Numerous antique dealers are being joined by art galleries, studios, regional specialty shops and distinctive restaurants. Just beyond, tranquil Bogue Falaya Park provides tree-shaded picnic areas along the banks of the river.

Fairview-Riverside State Park   (504)845-3318
6 mi. SW via LA 21 & LA 22

A shady bend of the Tchefuncta River features a boat dock, fishing pier, picnic facilities and a campground.

Fontainbleau State Park
8 mi. S via US 190 - Mandeville

A live oak alley forms a luxuriant entrance to this large park along the shore of Lake Pontchartrain. The former site of a sugar plantation has nature trails, a swimming pool, fishing, boating, picnicking and a complete campground.

H.J. Smith's Son   (504)892-0460
downtown at 308 N. Columbia St.

The Smith family has continuously operated this authentic old general store since 1876. A hand-carved cypress canoe, a cast-iron coffin and many household and farm items are displayed in the museum.

Lake Pontchartrain Causeway
7 mi. S on US 190

The world's longest bridge, opened in 1956, extends thirty miles between the north and south shores of Lake Pontchartrain. It isn't very scenic, but it does shave many miles off the drive to New Orleans.

Madisonville   (504)845-7311
5 mi. SW on LA 21

Hollywood couldn't have done better in creating a nostalgic Old South river town. The magnolia-scented village on a quiet meander of the Tchefuncta River is tiny. But it is real and romantic, with a cluster of one-of-a-kind shops, narrated boat cruise, museum, and several fine restaurants displaying captivating Louisiana cuisine (see listings).

Swamp Tours
24 mi. E via I-12 - Slidell

To really discover the primeval grandeur of one of America's wildest bayous, a narrated swamp tour is a must. Shallow-draft motorboats meander past photogenic moss-draped trees, cypress knees, fan palms and wildflowers during two-hour trips. Wildlife you may see includes alligators, boar, bear, beaver, deer, raccoons, turtles, and rare birds. Operators with reserved tours, food service and gift shops include:

Gator Swamp Tours   (504)484-6100   (800)875-4287
Honey Island Swamp Tours   (504)641-1769
Swamp Monster Tours   (504)641-5106   (800)245-1132

RESTAURANTS

Abita Brew Pub   *(504)892-5837   (800)737-2311*
2 mi. E at 72011 Holly St. - Abita Springs
B-L-D.   *Moderate*
A fine selection of zesty Louisiana pub grub is served with skillfully crafted brews made in the state's oldest microbrewery and served in a handsome old building with a tasting room, gift shop and brew pub.

Artesia   *(504)892-1662*
2 mi. E at 21516 Hwy. 36 - Abita Springs
L-D.   *Expensive*
A legendary chef, born in New Orleans, recently opened a superb culinary hideaway to critical acclaim. Fresh seasonal ingredients like wild local chanterelle mushrooms are masterfully transformed into dishes that are simply beautiful and richly flavorful. A Victorian hotel annex is now a plush inn with intimate firelit dining rooms.

Bechac's Restaurant   *(504)626-8500*
7 mi. S at 2025 Lakeshore Dr. - Mandeville
L-D.   *Moderate*
A local dining tradition for more than a century now offers updated Continental dishes with an appealing Louisiana topspin. Full linen enhances a dining room and bar with a Lake Pontchartrain view.

Coffee Rani   *(504)893-6158*
downtown at 234-A Lee Lane
B-L-D.   *Moderate*
Generous helpings of contemporary comfort foods include spectacular cinnamon rolls and other pastries, plus all kinds of coffees and teas. This spiffy coffee house with a dining deck is a deserved local favorite.

Coffee's Boilin' Pot   *(504)845-2348*
5 mi. SW at 305 Old Covington Hwy. (LA 21) - Madisonville
L-D.   *Low*
Roll up your sleeves and dig into platters of boiled crawfish, crabs and shrimp, or catfish or frog legs. The Gossey Cake is a perfect way to end a great feed at this authentic, rustic little roadhouse.

The Dakota Restaurant   *(504)892-3712*
3 mi. S at 629 N. Hwy 190
L-D.   *Expensive*
Here is a delightful source of contemporary Louisiana cuisine (picture soft-shelled crab stuffed with crawfish, shrimp and crabmeat fried and set on roasted pecan rice topped with creole sauce). The relaxed, tony dining room and lounge are an appropriately sophisticated backdrop.

Fusion Bistro   *(504)875-7620*
downtown at 321 N. Columbia St.
L-D.   *Expensive*
In 1996, an acclaimed local chef, born in New Orleans, opened an enchanting restaurant where Louisiana classics become fusion cuisine when blended with Southwestern, Asian and Mediterranean influences. Fresh, attractive dishes with exciting flavors are presented in a comfortably upscale bistro and garden court.

La Provence   *(504)626-7662*
13 mi. SE at 25020 Hwy. 190 - Lacombe
D only.   *Expensive*
One of Louisiana's best restaurants features top quality fresh local ingredients in an innovative mix of Southern French and Louisiana flavorings. The table d'hôte menu is a great way to experience grand cuisine in this intimate French country-style dinner house.

Licata's Restaurant and Seafood Market   *(504)893-1252*
3 mi. S at 1102 N. Hwy. 190
L-D.   *Moderate*
The catfish po' boy or gumbo are perfect ways to discover the simple delight of fried or boiled fresh real Louisiana seafood. The plain coffee shop/bar has a big seafood market next door.

Morton's Seafood Restaurant   *(504)845-4970*
5 mi. SW at 702 Water St. - Madisonville
L-D.   *Moderate*
Flavorful Louisiana dishes like freshly boiled crawfish or fried catfish have made this old-fashioned dining room/saloon a favorite for many years. An enclosed porch and open dining porch overlook a picturesque river.

Trey Yuen Cuisine of China   *(504)626-4476*
6 mi. S at 600 N. Causeway Blvd. - Mandeville
L-D.   *Moderate*
One of the South's best Chinese restaurants offers unique dishes that masterfully combine local seafoods with Oriental cooking techniques. (Consider marinated sliced gator meat stir-fried with mushrooms in a light oyster sauce!) Capacious, lavishly decorated dining rooms and a lounge overlook serene water-and-rock gardens.

Zazou Cafe   *(504)624-5235*
7 mi. S at 2101 Lakeshore Dr. - Mandeville
L-D.   *Moderate*
Creative creole cuisine has earned a loyal following for this casual bistro in an old house across a street from Lake Pontchartrain.

LODGING
Accommodations are surprisingly scarce and ordinary. Rates remain about the same throughout the year.

Courtyard by Marriott   *(504)871-0244*
3 mi. S at 101 Northpark Blvd. - 70433
90 units   *(800)321-2211*   *Moderate*
An indoor pool is a feature of this conventional motor hotel, and there is an exercise room and lounge. Each of the rooms is attractively furnished.

Holiday Inn   *(504)893-3580*
3 mi. S (near I-12) at 501 N. Hwy. 190 - 70433
156 units   *(800)465-4329*   *Moderate*
The area's largest lodging is a contemporary motor inn with an indoor/outdoor pool, whirlpool, exercise and recreation rooms, dining room and lounge. Each room is well furnished. One-bedroom suites also have a full kitchen.

Northpark Inn - Best Western   *(504)892-2681*
3 mi. S at 625 N. Hwy. 190 - 70433
74 units   *(800)528-1234*   *Moderate*
This modern motel has a pool, restaurant and lounge. Each unit is well furnished. The Magnolia Suite also has a whirlpool bath.

BASIC INFORMATION
Elevation: 25 feet   *Population (1990): 7,691*
Location: 40 miles North of New Orleans
Nearest airport with commercial flights: New Orleans - 42 miles
St. Tammany Parish Tourist & Convention Commission (504)892-0520
  5 mi. S at 68099 Hwy. 59 - Mandeville, LA 70471 (800)634-9443
Chamber of Commerce   (504)892-3216
  www.sttammanychamber.org

Bar Harbor, Maine

Bar Harbor is the East Coast's loveliest celebration of man and nature. It crowns a gentle rise by a bay on an island full of natural superlatives. The highest mountain on the Atlantic Coast and the only fiord south of Canada are here, in the oldest national park in the East. Although chartered in 1796 as a fishing village, tourism took hold before the Civil War. By 1880, it was a renowned summer resort. Soon after, some of America's wealthiest families—the Rockefellers, Astors, Pulitzers—began building palatial "cottages" as summer retreats, and donating land for what became Acadia National Park in 1919.

Today, most of the island is preserved in its natural state. Bar Harbor is the largest town. Blocks of trim human-scaled buildings house a wealth of galleries and specialty shops displaying renowned New England arts, crafts and gourmet products, plus diverse nightlife and enticing restaurants. Many historic and contemporary lodgings reflect genteel yesteryears in prime locations downtown and by the shore.

WEATHER PROFILE

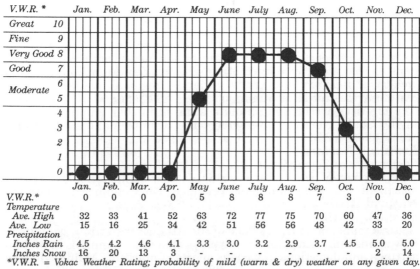

V.W.R. *		Jan.	Feb.	Mar.	Apr.	May	June	July	Aug.	Sep.	Oct.	Nov.	Dec.
Great	10												
Fine	9												
Very Good	8												
Good	7												
Moderate	6												
	5												
	4												
	3												
	2												
	1												
	0												

	Jan.	Feb.	Mar.	Apr.	May	June	July	Aug.	Sep.	Oct.	Nov.	Dec.
V.W.R.*	0	0	0	0	5	8	8	8	7	3	0	0
Temperature												
Ave. High	32	33	41	52	63	72	77	75	70	60	47	36
Ave. Low	15	16	25	34	42	51	56	56	48	42	33	20
Precipitation												
Inches Rain	4.5	4.2	4.6	4.1	3.3	3.0	3.2	2.9	3.7	4.5	5.0	5.0
Inches Snow	16	20	13	3	-	-	-	-	-	-	2	14

*V.W.R. = Vokac Weather Rating; probability of mild (warm & dry) weather on any given day.

ATTRACTIONS
Acadia National Park   *(207)288-3338*
just W on ME 3

The premier national park in the Northeast (circa 1919) includes more than half of Mount Desert Island, where Bar Harbor is located. Here is the quintessential rockbound coast of Maine. Massive granite cliffs, accessible sandy beaches, and the only fjord on the American east coast are backed by thick forests of hardwoods and pine. Inland on the fifty-square-mile island, Cadillac Mountain rises 1,530 feet above the surf. The highest summit on the Atlantic Coast can be reached by car via the Loop Road. Paved roads, and 120 miles of hiking and biking trails (including fifty miles of historic carriage paths), provide access to fresh and (cold) saltwater swimming beaches, historic sites, two campgrounds, and the visitor center (3 mi. NW at Hulls Cove).

Bicycling

There is no better way to experience the intimate grandeur of Acadia National Park and the rest of Mount Desert Island than on a bicycle. Mountain bikes and all related accessories can be rented by the half day or full day at:

Acadia Bike & Canoe   *(207)288-9605 (800)526-8615 (outside ME)*
Bar Harbor Bicycle Shop *(207)288-3886*

Boat Rentals

Exploring the spectacular coastline of the national park and nearby islands on your own or with a guide can be easily arranged downtown. For hourly or longer rentals and information, contact:

Acadia Bike & Canoe *(canoes)*   *(207)288-9605 (800)526-8615*
Acadia Outfitters *(tours, kayaks & canoes)*   *(207)288-8118*
Coastal Kayaking Tours *(tours & kayaks)* *(207)288-9605 (800)526-8615*
Harbor Boat Rentals *(powerboats)*   *(207)288-3757*

Boat Rides

Sightseeing cruises, whale and puffin watching trips, nature cruises and day sails can be arranged near the downtown pier at appropriate times of year. For information and reservations, call

Acadian Nature Cruise   *(207)288-3322*
Bar Harbor Whale Watch Co.   *(207)288-2386 (800)942-5374*
Frenchman Bay Nature Cruise   *(207)288-3322*

Downtown
around the Village Green at Mt. Desert & Main St.

The heart of Bar Harbor is the quintessence of man and nature in harmony. Blocks of historic and compatible newer buildings evoke a genteel past along tree-lined streets by tranquil Frenchman Bay. A wealth of fine art and crafts galleries, regional specialty shops, distinctive restaurants, quaint lodgings and a landmark inn are here. The district's picturesque human scale is further enhanced by an idyllic village green, lush sea-view park, town pier, and a serene and scenic shore path.

Fishing Charters
downtown at Town Pier

Several charter boats offer seasonal lobster-fishing and/or deep-sea sportfishing with all equipment provided. The Chamber has details.

Natural History Museum   *(207)288-5015*
just NW on ME 3

A stone mansion on the College of the Atlantic waterfront campus is now a museum with extensive displays of mounted animals in lifelike settings and depictions of various sports of maritime Maine. Visitors are encouraged to interact with a full-sized whale skeleton model.

Oceanarium & Lobster Hatchery   *(207)288-5005*
8 mi. NW on ME 3
Visitors can explore a living salt marsh, climb a viewing tower, or watch harbor seals. The **Maine Lobster Museum** offers interactive exhibits about lobsters, traps, boats, etc. At the **Lobster Hatchery** in town, guides narrate the process and display brood lobsters and tiny hatchlings to visitors. The original **Oceanarium** at Southwest Harbor has over twenty tanks with live sea animals, and a touch tank, plus interactive exhibits about the tides, fog and more.

RESTAURANTS

Bar Harbor Hotel - Bluenose Inn   *(207)288-3348*
1 mi. W on Route 3 at 90 Eden St.
B-D.   *Expensive*
The distinguished young hotel's acclaimed **Rose Garden Restaurant** presents creative and traditional New England cuisine in a plush-and-pretty setting where a gentleman can feel comfortable wearing a jacket.

Bar Harbor Inn   *(207)288-3351*
downtown on Newport Dr.
L-D.   *Expensive*
The posh hotel's dining room is **The Reading Room** (D only). New American cuisine with a Maine accent is presented in fresh innovative dishes like broiled haddock in smoked salmon slices or lobster pie with a buttered crumb topping. There are also luscious housemade desserts. Piano or harp entertainment contribute to the appeal of the relaxed, elegant setting. Panoramic views of the waterfront are also superb at the **Terrace Grill** (L-D), featuring lunch on the umbrella-shaded terrace.

The Bayview Inn   *(207)288-5861*
1 mi. W on Route 3 at 111 Eden St.
B-D.   *Expensive*
Innovative New England cuisine gets careful attention. The hotel's informally elegant dining room in a historic Georgian mansion overlooking Frenchman Bay has fine views and period decor.

Cottage Street Bakery & Deli   *(207)288-3010*
downtown at 59 Cottage St.
B-L-D.   *Moderate*
An array of baked goods is made fresh from scratch, on the premises, including seasonal Maine wild blueberry pie. Fresh hot popovers with homemade blueberry jam is one of many morning delights. In winter, the kitchen becomes a factory for all natural Maine berry condiments.

Duffy's Quarterdeck Restaurant   *(207)288-5292*
downtown at 1 Main St.
L-D.   *Moderate*
Fresh Maine lobster is featured in half a dozen different dishes described on a contemporary American menu. But, the real star in this casual restaurant with nautical decor is the view of Frenchman Bay from inside or on a deck.

Fisherman's Landing   *(207)288-4632*
downtown at 35 West St.
L-D.   *Low*
Here is a long-time favorite source for fresh succulent boiled Maine lobster. Other local treats can also be ordered from a blackboard menu and enjoyed on an outdoor deck or pavilion over the harbor.

Galyn's Galley   *(207)288-9706*
downtown at 17 Main St.
L-D.   *Moderate*
Fresh local fish are given serious attention along with slow-roasted
prime rib and hand-cut steaks. A Victorian boarding house has been
transformed to include relaxed, nautical dining rooms. There is also a
bar with periodic live entertainment, and a view deck.

George's Restaurant   *(207)288-4505*
downtown at 7 Stephens Lane
D only.   *Expensive*
Innovative Mediterranean cuisine is skillfully prepared with fresh
quality ingredients and described on a menu that invites you to dine
or simply graze. The lobster strudel is a delightful alterative to
steamed lobster (also served). Sophisticated decor in the house off the
main street complements the cuisine. There is also a dining terrace
and a piano bar.

The Golden Anchor Pier Restaurant   *(207)288-2110*
downtown at 55 West St.
B-L-D.   *Expensive*
Down-East fare includes seafood specialties like baked stuffed lobster.
Casual dining rooms and an open-air deck topside share a spectacular
view of the harbor and nearby islands from a choice waterfront
location.

Island Chowder House   *(207)288-4905*
downtown at 38 Cottage St.
L-D.   *Moderate*
Hearty portions of Down-East dishes like award-winning clam
chowder, Maine lobster and homemade blueberry pie are served in a
friendly, casual restaurant with a full bar and a model train circling
the dining room.

Jordan Pond House   *(207)276-3316*
10 mi. SW via Route 3 on Acacia National Park Loop Road
L-tea-D.   *Moderate*
Afternoon beverages with warm popovers made here is a must. The
homemade ice cream is a nice way to top off a meal of contemporary
New England cuisine. A flagstone fireplace warms the handsome
contemporary room, and expansive windows provide a panoramic view
of gardens, Jordan Pond, forests, and mountains. A covered terrace
shares the memorable view.

Maggie's Classic Scales   *(207)288-9007*
downtown at 6 Summer St.
D only.   *Moderate*
Fresh local fish and organic vegetables are consistently used for
meticulously prepared imaginative dishes. Breads and desserts are
also homemade from scratch. Guests can opt for an intimate relaxed
room or an enclosed sun porch overlooking lovely gardens.

The Porcupine Grill   *(207)288-3884*
just W at 123 Cottage St.
D only.   *Expensive*
Imaginative American cuisine features fresh quality ingredients
expertly prepared with a lot of extra touches. The dinner house is an
island favorite for delicious food and dignified-yet-casual decor that
includes many quality antiques in the bar and upstairs dining rooms.

LODGING

Accommodations are abundant, with a wealth of historic bed-and-breakfasts, inns, and motels. Many have choice waterfront sites or dramatic overlooks. Summer is high season. Many places close for the winter, and reduce their spring and fall rates 40% or more.

Atlantic Eyrie Lodge   *(207)288-9786*
1 mi. W on Route 3 to Highbrook Rd. - 04609
58 units   *(800)422-2883*   *Moderate-Expensive*
Perched atop a bluff overlooking the bay is a four-story modern motel with a pool. Each well-furnished unit has a private bay-view balcony.

Atlantic Oakes By-the-Sea   *(207)288-5801*
1 mi. W on Route 3 at 119 Eden St. (Box 3) - 04609
150 units   *(800)336-2463*   *Expensive*
This expansive motel includes a mansion and several modern buildings up to four stories with large outdoor and indoor pools, whirlpool, pebble beaches and boat dock, and (fee) five tennis courts. Each unit is well furnished. Most have a private deck with a bay view.

Balance Rock Inn   *(207)288-2610*
downtown at 21 Albert Meadow - 04609
21 units   *(800)753-0494*   *Very Expensive*
Balance Rock Inn is one of America's quintessential bed-and-breakfast hideaways. A turn-of-the-century mansion by the sea is secluded amid luxuriant landscaping. Amenities of the romantic inn include a historic waterfront path, an ocean view pool, and an exercise room. Full buffet breakfast and afternoon tea are complimentary. Each spacious room is individually luxuriously furnished with antiques and all contemporary conveniences. Most have an intimate ocean view, whirlpool bath, and a private porch. Some also have a fireplace and sauna.

Bar Harbor Hotel - Bluenose Inn   *(207)288-3348*
1 mi. W on Route 3 at 90 Eden St. - 04609
97 units   *(800)445-4077   Expensive-Very Expensive*
High atop a hillside overlooking the bay is a stylish four-story motor lodge with two pools (one indoor), whirlpool, exercise room, gourmet restaurant (see listing), plush firelit lounge, and a gift shop. Rooms are well furnished in the Stenna Nordica building. Most spacious, beautifully furnished rooms in Mizzentop share the fine bay view and also have a private balcony and gas fireplace.

Bar Harbor Inn   *(207)288-3351*
downtown on Newport Dr. (Box 7) - 04609
153 units   *(800)248-3351   Expensive-Very Expensive*
Bar Harbor's premier resort hotel has a perfect location on beautifully landscaped grounds by the harbor downtown. Amenities of the three-story complex include a pool, whirlpool, (fee) boat dock, small beach, historic waterfront path, gourmet restaurant (see listing) and lounge. Light breakfast and cookies are complimentary. Each room is beautifully furnished with all contemporary conveniences. Oceanfront Lodge rooms also have private balconies.

Bar Harbor Regency   *(207)288-9723*
1 mi. W on Route 3 at 123 Eden St. - 04609
221 units   *(800)234-6835*   *Expensive*
The area's largest hotel is on an attractively landscaped site by the bay. The four-story contemporary complex has a large view pool, whirlpool, sauna, tennis courts, putting green, exercise room, marina, bay-view restaurant and lounge, and gift shop. Each well-furnished room has a private balcony—most with a panoramic view of the bay.

Bar Harbor, Maine

The Bayview Inn (207)288-5861
1 mi. W on Route 3 at 111 Eden St. - 04609
38 units (800)356-3585 *Expensive-Very Expensive*
A white brick Georgian-style mansion perched above the harbor is now the heart of an elegant hotel complex. The secluded wooded setting includes a view pool, whirlpool, exercise room, fine restaurant (see listing) and lounge. Some of the beautifully furnished inn, hotel and townhouse rooms have a sea view, fireplace, and a whirlpool bath.

The Golden Anchor Inn & Pier (207)288-5033
downtown at 55 West St. - 04609
88 units (800)328-5033 *Expensive*
The harbor borders this modern motel by the heart of town, and there is a view pool. Buffet breakfast is complimentary. The pier also houses a bay-view restaurant (see listing), and day cruises. All of the well-furnished rooms have a private balcony with a superb waterfront view.

The Kedge Bed & Breakfast (207)288-5180
just W at 112 West St. - 04609
3 units (800)597-8306 *Moderate-Expensive*
Frenchman Bay is across a street from this graceful bed-and-breakfast in a transformed 1870 home. Full breakfast is complimentary. Each spacious, beautifully furnished room has period and contemporary decor, and a private bath, but no phone. Two have a gas fireplace.

The Ledgelawn Inn (207)288-4596
just W at 66 Mount Desert St. - 04609
33 units (800)274-5334 *Moderate-Expensive*
A baronial 1904 summer home was recently transformed into a nostalgic inn with stylish period pieces throughout, a nifty widow's walk, and a firelit bar. Full buffet breakfast is complimentary. Each beautifully furnished room in the mansion and carriage house blends antiques and all modern conveniences. Some also have a fireplace, private porch and/or whirlpool bath.

Primrose Inn (207)288-4031
just W at 73 Mount Desert St. - 04609
15 units (800)543-7842 *Moderate-Expensive*
A big 1878 summer cottage now serves as an appealing bed-and-breakfast. Full buffet breakfast and afternoon treats are complimentary. Each beautifully furnished room blends antiques and contemporary conveniences. Some also have a fireplace or whirlpool bath.

The Tides (207)288-4968
just W at 119 West St. - 04609
3 units *Very Expensive*
An 1887 oceanfront estate amid lovely lawns and gardens still conveys the luxury of another era in its role as a bed-and-breakfast. Full gourmet breakfast and afternoon tea and baked goods are complimentary. Each spacious two-room suite is individually luxuriously furnished with a thorough blend of nostalgic and contemporary conveniences, and has a bay view. Two also have a fireplace.

BASIC INFORMATION

Elevation: 20 feet *Population (1990): 4,443*
Location: 260 miles Northwest of Boston
Nearest airport with commercial flights: Trenton, ME - 12 miles
Bar Harbor Chamber of Commerce (207)288-5103
  downtown at 93 Cottage St. (Box 158) - 04609 (800)288-5103
  www.barharborinfo.com

Boothbay Harbor, Maine

Boothbay Harbor is one of New England's most beguiling seaport villages. It is sequestered along narrow winding streets and gentle hills above a snug harbor. Luxuriant stands of hardwoods and pine back the rockbound coastlines of islands and peninsulas that shelter the village and harbor from the ocean. The area was settled by fishermen in 1630. For the past century, it has been evolving into a recreation and leisure destination.

Nautical activities are as important as ever in one of the Northeast's preeminent natural harbors. Lobstering, fishing and boating attract hordes of sportsmen and tourists in summer and fall. So do quaint galleries and studios full of prime regional art and crafts, specialty shops displaying nautical gifts, and gourmet stands and restaurants featuring lobsters and blueberries. Lodgings are plentiful and delightfully one-of-a-kind, ranging from modern motor hotels to historic small inns and resorts. Most are on or near the waterfront.

WEATHER PROFILE

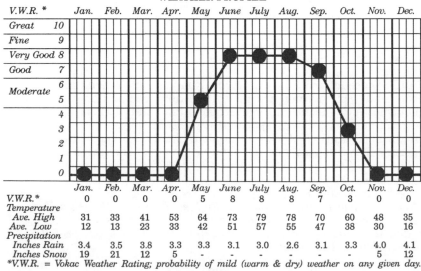

	Jan.	Feb.	Mar.	Apr.	May	June	July	Aug.	Sep.	Oct.	Nov.	Dec.
V.W.R.*	0	0	0	0	5	8	8	8	7	3	0	0
Temperature												
Ave. High	31	33	41	53	64	73	79	78	70	60	48	35
Ave. Low	12	13	23	33	42	51	57	55	47	38	30	16
Precipitation												
Inches Rain	3.4	3.5	3.8	3.3	3.3	3.1	3.0	2.6	3.1	3.3	4.0	4.1
Inches Snow	19	21	12	5	-	-	-	-	-	-	5	12

*V.W.R. = Vokac Weather Rating; probability of mild (warm & dry) weather on any given day.

ATTRACTIONS

Barrett Park
1 mi. E on Lobster Cove Rd.
Fishing, swimming (for the really robust), sunbathing, and picnicking are all popular in a park with 1,800 feet of shoreline on tranquil Lobster Cove. The rockbound coastal views are memorable.

Bicycling
  Tidal Transit Co.   *(207)633-7140*
  downtown at 49 Townsend Av.
The maritime beauty of the village and surrounding coastline are perfect for leisurely bike jaunts along byways and trails. Mountain bikes and related accessories can be rented in town here.

Boat Rentals
  Midcoast Boat Rentals   *(207)633-4188*
  downtown at Pier 8
This is the place to rent a powerboat by the hour or longer for exploring the inlets and islands of the picturesque coast.

Boat Rides
One hour and longer sightseeing cruises, whale and puffin watching trips, day sails, sunset and moolight cruises can be arranged at appropriate times of year at several downtown piers. For information and reservations, call:
  Appledore   *(207)633-6598*
  Balmy Days Cruises   *(207)633-2284*
  Cap'n Fish's Boat Cruises   *(207)633-3244* *(800)636-3244*
Boothbay Railway Village   *(207)633-4727*
  3 mi. N on ME 27
A town hall, railroad station, post office, general store and a one-room schoolhouse are among dozens of buildings in a re-created historic Maine village. Collections of railroad relics, antique cars, trucks, and fire equipment are displayed. A ride on a coal-fired narrow-gauge steam train is a highlight.

Downtown
around Townsend Av. & Commercial St.
The heart of Boothbay Harbor looks like a movie set of a Down-East coastal village. In fact, it was. Part of the musical "Carousel" was filmed here. Piers extend into the sheltered harbor, backed by narrow winding streets with quaint shops brimming with local art, jewelry, crafts and regional gourmet foods. Sea-view restaurants, lounges, and lodgings are plentiful. For intimate nautical views, walk across the unique landmark footbridge.

Fishing Charters
Several charter boats leave from the downtown piers for half-day and all-day deep-sea fishing with all necessary equipment provided. You might even be able to arrange a hands-on experience with lobster trap hauling. For more information, contact:
  Breakaway Sportfishing   *(207)633-6990*
  Cap'n Fish's Deep Sea Fishing   *(207)633-3244* *(800)636-3244*
Grimes Cove Beach
  5 mi. SE on ME 96
This beach is on Ocean Point, a scenic peninsula overlooking offshore islands and the open ocean. It's a popular place to watch boats coming and going from the village. The water is inevitably cold, but hardy locals even swim here.

RESTAURANTS

Andrews' Harborside Restaurant   *(207)633-4074*
downtown at W end of the footbridge
B-L-D.   *Moderate*
Big fresh-baked cinnamon rolls are a breakfast specialty, while homemade desserts accompany traditional New England dishes later. There is a light, bright nautical feeling about the casual dining room and deck overlooking the harbor.

Harbour High Restaurant   *(207)633-3444*
downtown at 23 Oak St.
L-D.   *Moderate*
Traditional and updated New England dishes are typified by lobster pie or honey-crumb scallops. The pleasant little dining room and lounge complement the sophisticated cuisine, and there is a view porch.

Lawnmeer Inn and Restaurant   *(207)633-2544*
3 mi. S on Route 27 - West Boothbay Harbor
B-D.   *Expensive*
Creative New England cuisine made with top quality local fresh fish and produce is skillfully presented. Top off the delicious entrees with luscious desserts like blueberries in puff pastry. Every table in the casually elegant dining room of the charming 1898 inn has a fine harbor view.

Lobstermen's Co-op   *(207)633-4900*   *(800)785-6370*
just S on Atlantic Av.
L-D.   *Moderate*
At the working lobster pound, "you pick 'em, we cook 'em." Steamed clams and other local seafood are also popular. You order at the counter, and eat at rows of picnic tables outdoors or in a two-story pavilion with a superb harbor view.

Newagen Seaside Inn   *(207)633-5242*
6 mi. S on Route 27 - Cape Newagen
D only.   *Expensive*
Continental and American classics and updated dishes feature regional produce. The inn's large, relaxed dining room has water views on two sides.

Ocean Point Inn   *(207)633-4200*
7 mi. SE on Shore Rd. (ME 96) - East Boothbay
B-D.   *Expensive*
Contemporary American cuisine is given careful attention in the relaxed, gracious atmosphere of the inn's waterfront dining room. Scenic picture-window views of the ocean and islands are memorable.

Robinson's Wharf   *(207)633-3830*
2 mi. S on Route 27 - Southport
L-D.   *Moderate*
Basic classics among Down-East fare like fish chowder, and lobster—in stew, rolls, or whole—are served with homemade pies and brownies. Long communal tables under cover and on the wharf give hordes of fans a fine waterway and drawbridge view.

Rocktide Inn   *(207)633-4455*
just SE at 35 Atlantic Av.
B-D.   *Expensive*
Down-East fisherman's fare is featured—from finnan haddie to steamed fresh local clams, along with a salad bar, hot popovers, and homemade desserts. There are three casual and two semi-formal (jackets required) dining rooms with panoramic town/harbor views.

Spruce Point Inn   *(207)633-4152*

2 mi. SE via Atlantic Av. & Spruce Point Rd.

B-D.   *Expensive*

Gourmet New England cuisine and periodic lobster bakes are specialties of the picturesque inn by the sea. The large and plush pine-paneled dining room suggests a degree of formality in keeping with the sophisticated cuisine and dramatic oceanfront site.

The Thistle Inn   *(207)633-3541*

downtown at 53 Oak St.

L-D.   *Expensive*

Thoughtfully prepared New England cuisine is served in an intimate dining room with the warmth of a Scottish pub. The restaurant is part of a small inn.

LODGING

Accommodations are plentiful. Many—from resorts to motels—sport waterfront locales, and there are historic inns. Summer is high season. Most places close in winter, or reduce their rates 20% or more.

Brown's Wharf Inn   *(207)633-5440*

1 mi. S at 121 Atlantic Av. - 04538

70 units   *(800)334-8110*   *Expensive*

The view of the village and harbor is lovely from this modern motel with a waterfront restaurant and lounge. Each of the well-furnished rooms has a sea view.

Eastland Harborside Resort   *(207)633-5381*

1 mi. W via Route 27 & Lakeview Rd. (Box 101) - 04538

33 units   *(800)235-5402*   *Moderate-Expensive*

Above the shore of West Harbor is a modern motel with one of the area's few sandy beaches. They also have a pool, and a dock with complimentary rowboats and canoes. Each spacious room is comfortably furnished and has a private balcony or deck with a water view.

Fisherman's Wharf Inn   *(207)633-5090*

downtown at 22 Commercial St. - 04538

54 units   *(800)628-6872 (outside ME) Moderate-Expensive*

Pier #6 juts into the harbor in the heart of town. It includes this modern motel with a big waterfront restaurant, lounge, and gift shop. Many well-furnished rooms have a balcony and harbor view.

Five Gables Inn   *(207)633-4551*

4 mi. SE via Route 96 on Murray Hill Rd. - East Boothbay 04544

16 units   *(800)451-5048*   *Moderate-Expensive*

A Victorian summer hotel overlooking Linekin Bay has been lovingly transformed into a bed-and-breakfast inn. A hearty breakfast buffet and afternoon beverages are complimentary. Each room has nostalgic touches, a water view and contemporary conveniences, including a private bath. Several have a fireplace.

Lawnmeer Inn   *(207)633-2544*

2 mi. S on Route 27 (Box 505) - West Boothbay Harbor 04575

32 units   *(800)633-7645*   *Moderate-Expensive*

Tucked away in a serene location by the water's edge is a three-story, century-old white clapboard inn. Broad decks and a fine restaurant (see listing) overlook the inlet. So do Adirondack chairs on an expansive lawn extending from the chef's garden to the dock. Each room is well furnished. There are no phones, but many rooms have water views, and some have a balcony.

Newagen Seaside Inn   *(207)633-5242*
6 mi. S on Route 27 (Box 88) - Cape Newagen 04552
26 units   *(800)654-5242*   *Expensive*
Far from the maddening crowds, at the forested tip of Southport
Island, is a classic rockbound-coast-of-Maine inn. Amenities include an
enormous saltwater pool by the ocean, a heated freshwater pool, two
tennis courts, a nature trail, tidal pools, a dock and rowboats, plus a
lounge and dining room (see listing). Bountiful breakfast buffet is
complimentary. Most of the well-furnished rooms offer ocean views
instead of TV and phone. Six rooms have private view decks.

Ocean Gate Inn   *(207)633-3321*
3 mi. S on Route 27 (Box 240) - West Southport 04576
67 units   *(800)221-5924*   *Moderate-Expensive*
Nestled in woods adjacent to the rockbound coast is a contemporary
motel with a pool, two tennis courts, exercise room, lawn games and a
dock with boats for guests. Full breakfast buffet is complimentary.
Each room is attractively furnished. Most have a private balcony by
the waterfront.

Ocean Point Inn   *(207)633-4200*
7 mi. SE on Shore Rd. (ME 96) (Box 409) - East Boothbay 04544
61 units   *(800)552-5554*   *Moderate-Expensive*
A lodge, motel and cottages are sprinkled along the point at the
entrance to Linekin Bay. There is a pool, restaurant (see listing), and
lounge. Most of the comfortably furnished units have an ocean view.
Some have a private balcony or porch or fireplace.

Rocktide Inn   *(207)633-4455*
just SE at 35 Atlantic Av. - 04538
98 units   *(800)762-8433*   *Expensive*
The area's biggest lodging is a modern motor inn built out over the
harbor overlooking downtown. The complex includes an indoor pool,
boat dock, view restaurant (see listing) and lounge. An elaborate buffet
breakfast is complimentary. Each room is attractively furnished. Some
have a private balcony with an intimate view of both the harbor and
village.

Spruce Point Inn   *(207)633-4152*
2 mi. SE via Atlantic Av. & Spruce Point Rd. (Box 237) - 04538
74 units   *(800)553-0289*   *Expensive-Very Expensive*
This recently renovated resort is on a wooded peninsula at the
entrance to Boothbay Harbor. Amenities include fresh and saltwater
pools, whirlpool, two tennis courts, fitness room, nature trails and
tidepools, dock and boats, gourmet restaurant (see listing) and lounge
with entertainment. (Modified American Plan rates include breakfast
and dinner in summer.) All of the units in the inn and cottages are
beautifully furnished. Many have fine ocean views. Some also have a
fireplace.

BASIC INFORMATION
Elevation: 12 feet   Population (1990):   2,347
Location: 165 miles Northeast of Boston
Nearest airport with commercial flights: Augusta - 33 miles
Boothbay Harbor Region Chamber of Commerce   (207)633-2353
*   just N on ME 27 at 192 Townsend Av. (Box 356) - 04538*
*   (800)266-8422*
www.boothbayharbor.com

Camden, Maine

Camden is one of America's most enchanting collaborations between man and nature. It is sequestered in luxuriant woodlands at the foot of gentle mountains that rise dramatically above a snug harbor. The lovely setting is further enhanced by a four-season climate that assures flamboyant fall colors. The town was settled during the late 19th century by shipbuilders and seafarers. From the beginning, artists and craftsmen were also attracted, and writers. Edna St. Vincent Millay began her career here.

Today, the mountains and shore are as splendid as ever. But, shipbuilders and mill workers have been replaced by sportsmen and vacationers. Downtown, a photogenic mix of proudly maintained historic buildings and compatible newer ones surround dramatic Harbor Park with its solid-rock cascade where a river meets the sea. Quality artwork, crafts, antiques and regional specialties are plentiful. So are restaurants and inns with memorable histories and nautical outlooks.

WEATHER PROFILE

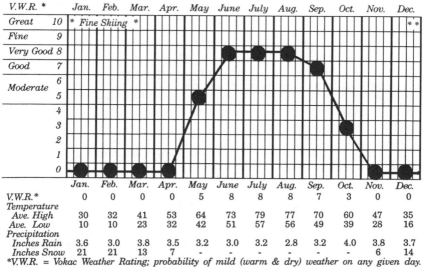

V.W.R. *		Jan.	Feb.	Mar.	Apr.	May	June	July	Aug.	Sep.	Oct.	Nov.	Dec.
Great	10	*	Fine Skiing	*									* *
Fine	9												
Very Good	8												
Good	7												
Moderate	6												
	5												

	Jan.	Feb.	Mar.	Apr.	May	June	July	Aug.	Sep.	Oct.	Nov.	Dec.
V.W.R.*	0	0	0	0	5	8	8	8	7	3	0	0
Temperature												
Ave. High	30	32	41	53	64	73	79	77	70	60	47	35
Ave. Low	10	10	23	32	42	51	57	56	49	39	28	16
Precipitation												
Inches Rain	3.6	3.0	3.8	3.5	3.2	3.0	3.2	2.8	3.2	4.0	3.8	3.7
Inches Snow	21	21	13	7	-	-	-	-	-	-	6	14

*V.W.R. = Vokac Weather Rating; probability of mild (warm & dry) weather on any given day.

Bicycling
Brown Dog Bike   *(207)236-6664*
downtown at 53 Chestnut St.
Spectacular coastlines backed by scenic mountains, forests, lakes and rivers are ideal for bike tours along byways and trails. Bicycle rentals, accessories, maps and information are available here.

Boat Rides
Both motor vessels and sailboats leave from Town Landing downtown for sightseeing or nature cruises ranging in length from one hour to all day. The Appledore, Olad and Surprise are big (more than fifty feet long) sailing schooners; Wendameen is a big windjammer featuring overnight sails with breakfast and dinner; and Betselma is a power excursion boat.

Appledore	*(207)236-8353*
Betsclma	*(207)236-4446*
Olad	*(207)236-2323*
Surprise	*(207)236-4687*
Wendameen	*(207)594-1751*

Camden is the windjammer capital of the world. Several, including some National Landmark Vessels, leave from here for trips of three to six days. The Chamber has details.

Camden Hills State Park   *(207)236-3109*
2 mi. N on US 1
This large park surrounds 1,380-foot Mount Megunticook, but the highlight is a road up 800-foot Mt. Battie to a splendid view of the village and coast. There are also hiking trails, picnic facilities and a complete campground.

Downtown
around Main & Bayview Sts.
Picture-postcard historic buildings line curving streets where a clear stream cascades down a massive granite slope to a snug harbor. A charming town park and landing enhance a waterfront overlooking picturesque islands and a peerless collection of windjammers. Galleries and studios, specialty shops and restaurants feature regional art, crafts and food, while attractively landscaped historic and contemporary buildings reflect the town's perfect human scale, good taste, and splendid nautical views.

Farnsworth Art Museum   *(207)596-6457*
8 mi. S via US 1 at 19 Elm St. - Rockland
The theme of this major art museum is artists with Maine ties, like Winslow Homer and Andrew, Jamie, and N. C. Wyeth. The permanent "Maine in America" collection includes outstanding works from the past two hundred years.

Laite Memorial Beach
just SE on Bayview St.
The nearest beach is small, and the water is cold. But it is scenic, and there are restrooms and picnic sites.

Old Conway House Complex   *(207)236-2257*
1 mi. S via US 1
An 18th century farmhouse has been fully restored and outfitted with authentic period pieces. The complex, open in July and August, also includes a barn with antique sleighs, carriages, and farm implements; a blacksmith shop; maple sugar house; herb garden; and the Mary Meeker Cramer Museum of local memorabilia.

Winter Sports
Camden Snow Bowl   *(207)236-3438*
4 mi. W via US 1 & John St.

The ocean is closer to Camden Snow Bowl than to any other lift-served alpine ski area in America. As a result, the view of Penobscot Bay less than four miles away is unforgettable from the 1,100-foot summit. The vertical rise is 950 feet, and the longest run is more than a mile. There is one chairlift. Basic facilities, service, and food service are at the base. Lodgings are in town. Ski season is mid-December to mid-March. There is also an ice skating pond. For a real thrill, don't miss the 400-foot toboggan run that whizzes you down a steep ramp onto the frozen pond.

RESTAURANTS

The Belmont Restaurant   *(207)236-8053*
downtown at 6 Belmont Av.
D only.   *Expensive*

Creative New England cuisine receives careful attention under the guidance of a well-known chef in a pleasant little inn with informal Victorian decor.

Camden Harbour Inn   *(207)236-4200*   *(800)236-4266*
downtown at 83 Bayview St.
B-D.   *Expensive*

Traditional and contemporary New England cuisine is presented in the candlelit dining room of an inn that captures the spirit of its 1870s roots from a hillside perch overlooking Camden Harbor.

Cappy's Chowder House   *(207)236-2254*
downtown at 1 Main St.
B-L-D.   *Moderate*

Here is the place for great lobster stew or chowder, and fresh local seafood and baked goods. (Don't miss the lobster roll on a homemade croissant.) Locals and visitors alike flock to this landmark with warm pub decor on two levels.

Chez Michel Restaurant   *(207)789-5600*
6 mi. N on US 1 - Lincolnville Beach
L-D.   *Moderate*

Fresh Maine lobsters and salmon, homemade chowders and desserts are featured among New England cuisine with a French accent. The simply comfortable restaurant has an outside deck overlooking Penobscot Bay.

Lobster Pound Restaurant   *(207)789-5550*
6 mi. N on US 1 - Lincolnville Beach
L-D.   *Moderate*

Lobster from their tanks is the specialty. Fresh seafood, turkey and steaks are also served indoors or outdoors. The enormous casual restaurant and bar border Penobscot Bay. There is also a gift shop.

Peter Ott's   *(207)236-4032*
downtown at 16 Bayview St.
D only.   *Moderate*

Fresh local seafood and black Angus beef highlight contemporary American fare served in a big bustling restaurant and lounge.

Samoset Resort   *(207)594-0774*   *(800)341-1650*
6 mi. S via US 1 & Waldo Rd. at 220 Warrenton St. - Rockport
B-D.   *Expensive*

The resort's handsome dining room is **Marcel's**, where Continental cuisine receives polished table service worthy of the semi-formal elegance of the setting overlooking Penobscot Bay.

Sea Dog Brewing Company   *(207)236-6863*
downtown at 43 Mechanic St.
L-D.   *Moderate*
Hearty helpings of Down-East homestyle cooking can be washed down
with their medal-winning lagers and ales. The big tavern in a
microbrewery overlooks the waterfall at historic Knox Mill.

Waterfront Restaurant   *(207)236-3747*
downtown at 40 Bayview St.
L-D.   *Moderate*
Fresh grilled fish and lobsters and a raw bar highlight the offerings
served in casual dining areas, bar and deck bordering Camden Harbor.

Whitehall Inn   *(207)236-3391*
just N on US 1 at 52 High St.
B-D.   *Expensive*
The inn's dining room specializes in traditional New England cuisine,
including housemade baked goods and desserts. The informal dining
room and lounge reflect the authentic appeal of this historic inn.

LODGING

Accommodations are plentiful in and around town. Historic inns and
bed-and-breakfasts predominate. Several border or overlook the bay.
Summer is high season. Many places close for the winter and reduce
their rates 30% or more in spring and fall.

Blue Harbor House, A Village Inn   *(207)236-3196*
downtown at 67 Elm St. - 04843
10 units   *(800)248-3196*   *Moderate-Expensive*
An 1810 home has been transformed into a classic New England bed-
and-breakfast inn. Full breakfast is complimentary. Each room is
beautifully furnished with antiques and most modern conveniences.
Whirlpool baths are available.

The Camden Riverhouse Hotel - Best Western   *(207)236-0500*
downtown at 11 Tannery Lane - 04843
36 units   *(800)755-7483*   *Expensive*
A footbridge connects this 1995 four-story motel to the heart of town.
There is an exercise room and complimentary light breakfast. Some of
the well-furnished rooms have a mini-kitchen and whirlpool.

The Country Inn at Camden - Rockport   *(207)236-2725*
1 mi. S on US 1 at 40 Commercial St. (Box 277) - 04843
28 units   *Expensive*
An indoor pool, whirlpool, sauna, and exercise room are features of
this newer motel. Continental breakfast and afternoon tea are
complimentary. Each room is well furnished. Some have a whirlpool.

Hawthorn Inn   *(207)236-8842*
just N at 9 High St. - 04843
10 units   *Expensive*
A stately turreted 1894 mansion (on the National Register) and
carriage house were restored to serve as a bed-and-breakfast. Full
breakfast is complimentary. Each room is beautifully furnished with
lovely antiques and all contemporary conveniences except a phone.
Some overlook the harbor. Two luxury rooms in the Carriage House
have a private view balcony, fireplace and two-person whirlpool bath.

The Inn at Sunrise Point   *(207)236-7716*
4 mi. N on US 1 (Box 1344) - 04843
7 units   *(800)435-6278*   *Expensive-Very Expensive*
A landscaped turn-of-the-century estate tucked away at the edge of
Penobscot Bay is now a luxury inn with cottages and a private

seashore. Full breakfast and afternoon appetizers served in a glass conservatory are complimentary. Each luxuriously furnished room has a fireplace, all conveniences including a large tub, and an ocean view. The cottages also have a private deck and double whirlpool.

The Lodge at Camden Hills   *(207)236-8478*
1 mi. N on US 1 (Box 794) - 04843
20 units   *(800)832-7058*   *Expensive*
Some of the most romantic rooms in New England are nestled in a park-like woodland setting. In the stylish complex of wood-trimmed buildings, each spacious, beautifully furnished room has every modern convenience, and a private deck with sea and wooded vistas. Deluxe cottages also have a kitchen, fireplace and two-person whirlpool.

Lord Camden Inn   *(207)236-4325*
downtown on US 1 at 24 Main St. - 04843
31 units   *(800)336-4325*   *Expensive*
One of downtown's landmarks is a restored 1893 brick building across a street from the harbor. Each well-furnished room in the four-story complex blends restored antique decor with all contemporary comforts. Most have a private balcony with a view of the village and harbor.

Norumbega   *(207)236-4646*
just N on US 1 at 61 High St. - 04843
13 units   *Very Expensive*
Norumbega is a fanciful Victorian castle-by-the-sea. Built in 1886 near Penobscot Bay, it served as a residence for a century. The meticulously restored five-story stone castle is now a truly baronial bed-and-breakfast on the National Historic Register. Complimentary full breakfast, afternoon beverages, and evening treats are served in dramatically wood-paneled public rooms with fireplaces and harbor views. Each beautifully furnished unit blends period and contemporary decor. Some units feature a fireplace, private view balcony or alcove, and clawfoot tub or whirlpool.

The Victorian By the Sea   *(207)236-3785*
4 mi. N via US 1 (Box 1385) - 04843
7 units   *(800)382-9817*   *Expensive*
A stately Victorian home by the sea is now an elegant bed-and-breakfast hideaway amid expansive lawns and gardens. Breakfast and evening sweets are complimentary. All of the beautifully furnished rooms have a fireplace. Most have a bay view.

Whitehall Inn   *(207)236-3391*
just N on US 1 at 52 High St. (Box 558) - 04843
50 units   *(800)789-6565*   *Expensive*
Camden's premier traditional country inn is on the National Historic Register. Antique wooden rockers on sprawling porches retain a nostalgic spirit dating back to 1834. So do public rooms including the restaurant (see listing) and lounge. Full breakfast is complimentary. There is also a breakfast and dinner plan. Guest rooms are simply, comfortably furnished. Some are small and share baths. None has a TV to mar the gentle appeal of this showcase of a time gone by.

BASIC INFORMATION

Elevation: 30 feet   *Population (1990):   5,060*
Location: 190 miles Northeast of Boston
Nearest airport with commercial flights: Rockland - 11 miles
Camden-Rockport-Lincolnville Chamber of Commerce (207)236-4404
  downtown at Public Landing (Box 919) - 04843   (800)223-5459
  www.camdenme.org

241

Freeport, Maine

Freeport is a delightful mix of early Americana and contemporary convenience. Forests blanket gentle hills and flatlands above tidewaters where the Harraseeket River meets the sea in scenic Casco Bay. By the late 18th century, the site proved ideal for settlement based on fishing, shipbuilding, farming and trade. L.L. Bean opened the modern era in 1912 with its retail and mail order business. In the 1980s, it was joined by a throng of retail outlet stores.

Today, Freeport is a preeminent destination for seafarers and sales-seekers. The Town Wharf is more compact and quiet than earlier, but still a vital starting place for nautical adventures. Downtown offers more than 100 stores, from L.L. Bean's recently expanded landmark sporting-goods-store-for-the-millennium, to upscale factory and designer outlets, plus one-of-a-kind Maine specialty shops. All of these, and a growing number of good restaurants and distinctive inns, are housed in restored historic buildings and compatible replicas.

WEATHER PROFILE

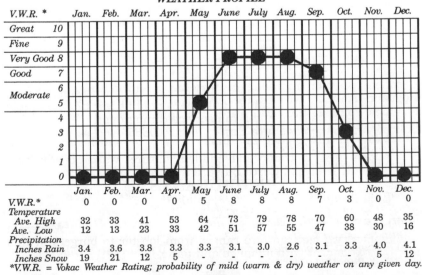

V.W.R. *		Jan.	Feb.	Mar.	Apr.	May	June	July	Aug.	Sep.	Oct.	Nov.	Dec.
Great	10												
Fine	9												
Very Good	8												
Good	7												
Moderate	6												
	5												
	4												
	3												
	2												
	1												
	0												

	Jan.	Feb.	Mar.	Apr.	May	June	July	Aug.	Sep.	Oct.	Nov.	Dec.
V.W.R.*	0	0	0	0	5	8	8	8	7	3	0	0
Temperature												
Ave. High	32	33	41	53	64	73	79	78	70	60	48	35
Ave. Low	12	13	23	33	42	51	57	55	47	38	30	16
Precipitation												
Inches Rain	3.4	3.6	3.8	3.3	3.3	3.1	3.0	2.6	3.1	3.3	4.0	4.1
Inches Snow	19	21	12	5	-	-	-	-	-	-	5	12

*V.W.R. = Vokac Weather Rating; probability of mild (warm & dry) weather on any given day.

ATTRACTIONS

Boat Rides

Atlantic Seal Cruises *(207)865-6112*
2 mi. S at 25 Main St. - South Freeport
Half-day cruises to Eagle Island and the museum home of Admiral Peary (first man to reach the North Pole), seal and osprey watches, and fall foliage trips can all be coupled with a fascinating lobstering demonstration.

Desert of Maine *(207)865-6962*
3 mi. W at 95 Desert Rd.
Sand left by the last ice age 8,000 years ago was exposed by overgrazing decades ago. A little natural "desert" has been growing ever since, with dunes even covering trees and small buildings. Narrated tours, museum, nature trails, large gift shop and complete campground are on-site.

Downtown
around Main & Bow Sts.
Two landmarks, the vast contemporary L.L. Bean store and the historic Harraseeket Inn, anchor one of the most unusual downtowns anywhere. Tree-lined, flowery streets are bordered by historic and modern buildings that proudly reflect New England-style architecture, and house one of America's great collections of outlet shops featuring brand-names and regional specialties. Even the McDonald's exudes Yankee Colonial charm in a contemporary building.

L.L. Bean *(800)341-4341*
downtown at 95 Main St.
The world famous sporting goods store began here in 1912 with the manufacture of hunting boots. Their giant retail outlet for outdoor equipment and clothing is now open 24 hours a day, every day of the year. The multilevel facility features handsome displays of all catalog products—from outdoor-related sporting goods to books and regional foods. Other features include an indoor trout pond where you can see a fly fishing demonstration, museum-quality exhibits, and more.

Mast Landing Sanctuary *(207)781-2330*
2 mi. SE on Upper Mast Landing Rd.
The Audubon Society operates this 140-acre preserve. More than three miles of marked trails access open fields, apple orchards, and a mature forest, plus a mill stream and marshes at the tideway of the Harraseeket River.

Winslow Memorial Park *(207)865-4198*
5 mi. S on Staples Point Rd.
Features of this tranquil coastal park include the town's sandy beach (the warmest for miles around, but much mud at low tide), a scenic self-guided nature trail, and a full-service campground.

Wolfe's Neck Woods State Park *(207)865-4465*
5 mi. SE on Wolfe's Neck Rd.
Self-guided hiking trails and guided nature walks overlooking Harraseeket River and Casco Bay are featured.

RESTAURANTS

Crickets Restaurant *(207)865-4005*
just S at 175 Lower Main St. (US 1)
L-D. *Moderate*
Contemporary American fare ranges from lobster to burgers in this modern restaurant with a lounge and patio.

15 Independence   *(207)865-1515*
1 mi. S at 15 Independence Dr.
B-L-D.   *Expensive*
Contemporary American cuisine and delicious housemade breads and
desserts are featured in recently-remodeled, comfortable dining rooms
of a converted 19th century home amid lovely gardens. A bakery/cafe
offers light fare earlier in a casual setting.

Harraseeket Inn   *(207)865-1085*
downtown at 162 Main St.
B-L-D.   *Expensive*
Freeport's landmark inn's main dining room (B-D) offers contemporary
New England cuisine with an emphasis on tastefully prepared fresh
local products. The elegant dining room is a gracious complement to
the gourmet fare. A casual tavern (L-D) features exhibition cookery and
a cheerful fireplace.

Harraseeket Lunch & Lobster Co.   *(207)865-4888*
2 mi. SE on Main St. at Town Wharf - South Freeport
L only.   *Moderate*
The lobsters are really fresh and simply, expertly prepared. So are
other seafoods in this funky eatery overlooking the waterfront.

Jameson Tavern   *(207)865-4196*
downtown at 115 Main St.
L-D.   *Expensive*
Fresh Maine seafood and steaks are given careful attention, and the
breads and desserts are homemade. A 1779 residence commemorated
as the "Birthplace of Maine" now has atmospheric dining rooms, a
more casual tap room, and a brick patio.

Lobster Cooker   *(207)865-4349*
downtown at 39 Main St.
L-D.   *Moderate*
Fresh-picked lobster and crabmeat rolls star among local seafoods
served in the casual dining room or garden patio of a historic building.

Ocean Farms Restaurant   *(207)865-3101*
downtown at 23 Main St.
L-D.   *Moderate*
"Keep it simple" is their culinary rule. It works for lobster from their
tanks and other fresh Maine seafood that highlight an extensive menu
offered for casual indoor, or covered porch, dining.

Wilbur's Ice Cream Parlor & Chocolate Factory   *(207)865-4071*
just S at 11 Independence Dr.
L-D.   *Moderate*
All kinds of sweet treats are served through a window at the factory,
and you can watch chocolates being made.

LODGING
Accommodations are plentiful in and near town. Historic inns and bed-
and-breakfasts predominate. June through October is high season.
Many places reduce rates 20% or more in winter.

Atlantic Seal Bed & Breakfast   *(207)865-6112*
2 mi. S at 25 Main St. (Box 146) - South Freeport 04078
3 units   *Moderate-Expensive*
An 1850 Cape Cod-style home is now a bed-and-breakfast inn in a
haven by a quiet harbor. Hearty sailor's breakfast is complimentary.
Your host is also a seafarer who runs narrated cruises (see listing).
Each cozy, comfortable room includes antiques. Two overlook the
harbor and offer a whirlpool or a fireplace, and a private bath.

Captain Josiah Mitchell House Bed & Breakfast   *(207)865-3289*
just N at 188 Main St. - 04032
7 units   *Moderate*
A Revolutionary-era sea captain's home is now a bed-and-breakfast inn
enhanced by many Oriental rugs, oil paintings and antiques. A
whirlpool tub is available to guests. Full breakfast is complimentary.
Each nicely furnished room has a private bath.

Freeport Inn   *(207)865-3106*
3 mi. S at 335 US 1 - 04032
82 units   *(800)998-2583*   *Moderate*
High on a hill above a tidal river is a modern motor inn with a pool,
cafe and water-view restaurant with entertainment. Each room is
comfortably furnished with all contemporary conveniences.

Harraseeket Inn   *(207)865-9377*
downtown at 162 Main St. - 04032
84 units   *(800)342-6423*   *Expensive-Very Expensive*
Freeport's foremost lodging is the Harraseeket Inn. The gracious
Colonial-style inn is a charming blend of historic and contemporary
structures on expansive, well-landscaped grounds. Features include an
indoor lap pool, exercise equipment, plush restaurant (see listing) and
a casual classy tavern. Sumptuous Maine breakfast, and tea, are
complimentary. Antiques enhance beautifully furnished rooms with all
contemporary amenities including a private whirlpool or standard bath
and special touches like a quarter-canopy bed. More than twenty rooms
also have a fireplace.

The Isaac Randall House   *(207)865-5295*
just S at 5 Independence Dr. - 04032
12 units   *(800)865-9295*   *Moderate-Expensive*
A Federal-style farmhouse (circa 1823) now serves as a nostalgic bed-
and-breakfast with numerous antique accents. Hearty breakfast is
complimentary. All rooms are well furnished, including a private bath and
all contemporary amenities. Some rooms have a fireplace.

Kendall Tavern Bed & Breakfast   *(207)865-1338*
just N at 213 Main St. - 04032
7 units   *(800)341-9572*   *Moderate-Expensive*
A restored pre-Civil War house amid spacious grounds is now a
comfortable bed-and-breakfast inn. There is an indoor whirlpool tub.
Full breakfast is complimentary. Each nicely furnished room is
embellished with antiques, and has a private bath.

181 Main Street Bed & Breakfast   *(207)865-1226*
just N at 181 Main St. - 04032
7 units   *(800)235-9750*   *Moderate*
An 1840s home has been transformed into a stylish bed-and-breakfast
with a wealth of furnishings and flourishes of that era. The grounds
are accented by gardens, and there is a pool. Full gourmet breakfast
is complimentary. Each room is well furnished to reflect the charm of
yesteryear, and has a private bath.

BASIC INFORMATION

Elevation: 130 feet   Population (1990):   6,905
Location: 125 miles Northeast of Boston
Nearest airport with commercial flights: Portland, ME - 22 miles
Freeport Merchants Association   (207)865-1212 (800)865-1994
  downtown at 23 Depot St. (Box 452) - 04032
www.freeportusa.com

Kennebunkport, Maine

Kennebunkport is the center of Maine's most usable oceanfront. Located where the Kennebunk River empties into the Atlantic Ocean, the coast is alternately rockbound headlands and sandy beaches backed by gentle forested hills. The village, and Kennebunk across the river, were settled by the mid-17th century, and prospered from shipbuilding. By the turn of this century, artists, writers and wealthy summer visitors began to discover the area's appeal for creativity and leisure.

Today, much of the grand architectural legacy is on the National Historic Register. Around Dock Square, proudly maintained remnants of the maritime past now serve as studios and galleries, regional specialty shops, and waterfront restaurants featuring Maine lobsters and other seafood. Numerous mansions retain their genteel spirit while serving as bed-and-breakfasts. Several major ocean-view inns combine the aura of Victorian grand hotels with contemporary facilities.

WEATHER PROFILE

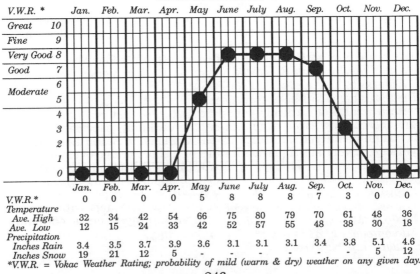

	Jan.	Feb.	Mar.	Apr.	May	June	July	Aug.	Sep.	Oct.	Nov.	Dec.
V.W.R.*	0	0	0	0	5	8	8	8	7	3	0	0
Temperature												
Ave. High	32	34	42	54	66	75	80	79	70	61	48	36
Ave. Low	12	15	24	33	42	52	57	55	48	38	30	18
Precipitation												
Inches Rain	3.4	3.5	3.7	3.9	3.6	3.1	3.1	3.1	3.4	3.8	5.1	4.6
Inches Snow	19	21	12	5	-	-	-	-	-	-	5	12

*V.W.R. = Vokac Weather Rating; probability of mild (warm & dry) weather on any given day.

246

Beaches   *(207)967-4304*
just E on Beach St.
Kennebunkport is near the middle of New England's finest array of
sandy ocean beaches. In town, smooth sand and captivating backdrops
can be enjoyed on either side of the Kennebunk River outlet. The water
is chilly, but, especially on warm days in August, people do swim here.
Along Ocean Avenue beyond Colony Beach, one of the most dramatic
and photogenic rockbound coasts anywhere includes Spouting Rock,
and a Blowing Cave within view of former President George Bush's
oceanfront estate.

Bicycling
Cape-able Bike Shop   *(207)967-4382*
1 mi. N via North St. on Arundel Rd.
Scenic shoreline roads and byways and trails into the gentle forested
hills and river valleys are ideally suited to bike riding. Any kind of
bicycle can be rented for a half day or longer, together with all
accessories, maps and information at this full-service shop.

Boat Rentals
Paddle the picturesque coastline, tidal rivers and streams on guided
kayak or solo canoe at:
Gone with the Wind   *(kayaks)*   *(207)283-8446*
Kennebunkport Marina   *(canoes)*   *(207)967-3411*

Boat Rides
Learn about lobsters and see them harvested during a one-and-a-half
hour narrated scenic trip aboard a lobster boat:
Second Chance   *(207)967-5507*   *(800)767-2628*
Whale watching is the main event, and it is complemented by expert
narration aboard boats that leave daily in summer:
Indian Whale Watch   *(207)967-5912*
Nautilus Whale Watch   *(207)967-0707*
A two-hour scenic sailing trip for up to six people aboard a traditional
rig schooner can be reserved from May into October:
Schooner Lazy Jack   *(207)967-8809*

Brick Store Museum   *(207)985-4802*
4 mi. NW at 117 Main St. - Kennebunk
An 1825 brick store and three adjacent 19th century buildings in
Kennebunk's National Historic Register district now serve as a
handsome showcase of local and regional art, textiles, furnishings, and
memorabilia. There is also a first-rate museum shop. The museum's
nearby **Taylor-Barry House** (circa 1803) has period furnishings
shown on guided tours.

Downtown   *(207)967-3686*
centered around Dock Square
The heart of town is compact and remarkably photogenic. Many
beautifully restored buildings on the National Historic Register line
narrow, flowery streets on both sides of a short bridge over the placid
tidewaters of the Kennebunk River. Shops full of quality local art,
crafts, antiques and regional gourmet delights; numerous atmospheric
restaurants with tranquil town and harbor views; plus genteel inns
and bed-and-breakfasts occupy old and new buildings with genuine
Down-East charm. The jaunty **Intown Trolley** offers a 45-minute
narrated tour of the area.

Fishing Charters

Sportfishing on the ocean or local tidal rivers can be reserved with all equipment provided. Half-day (or longer) trips leave from the town docks:

Lady J Sportfishing Charters Inc. *(207)985-7304*
Venture Inn Charters Inc. *(207)967-0005 (800)853-5002*

Ogunquit *(207)646-2939*
12 mi. S via ME 9 & US 1

The single best beach in Maine borders this flamboyant village with three miles of fine white sand. A mile-long shoreline path extends south to Perkins Cove—a beautiful little sheltered harbor spanned at its inlet by a colorful drawbridge. Daunting hordes of fun-lovers have discovered Ogunquit's artistic heart here amid quaint studios, shops and restaurants.

Old Orchard Beach *(207)934-2500*
18 mi. N via US 1 on ME 5

The wide, seven-mile-long sandy beach has been a major summer destination for many years for sunbathing and swimming. Other fun-seekers' diversions include a pier and **Palace Playland** amusement park on the beachfront. Inland, **Cascade Water and Amusement Park** and **Aquaboggen Water Park** (both in Seco) offer a variety of water slides, pools, bumper boats and more.

Seashore Trolley Museum *(207)967-2800*
3 mi. N via North St. on Log Cabin Rd.

The oldest and largest museum in the world preserving electric rail transit vehicles is a must-see. More than 225 antique electric trolleys from several continents have been collected here since 1939. A "Streetcar Named Desire" from New Orleans is a highlight among dozens of restored cars. A visitor gallery overlooks cars currently undergoing restoration. The premier barn displays the evolution of rail transit from horse-drawn vehicles to streamlined streetcars. A four-mile Main Line offers the nostalgic excitement of excursions in restored trolleys. Guided tours can also be arranged at the visitor center, where there is an orientation video, snack bar, and large museum store.

RESTAURANTS

Arrows Restaurant *(207)361-1100*
13 mi. SW via US 1 on Berwick Rd. - Ogunquit
D only.   *Very Expensive*

Fresh herbs and vegetables from their garden contribute to creative American dishes described on a menu that changes nightly. The acclaimed cuisine is served amid informally elegant atmosphere in an 18th-century country house on beautiful grounds.

Arundel Wharf Restaurant *(207)967-3444*
downtown at 43 Ocean Av.
L-D.   *Expensive*

Lobster rolls made here are outstanding. Six other lobster entrees and fresh regional seafoods are also served in imaginative, flavorful dishes that can match the delightful waterfront view from a nifty nautical dining room and shaded deck.

Cape Arundel Inn *(207)967-2125*
1 mi. SE on Ocean Av.
D only.   *Expensive*

Creative New England cuisine with an emphasis on flavor and freshness is served in a romantic setting where every table has a surf view. The ocean-view inn also serves drinks on a wraparound porch.

Chase Hill Bakery   *(207)967-2283*
downtown at 9 Chase Hill Rd. - Kennebunk
B-L.   *Moderate*
Tasty traditional and contemporary baked goods ranging from scones
to calzones are made here from scratch. This bakery and cafe with
light, fresh fare and outside seating is a local favorite.

Clay Hill Farm   *(207)361-2272*
14 mi. SW on Agamenticus Rd.
D only.   *Expensive*
Expertly prepared classic cuisine with a contemporary flair focusing on
fresh regional flavors and luscious desserts like raspberry pie have
made this one of the Maine coast's most renowned gourmet hideaways.
Informally elegant dining rooms enhance a large historic farmhouse
amid colorful gardens.

Federal Jack's Brew Pub   *(207)967-4322*
downtown at 8 Western Av. - Kennebunk
L-D.   *Moderate*
Some of the handcrafted ales are excellent. Light and lively pub grub
like ale-steamed shrimp is also served in a polished wood-trimmed pub
and on a deck overlooking the waterfront.

The Grey Gull   *(207)646-7501*
8 mi. SW via US 1 at 321 Webhannet Dr. - Wells
D only.   *Expensive*
Imaginative updates of classic New England cuisine like maple walnut
chicken are served in a nostalgic old shingled building near the ocean.
Dining rooms and a lounge have also been updated. Some of the now-
stylish tables offer a splendid view of the ocean.

Hurricane Restaurant   *(207)646-6348*
11 mi. SW via US 1 on Oarweed Ln. in Perkins Cove - Ogunquit
L-D.   *Expensive*
Unique treatments of fresh regional dishes can be very good, even in
support dishes like tossed salad with pistachios, or whole wheat
sourdough bread. But, it can't top the fabulous view of the coast from
two snazzy little dining rooms. The wait can be long.

The Lobster Pot   *(207)967-4607*
2 mi. NE at 62 Mills Rd. - Cape Porpoise
B-L-D.   *Moderate*
Twin lobsters with melted butter is an excellent selection in this big
rustic roadside restaurant. Family-style dining reigns.

Salt Marsh Tavern   *(207)967-4500*
downtown at 46 Western Av.
D only.   *Expensive*
Creative adaptations of traditional American cuisine are given skilled
attention. A large old barn was transformed into a place of elegant
rusticity thanks to candlelit tables dressed with linen, fine art, a big
picture window view of a tidal marsh, and piano music nightly.

Seascapes   *(207)967-8500*
2 mi. NE via Route 9 at 77 Pier Rd. - Cape Porpoise
L-D.   *Very Expensive*
One of the Maine coast's most renowned gourmet havens is Seascapes.
New American cuisine is expertly prepared from top-quality, fresh
ingredients of the season. Emphasis is on local seafood. Results are
inevitably flavorful. Desserts are similarly adventurous and delicious.
The dining room and piano bar are as pretty and pleasing as the
intimate view of lobster boats in the harbor.

Stage Neck Inn   *(207)363-3850 - York Harbor*
20 mi. SW via US 1 at 100 Stage Neck Rd.
B-L-D.   *Expensive*
Contemporary American cuisine results from expert preparation of top
quality fresh regional seafood and produce. But the appealing fare is
only half of the reason to be here for a special occasion. In addition,
guests are delighted by a window-wall ocean view on three sides of the
comfortably elegant **Harbor Porches** dining room. The more casual
Sandpiper Bar & Grille also has a shore view, and a well-played
grand piano.

The White Barn Inn   *(207)967-2321*
just S at 37 Beach St.
D only.   *Very Expensive*
The White Barn Inn is one of America's truly great restaurants. Here
is New American cuisine with a New England accent at its
quintessential best. Sumptuous offerings, which change weekly, are
typified by roasted halibut filet on a bed of forest mushrooms with
champagne sauce. Everything from several kinds of delicious bread to
luscious sorbets and sublime desserts is made here. Service is similarly
extraordinary—guests at each table are served simultaneously, one
waiter per plate. Jackets are appropriate for gentlemen in a romantic,
formally elegant dining room, where crystal, china, silver, fine linen
and flowers adorn each candlelit table; a pianist plays near the copper-
topped bar; and tiers of seasonally changed flowers are illuminated
beyond a dramatic twenty-foot-high picture window.

LODGING

Choices are abundant and diverse, including some of the most
picturesque inns and resorts in America. Several of the best feature
grand ocean views. Summer is high season. Most places cut their rates
by 30% and more in winter, or close for that season.

Bufflehead Cove   *(207)967-3879*
1 mi. NW via Route 35 on Gornitz Ln. (Box 499) - 04046
5 units   *Expensive*
Bufflehead Cove is one of the loveliest bed-and-breakfasts in New
England. Sequestered in deep woods by the Kennebunk River is a
romantic grey-shingled mansion with river-view porches and posh
public rooms. Expansive lawns and gardens slope to a boat dock. Full
gourmet breakfast and evening wine and cheese are complimentary.
Each room is luxuriously furnished with a blend of antiques and all
contemporary conveniences. Most have a private view balcony or deck.
"The Hideaway" is a spacious mostly-glass cottage out back that also
has a two-sided fireplace, a double whirlpool bath, and other special
touches worthy of your dreams.

The Captain Fairfield Inn   *(207)967-4454*
downtown at corner of Pleasant & Green Sts. (Box 1308) - 04046
9 units   *(800)322-1928*   *Expensive*
A Federal-style 1813 mansion on the National Historic Register is now
a handsome bed-and-breakfast amid trees, gardens, and other sea
captain's homes near the heart of town. Full gourmet breakfast and
afternoon tea and treats are complimentary. Each room is beautifully
furnished with a combination of antiques and all contemporary
amenities. Several have a fireplace. The Library Suite also has a large
whirlpool bath and a private porch.

The Cliff House   (207)361-1000
13 mi. SW via US 1 on Shore Rd. (Box 2274) - Ogunquit 03907
162 units   *Expensive*
One of Maine's grand old resorts sprawls along a dramatic oceanfront
headland called Bald Head Cliff as it has for 125 years. The six-story
complex has been thoroughly updated. Amenities include two pools
(one indoors), whirlpool, sauna, two tennis courts, exercise room, game
room including table tennis with a sea view, walking paths, plus a
circular dining room and lounge with an outdoor deck above the waves.
Most of the well-furnished rooms have private balconies with
memorable surf views.

The Colony Hotel   (207)967-3331
1 mi. S on Ocean Av. at King's Hwy. (Box 511) - 04046
125 units   (800)552-2363 *Expensive-Very Expensive*
The photogenic Colony Hotel on a rocky promontory above the mouth
of the Kennebunk River dates from 1914. Luxuriant lawns and
gardens surround the four-story complex on the National Historic
Register with a sandy beach across a road, big saltwater pool, putting
green, rental bicycles, stylish restaurant, entertainment lounge and gift
shop. Many of the well-furnished rooms have a grand ocean view.

1802 House Bed & Breakfast Inn   (207)967-5632
just N at 15 Locke St. (Box 646-A) - 04046
6 units   (800)932-5632 *Expensive-Very Expensive*
A handsome 19th century inn is surrounded by gardens in a secluded
spot by a golf course. A full country breakfast and afternoon treats are
complimentary. Each beautifully furnished room combines period and
contemporary amenities including a private bath. Most rooms have a
gas or wood fireplace. Two have a double whirlpool bath.

The Inn at Harbor Head   (207)967-5564
2 mi. NE via Route 9 at 41 Pier Rd. (RR 2, Box 1180) - 04046
5 units   *Expensive-Very Expensive*
One of the most romantic waterside hideaways in Maine is the Inn at
Harbor Head. The century-old picturesque bed-and-breakfast is nestled
in a garden on a knoll above the quiet harbor at Cape Porpoise.
Gourmet breakfast and evening refreshments are complimentary. Each
room is beautifully furnished with nostalgic and contemporary amenities (except TV). Some also have a private deck, fireplace or whirlpool tub.

The Maine Stay Inn & Cottages   (207)967-2117
downtown at 34 Maine St. (Box 500-A) - 04046
17 units   (800)950-2117   *Expensive*
A handsome 1860 home on the National Historic Register has been
transformed into a bed-and-breakfast and cottages amid gardens and
lawns. Full breakfast and afternoon tea are complimentary. Antiques
and period decor are blended with all contemporary conveniences
(except phone) in each beautifully furnished unit. Several have a
fireplace, while most cottages also have a kitchen.

The Nonantum Resort   (207)967-4050
just S at 95 Ocean Av. (Box 2626) - 04046
117 units   (800)552-5651   *Expensive*
The Nonantum has a delightful riverfront site between a nearby sandy
beach and downtown. The four-story inn, dating from 1883, and
adjacent contemporary lodge, reflect the era of grand hotels. Amenities
include a pool, fitness center, (fee) marina with lobster boat rides;
restaurant, lounge and gift shop. Many of the well-furnished rooms
have a private balcony and fine river view.

Old Fort Inn　　　*(207)967-5353*
1 mi. S via Ocean Av. on Old Fort Av. (Box M) - 04046
16 units　　　　　*(800)828-3678　Expensive-Very Expensive*
A historic carriage house and barn have been meticulously transformed into an elegant secluded bed-and-breakfast with a pool and tennis court. Buffet breakfast and some treats are complimentary. Each room is beautifully furnished with a blend of nostalgic and all contemporary conveniences (even wet bars/refrigerators and microwaves). Some also have a whirlpool bath.

The Shawmut Ocean Resort　　　*(207)967-3931*
2 mi. SE on Ocean Av. & Turbats Creek Rd. (Box 431) - 04046
82 units　　　　　*(800)876-3931　Moderate-Expensive*
This venerable 1913 inn has a spectacular oceanfront site. Expansive lawns extend from the sprawling three-story complex to a large saltwater pool by a sandy beach. The big pleasant dining room offers panoramic seascape views, and there is an entertainment lounge and gift shop. Each room is comfortably furnished. Some have a private balcony with a fine ocean view.

Stage Neck Inn　　　*(207)363-3850*
20 mi. SW via US 1 at 100 Stage Neck Rd. (Box 70) - York Harbor 03911
60 units　　　　　*(800)222-3238　Expensive-Very Expensive*
The Stage Neck Inn distinguishes one of New England's most spectacular locales. The handsome contemporary resort borders a rockbound coastline, a splendid long sandy beach, and a scenic tidal river and marina. Other amenities of the well-landscaped complex include two pools (one indoor), two tennis courts, whirlpool, sauna, fitness room, bicycles, gourmet restaurant (see listing), and grand piano bar. Each room is beautifully furnished and has a private balcony—many overlooking the ocean.

The White Barn Inn　　　*(207)967-2321*
just S at 37 Beach St. (Box 560-C) - 04046
24 units　　　　　　　　　*Expensive-Very Expensive*
The White Barn Inn is a preeminent source of gracious Maine hospitality. Nineteenth century buildings have been meticulously restored, upgraded and filled with New England period furnishings and fine art objects. There is also a swimming pool among shade trees and colorful gardens. The heart of the complex is a legendary restaurant (see listing). A gourmet Continental breakfast and bicycles are complimentary. Each room is luxuriously furnished with a blend of nostalgic country inn atmosphere and all contemporary conveniences, plus a wealth of subtle touches. Each of the spacious "Carriage House Suites" also has a fireplace and a large whirlpool bath.

BASIC INFORMATION

Elevation:　20 feet　　　　*Population (1990):　3,356*
Location:　85 miles Northeast of Boston
Nearest airport with commercial flights:　Portland, ME - 25 miles
Kennebunk-Kennebunkport Chamber of Commerce　(207)967-0857
　just W on Rt. 9 at 17 Western Av. (Box 740) - Kennebunk 04043
　www.kkcc.maine.org

St. Michaels, Maryland

St. Michaels is the most captivating village on Chesapeake Bay. It is sequestered around the end of a snug harbor. Hardwood forests and fields cover flatlands that extend to numerous nearby inlets and bays on the surrounding Eastern Shore peninsula. Settlement began in the late 17th century. Much later, the village prospered as a shipyard and shellfish processing center. In the 1960s, St. Michaels' unspoiled heritage and nautical appeal began to attract mariners and pleasure-seeking landlubbers in increasing numbers.

Shellfish and shipyards have been supplanted in importance by tidewater sports from sailing and fishing to waterfowl hunting (this is a major flyway). Restored brick Victorian buildings on tree-and-flower-lined streets house quaint shops featuring local art and crafts, and nautical gifts. Excellent restaurants offer Eastern Shore cuisine amid nostalgic furnishings, or by the water. Unusual historic bed-and-breakfasts are numerous, and there are three notable waterfront inns.

WEATHER PROFILE

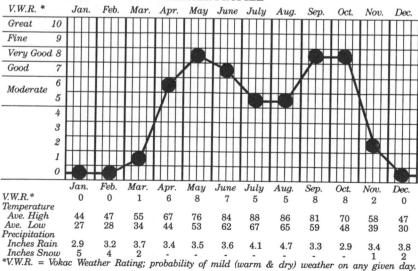

V.W.R.*		Jan.	Feb.	Mar.	Apr.	May	June	July	Aug.	Sep.	Oct.	Nov.	Dec.
Great	10												
Fine	9												
Very Good	8												
Good	7												
Moderate	6												
	5												

	Jan.	Feb.	Mar.	Apr.	May	June	July	Aug.	Sep.	Oct.	Nov.	Dec.
V.W.R.*	0	0	1	6	8	7	5	5	8	8	2	0
Temperature												
Ave. High	44	47	55	67	76	84	88	86	81	70	58	47
Ave. Low	27	28	34	44	53	62	67	65	59	48	39	30
Precipitation												
Inches Rain	2.9	3.2	3.7	3.4	3.5	3.6	4.1	4.7	3.3	2.9	3.4	3.8
Inches Snow	5	4	2	-	-	-	-	-	-	-	1	2

*V.W.R. = Vokac Weather Rating; probability of mild (warm & dry) weather on any given day.

253

Boat Rentals
St. Michaels Town Dock Marina   *(410)745-2400   (800)678-8980*
downtown at 305 Mulberry St.
Power boats can be rented here for three hours or all day.

Boat Ride
Patriot Cruises   *(410)745-3100*
downtown off Cherry St.
From enclosed or open-air decks of the 65-foot **Patriot**, you can watch watermen harvesting shellfish during one-hour narrated scenic tours.

Chesapeake Bay Maritime Museum   *(410)745-2916*
just E at E end of Mill St.
The only museum devoted to the heritage of the entire Chesapeake Bay is, appropriately, next to it. The expansive waterfront site includes nine exhibit buildings and the nation's largest collection (more than eighty) of historic Chesapeake Bay vessels. Dockside, a skipjack, tugboat, log-bottom bugeye, waterfowl-hunting boats and others trace the history of watercraft from sailing and steamboats to modern propelled vessels. Ongoing restorations can be viewed in the working Boat Yard. Displays include guns and waterfowl decoys; tools used for seafood harvesting; paintings; models and relics. The restored 1879 Hooper Strait Lighthouse is a photogenic landmark with a panoramic harbor view. There is also an extensive Museum Store.

Downtown
centered around Talbot St. & Carpenter St.
Restored brick and wood homes and stores, some dating to Colonial times, border narrow streets around a snug harbor. Many house distinctive restaurants; gourmet shops; stores featuring regional art, crafts, and antiques; and charming bed-and-breakfasts.

Food Specialties
Flamingo Flats   *(410)745-2053   (800)468-8841*
downtown at 100 Talbot St.
Generous samples of salsas, sauces and more are offered from 1,000-plus condiments displayed with related culinary items for sale here.

St. Mary's Square Museum   *(410)745-9561*
downtown on St. Mary's Square between Mulberry & Chestnut Sts.
A 200-year-old building of half-timber hewn with a broad axe was relocated here. Nearby is the "Cannonball House" (circa 1805). In a British attack during the War of 1812, a cannonball penetrated the roof and rolled down the attic stairway—no one was hurt. "The town that fooled the British" successfully repelled two attacks. Extinguishing all lights in town and hanging lanterns in tree tops led the British to believe the town was on a high bluff—and overshoot the houses. This was probably the first "blackout" in the history of warfare.

RESTAURANTS

Carpenter Street Saloon   *(410)745-5111*
downtown at corner of Talbot & Carpenter Sts.
B-L-D.   *Moderate*
Traditional Eastern shore fare is served in a family-friendly casual dining room and saloon.

The Crab Claw Restaurant   *(410)745-2900*
downtown at Navy Point Rd.
L-D.   *Moderate*
Fresh seafood (especially steamed Maryland blue crabs) has been the hallmark since 1965 of this casual eatery with fine harbor views.

The Inn at Perry Cabin   *(410)745-2200*
just N at 308 Watkins Lane
B-L-D.   *Very Expensive*
The Inn's dining room has some of the finest gourmet cuisine in the
region. Everything is prepared with classically derived creative skill
and top-quality fresh ingredients (including herbs from their garden),
and they do their own baking. The formally elegant firelit manor house
dining room opens onto a terrace (used seasonally).

Michael Rork's Town Dock Restaurant   *(410)745-5577*
downtown at 125 Mulberry St.
L-D.   *Expensive*
One of the region's great chefs has made the Town Dock Restaurant a
preeminent source of creative Eastern shore cuisine. Fresh Maryland
seafood is a highlight among expertly prepared dishes served in a
stylish multilevel dining room and terrace with a fine waterfront view.

Morsels   *(410)745-2911*
downtown at 205 N. Talbot St.
L-D.   *Moderate*
Gourmet goodies including homemade desserts are served at a few
tables in the casual cafe, outside on a brick alleyway and to go.

St. Michaels Crab House   *(410)745-3737*
downtown at 305 Mulberry St.
L-D.   *Moderate*
Steamed crab and shellfish are featured along with treats ranging from
crab balls or sweet potato fries to French silk pie. An 1830s oyster
shucking shed houses a relaxed dining room, bar and view patio.

St. Michaels Harbour Inn   *(410)745-5102*
just E at 101 N. Harbor Rd.
B L D.   *Expensive*
The inn's dining room, **Windows**, offers updated American fare with
a lovely harbor view from a comfortable setting.

208 Talbot   *(410)745-3838*
downtown at 208 N. Talbot St.
L-D.   *Expensive*
You may need a reservation to enjoy gourmet fare in one of the
Eastern Shore's most deservedly popular restaurants. Fresh seafood
stars along with housemade pastries and ice cream served in the firelit
dining room of a remodeled Victorian brick house with many antiques.

LODGING

Far from the nearest freeway, ordinary motels are scarce. But,
waterfront resorts, historic lodgings, and charming bed-and-breakfast
inns are numerous. Rates are highest on weekends from spring into
fall. Weekday winter rates may be at least 20% less.

Ashby Bed & Breakfast   *(410)822-4235*
13 mi. E via Goldsborough Neck Rd. (Box 45) - Easton 21601
8 units   *Very Expensive*
Ashby is one of America's landmark bed-and-breakfast inns. A splendid
Italianate manor house amid meticulous gardens and lawns crowns a
rise near the tranquil Miles River. The historic estate has a terraced
view pool, whirlpool, lighted tennis court, exercise room with tanning
bed, paddleboat, canoe, jogging and bike paths. Breakfast is complimentary. Careful renovation balanced the appeal of yesteryear and all
contemporary conveniences. The river can be seen from each individually luxuriously furnished room. Some also have a fireplace, whirlpool
tub, or private view balcony.

Barrett's Bed & Breakfast Inn *(410)745-3322*
downtown at 204 N. Talbot St. (Box 279) - 21663
9 units   *Expensive*
An 1860s Colonial-style brick house in the heart of town is now a romantic bed-and-breakfast. Full breakfast is complimentary. Each attractively furnished room blends period and modern furnishings, including a private bath and fireplace. Five rooms also have a double whirlpool tub in view of the fireplace.

Harbourtowne Golf Resort & Conference Center *(410)745-9066*
2 mi. NW on Rt. 33 at Martingham Dr. (Box 126) - 21663
111 units   *(800)446-9066*   *Expensive*
Chesapeake Bay adjoins this sprawling contemporary complex with a (fee) championship 18-hole golf course, driving range and putting green; bicycles; tennis; pool; exercise equipment; and restaurant. All comfortably furnished units have a private patio or balcony. Many have a bay view. Some suites have a fireplace or woodburning stove.

The Inn at Perry Cabin *(410)745-2200*
just N at 308 Watkins Lane - 21663
41 units   *(800)722-2949*   *Very Expensive*
One of the East's most distinguished small hotels is the Inn at Perry Cabin. The graceful complex opened in 1990, surrounded by manicured grounds on a cove of Chesapeake Bay. The inn, owned by Sir Bernard Ashley, is a showcase of Laura Ashley decor. Amenities include an indoor pool, sauna and steam room, exercise room, game room, and gourmet dining room (see listing). Full English breakfast and afternoon tea are complimentary. Many of the luxuriously furnished rooms have a fine bay view. Some also have a whirlpool bath.

Kemp House Inn *(410)745-2243*
downtown at 412 S. Talbot St. (Box 638) - 21663
8 units   *Moderate*
A large 1807 brick home is now a stylish inn. Continental breakfast is complimentary. Each well-furnished room combines period decor and modern conveniences. Four also have a working fireplace.

The Parsonage Inn *(410)745-5519*
downtown at 210 N. Talbot St. - 21663
8 units   *(800)394-5519*   *Expensive*
A late Victorian brick home is now a handsome bed-and-breakfast. A breakfast featuring homemade pastries, and bicycles, are complimentary. Each well-furnished room blends period decor and modern conveniences. Three also have a fireplace.

St. Michaels Harbour Inn & Marina *(410)745-9001*
just E at 101 N. Harbor Rd. - 21663
46 units   *(800)955-9001* *Expensive-Very Expensive*
This contemporary three-story hotel is on the harbor overlooking the village center. Amenities include a complete marina and dock, view pool, workout room, (rental) boats and bicycles, dining room (see listing), bar and store. All rooms are well furnished. Many have a harbor-view patio or balcony. Some have a whirlpool bath.

BASIC INFORMATION

Elevation: 10 feet   *Population (1990):* 1,301
Location: 68 miles Southeast of Baltimore, MD
Nearest airport with commercial flights: Baltimore - 60 miles
Talbot County Chamber of Commerce   *(410)822-4606 (888)229-7829*
9 mi. E at 201 Marlboro Rd., Suite 3 (Box 1366) - Easton 21601
http://internetconnection.com/talbot/

Chatham, Massachusetts

Chatham is the prettiest village on Cape Cod. Sequestered at "the elbow" of the arm-shaped peninsula, it is nearly surrounded by quiet harbors where the Atlantic Ocean and Nantucket Sound meet. Founded in 1656, the settlement soon prospered from farming and fishing. Growth has been slow and decorous, even after Cape Cod National Seashore was created in 1961.

Today, surrounding woodlands and shorelines of ocean beaches and bays remain unspoiled in spite of increasing demand for recreation. The past is proudly preserved in classic New England-style whitewashed churches, trim homes (many serving as bed-and-breakfasts) and gardens. Downtown is a delightful array of cosmopolitan restaurants, and shops featuring regional art, crafts, antiques and gourmet treats. Handsome historic inns, including a landmark inn by a popular park and a nearby major resort by a sandy beach, celebrate the timeless romance of the Cape Cod style.

WEATHER PROFILE

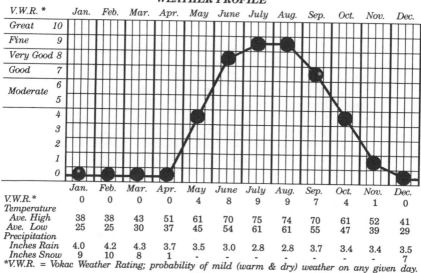

V.W.R.*		Jan.	Feb.	Mar.	Apr.	May	June	July	Aug.	Sep.	Oct.	Nov.	Dec.
Great	10												
Fine	9												
Very Good	8												
Good	7												
Moderate	6												
	5												
	4												
	3												
	2												
	1												
	0												

	Jan.	Feb.	Mar.	Apr.	May	June	July	Aug.	Sep.	Oct.	Nov.	Dec.
V.W.R.*	0	0	0	0	4	8	9	9	7	4	1	0
Temperature												
Ave. High	38	38	43	51	61	70	75	74	70	61	52	41
Ave. Low	25	25	30	37	45	54	61	61	55	47	39	29
Precipitation												
Inches Rain	4.0	4.2	4.3	3.7	3.5	3.0	2.8	2.8	3.7	3.4	3.4	3.5
Inches Snow	9	10	8	1	-	-	-	-	-	-	-	7

*V.W.R. = Vokac Weather Rating; probability of mild (warm & dry) weather on any given day.

ATTRACTIONS
Beaches   *(508)945-5180*
 2 mi. SE via MA 28
Several sandy beaches are scattered along the town's shoreline. Free parking, lifeguards and restrooms are at **Oyster Pond Beach** (by Stage Harbor Rd.) near the heart of town. **Harding, Ridgevale,** and **Cockle Cove Beaches,** two miles southwest overlooking Nantucket Sound, are also popular but charge to park.

Bicycling
Numerous byways in and around the village provide easy access to all scenic areas of the relatively flat cape. The Cape Cod Rail Trail is a thirty-mile-long separated bike path. Bicycles can be rented near town.

Boat Rentals
Sheltered bays and inlets surround Chatham, protected from the Atlantic Ocean by barrier islands. To explore the watery playground, watercraft rentals are available at several places, including:

Cape Water Sports   *(all boats)*   *Harwich Port* (508)432-7079
Monomoy Sail & Cycle *(paddle & sail) Chatham*   (508)945-0811
Offshore Water Sports *(jet boats)   Chatham*   (508)945-5700

Boat Rides   *(508)487-3424*
Several major villages on Cape Cod offer scenic boat rides, plus memorable whale-watching trips. Naturalists provide narratives during 2.5- to 4-hour trips by several companies from April into October.

Cape Cod National Seashore   *(508)349-3785*
 starts just E & along US 6
From the barrier islands by Chatham to the tip of Cape Cod beyond Provincetown, more than thirty miles of ocean beaches and sand dunes, plus woodlands, tidal marshes and freshwater ponds, are protected in a natural state. Six ocean beaches overseen by lifeguards feature swimming. The shore is also deservedly popular for beachcombing, fishing, hiking, bicycling, and picnicking. There are visitor centers with exhibits and programs in Eastham and Provincetown.

Chatham Light
 2 mi. N off MA 28
The picturesque lighthouse is one of a pair erected here in 1877. There is a panoramic view of an ocean inlet, sandbars, and the ocean beyond.

Fish Pier   *(508)945-5186*
 1 mi. NE at Shore Rd. & Barcliff Av.
The commercial fleet usually starts returning from fishing grounds up to one hundred miles offshore after noon. The photogenic scene can be viewed from a visitor's balcony. **The Water Taxi** also leaves from here to take visitors sightseeing or to the best barrier island beaches.

Old Atwood House Museum
 just S at 347 Stage Harbor Rd.
One of the oldest houses in Chatham (circa 1752) is now fully restored and maintained by Chatham Historical Society. Rooms are furnished in period antiques dating as far back as 1635, plus sea shell displays, photos, paintings and murals. An herb garden and lighthouse turret are on the grounds.

Old Grist Mill
 just S off Shattuck Pl. by Chase Park
The mill, built in 1797 to grind corn with wind power, is on the National Historic Register. It is free to the public in summer.

Provincetown   *(508)487-3424*

38 mi. NW on US 6

Provincetown was where the Pilgrims landed first in 1620—after trying and failing to get into the harbor at Chatham. Much of a 380-year history as a seafaring area is now preserved in a National Historic District. Also preserved is its legacy as a source of cosmopolitan hospitality—Provincetown is America's premier gay resort town. Attractions include secluded sand dunes and beaches, peerless whale watching opportunities (see Boat Rides), and the **Provincetown Museum** displaying the only pirate ship ever found. A wealth of restaurants, lodgings and swinging nightlife cater to gays and straights. Arts and crafts galleries display flamboyant local works. The town's most arresting feature is the Pilgrim Monument. The tallest all-granite obelisk in America towers 252 feet.

Railroad Museum

just N at 153 Depot St.

A classy little Victorian railroad station, on its original site, now displays railroad relics dating as far back as 1826, including a restored 1910 caboose, scale models, and a diarama.

RESTAURANTS

The Bistro   *(508)945-5033*

downtown at 595 Main St.

D only.   *Expensive*

The creative menu is typified by dishes like a warm lobster taco and others with a spicy accent. An open hardwood grill is popular in this relaxed upstairs bistro with big windows overlooking Main Street.

Chatham Bars Inn   *(508)945-0096*

just NE at 297 Shore Rd.

B L D.   *Expensive-Very Expensive*

The inn's **Main Dining Room** (B-D—Expensive) features creative regional cuisine like lobster and scallop saute or grilled veal T-bone with gracious elegance and a view of Nantucket Sound. Jackets are appropriate for gentlemen. The **Beach House Grill** (B-L—Expensive) offers light fare, fun, and great views of the beach and harbor.

The Chatham Squire   *(508)945-0945*

downtown at 487 Main St.

L-D.   *Moderate*

Seasonally fresh seafood stars in chowder redolent of clam, stuffed clam shells, and many other delicious dishes. After nearly thirty years, Chatham's first raw bar and always-busy dining room still radiate the convivial feeling of old Cape Cod.

Chatham Wayside Inn   *(508)945-5550*

downtown at 512 Main St.

B-L-D.   *Expensive*

Traditional Cape Cod and New England fare distinguishes the landmark inn's restaurant with dishes like cranberry pancakes with maple syrup for breakfast or lobster pie for dinner. The large dining room and tavern convey the simple comfort of yesteryear.

Christian's   *(508)945-3362*

downtown at 443 Main St.

D only.   *Expensive*

Fresh seafood stars in unique creations derived from many of the world's culinary styles. Everything from crusty French bread to luscious desserts is baked here. Downstairs is quietly upscale, while plush bistro style prevails upstairs around a piano bar.

The Impudent Oyster   (508)945-3545
downtown at 15 Chatham Bars Av.

L-D.   *Expensive*

A blend of major international culinary styles results in creative dishes with assertive appeal. Even local seafood specialties have unusually flavorful character. The casual dining room is a local favorite.

Pate's Restaurant   (508)945-9777
1 mi. W at 1260 Main St. (Route 28)

D only.   *Expensive*

Since 1957, Pate's has been popular for fresh local seafood, steaks, and lamb chops grilled on an open hearth and served in a casual setting.

Wequassett Inn   (508)432-5400
5 mi. NW on Route 28 at Pleasant Way

B-L-D.   *Expensive*

The historic inn's dining room showcases contemporary American cuisine. Fresh regional seafood, and skilled updates of beef tenderloin, game hen and other entrees can also be enjoyed with fine housemade desserts. Semi-formal attire is appropriate for evening dining in a gracious room with window-walls on three sides, piano entertainment, and a deck off the lounge with a bay view.

LODGING

Accommodations are numerous. Most are historic bed-and-breakfasts. There are two elegant waterfront inns. Summer is high season. Rates during the rest of the year may be reduced 30% or more.

Bradford Inn & Motel   (508)945-1030
downtown at 26 Cross St. (Box 750) - 02633

29 units   (800)242-8426   *Expensive*

Chatham's historic district includes an 1860 sea captain's house and other buildings in a landscaped complex with a pool, restaurant and fireplace lounge just off Main Street. Breakfast is complimentary. Each individually well-furnished room combines nostalgic decor and all contemporary conveniences. Some also have a fireplace or kitchen.

Captain's House Inn of Chatham   (508)945-0127
1 mi. N on Route 28 at 369 Old Harbor Rd. - 02633

19 units   (800)315-0728   *Expensive-Very Expensive*

An 1839 sea captain's mansion has been transformed into a classic New England bed-and-breakfast in a tranquil setting enhanced by colorful gardens. Full breakfast, English afternoon tea, and bicycles are complimentary. Quality antiques are blended with all contemporary conveniences except TV in each of the beautifully furnished rooms. Several also have a gas or pressed-wood fireplace and a two-person whirlpool bath.

Chatham Bars Inn   (508)945-0096
just NE at 297 Shore Rd. - 02633

152 units   (800)527-4884   *Expensive-Very Expensive*

One-quarter mile of private sandy beach "for surf and still water bathing" is the key to an elegant landmark dating from 1914. It is now a quintessential Cape Cod resort by a harbor with views to the ocean. Amenities of the newly upgraded inn-and-cottage complex include an adjacent (fee) 9-hole golf course plus a putting green, beachfront pool, three tennis courts, fitness room, gourmet restaurants (see listing) and lounges, and a gift shop. All of the beautifully furnished rooms combine period touches with all modern conveniences. Some feature a private water-view deck or balcony, and a gas fireplace.

Chatham Town House Inn   *(508)945-2180*
downtown at 11 Library Lane - 02633
29 units   *(800)242-2180   Expensive-Very Expensive*
An 1881 sea captain's estate in Chatham's historic district has become a charming bed-and-breakfast with a pool, whirlpool, and gourmet restaurant. Full breakfast is complimentary. Each room in the inn and cottages is well furnished. Some also have a fireplace.

Chatham Wayside Inn   *(508)945-5550*
downtown at 512 Main St. (Box 685) - 02633
56 units   *(800)391-5734   Expensive-Very Expensive*
Chatham's picturesque 1860 landmark inn in the heart of the historic district was meticulously upgraded and expanded in 1995. In a garden setting by the village park, there is a pool, restaurant (see listing) and tavern. Beautifully furnished rooms are in a variety of types and styles that convey vintage Cape Cod. Private balconies and whirlpool baths are also available.

Cranberry Inn at Chatham   *(508)945-9232*
downtown at 359 Main St. - 02633
18 units   *(800)332-4667   Expensive-Very Expensive*
Chatham's oldest inn has a traditional of hospitality going back nearly 170 years. The 1830 inn in the heart of the historic district was recently expanded and upgraded to include a glamorous firelit lounge, and gardens with a path that extends to a cranberry bog. Gourmet Continental breakfast and afternoon tea and pastries are complimentary. Each beautifully furnished room tastefully combines cranberry-related pieces, period decor, and all contemporary conveniences. Spacious fireplace suites are available, as are private balconies.

Cyrus Kent House Inn   *(508)945-9104*
downtown at 63 Cross St. - 02633
10 units   *(800)338-5368   Expensive-Very Expensive*
A 19th century sea captain's home was meticulously transformed into a bed-and-breakfast. Continental breakfast is complimentary. English antiques are blended with all contemporary amenities. Some of the spacious, well-furnished rooms have a fireplace.

Wequassett Inn   *(508)432-5400*
5 mi. NW on Route 28 at Pleasant Bay - 02633
104 units   *(800)225-7125*   *Very Expensive*
Some buildings are more than 200 years old in this beautifully landscaped secluded resort on a peninsula overlooking Pleasant Bay and Round Cove. The handsome complex of Cape Cod-style cottages and Colonial structures has a private beach, (fee) launch to Outer Beach, dock and rental boats, plus a large view pool, four tennis courts, exercise room, gourmet restaurant (see listing), lounge, and gift shop. Each spacious, luxuriously furnished room blends the New England heritage with all contemporary conveniences and has a private patio or balcony. Some have a fine water view, and a few also have a gas fireplace.

BASIC INFORMATION

Elevation: 40 feet   *Population (1990):   6,579*
Location: 95 miles Southeast of Boston
Nearest airport with commercial flights: Hyannis - 21 miles
Chatham Chamber of Commerce   (508)945-5199
downtown on Main St. near Cross St. (Box 793) - 02633 (800)715-5567

Charlevoix, Michigan

"Charlevoix the beautiful" easily lives up to its billing. Fine sand beaches distinguish the town's western boundary along Lake Michigan. Picturesque Round Lake and one of the world's shortest rivers border downtown, and lovely thirteen-mile-long Lake Charlevoix defines the eastern town limits. Earliest settlement as a fishing and trapping village was quickly replaced by genteel tourism after the arrival of a railroad in 1892.

For more than a century, natural attractions and civic pride have made Charlevoix an increasingly appealing travel destination. Numerous town parks enhance and preserve the natural beauty of lakes, stream, beaches and dunes. The main street is lined for miles with petunias. Downtown, handsome shops feature the works of local artists and craftsmen; there is a notable concentration of restaurants and lounges; and most of the best lodgings all reflect the town's delightful human scale and fun-loving character.

WEATHER PROFILE

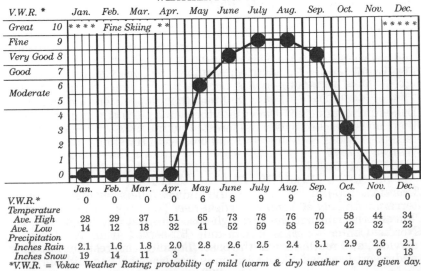

V.W.R. *	Jan.	Feb.	Mar.	Apr.	May	June	July	Aug.	Sep.	Oct.	Nov.	Dec.
V.W.R.*	0	0	0	0	6	8	9	9	8	3	0	0
Temperature												
Ave. High	28	29	37	51	65	73	78	76	70	58	44	34
Ave. Low	14	12	18	32	41	52	59	58	52	42	32	23
Precipitation												
Inches Rain	2.1	1.6	1.8	2.0	2.8	2.6	2.5	2.4	3.1	2.9	2.6	2.1
Inches Snow	19	14	11	3	-	-	-	-	-	-	6	18

*V.W.R. = Vokac Weather Rating; probability of mild (warm & dry) weather on any given day.

Downtown

One of the Midwest's most beautiful downtowns is centered along Bridge Street, above scenic Round Lake. Stylish regional arts, crafts, antiques and gourmet food stores; restaurant and lounges; and the area's best lodgings are further enhanced by double rows of multicolored petunias (part of four miles of flowers that are an annual source of great pride). At the north end, scenic walkways lining both sides of the tranquil Pine River Channel extend to Lake Michigan.

East Park   *(616)547-3253*
downtown by Bridge St.

This manicured greenbelt borders the Round Lake yacht basin. It is picturesque and peaceful, apart from frequent entertainment in the pavilion, and festivals. Nearby across Pine River Channel is Depot Beach where lifeguards oversee swimmers enjoying the relatively warm, calm water in summer.

Fisherman's Island State Park   *(616)547-6641*
3 mi. SW on Bells Bay Rd.

The area's largest park offers seven miles of primitive public beaches on Lake Michigan. Fishing is popular, and there are shoreline and woodlands hiking trails and a campground.

Fishing Charters

A rare combination of a great lake, stream, and sheltered inland lake make Charlevoix a major destination for anglers. Lake Michigan offers salmon and trout, while Lake Charlevoix adds bass and pike. Half-day or full day trips can be chartered at:

Blue Fin Sport Fishing Charters   *(616)547-6808*
Ward Brothers Charter Boats, Inc.   *(616)547-2371*

Food Specialties

South of town is a major fruit-growing area. The harvest begins with strawberries in June; then cherries; peaches; and finally, all sorts of apples. Two picturesque farms sell their bounty in a cornucopia of fresh and packaged displays. You can even pick your own fruit in season.

Elzinga Farm Market *10 mi. S on US 31 - Atwood (616)599-2604*
Friske Orchards   *12 mi. S via US 31 on C 48   (616)588-6185*

Lake Michigan Beach and Park   *(616)547-3253*
just W at Grant St. & Park Av.

A white sand beach is the highlight, and this is a good place to hunt for the fossilized rocks called Petoskey Stones. Lifeguards, concessions, and restrooms are provided seasonally.

Mount McSauba Recreation Area   *(616)547-3253*
1 mi. N on Mt. McSauba Rd.

The biggest of the rolling sand dunes that slope down to the shore of Lake Michigan north of town are the centerpiece of a primitive park that can be reached by several forested hiking trails. In the winter, the facility provides both downhill and cross-country skiing.

Winter Sports

Boyne Mountain   *(616)549-2441   (800)462-6963*
22 mi. SE via Hwys. 32 & 75

One of the top-rated ski areas in the Midwest offers surprisingly varied terrain with only 500 feet of vertical rise. The longest run is one mile. Ten chairlifts include the first high-speed six-seater in the nation. The Nordic Center features a four-mile lift-served trail. All facilities, services, and rentals are at the base, including fine restaurants, bars, and resort lodgings. Skiing season is late November to mid-April.

RESTAURANTS

Great Lakes Whitefish & Chips   *(616)547-4374*
downtown at 421 Bridge St.
L-D.   *Moderate*
Fresh and flavorful Lake Michigan whitefish and walleye have been
pleasing seafood lovers for many years. Results of the much-coveted,
but still secret, recipe can be enjoyed in this casual eatery or to go.

Grey Gables Inn   *(616)547-9261*
just E at 308 Belvedere Av.
D only.   *Expensive*
Since 1936, slow-roasted prime rib, center-cut pork chops with dried
cherry stuffing, and locally caught fresh fish have been featured along
with homemade desserts. Casually elegant Victorian decor
complements the American cuisine, and there is a lounge with
entertainment for dancing.

Juilleret's Restaurant   *(616)547-9212*
1 mi. S at 1418 S. Bridge St.
B-L.   *Moderate*
Home-baked breads and desserts accompany traditional American fare
in this locally popular coffee shop. The french toast is outstanding.

Karl's Pastry Shop   *(616)547-6431*
1 mi. S at 1200 S. Bridge St.
B-L.   *Moderate*
First-rate pastries (including Tom's Mom's cookies) and assorted deli
delights are served to go or at tables in this full-service bakery/deli.

Stafford's Weathervane Restaurant   *(616)547-4311*
downtown at 106 Pine River Lane
L-D.   *Moderate*
Fresh whitefish is featured on a creative American menu. The casually
elegant dining room, deck and lounge provide a delightful view of Pine
River Channel and Lake Michigan. But, it is the huge boulders around
the five fireplaces that make this a unique landmark.

Terry's Place   *(616)547-2799*
downtown at 101 Antrim St.
D only.   *Expensive*
Mainstream and updated Continental and American dishes including
local fresh perch, walleye and whitefish are skillfully prepared in this
pleasant dinner house.

Villager Pub   *(616)547-6925*
downtown at 413 Bridge St.
L-D.   *Moderate*
Fresh broiled whitefish stars among contemporary American dishes
served in a cozy corner pub with nostalgic 1950s decor.

LODGING

Accommodations are relatively scarce, but varied—from motels and
hotels to bed-and-breakfast inns. Some have historic decor or lovely
waterfront views. Summer is the high season. During the rest of the
year, apart from weekends, rates may be reduced by 30% or more.

Charlevoix Country Inn   *(616)547-5134*
just N at 106 W. Dixon Av. - 49720
10 units   *Moderate-Expensive*
Lake Michigan provides a fine backdrop to this country-style inn.
Continental-plus breakfast is complimentary. Each room is comfortably
furnished. Most have a private bath.

Edgewater Inn   *(616)547-6044*
  downtown at 100 Michigan Av. - 49720
  50 units   *(800)748-0424   Expensive-Very Expensive*
This all-suites motor lodge has a choice location by the water. The contemporary three-story complex has an indoor/outdoor pool, whirlpool, sauna, fitness room, boat slips, and a restaurant. Each well-furnished one- or two-bedroom suite has a kitchen, and a private deck with a waterfront view. Many have a fireplace. A few also have a large whirlpool bath.

Inn at Grey Gables Bed & Breakfast   *(616)547-2251*
  just E at 306 Belvedere Av. - 49720
  7 units   *(800)280-4667   Moderate-Expensive*
A century-old "cottage" with a wrap-around porch is a recently remodeled bed-and-breakfast near Round Lake and downtown. Full breakfast and evening snacks are complimentary. Each well-furnished room has nostalgic atmosphere and a private bath.

The Lodge Motel   *(616)547-6565*
  downtown at US 31 N at the Bridge (Box 337) - 49720
  40 units   *Moderate-Expensive*
A pool and a location a block from water distinguish this motel. Each room is comfortably furnished. Some have a private view balcony.

Pointes North Inn   *(616)547-0055*
  downtown at 101 Michigan Av. - 49720
  22 units   *(800)968-5433   Expensive*
A scenic location near the bridge and an indoor/outdoor pool are features of this all-suites motel. Each well-furnished one- or two-bedroom unit has a kitchen, private view deck, and a large whirlpool bath.

Sloop Inn Hotel   *(010)547-0300*
  just NE at 801 Petoskey Av. - 49720
  59 units   *(888)252-2505   Moderate-Expensive*
Among the newest places in town is a three-story motel with an indoor pool and whirlpool. Each room is comfortably furnished.

Water Street Inn   *(616)582-3000*
  15 mi. SE at 200 Front St. - Boyne City 49712
  27 units   *(800)456-4313   Expensive*
One of the region's most distinctive lodgings is an all-suites motel with turn-of-the-century antique decor on a beach at the other end of Lake Charlevoix. Each well-furnished one-bedroom suite has a kitchen, private lake-view deck, a whirlpool bath, and/or a fireplace.

Weathervane Terrace Hotel   *(616)547-9955*
  downtown at 111 Pine River Lane - 49720
  68 units   *(800)552-0025   Moderate-Expensive*
Lake Michigan, Round Lake, Pine River and downtown are all an easy stroll from this contemporary three-story motor lodge on a hill. The rock-trimmed landmark has a pool and whirlpool. Expanded Continental breakfast is complimentary. Each room is well furnished. One-bedroom units have a kitchenette, fireplace and lake-view private balcony. Nine units have a private lake-view balcony and a large in-room whirlpool.

BASIC INFORMATION

Elevation: 600 feet   Population (1990): 3,116
Location: 270 miles Northwest of Detroit
Nearest airport with commercial flights: Traverse City - 46 miles
Charlevoix Area Conv. & Visitors Bureau (616)547-2101 (800)367-8557
  downtown at 408 Bridge St. - 49720   www.charlevoix.org

Holland, Michigan

Holland is the heart of Dutch hospitality and heritage in America. Lake Michigan lies just beyond the sheltered site by scenic little Lake Macatawa. Attracted by fertile soil and abundant water, Dutch immigrants seeking religious freedom settled here in 1847.

Today, much of the population is of Dutch descent, and Holland exalts in its semblance of a Dutch town. Millions of tulips bloom in parks, gardens, and along eight miles of tulip lanes during the renowned May Tulip Time Festival. Authentic windmills, drawbridges, and wooden shoe factories also reflect the heritage. So do themed shopping complexes, restaurants, and lodgings. Downtown, an orderly mix of historic and modern buildings, flowery pocket parks, fountains, and sculptures line tree-shaded brick sidewalks. Numerous specialty shops feature regional and Dutch art, crafts, and collectibles. There are several good restaurants downtown, but lodgings are almost all farther out by the area's other cultural and recreation spots.

WEATHER PROFILE

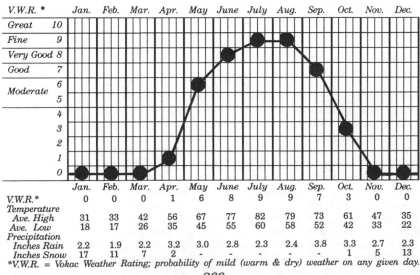

V.W.R. *		Jan.	Feb.	Mar.	Apr.	May	June	July	Aug.	Sep.	Oct.	Nov.	Dec.
Great	10												
Fine	9												
Very Good	8												
Good	7												
Moderate	6												
	5												

	Jan.	Feb.	Mar.	Apr.	May	June	July	Aug.	Sep.	Oct.	Nov.	Dec.
V.W.R.*	0	0	0	1	6	8	9	9	7	3	0	0
Temperature												
Ave. High	31	33	42	56	67	77	82	79	73	61	47	35
Ave. Low	18	17	26	35	45	55	60	58	52	42	33	22
Precipitation												
Inches Rain	2.2	1.9	2.2	3.2	3.0	2.8	2.3	2.4	3.8	3.3	2.7	2.3
Inches Snow	17	11	7	2	-	-	-	-	-	1	5	13

*V.W.R. = Vokac Weather Rating; probability of mild (warm & dry) weather on any given day.

Bicycling

Many miles of gentle bike paths link lakes, beaches and parks around town. Rentals and related equipment are available at:

Cross Country Cycle *just N at 137 N. River Av.* *(616)396-7491*
Lakeshore Cycle *3 mi. NW at 650 Riley St.* *(616)399-0414*

Downtown

Well-maintained historic and newer buildings and pocket parks with sculptures and fountains share flowery tree-lined streets. Wide brick sidewalks are heated in winter! The substantial core area includes numerous regional art galleries, collectibles shops, restaurants and lounges, plus summer repertory theater in adjoining Hope College.

Dutch Village *(616)396-1475*
3 mi. NE via US 31 on James St.

Authentic Dutch architecture distinguishes a re-created Netherlands village, along with manicured gardens, canals and windmills. Features include a giant wooden shoe slide, antique carousel, chair swing, and museum exhibits. Shops specialize in Old World gifts ranging from wooden shoes to Delft china. For food, there are Dutch treats.

The Holland Museum *(616)392-9084* *(888)200-9123*
downtown at 31 W. 10th St.

A restored classical revival building in Centennial Park showcases Netherlands Delftware, pewter, paintings and furniture. Other permanent and changing exhibits reflect the area's colorful heritage.

Holland State Park *(616)399-9390*
6 mi. W at 2215 Ottawa Beach Rd.

This large scenic park features a quarter-mile-long sandy beach on Lake Michigan, shore fishing on the channel connecting it to Lake Macatawa, and sheltered lake swimming. There are also picnic sites and two complete campgrounds. Watercraft rentals are nearby.

Saugatuck *(616)857-5801*
10 mi. SW via US 31

The Kalamazoo River borders this picturesque village. Beyond, sand dunes slope to beaches along Lake Michigan. Dune rides, hiking, swimming, fishing and boating are popular. Tiny Saugatuck has become a major Midwestern art colony. Regional arts, crafts and gourmet specialties abound, complemented by distinctive restaurants and lodgings.

Specialty Shops

De Klomp Wooden Shoe & Delftware Factory *(616)399-1900*
4 mi. NE at US 31 at 12755 Quincy St.

You can watch craftsmen create authentic wooden shoes using Dutch machines, and tour the only factory producing hand-painted blue and white Delftware in America. There is a large gift shop.

Wooden Shoe Factory *(616)396-6513*
1 mi. E at 447 US 31 at 16th St.

The most complete wooden shoe manufacturing plant in America uses European machines—some more than a century old. You can watch the process from logs to shoes, and buy the shoes and other Dutch gifts in a large colorful complex that has been in Holland since 1926.

Veldheer Tulip Gardens *(616)399-1900*
4 mi. NE at US 31 & 12755 Quincy St.

Next to the De Klomp factory (see listing) is a delightful touch of "Old Holland" with windmills, drawbridges and canals, and gardens with more than two million tulips and other flowers ablaze with color beginning in late April-May. Tulip bulbs are available for sale.

Windmill Island   *(616)396-5433*
just NE at 7th St. & Lincoln Av.
The only authentic Dutch windmill operating in the United States is
the centerpiece of a delightful park. The 18th century landmark, with
"sails" towering more than 100 feet, was relocated and refurbished with
special permission of the Dutch government in 1965. You can tour the
mill with costumed guides, and buy the whole wheat flour it grinds.
More than 100,000 tulips in bloom in the spring border canals and a
reproduction of a hand-raised drawbridge; authentic Dutch carousel;
museum in a re-created wayside inn; miniature village exhibit;
candlemaker studio; food and gift concessions.

RESTAURANTS

Alpenrose Restaurant & Pastry Shop   *(616)393-2111*
downtown at 4 E. 8th St.
B-L-D.   *Moderate*
Assorted fresh pastries can be enjoyed with American and Austrian
dishes in several dining rooms of a casual upscale Bavarian-style cafe.
Eighth Street Grille   *(616)392-5888*
downtown at 20 W. 8th St.
L-D.   *Moderate*
A soup bar, sandwiches, salads, pastas and more are served amid
historic surroundings in a casual gathering place.
Hatch Bar & Grille   *(616)399-9120*
5 mi. W at 1870 Ottawa Beach Rd.
L-D.   *Moderate*
Steaks, prime rib and seafood are specialties from the open-hearth
grill. The comfortable dinner house with nautical decor and indoor and
outdoor patio lounges is by a marina at Lake Macatawa.
Piper Restaurant   *(616)335-5866*
6 mi. W at 2225 S. Shore Dr.
D only.   *Expensive*
Contemporary American cuisine has real appeal in wood-fired pizza
and other dishes on a wide-ranging menu. The popular restaurant has
a casually elegant dining room, lounge and deck with a panoramic view
overlooking Lake Macatawa.
Queen's Inn at Dutch Village   *(616)393-0310*
3 mi. NE at 12350 James St.
L-D.   *Moderate*
Holland's premier Dutch restaurant offers traditional Dutch and
American dishes served by costumed waitresses amid comfortable Old
World atmosphere. Breakfast buffets are a weekend specialty, as they
have been for over thirty years.
Till Midnight   *(616)392-6883*
downtown at 208 College Av.
L-D.   *Expensive*
Contemporary American and international dishes with a fresh flair can
be accompanied by homemade breads and desserts. Patrons have a
choice of a cozy upscale dining room, lounge or sidewalk cafe.
Village Inn Pizza   *(616)392-1818*
2 mi. SW at 934 S. Washington Av.
L-D.   *Moderate*
The region's best pizza gives you a choice of hand-tossed or Chicago-
style deep dish. Both are excellent. So are support dishes like jalapeno
poppers and oven-baked ribs. The locally owned parlor has four casual
dining rooms, a long mahogany bar, and dining patio.

LODGING
There are numerous lodgings in town. A few bed-and-breakfast inns, motor hotels, and a lakeview motel are notable. Summer is high season. Non-weekend rates at other times may be reduced by 20% or more.

The Centennial Inn   *(616)355-0998*
downtown at 8 E. 12th St. - 49423
8 units   *Moderate-Expensive*
An 1889 home and carriage house were transformed into a bed-and-breakfast in 1995. Full breakfast is complimentary. Each well-furnished room has all contemporary conveniences, including a private bath. Six also have a freestanding Victorian fireplace.

Country Inn By Carlson   *(616)396-6677*
3 mi. NE (near US 31) at 12260 James St. - 49424
116 units   *(800)456-4000*   *Moderate*
The Dutch Village and Manufacturer's Marketplace are next to this handsome contemporary motel. An expanded Continental breakfast is complimentary. Each room is well furnished. Many have a large in-room whirlpool.

Dutch Colonial Inn   *(616)396-3664*
just S at 560 Central Av. - 49423
5 units   *Moderate-Expensive*
Holland's finest lodging is the Dutch Colonial Inn. An elegant home built in 1928 is now a charming bed-and-breakfast inn. Dutch hospitality and full breakfast are complimentary. Each room is beautifully furnished with both period decor and contemporary conveniences. Several also have an in-bath whirlpool tub for two.

Hampton Inn   *(616)399-8500*
3 mi. NE at 12427 Felch St. - 49424
116 units   *(800)426-7866*   *Moderate-Expensive*
A large indoor recreation area includes a big indoor pool, two whirlpools, exercise room, plus ping pong and pool tables. Continental breakfast buffet is complimentary. Kitchen units are available, and sixteen rooms have a long whirlpool tub.

Holiday Inn & Conference Center   *(616)394-0111*
2 mi. SE (by US 31) at 650 E. 24th St. - 49423
168 units   *(800)279-5286*   *Moderate-Expensive*
The area's largest lodging is a four-story contemporary motor hotel with an indoor pool amidst tropical greenery, whirlpool, sauna, exercise room, game room, dining room and nightclub. Each well-furnished room has a private view deck.

The Kingsley House   *(616)561-6425*
14 mi. S at 626 W. Main St. - Fennville 49408
8 units   *Moderate-Expensive*
A Queen Anne-style Victorian home is now a posh bed-and-breakfast. A full family-style breakfast on weekends (Continental weekdays) and afternoon treats are complimentary. Each room is beautifully furnished with antiques and contemporary conveniences, except phones. Three suites also have a whirlpool bath for two.

BASIC INFORMATION
Elevation: 610 feet   Population (1990):   30,745
Location: 150 miles Northeast of Chicago
Nearest airport with commercial flights: Grand Rapids - 35 miles
Holland Area Convention & Visitors Bureau (616)394-0000 (800)506-1299
downtown at 76 E. 8th St. - 49423   www.holland.org/hcvb
Town photo courtesy of Holland Area Convention & Visitors Bureau.

Petoskey, Michigan

Petoskey is a classic among genteel Midwestern towns. Luxuriant forested hills and farmlands surround this lively little city on a picturesque bay of Lake Michigan. Settlement began before the Civil War thanks to forests, fish and furs. But, more than a century ago, the village's role as a major recreation destination was already clear.

The great lake's timeless appeal, the natural beauty and winter recreation prospects of surrounding hills, and Petoskey's original heritage remain intact. From the remarkably preserved Victorian community of Bay View to lavish new resort developments at Bay Harbor, places for fun and culture are well represented. Downtown, the handsome Gaslight Shopping District and two landmark century-old hotels are near lovely lakefront parks. Numerous stores specialize in regional art, crafts, antiques and gourmet foods. Several restaurants feature fresh Michigan fish and farm products. Contemporary lodgings in town are augmented by elaborate condo hotels in nearby major ski resorts.

WEATHER PROFILE

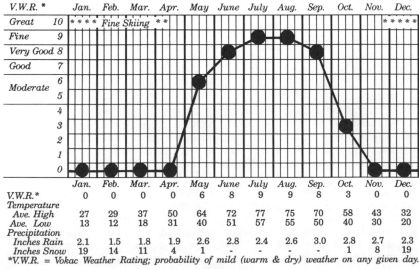

V.W.R.*		Jan.	Feb.	Mar.	Apr.	May	June	July	Aug.	Sep.	Oct.	Nov.	Dec.
V.W.R.*		0	0	0	0	6	8	9	9	8	3	0	0
Temperature													
Ave. High		27	29	37	50	64	72	77	75	70	58	43	32
Ave. Low		13	12	18	31	40	51	57	55	50	40	30	20
Precipitation													
Inches Rain		2.1	1.5	1.8	1.9	2.6	2.8	2.4	2.6	3.0	2.8	2.7	2.3
Inches Snow		19	14	11	4	1	-	-	-	-	1	8	19

*V.W.R. = Vokac Weather Rating; probability of mild (warm & dry) weather on any given day.

ATTRACTIONS

Bay View
just E
The summer colony of Bay View began in 1875 as a Methodist spiritual, cultural and educational retreat. A historic auditorium still hosts a swirl of concerts and other summer programs. The gentle, tree-shaded community of more than four hundred remarkably preserved Victorian homes is on the National Historic Register.

Bicycling
Scenic highways, byways and an impressive paved trail system access lake shores, streams and forested hills around town. For rentals and trail information, contact:
Adventure Sports	*(616)347-3041*
High Gear Sports	*(616)347-6118*

Downtown   *(616)347-4150*
downtown is centered around Mitchell & Howard Sts.
Petoskey's Gaslight District is a photogenic area of lovingly restored and maintained historic buildings. Numerous specialty shops feature regional collectibles. There are also distinctive restaurants and a charming historic inn. Nearby, waterfront parks provide a marina, museum, swimming beach, fishing sites, and the quiet beauty of Bear River where it tumbles into the bay.

Little Traverse Bay History Museum   *(616)347-2620*
downtown off Bayfront Dr.
A Victorian railroad depot near the waterfront is now a treasury of the area's history. Exhibits cover the Indian, pioneer and resort eras, and include memorabilia from two noted residents—Bruce Catton (the Civil War author), and Ernest Hemingway.

Petoskey State Park   *(616)347-2311*
6 mi. NE on MI 119
Amenities of this large lakeshore park include a swimming beach, fishing sites, hiking trails, picnicking, and a complete campground. The most noted feature, though, is "Petoskey stones." The fossilized coral comes in with storm waves each winter and is much sought by rockhounds each spring.

Winter Sports
Boyne Highlands   *(616)526-3000*   *(800)462-6963*
10 mi. NE via MI 119 on Highlands Dr. - Harbor Springs
One of the Midwest's most complete ski areas has 540 feet of vertical rise. The longest run is one mile. Eight chairlifts serve the area, and there is a complete Nordic facility, as well as tobogganing. All facilities, services, and rentals are at the base, including fine restaurants, bars and a resort hotel. Skiing season is late November to mid-April.

Nub's Nob Ski Area   *(616)526-2131*   *(800)754-6827*
11 mi. NE via MI 119 at 500 Nub's Nob Rd. - Harbor Springs
The vertical rise is 427 feet and the longest run is nearly one mile. There are seven chairlifts. All facilities, services and rentals are at the base, including food service. Ski season is late November into April.

RESTAURANTS

Andante   *(616)348-3321*
downtown at 321 Bay St.
D only.   *Expensive*
Creative American cuisine is showcased on an eclectic menu appealing to a wide range of tastes. The gourmet fare is skillfully combined with a spectacular view of the bay in the intimate dinner house.

Arboretum   *(616)526-6291*
12 mi. N on MI 119 (at Lake Shore Dr.) - Harbor Springs
D only.   *Expensive*
Fresh seasonal ingredients are carefully prepared for dishes like planked whitefish or big chargrilled porterhouse. Lovely desserts like raspberry-apple crisp are also served amid upscale surroundings.

City Park Grill   *(616)347-0101*
downtown at 432 E. Lake St.
L-D.   *Moderate*
A diversified menu of contemporary American and international fare includes whitefish in three different styles. The ornate black walnut/cherry back bar is more than a century old, and the pub was a favorite haunt of Ernest Hemingway.

Johan's Pastry Shop   *(616)347-3815*
downtown at 565 W. Mitchell St.
B-L.   *Moderate*
One of Michigan's great bakeries produces a delicious cherry Danish and a humongous cinnamon roll redolent of walnuts. These and more are served with coffee here or to go.

Stafford's Bay View Inn   *(616)347-2771*
1 mi. NE via US 31 at 613 Woodland Av.
B-L-D.   *Expensive*
New American cuisine is typified by dishes like sauteed chicken breast in a pecan crust or marinated grilled lamb with gooseberry-mint sauce. The classic Victorian inn's dining rooms retain their decorous tranquility and charming bay view.

Stafford's Perry Hotel   *(616)347-4000*
downtown at Bay & Lewis Sts.
B-L-D.   *Expensive*
The historic hotel's **H.O. Rose Room** offers an ambitious selection of updated international favorites ranging from New York strip buffalo steak to fricasseed rabbit on sun-dried tomato pasta. The landmark's comfortably upscale dining room also features a pianist and alfresco dining on the veranda.

Stafford's Pier Restaurant   *(616)526-6201*
10 mi. N at 102 Bay St. - Harbor Springs
L-D.   *Expensive*
Local perch fillets are served sauteed or fried, and there are creative American dishes like stewed buffalo sirloin or smoked chicken pie. A comfortably informal setting overlooks the yacht harbor.

Terrace Inn   *(616)347-2410*
1 mi. NE at 1549 Glendale Av.
D only.   *Moderate*
Planked whitefish, pan-fried walleye, and homemade desserts are specialties in the nostalgic Victorian dining room of a historic inn.

LODGING

There are more than two dozen area accommodations, including three historic hotels, a four-season resort, and bay-view motels. Summer is high season. Rates may be reduced by at least 30% at other times.

Apple Tree Inn   *(616)348-2900*
1 mi. S on US 131 at 915 Spring St. - 49770
40 units   *(800)348-2901*   *Moderate*
The distant bay can be seen from this contemporary four-story motel with an indoor pool and whirlpool. Each well-furnished room has a private bay-view balcony. Some also have a whirlpool bath.

Bay Winds Inn   *(616)347-4193*
1 mi. S on US 131 at 909 Spring St. - 49770
51 units   *(800)204-1748*   *Moderate-Expensive*
This recently remodeled motel has a large indoor pool, whirlpool, and exercise room. Many of the well-furnished room have a private patio or balcony. Some also have a two-person whirlpool or fireplace.

Best Western Inn   *(616)347-3925*
1 mi. S on US 131 at 1300 Spring St. - 49770
85 units   *(800)528-1234*   *Moderate-Expensive*
Amenities in this contemporary motel overlooking the bay include an indoor pool, whirlpool, sauna, exercise room, and game rooms. Each room is well furnished. Many feature an in-room whirlpool.

Boyne Highlands Resort   *(616)526-3000*
10 mi. N via Hwy. 119 at 600 Highlands Dr. - Harbor Springs 49740
385 units   *(800)462-6963*   *Expensive*
The area's most complete four-season resort is a lodge and condominium complex amid four 18-hole (fee) golf courses with driving range and putting green. In winter, chairlifts serve a complete (fee) ski area. Other amenities include two tennis courts, two pools, whirlpool, sauna, exercise room, game room, restaurant and entertainment lounge, and a gift shop. Each lodge room or condominium (up to four bedrooms) is well furnished. Many units have a private view balcony or patio, a kitchenette, and a gas fireplace.

Stafford's Bay View Inn   *(616)347-2771*
1 mi. NE via US 31 at 613 Woodland Av. - 49770
31 units   *(800)258-1886*   *Expensive*
Since 1886, this gracious country inn overlooking the bay has been a haven of tranquility with antique furnishings and decor. Full breakfast is complimentary, and there is fine dining (see listing). Each well-furnished room blends period and modern conveniences. Each room has a bath, but no TV or phone. Some of the newest suites have a sitting room with gas fireplace and bay view and a whirlpool bath.

Stafford's Perry Hotel   *(616)347-4000*
downtown at Bay & Lewis Sts. - 49770
81 units   *(800)737-1899*   *Moderate-Expensive*
Petoskey's first brick hotel opened in 1899. The three-story classic continues as a downtown landmark overlooking the bay. Amenities include two restaurants (see listing), lounge, whirlpool, and exercise equipment. Each attractively furnished unit has all contemporary conveniences. Some also have a private bay-view balcony.

Terrace Inn   *(616)347-2410*
1 mi. NE off US 31 at 1549 Glendale Av. (Box 266) - 49770
44 units   *(800)530-9898*   *Moderate*
The kinder, gentler Bay View district's other historic inn is a four-story hotel that opened in 1911. Antiques and period decor contribute to the nostalgic spirit, as does the dining room (see listing). None of the comfortably furnished room has a TV or phone, but each has a private bath.

BASIC INFORMATION

Elevation: 700 feet   *Population (1990): 6,056*
Location: 265 miles Northwest of Detroit
Nearest airport with commercial flights: Pellston - 19 miles
Petoskey/Harbor Springs/Boyne Country Visitors Bureau (616)348-2755
downtown at 401 E. Mitchell St. - 49770   *(800)845-2828*
www.boynecountry.com

Traverse City, Michigan

Traverse City is one of America's most complete four-season recreation and culture capitals. The two long arms of Lake Michigan's spectacular Grant Traverse Bay end in town. All around are hills with ski areas, small lakes, gentle rivers bordered by hardwoods, and extensive fruit orchards and vineyards. Nearby along the lake are some of America's largest sand dunes. The town began as a logging camp shortly before the Civil War. Growth was steady thanks to the development of cherry orchards and a wealth of recreation and cultural facilities.

Today, Traverse City is one of the world's top cherry-growing areas, and it is a flourishing travel destination. By a bayfront park, stylish historic and contemporary buildings line tree-shaded streets downtown with an outstanding array of specialty shops, galleries, restaurants, nightlife and a landmark hotel. Sandy beaches in town extend to all sorts of modish lodgings, including Michigan's largest resort.

WEATHER PROFILE

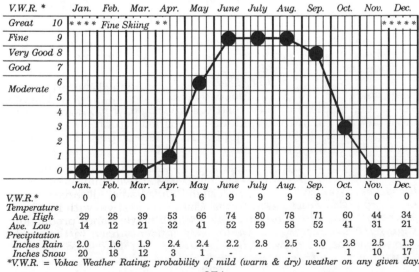

V.W.R.*	Jan.	Feb.	Mar.	Apr.	May	June	July	Aug.	Sep.	Oct.	Nov.	Dec.
V.W.R.*	0	0	0	1	6	9	9	9	8	3	0	0
Temperature												
Ave. High	29	28	39	53	66	74	80	78	71	60	44	34
Ave. Low	14	12	21	32	41	52	59	58	52	41	31	21
Precipitation												
Inches Rain	2.0	1.6	1.9	2.4	2.4	2.2	2.8	2.5	3.0	2.8	2.5	1.9
Inches Snow	20	18	12	3	1	-	-	-	-	1	10	17

*V.W.R. = Vokac Weather Rating; probability of mild (warm & dry) weather on any given day.

Bicycling
Many miles of relatively gentle byways and bike paths access orchards, forests, lakes and streams that make this one of the most scenic areas in the Midwest. Mountain bikes and cruisers can be rented by the hour or longer at:

Brick Wheels	*(616)947-4274*
McLain Cycling and Fitness	*(616)941-8855*

Boat Rentals
Fishing boats, ski-boats, pontoons, sailboats, paddle boats, and jet skis can be rented by the hour or longer in town for cruises on the bay. Several places in town have various kinds of boats and all related gear, including:

Sail and Power Boat Rental	*(616)922-3006*

Nearby are clear scenic rivers ideal for canoes or inner tubes. Contact:

Ranch Rudolph	*(616)947-9529*
Riverside Canoe Trips	*(616)325-5622*

Boat Rides
The photogenic beauty of Grand Traverse Bay can be enjoyed aboard a sailboat or powerboat. Several charter companies also take out parties for sportfishing. Contact:

Pisces Charter Boats		*(616)938-1562*
T. C. Charters	*(fishing only)*	*(616)947-6612*
Traverse Tall Ship Co. *(sailboat)*		*(616)941-2000*

Clinch Park
downtown at Grandview Pkwy. at Cass St.
One of the Midwest's best town parks borders the bay with sandy beaches, swimming areas, and a marina. A steam train tours the well-landscaped park. The **Con Foster Museum** (922-4905) has permanent and changing exhibits and presentations, and a museum shop. **Clinch Park Zoo** (922-4904) features native Michigan wildlife and a freshwater aquarium.

Downtown   *(616)922-2050*
centered around Front & Cass Sts.
A pleasing mix of historic and contemporary buildings lines tidy tree-lined streets just inland from the waterfront. The diverse and complete shopping and dining core sports a prodigious number of antique shops, galleries, specialty food stores, and restaurants that celebrate Michigan products. Appropriately, downtown's most distinctive landmark is a vital historic hotel.

Food Specialties   *(800)872-8377*
In all directions from town are nearby sources of regional produce in season. You can pick your own fruit, visit a cider mill, tour a maple sugar farm, and buy gourmet treats and gifts during drives into the bounteous countryside.

Interlochen Center for the Arts   *(616)276-6230*
16 mi. SW on US 31
Interlochen Arts Academy, America's premier private high school for the arts, is in a lovely sylvan setting between two small lakes. So is Interlochen Arts Camp and Interlochen Public Radio. All three support the internationally acclaimed Interlochen Arts Festival with hundreds of concerts (featuring famed guest artists), plays, dance productions and visual art exhibits by faculty and students open to the public during much of the year.

Interlochen State Park   *(616)276-9511*
16 mi. SW via US 31 on Hwy. 137
Swimming areas and sand beaches distinguish this park on Duck and Green Lakes next to the National Music Camp. Fishing, boat rentals, picnicking and a complete campground are also available.
Music House   *(616)938-9300*
9 mi. NE at 7377 US 31 North - Acme
Beautifully restored antique musical instruments—theater and dance organs, music boxes, nickelodeons, pianos, phonographs, and radios—are showcased in elaborate re-creations of a Victorian theater, saloon and general store. All major instruments are played as a highlight of each guided tour.
Sleeping Bear Dunes National Lakeshore   *(616)326-5134*
25 mi. W on MI 72 at 9922 Front St. - Empire
More than 35 miles of the Lake Michigan shoreline west of town are protected in a spectacular natural playground. A barefoot romp up the fine-sand slope of a 150-foot-high dune rewards climbers two ways—with a panoramic view of Glen Lake, surrounding dunes, and hardwood forests, plus a much easier, and typically faster, trip down. The nearby seven-mile-long Pierce Stocking Drive is an especially scenic loop. The visitor center at Headquarters in Empire has exhibits and information on hiking, fishing, canoeing and tubing, and complete campgrounds.
Traverse City State Park   *(616)922-5270*
3 mi. E on US 31
A long sandy beach is the major attraction of the state's in-town scenic park along East Bay. Swimming and fishing, a beach house, picnic area, and large complete campground are very popular.
Wineries
There is a concentration of wineries in the Grand Traverse area. Several offer tours, tasting, and sales including three wine producers on the Old Mission Peninsula a few miles north of town:
   Bowers Harbor Vineyard   *(616)223-7615*
   Chateau Chantal   *(616)223-4110*
   Chateau Grand Traverse   *(616)223-7355*
Winter Sports
   Crystal Mountain Resort   *(616)378-2000   (800)968-7686*
   30 mi. SW via MI 115 at 12500 Crystal Mt. Dr. - Thompsonville
This ski area is a family favorite, with 375 feet of vertical rise and runs up to one-half mile long. There are five chairlifts plus an extensive Nordic trail network. All facilities, services and rentals are at the base, including a complete year-round resort. The ski season is from late November into April.
   Shanty Creek/Schuss Mountain   *(616)533-8621   (800)678-4111*
   35 mi. NE on Shanty Creek Rd. - Bellaire
Two nearby ski areas are combined, with 420 feet of vertical rise. The longest run is one mile. There are six chairlifts, plus extensive Nordic trails. All facilities, services and rentals are at the base, including an elaborate year-round resort. Ski season is late November into April.
   Sugar Loaf Resort   *(616)228-5461   (800)952-6390*
   20 mi. NW at 4500 Sugarloaf Mt. Rd. - Cedar
Views of Lake Michigan are outstanding. With 500 feet of vertical rise, the longest run is one mile. There are six chairlifts, plus extensive Nordic trails. All facilities, services and rentals are at the base, including food service. Ski season is late November to mid-March.

RESTAURANTS

Bowers Harbor Inn   *(616)223-4222*
10 mi. NE at 13512 Peninsula Dr.
D only.   *Expensive*
"Fish in a bag" is a specialty among imaginative American dishes that achieve distinction in this deservedly popular gourmet haven. A historic Victorian mansion overlooking the bay complements the cuisine with informally elegant decor and classical music on weekends.

The Bowery   *(616)223-4333*
10 mi. NE at 13512 Peninsula Dr.
D only.   *Moderate*
The ribs are delicious, and there are first-rate contemporary American comfort foods, too, in this casual, comfortable neighbor to Bowers.

Grand Traverse Resort   *(616)938-5455*
7 mi. NE at 100 Grand Traverse Village Blvd. - Acme
B-L-D.   *Expensive*
Innovative American regional cuisine including wild game and local fresh fish is featured in **Trillium Restaurant** (D only). The elegant dining room atop the resort's seventeen-story tower provides a delightful outlook on the distant bay. There is also live music for dancing.

Hattie's   *(616)271-6222*
15 mi. N via Hwy. 22 at 111 St. Joseph - Suttons Bay
D only.   *Expensive*
A limited menu presents creative regional American dishes like morel ravioli or grilled range hen with cherry sauce. The decor is as skillfully brought off and simply elegant as the cuisine.

La Cuisine Amical   *(616)941-8888*
downtown at 229 E. Front St.
B-L-D.   *Moderate*
European-style pastries and breads are as good as they look in this stylish young European bakery cafe. Light flavorful fare at all meals (like rotisserie chicken) further contribute to the popularity.

Mabel's   *(616)947-0252*
2 mi. E on US 31 at 472 Munson Av.
B-L-D.   *Moderate*
Traditional American fare is enhanced by homemade breads, rolls, and desserts (including cherry pie) served in a big genial restaurant.

Mountain Jack's   *(616)938-1300*
6 mi. NE at 5555 US 31 North - Acme
D only.   *Expensive*
Prime rib, steaks, and hickory-smoked salmon are specialties served in a cozy dinner house with a waterside view.

Omelette Shoppe & Bakery   *(616)946-0912*
downtown at 124 Cass St.
B-L.   *Moderate*
The Omelette Shoppe & Bakery serve some of the best breakfasts in the Midwest. Omelettes are tender works of art, the cherry pecan sausage is a stellar regional specialty, and the fresh thin-wrapped walnut-laden cinnamon rolls are splendid. At times there may be a line to get into ever-popular dining areas beyond displays of baked goods.

Poppycocks   *(616)941-7632*
downtown at 128 E. Front St.
L-D.   *Moderate*
Everything is made in-house, including fresh baked goods and pastas. The relaxed restaurant is a local favorite for light creative meals.

Sleder's Family Tavern   *(616)947-9213*
just W at 717 Randolph St.
L-D.   *Moderate*
Michigan's oldest continuously operating tavern opened in 1882. They
now serve dishes ranging from fresh whitefish to buffalo burgers amid
authentically old-time tavern decor.

Waterfront Inn   *(616)938-2321*
4 mi. E at 2061 US 31 North
B-L-D.   *Expensive*
Atop the hotel is **Reflections**, a fine dining room where fresh local fish
and seafood specialties are featured on a contemporary American
menu. Casual upscale decor is enhanced by a window-wall bird's-eye
view of a beach and Grand Traverse Bay.

Windows   *(616)941-0100*
6 mi. N on Hwy. 22 at 7677 West Bay Shore Dr.
D only.   *Expensive*
One of Michigan's finest dinner houses presents skillfully prepared
New American cuisine with both a French and Cajun influence.
Chocolate dessert specialties and their own ice creams are also
delicious in this plush gourmet haven with a sterling view by the bay.

LODGING

Accommodations are abundant—in all categories. There are more
lakefront lodgings here than in any town in the Midwest. Summer is
high season. Rates may be reduced 40% or more at other times.

Bayshore Resort   *(616)935-4400*
just E at 833 E. Front St. - 49686
120 units   *(800)634-4401   Expensive-Very Expensive*
One of the region's newest and most complete waterfront lodgings is
this four-story Victorian-style motel. Amenities include a fine sandy
beach, indoor pool, whirlpool and exercise room. An expanded
Continental breakfast is complimentary. All of the well-furnished
rooms have a private patio or balcony—many overlooking the beach.
Spa rooms also have a large in-room whirlpool, and corner suites have
a gas fireplace and whirlpool-for-two in a separate room.

Grand Beach Resort Hotel   *(616)938-4455*
4 mi. E at 1683 US 31 North - 49686
95 units   *(800)968-1992*   *Expensive*
A fine sandy beach borders this stylish 1990s three-story motel, and
there is an indoor pool, whirlpool, and exercise room. Expanded
Continental breakfast is complimentary. Many of the well-furnished
rooms have a large private balcony or patio by the beach. Some
spacious rooms by the courtyard also have a two-person whirlpool.

Grand Traverse Resort   *(616)938-2100*
7 mi. NE at 100 Grand Traverse Village Blvd. (Box 404) - Acme 49610
660 units   *(800)748-0303   Expensive-Very Expensive*
Michigan's biggest and most complete four-season getaway is the
Grand Traverse Resort. The enormous seventeen-story complex on a
well-landscaped rise above lake Michigan includes two (fee)
championship 18-hole golf courses and all related facilities, nine tennis
courts (five indoors), racquetball courts, and a fitness center, plus two
indoor and two outdoor pools, whirlpools, saunas, exercise room,
several restaurants (see listing) and lounges, and a gallery of specialty
shops. There is a beach and on/in water recreation in abundance in
summer and cross-country skiing, ice skating, sleigh rides,
snowmobiling, sledding and more in winter. All hotel, tower and

condominium units (up to three bedrooms) are beautifully furnished. Tower rooms also have a grand view and whirlpool bath.

Holiday Inn   *(616)947-3700*
just E at 615 E. Front St. - 49686
179 units   *(800)888-8020*   *Expensive*
This modern four-story motor hotel by the bay has a beach, indoor and outdoor pool, whirlpool, sauna, exercise room, restaurant and entertainment lounge, and gift shop. Many well-furnished rooms have a bayfront view. Some have a big in-room whirlpool.

Park Place Hotel   *(616)946-5000*
downtown at 300 E. State St. - 49684
140 units   *(800)748-0133*   *Expensive*
Downtown's most distinctive landmark opened in 1930. The ten-story brick hotel now has an indoor pool, whirlpool, sauna, exercise room, rental bikes, restaurant and lounge, and gift shop. Each attractively furnished room was recently redecorated. Some have a private balcony, a panoramic view to the lake, and a whirlpool bath.

Pointes North Inn   *(616)938-9191*
4 mi. E at 2211 US 31 North - 49686
52 units   *(800)968-3422*   *Expensive*
Three hundred feet of fine sandy beach border this contemporary three-story all-suites motel with an outdoor view pool. Each well-furnished suite has a mini-kitchen, private balcony or patio overlooking the bay, and a large in-room whirlpool.

Sugar Beach Resort Hotel   *(616)938-0100*
4 mi. E at 1773 US 31 North - 49686
95 units   *(800)509-1995*   *Expensive*
A fine sandy beach borders this 1995 motel, and there is an indoor pool, whirlpool and exercise room. Continental breakfast is complimentary. All of the well-furnished rooms have a private patio or balcony. Most are by the sand. Some of the rooms off the lake front have a large in-room whirlpool.

Traverse Beach Motel-Condominium   *(616)946-5262*
just E at 877 Munson Av. (US 31 North) - 49686
87 units   *(800)634-6113*   *Expensive*
A long sugar-sand beach adjoins this modern three-story complex that also has an indoor pool, whirlpool, and fitness room. Each of the comfortably furnished motel and condominium rooms has a private patio or balcony overlooking the beach. Suites also have a mini-kitchen and a whirlpool bath.

Waterfront Inn   *(616)938-1100*
4 mi. E at 2061 US 31 North (Box 1736) - 49685
128 units   *(800)551-9283*   *Expensive*
Nearly 800 feet of sugar-sand beach borders this modish four-story hotel that also has a large indoor pool, whirlpool, saunas, exercise room, rental watercraft, restaurant (see listing) and lounge. Most of the beautifully furnished rooms have a splendid beach and bay view. Eight rooms also have an in-room two-person whirlpool.

BASIC INFORMATION

Elevation: 600 feet   Population (1990):   15,155
Location: 250 miles Northwest of Detroit
Nearest airport with commercial flights: in town
Traverse City Convention & Visitors Bureau (616)947-3134 (800)872-8377
* downtown at 101 W. Grandview Pkwy. - 49684*

New Ulm, Minnesota

New Ulm is a beguiling blend of Midwestern charm and Old World heritage. Forested bluffs frame this well-built town in the serene Minnesota River valley. German immigrants began settling here in 1854, drawn by rich prairie soil and a navigable river. After surviving the Dakota Indian battles of 1862, the town grew steadily.

Today, one of the Midwest's few planned communities still prospers from a precise layout of wide streets and diverse parks. The Teutonic background is celebrated in distinctive architecture, trim lawns and gardens, and orderly houses and storefronts. Emphasis on family values is displayed in well-used parks, including a recreation center with an Olympic pool, ice arena, racquetball courts, and a fitness facility. Downtown is a highly strollable mix of shops featuring regional and German crafts, antiques and culinary treats. In spite of a rich legacy of charming Victorian buildings and a wealth of recreation and cultural opportunities, restaurants and lodgings are surprisingly scarce.

WEATHER PROFILE

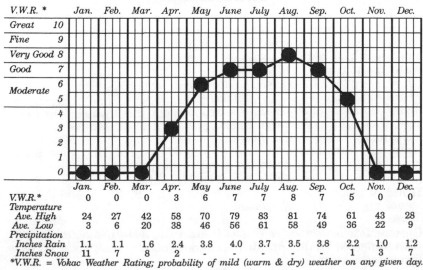

V.W.R.*		Jan.	Feb.	Mar.	Apr.	May	June	July	Aug.	Sep.	Oct.	Nov.	Dec.
V.W.R.*		0	0	0	3	6	7	7	8	7	5	0	0
Temperature													
Ave. High		24	27	42	58	70	79	83	81	74	61	43	28
Ave. Low		3	6	20	38	46	56	61	58	49	36	22	9
Precipitation													
Inches Rain		1.1	1.1	1.6	2.4	3.8	4.0	3.7	3.5	3.8	2.2	1.0	1.2
Inches Snow		11	7	8	2	-	-	-	-	-	1	3	7

*V.W.R. = Vokac Weather Rating; probability of mild (warm & dry) weather on any given day.

280

ATTRACTIONS

August Schell Brewery, Garden & Deer Park   *(507)354-5528*
2 mi. SE via Broadway & 18th Sts. on Schell Rd.
The August Schell Brewing Company, founded in 1860, is New Ulm's oldest industry. The award-winning family-owned brewery, housed in the original brick buildings, exudes Old World charm. It is open for (fee) tours. Grounds around the (private) family mansion include formal flower gardens, a deer park, Museum of Brewing and gift shop.

Brown County Historical Museum   *(507)354-2016*
downtown at 2 N. Broadway
The baroque German Renaissance-style structure was erected as a post office in 1910. Now on the National Historic Register, it contains three floors of exhibits highlighting area pioneer and American Indian life, plus an interactive children's area, research library and gift shop.

Cathedral of the Holy Trinity   *(507)354-4158*
just NW at 605 N. State St.
This imposing stone church (circa 1893) reflects a German baroque influence in dark heavy colors and gold ornamentation of the interior decorations. The four sides of the top of the sky-scraping bell tower have working clocks visible for many miles.

Flandrau State Park   *(507)354-3519*   *(800)246-2267*
2 mi. S at 1300 Summit Av.
One of the Midwest's most complete parks includes grassy expanses and woodlands between steep bluffs that confine the scenic Cottonwood River. A swimming pool with a sand bottom and beach house is a highlight, along with tubing; fishing; hiking trails; elaborate picnic, camping, and play areas; and (in winter) ski and snowshoe trails.

The Glockenspiel   *(507)359-8344*
downtown at 4th St. & Minnesota St.
One of the world's largest free-standing carillon clock towers is a 45-foot-tall landmark in a lovely little park. Since 1979, bells weighing up to 600 pounds have been programmed to play each afternoon while animated figurines appear from behind sliding doors and perform.

Hermann Monument   *(507)359-8344*
1 mi. SW at Center & Monument Sts.
A heroic statue towers 102 feet over a scenic blufftop park above the city. It was erected in 1897 to commemorate a Teutonic warrior who united Germany in 9 A.D. A winding stairway leads to fine city views.

RESTAURANTS

The Backerei & Coffee Shop   *(507)354-6011*
downtown at 27 S. Minnesota
B-L.   *Low*
A very good assortment of pastries (the nut roll is fine), bagels, and other morning delights are served with light fare in the shop, or to go.

DJ's Restaurant   *(507)354-3843*
just NW at 1200 N. Broadway
B-L-D.   *Low*
German and American dishes from bratwurst with sauerkraut to broasted chicken are served in a family-oriented coffee shop.

Holiday Inn   *(507)359-2941*
2 mi. SE at 2101 S. Broadway
B-L-D.   *Moderate*
German fare is featured, along with American dishes, in a dining room with some Old World appeal. The friendly nearby lounge has periodic live entertainment.

The Sausage Shop   *(507)354-3300*
downtown at 3rd North & Broadway
B-L.   *Moderate*
The town's German tradition is attractively displayed here. You can get
all sorts of sausages, plus their hams and maple-cured slow-smoked
dried beef, to go with salads, luncheon loaves, and more.
Ulmer Cafe   *(507)354-8122*
downtown at 115 N. Minnesota St.
B-L.   *Low*
Homemade specialties have made this casual cafe a popular local
choice for breakfast or lunch.
Veigel's Kaiserhoff   *(507)359-2071*
downtown at 221 N. Minnesota St.
L-D.   *Moderate*
Barbecued ribs are a specialty, along with a good assortment of
German dishes that include homemade strudel. Warm wood-toned
Bavarian decor in the dining rooms and lounge contribute to the
appeal of a restaurant that has been the local favorite for sixty years.

LODGING

Accommodations are remarkably scarce, prosaic, and inexpensive.
Almost all of the half-dozen lodgings are part of a chain or ordinary
motels in spite of the many splendid Victorian buildings in town. There
is no "high season," but rates may be as much as 10% less on
weekdays.
Budget Holiday Motel   *(507)354-4145*
just NW at 1316 N. Broadway - 56073
44 units   *Low-Moderate*
In this modern motel, each newly remodeled room is simply furnished.
Colonial Inn   *(507)354-3128*
just NW at 1315 N. Broadway - 56073
24 units   *Low*
This modern motel was refurbished for the 1990s. Rooms ranging from
small to standard are comfortably furnished.
Holiday Inn   *(507)359-2941*
2 mi. SE at 2101 S. Broadway - 56073
126 units   *(800)465-4329*   *Moderate*
There is no competition for New Ulm's biggest and most complete
lodging. The chain has done a nice job of reflecting the town's German
heritage in architecture and decor. Amenities include an indoor pool,
whirlpool, sauna, exercise room, game room, restaurant (see listing),
and lounge. All rooms are well furnished.
Super 8 Motel - New Ulm   *(507)359-2400*
2 mi. S at 1901 S. Broadway - 56073
62 units   *(800)800-8000*   *Low-Moderate*
The chain's local representative is simply contemporary. Each room is
comfortably furnished. In-bath whirlpools are also available.

BASIC INFORMATION

Elevation: 900 feet   Population (1990):   13,132
Location: 90 miles Southwest of Minneapolis
Nearest airport with commercial flights: Mankato, MN - 35 miles
New Ulm Area Chamber of Commerce (507)354-4217   (888)463-9856
*   downtown at 1 N. Minnesota St. (Box 384) - 56073*
www.ic.new-ulm.mn.usa

Red Wing, Minnesota

Red Wing is a classic Midwestern community with a rich heritage and a favored locale. Forested limestone bluffs tower over this handsome town at the heart of the broad upper Mississippi River valley. Settlement began about 1850. Soon, Red Wing was the world's largest primary wheat market. By 1900, it was also renowned for footwear and pottery, and thanks to newfound wealth, as a leader in the era's "City Beautiful" movement.

Red Wing's authentic heritage of Midwestern industry and abundance is delightfully intact. Waterfront parks border the river. Downtown, flowers cascade from lamppost baskets. Well-kept brick and stone buildings house a wealth of restaurants, lounges and specialty shops, and a grand hotel, historic theater and other civic landmarks share the skyline with gargantuan grain elevators. Numerous romantic bed-and-breakfast inns and modern lodgings serve visitors here for the area's recreational and cultural charms.

WEATHER PROFILE

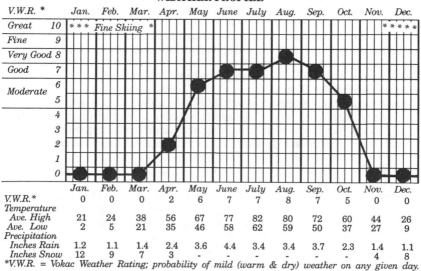

V.W.R. *		Jan.	Feb.	Mar.	Apr.	May	June	July	Aug.	Sep.	Oct.	Nov.	Dec.
V.W.R.*		0	0	0	2	6	7	7	8	7	5	0	0
Temperature													
Ave. High		21	24	38	56	67	77	82	80	72	60	44	26
Ave. Low		2	5	21	35	46	58	62	59	50	37	27	9
Precipitation													
Inches Rain		1.2	1.1	1.4	2.4	3.6	4.4	3.4	3.4	3.7	2.3	1.4	1.1
Inches Snow		12	9	7	3	-	-	-	-	-	-	4	8

*V.W.R. = Vokac Weather Rating; probability of mild (warm & dry) weather on any given day.

283

Barn Bluff
just E via 5th St.
The view of Red Wing and the Mississippi River valley is outstanding from the top of this 200-foot-high promontory on the National Register of Geological Sights. The only way up is via a well-groomed trail and stairways with informative markers along the way.

Bay Point Park
just W via Levee Rd.
This lovely little park juts into the apex of the sharpest bend of the Mississippi River. There are picnic facilities and a jogging path. Boathouse Village adjoins, where picturesque boathouses ride up and down on now-rare "gin poles" to accommodate changing water levels.

Boat Rentals
Welch Mill Canoeing and Tubing *(651)258-4469 (800)421-0699*
12 mi. W via Hwy. 61 at 14818 264th St. Path - Welch
Rent canoes, tubes and related equipment here and get free shuttle service for quiet floats on the scenic Cannon River.

Colvill Park
1 mi. E on US 61
Red Wing's most complete riverfront park has a marina, fishing sites, municipal swimming pool, tennis courts, and riverview paths.

Downtown
centered around East and West Avenues and Main St.
Flowers accent a walkway along the Mississippi River in lovely Levee Park, at the northern edge of downtown. Up a gentle slope is the venerable St. James Hotel (see listing) surrounded by rows of substantial brick and stone buildings housing specialty shops featuring local crafts and antiques, plus atmospheric restaurants and lounges. Colorful pocket parks reinforce the "City Beautiful" heritage. Visitors can enjoy self-guided walking tours or (in summer) a narrated tour aboard a San Francisco-style trolley.

Frontenac State Park *(651)345-3401*
10 mi. SE on US 61
The north shore of Lake Pepin on the Mississippi River borders this large four-season park. Fishing and boating, trails and scenic overlooks, and a public golf course are enjoyed in summer. In winter, cross-country ski and snowmobile trails are maintained. Mt. Frontenac has a vertical rise of 400 feet, and the longest run is nearly one mile. There are three chairlifts, a ski school, rentals and food service at the base.

Goodhue County Historical Museum *(651)388-6024*
just SW at 1166 Oak St.
This expansive museum is on a hilltop overlooking the town and river. Permanent exhibits depict the area's evolution from prehistoric times to the booming era when Red Wing was the world's largest primary wheat market, and a renowned source of pottery and shoes. There is also a museum store.

The Sheldon Auditorium Theatre *(651)385-3667 (800)899-5759*
downtown at 443 W. 3rd St.
America's first municipal theater opened in 1904. The classic gray brick building has been restored to include its original "jewel box" interior. Tours include a multimedia presentation about Red Wing's history. Diverse performing, cinematic and visual arts events are scheduled year-round in the 466-seat auditorium.

Winter Sports
Welch Village Ski Area   *(651)258-4567   (800)421-0699*
11 mi. W via US 61 at 26685 County 7 Blvd. (RR 1, Box 146) - Welch
Southern Minnesota's largest ski area has a vertical rise of 360 feet,
and the longest run is about 4,000 feet. There are eight chairlifts. All
facilities, services and rentals are available at the base, along with
restaurants and bars.

RESTAURANTS

Bev's Cafe   *(651)388-5227*
downtown at 221 Bush St.
B-L.   *Low*
Good old-fashioned home cooking shows up in everything from hash to
real mashed potatoes. Portions are generous, too, in this unassuming
cafe with a loyal following.

Braschler's Bakery & Coffee Shop   *(651)388-1589*
downtown at 410 W. 3rd St.
B-L.   *Low*
Fresh baked goods and desserts are featured, along with light fare and
a salad bar, in the cozy coffee shop.

Liberty's Restaurant and Lounge   *(651)388-8877*
downtown at 303 W. 3rd St.
B-L-D.   *Moderate*
Traditional American steaks, prime rib and seafood star on a wide-
ranging eclectic menu. Comfortable rooms are decorated with antiques
and pictures from the town's earlier times.

Old Fashioned Foods   *(651)388-8916*
1 mi. W at 1920 W. Main St.
B-L-D.   *Low*
Everything from soup to pies and bundt cake is homemade in this
casual take-out/eat-in place at the Pottery Salesroom location.

St. James Hotel   *(651)388-2846*
downtown at 406 Main St.
B-L-D.   *Moderate-Expensive*
The hotel's **Port of Red Wing Restaurant** (L-D—Expensive) offers
contemporary American cuisine in an informally elegant setting that
reflects the charm of the riverboat era.   The **Veranda Restaurant**
(B-L—Moderate) has American favorites in an enclosed veranda with
a fine view of the Mississippi River.

Stag Head   *(651)388-6581*
downtown at 219 Bush St.
L-D.   *Moderate*
One of the region's newest restaurants has earned critical acclaim for
contemporary American and Italian dishes. They also serve their own
pastries and desserts in a handsome dining room with a bar and a
comfortable feeling of yesteryear.

LODGING

There are about a dozen accommodations, including a historic hotel
and several distinctive bed-and-breakfast inns. There is no "high
season," but rates may be reduced 10% or more apart from weekends.

AmericInn Motel   *(651)385-9060*
1 mi. W at 1819 Old W. Main St. - 55066
43 units   *(800)634-3444*   *Moderate-Expensive*
One of Red Wing's newest lodgings is a motel with an indoor pool,
whirlpool and sauna. Each room is well furnished. Three "King Spa"
rooms also have a whirlpool-for-two near the bed.

The Candlelight Inn   *(651)388-8034*
downtown at 818 W. 3rd St. - 55066
5 units   *Expensive*
An 1877 home has been lovingly transformed into a gracious bed-and-breakfast with original handblown lighting fixtures, exceptional hardwood decor and distinctive fireplaces. A full breakfast is complimentary. All rooms are beautifully furnished with Victorian antiques and a private bath, but no phones. Most rooms have a gas fireplace. Some also have a whirlpool tub.

Days Inn   *(651)388-3568*
1 mi. SE on US 61 at 955 E. 7th St. - 55066
49 units   *(800)329-7466*   *Moderate*
This contemporary motel has a large indoor pool and whirlpool, and there is a popular park and marina opposite. Each room is comfortably furnished. Some also have a whirlpool tub.

Golden Lantern Inn   *(651)388-3315*
just S at 721 East Av. - 55066
5 units   *Moderate-Expensive*
A historic Tudor Revival home lavishly furnished with hardwoods and fireplaces is now a romantic bed-and-breakfast inn. There is a whirlpool in the back yard. Full breakfast and afternoon snacks are complimentary. Each room is attractively furnished and has a private bath. Two also have a double whirlpool and a fireplace.

Quiet House Suites - Best Western   *(651)388-1577*
1 mi. W on US 61 at 752 Withers Harbor Dr. - 55066
51 units   *(800)528-1234*   *Moderate-Expensive*
One of Minnesota's most romantic motels has the charm of a country inn, plus contemporary amenities like an indoor/outdoor pool, whirlpool and exercise equipment. Each room is beautifully furnished. Many are uniquely decorated theme suites (Oriental, art deco, Vintage Cabin, Roman Bath, etc.) with an in-room whirlpool for two.

St. James Hotel   *(651)388-2846*
downtown at 406 Main St. - 55066
60 units   *(800)252-1875*   *Expensive*
The heart of Red Wing is the St. James Hotel. Overlooking the Mississippi River beyond a scenic park is a five-story red brick complex listed on the National Register that has been restored to its full Victorian elegance. Amenities include fine restaurants (see listing) and a lounge, plus distinctive specialty shops. Each beautifully furnished room is individually decorated with Victorian antiques and reproductions, plus a handmade quilt and all modern conveniences. Some also have a whirlpool tub, and a fine view of the river.

BASIC INFORMATION

Elevation: 710 feet   Population (1990):   15,134
Location: 55 miles Southeast of Minneapolis
Nearest airport with commercial flights: Minneapolis - 48 miles
Red Wing Visitors & Convention Bureau (651)385-5934 (800)498-3444
   downtown at 418 Levee St - 55066
   www.redwing.org

Natchez, Mississippi

Natchez is a peerless treasury of the "Old South." Rich lands behind high bluffs along the Mississippi River caused the French to establish a fort here in 1716. After the area became part of the United States in 1798, cotton and steamboats made Natchez a boomtown, with more millionaires per capita than anywhere in the country. Following the Civil War, a long period of genteel decline began.

Today in the oldest settlement on the Mississippi, horse-drawn carriages are popular again, gambling is back along the riverfront, charming restaurants serve classic Southern dishes, and downtown is coming back from a long torpor. Many spectacular plantation mansions and townhouses in America's largest collection (about 500) of antebellum homes and buildings are fully restored. Outfitted with elegant period furnishings and showcased amid beautiful gardens, numerous romantic houses now serving as plush bed-and-breakfast inns are custodians of a proud heritage and Natchez's major attractions.

WEATHER PROFILE

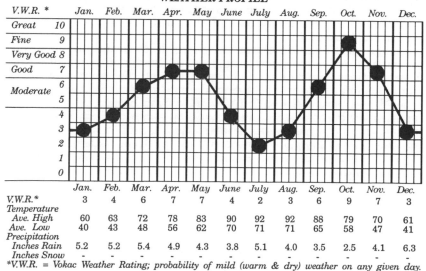

V.W.R. *		Jan.	Feb.	Mar.	Apr.	May	June	July	Aug.	Sep.	Oct.	Nov.	Dec.
V.W.R.*		3	4	6	7	7	4	2	3	6	9	7	3
Temperature													
Ave. High		60	63	72	78	83	90	92	92	88	79	70	61
Ave. Low		40	43	48	56	62	70	71	71	65	58	47	41
Precipitation													
Inches Rain		5.2	5.2	5.4	4.9	4.3	3.8	5.1	4.0	3.5	2.5	4.1	6.3
Inches Snow		-	-	-	-	-	-	-	-	-	-	-	-

*V.W.R. = Vokac Weather Rating; probability of mild (warm & dry) weather on any given day.

Downtown
centered around Canal & Franklin Sts.
Multistoried landmarks of brick and stone, magnolia-scented gardens, monuments, fountains, occasional brick pavement and iron-filigree evince Natchez's golden age. A few specialty shops and restaurants, plus a historic hotel, distinguish a district that also has blocks needing attention to reclaim them from genteel decay.

Homochitto National Forest   *(601)384-5876*
20 mi. E via US 84
Much of the southwestern corner of Mississippi is in this forest. Swimming, fishing, and hiking are popular, and there are numerous picnic areas and a complete campground.

Natchez Carriage Company   *(601)446-6631*   *(800)647-6742*
downtown at 201 S. Canal St.
Horse-drawn carriages are abundantly available for narrated 45-minute tours of picturesque downtown Natchez and surroundings.

Natchez National Historical Park   *(601)442-7047*
1 mi. E at 1 Melrose-Montebello Pkwy.
This park, established in 1988, features the **Melrose Estate**, an 1845 Greek Revival mansion with original furnishings surrounded by outbuildings and gardens. Other historic buildings are being added.

Natchez Pilgrimage Tours   *(601)446-6631*   *(800)647-6742*
downtown at Canal & State Sts.
More than a dozen nationally recognized antebellum mansions surrounded by luxuriant gardens may be toured individually on a daily basis year-round. Throughout renowned spring and fall pilgrimages, these and many other historic homes are shown by natives in period costume during scheduled combination tours. Most are furnished with quality antiques and original heirlooms. Several also serve as nostalgic bed-and-breakfast inns (see listings).

Natchez State Park   *(601)442-2658*
10 mi. NE
A popular bass-fishing lake with boat rentals is the centerpiece of a large park. Hiking, biking and horseback riding trails, picnic facilities, cabins and a complete campground are also available.

Natchez Trace Parkway   *(601)842-1572*
8 mi. NE via US 61
Animals and (later) American Indians "traced" a route that evolved into one of the most important pioneer highways of the early 1800s. The current parkway closely follows the route for nearly 450 miles from Natchez to Nashville. A pristine two-lane highway bordered by mowed greensward fits seamlessly into sylvan countryside unspoiled by intrusive billboards or developments. Wayside exhibits, hiking and nature trails, numerous picnic areas and several campgrounds are provided. At **Emerald Mound** (11 miles from Natchez), temple mounds built by prehistoric Indians around 1300 A.D. are among the largest in America. **Mount Locust** (15 miles from Natchez), the only remaining inn on the Trace, has been restored to its early 1800s appearance. There are historic exhibits and interpretive programs.

Natchez Under-the-Hill   *(601)445-0605*   *(800)722-5825*
just SW at 21 Silver St.
The Lady Luck, a replica of a steamboat permanently docked by the Mississippi River, is a 24-hour-a-day casino. Nearby are a riverwalk, plus several restaurants, bars and shops on a once-lusty waterfront.

RESTAURANTS

Carriage House Restaurant   *(601)445-5151*
downtown at 401 High St.
L only.   *Moderate*
Classic Southern fried chicken with tiny biscuits and pecan pie with whipped cream are deservedly famous specialties. In this Natchez favorite, full linen enhances a large dining room and lounge in the carriage house of Stanton Hall, a grand antebellum mansion.

Liza's Contemporary Cuisine   *(601)446-6368*
1 mi. SW at 657 S. Canal St.
D only.   *Expensive*
New American cuisine with a Southern accent stars in dishes like pan-fried catfish with beurre blanc hot sauce and black-eyed pea relish. Housemade desserts are a first rate finish to gourmet dining amidst casual elegance in a historic home, with Mississippi River views.

Monmouth Plantation   *(601)442-5852*
1 mi. E via John Quitman Pkwy. at 36 Melrose Av.
D only.   *Very Expensive*
Fixed-price five-course gourmet dinners are made truly special by the setting in Monmouth Plantation. Semi-formal attire is appropriate in a magnificent dining room filled with opulent antiques basking in the romantic glow of candles and a splendid gaslight chandelier.

Natchez Landing   *(601)442-6639*
just SW at 35 Silver St. - Under-the-Hill
L-D.   *Moderate*
Hickory-smoked barbecued meats and fried catfish are specialties of a comfortably rustic dining room and bar overlooking the river.

Scrooge's   *(601)446-9922*
downtown at 315 Main St.
L-D.   *Moderate*
Broccoli fritters or popcorn shrimp may be among the contemporary regional dishes served amid upscale pub-style decor in this notable newer addition to downtown dining and drinking.

Wharf Master's House   *(601)445-6025*
just SW at 57 Silver St. - Under-the-Hill
L-D.   *Moderate*
Seafood, steak and Southern specialties have won a following of both natives and visitors. The casual family-oriented dining room and bar are in a historic building near the Mississippi River.

LODGING
One of America's finest concentrations of antebellum buildings and mansions on the National Register of Historic Places is in Natchez. Many offer tours and have become charming bed-and-breakfast inns. March and October are high season. Most places have the same rates year-round, but a few reduce rates 10% or more at other times.

The Briars   *(601)446-9654*
1 mi. SW via Canal St. at 31 Irving Lane (Box 1245) - 39120
14 units   *(800)634-1818*   *Expensive*
Crowning a promontory above the Mississippi River, The Briars is one of America's best plantation-style bed-and-breakfast inns. Acres of lush gardens surround the main house which exudes the elegance and grace of its 1818 origin. There is a pool. A complimentary plantation breakfast is served in a river-view pavilion. Each luxuriously furnished spacious room showcases quality antiques and has a private bath and all contemporary amenities. Two suites also have a gas fireplace.

The Burn   *(601)442-1344*
just N at 712 N. Union St. - 39120
    7 units   *(800)654-8859*   *Moderate-Expensive*
A handsome 1834 mansion with a spectacular spiral staircase and a
pool in a formal garden is now a romantic bed-and-breakfast inn. Full
breakfast and evening treats are complimentary. Fine antiques are
combined with all present day comforts (except phone) in each
beautifully furnished room.

Governor Holmes House   *(601)442-2366*
downtown at 207 S. Wall St. - 39120
    4 units   *(888)442-0166*   *Moderate*
One of the oldest (1794) homes in downtown Natchez is now an
appealing bed-and-breakfast. Full Southern breakfast is complimentary.
Each room is attractively furnished with period antiques and paintings,
plus modern conveniences (except phone) including a private bath.

Linden   *(601)445-5472*
1 mi. E via John Quitman Pkwy. at 1 Linden Pl. - 39120
    7 units   *(800)254-6336*   *Moderate-Expensive*
A stately (1800) Federal-style plantation home is now a dignified bed-
and-breakfast on a gentle slope behind moss-draped oaks. A Southern
plantation breakfast is complimentary. Each room is attractively
furnished with period antiques, canopied bed, and private bath, but no
phone or TV.

Monmouth Plantation   *(601)442-5852*
1 mi. E via John A. Quitman Pkwy. at 36 Melrose Av. - 39120
    28 units   *(800)828-4531*   *Expensive*
The grandeur and grace of the antebellum South is epitomized by the
skilled restoration of Monmouth. The hilltop mansion (circa 1818) and
outbuildings on the National Register are surrounded by 26 acres of
luxuriant lawns, moss-draped oaks, extensive flower gardens, and
paths leading to a tranquil pond. Elegant Southern breakfast and
afternoon appetizers are complimentary. Formal fixed-price dinners
(see listing) showcase the romance of enduring treasures and genuine
Southern hospitality. Each beautifully furnished room combines
luxurious period antiques with all contemporary amenities.

Natchez Eola Hotel   *(601)445-6000*
downtown at 110 N Pearl St. - 39120
    125 units   *(800)888-9140*   *Moderate*
Downtown's largest building is the seven-story Eola Hotel (on the
National Register). The somewhat refurbished 1927 complex has
glimmerings of a posh past in its dining room and bars. Some of the
simply furnished rooms have river-view balconies.

Ramada Inn Hilltop   *(601)446-6311*
1 mi. SW at 130 John R. Junkin Dr. (US 84) - 39120
    162 units   *(800)256-6311*   *Moderate*
Natchez's largest lodging is a contemporary motor hotel on a bluff
overlooking the Mississippi River and bridges. Amenities include a
river-view pool, dining room and lounge. All rooms are well furnished.
Some have a private balcony with a river view.

BASIC INFORMATION

Elevation: 210 feet   *Population (1990): 19,460*
Location: 170 miles Northwest of New Orleans
Nearest airport with commercial flights: Alexandria, LA - 70 miles
Natchez Convention & Visitors Bureau   (601)446-6345   (800)647-6724
    downtown at 422 Main St. (Box 1485) - 39121 www.bkbank.com\ncvb\ncvb

Vicksburg, Mississippi

Vicksburg is an enduring cornerstone of the history, heritage and hospitality of the "Old South." A high bluff and rich flatlands by the Mississippi River led to settlement in 1811. Steamboats, a railroad and cotton all contributed to rapid growth and prosperity until the Civil War. On July 4, 1863, after a 47-day siege, the "Gibraltar of the Confederacy" was surrendered. Tourism finally joined trade as the keystone to Vicksburg's resurgence more than a century later.

Riverboat gambling has revitalized the waterfront in recent years. Downtown, a few specialty shops, antiques stores and restaurants are helping to restore the once-vital district. Horse-drawn carriages again clop along oak-and-magnolia-shaded streets where proudly restored Victorian homes showcase authentic heritage pieces and Southern hospitality to visitors and overnight guests. North and east of town, one of the nation's most beautiful military parks is a soul-stirring memorial to a great turning point in American history.

WEATHER PROFILE

V.W.R. *		Jan.	Feb.	Mar.	Apr.	May	June	July	Aug.	Sep.	Oct.	Nov.	Dec.
Great	10												
Fine	9												
Very Good	8												
Good	7												
Moderate	6												
	5												
	4												
	3												
	2												
	1												
	0												

	Jan.	Feb.	Mar.	Apr.	May	June	July	Aug.	Sep.	Oct.	Nov.	Dec.
V.W.R.*	1	2	6	7	7	5	3	4	7	9	6	3
Temperature												
Ave. High	57	60	70	75	82	88	90	90	86	77	68	60
Ave. Low	40	43	47	56	63	69	70	70	65	57	47	40
Precipitation												
Inches Rain	5.1	4.8	5.5	4.7	4.3	3.8	4.4	3.6	3.0	2.6	3.7	5.2
Inches Snow	1	1	-	-	-	-	-	-	-	-	-	-

*V.W.R. = Vokac Weather Rating; probability of mild (warm & dry) weather on any given day.

ATTRACTIONS

Biedenharn Museum of Coca-Cola Memorabilia *(601)638-6514*
downtown at 1107 Washington St.
The world's first bottling of Coca-Cola took place in 1894 in this Victorian brick building. The restored complex includes Coca-Cola memorabilia, an old-fashioned homemade candy store and soda fountain (Cokes are featured), and a gift shop.

Boat Ride
  Mississippi River Adventure   *(601)638-5443*   *(800)521-4363*
  downtown at foot of Clay St.
The captain narrates over 500 years of history during a one-hour jet-boat cruise. Highlights include views of Grant's Canal and Confederate artillery defenses from the Civil War siege, modern-day boat traffic, and riverbank wildlife.

Cairo Museum   *(601)636-2199*
  1 mi. N opp. National Cemetery entrance
The U.S.S. Cairo was a Union ironclad sunk in the Yazoo River north of town in 1862. It was the first vessel in history sunk by an electrically detonated mine. The gunboat was salvaged in the 1960s, restored, and is on display next to a museum full of recovered artifacts.

Gray and Blue Naval Museum   *(601)638-6500*
  downtown at 1102 Washington St.
Here is the world's largest collection of Civil War gunboat models. Paintings, reference materials, and artifacts also support the museum's presentation of the naval history of the Civil War.

Historic Houses
Many elegant mansions and townhouses built during the 1800s in Vicksburg have been fully restored and furnished with museum-quality period antiques. Most are surrounded by giant hardwoods and colorful gardens, and are on the National Historic Register. The Vicksburg Spring and Fall Pilgrimages are deservedly the town's main events. The best antebellum homes open to self-guided tours include: the **Cedar Grove** and **The Duff Green Mansion** (see lodging listings), and **Balfour** (with a remarkable three-story elliptical staircase), plus **Martha Vick House** (built for the daughter of the town's founder) and **McRaven Home** (complete with cannon damage from the siege).

Old Court House Museum   *(601)636-0741*
  downtown at 1008 Cherry St.
Vicksburg's preeminent landmark, built in 1858 by skilled slave labor, is centered on a square block on the highest hill in town. Thirty-foot Ionic columns support massive stone porticos on each of four sides. Jefferson Davis launched his political career here, and on July 4, 1863, Union troops raised the American flag, signifying the end of the 47-day siege. The building has been a museum since 1948 housing thousands of artifacts reflecting Southern heritage. There is a gift shop.

Riverboat Gambling
  downtown and south along the Mississippi River
Riverboat gambling returned to Vicksburg in 1993. There are now four major casinos on the waterfront open 24 hours every day. All have affiliated restaurants, bars, and lodgings.
  Ameristar Casino   *3 mi. S at 4146 S. Washington (800)700-7770*
  Harrah's Casino Vicksburg *downtown at 1310 Mulberry St. (800)427-7247*
  Isle of Capri Casino *3 mi. S at 3990 S. Washington (800)946-4753*
  Rainbow Casino   *4 mi. S at 1380 Warrenton Rd. (800)503-3777*

Vicksburg National Military Park   *(601)636-0583*
2 mi. E via Clay St. (US 80)

One of America's most evocative historic parks includes the sites of Union siege lines and Confederate defenses for several miles along the eastern and northern outskirts of Vicksburg. The visitor center has museum exhibits and a related film. The self-guided sixteen-mile driving tour is a memorable way to visualize and understand one of the most important battles ever fought in America. Fortifications, artillery and trenches have been recreated on actual sites. The hallowed grounds include more than one thousand monuments, memorials, and markers. Some, like the Illinois Memorial, are truly grand. Many are soul-stirring.

RESTAURANTS

Cedar Grove Mansion Inn   *(601)636-1000*
1 mi. S at 2200 Oak St.
D only.   *Expensive*
Andre's offers skillfully prepared New Orleans-style cuisine ranging from catfish to filet mignon. Vicksburg's most elegant dining room and lounge capture romance with lavish period furnishings in the 1840 mansion, and in a candlelit courtyard.

Delta Point Restaurant   *(601)638-1000*
3 mi. S at 4144 Washington St.
D only.   *Expensive*
Contemporary American cuisine is served in a plush, completely renovated setting overlooking the river.

Duff's Tavern and Grille   *(601)638-0169*
downtown at 1306 Washington St.
L-D.   *Moderate*
Contemporary American cuisine includes regional delights like cajun shrimp amid upscale pub-style decor in downtown's toniest restaurant.

Goldie's Trail Bar-B-Que   *(601)636-9839*
3 mi. S at 4127 S. Washington St.
L-D.   *Low*
Pit barbecued ribs, chicken, beef, pork, or sausage and all the right side dishes have starred in this real down-home Q-parlor since 1960.

Top O' the River   *(601)634-0450*
2 mi. E on E. Clay St. at 1425 Lum Dr.
D only.   *Moderate*
Half-pound catfish filet with hush puppies, cornbread and fried dill pickles (!) is the specialty of a relaxed restaurant that shares a location with "the Dock" Seafood Buffet.

Walnut Hills Restaurant   *(601)638-4910*
just E at 1214 Adams St.
L-D.   *Low*
Acclaimed fried chicken tops Southern home-cooked dishes served family-style or a la carte amidst nostalgic decor of a Victorian home.

LODGING

Numerous antebellum mansions in Vicksburg offer tours and have become romantic bed-and-breakfast inns. High season is spring through fall. In winter, some places reduce their rates 10% or more.

Annabelle   *(601)638-2000*
1 mi. S at 501 Speed St. - 39180
8 units   *(800)791-2000*   *Moderate-Expensive*
A handsome Victorian brick house (circa 1868) became a bed-and-breakfast inn in the 1990s. A Southern breakfast is complimentary, as

293

is use of the pool. Each room is beautifully furnished with original art and antiques and all contemporary conveniences.

Belle of the Bends　　*(601)634-0737*
1 mi. S at 508 Klein St. - 39180
5 units　　　　*(800)844-2308*　　　*Moderate-Expensive*
This bed-and-breakfast (circa 1876) occupies an elaborate Victorian Italianate residence replete with oval arched woodwork. It is surrounded by shade trees and gardens. Full country breakfast is complimentary. Each beautifully furnished room is embellished in quality antiques and contemporary conveniences except phones.

Cedar Grove Mansion Inn　　*(601)636-1000*
1 mi. S at 2200 Oak St. - 39180
30 units　　　　*(800)862-1300*　　　*Moderate-Expensive*
Vicksburg's biggest antebellum mansion (circa 1840) was skillfully restored to serve as a romantic bed-and-breakfast inn. Amenities of the five-acre complex on the National Register include formal gardens with gazebos; fountains and courtyards; pool; tennis court; exercise room; and gourmet restaurant (see listing). Full Southern breakfast is complimentary. Each room is beautifully furnished with period antiques and all modern conveniences.

The Corners　　*(601)636-7421*
1 mi. S at 601 Klein St. - 39180
15 units　　　　*(800)444-7421*　　　*Moderate-Expensive*
The city's only river-view bed-and-breakfast occupies a distinctive 1872 complex on the National Register. Full plantation breakfast is complimentary. Each room is beautifully furnished with period antiques and all modern conveniences. Several have distant river views, gas fireplace and whirlpool bath.

Days Inn at Rainbow Casino　　*(601)638-7111*
4 mi. S at 1350 Warrenton Rd. - 39180
96 units　　　　*(800)667-4657*　　　　　*Moderate*
This motel opened in the 1990s with an indoor pool, whirlpool, sauna and exercise room next to the Mississippi River, the Rainbow Casino and a family fun park. Each room is attractively furnished and there are whirlpool suites.

The Duff Green Mansion　　*(601)636-6968*
just NE at 1114 First East St. - 39180
7 units　　　　*(800)992-0037*　　　*Moderate-Expensive*
Splendid Paladian architecture distinguishes this 1856 mansion on the National Register, and there is a pool. Full breakfast is complimentary. Each room combines beautifully furnished period decor, a gas fireplace, and all contemporary conveniences.

Harrah's Casino Hotel Vicksburg　　*(601)636-3423*
downtown at 1310 Mulberry St. - 39180
117 units　　　　*(800)427-7247*　　　*Moderate-Expensive*
For "the action," Harrah's 1990s seven-story hotel has the best location—by a riverboat casino on the Mississippi and a short stroll from downtown. There is a restaurant and lounge. Each well-furnished room has a view of the river or downtown.

BASIC INFORMATION

Elevation: 210 feet　　　　*Population (1990): 20,908*
Location: 220 miles North of New Orleans
Nearest airport with regular flights: Jackson, MS - 50 miles
Vicksburg Convention & Visitors Bureau (601)636-9421 (800)221-3536
1 mi. E at Clay St. / Old Hwy. 27 (Box 110) - 39181 www.vicksburg.org / cvb

Branson, Missouri

Branson is the recreation and entertainment capital of America's heartland. Gentle woodlands and folds of the Ozark Mountains surround the choice locale along the picturesque banks of a historic reservoir. A relatively mild four-season climate, clear streams and lush forests first attracted vacationers a century ago. But, it wasn't until the 1960s that music theaters began to transform Branson.

Today, one of America's most glittering arrays of entertainment showplaces line "The Strip" for five miles west of downtown. Top-name recording artists headline elaborate theaters with music and comedy styles that appeal to all ages and tastes. Traditional Ozark arts and crafts, and country cooking, are abundantly available, especially downtown and in Silver Dollar City. A full range of lodgings serves both show-goers and outdoor enthusiasts enjoying expansive lakes and sylvan hills and hollows of the surrounding Mark Twain National Forest.

WEATHER PROFILE

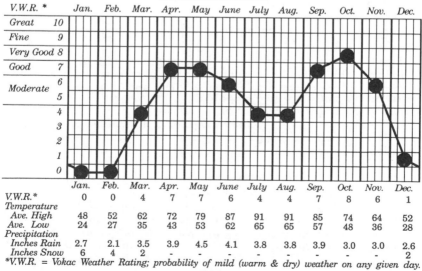

V.W.R. *		Jan.	Feb.	Mar.	Apr.	May	June	July	Aug.	Sep.	Oct.	Nov.	Dec.
V.W.R.*		0	0	4	7	7	6	4	4	7	8	6	1
Temperature													
Ave. High		48	52	62	72	79	87	91	91	85	74	64	52
Ave. Low		24	27	35	43	53	62	65	65	57	48	36	28
Precipitation													
Inches Rain		2.7	2.1	3.5	3.9	4.5	4.1	3.8	3.8	3.9	3.0	3.0	2.6
Inches Snow		6	4	2	-	-	-	-	-	-	-	-	2

*V.W.R. = Vokac Weather Rating; probability of mild (warm & dry) weather on any given day.

295

ATTRACTIONS
Branson Scenic Railway　　*(417)334-6110*　　*(800)287-2462*
downtown at 206 E. Main St.
For a scenic and sentimental journey, the nearly two-hour trip that leaves the downtown depot several times daily is a winner. Restored Vista-Dome and other posh passenger cars provide comfort for a narrated forty-mile round-trip through virtually inaccessible foothills and river valleys.

College of the Ozarks　　*(417)334-6411*
3 mi. SW via US 65
Students work, rather than pay, for their education in this small liberal arts college. The Ralph Foster Museum features Ozark-area memorabilia. Edwards Mill, a working reproduction of a 19th century water-powered grist mill, produces whole grain meal. A weaving studio, store, and food service are also available.

Lake Tenaycomo　　*(417)334-3015*
downtown on Lake Dr.
Missouri's first major manmade lake (1913) extends more than twenty miles below Table Rock Lake. A scenic park lines the reservoir's banks downtown. There are also facilities for trout fishing, boating, picnicking and camping. The "Lake Queen" departs from a downtown dock for narrated sightseeing cruises, plus breakfast or dinner cruises.

Live Theater
W of downtown, primarily along Main St. (MO 76)
Diverse, star-studded venues offer all styles of music from country and bluegrass to pop and jazz, plus homespun or sophisticated comedy. Several dozen elaborate live theaters that line the main thoroughfare for five miles have made Branson a contender for the Show Business Capital of America. The author's favorites are:

Andy Williams Moon River Theatre		*(417)334-4500*
Bobby Vinton Theatre	*(800)872-6229*	*(417)334-2500*
Jim Stafford Theatre		*(417)335-8080*
Lawrence Welk Champagne Theatre	*(800)505-9355*	*(417)337-7469*
Mickey Gilley Theatre	*(800)334-1936*	*(417)334-3210*
Roy Clark Celebrity Theatre		*(417)334-0076*
Shoji Tabuchi Theatre		*(417)334-7469*
Yakov Smirnoff	*(800)336-6542*	*(417)336-6542*

Ozarks Discovery IMAX Theater　*(417)335-4832*　*(800)419-4832*
5 mi. W on Shepherd of the Hills Pkwy.
The history, legends and music of the Ozarks are skillfully blended in a dramatic, giant-screen presentation that is a must-see for anyone interested in understanding the spirit of this special place.

Ride the Ducks　　*(417)334-3825*
2 mi. W on MO 76
Climb aboard a restored World War II amphibious vehicle (a "duck") for a narrated land and lake excursion.

Shepherd of the Hills　　*(417)334-4191*
8 mi. W on MO 76
The area featured in Harold Bell Wright's novel "The Shepherd of the Hills" is a working homestead. Guided tours pass authentically furnished Old Matt's cabin (home of the leading characters), and a working steam-powered saw and grist mill. A 230-foot Inspiration Tower, craft demonstrations, music shows, wagon rides, and an outdoor amphitheater are nearby.

Showboat Branson Belle   *(417)336-7171*   *(800)227-8587*
9 mi. SW via MO 165

A mighty sternwheeler offers a scenic two-hour cruise of Table Rock Lake, plus breakfast, lunch or dinner, and a rollicking live show.

Silver Dollar City   *(417)336-7180*   *(800)952-6626*
9 mi. W on MO 76

Silver Dollar City is one of America's best theme parks. An 1890s-style Ozark settlement seamlessly shares an expansive site full of towering trees and colorful gardens with a dozen stage shows, and major thrill rides as scenic as they are exciting. More than 100 resident craftsmen demonstrate traditional artistry from wood carving to glass blowing, and country cooking. Comedy skits and country bluegrass, gospel and Dixieland music are performed throughout the park in dozens of shows daily. The largest theater is the 3,000-seat Echo Hollow Amphitheater. Several major festivals are also held here annually, from the Spring Flower Show through the fall National Festival of Craftsmen and Musicians. Under Silver Dollar City is **Marvel Cave**—the original attraction. A highlight is an enormous twenty-story-high "room."

Table Rock Lake   *(417)334-4865*
9 mi. SW via MO 165

The visitor center has a good view of the dam and lake, and related displays. Bass, crappie, and walleye fishing are popular, as are swimming, scuba diving, boating, and water skiing. Boat rentals are available, and there are numerous camping and picnicking facilities. Nearby is Missouri's largest trout hatchery, and a visitor center.

White Water   *(417)334-7487*
4 mi. W on MO 76

A wave pool, water slides and flumes, inner-tube rapids, streams and pools are some of the features in the area's most elaborate water park.

RESTAURANTS

Big Cedar Lodge   *(417)335-2777*
9 mi. SW via US 65 at 612 Devil's Pool Rd.
B-L-D.   *Expensive*

The **Devil's Pool Restaurant** features a tasty breakfast buffet and regional specialties amid perfect Ozark decor. The imposing room is marked by a huge stone fireplace, bark-covered pine posts, exposed log rafters and oak plank floors. Trophy animal and fish mounts and classic sporting gear adorn the walls, and picture windows frame a forested lake. The stylish **Truman Smokehouse** features lighter fare.

Bob Evans Restaurant & General Store   *(417)336-2023*
just W at 801 W. Main St.
B-L-D.   *Moderate*

Homestyle American fare includes local specialties and baked goods in a casual old-fashioned restaurant with a well-stocked general store.

Branson Cafe   *(417)334-3021*
downtown at 102 Main St.
B-L-D.   *Moderate*

Good old-fashioned country cookin' backed by homemade biscuits, cinnamon rolls and pies stars in the area's oldest eatery..

Buckingham's Restaurant & Oasis   *(417)337-7777*
3 mi. W at 2820 W. Highway 76
D only.   *Expensive*

Contemporary Continental cuisine is given expert attention in dishes like steak Diane. Tableside cooking, full linen, and hand-painted wall murals and African art contribute to a swanky safari feeling.

Candlestick Inn   *(417)334-3633*
1 mi. E via Hwy. 76 at 127 Taney St.
L-D.   *Expensive*
Contemporary American cuisine is skillfully presented in fresh seafood
and aged beef entrees and support dishes like stuffed sweet potatoes.
Specialties like prime rib compete with an outstanding view of Lake
Taneycomo from the casually elegant hilltop aerie.
Dimitri's   *(417)334-0888*
downtown at 500 E. Main St.
D only.   *Expensive*
Greek and Continental dishes are given careful attention. A tableside
Caesar salad and spectacular flaming desserts are dramatic ways to
start and end meals here. Posh dining rooms in the floating restaurant
offer intimate views of the lake.
Dixie Stampede   *(417)336-3000*   *(800)520-5544*
2 mi. W at 1525 W. Highway 76
D only.   *Expensive*
Branson's biggest restaurant features four-course feasts of down-home
delights served to 1,000 guests at tiered tables around an arena.
Dozens of costumed performers and horses present an action-packed
show that assures fun and excitement for the whole family.
The Friendship House   *(417)334-6411*
2 mi. S via US 65 on V-Highway
B-L-D.   *Low*
Ozark country-style cooking is featured in this big family-oriented
student-operated restaurant overlooking the College of the Ozarks. The
gift shop offers student-made gourmet goods and art items.
Outback Steak and Oyster Bar   *(417)334-6306*
2 mi. W at 1914 W. Highway 76
L-D.   *Expensive*
The best overall dining adventure in Branson can be enjoyed at the
Outback Steak and Oyster Bar. Try a fried gator appetizer, delicious
fresh tilapia entree (a delicate flavorful fish) and key lime pie for
dessert. Fine Australian beers and wine, hearty portions, warm and
friendly museum-quality Outback decor and shady dining verandas all
contribute to the fun in this delightful dining complex.
Pie Annie's   *(417)335-8080*
4 mi. W on W. Highway 76
L-D.   *Moderate*
Soups, salads, sandwiches and other light dishes are served, along with
nifty desserts. Comfortable, distinctive decor is as whimsical as Jim
Stafford's delightful show downstairs.
Rocky's Italian Restaurant   *(417)335-4765*
downtown at 120 N. Sycamore St.
L-D.   *Moderate*
Generous portions of flavorful Italian classics are served in a converted
turn-of-the-century feed mill outfitted with distinctive art and sculpture
in a relaxed setting.
The Shack Cafe   *(417)334-3490*
downtown at 108 S. Commercial St.
B-L-D.   *Moderate*
Country comfort foods have made this plain old-fashioned cafe a local's
favorite for decades. Natives and visitors alike are drawn to the dessert
display showcasing mile-high meringue pies.

LODGING

Accommodations are superabundant in and around town. Most are moderately priced, and range from plush resorts by the lakes to large hotels and motels near the theaters. Late spring through early fall is prime time. Winter rates are often reduced 40% or more.

Big Cedar Lodge   *(417)335-2777*
  9 mi. SW via US 65 at 612 Devil's Pool Rd. - Ridgedale 65739
  246 units   *Expensive-Very Expensive*
Big Cedar Lodge is the Ozarks' premier resort. Deep in a lush forest by peaceful Table Rock Lake is a complex that is both rustic and majestic. Richly grained woods and rough stone distinguish dozens of buildings up to four stories surrounded by expansive grounds that look natural rather than manicured, accented with ponds and waterfalls, wooden bridges and stone paths. Amenities include a (fee) marina with all sorts of boat rentals, stables with horseback riding and carriage rides, and an 18-hole golf course (nearby), plus tennis courts, mini-golf course, jogging, nature, and hiking trails; large view pool, whirlpool, sauna, fitness center, bicycles, fine dining (see listing) and lounge; plus resort shop. Quality artwork, crafts and antiques are used throughout. Each luxuriously furnished room captures the spirit of the wilderness while providing all contemporary conveniences. Many romantic knotty pine cabins also have a large private view deck, plus a two-person whirlpool and stone fireplace in view of the king bed.

Branson Hotel Bed & Breakfast Inn   *(417)335-6104*
  downtown at 214 W. Main St. - 65616
  9 units   *Moderate-Expensive*
A turn-of-the-century small hotel has been artistically restored and now serves as a gracious bed-and-breakfast. Full breakfast and afternoon repast are complimentary. Each well-furnished room blends antiques and Victorian decor with all contemporary conveniences.

Cascades Inn   *(417)335-8424*
  4 mi. W at 3226 Shepherd of the Hills Exp. - 65616
  160 units   *(800)588-8424*   *Moderate*
A big indoor pool, whirlpool, sauna, steam room, exercise room, game room and gift shop distinguish this contemporary motel. Each room is well furnished, and some have a whirlpool bath.

Crowne Plaza Branson   *(417)335-5767*
  3 mi. W via Hwy. 76 at 120 S. Wildwood Dr. - 65616
  500 units   *(888)566-5290*   *Moderate-Expensive*
Branson's biggest hotel is in the heart of the theater action. The contemporary ten-story complex has an indoor/outdoor pool, whirlpool, sauna, exercise room, restaurant, lounge, salon and gift shops. Each room is well furnished. Many suites also have a balcony and whirlpool.

Emery Creek Bed and Breakfast   *(417)334-3805*
  5 mi. N via US 65 at 143 Arizona Dr. - 65616
  6 units   *(800)362-7404*   *Moderate-Expensive*
A forest path winds down a hillside to the creek from this stylish bed-and-breakfast with a gift shop. Full breakfast is complimentary. Each room is individually beautifully furnished with a tasteful blend of nostalgic and contemporary decor, including a large whirlpool bath. Four rooms also have a gas fireplace.

Hotel Grand Victorian   *(417)336-2935*
  3 mi. W at 2325 W. Hwy. 76 - 65616
  152 units   *(800)324-8751*   *Moderate*
This handsome five-story motel has a large indoor and an outdoor pool,

whirlpool, and a gift shop. An expanded Continental breakfast is complimentary. Each room is well furnished with a Victorian theme, and most have a private balcony. Deluxe whirlpool suites are spacious and have a kitchenette and two-person in-room whirlpool.

Mountain Music Inn   *(417)335-6625*
5 mi. W via Hwy. 76 at 300 Schaefer Dr. - 65616
140 units   *(800)888-6933*   *Moderate*
Several theaters are within walking distance of this contemporary three-story motel with two pools (one indoor), whirlpool and exercise room. Each room is well furnished. Some have an in-room whirlpool.

Palace Inn   *(417)334-7666*
3 mi. W at 2820 W. Hwy. 76 (Box 6004) - 65615
165 units   *(800)725-2236*   *Moderate*
Theaters are a stroll from this attractive contemporary seven-story hotel with two pools (one indoor), whirlpools, sauna, five restaurants (see Buckingham's) and lounge, and salon. Each well-furnished room has a private view balcony. Some also have a whirlpool bath.

Pointe Royale Condominium Rentals   *(417)334-5614*
6 mi. SW via Hwys. 76 & 165 at 158-A Pointe Royale Dr. - 65616
267 units   *(800)962-4710*   *Moderate-Expensive*
Amenities in this modern condominium complex include a (fee) 18-hole golf course, plus two tennis courts, two large pools, saunas, two restaurants and a lounge. Many of the well-furnished condos have a private balcony. Some also have a fireplace and a whirlpool bath.

Rock Lane Resort   *(417)338-2211*
12 mi. SW via Hwy. 76 on Indian Point Rd. (Star Rt. 1, Box 920) - 65616
128 units   *(800)704-1888*   *Moderate-Expensive*
Table Rock Lake almost surrounds the area's best condominium resort. The contemporary four-story complex includes a (fee) marina and rental boats, plus a half-mile of shoreline, two tennis courts, two pools, fine view restaurant, and a lounge. Most well-furnished rooms have a private lake-view balcony, and there are condos up to three bedrooms.

Settle Inn   *(417)335-4700*
4 mi. W via Hwy. 76 at 3050 Green Mountain Dr. - 65616
300 units   *(800)677-6906*   *Moderate-Expensive*
Thirty-two whirlpool theme rooms star in this contemporary four-story motor inn with two indoor pools and whirlpools, restaurant and bar; and free breakfast show. Each room is well furnished. The theme rooms feature a private balcony, large in-room whirlpool, and creative fun decor ranging from Taj Mahal to tropical jungle.

The Woods Resort   *(417)334-2324*
3 mi. W at 2201 Roark Valley Rd. - 65616
360 units   *(800)935-2345*   *Moderate-Expensive*
This picturesque log lodge and cabins in a forest includes a large pool and walking trails. Breakfast bar is complimentary. Each well-furnished room displays the Ozark country style and includes a stone fireplace, kitchen, private deck and whirlpool bath.

BASIC INFORMATION

Elevation: 722 feet   Population (1990):   3,706
Location: 220 miles South of Kansas City, MO
Nearest airport with commercial flights: Springfield, MO - 48 miles
Branson/Lakes Area Chamber of Commerce (417)334-4136 (800)214-3661
1 mi. N on MO 248 near US 65 (Box 1897) - 65615
www.branson.cvv.com
Town photo courtesy of Kim Kulish & Branson/Lakes Area C of C.

Bigfork, Montana

Bigfork is one of the hidden treasures of the Rocky Mountains. The village is sequestered along a picturesque bay in a remote corner of a huge high country lake. A luxuriant pine forest shelters the town, and slopes along the shore to the south are covered with fruit orchards. Precipitous mountains extend eastward to glacier-dotted peaks. Bigfork was a tiny crossroad until the 1970s, when the long-overdue "discovery" of one of the West's great leisure sites began.

Today, the little main street has a picture-postcard appeal, with a flower-bordered lineup of rustic Western-style buildings housing sophisticated art galleries, gourmet food shops and restaurants, a well-regarded summer theater and saloons with beguiling Old West decor. Lodgings are relatively scarce, but there are several fine lakefront resorts and romantic bed-and-breakfasts. Every imaginable lake and river-oriented recreation can be enjoyed in town, along with all sorts of alpine activities in the adjacent mountains.

WEATHER PROFILE

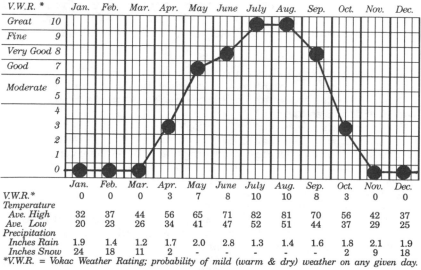

V.W.R. *		Jan.	Feb.	Mar.	Apr.	May	June	July	Aug.	Sep.	Oct.	Nov.	Dec.
Great	10												
Fine	9												
Very Good	8												
Good	7												
Moderate	6												
	5												
	4												
	3												
	2												
	1												
	0												

	Jan.	Feb.	Mar.	Apr.	May	June	July	Aug.	Sep.	Oct.	Nov.	Dec.
V.W.R.*	0	0	0	3	7	8	10	10	8	3	0	0
Temperature												
Ave. High	32	37	44	56	65	71	82	81	70	56	42	37
Ave. Low	20	23	26	34	41	47	52	51	44	37	29	25
Precipitation												
Inches Rain	1.9	1.4	1.2	1.7	2.0	2.8	1.3	1.4	1.6	1.8	2.1	1.9
Inches Snow	24	18	11	2	-	-	-	-	-	2	9	18

*V.W.R. = Vokac Weather Rating; probability of mild (warm & dry) weather on any given day.

ATTRACTIONS

Everit L. Sliter Memorial Park
downtown on S side of Swan River Bridge
Rapids of the Swan River border this lovely little park with picnic tables shaded by huge pine and broadleaf trees. Precipitous steps up the adjacent dam lead to a great view of Flathead Lake.

Flathead Lake
adjacent to town on the west
The largest freshwater lake west of the Mississippi is about thirty miles long and fifteen miles wide. During summer, numerous lakefront parks have most kinds of water recreation. Marinas in town and nearby offer boat rentals, plus narrated cruises on the lake. Summer silver salmon fishing is renowned. A scenic paved loop drive of nearly ninety miles provides panoramic views and access to numerous campgrounds, picnic areas, hiking trails, and orchards.

Flathead National Forest   *(406)837-5081*
around town
Some of the nation's largest and most spectacular wilderness areas have more than a thousand miles of summer trails. The Flathead Wild and Scenic River system is renowned for half-day to multi-day whitewater river adventures. In winter, cross-country skiing, snowmobiling, and ice fishing are popular, and Big Mountain is one of the state's major downhill ski areas.

Food Specialties
Eva Gates Homemade Preserves   *(800)682-4283*
Viki's Montana Classics   *(800)248-1222*
Wild huckleberry preserves and syrups are a specialty of these fine manufacturers of gourmet fruit products. Both have delightful tasting and sales rooms in Bigfork.

Glacier National Park   *(406)888-7800*
38 mi. N via MT 35 & US 2
(See Whitefish, Montana attractions regarding this natural wonder.)

Jewel Basin Hiking Area   *(406)758-5200*
10 mi. NE via MT 35, MT 83 & Echo Lake Rd.
A pristine little section of Rocky Mountain high country has been specially designated as a backcountry hiking area. Thirty-five miles of trails connect dozens of picturesque high mountain lakes, clear cold streams, and waterfalls accessible only to energetic walkers.

Orchards
start 4 mi. S on MT 35
Several miles of gentle slopes above the eastern shore of Flathead Lake are covered with cherry trees and other kinds of fruit orchards. Roadside stands display and sell the harvest in summer and fall.

Warm Water Feature
Big Sky Waterslide   *(406)892-2139*
22 mi. N at jct. US 2/MT 206
Nearly a dozen water slides, a very popular inner-tube river run, and hot tubs distinguish this aquatic family fun center. Sunny and shaded picnic areas, and concessions, are also available.

Wayfarer State Park
1 mi. SW just W of MT 35
A beach, dock, boat ramp, picnic areas and camping facilities have been added to a pine forest along the shore of Flathead Lake. Boating, swimming, fishing, and water-skiing are popular.

RESTAURANTS

Bigfork Inn   *(406)837-6680*
downtown at 604 Electric Av.
D only.   *Moderate*
International specialties ranging from chicken breast parmigiana to breaded Flathead Lake whitefish are prepared with seasonally fresh ingredients. Comfortable country-inn style dining rooms, a bar with frequent live entertainment and dancing, and outdoor dining (in summer) all contribute to the landmark's continuing popularity.

Bridge Street Gallery & Wine Cafe   *(406)837-5825*
downtown at 408 Bridge St.
L-D.   *Expensive*
Creative contemporary dishes are expertly prepared, including luscious desserts made here. Intimate sophisticated dining rooms are also ideal showcases for quality local art objects available for sale.

Brookies Cookies   *(406)837-2447*   *(800)697-6487*
downtown at 191 Mill St.
B-L.   *Moderate*
Every morning, the aroma of fresh-baked cinnamon rolls, scones, cookies and other tasty baked goods draws natives and visitors alike to enjoy a hot treat with coffee or espresso on the cheerful river-view deck or to go.

Coyote Roadhouse Restaurant   *(406)837-1233*
6 mi. E via MT 209 at 602 Three Eagle Lane
D only.   *Expensive*
An eclectic selection of creative gourmet fare is prepared by the acclaimed chef/owner. Refined rusticity contributes to the country charm of the secluded roadhouse/inn with a tranquil view of the Swan River past flower gardens.

Hale's Lake House   *(406)837-7377*
downtown at 425 Grand Av.
B-L-D.   *Moderate*
One of the West's great chefs owns a place that mixes fun, food, and drinks with a lake view. Some nifty Hawaiian dishes reflect his roots, from Portuguese french toast with coconut; or Kahuna burgers with beef patty, Portuguese sausage and cheese; to a pu pu platter. There is a warm and cheerful dining room and lounge downstairs, and an umbrella-shaded deck overlooking the bay upstairs.

Marina Cay Resort   *(406)837-5861*
downtown at 180 Vista Lane
B-L-D.   *Moderate-Expensive*
The resort's dinner house is **Quincy's** (D only—Expensive), where New Western cuisine is served in a casually elegant dining room overlooking the water. A plush entertainment lounge shares the view. Downstairs, **Champs** and the **Tiki Bar** (B-L-D—Moderate) offer distinctive treats like beer-battered asparagus and lake whitefish & chips in a comfortable lounge or on a waterside shaded deck.

The Raven Brewpub and Grill   *(406)837-2836*
5 mi. S at 25999 MT 35
L-D.   *Moderate*
Bigfork's own brew pub, opened in 1996, serves their full-bodied premium ales, and uses them in support of fine pub grub like mussels steamed in beer or New Orleans-style shrimp po' boy sandwich. A popular bar and a shaped-up dining deck have a panoramic lake view.

Showthyme   *(406)837-0707*
downtown at 548 Electric Av.
L-D.   *Moderate*
Superb rack of lamb and a chicken rellano with shrimp sauce reflect
the chef/owner's creative genius. A huckleberry ice cream crepe floating
on huckleberry sauce is just one of the luscious desserts that showcase
local ingredients in innovative Western cuisine. Hardwood tables and
chairs in a room with antique brick walls and a stamped-tin ceiling
provide a sophisticated setting. So does a downstairs dining room by
a wine-cellar bank vault, and a garden patio.

Swan River Cafe   *(406)837-5618*
downtown at 360 Grand Av.
B-L-D.   *Expensive*
Hearty helpings of skillfully prepared contemporary European and
American dishes are served in the romantic inn's cafe. Guests have a
choice of a cozy firelit lounge, a light and bright dining room with art
and greenery, or an umbrella-shaded deck overlooking beautiful Swan
River and the lake.

Tuscany's   *(406)837-2505*
downtown at 331 Bridge St.
L-D.   *Expensive*
New owners in 1998 are continuing a tradition of classic and creative
Italian cuisine served in a colorful trattoria and on a flower-backed
deck near the Swan River.

LODGING

Accommodations in and near town are surprisingly scarce, but
uniformly distinctive. Two of the best places are by Flathead Lake, and
several bed-and-breakfasts reflect Montana style and hospitality. High
season is June into September. Rates are usually reduced by 20% or
more at other times.

Coyote Roadhouse Inn   *(406)837-4250*
6 mi. E via MT 209 at 602 Three Eagle Lane (Box 1166) - 59911
6 units   *Moderate-Expensive*
Antiques enhance this lodge in a garden near scenic Swan River, and
there is a gourmet dining room (see listing). Full breakfast is
complimentary. Each well-furnished room has a mountain view. There
are no room phones. Two rooms share a bath. Two suites have a
private bath with a whirlpool tub. Riverside cabins have a kitchenette
and whirlpool bath.

Flathead Lake Lodge   *(406)837-4391*
1 mi. S via MT 35 (Box 248) - 59911
40 units   *Very Expensive*
Flathead Lake Lodge is the crown jewel among Western luxury dude
ranches. Handsome log-and-rock buildings are secluded among
spacious landscaped grounds along the shore of Flathead Lake. Guests
are pampered with a remarkable diversity of on-site amenities and
activities. One inclusive cost covers a large outdoor heated lakeview
pool, whirlpool, saunas, four tennis courts, recreation room, ping pong
table, rifle range, private beach, marina with all kinds of boating and
fishing opportunities, plus horseback riding, rodeos, and cookouts. All
of the above and beautifully appointed rustic Western units are rented
for a minimum stay of one week. The rate includes three gourmet
meals served daily in polished, wood-trimmed dining rooms that
showcase Rocky Mountain style and hospitality.

Marina Cay Resort   *(406)837-5861*
downtown on Bigfork Loop at 180 Vista Lane (Box 663) - 59911
120 units   *(800)433-6516*   *Expensive*
Marina Cay Resort is Flathead Lake's best waterfront resort. The contemporary wood-trim complex has a long pool, whirlpool, lake-view restaurants and bars (see listing), marina (with boat rentals), and a private lawn/beach area on sheltered Bigfork Bay next to downtown. Each spacious hotel room or condo (up to three bedrooms) is well furnished and has big view windows. Many have a pitched roof, skylight, lake-view deck and gas fireplace. Three Marina Suites also have a large whirlpool with a view.

The O'Duachain Country Inn   *(406)837-6851*
6 mi. E at 675 Ferndale Dr. - 59911
5 units   *(800)837-7460*   *Expensive*
A wraparound deck overlooks a tranquil alpine landscape beyond the dramatic log lodge. In the valley's original bed-and-breakfast, full gourmet breakfast and hot tub are complimentary. Most well-furnished rooms have a private bath and feature Western artifacts.

Osprey Inn   *(406)857-2042*
12 mi. W via MT 82 at 5557 Hwy. 93 South - Somers 59932
5 units   *(800)258-2042*   *Moderate*
A state beach park is just a stroll from Osprey Inn. The contemporary log-trim bed-and-breakfast on a slope next to Flathead Lake has a dock, swimming off a public beach, and a view hot tub. Full breakfast is complimentary. Each cozy room is well furnished and has a private bath (but no phone or TV). Two have a fine lake view.

Soiree Lodge   *(406)257-5770*
8 mi. N via MT 35 at 10 Sky Lane   Kalispell 59901
4 units   *Moderate-Expensive*
In 1997, a luxurious bed-and-breakfast hideaway opened in a private game/forest preserve overlooking meadows and mountains. Full gourmet breakfast and afternoon refreshments are complimentary. Each spacious room is beautifully furnished with all contemporary conveniences. The suite also has a large whirlpool bath with a tranquil picture-window view.

Swan River Inn   *(406)837-2220*
downtown at 360 Grand Av. - 59911
3 units   *Expensive*
In 1996, this romantic bed-and-breakfast inn opened in the heart of town. Complimentary breakfast for two is served upstairs in the cafe (see listing). Each room is individually beautifully furnished in a whimsical theme and has a tranquil lake view. One has a whirlpool; another has a gas fireplace and clawfoot tub.

Timbers Motel   *(406)837-6200*
just S at 8540 MT 35 (Box 757) - 59911
40 units   *(800)821-4546*   *Moderate*
A small pool with mountain views, a whirlpool, and saunas are features of this modern motel. Each spacious room is nicely furnished.

BASIC INFORMATION

Elevation: 2,980 feet   *Population (1990): 1,000*
Location: 490 miles East of Seattle
Nearest airport with commercial flights: Kalispell, MT - 20 miles
Bigfork Area Chamber of Commerce   (406)837-5888
  just N at 8155 Montana Highway 35 (Box 237) - 59911

Red Lodge, Montana

Red Lodge is an authentic Old West gateway to the Rocky Mountains. Colorful Victorian buildings fill a pretty little valley surrounded by sagebrush-covered rangeland that ends abruptly at the awesome escarpment of the Beartooth Mountains. More than a century ago, coal mines fueled a period of prosperity. By the Depression, however, the mines began to close. Then, the breathtaking Beartooth Highway opened, linking Red Lodge with Yellowstone National Park, and paving the way to the era of tourism.

Today, the mines are all gone. The town's heritage of hard-working, hard-drinking miners is well preserved in a legacy of Victorian structures on main street, which sports numerous good restaurants, galleries and specialty shops featuring local arts and crafts, and one of the West's outstanding concentrations of unspoiled saloons and legal gambling halls. A restored landmark hotel and several distinctive lodgings accommodate increasing numbers of summer and winter visitors.

WEATHER PROFILE

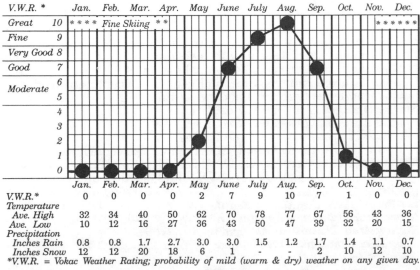

V.W.R.*		Jan.	Feb.	Mar.	Apr.	May	June	July	Aug.	Sep.	Oct.	Nov.	Dec.
Great	10	* * * * Fine Skiing * *										* * * * * *	
Fine	9												
Very Good	8												
Good	7												
Moderate	6 / 5												
	4												
	3												
	2												
	1												
	0												

	Jan.	Feb.	Mar.	Apr.	May	June	July	Aug.	Sep.	Oct.	Nov.	Dec.
V.W.R.*	0	0	0	0	2	7	9	10	7	1	0	0
Temperature												
Ave. High	32	34	40	50	62	70	78	77	67	56	43	36
Ave. Low	10	12	16	27	36	43	50	47	39	32	20	15
Precipitation												
Inches Rain	0.8	0.8	1.7	2.7	3.0	3.0	1.5	1.2	1.7	1.4	1.1	0.7
Inches Snow	12	12	20	18	6	1	-	-	2	10	12	10

*V.W.R. = Vokac Weather Rating; probability of mild (warm & dry) weather on any given day.

ATTRACTIONS

Absaroka-Beartooth Wilderness   *(406)446-2103*
13 mi. W via US 212 & Lake Fork Rd.
The wilderness portion of Montana's Custer National Forest starts a few miles from town and extends to Yellowstone National Park. It is a ruggedly beautiful series of glacier-dotted plateaus and jagged mountains that includes Granite Peak (12,799 feet), the highest point in the state. Nearby, millions of grasshoppers are embedded in the ice of mile-long Grasshopper Glacier. Hundreds of crystal-clear lakes, shimmering glaciers, cascades and waterfalls, deep valleys, and pine forests appeal to hikers, backpackers, horseback riders, campers, hunters, and fishermen.

Beartooth Highway
US 212 for 69 mi. to Yellowstone Park
"The most scenic drive in America," according to Charles Kuralt, among others, is a paved two-lane roadway that connects Red Lodge with Yellowstone National Park in sixty-nine breathtaking miles. Via a series of awesome switchbacks on a sheer canyon wall, travelers surmount the 11,000 foot Beartooth Plateau. For the next several miles the highway provides rare auto access to a vast alpine tundra as it winds past snowfields, dozens of tiny lakes, and fields of flowers high above timberline. Farther along, the roadway descends back into a dense pine forest rich with waterfalls and streams. Picnic areas, campgrounds, trailheads, and fishing accesses are plentiful. The road is open from late May into October, weather permitting.

Historic District
downtown on Broadway
A reputation as an unspoiled, lively Western town is one of Red Lodge's most enduring attributes. The welter of Victorian-era saloons and uninhibited drinking places that line the main street (Broadway) still come alive with Western music, dancing, and legal gambling each evening as they have for more than a century. Other brick buildings along the photogenic thoroughfare now house notable restaurants, galleries and specialty shops, as well as a landmark Victorian hotel, Western ware and sporting goods stores that have served residents and visitors for decades.

Horseback Riding
Horses can be rented for hourly and longer scenic rides into the Custer Nation Forest at several local outfitters.

River Running
33 mi. N on MT 78 near Absarokee
Whitewater day and half-day trips on the scenic Stillwater River (less than an hour by car) can be reserved in summer at several outfitters.

Winter Sports
Red Lodge Mountain Resort   *(800)444-8977*
6 mi. W via US 212 & Forest Rd.
After a major recent expansion of the ski area, the vertical rise is 2,400 feet and the longest run is over two miles. Elevation at the top is 9,416 feet. There are seven chairlifts. All facilities, services and rentals are available at the base for downhill and cross-country skiing. A restaurant, cafeteria and bar are at the mountain. Lodgings are in town. The skiing season is mid-November to mid-April.

Yellowstone National Park   *(307)344-7311*
69 mi. SW on US 212
(See Cody, Wyoming attractions for description.)

Bogart's   *(406)446-1784*
downtown at 11 S. Broadway
L-D.   *Moderate*
Italian, Mexican, and American comfort foods are served in a Western-style dining room and saloon with Bogie memorabilia.

City Bakery   *(406)446-2100*
downtown at 104 S. Broadway
B-L.   *Low*
One of the Northern Rockies' premier bakeries has display cases brimming with distinctive breads like multigrain and prairie bread, pastries (don't miss the sticky buns) and some awesome Napoleons and cream puffs among desserts.

Natali Italian Pasta and Steak House   *(406)446-4025*
downtown at 115 S. Broadway
D only.   *Moderate*
A two-pound T-bone steak is a mighty crowd-pleaser among a wide selection of steaks and Italian dishes served in a comfortably upscale hideaway off Broadway.

P.D. McKinney's   *(406)446-1250*
just S at 407 S. Broadway
B-L.   *Low*
Sourdough pancakes and homemade cinnamon rolls are among hearty American fare that has been popular for years in this plain little cafe.

The Pollard   *(406)446-0001*
downtown at 2 N. Broadway
B-L-D.   *Expensive*
Greenlee's at the Pollard features contemporary gourmet cuisine with a charming Western accent, plus fine housemade baked goods and desserts. The refined dining room is tops for special occasions.

Red Lodge Cafe   *(406)446-1619*
downtown at 16 S. Broadway
B-L-D.   *Moderate*
Traditional Western meals are accompanied by a salad bar and desserts like a mile-high lemon meringue pie. The Old-West-style cafe with colorful murals has been a family favorite for decades.

Red Lodge Pizza Company   *(406)446-3333*
downtown at 123 S. Broadway
L-D.   *Moderate*
All kinds of traditional and creative hand-thrown pizzas, plus a full range of flavorful comfort foods, are served in a cheerful wood-trimmed parlor and pub.

Rock Creek Resort   *(406)446-1196*
5 mi. S on US 212
B-L-D.   *Expensive*
Old Piney Dell (D only), and the **Kiva Restaurant** (B-L) feature contemporary Western fare by Rock Creek in stylish dining rooms with an intimate view of the rushing stream.

Serrano's   *(406)446-2900*
downtown at 17 S. Broadway
D only.   *Moderate*
Traditional Mexican and innovative Southwestern dishes are typified by enchiladas especial (layers of chicken, jack cheese, and blue corn tortillas topped with salsa verde and sour cream), Indian fry bread or sopaipillas. Knotty pine booths line the congenial 1996 cantina.

Lodgings are relatively scarce, but distinctive. High seasons are both winter and summer. Rates are usually reduced as much as 30% in spring and fall.

Chateau Rouge   *(406)446-1601*
1 mi. S on US 212 at 1505 S. Broadway (HC-49, Box 3410) - 59068
24 rooms   *(800)926-1601*   *Moderate-Expensive*
An indoor pool and whirlpool are features of this modern chalet complex. Each well-furnished condominium unit has a complete kitchen. Two-bedroom units also have a wood-burning fireplace.

Inn on the Beartooth   *(406)446-3555*
2 mi. S on US 212 (Box 1515) - 59068
5 units   *(888)222-7686*   *Moderate*
This fine new log inn was designed to serve as a bed-and-breakfast with a Western spirit and a mountain view. Full breakfast and a sauna are complimentary. Warm lodgepole decor blends with all contemporary conveniences in each beautifully furnished room.

Lu Pine Inn - Best Western   *(406)446-1321*
just S at 702 S. Hauser (Box 30) - 59068
46 rooms   *(800)528-1234*   *Moderate*
A small indoor pool, whirlpool, sauna, exercise room, and game room are features in this modern motel. Each room is well furnished. Some have a large whirlpool tub.

The Pollard   *(406)446-0001*
downtown at 2 N. Broadway (Box 650) - 59068
38 rooms   *(800)765-5273*   *Moderate-Expensive*
Red Lodge's turn-of-the-century three-story landmark hotel, listed on the National Historic Register, reopened in 1994 after a thorough restoration and enhancement. Features include a whirlpool, saunas, racquetball courts and exercise room, plus a fine dining room (see listing) and gift shop. Full breakfast is complimentary. Each beautifully furnished room has refined Western decor and all contemporary amenities. Ten suites have a large whirlpool tub.

Rock Creek Resort   *(406)446-1111*
5 mi. S on US 212 (HC 49, Box 3500) - 59068
88 rooms   *(800)667-1119*   *Moderate-Expensive*
Overlooking Rock Creek where it tumbles out of the mountains is a resort condominium complex with an outdoor pool, whirlpool, sauna, exercise room, tennis, fishing, and nature trails, plus rental bikes and restaurants (see listing) in an attractively landscaped setting. Each spacious unit is well furnished. Some suites have a kitchen, gas or wood fireplace and/or whirlpool tub, and private creek-view deck.

Willows Inn   *(406)446-3913*
just S at 224 S. Platt Av. - 59068
7 units   *Moderate*
Turn-of-the-century Western style lives on in a skillfully restored little inn on the quiet side of downtown. Homebaked pastries in a Continental-plus breakfast, and afternoon beverages, are complimentary. Most of the comfortably furnished rooms have a private bath.

BASIC INFORMATION
Elevation: 5,553 feet   Population (1990): 1,958
Location: 540 miles Northwest of Denver, CO
Nearest Airport with regular flights: Billings, MT - 63 miles
Red Lodge Area Chamber of Commerce   (406)446-1718 (888)281-0625
just N at 601 N. Broadway (Box 988) - 59068 www.wtp.net/redlodge

Whitefish, Montana

Whitefish is the Wild West at its friskiest in a classic Rocky Mountain setting. It occupies a luxuriant pine forest along the shore of a sheltered mountain-rimmed lake. Nearby to the east are the ragged peaks of Glacier National Park. The town prospered after the arrival of the transcontinental railroad in the late 19th century as both a switchyard and logging center. Much later, construction of a major ski area and major lakeside parks finally established Whitefish as a year-round visitor destination.

The big railroad switchyard still anchors downtown. Rustic wood-trimmed buildings include saloons featuring drinking, dancing, and legal gambling; and atmospheric restaurants and specialty shops that reflect Western style. Newer motels, bed-and-breakfast inns and resorts are sprinkled downtown, by a golf course, on the lakefront, along the river, and at the ski area to better serve visitors enjoying a wide range of recreation opportunities.

WEATHER PROFILE

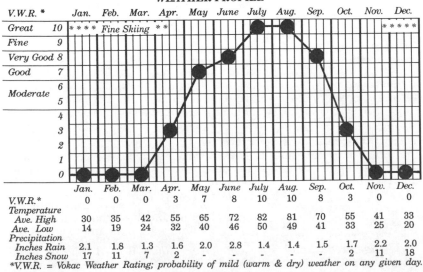

V.W.R. *		Jan.	Feb.	Mar.	Apr.	May	June	July	Aug.	Sep.	Oct.	Nov.	Dec.
Great	10	* * * Fine Skiing * *						●	●			* * * * *	
Fine	9												
Very Good	8						●			●			
Good	7					●							
Moderate	6												
	5												
	4												
	3				●						●		
	2												
	1												
	0	●	●	●								●	●

	Jan.	Feb.	Mar.	Apr.	May	June	July	Aug.	Sep.	Oct.	Nov.	Dec.
V.W.R.*	0	0	0	3	7	8	10	10	8	3	0	0
Temperature												
Ave. High	30	35	42	55	65	72	82	81	70	55	41	33
Ave. Low	14	19	24	32	40	46	50	49	41	33	25	20
Precipitation												
Inches Rain	2.1	1.8	1.3	1.6	2.0	2.8	1.4	1.4	1.5	1.7	2.2	2.0
Inches Snow	17	11	7	2	-	-	-	-	-	2	11	18

*V.W.R. = Vokac Weather Rating; probability of mild (warm & dry) weather on any given day.

Aerial Tramway
Big Mountain Chairlift/Gondola   *(800)858-5439*
8 mi. N on County Road 487
Visitors can ride the gondola at Big Mountain to the summit for panoramic views of the entire Flathead Valley and see spectacular peaks in Glacier Park and the Canadian Rockies. Winter skiers are replaced by sightseers, hikers and mountain bikers in summer.

Glacier National Park   *(406)888-7800*
26 mi. E via US 93 & MT 40 on US 2
More than a million acres of the majestic Northern Rocky Mountains are preserved much as they were before man first saw them. Shimmering glaciers and emerald-green lakes, cascading waterfalls, fields of wildflowers, dense forests, and abundant wildlife are all part of the spectacle. For fifty miles, the Going-to-the-Sun Highway is one of the world's renowned drives. All roads and trails, and accommodations from campgrounds to historic lodges, are usually open from June into September, depending on snow conditions.

Hungry Horse Dam
19 mi. SE via US 93 & MT 40
One of America's highest (564 feet) concrete dams impounds a thirty-four-mile-long reservoir in a narrow canyon with forested campgrounds and recreation sites. A visitor center, self-guided tours, and displays are open daily in summer.

River Running
23 mi. E via US 93 & MT 40 on US 2 - West Glacier   (800)338-5072
The national Wild and Scenic River system includes 219 miles of the North and Middle Forks of the Flathead River by Glacier National Park. Guided half- to six-day trips ranging from tranquil scenic floats to thrilling whitewater runs can be arranged, with all equipment provided, during July and August.

Whitefish Lake
1 mi. NW via County Rd. 487 & Skyles Place
Mountains and dense pine forests surround a picturesque lake seven miles long and two miles wide. In town, City Beach Park provides a well-maintained sandy beach overseen by lifeguards in summer. Swimming, sunbathing, sailing, sailboarding, fishing, power boating, and picnicking are all popular.

Whitefish State Park
3 mi. NW via West 2nd St. on State Park Rd.
The view from the sandy beach across Whitefish Lake to forested mountains epitomizes the natural grandeur of the Northwest. Pine-shaded picnic tables share the panorama with a swimming and sunbathing beach, a boat ramp and dock, and a complete campground just beyond. Fishing and sailing are also popular.

Winter Sports
Big Mountain Ski & Summer Resort *(406)862-1960 (800)859-3526*
8 mi. N on County Rd. 487
One of Montana's two largest ski areas overlooks the lake and downtown Whitefish. The vertical rise is 2,200 feet and the longest run is 2.5 miles. Elevation at the top is 7,000 feet. There are nine chairlifts. All facilities, services, and rentals are available at the area for both downhill and cross-country skiing. Restaurants, bars and lodgings are at the base, and there are also sleigh rides and snowmobiling. The skiing season is Thanksgiving to mid-April.

Buffalo Cafe   *(406)862-2833*
  downtown at 514 Third St. East
  B-L.   *Low*
Abundant platefuls of dishes like "buffalo pie" and many Western standards have made this big cheerful coffee shop with wood trim and Western artifacts one of two best breakfast places in town.

Dire Wolf Pub   *(406)862-4500*
  1 mi. N at 845 Wisconsin Av.
  L-D.   *Moderate*
All kinds of designer or create-your-own pizzas are served along with comfort foods and beverages, including nearly a dozen tap beers, in a big family-friendly pub.

Great Northern Bar & Grill   *(406)862-2816*
  downtown at 128 Central Av.
  L-D.   *Low*
Assorted ⅓-pound burgers are the specialty along with various baked potatoes and other dishes that can be washed down with a dozen tap beers. The big saloon with a bar, games, and a nifty patio has been a local favorite for years.

Grouse Mountain Lodge   *(406)862-3000*
  1 mi. W at 1205 US 93N
  B-L-D.   *Expensive*
The resort's **Logan's Grill** is Whitefish's mainstay for contemporary and creative American cuisine. Wild game is a specialty, from fresh local whitefish to exotic emu. The casually elegant dining room showcases trophy game heads, a thirty-foot-high river-rock see-through fireplace and monumental glass etchings. A polished entertainment lounge adjoins.

Out of the Blue Bakery Cafe   *(406)862-6232*
  downtown at 244 Spokane Av.
  B-L.   *Moderate*
Some of the best breakfasts in the Northern Rockies are in Out of the Blue. Stellar offerings range from specialty scrambles to build-your-own omelets with delectable add-ons like warm green pork chile sauce, plus huge, delicious pastries like seven-grain cinnamon rolls, croissants or stuffed brioche. The split-level coffee shop is surrounded by distinctive wall art, greenery and cases full of baked goods.

Spencer & Co.   *(406)756-8941*
  7 mi. S at 4010 Hwy. 93 North - Kalispell
  D only.   *Moderate*
The best steakhouse in the valley has the right idea—keep it simple and cook it carefully. Half a dozen superb steaks from a small center cut sirloin to a twenty-ounce T-bone are served with plenty of Texas toast, spaghetti, and a crisp garden salad. That's it, and it's enough to fill the friendly little dining areas and bar every night.

Tupelo Grille   *(406)862-6136*
  downtown at 17 Central Av.
  L-D.   *Moderate*
Whitefish's most sophisticated cuisine is enjoyed at Tupelo Grille. Louisiana cuisine tops the menu with specialties like crawfish cakes, etoufee, gumbo, and bread pudding for dessert. Dishes are authentic and excellent, as are the po' boys and muffelattas for lunch. The warm and friendly little dining room is a pleasant backdrop.

Whitefish Lake Restaurant   *(406)862-5285*
1 mi. W on US 93N
L-D.   *Expensive*
The combination of hearty American fare and a big genial old log lodge
by the Whitefish Golf Course have made this a long-time local favorite.
Lunch is served in a casual clubby dining area next door.

LODGING

Whitefish has nearly two dozen places to stay, including impressive
accommodations by the lake and the ski lifts. High season is summer
in town and winter at the ski area. Spring and fall rates are usually
about 30% less.

Alpinglow Inn   *(406)862-6966*
8 mi. N at 3900 Big Mountain Rd. (Box 1770) - 59937
54 units   *(800)754-6760*   *Expensive*
At the base of the ski lifts and groomed slopes on Big Mountain, this
modern three-story motor lodge is ideally situated in winter. Amenities
include two whirlpools, saunas, restaurant (B-L-D—Moderate) with
contemporary Western fare and a great panoramic valley view, bar,
and gift shop. Comfortable rooms on the south side have awesome
views of the Flathead Valley.

Duck Inn   *(406)862-3825*
1 mi. SE at 1305 Columbia Av. - 59937
10 units   *(800)344-2377*   *Moderate*
The scenic little Whitefish River runs past this contemporary wood-
trimmed lodge with a whirlpool. Homemade Continental breakfast is
complimentary. Each room is well furnished and has a private bath
with a deep soaking tub. Most also have a fireplace and private view
patio or balcony.

The Garden Wall Inn   *(406)862-3440*
just S at 504 Spokane Av. - 59937
5 units   *(888)530-1700*   *Moderate-Expensive*
A well-landscaped 1920s house a stroll from downtown has been
skillfully transformed into a bed-and-breakfast inn. A bountiful three-
course breakfast and use of bicycles are complimentary. Each compact
room is attractively furnished with period antiques. Most have a
private bath.

Good Medicine Lodge   *(406)862-5488*
just N at 537 Wisconsin Av. - 59937
9 units   *(800)860-5488*   *Moderate-Expensive*
This contemporary log bed-and-breakfast inn with a whirlpool is by the
road to the lake and Big Mountain. A fresh-baked breakfast and
evening beverage are complimentary. Each cozy room is well furnished,
including lodgepole-pine bed and a private bath.

Grouse Mountain Lodge   *(406)862-3000*
1 mi. W on US 93N at 2 Fairway Dr. - 59937
144 units   *(800)321-8822*   *Expensive*
The Valley's largest and most luxurious resort hotel is a contemporary
showcase of native Montana architecture and decor overlooking two
adjacent (fee) 18-hole golf courses. Landscaped grounds include an
indoor pool, three whirlpools, a game room, and sauna; and there are
tennis courts, a gourmet restaurant (see listing), lounge with live
entertainment, and a gift shop. Each spacious room is attractively
furnished. Some have a private balcony with a mountain view and a
large in-bath whirlpool.

Kandahar Lodge *(406)862-6098*
8 mi. N at 3824 Big Mountain Rd. (Box 1659) - 59937
48 units *(800)862-6094* *Expensive*
Big Mountain's ski slopes are connected by groomed trails to the stylish wood-trimmed lodge in the pines on Big Mountain. There is a whirlpool and sauna, and a popular restaurant and lounge near a dramatic rock fireplace. Each unit is tastefully furnished, and kitchens are available.

Lazy Bear Lodge *(406)862-4020*
2 mi. S at 6390 S. US 93 - 59937
65 units *(800)888-4479* *Moderate-Expensive*
The ninety-foot indoor waterslide is a fun-filled crowd-pleaser that is unique in Whitefish. A pool and three whirlpools are other features of this newer motel set back from the highway. Each room is comfortably furnished.

Pine Lodge Quality Inn *(406)862-7600*
1 mi. S on US 93 at 920 Spokane Av. - 59937
76 units *(800)305-7463* *Moderate-Expensive*
Whitefish's best motel has an indoor/outdoor pool with the additional high-tech appeal of exercise jets, as well as a whirlpool and exercise room. In the contemporary log-framed building, each room is well furnished in a warm Western style. Full suites have a mini-kitchen, in-bath whirlpool, and gas fireplace. Many units also have a private river-view balcony.

Rocky Mountain Lodge - Best Western *(406)862-2569*
2 mi. S at 6510 US 93S - 59937
79 units *(800)862-2569* *Moderate-Expensive*
Natural wood and stone decor touches distinguish one of the area's newer motels which also has a small pool, whirlpool and exercise room. All rooms are well furnished. Several have a kitchenette and two-person in-bath whirlpool and/or gas fireplace.

Whitefish Lake Lodge *(406)862-2929*
1 mi. N at 1399 Wisconsin Av. (Box 2040) - 59937
40 units *(800)735-8869* *Expensive*
The only overnight lodging on the shore of Whitefish Lake is a charming contemporary four-story condominium resort. Amenities of the well-landscaped complex include a sandy beach and swimming area, marina with all sorts of watercraft rentals, large view pool and three whirlpools. There are a few comfortable (non-lake-view) lodge rooms. All of the attractively furnished one- to three-bedroom units have a kitchen, gas fireplace, and big private balcony (many with a fine lake view).

BASIC INFORMATION

Elevation: 3,033 feet *Population (1990): 4,368*
Location: 500 miles East of Seattle, WA
Nearest Airport with regular flights: Kalispell, MT - 10 miles
Whitefish Area Chamber of Commerce *(406)862-3501*
downtown on North Central Av. at BN Depot, Suite 303 (Box 1120) - 59937
Flathead Convention and Visitor Association *(800)543-3105*
www.whitefishmt.com

North Conway, New Hampshire

North Conway is the peerless gateway to New England's biggest mountain playground. The Northeast's highest peak, Mt. Washington, is a perfect backdrop to the village in a broad valley rimmed by leafy green mountains. Settlement began about 200 years ago, but the area's appeal to visitors began in the 1860s after development of a road and cog railway to the top of Mt. Washington. Four-season status was assured by creation of one of the country's first ski areas in town in 1938.

Unspoiled high country and historic attractions are still here, along with many others now vying for travelers' attention. Covered bridges, a colorful depot, a whitewashed landmark inn and other evidence of earlier times are as beguiling as ever. There are also plenty of contemporary restaurants and lodgings, along with an abundance of notable art galleries, crafts centers, antiques and regional specialty shops. Along the main road into town is one of America's largest selection of tax-free factory outlet and name-brand stores.

WEATHER PROFILE

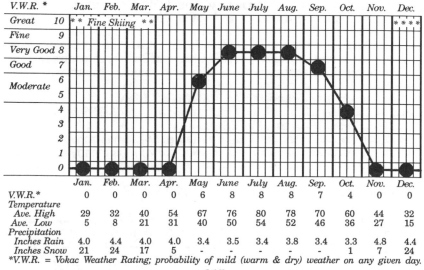

V.W.R. *		Jan.	Feb.	Mar.	Apr.	May	June	July	Aug.	Sep.	Oct.	Nov.	Dec.
Great	10	** Fine Skiing **											****
Fine	9												
Very Good	8												
Good	7												
Moderate	6												
	5												
	4												
	3												
	2												
	1												
	0												

	Jan.	Feb.	Mar.	Apr.	May	June	July	Aug.	Sep.	Oct.	Nov.	Dec.
V.W.R.*	0	0	0	0	6	8	8	8	7	4	0	0
Temperature												
Ave. High	29	32	40	54	67	76	80	78	70	60	44	32
Ave. Low	5	8	21	31	40	50	54	52	46	36	27	15
Precipitation												
Inches Rain	4.0	4.4	4.0	4.0	3.4	3.5	3.4	3.8	3.4	3.3	4.8	4.4
Inches Snow	21	24	17	5	-	-	-	-	-	1	7	24

*V.W.R. = Vokac Weather Rating; probability of mild (warm & dry) weather on any given day.

315

ATTRACTIONS
Attitash Bear Peak   *(603)374-2368   (800)223-7669*
10 mi. NW on US 302 - Bartlett
Attitash has something for everyone in summer. Take a ride on an
alpine slide. Rent a mountain bike. Ride a scenic chairlift to the White
Mountain Observation Tower. On hot days, there are waterslides. At
the Fields of Attitash are guided horseback rides. In winter, the state's
largest skiable area is served by eleven chairlifts accessing 1,750 feet
of vertical rise with runs as much as two miles long. All necessary
rentals, plus sleigh rides, food, lodgings, and more are at the complex.
Boat Rentals
Saco Bound on the Saco River   *(603)447-2177*
7 mi. SE on US 302 in Center Conway
In summer, the gentle Saco River beckons with clear water, sandy
beaches, and fine scenery. At their seasonal information center, you
can arrange for one-day canoe rentals and pick-ups, touring kayaks
and accessories, or a guided trip.
Conway Scenic Railroad   *(603)356-5251   (800)232-5251*
downtown at Depot by Main St. (NH 16)
Restored vintage coaches pulled by steam or early diesel locomotives
depart from downtown's colorful Victorian depot. Trains leave several
times daily for trips of various lengths into the luxuriant countryside.
Dining car service is (selectively) available. The depot also has a
railroad museum, gift shop and outdoor displays.
Diana's Baths
3 mi. W on US 302
Monumental granite basins; deep, clear pools; and cascading waterfalls
make this one of New England's most delightful swimming holes. Ask
for directions. Cars park by the road. "The baths" are about a half mile
from the road.
Echo Lake State Park   *(603)356-2672*
2 mi. W via US 302 on West Side Rd.
A picturesque little lake is the centerpiece of this park. Swimming from
a sandy beach is the main attraction. There are also picnic sites and
hiking trails. Nearby, a scenic road on Cathedral Ledge, 700 feet above
the valley, offers panoramic views of the White Mountains.
Heritage - New Hampshire   *(603)383-9776*
5 mi. N on NH 16 - Glen
High-tech audiovisual and animation techniques let visitors experience
sights, sounds and events through 350 years of New Hampshire history
beginning in 1634 as they walk along a path among theatrical sets. A
simulated steam train ride through Crawford Notch at the peak of
foliage season is the capper.
League of New Hampshire Craftsmen   *(603)356-2441*
just S at 2526 Main St. (NH 16)
One of America's finest craft leagues (since 1932) has a popular local
store with extensive displays of jewelry, blown glass, pottery, leather
goods and other premium handicrafts. All have been juried for quality,
and are available for sale.
Mt. Washington Auto Road   *(603)466-3988*
28 mi. N on NH 16
You can drive your own car or arrange for a guided tour up a steep
eight-mile toll road to the top of Mt. Washington. The summit, above
timberline at 6,288 feet, is the highest in the Northeast. On a clear

day, you can see three states, Canada and the Atlantic Ocean. Weather here is notoriously capricious, and often breezy. For example, the highest wind velocity ever recorded—231 mph—occurred in April 1934. The Summit Museum offers exhibits related to the mountain.

Mt. Washington Cog Railway   *(603)278-5404*   *(800)922-8825*
36 mi. NW via US 302
Authentic coal-fired steam trains leave several times daily to climb one of the steepest tracks in the world during a three-hour round trip to the top of Mt. Washington. On a clear day, the journey can be as unforgettable as the view. The Marshfield Base Station has a museum, restaurant and gift shop. Advance ticket purchase is recommended.

Story Land   *(603)383-4186*
5 mi. N on NH 16 - Glen
Well over a dozen themed rides include Bamboo Chutes (an Oriental-themed water flume ride) and an exciting river raft ride. Shade trees, lawns and gardens accent the rides, attractions, theater, and World Food Plaza. The park has provided fun for children and the young at heart for nearly half a century.

White Mountain National Forest   *(603)447-5448*
just W & N via US 302
Mt. Washington, 6,288 feet above sea level, is the highest summit in the Northeast. It and most of the rest of the White Mountains are in this vast forest. Most of the state's major ski areas are here. In summer, clear streams, picturesque waterfalls, and tranquil ponds in lush hardwood forests are popular for hiking, biking, swimming, fishing, boating, picnicking and camping.

Winter Sports
Cranmore Mountain Resort   *(603)356-8500*   *(800)786 6754*
just E off NH 16 on Skimobile Rd.
One of the few major "in-town" ski areas in New England is also one of the country's oldest, founded in 1938. The vertical rise is 1,200 feet. The longest run is nearly two miles. There are seven chairlifts. (A chairlift takes visitors up to great town/mountain views in summer, too.) All facilities, services and rentals are at the base for alpine and nordic skiing. Restaurants, bars, and lodgings are at the slopes, with many more downtown. Ski season is December through March.

RESTAURANTS

Bagels Plus   *(603)356-7400*
downtown on Main St.
B-L.   *Moderate*
All sorts of traditional and creative bagels are made here from scratch and baked fresh daily. They're served to go or with a selection of beverages and other light fare in a casual coffee shop.

Bellini's   *(603)356-7000*
downtown at 33 Seavey St.
D only.   *Moderate*
Lasagna with homemade noodles is a specialty among carefully prepared generous Italian dishes served with a bottomless salad and homemade bread. Guests have a choice of a comfortably casual dining room, lounge or alfresco seating.

Bernerhof Inn   *(603)383-9131*
8 mi. N on US 302 - Glen
D only.   *Expensive*
Acclaimed Swiss cuisine ranges from traditional (cheese fondue) to

unique (rice-crust pizzas!) on a changing menu that reflects fresh seasonal ingredients and the talented chef's whims. Desserts are luscious, too, in the inn's gracious Old World setting. Microbrews and other drinks are served with lighter fare in the Black Bear Pub.

The Inn at Thorn Hill   *(603)383-4242*
9 mi. N via Route 16-A on Thorn Hill Rd. - Jackson
D only.   *Very Expensive*
Creative American cuisine is expertly presented in fresh and flavorful seasonal dishes. Delicious housemade desserts like frozen Grand Marnier souffle also contribute to the appeal of a congenial dining room with an elegant country look.

New England Inn   *(603)356-5541*
4 mi. N on Route 16-A at the Intervale
B-D.   *Moderate*
New England's traditional cuisine is celebrated in cranberry pot roast, roast duckling, lobster casserole pie and other regional delights like housemade Toll House pie for dessert. Casual country atmosphere in the inn's dining room and cozy tavern are the right backdrop.

Scottish Lion Inn & Restaurant   *(603)356-6381*
1 mi. N on US 302
L-D.   *Expensive*
Traditional dishes from the British Isles include a notable highland game pie. There is also a creative array of international menu items, and they do their own baking. The country inn has both a dining room and firelit pub in the Scottish tradition.

The 1785 Inn   *(603)356-9025*
2 mi. N on US 302 at 3582 N. White Mountain Hwy.
D only.   *Expensive*
New American cuisine is expertly prepared in dishes like boned rabbit in cream sherry sauce or seared veal rib chop with mushroom butter. Homebaked breads and desserts are excellent. The inn's authentic Colonial atmosphere, antique fireplaces, and mountain views make the dining room a fine choice for a romantic gourmet getaway.

Stonehurst Manor   *(603)356-3113*
1 mi. N on US 302
B-D.   *Expensive*
Traditional and innovative American cuisine is typified by a baked stuffed lobster entree or lobster spring rolls appetizer. Assorted designer pizzas from a wood-fired stone oven are also featured on a grazing menu. The inn has gracious dining rooms, a screened summer porch with mountain panoramas, and the Library Lounge.

The Wentworth   *(603)383-9700*
9 mi. N on Route 16-A - Jackson
B-D.   *Expensive*
New American cuisine is expertly prepared using top quality produce from the kitchen garden and local farms, regional seafood, and other fresh seasonal ingredients. The landmark hotel's casually elegant dining room is a delightful setting for gourmet adventures.

The White Mountain Hotel & Resort   *(603)356-7100*
2 mi. NW on West Side Rd.
B-L-D.   *Expensive*
Contemporary American dishes might include a wild mushroom pie appetizer and a seafood casserole entree. The landmark hotel's casually elegant dining room is further enhanced by live piano entertainment and panoramic valley views.

Wildcat Inn & Tavern   *(603)383-4245*
9 mi. N via Route 16-A - Jackson
B-L-D.   *Expensive*
Ham-and-cheese-stuffed chicken breast in puff dough with mustard
sauce typifies the creative country cuisine featured in the historic inn's
informal dining room. The tavern is a good bet for light fare.
Yesterdays   *(603)383-4457*
9 mi. N via Route 16-A - Jackson
B-L-D.   *Low*
Breakfast is featured in a good selection of homecooked standards
supported by nifty touches like pure maple syrup, and breads, muffins
and pies made here in a cheerful down-East coffee shop.

LODGING

Lodgings are abundant, including one of New England's best collections
of historic village inns, bed-and-breakfasts, and small resorts. Early fall
(leaf-peeper time) is high season, with summer and winter close
behind. Early spring rates may be reduced 30% or more.
Bernerhof Inn   *(603)383-9131*
8 mi. N on US 302 (Box 240) - Glen 03838
9 units   *(800)548-8007*   *Moderate-Expensive*
A stylish three-story Victorian home is now a small elegant country inn
with a fine restaurant (see listing) and lounge, and cooking school. A
full gourmet breakfast is complimentary. Each room is a beautifully
furnished blend of nostalgic and contemporary conveniences (except
phone). Several rooms also have a two-person in-room whirlpool. Three
of these are in a window alcove.
Christmas Farm Inn   *(603)383-4313*
10 mi. N on Route 16-B (Box CC) - Jackson 03846
33 units   *(800)443-5837*   *Expensive*
On a hillside overlooking the White Mountains is a rambling historic
complex that has become a charming country inn. Beautifully
landscaped grounds include a putting green, pool, sauna, a big game
room with ping pong, a fine dining room with housemade desserts, and
a cozy lounge. Period and contemporary touches fill each beautifully
furnished room in the inn, outbuildings and cottages. Some also have
an in-room two-person whirlpool or a fireplace.
Eagle Mountain House   *(603)383-9111*
10 mi. N via Route 16-B on Carter Notch Rd. (Box E) - Jackson 03846
93 units   *(800)966-5779*   *Expensive*
Past a waterfall high on a hill stands a grand old New England style
resort surrounded by the White Mountains. The five-story main inn
was built in 1915, lovingly restored in 1986 and is now on the National
Historic Register. It reflects the quaint charm of yesteryear with a 280-
foot veranda scattered with antique rockers and a lobby and library
with fireplaces. Amenities include a (fee) 9-hole golf course, plus two
tennis courts, pool, whirlpool, saunas, exercise room, congenial
restaurant and tavern. Each comfortably furnished room has a private
bath and distinctive country atmosphere.
Eastern Slope Inn Resort   *(603)356-6321*
downtown on Main St. (Route 16) (Box 359) - 03860
145 units   *(800)258-4708*   *Moderate-Expensive*
Part of the heart of North Conway for more than a century has been
this classic three-story New England resort on the National Historic
Register. Amenities include two tennis courts, a big indoor pool,

whirlpool, sauna, restaurant and pub. Each room is comfortably furnished. Some have a whirlpool bath.

Ellis River House   *(603)383-9339*
10 mi. N on Route 16 (Box 656) - Jackson 03846
18 units   *(800)233-8309*   *Expensive*
Trout fishing in summer and cross-country skiing in winter are on-site features of this stylish bed-and-breakfast in a quiet setting by a river. There is also a pool and indoor whirlpool with a river view. Full hearty breakfast is complimentary. Period antiques are combined with contemporary conveniences in well-furnished rooms. Three rooms have a shared bath. Many of the rooms with a private bath also have a fireplace. Two rooms have a two-person whirlpool and a gas fireplace.

Four Points Hotel by ITT Sheraton   *(603)356-9300*
2 mi. S on US 302 (Box 3189) - 03860
200 units   *(800)648-4397*   *Expensive*
You can shop 'til you drop at Sheraton's contemporary four-story hotel, with more than forty tax-free outlet stores on premises. Other amenities include six (fee) tennis courts, plus an indoor pool, whirlpool, saunas, fitness facilities, (in winter) an ice skating rink, restaurant, and lounge. Each room is well furnished.

Fox Ridge Motor Inn   *(603)356-3151*
1 mi. S on US 302 & Route 16 (Box 990) - 03860
136 units   *(800)343-1804*   *Expensive*
In 1995 a well-outfitted motor inn opened amid expansive lawns on a wooded hill. Amenities include three tennis courts, two big pools (one indoors), whirlpool, saunas, miniature golf, and game center. Each tastefully furnished room has a porch or balcony. Many have a fine distant mountain view.

The Inn at Thorn Hill   *(603)383-4242*
9 mi. N via Route 16-A on Thorn Hill Rd. (Box A) - Jackson 03846
19 units   *(800)289-8990   Expensive-Very Expensive*
Stanford White designed this mansion in the mountains in 1895. It is now a classic New England bed-and-breakfast with superb mountain views, a romantic restaurant (see listing) and cozy firelit pub, pool and whirlpool. Full gourmet breakfast is complimentary. Each room in the inn and cottages is uniquely beautifully furnished and has a private bath but no phone or TV to detract from the plush Victorian atmosphere. The cottages also have a gas fireplace and whirlpool bath.

Nestlenook Farm Resort   *(603)383-9443*
9 mi. N via Route 16-A on Dinsmore Rd. (Box Q) - Jackson 03846
7 units   *(800)659-9443   Expensive-Very Expensive*
Nestlebrook Farm is the quintessential New England country inn. A resplendent Victorian gingerbread mansion serves as the bed-and-breakfast centerpiece of a Currier and Ives painting-come-to-life estate with arched bridges and willow trees by a pond and stream, colorful flower gardens and lawns extending to pastures, forests and majestic mountain backdrops. Summer features a pool with swim jets, a carriage ride, mountain biking, hiking, fishing, and boating. Winter means an idyllic sleigh ride, ice skating and cross-country skiing. There is also a state-of-the-art (electronic and mechanical) game room. Full country breakfast and afternoon wine and treats are complimentary. Each room is individually beautifully furnished with Victorian and contemporary decor including a two-person whirlpool bath. One room also has a fireplace.

Red Jacket Mountain View - Best Western   *(603)356-5411*
 1 mi. S on US 302 & Route 16 (Box 2000) - 03860
 152 units   *(800)752-2538*   *Expensive*
This contemporary three-story motor lodge on a well-landscaped hillside has two big pools (one indoors), whirlpool, saunas, two tennis courts, exercise facilities, mountain-view restaurant, entertainment lounge, and gift shop. Many of the well-furnished rooms have a private patio or balcony with a mountain view. Four rooms have a two-person in-room whirlpool.

Stonehurst Manor   *(603)356-3113*
 1 mi. N on US 302 (Box 1937) - 03860
 24 units   *(800)525-9100*   *Moderate-Expensive*
A baronial turn-of-the-century mansion in a pine forest on a hill overlooking the mountains has been a lodging landmark for half a century. It has a large pool and (fee) whirlpool, hiking trails, gracious dining (see listing) and a firelit lounge. Each beautifully furnished room has a private bath and reflects Victorian craftsmanship and touches (no phone). Seven rooms also have a fireplace.

The Wentworth   *(603)383-9700*
 9 mi. N on Route 16-A (Box M) - Jackson 03846
 58 units   *(800)637-0013*   *Moderate-Expensive*
The Wentworth has been the heart of picturesque Jackson for more than 150 years. The stylish four-story complex includes a (fee) 18-hole golf course, pool, tennis court, and (in winter) cross-country skiing, ice skating and (fee) sleigh rides, plus gourmet restaurant (see listing) and lounge. Each beautifully furnished room combines the romance of yesteryear with all contemporary conveniences. Some also have a gas fireplace and/or two-person whirlpool.

The White Mountain Hotel & Resort   *(603)356-7100*
 2 mi. NW on West Side Rd. (Box 1828) - 03860
 80 units   *(800)533-6301*   *Moderate-Expensive*
High on a hill near the base of an enormous stone escarpment is a handsome historic resort. A luxuriant forest surrounds the landscaped three-story complex with a (fee) 9-hole golf course and putting green, plus a tennis court, view pool, whirlpool, saunas, exercise room, hiking trails, fine restaurant (see listing) and lounge. Each attractively furnished room has a mountain view.

BASIC INFORMATION

Elevation: 530 feet   *Population (1990):   2,104*
Location: 140 miles North of Boston
Nearest airport with commercial flights: Portland, ME - 60 miles
Mt. Washington Valley Chamber of Commerce   (603)356-5701
 downtown on N. Main St. (Box 2300) - 03860   (800)367-3364
 www.4season-resort.com

Wolfeboro, New Hampshire

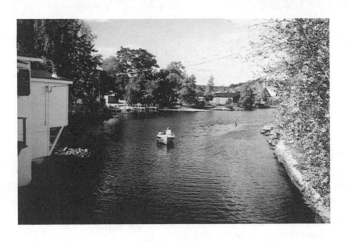

Wolfeboro is America's oldest summer resort. It is ensconced along the shore of Lake Winnipesaukee, New England's second largest lake. All around, a lush hardwood forest blankets gentle mountains that are outliers of the vast White Mountains to the north. The beauty of this setting attracted the last English Colonial governor, who built a palatial summer home. Other elaborate retreats and resorts followed.

The original estate is gone. But, the charm of the spot where the lake meets the mountains remains, and Wolfeboro proudly reflects its genteel colonial heritage. Downtown has the compact appearance of an idyllic New England village, bordered by a photogenic park and docks on the lakefront, and a tranquil back bay reached by an inlet through town. Carefully maintained historic buildings and trim contemporary ones house regional art, crafts, antiques and gourmet specialty shops. While there are several notable restaurants and a venerable landmark inn, lodgings are among the scarcest in any great town.

WEATHER PROFILE

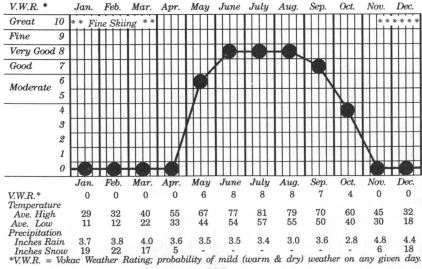

V.W.R.*	Jan.	Feb.	Mar.	Apr.	May	June	July	Aug.	Sep.	Oct.	Nov.	Dec.
V.W.R.*	0	0	0	0	6	8	8	8	7	4	0	0
Temperature												
Ave. High	29	32	40	55	67	77	81	79	70	60	45	32
Ave. Low	11	12	22	33	44	54	57	55	50	40	30	18
Precipitation												
Inches Rain	3.7	3.8	4.0	3.6	3.5	3.5	3.4	3.0	3.6	2.8	4.8	4.4
Inches Snow	19	22	17	5	-	-	-	-	-	-	6	18

*V.W.R. = Vokac Weather Rating; probability of mild (warm & dry) weather on any given day.

Boat Rentals
Various kinds of boats can be rented at several locations in town to enjoy the scenery on Lake Winnipesaukee, New Hampshire's largest lake, including:

Goodhue & Hawkins Navy Yard   *(603)569-2371*   *(800)689-2628*
Wolfeboro Marina   *(603)569-3200*

Boat Rides
MS Mount Washington   *(603)366-5531*
downtown at Town Docks

A trim 280-foot-long excursion ship with a capacity of 1,250 passengers continues a tradition of Lake Winnipesaukee excursions started in 1872. Daily two- and three-hour scenic cruises are supplemented by less frequent dinner/dance cruises and evening special theme cruises.

Winnipesaukee Belle   *(603)569-3016*
downtown at Town Docks

Sightseeing cruises of southern Lake Winnipesaukee aboard an excursion boat that began serving the lake in 1998 depart daily in summer.

Brewster Beach
just E via Main St. & Clark Rd.

A sandy swimming beach, restrooms and picnic tables are near the heart of town by the big picturesque lake.

Clark House Museum   *(603)569-4997*
just S on Main St.

A Colonial home, an 1820 one-room schoolhouse, and a Victorian firehouse replica are included in the Wolfeboro Historical Society museum complex. All are clustered on a village green and outfitted with period furnishings and memorabilia.

Hampshire Pewter Company   *(603)569-4944*
downtown at 43 Mill St.

The Colonial pewterer's craft was revived here in 1974. Casting, soldering and buffing can be observed during a guided tour of the factory where ancient techniques once again produce goblets, tankards, candlesticks, spoons and ornaments of lasting value. All are sold in the Tabletop Shop.

League of New Hampshire Craftsmen   *(603)569-3309*
just N at 64 Center St.

Jewelry, blown glass, pottery, leather goods, woodwork and other premium handicrafts made in New Hampshire are displayed and sold. All have been juried for quality.

Weirs Beach   *(603)524-5531*
29 mi. W via NH 28 & NH 11

Sprawled along the shore of Lake Winnipesaukee at Weirs Beach are amusement rides, a boardwalk, waterslide complexes (including the longest slide in New England), scenic train rides, and complete facilities for swimming, boating, and other water sports.

Wentworth State Park
5 mi. E on NH 109

A small swimming beach is the centerpiece of this park on Wentworth Lake. A bathhouse and picnic sites are available.

Winter Sports
Gunstock Ski Area   *(603)293-4341*   *(800)486-7862*
25 mi. W on NH 11A - Gilford

At this year-round resort, cross-country and downhill skiing and fine lake views are enjoyed in winter. With 1,400 feet of vertical rise, the longest run is over two miles. There are five chairlifts. All facilities, services and rentals are at the base. Restaurants, bars and lodgings are nearby. Ski season is mid-November through March.

Wright Museum   *(603)569-1212*
just NE at 77 Center St.

American life and major events during World War II from 1939 to 1945 are displayed in an extensive collection of memorabilia and vehicles, plus related films, broadcasts and music.

RESTAURANTS

Bailey's   *(603)569-3662*
just S on S. Main St. (Route 28)
B-L-D.   *Moderate*
For sixty years, Bailey's has offered a fine selection of all-American standards. They also make their own ice creams, fudge, butterscotch and penuche sauces for all sorts of delicious dairy treats. Comfortable, cheerful dining areas are often full in the area's biggest and best place for casual family dining.

The Cider Press   *(603)569-2028*
3 mi. S on Route 28 at 10 Middleton Rd.
D only.   *Moderate*
Traditional and updated American dishes and housemade desserts are served in several candlelit barnwood rooms and a cozy firelit lounge. Don't miss the spiked hot apple cider.

Jo Green's   *(603)569-8668*
downtown at 33 Dockside St.
L-D.   *Moderate*
All kinds of coffees, beer, wine or blender drinks can be enjoyed with contemporary comfort foods and close-up views of the lake.

The Lakeview Inn   *(603)569-1335*
just N at 120 N. Main St.
D only.   *Moderate*
Rack of lamb, Chateaubriand and other Continental classics share a menu with regional updates like broiled scrod in one of the area's favorite dinner houses. The inn's dining room is casually elegant, and a lighter menu is served in the cozy lounge.

Love's Quay   *(603)569-3303*
downtown at Bayside Village #1 on Bay St.
L-D.   *Moderate*
One of the region's newest destinations for fine dining features fresh seafood on an eclectic menu of contemporary international fare. Breads and a wide selection of luscious desserts are also made here and served in a comfortable stylish dining room, on a screened porch, and on a patio by the water.

P.J.'s Dockside Restaurant   *(603)569-6747*
downtown at the Town Docks
B-L-D.   *Moderate*
Pan-cooked omelets for breakfast, or lobster or clam rolls and all kinds of ice cream dishes later, are among the comfort foods that make this a family favorite overlooking the docks and lake.

Strawberry Patch   *(603)569-5523*
downtown at 30 N. Main St.
B-L.   *Moderate*
Strawberries are taken seriously in dishes like strawberry pancakes and in all kinds of decor touches. Tasty light fare, a cheerful setting, and a gift shop all contribute to the appeal.

The Wolfeboro Inn   *(603)569-3016*
downtown at 90 N. Main St.
B-L-D.   *Moderate*
The landmark inn's **1812 Room** specializes in slow-roasted prime rib, and fresh seafood presented as traditional and creative New England dishes served in a country-elegant firelit room. **Wolfe's Tavern** serves the right stuff to complement the delightful spirit of a cozy old New England pub.

LODGING

Accommodations are remarkably scarce, but distinctive, since there are no chain lodgings. The inn and a few small motels have lake views. Summer is high season. Among places that don't close in winter, rates are often reduced 20% or more.

The Lake Motel   *(603)569-1100*
just S on S. Main St. (Route 28) (Box 887) - 03894
35 units   *Moderate*
Lush green lawns extend to a private sandy beach on Crescent Lake. The modern one-story motel has a dock, rental boats and a tennis court. Many of the well-furnished rooms have a deck and a peaceful lake view. Some also have a kitchen.

The Lakeview Inn & Motor Lodge   *(603)569-1335*
just N at 200 N. Main St. (Box 713) - 03894
17 units   *Moderate*
This pleasant motor lodge has one of the area's best restaurants (see listing) and a lounge. Trees block the lake view, but each unit is comfortably furnished with all contemporary conveniences. There are three inn rooms with Colonial flourishes, and motel rooms with a patio or balcony.

Piping Rock Motel & Cottages   *(603)569-1915*
3 mi. N at 680 N. Main St. - 03894
22 units   *(800)317-3864*   *Moderate-Expensive*
A sandy beach and dock on Lake Winnipesaukee are the features here. All units are comfortably furnished. Motel rooms have a private lake-view patio or balcony. Housekeeping cottages with a kitchen and two-plus bedrooms are rented weekly.

The Wolfeboro Inn   *(603)569-3016*
downtown at 90 N. Main St. (Box 1270) - 03894
44 units   *(800)451-2389*   *Expensive-Very Expensive*
The Wolfeboro Inn is the heart of town. The three-story classic New England inn crowns a rise by the lake. Amenities include a private sandy beach, boat dock, fine dining room (see listing), tavern and lounge. A 1½-hour cruise on a picturesque excursion boat, the Winnipesaukee Belle (see boat rides), and Continental buffet breakfast are complimentary. Each room is beautifully furnished. A few have a private balcony and a romantic lake view.

BASIC INFORMATION

Elevation: *570 feet*   *Population (1990):*   *4,807*
Location: *105 miles North of Boston*
Nearest airport with commercial flights: Laconia, NH - 27 miles
Wolfeboro Chamber of Commerce   *(603)569-2200*
   downtown at 32 Central Av. (Box 547) - 03894   *(800)516-5324*

Taos, New Mexico

Taos is America's oldest village. It is an enchanting blend of a spectacular location, diverse cultures, and an artistic temperament. Almost 7,000 feet above sea level, Taos lies near the edge of an enormous river basin at the base of the state's highest mountains. Ancient Indians chose the sheltered site by year-round streams for the pueblo hundreds of years before Spanish Colonists arrived. In turn, the Spanish presence existed for centuries before the region became part of America in 1846. The cultural mix, splendid isolation and natural grandeur began to attract artists and dreamers in the 1890s.

They are still coming to this remarkable concentration of ancient adobes, romantic courtyards shaded by enormous old trees, and narrow winding streets. Around the venerable little Plaza are outstanding museums, arts and crafts studios, and galleries. In addition, a wealth of bars, restaurants and lodgings showcase the unique Taos style—an artful blend of natural materials, Old World refinement and frontier rusticity.

WEATHER PROFILE

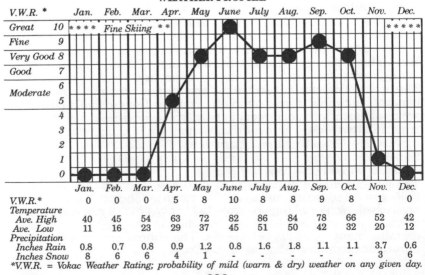

		Jan.	Feb.	Mar.	Apr.	May	June	July	Aug.	Sep.	Oct.	Nov.	Dec.
Great	10												
Fine	9												
Very Good	8												
Good	7												
Moderate	6												
	5												

	Jan.	Feb.	Mar.	Apr.	May	June	July	Aug.	Sep.	Oct.	Nov.	Dec.
V.W.R.*	0	0	0	5	8	10	8	8	9	8	1	0
Temperature												
Ave. High	40	45	54	63	72	82	86	84	78	66	52	42
Ave. Low	11	16	23	29	37	45	51	50	42	32	20	12
Precipitation												
Inches Rain	0.8	0.7	0.8	0.9	1.2	0.8	1.6	1.8	1.1	1.1	3.7	0.6
Inches Snow	8	6	6	4	1	-	-	-	-	-	3	6

*V.W.R. = Vokac Weather Rating; probability of mild (warm & dry) weather on any given day.

ATTRACTIONS

Carson National Forest   *(505)758-6200*
surrounding town

The preeminent attraction in this forest is Wheeler Peak. At 13,161 feet, it is the highest point in the state. The Wheeler Peak Wilderness Area can be accessed from Taos Ski Valley a few miles northwest of town. Four other wilderness areas and sections of the majestic Sangre de Cristo Mountains are also popular for hiking, backpacking, mountain biking, hunting, fishing, and water sports. Information and maps can be obtained at the Supervisor's office in town.

Museums   *(505)758-0505*

Several of Taos' most notable architectural landmarks on the National Historic Register are museums. Most are downtown. The **Ernest L. Blumenschein Home**, an adobe with portions dating back to 1790, was the home of the co-founder of the famous Taos Society of Artists. In addition to containing original antique furnishings, it also showcases paintings by prominent local artists. The **Governor Bent House and Museum** was the home of New Mexico's first American governor after the territory was annexed to the U.S. in 1846. He was killed here a year later by an angry mob protesting American rule. Today the old adobe houses a museum of his and Southwestern memorabilia. **Harwood Foundation Museum** is a group of historic adobe buildings that house an excellent gallery featuring many paintings by famous early artists of Taos. The **Kit Carson Home and Museum** was from 1843 until he died in 1868, the permanent residence of one of the West's most famous frontiersmen. Several rooms have been furnished as they might have been, and there are many mementoes. **Martinez Hacienda** (2 mi. W on NM 240) is a classic Spanish-Colonial hacienda—built in 1804 around two courtyards for protection from unfriendly outsiders. The restored complex features period furnishings and living history demonstrations. **Millicent Rogers Museum** (4 mi. N via NM 3) is an outstanding collection of Spanish-Colonial and Indian arts and crafts displayed in a well-preserved Spanish adobe hacienda.

Rio Grande Gorge Bridge
11 mi. NW on US 654

One of the highest highway bridges in the country spans a precipitous chasm 650 feet above the Rio Grande. Elevated sidewalks, observation platforms, and picnic areas have been provided.

Rio Grande Gorge Wild River Recreation Area   *(505)758-8851*
N & S of town

The banks of spectacular sections of the Rio Grande gorge now include camping and picnic areas, hiking trails, trout fishing, and a steep and narrow chasm with some thrilling and scenic whitewater rafting. For trips up to three days with all transportation and equipment provided, contact **Rio Grande Rapid Transit** at (800)222-7238.

San Francisco de Asis Church   *(505)758-2754*
4 mi. S on NM 68 - Ranchos de Taos

The most painted and photographed church in America may well be this gem of Spanish mission architecture. The massive, heavily buttressed adobe building, constructed between 1710 and 1755, is one of the oldest continuously-used churches in the West. The interior contains many religious art objects. The church rectory houses the miraculous painting "Shadow of the Cross."

Taos Pueblo   *(505)758-9593*
2 mi. N on N. Pueblo Rd.
Taos Pueblo is not a ruinsite of ancient peoples. It is the heart of a village of more than 1,000 Taos Indians that has been inhabited continuously for at least 800 years. A masterpiece of Indian architecture, it has changed little since the first Spaniards saw it in 1540. The two large, five-level adobe structures are the oldest "apartment buildings" and the highest pueblos in the country.

Winter Sports
Taos Ski Valley   *(505)776-2291*   *(800)776-1111*
19 mi. NE via NM 3 & NM 150
The vertical drop is 2,612 feet and the longest run (5.3 miles) is one of the West's longest. Runs plunge into a cluster of condominiums on a steep slope by the base of the ten chairlifts that serve the area. All facilities, services and rentals are available at the base for downhill skiing, along with numerous restaurants and bars. Skiing season is from late November into April.

RESTAURANTS

Apple Tree Restaurant   *(505)758-1900*
1 block N at 123 Bent St.
L-D.   *Moderate*
Delicious New Southwestern cuisine including homemade bread and desserts continues in one of Northern New Mexico's most time-honored destinations for fine dining. A picturesque historic adobe has several romantic firelit rooms showcasing quality local art, and there is a delightful garden patio.

Casa Cordova   *(505)776-2500*
9 mi. NE on NM 150 - Arroyo Seco
D only.   *Expensive*
Fresh, contemporary fare and on-premises baking are featured in this long-established restaurant in a quiet country location. The spare elegance of the firelit dining rooms in a lovely 150-year-old Spanish-Colonial home is a classic example of the Taos style.

The Historic Taos Inn   *(505)758-1977*
2 blocks N at 125 Paseo del Pueblo Norte
B-L-D.   *Moderate*
Doc Martin's, the historic inn's restaurant, is a quintessential source of New Mexican specialties in an enchanting setting. Several intimate dining rooms have kiva fireplaces, rough-hewn wood ceilings, and premium-quality art objects showcased against whitewashed adobe walls and sconces. The **Adobe Bar** is a similarly atmospheric gathering place in one of the most romantic examples of the Taos style.

House of Taos French Restaurant   *(505)758-3456*
3 mi. N at 1587 Paseo del Pueblo Norte
D only.   *Very Expensive*
Four-course dinners reflecting classic French orientation and a contemporary New Mexican outlook are prepared and served by the chef/owners in a historic adobe in the country. Local art enhances the casually elegant decor.

La Luna Ristorante   *(505)751-0023*
just S at 223 Paseo del Pueblo Sur
D only.   *Moderate*
Pizza from a woodburning oven and hearty helpings of pasta, seafood and steaks, plus tempting desserts, distinguish this comfortably modish trattoria.

Lambert's Restaurant   *(505)758-1009*
just S at 309 Paseo del Pueblo Sur
L-D.   *Moderate*
Creative American cuisine reflects expert attention given to seasonally fresh ingredients, and to housemade desserts. Intimate, upscale rooms are a good setting for casual fine dining.

Michael's Kitchen   *(505)758-4178*
just N at 304 Paseo del Pueblo Norte
B-L-D.   *Moderate*
Display cases brim with flavorful pastries, donuts, and other notable accompaniments to hearty American and regional dishes. This acclaimed Taos-style coffee shop and bakery has been a Southwestern landmark for many years.

Northtown Restaurant   *(505)758-2374*
1 mi. N on US 64
B-L.   *Low*
Skillfully prepared American and New Mexican dishes are served with delicious homemade pastries and desserts in this appealing little coffee shop with knotty pine decor and Taos art.

Sagebrush Inn   *(505)758-2254*
3 mi. S on NM 68 at 1508 Paseo del Pueblo Sur (NM 68)
B-D.   *Moderate*
Steaks and prime rib are featured in the inn's casually elegant **Los Vaqueros** room (D only). Hearty American breakfasts are served in the **Sagebrush Dining Room** (B only), with its skylit alcove full of vibrant greenery. Both rooms exude traditional Taos style, enhanced by museum-quality art objects and fireplaces. The firelit lounge offers the same refined rusticity, plus live entertainment for dancing.

Villa Fontana   *(505)758-5800*
5 mi. N on NM 522
D only.   *Very Expensive*
Northern Italian cuisine is given expert attention in classic and innovative dishes enhanced by wild mushrooms gathered in nearby mountains in summer, and top-quality fresh ingredients year-round. Service is tableside in intimate, upscale dining rooms.

LODGING

Lodgings are plentiful. Most are bed-and-breakfast inns that exude history and cultural appeal. Most places keep the same rates all year. For some, spring and fall rates may be 20% less.

Alma del Monte Bed & Breakfast   *(505)776-2721*
10 mi. NW at 372 Hondo Seco Rd. (Box 1434) - 87571
5 units   *(800)273-7203*   *Expensive*
A large contemporary hacienda reflects the Taos style in a quiet setting surrounded by sagebrush and panoramic mountain vistas. Full gourmet breakfast and afternoon refreshments are complimentary. Each spacious, beautifully furnished room has a kiva gas fireplace, skylight and whirlpool bath.

American Artists Gallery House Bed & Breakfast *(505)758-4446*
1 mi. S at 132 Frontier Lane (Box 584) - 87571
10 units   *(888)410-9364*   *Moderate-Expensive*
Taos architecture and decor are artistically displayed in this romantic hacienda. A gourmet breakfast and whirlpool for star-gazers are complimentary. Each beautifully furnished room has a kiva fireplace. Three have a large whirlpool bath.

Casa de las Chimeneas *(505)758-4777*
just S at 405 Cordoba Rd. (Box 5303) - 87571
6 units   *Expensive*
One of Taos' best bed-and-breakfasts is in a classic New Mexican adobe surrounded by spectacular gardens. A high adobe wall contributes to the serenity, and there is a whirlpool, sauna and exercise room. Gourmet breakfast and afternoon appetizers and beverages are complimentary. Each room is a beautiful blend of artistic Taos decor and all contemporary conveniences and has a woodburning or gas fireplace.

Casa Europa Inn & Gallery   *(505)758-9798*
1 mi. SW at 840 Upper Ranchitos Rd. (HC 68, Box 3F) - 87571
7 units   *(888)758-9798*   *Moderate-Expensive*
Giant cottonwoods shade a classic 17th century adobe estate that is now an elegant bed-and-breakfast with a whirlpool and sauna. Gourmet breakfast and evening appetizers are complimentary. Each beautifully furnished room has a fireplace and a marble bath. Private whirlpool rooms are also available.

El Pueblo Lodge   *(505)758-8700*
just N at 412 Paseo del Pueblo Norte - 87571
60 units   *(800)433-9612*   *Moderate*
A year-round pool and whirlpool are features of this modern pueblo-style motel. Each nicely furnished unit has some New Mexican decor. Several condos (up to three bedrooms) have a fireplace.

El Rincon Bed and Breakfast   *(505)758-4874*
1 block E at 114 Kit Carson - 87571
16 units   *Moderate-Expensive*
Modified pueblo architecture and adobe-and-wood decor are skillfully combined in a century-old complex that now serves as a bed-and-breakfast inn filled with handcrafted furnishings and local art. Breakfast is complimentary. Each beautifully furnished unit has a private bath and many whimsical extras. Some also have a gas fireplace, private mountain view terrace, or whirlpool bath.

Hacienda del Sol   *(505)758-0287*
1 mi. N at 109 Mabel Dodge Ln. (Box 177) - 87571
10 units   *Moderate-Expensive*
Hacienda del Sol is the quintessence of Taos style. Huge cottonwood trees shade spacious grounds in a tranquil setting by Pueblo Indian lands. Lovely gardens surround a 180-year-old adobe, and there is an enchanting view of Taos Mountain from an outdoor whirlpool deck. Memorable gourmet breakfast and afternoon treats are complimentary. All of the romantic old and newer adobe rooms are luxuriously furnished with Southwestern art, antiques and handcrafted furniture. Most have a private bath, mountain views, and a kiva fireplace. "Los Amantes" also has a room-sized whirlpool with a skylight. "Adobe" has a private steam room.

The Historic Taos Inn   *(505)758-2233*
1 block N at 125 Paseo del Pueblo Norte - 87571
36 units   *(800)826-7466*   *Moderate-Expensive*
Downtown's landmark inn, on the National Register, is an artistically restored century-old adobe complex. Courtyards sequester a pool and whirlpool, and delightful public rooms include an enchanting restaurant (see listing) and lounge. The lobby has a high viga ceiling with a skylight, a sunken kiva fireplace sitting area, and a library where "meet the artist" events occur. Each room is individually beautifully furnished by Taos artisans. Many have a kiva fireplace.

Inn on La Loma Plaza   *(505)758-1717*
  just SW at 315 Ranchitos Rd. (Box 4159) - 87571
  7 units   *(800)530-3040*   *Moderate-Expensive*
Huge shade trees surround this walled estate on the National Historic Register amid fountains and flowers. Gourmet breakfast and afternoon snacks are complimentary. Each room is individually beautifully decorated with local art and handcrafted furniture, and has all contemporary conveniences including a private bath and fireplace.

La Posada de Taos   *(505)758-8164*
  2 blocks W at 309 Juanita Ln. (Box 1118) - 87571
  6 units   *(800)645-4803*   *Moderate-Expensive*
An old adobe with foot-thick walls and rough-hewn beams was Taos' first bed-and-breakfast inn. A full breakfast is complimentary. Each artistically decorated room has a private bath. Some rooms also have a whirlpool and/or a fireplace.

Quail Ridge Inn Resort   *(505)776-2211*
  5 mi. NE on NM 150, Ski Valley Rd. (Box 707) - 87571
  110 units   *(800)624-4448*   *Moderate-Expensive*
Taos' most complete resort is a pueblo-style condominium complex on expansive grounds. Full breakfast is complimentary. Amenities include a large year-round pool, two whirlpools, saunas, eight tennis courts, four racquetball courts, plus a restaurant and lounge. Each unit (up to three bedrooms) is tastefully furnished and has a fireplace. Studios also have a kitchen.

Sagebrush Inn   *(505)758-2254*
  3 mi. S on NM 68 at 1508 Paseo del Pueblo Sur (Box 557) - 87571
  100 units   *(800)428-3626*   *Moderate-Expensive*
Taos' landmark motor hotel is a venerable pueblo-style complex. The main building opened in 1929. Amenities include a large outdoor pool and two whirlpools, plus charming restaurants (see listing) and an entertainment lounge. Full breakfast is complimentary. Each comfortable room showcases the Taos style. Some also have a kiva fireplace and a private mountain-view balcony.

Touchstone Bed & Breakfast Inn   *(505)758-0192*
  1 mi. N at 110 Mabel Dodge Ln. (Box 2896) - 87571
  8 units   *(800)758-0192*   *Moderate-Expensive*
A nearly 200-year-old hacienda on lush grounds bordering Pueblo Indian lands recently became one of the area's finest bed-and-breakfast inns. Towering cottonwoods shade wildflower gardens and an outdoor whirlpool. A massage room is the beginning of a full spa. Gourmet vegetarian breakfast is complimentary. Each of the beautifully furnished rooms blends classic New Mexican art and all contemporary conveniences. Most have a fireplace. Several have a large in-room whirlpool.

BASIC INFORMATION

Elevation: 6,950 feet   *Population (1990):   4,065*
Location: 130 miles Northeast of Albuquerque
Nearest airport with commercial flights: Santa Fe - 77 miles
Taos County Chamber of Commerce   (505)758-3873   (800)732-8267
  2 mi. S at 1139 Paseo del Pueblo Sur (P.O. Drawer I) - 87571
  http:\\taosweb.com\TAOS

Cooperstown, New York

Cooperstown is the urban embodiment of truth, beauty, and the American way. It is on a gentle slope by the end of a long lake and the headwaters of a calm river. Hardwood forests and lush farmlands cover rolling hills all around. The town was founded in 1786 by Judge William Cooper, father of James Fenimore Cooper—America's first famous novelist. Legend has it that baseball was invented here in 1839 by another famed resident—Abner Doubleday. Regardless, a century later, the National Baseball Hall of Fame became a reality downtown.

Today, the surroundings are as beautifully bucolic as ever. In town, residents' pride in their long, rich legacy is reflected in the postcard charm of tree-lined streets, manicured lawns and gardens, and tidy Victorian homes. Downtown is compact and vital, with solid blocks of historic buildings housing shops full of regional arts, crafts, antiques and collectibles; diverse restaurants; distinctive lodgings; and the renowned museum—now joined by two others a mile north.

WEATHER PROFILE

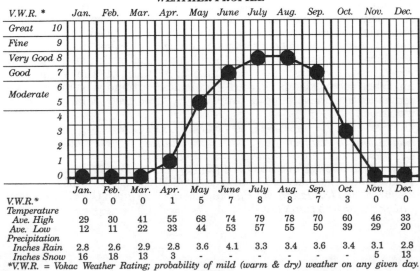

V.W.R.*		Jan.	Feb.	Mar.	Apr.	May	June	July	Aug.	Sep.	Oct.	Nov.	Dec.
Great	10												
Fine	9												
Very Good	8												
Good	7												
Moderate	6 5												
	4												
	3												
	2												
	1												
	0												

	Jan.	Feb.	Mar.	Apr.	May	June	July	Aug.	Sep.	Oct.	Nov.	Dec.
V.W.R.*	0	0	0	1	5	7	8	8	7	3	0	0
Temperature												
Ave. High	29	30	41	55	68	74	79	78	70	60	46	33
Ave. Low	12	11	22	33	44	53	57	55	50	39	29	20
Precipitation												
Inches Rain	2.8	2.6	2.9	2.8	3.6	4.1	3.3	3.4	3.6	3.4	3.1	2.8
Inches Snow	16	18	13	3	-	-	-	-	-	-	5	13

*V.W.R. = Vokac Weather Rating; probability of mild (warm & dry) weather on any given day.

332

ATTRACTIONS

Boat Ride
   Lake Otsego Boat Tours   *(607)547-5295*
   downtown at foot of Fair St.
Two classic wooden boats that cruised here at the turn of the century have been fully restored. One-hour narrated tours of the scenic lake are offered from May into October.

Downtown
   centered around Main St. & Pioneer St.
Remarkably photogenic blocks of proudly maintained Victorian and Edwardian buildings face each other along narrow tree-lined Main Street. Just beyond is a lovely little park where the Susquehanna River leaves Otsego Lake. **The National Baseball Hall of Fame** (see listing) is a red-brick landmark at one end, and many stores sport baseball souvenirs, as well as regional antiques and crafts. **Gallery 53 Artworks** (118 Main St.) has an impressive array of regional folk, baseball, and modern art for browsers and collectors. There are also plenty of places to eat and drink, and nostalgic 19th century lodgings.

The Farmers' Museum & Village Crossroads   *(607)547-1410*
   1 mi. N on NY 80
Here is one of America's great living history museums of rural life in early times. A massive stone barn, the main museum, is full of agricultural artifacts. Beyond, the Village Crossroads has more than a dozen early 19th century buildings. In appropriately furnished shops, artisans in period dress present blacksmithing, weaving, printing, open-hearth cooking and more. A must-see exhibit is the "Cardiff Giant"—the so-called petrified prehistoric man (dug up in a nearby field after the Civil War) that turned out to be one of the most infamous hoaxes of all time. Quality handicrafts and reproductions are sold in the General Store, and there is a gift shop and food service.

Fenimore House Museum   *(607)547-1410*
   1 mi. N on NY 80
A graceful 1930s neo-Georgian mansion overlooking Otsego Lake is now a museum displaying one of the nation's major collections of American crafts; folk, fine and Indian art. Memorabilia of James Fenimore Cooper, America's first acclaimed novelist, is suitably represented. The Browere life masks of prominent early Americans project an eerie vitality. There is also an excellent museum store.

Fly Creek Cider Mill & Orchard   *(607)547-9692*
   3 mi. NW via Route 28 - Fly Creek
From mid-August to November, apple cider is made the same way it has been since 1856 in the area's oldest water-powered cider mill. Hot spiced cider goes well with their homemade apple pie, apples rolled in puff pastry and gourmet specialties like horseradish cheddar cheese. Upstairs is a gift shop full of country gifts and crafts.

Glimmerglass Opera   *(607)547-2255*
   7 mi. N on NY 80
Opera buffs from around the world flock to the Alice Busch Opera Theater each summer. Acclaimed performances are staged in a simply grand contemporary building with sliding walls that open on balmy nights to peaceful meadows beside glimmering Otsego Lake.

Glimmerglass State Park   *(607)547-8662*
   8 mi. N on Route 31
Near the north end of the lake is the area's most complete park. Amenities include a swimming beach and bathhouse, fishing, hiking

and biking trails, picnic areas, and a campground.

National Baseball Hall of Fame & Museum   *(607)547-7200*
downtown on Main St.   *(888)425-5633*
The ultimate celebration of baseball is this renowned museum that chronicles the history of the game and its players. Plaques honor all-time greats, while exhibits showcase the World Series, ballparks, the evolution of equipment, and baseball today with photos, statues, video, interactive computers, and memorabilia. A theater presents a multimedia show that captures the spirit of the game. The complex also sports a library, archive and gift shop.

RESTAURANTS

The Lake Front Restaurant   *(607)547-8188*
downtown at 10 Fair St.
B-L-D.   *Moderate*
An extensive menu of all-American fare is offered in a pleasant dining room with a window wall and deck overlooking beautiful Otsego Lake. A comfortable modern motel adjoins.

The Otesaga Resort Hotel   *(607)547-9931*
just N at 60 Lake St.
B-L-D.   *Moderate-Expensive*
The hotel's **Otesaga Dining Room** (B-D—Expensive) has traditional American cuisine in morning buffets, and prix fixe candlelit dinners accompanied by piano music. **The Hawkeye Bar & Grill** (L-D—Moderate) offers regional grill fare with housemade breads and desserts in a relaxed setting near the lake. There is also an entertainment lounge.

The Pepper Mill   *(607)547-8550*
just S on Chestnut St (Route 28)
L-D.   *Moderate*
Fresh beer-battered haddock or charbroiled pork ribs typify the wide selection of contemporary American dishes, along with housemade baked goods, in this comfortable family-oriented place.

The Red Sleigh Restaurant   *(607)547-5581*
8 mi. N on Lake Rd. (Route 80)
B-L-D.   *Moderate*
Slow-roasted prime rib and seafood bisque are a couple of appealing specialties on an extensive menu of contemporary international dishes. Homemade desserts are also served in the popular, relaxed restaurant.

Sal's Pizzeria   *(607)547-5721*
downtown at 110 Main St.
L-D.   *Low*
The best pizza and calzone in town are served along with all kinds of family comfort foods in a cheerful dining room or on an outside deck.

TJ's Place Restaurant   *(607)547-4040*
downtown at 124 Main St.
B-L-D.   *Moderate*
Their homemade breads make tasty french toast in the morning and sandwiches later in this big friendly coffee shop that also sports a gift shop with many one-of-a-kind pieces of memorabilia.

The Tunnicliff Inn   *(607)547-9611*
downtown at 34-36 Pioneer St.
L-D.   *Moderate*
In addition to lodgings, the inn, built in 1802, offers Italian favorites like veal marsala or seafood primavera served in a pleasant upstairs dining room or downstairs amid more casual pub style atmosphere.

LODGING

There are nearly two dozen accommodations in and around town. Many are bed-and-breakfasts in restored historic buildings. Happily, no major chains are present among motels or hotels. Summer is high season. Winter rates are as much as 20% less.

The Bassett House Inn   (607)547-7001
downtown at 32 Fair St. - 13326
5 units   *Expensive*
An American clock collection and a century-old billiard table are part of the charm of this inn built in 1816. The fully restored three-story building blends antiques and (except for phones) all contemporary conveniences. Continental breakfast is complimentary. Each well-furnished room is individually decorated.

The Inn at Cooperstown   (607)547-5756
downtown at 16 Chestnut St. - 13326
18 units   *Moderate*
The inn was built in 1874 as an annex to the Hotel Fenimore. The restored three-story building with a sweeping veranda and nostalgic public rooms is a centerpiece of the historic district near the lake. Each comfortably furnished room has a private bath, but no phone or TV.

Inn at the Commons - Best Western   (607)547-9439
3 mi. S on Route 28 at 50 Commons Dr. - 13326
62 units   (800)528-1234   *Moderate-Expensive*
New in 1995, this motel has an indoor pool, whirlpool and exercise room. Continental breakfast is complimentary. Each room is well furnished. Some also have a large whirlpool bath.

Lake 'N Pines Motel   (607)547-2790
7 mi. N on Lake St. (Route 80) (RR 2, Box 784) - 13326
24 units   (800)615-5253   *Moderate*
Set back off the road in the pines by Otsego Lake is a motel with a sandy beach, free rowboats and paddleboats; plus two pools (one indoors), whirlpool, sauna and game room. Some of the comfortably furnished rooms have a lake view and balcony.

Lake View Motel & Cottages   (607)547-9740
6 mi. N on Lake St. (Route 80) (RD 2, Box 932) - 13326
14 units   (888)452-5384   *Moderate*
Down the hill from the shaped-up little motel are a beach and dock for lake swimming and rental boats. Each room is nicely furnished.

The Otesaga Resort Hotel   (607)547-9931
just N at 60 Lake St. (Box 311) - 13326
138 units   (800)348-6222   *Very Expensive*
Since 1909, the Otesaga has been Cooperstown's lodging landmark. Amenities of the stately six-story brick complex (closed in winter) include a famed 18-hole (fee) golf course by the lake, and rental boats, plus lake swimming and fishing, a pool, tennis, fine dining (see listing) and an entertainment lounge. Rates include breakfast and dinner—modified American plan. Each room is nicely furnished and has a private bath and most conveniences.

BASIC INFORMATION

Elevation: 1,260 feet   Population (1990):   2,180
Location: 210 miles Northwest of New York City
Nearest airport with commercial flights: Utica, NY - 50 miles
Cooperstown Chamber of Commerce   (607)547-9983
  downtown at 31 Chestnut St. - 13326
  www.cooperstownchamber.org

Lake Placid, New York

Lake Placid is one of the premier summer and winter playgrounds of America. Surrounded by the highest summits of the Adirondack Mountains, it is located by two of the prettiest small lakes in the heart of the East's largest park. From its founding before the Civil War, the village was supported by tourists. Prosperity and world-renown were confirmed with the Winter Olympics here in 1932 and in 1980.

Abundant natural endowments are now coupled with a wealth of cultural enhancements. World-class alpine and nordic winter sports facilities are open to everyone—as participants or viewers. All sorts of recreation vehicles provide access to forests, mountains, lakes, and rivers. The tranquil shoreline of Mirror Lake is just below downtown's Main Street. Solid blocks of buildings varying greatly in age and style occasionally give way to lakeview and beach parks. Adirondack art, crafts and mementoes are well represented in many specialty shops. So are restaurants, lounges, nightlife, museums, and lodgings.

WEATHER PROFILE

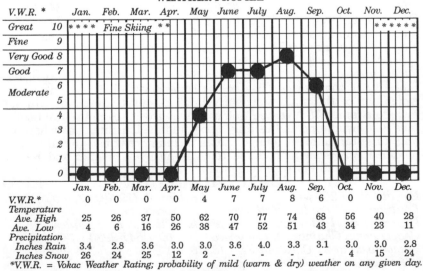

V.W.R. *		Jan.	Feb.	Mar.	Apr.	May	June	July	Aug.	Sep.	Oct.	Nov.	Dec.
Great	10	* * * *	Fine Skiing	* *								* * * * * *
Fine	9												
Very Good	8												
Good	7												
Moderate	6												
	5												
	4												
	3												
	2												
	1												
	0												

	Jan.	Feb.	Mar.	Apr.	May	June	July	Aug.	Sep.	Oct.	Nov.	Dec.
V.W.R.*	0	0	0	0	4	7	7	8	6	0	0	0
Temperature												
Ave. High	25	26	37	50	62	70	77	74	68	56	40	28
Ave. Low	4	6	16	26	38	47	52	51	43	34	23	11
Precipitation												
Inches Rain	3.4	2.8	3.6	3.0	3.0	3.6	4.0	3.3	3.1	3.0	3.0	2.8
Inches Snow	26	24	25	12	2	-	-	-	-	4	15	24

*V.W.R. = Vokac Weather Rating; probability of mild (warm & dry) weather on any given day.

Bicycling
Many miles of scenic high country roads and trails are accessible by assorted bikes that can be rented at several places in town.

Boat Rentals
Only canoes and other non-motorized boats are allowed on picturesque Mirror Lake downtown. Nearby, Lake Placid and many miles of wild and tame rivers extend into the forested high country. All kinds of watercraft can be rented by the hour or longer at several places.

Boat Rides
Lake Placid Marina   *(518)523-9704*
just N on Mirror Lake Dr.
A distinctive enclosed boat provides a one-hour narrated tour of the classic Adirondack mountain lake anytime from May into October.

High Falls Gorge   *(518)946-2278*
8 mi. NE on NY 86 - Wilmington
The Ausable River has cut a deep chasm at the base of Whiteface Mountain. Pathways, bridges and observation decks overlook photogenic waterfalls, rapids and potholes. Notable mineral displays, a rock shop, gift shop, food service and picnic facilities are provided.

John Brown Farm State Historic Site   *(518)523-3900*
3 mi. S via NY 73
The last home of the noted abolitionist has been restored to its original appearance, and outfitted with appropriate mementoes. His grave is part of the self-guided free tour of the grounds.

Lake Placid Center for the Arts   *(518)523-2512*
just W at 93 Saranac Av.
This year-round cultural center offers live theater, concerts, film series, dance, and art exhibits. Next door is the **Adirondack North Country Crafts Center & Store** displaying and selling locally produced works of over 200 artists and craftsmen.

Lake Placid Historical Museum   *(518)523-1608*
1 mi. S on Averyville Rd.
Artifacts from the 1932 and 1980 Olympics, and nearly 200 years of memorabilia, are displayed in a restored railroad station.

Olympic Attractions   *(518)523-1655   (800)462-6236*
E on NY 73 & NY 86
All major Olympic facilities (except the downtown center) are east of town. The **Jumping Complex** (3 mi. SE on NY 73) is used year-round for training and competition. A chairlift and glass-enclosed elevator rises 250 feet to an enclosed deck with grand views of the jumps and mountains. The **Sports Complex at Mt. Van Hoevenberg** (7 mi. SE on NY 73) features cross-country, luge and bobsled facilities (all open to the public in winter), and a biathlon range. In summer, there are hiking and biking trails, horseback rides, guided trolley tours of the track areas, and a thrilling (wheeled) bobsled ride piloted by professionals. **Whiteface Mountain** (16 mi. NE on NY 86) is the downhill ski site. Two summer chairlifts provide spectacular views from the summit of Little Whiteface.

Olympic Center   *(518)523-1655   (800)462-6236*
downtown on Main St.
In 1980, Eric Heiden captured five gold medals in speed skating in the oval near this building where a young American hockey team beat the Soviet pros in 1980. Today, the center houses four indoor ice skating

rinks now used for practice, public skating, ice shows, hockey games and concerts. The **Lake Placid Winter Olympic Museum** features memorabilia and video exhibits from the 1932 and 1980 Olympics. To catch the spirit in winter, climb a nearby fifty-foot tower by Mirror Lake, take a toboggan down the chute at forty miles an hour, and skitter far out onto the frozen lake.

Uihlein Sugar Maple Field Station　　　*(518)523-9337*
3 mi. S on Bear Cub Rd.
Cornell University has developed a scientific method using plastic tubing to gather sugar sap from thousands of maple trees into a single collecting tank. The Sugarhouse has free exhibits and maple syrup demonstrations. Sap usually runs in March and April.

Whiteface Veterans Memorial Highway　　　*(518)946-7175*
25 mi. NE via NY 86 - Wilmington
On a clear day, the panoramic view from the summit of Whiteface Mountain, one of the highest peaks in the Northeast at 4,865 feet, is remarkable. A stone building with a gift shop and snacks is a short hike or an elevator ride through the mountain to the top.

Winter Sports
Whiteface Mountain Ski Area　　*(518)523-1655*　*(800)462-6236*
10 mi. NE on NY 86 - Wilmington
The site of Olympic downhill skiing in 1980 has the highest vertical rise (3,216 feet) in eastern America. The panoramic views are superb, and the longest run is 3.5 miles. There are ten chairlifts. All facilities, services and rentals are available at the base. Food and drink are limited, but abundant in Lake Placid. Ski season is mid-November to mid-April. World-class Nordic facilities are available nearby at Mt. Van Hoevenberg (see Olympic attractions).

RESTAURANTS

Alpine Cellar　　　*(518)523-2180*
1 mi. E on NY 86 near jct. NY 73
D only.　　　　　　　　　　　　　　　　　　　　　*Moderate*
Authentic Bavarian dishes range from Swiss fondue and homemade bread to sauteed venison medallions with wild mushrooms. Alpine artifacts and decor distinguish the popular restaurant and tavern.

The Artist's Cafe　　　*(518)523-9493*
downtown at 1 Main St.
L-D.　　　　　　　　　　　　　　　　　　　　　　*Moderate*
Light, contemporary American fare provides an excuse to check out this convivial little cafe by a park. There are a few tables with a fine lakefront view on an enclosed porch.

The Charcoal Pit　　　*(518)523-3050*
1 mi. W on Saranac Av. (NY 86)
D only.　　　　　　　　　　　　　　　　　　　　　*Expensive*
Prime rib and rack of lamb top a menu that also features some Greek dishes. Generous, tasty portions, comfortable rooms, and a garden-view solarium have made this a local favorite for over forty years.

The Cottage Cafe　　　*(518)523-9845*
just N on Mirror Lake
L-D.　　　　　　　　　　　　　　　　　　　　　　*Moderate*
All sorts of big sandwiches and salads are served. But, the view is the thing. High peaks of the Adirondacks rise dramatically from picturesque Mirror Lake. The scene is especially peaceful from the birch-shaded lakefront deck.

Lake Placid Lodge   *(518)523-2700*
3 mi. NW via NY 86 & Whiteface Inn Rd.
B-L-D.   *Very Expensive*
The luxuriously rustic lodge's dining room is a prime source of innovative American cuisine with an Adirondack flair. The menu changes frequently to feature fresh seasonal produce, game and seafood. Desserts are truly irresistible. Proper attire is requested for the sophisticated hideaway's plush dining room. There is also a scenic lake-view terrace and an intimate firelit pub that perfectly convey the Adirondack style.

Lake Placid Resort Holiday Inn   *(518)523-3339*
downtown at 1 Olympic Dr.
B-L-D.   *Moderate-Expensive*
The resort's **La Veranda** (D only—Expensive) offers contemporary American fare and housemade desserts in the informally elegant, firelit setting of a transformed house with an imposing veranda. A more casual restaurant features all meals.

Mirror Lake Inn   *(518)523-2544*
downtown at 5 Mirror Lake Dr.
B-L-D.   *Expensive*
The elegant resort hotel includes the **Averil Conwell Dining Room**, where creative American cuisine is excellent in dishes ranging from wild mushroom bisque with bourbon to home-smoked seafood and luscious desserts like peanut butter pie. Two gracious dining areas have a lovely picture-window view of Mirror Lake.

Upper Crust Bakery & Cafe   *(518)523-2269*
just S at 215 Main St.
B-L.   *Moderate*
All kinds of morning delights and a few specialties like blueberry pancakes are popular in this very casual cafe/takeout shop.

The Woodshed Restaurant   *(518)523-9470*
just S at 237 Main St.
D only.   *Moderate-Expensive*
Contemporary American fare served in a warm and rustic setting has made this a local favorite.

LODGING

Lodgings are plentiful and varied. Many are by or near a lake or winter sports facilities. Summer, "leaf peeper" season, and winter share high season honors. Spring and late fall may be at least 20% less.

Golden Arrow Hotel - Best Western   *(518)523-3353*
downtown at 150 Main St. - 12946
134 units   *(800)582-5540*   *Moderate-Expensive*
Here is the best setting by Mirror Lake in town. The contemporary four-story hotel has a lovely white sand beach, lake swimming, a dock with boats and canoes, putting green, indoor pool, whirlpools, saunas, exercise center, racquetball, restaurant, nightclub and shops. All of the well furnished rooms have a private balcony or terrace. Many have superb lake/mountains views. Some also have a whirlpool tub.

Interlaken Inn   *(518)523-3180*
just N at 15 Interlaken Av. - 12946
11 units   *(800)428-4369*   *Expensive*
This authentic country inn with a pleasant Victorian feeling is a stroll from two lakes. Full breakfast, afternoon tea and treats and gourmet dinner are included. Each attractively furnished room features some antiques and has a private bath, but no phone or TV.

Lake Placid Hilton Resort   *(518)523-4411*
downtown at 1 Mirror Lake Dr. - 12946
178 units   *(800)445-8667*   *Expensive*
There are some lakeside rooms in this modern five-story hotel. Amenities include four pools (two indoor), whirlpools, exercise room, boats, restaurant, and an entertainment lounge. Most of the well furnished rooms have a private balcony facing the lake and mountains.

Lake Placid Lodge   *(518)523-2700*
3 mi. NW via NY 86 & Whiteface Inn Rd. (Box 550) - 12946
37 units   *Very Expensive*
Set alongside a lovely mountain lake deep in a forest is an incomparable Adirondack retreat. The lodge is a romantic celebration of rustic wood and stone and sumptuous furnishings. There is a sandy beach, swimming area and dock, canoes, bicycles, forested trails, a gracious dining room (see listing), cozy firelit pub and a billiard room. Gourmet breakfast is included. Each room is luxuriously furnished with Adirondack arts and crafts and all contemporary conveniences. Most also have a dramatic stone fireplace and a large soaking tub.

Lake Placid Resort Holiday Inn   *(518)523-2556*
downtown at 1 Olympic Dr. - 12946
210 units   *(800)874-1980*   *Moderate-Expensive*
Crowning a hill overlooking Mirror Lake is a contemporary four-story resort hotel. Amenities include a putting green, eleven tennis courts, indoor pool, whirlpool, sauna, restaurants (see listing), entertainment lounge, and gift shop. Most of the well-furnished rooms have a private view balcony. Some also have a gas or wood fireplace and whirlpool tub.

The Lakeshore Motel   *(518)523-2261*
just NW at 54 Saranac Av. - 12946
16 units   *Moderate*
A private beach and boats for guests are features of this modern little motel. Newer rooms by the lake are comfortably furnished.

Mirror Lake Inn   *(518)523-2544*
downtown at 5 Mirror Lake Dr. - 12946
128 units   *Expensive-Very Expensive*
Lake Placid's lodging landmark is an elegant four-story whitewashed resort with frontage on scenic Mirror Lake. Facilities include a private sandy beach, boats and a dock, wooded trails, indoor and outdoor pools, tennis court, whirlpool, sauna, bicycles, exercise equipment, (fee) complete spa, fine lake view dining (see listing), lounge, and gift shop. Each room is beautifully furnished. Most have a lake-view balcony. Some also have a large in-room whirlpool.

Wildwood on the Lake   *(518)523-2624*
just NW at 88 Saranac Av. - 12946
35 units   *(800)841-6378*   *Moderate-Expensive*
The lake is too shallow for swimming here, but there is a spring-fed natural pool with a small beach, plus a small pool, whirlpool and sauna, and boats for guests. The modern motel offers well-furnished rooms, many with private lake-view balconies.

BASIC INFORMATION

Elevation: 1,890 feet   Population (1990):   2,485
Location: 290 miles North of New York City
Nearest airport with commercial flights: Saranac Lake - 17 miles
Lake Placid / Essex County Visitors Bureau   (518)523-2445
*   downtown in Olympic Arena at 216 Main St. - 12946   (800)447-5224*
www.lakeplacid.com

Saratoga Springs, New York

Saratoga Springs is America's oldest sybaritic playground. Woodlands and gentle hills around town rise above a great bend of the tranquil Hudson River. Nearby to the north and west are the Adirondack Mountains. But, it was abundant mineral springs that launched the first hotel almost two hundred years ago. Soon, the rich and famous were drawn by the health-giving benefits. By 1900, elegant hotels, splendid thoroughbred and harness race tracks, and grand casinos all contributed to the town's world-renown.

Today, more than 1,000 buildings on the National Historic Register, interspersed with more prosaic buildings, house numerous galleries, specialty shops, restaurants, museums and hotels in a large downtown district. Beyond, toward the peerless racetracks, some stately homes on tree-lined streets now serve as sumptuous bed-and-breakfast inns. At Saratoga Spa State Park, you can swim, get a mineral water bath and massage, and enjoy performing arts.

WEATHER PROFILE

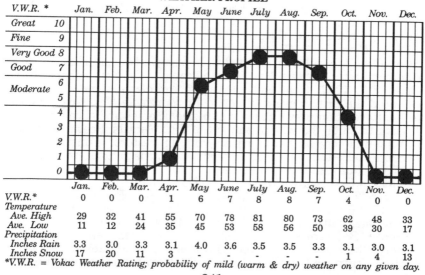

	Jan.	Feb.	Mar.	Apr.	May	June	July	Aug.	Sep.	Oct.	Nov.	Dec.
V.W.R.*	0	0	0	1	6	7	8	8	7	4	0	0
Temperature												
Ave. High	29	32	41	55	70	78	81	80	73	62	48	33
Ave. Low	11	12	24	35	45	53	58	56	50	39	30	17
Precipitation												
Inches Rain	3.3	3.0	3.3	3.1	4.0	3.6	3.5	3.5	3.3	3.1	3.0	3.1
Inches Snow	17	20	11	3	-	-	-	-	-	1	4	13

*V.W.R. = Vokac Weather Rating; probability of mild (warm & dry) weather on any given day.

ATTRACTIONS

Congress Park   *(518)584-6920*
downtown at Broadway & Congress St.
Towering broad-leaved trees shade expansive lawns, gardens, tranquil duck ponds and spring-water fountains in a landmark Victorian park. An imposing 1870 casino houses the **Historical Society's Museum** and the **Walworth Memorial Museum** highlighting the mineral springs, gambling, opulent hotels and major personalities in the town's evolution from a rustic village to a renowned resort.

Downtown
centered around Broadway & Lake Av.
Much of the Victorian splendor of Saratoga Springs' flamboyant past is still on display along Broadway. Some buildings serve as they did a century ago, and you can still taste the famous water. Art galleries, antique and specialty shops, restaurants and hotels are numerous.

The Great Escape & Splashwater Kingdom   *(518)792-3500*
21 min N on US 9 - Glen Falls
New York's largest fun park has more than 100 rides, shows and attractions. The spacious, landscaped site includes one of America's top-rated wooden roller coasters; a circus; Western-themed area; plus log flume, river rapids and all sorts of water rides. Elaborate stage shows are also featured.

Racing
Saratoga Harness Racing   *(518)584-2110*
1 mi. S on Nelson Av.
Saratoga Race Course   *(518)584-6200*
1 mi. SE on Union Av.
Thoroughbreds reign in Saratoga Springs, as they have for more than 150 years. Visitors to the **Harness Racing Museum and Hall of Fame** learn that "The Old Grey Mare" (of song) raced in harness in 1847 at the adjoining Saratoga Raceway—now one of the world's prettiest harness tracks. Thoroughbred racing began during the Civil War at nearby Saratoga Race Course. It is now the world's oldest continuous meet. The **National Museum of Racing and Hall of Fame** exhibits the history and future of thoroughbred racing, and celebrates famous horses, jockeys, and trainers. Both museums have well-stocked gift shops.

Saratoga National Historic Park   *(518)664-9821*
16 mi. E on US 4 - Schuylerville
Several square miles of forested hills just west of the Hudson River commemorate the two Battles of Saratoga. On September 19 and October 7, 1777, Gen. Horatio Gates' American soldiers decisively defeated the British army of Gen. John Burgoyne. This turning point of the Revolution prevented a split of the colonies and encouraged the French to enter the war in support of the colonists. Features include a nine-mile scenic drive with exhibits; restored American staff headquarters and costumed battlefield demonstrations (in summer); plus a visitor center and museum.

Saratoga Spa State Park   *(518)584-2535*
1 mi. SW via S. Broadway (US 9) & Avenue of Pines
One of America's most popular state parks offers a delightful diversity of aesthetic, cultural and recreational attractions. The **Roosevelt and Lincoln Bathhouses** offer mineral water baths and massage in restored facilities. Both are on the National Historic Register, as is the **Gideon Putnam Hotel** (see listing). The **Saratoga Performing Arts**

Center is the summer home of the New York City Opera and Ballet, and the Philadelphia Orchestra, plus special events. The **Spa Little Theatre** offers intimate theater and dance. Nearby is the **National Museum of Dance**. There are also restaurants, shops, two major swimming pools, a championship 18-hole golf course, tennis courts, miles of hiking trails, plus mineral springs and geysers.

RESTAURANTS

The Bread Basket   *(518)587-4233*
   downtown at 65 Spring St.
   B-L.   *Low*
One of New York's best bakeries makes everything from scratch daily. Traditional pastries like cinnamon rolls with raisins and nuts, designer delights like jalapeno cheddar scones and a tantalizing array of breads, rolls and desserts are all as delicious as they look in the display cases of this little gourmet hideaway.

Chez Sophie Bistro   *(518)583-3538*
   4 mi. S at 2853 Route 9 - Malta
   L-D.   *Moderate*
Updated French dishes have been offered for many years on a seasonal menu that features local herbs and produce from the garden. Luscious desserts are housemade in this restored classic 1940s diner.

Country Corner Cafe   *(518)583-7889*
   downtown at 25 Church St.
   B-L.   *Moderate*
Fresh baked breads and muffins served with homemade preserves, and fresh fruit pancakes with pure maple syrup, are among breakfast favorites served all day every day in a warm and cozy cafe.

Eartha's Kitchen   *(518)583-0602*
   just E at 60 Court St.
   D only.   *Expensive*
New American cuisine features creative mesquite-grilled specialties like salmon with pink grapefruit. The eclectic menu changes weekly. Rotating art gallery displays contribute to the relaxed sophistication of the well-liked dining room.

43 Phila Bistro   *(518)584-2720*
   downtown at 43 Phila St.
   L-D.   *Expensive*
One of the region's finest young restaurants displays a creative regional flair with contemporary American cuisine like squash and maple bisque. Even support dishes like sweet potato chips are carefully prepared. A sleek blonde-wood bar distinguishes the simply posh art deco style bistro.

Lillian's Restaurant   *(518)587-7766*
   downtown at 408 Broadway
   L-D.   *Moderate*
Original chicken dishes, steaks, and a wide variety of contemporary American fare has been served in this relaxed, comfortable restaurant for a quarter of a century.

The Olde Bryan Inn   *(518)587-2990*
   downtown at 123 Maple Av.
   L-D.   *Moderate*
Contemporary American fare includes center cuts of beef and fresh Atlantic seafood on an extensive menu offered in one of the town's oldest buildings. It's firelit in winter and there is an outside patio with live entertainment in summer.

Saratoga Springs, New York

Sperry's   *(518)584-9618*
downtown at 30½ Caroline St.
L-D.   *Expensive*
Maryland crabcakes and fresh (seasonal) soft shell crabs top the grilled
seafood specialties, and there are homemade pastries and desserts.
Polished hardwoods enhance the Edwardian-style dining room and bar,
and there is a tree-shaded dining deck.

The Springwater Inn   *(518)584-6440*
just E at 139 Union Av.
D only.   *Expensive*
Contemporary American dishes ranging from designer pizzas to fresh
grilled seafood are offered on an eclectic menu, and acclaimed desserts
are homemade. The relaxed firelit Adirondack tavern is a classic, and
the old-fashioned wraparound porch is charming.

Wheatfields   *(518)587-0534*
downtown at 440 Broadway
L-D.   *Moderate*
They make all of their pasta fresh every day, along with homebaked
bread, pastry and desserts. Patrons have a choice of relaxed
atmosphere inside, or an outdoor sidewalk cafe.

LODGING

There are more than forty accommodations in and around town. Only
two places feature mineral-spring baths. But, the selection of bed-and-
breakfasts and inns in restored Victorians includes some of America's
finest. The summer racing season is prime time. Rates are often
reduced at least 50% at other times.

Adelphi Hotel   *(518)587-4688*
downtown at 365 Broadway - 12866
38 units   *Expensive-Very Expensive*
High Victorian architecture distinguishes this small hotel, erected in
1877. The last of the once-posh hotels that lined Broadway is still rich
in decor and memorabilia of yesteryear. There is a pool and gardens,
and a seasonal restaurant and bar. Each comfortably furnished high-
ceiling room includes some period decor and a private bath.

Batcheller Mansion Inn   *(518)584-7012*
just SE at 20 Circular St. - 12866
9 units   *(800)616-7012   Expensive-Very Expensive*
The Batcheller Mansion is America's quintessential Victorian bed-and-
breakfast. With its colorful minarets, towers and turrets, it is a
peerless tribute to an opulent era when creative architectural master
builders, carvers, and cabinet makers made lavish use of rare woods
and stone that couldn't be duplicated today. Exquisite period pieces are
displayed throughout. Gourmet breakfast is complimentary. Each room
is individually luxuriously outfitted with nostalgic furnishings and all
contemporary conveniences. The vast Diamond Jim Brady room sports
a regulation-sized pool table and a double whirlpool bath. Some other
rooms also have whirlpool baths, or a private curved porch.

Gideon Putnam Hotel   *(518)584-3000*
1 mi. SW via S. Broadway in Spa State Park (Box 476) - 12866
132 units   *(800)732-1560*   *Very Expensive*
A large tranquil park in a forest surrounds a five-story Georgian-style
brick hotel built in 1930. The resort offers (fee) 27 holes of golf, eight
tennis courts, mineral baths and massage, rental bicycles, plus hiking
and cross-country ski trails, three pools, a gourmet restaurant, entertainment lounge and resort shop. Each room is well furnished.

Grand Union Motel   *(518)584-9000*
just S at 92 S. Broadway - 12866
64 units   *(800)735-2909*   *Expensive*
The Crystal Spa Mineral Bathhouse here is the state's only private mineral bath spa offering (fee) relaxing mineral baths, massages and other services. There is also a pool and whirlpool. Each of the modern motel's rooms is comfortably furnished.

Saratoga Bed & Breakfast   *(518)584-0920*
2 mi. NW at 434 Church St. - 12866
18 units   *(800)584-0920*   *Moderate-Expensive*
A pre-Civil War house and farmhouse have been transformed into a bed-and-breakfast inn (with a motel next door). Full Irish breakfast is complimentary. Each well-furnished room combines period and contemporary conveniences, including a private bath. Some of the rooms also have a phone, TV and gas fireplace.

Sheraton Saratoga Springs Hotel   *(518)584-4000*
downtown at 534 Broadway - 12866
240 units   *(800)325-3535*   *Expensive-Very Expensive*
The area's largest lodging is a stylish newer conference center hotel. The five-story complex has an indoor pool, sauna, exercise equipment, restaurant, entertainment lounge and gift shop. Each room is well furnished. Some of the rooms also have a private balcony and a whirlpool bath.

Union Gables Bed & Breakfast   *(518)584-1558*
just E at 55 Union Av. - 12866
10 units   *(800)398-1558*   *Expensive-Very Expensive*
A splendid Queen Anne Victorian home (circa 1901) recently was transformed into a delightful bed-and-breakfast. The mansion, on the National Historic Register, has a grand "Saratoga porch," whirlpool, exercise equipment and bicycles. A light breakfast is complimentary. Each individually, beautifully furnished room combines period and all contemporary conveniences including a private bath.

The Westchester House   *(518)587-7613*
just S at 102 Lincoln Av. (Box 944) - 12866
7 units   *(800)581-7613*   *Expensive-Very Expensive*
A gracious Queen Anne-style house (circa 1885) in a residential area now serves as a bed-and-breakfast inn. An elaborate Continental breakfast is complimentary. Each attractively furnished room combines some period decor with all contemporary conveniences, including a private bath.

BASIC INFORMATION

Elevation: 320 feet   Population (1990):   25,001
Location: 170 miles North of New York City
Nearest airport with commercial flights: Albany - 28 miles
Saratoga County Chamber of Commerce   (518)584-3255
*   downtown at 28 Clinton St. - 12866   (800)526-8970*
*   www.saratoga.org*

Beaufort, North Carolina

Beaufort is an unspoiled seaport village with a proud heritage. Long narrow barrier islands of the Outer Banks provide shelter from the Atlantic Ocean a mile away. North Carolina's third oldest town was settled in the early 1700s along one of the East Coast's few south-facing waterfronts. It prospered as a fishing village and port of entry—in spite of Blackbeard the Pirate and other swashbucklers who prowled these waters. Recently, the ocean, calm estuaries, and superb beaches began to attract travelers drawn by a mild climate at the northern end of the coastline where alligators and palm trees can flourish.

Today, much of the lively past is preserved. More than one hundred buildings have been restored along tree-lined streets. The harbor downtown features a boardwalk by colorful marinas, parks, and museums. Shops emphasize Southern arts, crafts and gourmet treats. Numerous restaurants specialize in Southern coastal cuisine, and some have marine views. Lodgings are uniformly small and distinctive.

WEATHER PROFILE

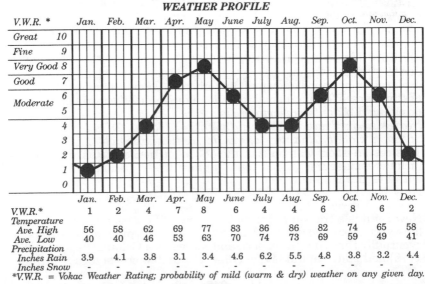

V.W.R. *	Jan.	Feb.	Mar.	Apr.	May	June	July	Aug.	Sep.	Oct.	Nov.	Dec.
V.W.R.*	1	2	4	7	8	6	4	4	6	8	6	2
Temperature												
Ave. High	56	58	62	69	77	83	86	86	82	74	65	58
Ave. Low	40	40	46	53	63	70	74	73	69	59	49	41
Precipitation												
Inches Rain	3.9	4.1	3.8	3.1	3.4	4.6	6.2	5.5	4.8	3.8	3.2	4.4
Inches Snow	-	-	-	-	-	-	-	-	-	-	-	-

*V.W.R. = Vokac Weather Rating; probability of mild (warm & dry) weather on any given day.

ATTRACTIONS

Atlantic Beach
4 mi. SW via US 70 & Atlantic Beach Rd.
The Atlantic Ocean washes against miles of south-facing beaches along the nearest barrier island accessible by car from Beaufort. Jaunty little Atlantic Beach is a major destination for ocean swimming, fishing, and boating. Amenities include fine sandy beaches, a boardwalk, piers, marinas, restaurants and the area's largest concentration of lodgings.

Beaufort Historic Site   *(252)728-5225*
downtown at 130 Turner St.
Beaufort was planned in 1713. A twelve-block area by the waterfront in the heart of town is on the National Historic Register. The site contains several restored and furnished buildings, including the 1796 Courthouse, a one-cell County Jail built in 1829, an 1859 apothecary shop, a fisherman's cottage, a stylish townhouse from the 1700s, and the old burial grounds. Guided hour-plus tours leave from the Welcome Center and gift shop several times daily.

Boat Rentals
Some of the picturesque barrier islands around Beaufort can only be reached by boat. To explore them, and nearby rivers, sounds, and the Intracoastal Waterway, power or sail boats can be rented at several places in town and in Atlantic Beach.

Boat Rides
Mystery Tours   *(252)728-7827*
downtown on Beaufort Waterfront
Scenic harbor tours leave several times daily. You may get close to wild horses, dolphins, birds—and pirates. Moonlight cruises and half-day fishing trips can also be arranged.

Cape Lookout National Seashore   *(252)728-2250*
1 mi. S of Beaufort Waterfront
Long, thin barrier islands extend for more than fifty miles north from Beaufort Inlet. On the undeveloped islands reachable by boat, surf fishing, hiking, seashell collecting, and primitive camping are popular. The 1859 lighthouse near Cape Lookout Point is still operational.

Croatan National Forest   *(252)638-5628*
starts 8 mi. W on US 70
The only coastal national forest between North Carolina and Canada has a second distinction. It is the northernmost natural habitat of the alligator. Numerous saltwater and freshwater channels backed by dense stands of pines and swamp hardwoods are ideally suited to exploration by canoe and small motorboats. There are many waterfowl nesting areas and unusual plants (like Venus flytrap), and a few designated beach recreation areas.

Fort Macon State Park   *(252)726-3775*
5 mi. S via US 70 & Ft. Macon Rd. - Atlantic Beach
This restored fort was built in the 1830s for harbor defense. Features include a museum, guided tours, nature trails, fishing, and a beach with lifeguards in summer.

New Bern   *(252)637-9400   (800)437-5767*
38 mi. NW on US 70
New Bern is a treasury of three centuries of Southern landmarks and lifestyles. Founded in 1710 by Swiss and German adventurers, it eventually thrived as a seaport, and served as a Colonial capital (1766-1776) and state capital (1776-1794). The architectural legacy includes

dozens of original and restored buildings on the National Historic Register. **Tryon Palace** (circa 1770) was the Colonial capitol of North Carolina and home of the Royal Governor. After the Revolutionary War, it served as the state capitol. The "most beautiful public building in Colonial America" was authentically reconstructed and furnished with outstanding period antiques and art. Extensive grounds are superbly landscaped in the 18th century English style, ranging from formal gardens to a wilderness walk. The complex also includes three elegant mansions furnished with period antiques. Costumed interpreters conduct tours and demonstrate Colonial crafts. The reception center has an orientation film, and there are crafts and gift shops. Historic blocks of buildings on tree-lined streets downtown house an array of specialty shops and restaurants. Most notable are **The Chelsea** (L-D—Moderate) in the building where Pepsi Cola was first made, plus **Harvey Mansion Historic Inn** (D only—Expensive) and **Henderson House** (D only—Very Expensive), dinner houses where chef/owners showcase their talent with fresh seasonal fare in artistically transformed 18th century buildings. On the downtown riverfront is the **Sheraton Grand New Bern**. The area's biggest and best hotel is a contemporary five-story brick complex with a large marina, view pool, exercise room, rental boats and bicycles, restaurant, and pub. All beautifully furnished rooms have a fine riverfront view. **The Aerie, Harmony House Inn**, and **King's Arms** are bed-and-breakfast inns and excellent sources of 19th century style, today's conveniences and Southern hospitality.

North Carolina Maritime Museum　　　*(252)728-7317*
downtown at 315 Front St.
Maritime and coastal natural heritage of the region are featured. Exhibits include saltwater aquariums; a major shell collection; fish, birds, decoys; ship models and full-sized craft. Field trips, excursions, and special programs are also offered, and there is a museum store.

The Rachel Carson Reserve　　　*(252)728-2170*
just S of Beaufort Waterfront
Carrot Island is easily visible from downtown but accessible only by boat. It is an unspoiled national sanctuary for wild horses and other wildlife. Hiking and beachcombing, fishing, clamming, swimming and primitive camping are popular.

RESTAURANTS

Anchor Inn　　　*(252)726-2156*
4 mi. W on Hwy. 70 at 109 N. 28th St. - Morehead City
B-L-D.　　　　　　　　　　　　　　　　　　　　*Moderate*
Hearty breakfasts range from create-your-own omelets through skillet dishes to creamed chipped beef on toast. Dinner options are also diverse in this casual family-oriented restaurant.

Beaufort Grocery Co.　　　*(252)728-3899*
downtown at 117 Queen St.
L-D.　　　　　　　　　　　　　　　　　　　　*Expensive*
The Beaufort Grocery Co. produces some of the best New Southern cuisine in America. The shrimp gougere alone would be worth a long detour. Everything reflects the talented staff's preoccupation with fresh quality ingredients used in remarkably creative ways—right down to the homemade sweet potato chips. And the desserts! Bordering the simply stylish wood-trimmed dining room are deli cases brimming with culinary delights.

Clawson's 1905 Restaurant   *(252)728-2133*
downtown at 429 Front St.
L-D.   *Moderate*
Slow-cooked baby back ribs or sauteed seafood are specialties on a
contemporary American menu. Tasty dishes prepared to order account
for part of Clawson's considerable popularity. The comfortable, recently
expanded two-level dining rooms and bar filled with Beaufort
memorabilia also contribute to the congenial feeling of a historic former
general store.
Loughry's Landing   *(252)728-7541*
downtown at 510 Front St.
L-D.   *Moderate*
Local seafood and steak are offered in a comfortable family-oriented
dining room and upper deck lounge that share a nifty view from a
waterfront location.
The Net House   *(252)728-2002*
downtown on Turner St. (between Front & Ann Sts.)
L-D.   *Moderate*
Creative Southern coastal cuisine is featured in creamy seafood bisque,
stuffed soft crabs and lightly batter-fried and broiled seafood served in
a very casual setting.
Sanitary Fish Market and Restaurant Inc.   *(252)247-3111*
3 mi. W at 501 Evans St. - Morehead City
L-D.   *Moderate*
The area's oldest seafood restaurant has been family-owned and
operated here since 1938. The deluxe shore dinner is a genuine
extravaganza. For regular meals, fresh fish and crustaceans are
prepared every which way and supported by homemade hush puppies
and desserts. Three enormous dining rooms overlook the Intracoastal
Waterway.
The Spouter Inn Restaurant   *(252)728-5190*
downtown at 218 Front St.
L-D.   *Moderate*
Fresh seafood is served in a comfortable dining room with a delightful
view of Beaufort Inlet. A waterfront patio is especially popular in
pleasant weather.

LODGING

Accommodations in Beaufort are relatively scarce and small, but
distinctive. They are much more numerous and prosaic nearby, where
several modern lodgings front on an Atlantic Ocean beach. Rates are
highest in summer, and scale down substantially in winter with
reductions of as much as 50%.
Atlantic Beach Holiday Inn   *(252)726-2544*
9 mi. W on Hwy. 58 (Salter Path Rd) (Box 280) - Atlantic Beach 28512
114 units   *(800)465-4329*   *Moderate-Expensive*
Holiday Inn found a fine oceanfront site for this modern five-story
motor hotel with a long sandy beach, pool, dining room and lounge.
Each comfortable unit has a private view balcony. Some overlook surf.
Beaufort Inn   *(252)728-2600*
just NW at 101 Ann St. - 28516
44 units   *(800)726-0321*   *Expensive*
The Beaufort Channel adjoins this handsome motel. There is an exercise
room, (fee) docking facilities and bicycles. Each room is well furnished and
has a private balcony.

The Cedars Inn   *(252)728-7036*

downtown at 305 Front St. - 28516

11 units   *Moderate-Expensive*

Cedars Inn is the central North Carolina coast's finest bed-and-breakfast. Two attractively landscaped buildings include a main house built in 1768. Both match the coastal charm of the historic downtown waterfront only steps away. Full Southern breakfast is complimentary. Each room is individually beautifully furnished with a blend of period pieces and all contemporary conveniences. Some rooms have a gas fireplace. One also has a large whirlpool bath.

Inlet Inn   *(252)728-3600*

downtown at 601 Front St. - 28516

37 units   *(800)554-5466*   *Expensive*

New for the 1990s is a three-story motel that captures Beaufort's architectural style in a fine location facing the waterfront by the heart of town. Most of the attractively furnished units have large private balconies overlooking the harbor. Some also have a wood-burning fireplace.

Pecan Tree Inn   *(252)728-6733*

downtown at 116 Queen St. - 28516

7 units   *Moderate-Expensive*

A stately Victorian home shaded by centuries-old pecan trees in the heart of town is now a charming bed and breakfast. Guests also enjoy the English flower and herb garden. An expanded Continental breakfast and afternoon beverages are complimentary. Many antiques enhance individually well-furnished rooms with modern conveniences including a private bath. Some have a fireplace. The "Bridal Suite" also has a large whirlpool bath.

Sheraton Atlantic Beach Oceanfront Hotel   *(252)240-1155*

9 mi W on Hwy 58 at 2717 W Fort Macon Rd(Bx 3040)-Atlantic Bch 28512

200 units   *(800)624-8875*   *Expensive*

A fine Atlantic Ocean beach frames the area's largest lodging. The contemporary nine-story complex also has a private pier, indoor and outdoor pools, whirlpool, exercise room, restaurant, bar, nightclub, and gift shop. Many of the well-furnished units have private surf views. Several have a whirlpool bath.

BASIC INFORMATION

Elevation: 7 feet   Population (1990):   3,808

Location: 142 miles Southeast of Raleigh, NC

Nearest airport with commercial flights: New Bern - 35 miles

Carteret County Tourism Development Bureau   (252)726-8148

3 mi. W at 3409 Arendell St. - Morehead City 28557

www.sunnync.com   (800)786-6962

Blowing Rock, North Carolina

Blowing Rock is a refined mountain village for all seasons. It is sequestered in a verdant hardwood forest atop one of the most spectacular rims in the Blue Ridge Mountains. Nearby is the highest peak and the deepest gorge in the East. The town, founded in the 1880s, was oriented toward vacationers from the lowlands since the beginning.

Gorgeous panoramas, crisp mountain air, and diverse recreation and cultural opportunities in Blowing Rock are more popular than ever in summer, thanks to a choice site by the renowned Blue Ridge Parkway. Travelers now also come here to enjoy dazzling fall colors; nearby ski areas in winter; and flowering dogwoods, azaleas and rhododendrons in spring. The picture-postcard village center is a stroller's delight with a lovely town park bordering many quaint shops featuring quality regional handicrafts and gifts. Colorful flower boxes accent notable restaurants and romantic inns. Nearby are historic and modern small resorts in picturesque settings.

WEATHER PROFILE

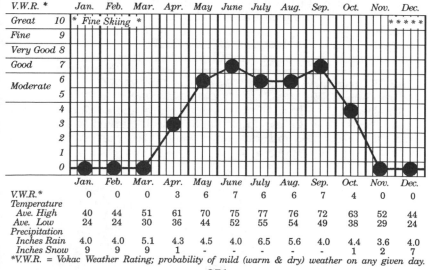

V.W.R.*		Jan.	Feb.	Mar.	Apr.	May	June	July	Aug.	Sep.	Oct.	Nov.	Dec.
Great	10	* Fine Skiing *										* * * * *	
Fine	9												
Very Good	8												
Good	7												
Moderate	6												
	5												
	4												
	3												
	2												
	1												
	0												

	Jan.	Feb.	Mar.	Apr.	May	June	July	Aug.	Sep.	Oct.	Nov.	Dec.
V.W.R.*	0	0	0	3	6	7	6	6	7	4	0	0
Temperature												
Ave. High	40	44	51	61	70	75	77	76	72	63	52	44
Ave. Low	24	24	30	36	44	52	55	54	49	38	29	24
Precipitation												
Inches Rain	4.0	4.0	5.1	4.3	4.5	4.0	6.5	5.6	4.0	4.4	3.6	4.0
Inches Snow	9	9	9	1	-	-	-	-	-	1	2	7

*V.W.R. = Vokac Weather Rating; probability of mild (warm & dry) weather on any given day.

351

ATTRACTIONS

Appalachian Heritage Museum   *(828)264-4726*
2 mi. N on US 321
A Victorian house portrays the cultural heritage of the Blue Ridge Mountain people with authentic 18th and 19th century furnishings, exhibits of area artifacts and antiques, and occasional related demonstrations.

The Blowing Rock   *(828)295-7111*
2 mi. SE on US 321
A large rock formation 4,000 feet above sea level overhangs John's River Gorge almost 3,000 feet below. When prevailing winds are right, light objects cast from the ledge will return to the thrower. Ripley's Believe It or Not said this is "the only place where it snows upside down." Nearby are gardens, an observation tower, and a well-stocked gift shop.

Blue Ridge Parkway   *(828)298-0398*
1 mi. N via US 321
One of America's most scenic drives extends 469 toll-free miles between Shenandoah National Park in Virginia and Great Smoky Mountains National Park in North Carolina and Tennessee. The pristine two-lane highway winds along the crest of the Blue Ridge and other mountains, topping out more than 6,000 feet above sea level on the slopes of Mt. Mitchell—the highest peak in the Eastern United States at 6,684 feet. It is lined with a natural bonanza of unspoiled woodlands, sparkling streams, wildlife, and meadows festooned with wildflowers. When rhododendrons bloom in June and fall foliage is at its most flamboyant in October, hiking trails, picnic sites, campgrounds, and overlooks are especially popular. Visitor centers, food and lodgings are well spaced along the corridor.

Grandfather Mountain   *(828)733-4337   (800)468-7325*
10 mi. S via US 221 at Blue Ridge Pkwy. - Linville
One of the highest peaks in the Blue Ridge (5,964 feet above sea level) has massive rock outcroppings amid dense hardwood and pine forests, and spectacular panoramas. Features include the Mile High Swinging Footbridge; native panthers, deer, bear and more in natural habitats; a visitor center and nature museum with food service and a gift shop; plus hiking trails and picnic areas.

Horseback Riding
Blowing Rock Stables   *(828)295-7847*
Miles of scenic trails wind through forested mountains. This is the nearest stables offering hour or longer guided horseback rides.

Linville Caverns   *(828)756-4171   (800)419-0540*
24 mi. S on US 221
North Carolina's only natural caverns feature underground streams with schools of sightless trout, and a well-marked trail among impressive stalactites and stalagmites. Guided tours are available, and there is a gift shop.

Linville Gorge   *(828)652-2144*
20 mi. SW on the Blue Ridge Pkwy.
A half-mile trail through rhododendrons connects a parking area at Milepost 316 with Linville Falls, which plunges more than 100 feet in two falls into the 2,000-foot-deep Linville Gorge Wilderness. The spectacular natural area far below in Pisgah National Forest is accessible by foot trails only.

Moses Cone Memorial Park   *(828)295-7938*
2 mi. N on the Blue Ridge Pkwy.

The former summer estate of a textile magnate now has a crafts center, and twenty-five miles of bridle paths and hiking trails through woodlands with trout streams and small lakes.

River Running

Blowing Rock is near three of the most scenic mountain streams in the South. The Nolichucky River to the west is a free-flowing river with miles of rapids in one of the East's deepest gorges. The close-by Watauga River offers mild rapids and bucolic beauty. The South Fork New River (actually the second oldest in the world after the Nile) is a designated "Natural Scenic River" that is ideal for canoeing. For details and reservations, contact:

Edge of the World *Banner Elk*   *(828)898-9550*   *(800)789-3343*

High Mountain Expeditions *Blowing Rock* 295-4200 (800)262-9036

Tweetsie Railroad   *(828)264-9061*   *(800)526-5740*
4 mi. N on US 321

A restored coal-fired steam locomotive makes a three-mile narrow-gauge rail excursion—complete with mock robberies. The turn-of-the-century-themed railroad town has a general store; sheriff's office and jail; old-time saloon with live entertainment; crafts demonstrations; petting zoo; rides; food service; and shops.

Winter Sports

Appalachian Ski Mountain   *(828)295-7828*   *(800)322-2373*
4 mi. N via US 321 on Ski Mountain Rd.

The largest concentration of major ski areas in the South is within twenty miles of Blowing Rock. Appalachian is the nearest. The vertical rise is less than 400 feet, but the longest run is more than one-half mile. There are three chairlifts, plus all facilities, services, rentals, a restaurant, and ice skating rink. Skiing season is from Thanksgiving into March.

RESTAURANTS

Blowing Rock Cafe   *(828)295-9474*
downtown at 349 Sunset Dr.
B-L-D.   *Moderate*

The strawberry-walnut bran muffin is a superb introduction to some of the high country's best breakfasts. A wide-ranging menu of contemporary American dishes is enhanced later by dishes like fresh trout or country ham, and fine homemade desserts. Guests can dine in a casually comfortable dining room or on the patio.

Chetola Resort at Blowing Rock   *(828)295-5500*
1 mi. N on N. Main St.
B-L-D.   *Expensive*

The resort showcases **The Manor House**, where contemporary American cuisine is skillfully presented in fresh and flavorful dishes. Refined cuisine is coupled with plush decor. Nearby is a warm, relaxed pub that opened in 1998.

Crippen's Country Inn & Restaurant   *(828)295-3487*
downtown at 239 Sunset Dr.
D only.   *Expensive*

Creative American cuisine has earned critical acclaim for the inn's restaurant. The menu changes daily and might include a pistachio-crusted black grouper with spinach-fennel salad. All breads, desserts and ice creams are housemade. The upscale dining room and bar complement the sophisticated fare.

Dockside Ira's   *(828)295-4008*
just W at 3148 Wonderland Trail
D only.   *Moderate*
Fresh seafood, steaks, ribs and chicken are served amidst nautical
decor in the dining room, bar and covered porch of a family-oriented
roadhouse in the woods.

Original Emporium Restaurant   *(828)295-7661*
2 mi. S on Hwy. 321
L-D.   *Low*
All kinds of American and Mexican comfort foods are served in a big
casual dining room, bar, and deck that share an awesome mountain view.

The Riverwood   *(828)295-4162*
just SE at 7179 Valley Blvd.
D only.   *Expensive*
Skillfully prepared New American cuisine includes fine regional
specialties like grilled fresh mountain trout, and desserts made on the
premises. The dinner house offers a setting of refined rusticity, and
there is a lounge.

Twig's   *(828)295-5050*
just SE on US 321 Bypass
D only.   *Expensive*
Fresh seafood, fowl and lamb are carefully prepared for a menu of
American and Continental dishes served in a simply sophisticated
dining room and on the porch in summer.

The Woodlands BBQ   *(828)295-3651*
just SE on US 321 Bypass
L-D.   *Low*
Chopped and sliced pork and beef barbecue has won a loyal following
for this big rustic Q parlor where live entertainment also happens.

LODGING

Accommodations are plentiful in and around the village and range
from quaint inns to posh resorts. June through October is high season.
Rates may be reduced 20% or more at other times.

Brookside Inn   *(828)295-3380*
just E on Hwy. 321 Bypass at Sunset Dr. (Box 372) - 28605
22 units   *(800)441-5691*   *Moderate-Expensive*
Here is a fashionable motel in a garden setting by a brook. Each unit
is well furnished with an appealing yesteryear motif. Two cottage-style
units by the creek also have a gas fireplace.

Chetola Resort at Blowing Rock   *(828)295-5500*
1 mi. NE on North Main St. (Box 17) - 28605
42 units   *(800)243-8652*   *Expensive*
The area's most complete lodge and conference center is in a park-like
setting on a hill overlooking a small lake. Amenities include an indoor
pool, whirlpool, sauna, racquetball courts, a fitness center, nature
trails, five tennis courts, plus (rental) canoes, boats and bicycles. There
is also a romantic restaurant (see listing) and lounge. Each spacious
unit is beautifully furnished. Many have a private lake-view balcony.
The "Lakeview Crown Suite" corner units also have a large whirlpool
bath. There are also condos.

Cliff Dwellers Inn   *(828)295-3121*
1 mi. NE near US 321 Bypass / US 221 at 116 Lakeview Ter. (Box 366)-28605
20 units   *(800)322-7380*   *Moderate-Expensive*
This modern motel on a hill has a pool and whirlpool overlooking
scenic high country. Some of the well-furnished units have a whirlpool.

Crippen's Country Inn & Restaurant   *(828)295-3487*
  downtown at 239 Sunset Dr. (Box 528) - 28605
  9 units   *Expensive*
A historic building has been carefully restored to house an elegant restaurant (see listing) and lounge and an inn that blends period pieces with contemporary conveniences. Each room is individually, attractively furnished and has a private bath.

Green Park Inn   *(828)295-3141*
  2 mi. SE on U.S. Hwy. 321 (Box 7) - 28605
  88 units   *(800)852-2462*   *Moderate-Expensive*
The big white framed building, on the National Register, may be (at 4,300 feet) the highest hotel in the East. Established in 1882, it is also one of the oldest inns in the South. Amenities include a pool, dining room, classic pub, and vestiges of a bygone era in touches like wicker furniture on the big porch. Each comfortably furnished room has a private bath. Some rooms also have a private balcony with a golf course view.

The Inn at Ragged Gardens   *(828)295-9703*
  downtown at 203 Sunset Dr. (Box 1927) - 28605
  12 units   *Expensive*
A turn-of-the-century bed-and-breakfast inn is surrounded by rock-walled formal gardens. Full breakfast is complimentary. All of the beautifully furnished rooms have a private bath and a gas fireplace. Most also have a whirlpool bath. Rooms in the 1998 wing are more spacious, and also have a private deck.

Maple Lodge   *(828)295-3331*
  downtown at 152 Sunset Dr. (Box 1236) - 28605
  11 units   *Moderate-Expensive*
Blowing Rock's oldest continuously operating bed-and-breakfast inn opened in 1946. Full buffet breakfast is complimentary. Country antiques, handmade quilts, and family heirlooms blend with contemporary conveniences, including a private bath.

Meadowbrook Inn   *(828)295-4300*
  downtown at 711 N. Main St. (Box 2005) - 28605
  61 units   *(800)456-5456*   *Expensive*
The village's most elaborate motor lodge is a contemporary four-story complex on a rise above a garden pond. Amenities include an indoor pool, whirlpool, exercise room, lounge, and casually elegant view dining room. Each room is beautifully furnished. Many have a panoramic view of the countryside. Several also have a gas fireplace and a large whirlpool tub.

BASIC INFORMATION

Elevation: 3,580 feet   Population (1990):   1,257
Location: 90 miles Northwest of Charlotte, NC
Nearest airport with commercial flights: Hickory, NC - 37 miles
Blowing Rock Chamber of Commerce   (828)295-7851   (800)295-7851
  downtown at 1038 Main St. (Box 406) - 28605
  www.blowingrock.com

Manteo, North Carolina

Manteo is the gateway to a vast saltwater playground. Secluded in a forest at the northern end of Roanoke Island, it is linked to the mainland and to the Outer Banks by bridges. These barrier islands provide a buffer more than 100 miles long between the Atlantic Ocean and sheltered sounds around Manteo's island. The town adjoins "the Lost Colony" site. Settled in 1585 by the first English colonists in the New World, it was mysteriously abandoned by 1590. Manteo was resettled nearly 300 years later.

Today Manteo is a vital village. Historic sites are proudly maintained, along with contemporary recreation facilities like scenic bike paths, waterfront parks and marinas. The picturesque town center by a sheltered bay has a few specialty shops, good restaurants and two of the region's best lodgings. Nearby to the east, villages sprinkled between ocean beaches and broad sounds on the Outer Banks have many additional facilities for visitors.

WEATHER PROFILE

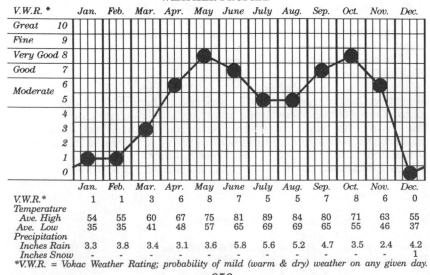

V.W.R. *	Jan.	Feb.	Mar.	Apr.	May	June	July	Aug.	Sep.	Oct.	Nov.	Dec.
V.W.R.*	1	1	3	6	8	7	5	5	7	8	6	0
Temperature												
Ave. High	54	55	60	67	75	81	89	84	80	71	63	55
Ave. Low	35	35	41	48	57	65	69	69	65	55	46	37
Precipitation												
Inches Rain	3.3	3.8	3.4	3.1	3.6	5.8	5.6	5.2	4.7	3.5	2.4	4.2
Inches Snow	-	-	-	-	-	-	-	-	-	-	-	1

*V.W.R. = Vokac Weather Rating; probability of mild (warm & dry) weather on any given day.

ATTRACTIONS

Beaches
6 mi. E via US 64 & NC 12
North Carolina Highway 12 extends for more than 100 miles along barrier islands that separate the Atlantic Ocean from the mainland. These Outer Banks, often less than one mile wide, are lined with seemingly endless miles of sandy oceanfront beaches suitable for swimming, surfing, beachcombing and fishing.

Bicycling
A six-mile bike path crosses Roanoke Island through Manteo. This and other separated paths and byways make the Outer Banks ideal for easy shoreline touring. Several shops offer hourly rentals and all accessories.

Boat Rentals
The sounds around Roanoke Island and the Outer Banks offer many miles of scenic sheltered waterways. Several places collectively offer hourly and longer rentals of nearly everything that floats—from aquacycles, windsurfers, kayaks or catamarans to jet skis or powerboats.

Boat Rides
The picturesque, protected waters of Roanoke Sound and beyond can be enjoyed during narrated cruises aboard a variety of passenger vessels in the area. Both daytime tours or an evening under the stars are offered.

Cape Hatteras National Seashore   *(252)473-2111*
6 mi. E via US 64 on NC 12
America's first national seashore extends more than seventy miles south from where US 64 ends at the Whalebone Junction Information Center in South Nags Head to Ocracoke Island. Long stretches of undeveloped coastline with fine sandy beaches; a wildlife refuge; lighthouses (including Cape Hatteras Lighthouse-circa 1870-at 208 feet, America's tallest); a free ferry; eight villages; and wild ponies on Ocracoke Island are all linked by NC 12. Nature trails, fishing piers, visitor centers and campgrounds are at various locations.

Elizabeth II State Historic Site   *(252)473-1144*
downtown on Dare St.
Across from Manteo's waterfront is a replica of a 69-foot square-rigged sailing vessel like those used to transport England's first colonists to the New World in 1585. The visitor center has exhibits, a multimedia presentation, guided tours and (in summer) interpreters in Elizabethan costumes portraying colonists and mariners.

Fishing Charters   *(800)446-6262*
downtown & SE on US 64
More than half of the state's saltwater sportfishing records were made off the Outer Banks. The Gulf Stream is only twelve miles offshore to the east, closer than anywhere north of Florida. Five sounds lie sheltered to the west, including Pamlico Sound (the largest inland body of water on the East Coast). Surf casting, pier and (around Manteo) bridge fishing are popular. For offshore fishing trips (complete with tackle, boat and ice) there are four marinas in and near town offering daily charter service. Several dive shops also offer charters offshore for wreck diving.

Fort Raleigh National Historic Site   *(252)473-5772*
3 mi. NW off US 64
A fort was built here in 1585 and expanded in 1587 by Sir Walter Raleigh's colonists—the first English settlers in the New World. When

Colonial Governor John White returned after a three-year absence, all he found was the word "Croatan." The fate of the "Lost Colony" remains an unsolved mystery. The fort has been reconstructed. The drama of "The Lost Colony" is re-enacted nightly in summer in the nation's oldest outdoor theater. **Lindsay Warren Visitor Center** has museum relics and displays, a film, (in summer) costumed interpreter programs, and a gift shop. Nearby **Elizabethan Gardens** is an Elizabethan-style memorial to the ill-fated colonists. Features include a Tudor-style gatehouse with period furniture and English portraits; Shakespearean herb garden, Queen's Rose Garden, Sunken Garden with ancient fountain and statues; a gazebo overlooking Roanoke Sound; and a great lawn encircled by camellias and azaleas.

Jockey's Ridge State Park   *(252)441-7132*
11 mi. NE off US 158 bypass
The largest natural sand dunes on the East Coast rise well over 100 feet above the nearby ocean and sound. You can hike to the top for a great view, but the real appeal is hang gliding. Steady breezes and soft sand dunes, and the largest hang gliding school in the world, make this the ultimate site to learn to fly. Re-live the Wright Brothers' airborne thrill (as a hang glider, not in a plane) with your own flight adventure by making arrangements with **Outer Banks Outdoors** at (252)441-4124 or (800)334-4777.

North Carolina Aquarium on Roanoke Island   *(252)473-3493*
3 mi. W via US 64 on Airport Rd.
Loggerhead turtles, sharks, and other live local marine creatures are displayed. A touch table provides a hands-on experience with starfish, crabs, sea urchins, and other small sea life. Films and educational programs are also offered.

Wright Brothers National Memorial   *(252)441-7430*
18 mi. NE on US 158 bypass
On December 17, 1903, the world's first sustained powered flight occurred here. Markers show where the aircraft took off and landed. A visitors center has a replica of the plane and exhibits detailing the story of their invention. Their living quarters and hangar buildings have been reconstructed nearby.

RESTAURANTS

Clara's Seafood   *(252)473-1727*
downtown on Queen Elizabeth St.
L-D.   *Moderate*
Long-standing family tradition continues to offer steamed, grilled, broiled, sauteed or fried seafood in a dining room and lounge with period accents and a charming harbor view.

Dunes Restaurant   *(252)441-7513*
10 mi. NE (Mile Post 16.5) on US 158 Bypass - Nags Head
B-L-D.   *Moderate*
Traditional American breakfast specials have made this casual coffee shop a popular stop near the beach.

1587 Restaurant   *(252)473-1587*
downtown at 405 Queen Elizabeth St.
D only.   *Expensive*
Some of the region's best cuisine distinguishes the 1587 Restaurant in the Tranquil House Inn. Hopefully, this gourmet haven will always feature the fresh Southern seafood with creative contemporary touches that made it famous. The sophisticated wood-trimmed dining room has a serene view of the waterfront.

Owens' Restaurant   *(252)441-7309*
10 mi. NE (Mile Post 16.5) on Beach Rd. - Nags Head
D only.   *Expensive*
Southern coastal cuisine with an emphasis on fresh fish has made this
family-owned restaurant and lounge a favorite for more than half a
century. Extensive nautical memorabilia enlivens the comfortable
setting.

Penguin Isle Soundside Grill & Bar   *(252)441-2637*
10 mi. NE (Mile Post 16) at 6708 S. Croatan Hwy. - Nags Head
D only.   *Expensive*
Mesquite-grilled coastal seafood and steaks are a specialty, along with
housemade pasta and breads. Fine desserts are also made here. The
big inviting dining room and lounge provide a scenic sunset view of
Roanoke Sound.

The Weeping Radish Brewery & Restaurant   *(252)473-1157*
1 mi. S on US 64
L-D.   *Moderate*
Here is an authentic German microbrewery where you can enjoy a tall
chilled glass of fine draft beer with a soft salted pretzel and spicy
mustard in the lounge or cozy Gingerbread House. German specialties
including luscious homemade desserts are served in the Bavarian-style
dining room below, and in a pine-shaded beer garden.

Windmill Point Restaurant   *(252)441-1535*
10 mi. NE (Mile Post 16.5) on U.S. 158 Bypass - Nags Head
D only.   *Expensive*
Contemporary American cuisine is skillfully prepared using fresh local
seafood plus choice prime rib, steaks, and fowl. Herb bread and
decadent desserts like Grand Marnier cake are housemade. The big
casually elegant dining rooms and lounge are decorated with the
largest collection of memorabilia from the S.S. United States luxury
liner, and they overlook Roanoke Sound.

LODGING

Accommodations are relatively scarce in Manteo and abundant a few
miles east near the beaches of the Outer Banks. Summer is high
season. Rates may be reduced 40% and more during fall and winter.
(Many places close during this time.)

Elizabethan Inn   *(252)473-2101*
1 mi. N at 814 US 64 (Box 549) - 27954
80 units   *(800)346-2466*   *Moderate*
This contemporary motel has a fitness center with indoor and outdoor
pools, whirlpool, sauna, exercise facilities and (fee) racquetball and
massage, plus a restaurant. Each unit is well furnished. Two also have
a two-person whirlpool bath.

First Colony Inn   *(252)441-2343*
10 mi. NE (M.P. 16) at 6720 S. Virginia Dare Trail - Nags Head 27959
26 units   *(800)368-9390   Expensive-Very Expensive*
An artistically restored and relocated 1932 classic inn with a sweeping
roof and encircling verandas is now a stylish bed-and-breakfast on the
National Register. An ocean beach is nearby, and there is a pool.
Expanded Continental breakfast and afternoon tea are complimentary.
Each beautifully furnished room blends fine period antiques and all
contemporary conveniences. Some have a private view porch and/or a
large whirlpool tub.

Nags Head Inn   *(252)441-0454*
12 mi. NE (M.P.14) at 4701 S. Virginia Dare Tr. (Bx 1599) - Nags Head 27959
  100 units   *(800)327-8881*   *Expensive*
A fine oceanfront beach adjoins this five-story motel with an
indoor/outdoor pool and whirlpool. Each room is well furnished and has
a private view balcony. Some also have a whirlpool tub.

Ocean Reef Suites - Best Western   *(252)441-1611*
  17 mi. NE (M.P.8.5) at 107 Virginia Dare Tr.(Box 1440)-Kill Devil Hills 27948
  70 units   *(800)528-1234*   *Expensive*
One of the Outer Banks' best all-suites hotels is a contemporary five-
story complex on the beach with a pool, whirlpool, sauna, exercise room
and restaurant. Each comfortably furnished suite has a bedroom, living
room, kitchen and a private oceanfront balcony.

Sanderling Inn Resort   *(252)261-4111*
  28 mi. NE at 1461 Duck Rd. - Duck 27949
  117 units   *(800)701-4111   Expensive-Very Expensive*
The Outer Banks' most luxurious resort hotel is a contemporary
oceanfront complex with a beach, large indoor and outdoor pool,
whirlpools, saunas, health club and two (fee) tennis courts, plus a
gourmet restaurant. Continental breakfast and afternoon tea are
complimentary. Many of the beautifully furnished units have an ocean
view. Some suites also have efficiencies, or a whirlpool bath.

Surf Side Motel   *(252)441-2105*
  10 mi. NE (M.P.16) at 6701 S. Virginia Dare Tr. (Bx 400) - Nags Head 27959
  76 units   *(800)552-7873*   *Expensive*
The ocean and a fine sand beach abut this modern five-story motel
with an indoor and outdoor pool and whirlpool. Continental breakfast
and afternoon tea are complimentary. Each well-furnished unit has a
private balcony—most with an ocean view. Some also have an
efficiency and/or a two-person whirlpool tub.

Tranquil House Inn   *(252)473-1404*
  downtown at 405 Queen Elizabeth St. (Box 2045) - 27954
  25 units   *(800)458-7069*   *Expensive*
At the heart of the photogenic village, on the waterfront by a marina
is this stylish wood-trimmed three-story inn. The outstanding 1587
Restaurant (see listing) is downstairs. Continental breakfast, and wine
reception each evening, are complimentary. Guests can also use the
inn's bicycles. Each room is beautifully, individually decorated.

The White Doe Inn   *(252)473-9851*
  downtown at 319 Sir Walter Raleigh St. (Box 1029) - 27954
  7 units   *(800)473-6091*   *Expensive*
A century-old Queen-Anne-style home (on the National Register) was
renovated and expanded in 1994 into a sumptuous bed-and-breakfast
inn in a tranquil setting near the heart of the village and the bustling
waterfront. Full breakfast and afternoon tea are complimentary, as are
bicycles for guests. Each room is individually luxuriously decorated
with period furnishings seamlessly blended with contemporary
conveniences except TV. Every room has a private bath (some have a
whirlpool) and a gas fireplace.

BASIC INFORMATION

Elevation: 5 feet   Population (1990):   991
Location: 90 miles South of Norfolk, VA
Nearest airport with commercial flights: Norfolk - 90 miles
Dare County Tourist Bureau   (252)473-2138   (800)446-6262
  just S at 704 Hwy. 64 (Box 399) - 27954   www.outer-banks.com / visitor-info

Waynesville, North Carolina

Waynesville is the unheralded gateway to the loftiest mountains in Eastern America. It is the major town nearest both Great Smoky Mountains National Park and the southern end of the Blue Ridge Parkway. The two highest summits east of the Mississippi River and the highest point on the Parkway are nearby. Northwest European farmers settled here more than two centuries ago. Growth was assured in modern times with heavy manufacturing.

Waynesville only recently began to be discovered as a major vacation destination. Impressive public buildings and monuments, shops featuring mountain handicrafts and culinary treats, and down-home restaurants are clustered along tree-lined streets downtown. Distinctive lodgings ranging from rustic to elegant are scattered around town on the way to the national parks and forests that assure Waynesville's ultimate role as a year-round recreation and leisure capital of the mountains.

WEATHER PROFILE

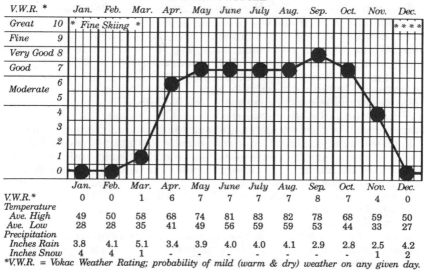

V.W.R.*		Jan.	Feb.	Mar.	Apr.	May	June	July	Aug.	Sep.	Oct.	Nov.	Dec.
Great	10	* Fine Skiing *											* * * *
Fine	9												
Very Good	8												
Good	7												
Moderate	6												
	5												
	4												
	3												
	2												
	1												
	0												

	Jan.	Feb.	Mar.	Apr.	May	June	July	Aug.	Sep.	Oct.	Nov.	Dec.
V.W.R.*	0	0	1	6	7	7	7	7	8	7	4	0
Temperature												
Ave. High	49	50	58	68	74	81	83	82	78	68	59	50
Ave. Low	28	28	35	41	49	56	59	59	53	44	33	27
Precipitation												
Inches Rain	3.8	4.1	5.1	3.4	3.9	4.0	4.0	4.1	2.9	2.8	2.5	4.2
Inches Snow	4	4	1	-	-	-	-	-	-	-	1	2

*V.W.R. = Vokac Weather Rating; probability of mild (warm & dry) weather on any given day.

ATTRACTIONS

Blue Ridge Parkway *(see Blowing Rock, NC)*
6 mi. SW via US 23
The highest point along the 469-mile parkway is at nearby Richland Balsam—6,047 feet above sea level.

Downtown *(828))456-3517*
centered around Main & Miller Sts.
Drinking fountains reward thirsty strollers and shoppers with some of the best-tasting water in the South. Brick sidewalks, comfortable wooden benches, colorful flower boxes and glimpses of mountains also contribute to the appeal of a vital town center. Tree-lined streets shade a handsome blend of new and old buildings. Many house specialty shops; art galleries; antique stores; restaurants; and nostalgic surprises like a genuine soda fountain and an old-time general store.

Ghost Town in the Sky *(828))926-1140   (800)446-7886*
9 mi. W on US 19 at 890 Soco Rd. - Maggie Valley
A chairlift, incline railway, and shuttle buses carry visitors to an "Old West" themed frontier town high in the mountains. There are gun fights; saloon and country music shows; plus numerous thrill rides like a looping mountainside roller coaster. Restaurants, snack bars and gift shops are at several locations.

Great Smoky Mountains National Park *(see Gatlinburg, TN)*
16 mi. W via US 19

Great Smoky Mountains Railway *(828))586-8811   (800)872-4681*
18 mi. SW on US 74 - Dillsboro
Round-trip excursions in reconditioned coaches, dining cars, cabooses, and open cars provide scenic views from foothills, forests, rivers and lakes to the Great Smoky Mountains. Sightseeing, dinner trips and raft 'n' rail trips range from 2½ to 7 hours. The **Historic Railway Museum** displays extensive railroad memorabilia in a building next to the Dillsboro Depot.

Horseback Riding
Riding a horse into the mountains is an ideal way to experience the romance of the high country. Numerous stables in and around town offer trips ranging from one hour to all day, by reservation.

Museum of North Carolina Handicrafts *(828))452-1551*
just S at 307 Shelton St.
The Shelton House (circa 1880), listed on the National Historic Register, is now a handsome showcase for traditional handicrafts created by some of the state's most acclaimed artisans. Wood carvings, pottery, braided rugs and more are displayed. The gift shop has a fine selection of handicrafts for sale.

Nantahala National Forest *(828))524-6441*
7 mi. W on US 23
Dense forest of hardwoods blanket mountains (many more than a mile above sea level) just south of Great Smoky Mountains National Park. A spectacular gorge, plus numerous lakes, rivers, and waterfalls accessible by hundreds of miles of roads and trails (including part of the Appalachian Trail) offer all sorts of recreation, and campgrounds.

Pisgah National Forest *(828))257-4200*
3 mi. S on US 276
Mount Mitchell (6,684 feet), the highest summit east of the Mississippi River, is here, along with twenty other 6,000-foot-plus mountains. Several wilderness areas can be accessed by hundreds of miles of trails, including part of the Appalachian Trail. Deep gorges, sparkling water-

falls (including Sliding Rock, a natural waterslide), rivers and lakes amid luxuriant forests offer a wealth of opportunities for recreation and camping.

River Running
Raft adventures on the nearby Pigeon and Nantahala Rivers have been thrilling paddlers for many years with the quiet grandeur of gorges near the Great Smoky Mountains. Professional guides lead half-day trips throughout the summer with enough whitewater for everyone. For reservations, call:

Nantahola Outdoor Center   *(828))488-2175   (800)232-7238*
Wildwater, Ltd.   *(828))488-0252   (800)762-2463*

Winter Sports
Cataloochee Ski Area   *(828))926-0285   (800)768-0285*
12 mi. W off US 19 at 1080 Ski Lodge Rd. - Maggie Valley
The vertical rise is 740 feet, the longest run is about 4,000 feet, and the view of the Great Smoky Mountains is terrific. There are two chairlifts. All facilities, services, rentals and food service are at the base. Lodgings are nearby in the valley. Ski season is December to March.

RESTAURANTS

Balsam Mountain Inn   *(828))456-9498*
8 mi. SW via US 23 near Mile Post 443 of Blue Ridge Pkwy. - Balsam
B-D.   *(800)224-9498*   *Moderate*
Contemporary American fare is served to overnight guests, and others by reservation, in a delightfully refurbished turn-of-the-century inn. Fireplaces, wicker furniture and other period furnishings and sylvan views distinguish the hillside haven.

Clyde's Restaurant   *(828))456-9135*
2 mi. SW on U.S. 23 at 1231 Balsam Rd.
B-L-D.   *Low*
The homestyle all-American meals are the reason why this casual coffee shop is, by their reckoning, "where the home folks eat."

DuVall's Restaurant   *(828))452-9464*
just N at 1104 N. Main St.
B-L-D.   *Low*
Large portions of uncomplicated country cooking—including mile-high pies—get diners into this homespun coffee shop.

J. Arthur's Restaurant   *(828))926-1817*
8 mi. NW on U.S. 19 at 801 Soco Rd. - Maggie Valley
D only.   *Moderate*
Prime rib, trout, and lamb star in a family-oriented dinner house and lounge with fireplaces and pine-panelled mountain decor.

The Old Stone Inn   *(828))456-3333*
1 mi. N at 900 Dolan Rd.
D only.   *Expensive*
Innovative Southern mountain cuisine has been served for more than half a century to overnight guests and others by reservation. The rustic candlelit dining room is just right, with a polished hardwood floor, log beam ceiling and a massive stone fireplace.

Pisgah Inn   *(828))235-8228*
21 mi. SE via U.S. 276 at Blue Ridge Pkwy., Mile Post 408
B-L-D.   *Moderate*
"From scratch" American country cooking is good, but the window-wall panoramic mountain view from the comfortable wood-toned dining room is grand. The complex (at 5,000 feet) also has a big gift shop featuring local crafts, a motel with view rooms, and a campground.

The Swag   *(828))926-0430*
12 mi. NW via US 276 & Hemphill Rd. at 2300 Swag Rd.
L-D.   *Very Expensive*
Four-course candlelit dinners of authentic regional cuisine at the Swag have won critical acclaim. Non-guests, by reservation, can enjoy seasonal garden-fresh soups and salads, entrees like grilled rainbow trout, and homemade desserts like Kentucky Derby pie. A massive stone fireplace, hand-hewn logs, and original mountain art contribute to the rustic elegance of the setting.

Whitman's Bakery & Sandwich Shoppe   *(828))456-8271*
downtown at 18 N. Main St.
B-L.   *Low*
Whitman's is one of North Carolina's best bakeries. They have been doing the right thing with pastries (try the bear claw) for years, and desserts like mile-high pies are as impressive as they are delicious.

LODGING

Conventional motels and hotels are relatively scarce. But, bed-and-breakfast inns that reflect the charm of the mountain setting are numerous. Summer and early fall are high season. Rates in some places may be reduced by 30% or more at other times.

Balsam Mountain Inn   *(828))456-9498*
8 mi. SW via US 23 near Blue Ridge Pkwy. (Box 40) - Balsam 28707
50 units   *Moderate-Expensive*
A classic small Victorian hotel, opened in 1908, was skillfully restored in the 1990s. Gracefully perched high on a mountain slope, it is on the National Historic Register. Full breakfast is complimentary in the authentic period dining room (see listing). Comfortably furnished rooms offer nostalgic appeal and a private bath, but no TV or phone.

Cataloochee Ranch   *(828))926-1401*
13 mi. NW on Fie Top Rd. Rt. 1 (Box 500) - Maggie Valley 28751
25 units   *(800)868-1401*   *Expensive*
Great Smoky Mountains National Park adjoins this ranch crowning a ridge 5,000 feet above sea level. Modified American Plan rates include breakfast and dinner (the dining room is open to the public), plus use of the swimming pool, whirlpool and amenities like tennis, pond fishing and (fee) horseback rides. The well-landscaped complex gracefully blends historic structures and contemporary amenities. Lodgings range from comfortably furnished ranch house rooms to cabins with fireplaces.

Jonathan Creek Inn   *(828))926-1232*
8 mi. W on US 19 at 4224 Soco Rd. (Box 66) - Maggie Valley 28751
43 units   *(800)577-7812*   *Moderate-Expensive*
A creek in a park-like setting is behind this contemporary wood-trim motel, along with a glass-enclosed pool. Many well-furnished rooms have a balcony overlooking the creek. Some have a kitchenette and a two-person whirlpool in the bathroom or bedroom.

Maggie Valley Resort & Country Club   *(828))926-1616*
8 mi. NW via US 19 at 340 Country Club Rd. - Maggie Valley 28751
75 units   *(800)438-3861*   *Expensive*
The Blue Ridge and Great Smoky Mountains surround this handsome contemporary resort with a (fee) championship 18-hole golf course, driving range and putting green, plus two tennis courts, a pool, and a mountain-view dining room and entertainment lounge. Each well-furnished room has a private view balcony.

Mountain Creek Bed & Breakfast   *(828))456-5509*
3 mi. S at 100 Chestnut Walk - 28786
6 units   *(800)557-9766*   *Moderate*
One of the most romantic lodgings in the mountains opened in 1995.
A distinctive historic building was artistically updated and converted
into a bed-and-breakfast amid lush trees and rhododendrons. In a
manicured clearing below the house, a stream turns an old mill wheel
by a trout pond. Full gourmet breakfast and afternoon treats are
complimentary. Each room is individually, beautifully furnished. Some
have a private view balcony, and two have an in-bath whirlpool.

The Old Stone Inn   *(828))456-3333*
1 mi. N at 900 Dolan Rd. - 28786
22 units   *(800)432-8499*   *Moderate*
A profusion of trees and flowering bushes surrounds this half-century-
old authentic mountain lodge. Rates include fresh-baked goods and a
bountiful breakfast. Candlelit gourmet dinners are served to guests
and the public in the appealing dining room (see listing). Each
comfortably furnished room combines a warm rustic feeling with
modern conveniences, except phones.

The Swag   *(828))926-0430*
12 mi. NW via US 276 at 2300 Swag Rd. - 28786
15 units   *(800)789-7672   Expensive-Very Expensive*
The Swag is an elegant aerie atop a 5,000-foot mountain. Several
original Appalachian buildings were moved here and upgraded to
showcase hand-hewn logs, stone work, and North Carolina furniture
and crafts. Amenities include a sauna, racquetball court, spring-fed
swimming pond, gourmet dining (see listing), and a gift shop. All
American Plan rates include three meals each day. Every room is
beautifully furnished with unique arts and crafts and contemporary
conveniences. Some, like the "Hideaway," also have a fireplace, private
balcony and whirlpool tub with a view.

Ten Oaks Bed & Breakfast Home   *(828))452-9433*
1 mi. N at 803½ Love Lane - 28786
4 units   *(800)563-2925*   *Moderate*
An 1898 Queen Anne Revival home amid leafy shade trees has been
restored for a return to yesteryear as a bed-and-breakfast inn. Full
Southern breakfast and an afternoon treat and beverages are
complimentary. Each well-furnished room has a fireplace and private
bath, plus TV and phone on request.

Waynesville Country Club Inn   *(828))456-3551*
2 mi. S on Main St. to Country Club Dr. (Box 390) - 28786
94 units   *(800)627-6250*   *Expensive*
Nestled between the Smokies and Blue Ridge Mountains is a
contemporary resort inn. Amenities include a scenic (fee) 27-hole golf
course, putting green, pool, tennis court, restaurant and lounge. Each
room is well furnished. Many have a private porch or balcony. There
are also private cottages and villas on the golf course.

BASIC INFORMATION

Elevation: 2,640 feet   Population (1990):   6,758
Location: 130 miles West of Charlotte, NC
Nearest airport with commercial flights: Asheville - 33 miles
Haywood County Chamber of Commerce (828)456-3021 (800)334-9036
*   1 mi. NE at 107 Woodland Dr. (P.O. Drawer 600) - 28786*
www.smokeymountains.net

Marietta, Ohio

Marietta has the most appealing mix of history and natural beauty of any town in the Ohio River valley. The choice forested site at the confluence of the Ohio and Muskingum Rivers is backed by foothills of the Appalachian Mountains. The first organized settlement in the Northwest Territory began here in 1788, marking the starting point of America's westward expansion. For a century after steamboats appeared in 1811, Marietta was a prosperous riverboat town. Boom-times ended but the town carried on with cheerful determination.

Today, Marietta is becoming a major destination for recreation and culture. Downtown, on the National Historic Register, is now separated from the two rivers by picturesque waterfront parks. Shops feature regional art, crafts, antiques and unique collectibles, and there are some good restaurants and live entertainment. Lodgings are surprisingly scarce and prosaic. The best is the oldest—a historic landmark hotel overlooking the rivers from the original heart of town.

WEATHER PROFILE

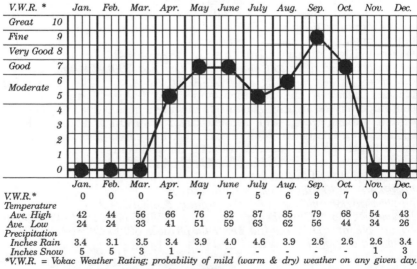

V.W.R. *		Jan.	Feb.	Mar.	Apr.	May	June	July	Aug.	Sep.	Oct.	Nov.	Dec.
Great	10												
Fine	9												
Very Good	8												
Good	7												
Moderate	6 5												
	4												
	3												
	2												
	1												
	0												

	Jan.	Feb.	Mar.	Apr.	May	June	July	Aug.	Sep.	Oct.	Nov.	Dec.
V.W.R.*	0	0	0	5	7	7	5	6	9	7	0	0
Temperature												
Ave. High	42	44	56	66	76	82	87	85	79	68	54	43
Ave. Low	24	24	33	41	51	59	63	62	56	44	34	26
Precipitation												
Inches Rain	3.4	3.1	3.5	3.4	3.9	4.0	4.6	3.9	2.6	2.6	2.6	3.4
Inches Snow	5	5	3	1	-	-	-	-	-	-	1	3

*V.W.R. = Vokac Weather Rating; probability of mild (warm & dry) weather on any given day.

Boat Rides
Valley Gem Sternwheeler   *(740)373-7862*
downtown at Washington St. Bridge & Front St. Landing
Narrated sightseeing excursions and dinner cruises on the Ohio and
Muskingum Rivers are regularly scheduled from May through October
aboard an authentic stern-wheeler. The 300-passenger boat has gift
and snack areas.

Campus Martius Museum   *(740)373-3750   (800)860-0145*
downtown at 601 Second St.
The first organized American settlement in the "Northwest Territory"
(the vast land west of the Ohio River) began with a civilian fort on this
site in 1788. The museum features the Putnam House, the only
surviving dwelling on its original site, and the oldest residence in Ohio.
Exhibits cover the early settlement and subsequent development of
Marietta and the territory.

The Castle   *(740)373-4180*
downtown at 418 Fourth St.
With its octagonal tower, arched doorways, and floor-to-ceiling bay
windows, the 1855 mansion is an outstanding example of Gothic
Revival architecture. Fine craftsmanship is on display throughout the
main building and adjacent carriage house. The Castle is open to the
public for tours, exhibits and special programs.

Downtown   *(740)373-5178*
centered around Third & Putnam Sts.
Downtown, just inland from parks along the Ohio and Muskingum
Rivers, has the look of a much bigger city. A surprising number of
multistory brick and stone buildings line the broad, tree-lined main
thoroughfare. Much of downtown is a designated National Historic
District. Restored and renovated landmarks house many shops
featuring antiques and collectibles, a few notable restaurants, and a
grand old landmark hotel. **Trolley Tours** (at 127 Ohio St.) offer
narrated hour-long trips around the historic district aboard 1900-style
trolleys. Horse-drawn carriages leave from the Lafayette Hotel for
romantic half-hour rides in the evening.

Fenton Art Glass   *(740)375-7772*
4 mi. S at 420 Caroline Av. - Williamstown, WV
Free forty-minute tours of the factory give visitors a chance to watch
master craftsmen blow and hand-form glass into artistic and functional
shapes. The glass museum displays heirlooms produced since its
beginning in 1905. The big factory outlet and gift store feature
complete selections of first-quality Fenton glass, plus factory seconds,
and world-wide glassware collectibles.

Marietta College   *(740)376-4643*
downtown at Putnam & Fourth Sts.
Chartered in 1835, this is one of the oldest colleges in Ohio. Enrollment
is about 1,200. The tranquil tree-shaded campus includes buildings on
the National Historic Register like Erwin Hall, with a clock tower that
has been a town landmark since 1850.

Mound Cemetery
downtown at Fifth & Scammel Sts.
The thirty-foot-high Conus Mound is a striking example of prehistoric
Moundbuilder's art. Nearby are the graves of 24 Revolutionary War
officers.

Muskingum Park   *(740)373-5178*
downtown between Front St. & Muskingum River
This delightfully strollable waterfront park includes some significant monuments. The "Memorial to the Start Westward" showcases a dramatic statue of three pioneers done in 1938 by Gutzon Borglum, who later sculpted Mount Rushmore. The "Civil War Monument" was erected in 1875 to honor more than 4,000 area soldiers. "Bicentennial Pavilion" is a center for community performances.

Ohio River Museum   *(740)373-3750   (800)860-0145*
downtown at 601 Front St.
The state museum honors the key role of the Ohio River in the development of a nation. While exhibits span three centuries, the Golden Age of Steamboats stars in a wealth of models and artifacts—including a full-sized calliope. Life on the river is presented in a half-hour video presentation. You can also go aboard the W.P. Snyder Jr. Moored by the museum, it is America's only remaining stern-wheeled steam towboat.

Wayne National Forest   *(740)373-9055*
just E & W via Hwy. 7
Rugged foothills of the Appalachian Mountains are covered with dense mixed forests of hardwoods and pine. Dogwoods in bloom in spring, and fall foliage are memorable. Several covered bridges lend to the area's charm. The Little Muskingum River offers canoeing and fishing. There are many miles of scenic hiking, riding and biking trails, plus primitive and developed campgrounds.

RESTAURANTS

Becky Thatcher Restaurant and Lounge   *(740)373-4130*
downtown at 237 Front St.
L-D.   *Moderate*
Prime rib and seafood top traditional American dishes served aboard a historic riverboat listed on the National Historic Register. Everyone can experience the ambiance of an authentic stern-wheeler in the casual dining room and lounge. Authentic showboat melodramas are presented in summer, and a musical revue each fall, in the theater.

Betsey Mills Club   *(740)373-3804*
downtown at 300 Fourth St.
L-D.   *Low*
Homestyle traditional American fare like chicken pies, stews, steaks and chops, plus cream pies for dessert, are served in the **Victorian Window Restaurant** amid casual Early American decor in a historic landmark.

First Settlement Square   *(740)373-8493*
downtown at 124 Putnam St.
B-L-D.   *Low*
Homemade ice cream stars among uncomplicated American dishes offered amid relaxed family atmosphere.

The Lafayette Hotel   *(740)373-5522*
downtown at 101 Front St.
B-L-D.   *Moderate*
The landmark's **Gun Room Restaurant** is the area's best known dining room. An extensive traditional American menu includes some treats like rum-battered french toast for breakfast and prime rib for dinner. Big dining areas and the lounge sport elaborate Gay 90s riverboat decor.

Levee House Cafe   *(740)374-2233*
downtown at 127 Ohio St.
B-L-D.   *Moderate*
Contemporary American meals are carefully, individually prepared.
Creative pasta dishes and desserts like chocolate chip-walnut pie are
especially notable. Diners can enjoy the comfortably restored interior
of an 1826 building, or a sidewalk cafe also overlooking the Ohio River.

Tally Ho   *(740)374-5228*
downtown at 211 Second St.
B-L-D.   *Moderate*
Charbroiled steaks top a varied menu in a casual dining room of a
complex that also features a pizza parlor and pub.

LODGING

Accommodations are relatively scarce and prosaic, with some
exceptions described below. Most rates remain the same year-round.

Best Western Marietta   *(740)374-7211*
2 mi. N at 279 Muskingum Dr. - 45750
47 units   *(800)528-1234*   *Moderate*
This modern motel is right on the Muskingum River. There is free boat
dockage, and (fee) water taxi to downtown. Fishing and waterskiing
are popular. Each unit is comfortably furnished.

The Buckley House   *(740)373-3080*
downtown at 332 Front St. - 45750
3 units   *Moderate*
A historic Victorian home has been converted into a bed-and-breakfast
inn with a peaceful garden with a gazebo and a whirlpool. There is a
river view from the two-tier front porch. Continental-plus breakfast is
complimentary. Each nicely furnished room has a private bath.

Comfort Inn   *(740)374-8190*
2 mi. E (near I-77) at 700 Pike St. - 45750
121 units   *(800)537-6858*   *Moderate*
This well-landscaped motel near the Ohio River was recently
remodeled. Amenities now include a restaurant, lounge, indoor pool,
whirlpool and exercise room. Each room is well furnished.

Holiday Inn   *(740)374-9660*
2 mi. E (near I-77) at 701 Pike St. - 45750
109 units   *Moderate*
Holiday's local contemporary motor hotel has a pool, wading pool,
dining room and lounge. Each room is comfortably furnished.

The Lafayette Hotel   *(740)373-5522*
downtown at 101 Front St. - 45750
78 units   *(800)331-9336; (800)331-9337 (OH)*   *Moderate-Expensive*
Marietta's best lodging is a classic riverboat era hotel. The five-story
brick hotel, on the National Register, was built in 1918 by the Ohio
River. There is a nostalgic dining room (see listing), a river-view
lounge, and a gift shop. Each of the recently renovated rooms is
comfortably furnished. Many have a river view. Some also have a
private view balcony.

BASIC INFORMATION

Elevation: 616 feet   *Population (1990):   15,026*
Location: 125 miles Southeast of Columbus
Nearest airport with commercial flights: local, 6 miles
Marietta/Washington County Convention & Visitors Bureau
  (740)373-5178   (800)288-2577
  downtown at 316 Third St. - 45750   www.rivertowns.org

Ashland, Oregon

Ashland is a great Western crossroads of culture and recreation. One of America's finest theatrical complexes and Shakespearean festivals, and a flourishing university, are driving forces. In a luxuriant mixed forest high on the southern rim of the Rogue River country, the town overlooks a broad pastoral valley surrounded by impressive peaks. A year after gold was discovered in nearby Jacksonville in 1851, Ashland was founded. It grew slowly until 1935, when success of a Shakespearean production led to a Festival Association.

Today, the Festival runs most of the year in a complex of three fine live theaters. Spectacular Lithia Park and the heart of town adjoin the Festival grounds. Many shops and galleries feature regional arts, crafts, and specialty foods. Fine restaurants are plentiful. One of America's greatest proliferations of bed-and-breakfast inns delight theater-goers, and outdoor enthusiasts here to enjoy nearby rivers, lakes, and mountains, and a mild four-season climate.

WEATHER PROFILE

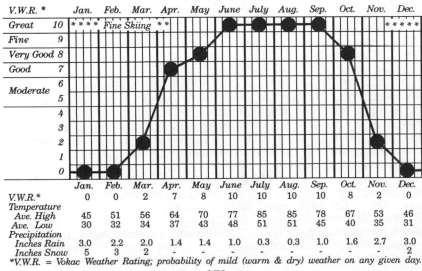

		Jan.	Feb.	Mar.	Apr.	May	June	July	Aug.	Sep.	Oct.	Nov.	Dec.
V.W.R.*		0	0	2	7	8	10	10	10	10	8	2	0
Temperature													
Ave. High		45	51	56	64	70	77	85	85	78	67	53	46
Ave. Low		30	32	34	37	43	48	51	51	45	40	35	31
Precipitation													
Inches Rain		3.0	2.2	2.0	1.4	1.4	1.0	0.3	0.3	1.0	1.6	2.7	3.0
Inches Snow		5	3	2	-	-	-	-	-	-	-	-	2

*V.W.R. = Vokac Weather Rating; probability of mild (warm & dry) weather on any given day.

Bicycling

Bicycles may be rented by the hour or longer to explore miles of separated bikeways and scenic byways in the lush, gentle valley.

Emigrant & Howard Prairie Lakes   *(541)776-7001; (541)482-1979*
5 mi. & 20 mi. E

These scenic nearby reservoirs offer swimming areas, plus boating (including rentals), water-skiing, and fishing. Both have shaded picnic areas and improved campgrounds.

Harry and David's   *(541)776-2277   (800)547-3033*
12 mi. N via I-5 & Barnett Rd. at 1314 Center Dr. - Medford

A Rogue Valley tradition since 1934 continues in a colorful market with luscious Comice (the famed "Royal Riviera") pears and other locally grown fruit. Northwestern gourmet products, crafts and clothing are also sold. Nearby is the packing plant and headquarters for the international distribution of gourmet food baskets and boxes next to **Jackson & Perkins'** multicolored rose test gardens.

Jacksonville   *(541)899-8118*
15 mi. NW via US 99 & OR 238

Gold was discovered here in 1851 in one of the state's first strikes. Many brick and stone buildings were constructed before the gold played out in the 1920s. The whole town is now a National Historic Landmark. Many well-preserved original buildings house specialty stores, galleries, and restaurants. The old County Courthouse (1884) is a museum displaying Oregon history. The **Peter Britt Music Festival** ((541)779-0847) and gardens are a short stroll up a hill. A brochure is available for a self-guided walking tour of town.

Lithia Park   *(541)488-5340*
downtown along Ashland Creek on Pioneer St.

One of the nation's grandest achievements among town parks borders the theater complex downtown and extends for more than a half mile along Ashland Creek. An enchanting forest shelters formal rose and rhododendron gardens, a landscaped pond with resident swans, meandering pathways, a band shell, tennis courts, imaginative play equipment, emerald-green lawns, playing fields, and secluded picnic sites. Drinking fountains on the adjacent plaza provide Lithium water from the nearby mountains. It *is* different.

Oregon Shakespeare Festival   *(541)482-4331*
downtown at 15 S. Pioneer St.

After more than sixty years, the Oregon Shakespeare Festival is world-famous. From February through October, the Tony Award-winning complex features major plays by the Bard and others in three splendid theaters. The outdoor Elizabethan Theatre, with a stage and auditorium inspired by the original Globe Theatre of Shakespeare's time, was recently given a multimillion dollar renovation and enhancement. Guided backstage tours let visitors see what goes on behind the scenes at the Festival's theaters. At the Exhibit Center, you can touch props, and try on costumes. The Tudor Guild Shop offers a wealth of gifts related to Elizabethan times and Ashland.

Rogue River National Forest   *(541)482-3333*
3 mi. SE on US 66 at 645 Washington St.

National Forest lands bordering Ashland and beyond have unlimited opportunities for hiking, fishing, boating, camping, and (in winter) alpine and cross-country skiing. The Ashland Ranger District Welcome Center has a large selection of trail guides, books and maps.

Southern Oregon University   *(541)552-6346*
1 mi. S at 1250 Siskiyou Blvd.
Chartered in 1926, this is the largest university in Southern Oregon.
Enrollment is about 4,300. Impressive buildings on tranquil, tree-shaded
grounds include a big recently-built student union, and two intimate
theaters presenting several plays for the public each academic year.
Wineries
  Ashland Vineyards *2 mi. E at 2775 E. Main St.*   *(800)503-9463*
  Valley View *23 mi. W at 1000 Upper Applegate Rd.*   *(800)781-9463*
  Weisinger's *4 mi. S at 3150 Siskiyou Blvd.*   *(800)551-9463*
These wineries are the best area producers of Northwestern wines.
Each has a stylish tasting area, wine and gift shop and tours.
Winter Sports
  Mt. Ashland Ski Area   *(541)482-2897*
  19 mi. SW via I-5 & Mt. Ashland Rd.
The vertical rise in 1,150 feet and the longest run is one mile.
Elevation at the top is 7,500 feet. There are four chairlifts. All essential
services, facilities, and rentals are available at the base for downhill
skiing. There is some food and drink at the base, but no lodgings. The
skiing season is late November into April.

RESTAURANTS

Back Porch BBQ   *(541)899-8821*
15 mi. NW via OR 99 & OR 238 at 605 N. 5th - Jacksonville
L-D.   *Moderate*
For authentic Texas barbeque, try Back Porch BBQ, where meats are
smoked on the premises and served with all the trimmings. The down-
home delight in a rustic setting also offers Tex-Mex dishes and
microbrewed beers.

Beasy's on the Creek   *(541)488-5009*
downtown at 51 Water St.
D only.   *Expensive*
Contemporary American dishes are served in a young restaurant in a
stylish setting enhanced by a fireplace and a fine view (shared by an
umbrella-shaded deck) overlooking the creek and mountains.

Bella Union Restaurant & Saloon   *(541)899-1770*
15 mi. NW via OR 238 at 170 W. California - Jacksonville
L-D.   *Moderate*
American comfort foods are served in colorful relaxed dining rooms, on
a vine-covered patio, and in a saloon with much-trod wooden
floorboards that evoke the building's Victorian heritage.

Chateaulin Restaurant   *(541)482-2264*
downtown at 50 E. Main St.
D only.   *Expensive*
Classical and creative French dishes star in Chateaulin, the region's
premier dinner house. Everything from full gourmet meals to light cafe
fare is expertly prepared with seasonally fresh ingredients. Housemade
desserts are exquisite, too. The polished wood-trimmed dining areas
and bar are inevitably crowded with theater-goers and others here to
enjoy sophisticated food and ambiance. A first-rate wine and gourmet
shop adjoins, complete with wine and cheese tasting daily.

The Firefly   *(541)488-3212*
downtown at 15 N. First St.
D only.   *Very Expensive*
The most assertively creative international cuisine in Southern Oregon
is the Firefly. Every dish is visually dramatic and engaging of every

sense. Cosmopolitan post-modern decor complements the adventurous culinary experience.

Hardware Cafe   *(541)482-0855*
  just E at 340 A St.
  B-L.   *Moderate*
Peerless pecan cinnamon rolls, orange bear claws, raspberry scones, and jalapeno cheddar bagels are among the wondrously creative and traditional pastries and breads made and displayed here. Enjoy them with coffee at a few tables, or to go, at this tucked-away tribute to morning delights.

Il Giardino Cucina Italiana   *(541)488-0816*
  downtown at 5 Granite St.
  D only.   *Expensive*
Ashland's favorite Italian restaurant serves consistently authentic Northern Italian cuisine in a casual little trattoria.

Jacksonville Inn   *(541)899-1900*   *(800)321-9344*
  15 mi. NW via OR 238 at 175 E. California St. - Jacksonville
  B-L-D.   *Expensive*
Acclaimed Continental cuisine has been served for many years amidst Victorian elegance in a romantic candlelit cellar or upstairs. The nostalgic Civil War-era building also houses a gourmet food and wine shop, and eight charming hotel rooms with Western antiques.

Monet Restaurant   *(541)482-1339*
  downtown at 36 S. Second St.
  L-D.   *Expensive*
Traditional gourmet French cuisine like steak au poivre share the menu with updates like roast pork tenderloin with a kiwi sauce, plus refined vegetarian dishes. In the posh, peaceful dining room, the mood is Monet. Outside, dine in Monet's garden.

Munchies   *(541)488-2967*
  downtown at 59 N. Main St.
  B-L-D.   *Moderate*
The desserts are delightful at Munchies. Displayed in cases by the entrance, pies, cakes and cookies are as good as they look. Breakfast pastries made here are also fine, along with scrambles and other casual American fare served in a congenial cellar.

New Sammy's Cowboy Bistro   *(541)535-2779*
  3 mi. N at 2210 S. Pacific Hwy. - Talent
  D only.   *Expensive*
The valley's most unusual dining experience features innovative American dishes expertly prepared and served in a quirky cottage where management has an attitude. The food has a major following.

Omar's   *(541)482-1281*
  1 mi. SE on US 99 at 1380 Siskiyou Blvd.
  L-D.   *Moderate*
In Ashland's oldest continuously operating restaurant and lounge, charbroiled steaks, fresh seafood and homemade desserts have been crowd-pleasers for more than half a century. The local landmark has two comfortable dining areas and a cozy lounge.

Primavera   *(541)488-1994*
  downtown at 241 Hargadine St.
  D only.   *Expensive*
Creative Northwest cuisine is expertly prepared using seasonal local and organic produce. Housemade desserts can be as dramatic as the artistic upscale decor. A romantic garden patio adjoins.

Standing Stone Brewing Company   *(541)482-2448*
downtown at 101 Oak St.
L-D.   *Moderate*
Ashland's first premium brew pub opened in 1997. Breads and desserts
made here are excellent, along with contemporary American fare.
Diners in the pub and back room have a great view of stainless-steel
kettles. Out back is a mountain-view dining deck.

The Winchester Country Inn   *(541)488-1115*
downtown at 35 S. Second St.
D only.   *Expensive*
Contemporary American cuisine is given careful attention in a long-
time favorite among Ashland's gourmet restaurants. Dinner guests in
the lavishly restored Victorian mansion look out on colorful flower
gardens from spring through fall.

LODGING

Lodgings are plentiful, including one of America's great concentrations
of premium bed-and-breakfasts. Nearby Medford is the source for
inexpensive lodgings. High season is late spring to early fall. Winter
prices are usually reduced at least 30%.

Bard's Inn - Best Western   *(541)482-0049*
downtown at 132 N. Main St. - 97520
89 units   *(800)528-1234*   *Moderate-Expensive*
Theaters are a stroll from this contemporary motel with a pool and
whirlpool. Each room is well furnished. Two have an in-room whirlpool.

Coolidge House   *(541)482-4721*
just N at 137 N. Main St. - 97520
6 units   *(800)655-5522*   *Moderate-Expensive*
A handsome Victorian home, on the National Historic Register, has
been skillfully transformed into a gracious bed-and-breakfast amid
colorful gardens. Full breakfast is complimentary. Each room is
beautifully furnished. Two also have a gas fireplace and whirlpool.

Country Willows Bed-and-Breakfast Inn   *(541)488-1590*
2 mi. SE at 1313 Clay St. - 97520
9 units   *(800)945-5697*   *Moderate-Expensive*
Country Willows Bed-and-Breakfast Inn is enchanting. A century-old
farmhouse, a cottage, and barn on a peaceful hillside share luxuriant
grounds with a view pool, whirlpool, and forest trails. Full gourmet
breakfast and bicycles are complimentary. Each beautifully furnished
room has a private bath, serene Northwest decor touches, and views.
The spacious "Sunrise" and "Pine Ridge" suites also have a gas
fireplace and posh baths with big tubs and showers.

Lithia Springs Inn   *(541)482-7128*
2 mi. N at 2165 W. Jackson Rd. - 97520
14 units   *(800)482-7128*   *Moderate-Expensive*
This gracious contemporary bed-and-breakfast inn is on colorfully
landscaped grounds that include a natural hot spring. Use of a
neighboring historic hot springs pool is complimentary to guests, along
with a full breakfast, beverages and cookies. Each room is individually
beautifully furnished including all contemporary conveniences. Almost
all feature an in-room two-person whirlpool with the added benefits of
mineral spring water.

Morical House Garden Inn   *(541)482-2254*
1 mi. N at 668 N. Main St. - 97520
7 units   *(800)208-0960*   *Expensive*
An 1880s farmhouse has been transformed into a stylish bed-and-

breakfast inn amid lawns and luxuriant gardens. Full breakfast and afternoon refreshments are complimentary. Each beautifully furnished room has a private bath and quality Victorian appointments. Two new garden rooms have a kitchenette, fireplace and a large whirlpool.

Mount Ashland Inn   *(541)482-8707*
 16 mi. S at 550 Mt. Ashland Rd. - 97520
 5 units   *(800)830-8707*   *Moderate-Expensive*
This handcrafted four-story log inn is nestled high in the pines a few miles from the Mt. Ashland Ski Area. Hearty breakfast and afternoon beverages are complimentary. Cedar log interiors, handicrafts, antiques, and mountain views distinguish each well-furnished room. There are no phones or TVs, but most rooms have a private bath. "Sky Lakes Suite" also has an in-room two-person whirlpool.

The Peerless Hotel   *(541)488-1082*
 just SE at 243 Fourth St. - 97520
 7 units   *(800)460-8758*   *Expensive*
A tiny hotel in the historic Railroad District has been lovingly restored. The inn, built in 1900, is now on the National Historic Register. Full breakfast in the new public dining room and use of bicycles are complimentary. Each room is beautifully furnished with an eclectic mixture of antiques and a private bath with a two-person shower or whirlpool, or dual clawfoot tubs.

Romeo Inn   *(541)488-0884*
 just S at 295 Idaho St. - 97520
 6 units   *(800)915-8899*   *Expensive*
A charming Cape Cod-style house is now a grand bed-and-breakfast inn set amid noble trees on an expansive lawn. Landscaped grounds also include a tranquil pool and whirlpool. A full breakfast is complimentary. Each spacious room is beautifully furnished with a blend of antiques and traditional decor. Three rooms have a fireplace. The "Stratford Suite" also has a kitchen and large whirlpool bath.

The Winchester Country Inn   *(541)488-1113*
 downtown at 35 S. Second St. - 97520
 18 units   *(800)972-4991*   *Expensive*
Spectacular gardens distinguish this bed-and-breakfast inn built around a restored Victorian on the National Register. There is an elegant restaurant (see listing) and a gift shop. A full breakfast is complimentary. Authentic period decor blends with contemporary conveniences in each beautifully furnished room. Several rooms have a private patio or balcony, gas fireplace, or large whirlpool bath.

Windmill's Ashland Hills Inn & Suites   *(541)482-8310*
 3 mi. SE on US 66 at 2525 Ashland St. - 97520
 230 units   *(800)547-4747*   *Moderate-Expensive*
Ashland's largest lodging is the area's only full-service resort hotel. Amenities of the contemporary three-story complex include a large pool and whirlpool in a landscaped courtyard, two tennis courts, jogging path, fitness room, bicycles, restaurant and lounge. Many of the spacious, well-furnished rooms have a private view balcony.

BASIC INFORMATION

Elevation: 1,951 feet   *Population (1990): 16,252*
Location: 268 miles South of Portland
Nearest airport with commercial flights: Medford, OR - 20 miles
Ashland Chamber of Commerce   *(541)482-3486*
 downtown at 110 E. Main St. (Box 1360) - 97520
Southern Oregon Reservation Center   *(541)488-1011   (800)547-8052*

Bandon, Oregon

Bandon is an inviting blend of natural grandeur and urbane renewal. The town extends to Pacific Ocean promontories that fall away to a smooth sandy beach accented by the West's most fanciful array of natural seagirt monoliths. At the base of sheltering bluffs by a tiny harbor along the Coquille River lies Old Town where settlement began shortly before the Civil War. Bandon survived devastating fires in 1914 and in 1936, but languished until the 1980s when it began to fulfill its destiny as a major leisure destination.

Today, the Coquille River waterfront and Old Town are more desirable than ever. A cheese factory, cranberry candy factory, and fresh seafood markets attest to interest in local gourmet foods. Studios, galleries, and myrtlewood factories reflect burgeoning interest in arts and crafts. Newer lodgings within a stroll of the historic district or the ocean serve crowds attracted in summer by the recreation and leisure appeal of the beaches and the river.

WEATHER PROFILE

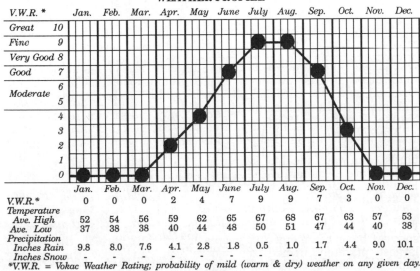

V.W.R.*		Jan.	Feb.	Mar.	Apr.	May	June	July	Aug.	Sep.	Oct.	Nov.	Dec.
V.W.R.*		0	0	0	2	4	7	9	9	7	3	0	0
Temperature													
Ave. High		52	54	56	59	62	65	67	68	67	63	57	53
Ave. Low		37	38	38	40	44	48	50	51	47	44	40	38
Precipitation													
Inches Rain		9.8	8.0	7.6	4.1	2.8	1.8	0.5	1.0	1.7	4.4	9.0	10.1
Inches Snow		-	-	-	-	-	-	-	-	-	-	-	-

*V.W.R. = Vokac Weather Rating; probability of mild (warm & dry) weather on any given day.

Bandon Beach State Park
for parts of 6 mi. along Beach Loop Dr.

Broad sandy beaches, Face Rock and a myriad other seagirt outcroppings, grassy headlands, and low sand dunes are enchanting attractions along this scenic byway. State park viewpoints, beach accesses, and picnic sites abound.

Bullards Beach State Park   *(541)347-2209*
3 mi. N via US 101

Miles of ocean beaches, low dunes, and a photogenic lighthouse on the tranquil north bank of the Coquille River by the ocean distinguish this park. Ocean and river fishing, beachcombing and dune hikes, picnic facilities and a first-rate campground are all popular.

Cape Blanco State Park   *(541)332-6774*
25 mi. S on US 101

Here is the most westerly park in the continental United States. It includes Oregon's highest lighthouse (250 feet above the sea), a campground, and a long section of near-wilderness beach.

Food Specialties

Bandon's Cheddar Cheese   *(541)347-2456*   *(800)548-8961*
downtown at 680 E. 2nd St.

Some of the West's finest cheddar (from mild to extra sharp) and jack cheeses are produced here. Samples are generously offered of each type of cheese. In the well-organized retail shop, visitors can taste, buy cheeses in various sizes, watch cheese being made through picture windows, or buy other Oregon food specialties.

Cranberry Sweets Co.   *(541)347-9475*
downtown at 1st St. / Chicago Av.

One of Oregon's most distinctive and delicious regional specialties is the cranberry-flavored candy produced here. Samples of many flavors (including the original favorite—cranberry nut) are offered, and sold along with Oregon food specialties.

Old Town   *(541)347-9616*
downtown at 2nd St. / Chicago Av.

The century-old heart of Bandon on a choice level site by the Coquille River near the ocean now offers arts and crafts shops, restaurants, night spots, lodgings, fishing charters, and sternwheel riverboat trips.

Shore Acres Arboretum   *(541)888-3732*
24 mi. N via US 101 & Beaver Hill Rd.

One of the Northwest's most beautiful public gardens is meticulously maintained by the state on estate grounds that include formal, Oriental, and rose gardens, plus rarities like bamboo and fan palms that attest to the "banana belt" micro-climate.

Sunset Bay State Park   *(541)888-4902*
23 mi. N via US 101 & W. Beaver Hill Rd.

A large cove with a curving fine-sand beach sheltered by forested bluffs, calm water ideal for swimming, and dramatic rock outcroppings offshore are elements of the quintessential Pacific Northwest scene. Facilities include picnic tables, a campground, and bathhouse.

West Coast Game Park   *(541)347-3106*
7 mi. S on US 101

For years, hundreds of free-roaming animals and birds (over seventy species) have been meeting people face-to-face here in the world's largest privately owned zoo where you can enjoy the exciting experience of both observing and touching wild animals.

RESTAURANTS

Bandon Boatworks   *(541)347-2111*
1 mi. W on S. Jetty Rd. at 275 Lincoln Av. SW
L-D.   *Moderate*
Fresh seafoods are featured, along with a salad bar and fresh bread. The little wood-toned upstairs dining room is comfortable, and has a panoramic view of the beach, harbor and lighthouse.

Bandon Fish Market   *(541)347-4282*
downtown at 249 1st St.
L-D.   *Moderate*
Their fresh seasonal fish and shellfish are all cooked to order. Locally caught, canned and smoked fish are also delicious. The thriving carryout features crab croissants, seafood cocktails, fish and chips, and chowder. There are picnic tables by the street.

Christophe's at Face Rock   *(541)347-3261*
3 mi. SW at 3225 Beach Loop Dr.
D only.   *Expensive*
Contemporary American fare is served in a light, bright split-level dining room with an atrium view of coastal surf across a highway.

Complements Coffee House   *(541)347-9440*
downtown at 160 2nd St.
B-L.   *Low*
Cranberry creations highlight an assortment of baked goods made and displayed here. They are served with light fare and assorted beverages in a country-style coffeehouse, or to take out.

Fraser's Restaurant & Lounge   *(541)347-3141*
just S on US 101
B-L-D.   *Low*
Old-fashioned American fare includes regional ice creams and cranberry pancakes served with brandied cranberry syrup in the comfortable cafe or the no-frills "Bandon mural" dining room.

Lord Bennett's Restaurant & Lounge   *(541)347-3663*
2 mi. SW at 1695 Beach Loop Rd.
L-D.   *Expensive*
Lord Bennett's is one of the Oregon coast's best restaurants. Fresh seafood stars in creative dishes like sauteed Dungeness crab legs with a Thai peanut sauce or petrale sole stuffed with shrimp. Housemade desserts are also delicious. The casually elegant upstairs dining room offers gorgeous views of the ocean from a blufftop site. There is also a snazzy lounge.

Minute Cafe   *(541)347-2707*
downtown at 145 N. 2nd St.
B-L-D.   *Low*
Minute Cafe serves the best breakfasts for many miles. Buttermilk or whole wheat pancakes with a choice of fruit in them, designer omelets, biscuits and gravy, and other American comfort foods are fresh and flavorful. Generous portions are another hallmark at all meals served in the cheerful little cafe with picnic-style dining in a garden patio.

The Wheelhouse   *(541)347-9331*
downtown at 125 Chicago St.
L-D.   *Moderate*
Oregon lamb, seafood, chicken and beef are served in generous portions. Diners in the nautical wood-trimmed dining room or in the upstairs pub have a view of fishing boats in the harbor across a street.

LODGING

Several distinctive lodgings have an ocean view. Summer is high season. Prices at other times may be as much as 30% lower.

Bandon Beach House   *(541)347-1196*
 3 mi. SW at 2866 Beach Loop Dr. - 97411
 2 units   *Expensive*
The Beach House is a delightful contemporary bed-and-breakfast on a bluff by a scenic ocean beach. Full breakfast is complimentary. The two spacious rooms are beautifully furnished. Each has a private bath, a fireplace, and a picture-window view of the surf below.

Gorman Motel   *(541)347-9451*
 1 mi. SW on Beach Loop Dr. at 1110 11th St. SW - 97411
 25 units   *Moderate*
Spectacular ocean views, access to a splendid beach, and a whirlpool distinguish this newer blufftop motel with comfortable rooms.

Harbor View Motel   *(541)347-4417*
 downtown at 355 US 101 (Box 1409) - 97411
 59 units   *(800)526-0209*   *Moderate*
This contemporary blufftop motel lives up to its name with a panoramic backdrop of the historic Old Town district just below, and the harbor beyond. There is a whirlpool. Each room is nicely furnished. Many have a small private balcony and a big harbor view.

The Inn at Face Rock   *(541)347-9441*
 3 mi. SW at 3225 Beach Loop Rd. - 97411
 55 units   *(800)638-3092*   *Moderate-Expensive*
Southern Oregon's only seaside resort is on a bluff across a highway from a superb ocean beach. A (fee) 9-hole golf course adjoins, and there is a whirlpool, Christophe's ocean-view restaurant (see listing), and lounge. Each spacious room is attractively furnished. Suites have a kitchenette, fireplace and private view deck. Five spacious, beautifully furnished "spa suites" also have a large in-room whirlpool.

Lighthouse Bed & Breakfast   *(541)347-9316*
 just W at 650 Jetty Rd. (Box 24) - 97411
 5 units   *Moderate-Expensive*
A contemporary residence on the river overlooking the lighthouse and ocean is the premier bed-and-breakfast inn in Bandon. It's a short walk to either the beach or Old Town after a complimentary gourmet breakfast. Each of the luxuriously furnished rooms has an ocean or river view and all contemporary amenities. The "Grey Whale Room" has a fireplace and a big whirlpool with an unforgettably romantic view.

Sunset Oceanfront Accommodations   *(541)347-2453*
 2 mi. SW at 1755 Beach Loop Rd. (Box 373) - 97411
 56 units   *(800)842-2407*   *Moderate-Expensive*
Some of the units in this motel/cabin/condo complex are built into a slope facing hauntingly beautiful rock monoliths along a sandy beach. Amenities include a whirlpool, sauna, and Lord Bennett's (see listing) adjacent restaurant. Well-furnished units range from motel rooms to romantic suites with private view decks, kitchens and fireplaces.

BASIC INFORMATION
Elevation: 60 feet   *Population (1990): 2,215*
Location: 230 miles Southwest of Portland
Nearest airport with commercial flights: Coos Bay, OR - 28 miles
Bandon Chamber of Commerce   (541)347-9616
  in Old Town at 2nd St. / Chicago Av. (Box 1515) - 97411
  www.harborside.com / Bandon

Bend, Oregon

Bend is the heart of one of America's finest year-round recreation wonderlands. Nearby, majestic glacier-clad peaks of the central Cascade Range tower over an evergreen forest. A seemingly endless assortment of crystal-clear lakes and streams grace the sylvan landscape. Bizarre remnants of recent volcanism also punctuate the unspoiled countryside. Bend was founded in 1900. A railroad and lumber milling sustained the town until recent years, when tourism transformed Bend into a burgeoning year-round recreation and leisure center.

Today, a bend of the Deschutes River is showcased in one of the West's loveliest parks. The center of town, only a block away, houses distinctive specialty shops and galleries, restaurants, lounges, and theaters in a compact district with a wealth of public improvements. Abundant lodgings in and around town, including some lavish resorts, serve visitors enjoying a remarkable diversity of outdoor recreation opportunities.

WEATHER PROFILE

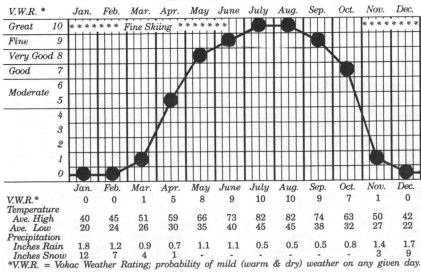

V.W.R.*	Jan.	Feb.	Mar.	Apr.	May	June	July	Aug.	Sep.	Oct.	Nov.	Dec.
V.W.R.*	0	0	1	5	8	9	10	10	9	7	1	0
Temperature												
Ave. High	40	45	51	59	66	73	82	82	74	63	50	42
Ave. Low	20	24	26	30	35	40	45	45	38	32	27	22
Precipitation												
Inches Rain	1.8	1.2	0.9	0.7	1.1	1.1	0.5	0.5	0.5	0.8	1.4	1.7
Inches Snow	12	7	4	1	-	-	-	-	-	-	3	9

*V.W.R. = Vokac Weather Rating; probability of mild (warm & dry) weather on any given day.

380

Bicycling

Scenic, relatively level terrain abounds in the pine forests around Bend. Miles of bicycle paths are available in town and at Sunriver Resort. Bicycles can be rented by the hour or longer in both places.

Cove Palisades State Park   *(541)546-3412*
39 mi. N off US 97

One of central Oregon's most popular parks borders the southern shore of Lake Chinook near the confluence of the Crooked and Deschutes Rivers. Volcanic cliffs tower above narrow watery fingers that stretch back to shaded campgrounds, picnic, fishing, and swimming areas, and a marina with rental boats.

Deschutes National Forest   *(541)388-5664*
S & W of town

This giant pine forest includes Century Drive—a 100-mile paved scenic loop past some of the Northwest's finest glacier-shrouded peaks and dozens of small, clear lakes; several notable volcanic areas; parts of the Mt. Jefferson, Mt. Washington, Three Sisters, and the Diamond Peak wilderness areas; and the state's biggest winter sports facility—the Mt. Bachelor Ski Area. A good system of paved and dirt roads is backed by hundreds of miles of trails including part of the Pacific Crest National Scenic Trail. Hiking, backpacking, horseback and pack trips, boating, fishing, swimming, river running, and camping are popular. All kinds of snow sports are enjoyed in winter. Information and maps can be obtained at the Supervisor's office in town.

Drake Park   *(541)389-7275*
downtown on Riverside Blvd.

Pine-shaded lawns slope to a placid stretch of the Deschutes River and frame splendid views of distant peaks. This is an enchanting place for a picnic near the heart of town. Canoeing is also popular. A half mile downstream is another picturesque haven, Pioneer Park, with shaded lawns, rock gardens, and flower beds by the river.

The High Desert Museum   *(541)382-4754*
7 mi. S on US 97

The cultural and natural history of the arid region of central and eastern Oregon is the focus of a substantial "living museum" opened in 1982. Among interactive features are "touch tables" and pioneer history demonstrations. Other buildings include a Forestry Learning Center where a tree's entire root system dangles dramatically overhead. Trails meandering through a forest pass streams full of trout, and wildlife exhibits including an otter pond with underwater and den-view areas.

Horseback Riding

Several area stables rent horses by the hour or longer. Some will also arrange extended pack trips into the national forest wilderness areas. For information and reservations, contact:

Inn of the 7th Mountain *7 mi. SW on Century Dr. Hwy.* 389-9458
Sunriver Resort   *16 mi. SW off US 97 - Sunriver*   593-6995
Metolius River Recreation Area   *(541)388-5664*
35 mi. NW: 31 mi. on US 20 & 4 mi. on (paved) Camp Sherman Rd.
The Metolius River abruptly appears out of the side of a pine-shaded hill near a well-marked parking lot/picnic area. It flows crystal-clear for a few miles and is one of the nation's most popular fly-fishing-only trout streams. Several cabin complexes, a campground, and a general store line the forested banks.

Newberry National Volcanic Monument   *(541)593-2421*
12 mi. S on US 97

The Lava Lands Visitor Center has automated displays, slide shows, and interpretive trails describing the remarkable geology of the area. Just north, a road winds to the top of Lava Butte, a cinder cone 500 feet high. At the top, an observation tower has panoramic views of the central Cascades. Across the highway, another paved road leads to lava river caves, where the highlight is a lava tunnel a mile long. Lanterns can be rented. There are also ice-filled caves. Two miles further south on US 97 is the eerie lava-cast forest, a fascinating collection of tree molds—or casts—which were formed when flowing molten lava surrounded and destroyed living trees 6,000 years ago. It can be viewed from a mile-long paved interpretive trail. Twenty-seven miles beyond is Newberry Crater. Within the caldera (giant crater) of this enormous volcano that collapsed upon itself are waterfalls, streams, and two pretty little lakes. Boat ramps and rentals, campgrounds, rustic resorts, and hiking trails have been provided. A magnificent panoramic view is enjoyed from the easily reached summit of Paulina Peak. One of the world's largest obsidian (volcanic glass) flows is accessed by a short interpretive trail.

River Running
Several river guide services in and near town offer two hour, all day, or longer rafting trips on the Deschutes River near town, and on nearby streams during the summer. All equipment and meals are provided for scenic, and whitewater, trips. For information and reservations, contact:

Cascade River Adventures   *(541)382-6277 (800)770-2161*
Fantastic Recreation Rentals   *(541)389-5640 (800)524-1918*
Sun Country Tours   *(541)382-6277 (800)770-2161*

Sisters
Sisters has always been a cute send-up of a wild Western town. Now it's becoming a real destination. **Sisters Bakery** is where the locals hang out and drink coffee with humongous donuts and other morning delights. **Sisters Brewing Company Restaurant & Pub** and **Hotel Sisters Restaurant & Saloon** are good bets for lunch or dinner. **Sisters Drug Company** offers wine tasting and has an Oregon products store. Nearby are several arts and crafts galleries to explore, and unique public sculptures.

Tumelo State Park   *(541)388-6055*
6 mi. NW on US 20

This park of shade trees, lawns, and (upstream) rock grottoes along the clear, gentle Deschutes River is an ideal locale for hiking, swimming, and fishing. Streamside picnic facilities and a complete campground are outstanding.

Winter Sports
Mt. Bachelor Ski Resort   *(541)382-2607*
22 mi. SW on Cascade Lakes Hwy.

With a chairlift to the mountain's 9,065-foot summit, the vertical rise in Oregon's biggest skiing complex is 3,100 feet and the longest run is two miles. There are ten chairlifts. All services, facilities, and rentals are available at the base for both downhill and cross-country skiing. Restaurant and lounge facilities have been provided at the area, but no lodgings. The skiing season is one of the longest in the West—from November through June.

RESTAURANTS
Alpenglow Cafe   *(541)383-7676*
downtown at 1040 NW Bond St.
B-L.   *Moderate*
Freshness reigns (they post a "freshness pledge") along with quality local ingredients like custom-smoked bacon. Their giant cinnamon rolls and luscious coffee cakes complement all sorts of contemporary Northwestern dishes in a cheerful wood-trimmed room with lots of regional art and greenery.

Broken Top Dining Room   *(541)383-8200*
2 mi. SW at 61999 Broken Top Dr.
L-D.   *Expensive*
Fresh regional ingredients are given expert attention for innovative American cuisine. The elegant dining room in the clubhouse of the Broken Top Golf Course is a showcase of fine regional decor. There is a spectacular mountain view beyond a lake and golf course from the dining rooms, deck and lounge.

Coho Grill   *(541)388-3909*   *(888)388-2646*
3 mi. SE at 61525 Fargo Lane
L-D.   *Expensive*
Contemporary Northwestern cuisine gets creative touches in dishes like wild rice banana cakes with mango salsa or roast pork tenderloin with peach chipotle marmalade. The comfortably upscale dining room overlooks a golf course and mountains.

Deschutes Brewery & Public House   *(541)382-9242*
downtown at 1044 NW Bond St.
L-D.   *Moderate*
Bend's first and finest brewery produces an array of handcrafted ales served with a goodly selection of pub grub favorites in wood-trimmed rooms in view of the brew process.

Giuseppe's Restaurant   *(541)389-8899*
downtown at 932 NW Bond St.
D only.   *Expensive*
Giuseppe's is a deservedly popular little trattoria with an appealing range of skillfully prepared Italian dishes including mozzarella bread sticks and hand-rolled pastas made fresh daily. Guests are served in a cheerful wood-and-plant-trimmed front room with a handsome hardwood bar or in cozy padded wood booths.

Goody's Soda Fountain   *(541)389-5185*
downtown at 957 NW Wall St.
L-D.   *Moderate*
One of the West's great soda fountains features assorted homemade ice creams and toppings (and even cones made here) in all sorts of dairy delights. Their chocolates are also displayed and served in the charming corner parlor with a classic old-fashioned soda fountain/bar and counters overlooking main street.

Honkers Restaurant   *(541)389-4665*
just S at 805 SW Industrial Way
L-D.   *Moderate*
Contemporary Northwest cuisine includes winners like assorted game dishes, cheesy twice-baked "gooey" potatoes or rum cake. You might see Canadian geese fly by riverside windows in the comfortable dining room and firelit lounge of a transformed sawmill.

McKenzie's Restaurant & Bar   *(541)388-3891*
downtown at 1033 NW Bond St.
D only.   *Moderate*
A varied menu of contemporary American fare ranges from pastas and pizzas to large sandwiches and steaks, plus a fine selection of premium microbrews on tap. A historic brick building houses the comfortable dark-wood dining room and bar enhanced by greenery.

Mexicali Rose   *(541)389-0149*
just E at 301 NE Franklin Av.
D only.   *Moderate*
Oregon's best Mexican restaurant offers skillfully prepared traditional dishes like fajitas, and creative Mexican cuisine like Dungeness crab enchiladas. The popular dinner house, ensconced in a historic lava rock building, has several relaxed, colorful dining rooms.

Pine Tavern Restaurant   *(541)382-5581*
downtown at 967 NW Brooks St.
L-D.   *Moderate*
In Bend's oldest restaurant (built in 1936), splendid sourdough scones are a unique introduction to fine Northwestern cuisine. Request the Garden Room where two giant living ponderosa pines highlight comfortably woodsy decor. Diners have an outstanding view of Drake Park and the river from inside or on the garden patio.

Rosette   *(541)383-2780*
downtown at 150 NW Oregon Av.
L-D.   *Expensive*
Distinctive Pacific Northwest dishes, and an assortment of desserts made here daily, are served in an intimate upscale dining room.

Scanlon's   *(541)382-8769*
3 mi. SW at 61615 Mt. Bachelor Dr.
L-D.   *Expensive*
An exhibition-style kitchen showcases creative Northwestern cuisine. Plants and wood trim enhance the upscale restaurant and bar.

Sunriver Resort   *(541)593-3740*
16 mi. SW via US 97 at Center Dr. - Sunriver
B-L-D.   *Expensive-Very Expensive*
The Meadows (B-L-D—Expensive) features updated Northwestern cuisine in the lodge's big, casually posh dining room with a golf course view. At **The Grille at Crosswater** (L-D—Very Expensive)(open only to guests of Sunriver Resort), innovative Northwestern cuisine can be extraordinary. The dining room is the epitome of elegant rusticity, and the picture-window view is memorable.

Toomie's Thai Cuisine   *(541)388-5590*
downtown at 119 NW Minnesota Av.
L-D.   *Moderate*
A wide range of authentic Thai dishes has made this young restaurant a popular destination for out-of-the-ordinary fare. Fresh flowers and live greenery enhance tasteful Thai decor.

Westside Bakery & Cafe   *(541)382-3426*
1 mi. W at 1005 NW Galveston Av.
B-L.   *Moderate*
The Westside is one of the finest bakery/coffee shops in the West. A vast array of decadent delights is displayed out front. These can be enjoyed with a delicious selection of egg scrambles, omelets, pancakes, waffles and other American breakfast classics in several casual dining areas decorated with all sorts of whimsical toys.

Lodgings are plentiful, including many low-cost motels along US 97 through town. Most of the area's finest accommodations are by the Deschutes River in or near town. Summer is high season. Many places reduce their rates 20% or more at other times.

Bend Riverside Motel   *(541)389-2363*
just N at 1565 NW Hall St.- 97701
  186 units   *(800)284-2363*   *Moderate-Expensive*
The scenic Deschutes River adjoins this contemporary motel complex next to lovely Pioneer Park. Landscaped grounds include a large indoor pool, whirlpool, saunas, and a tennis court. Each spacious room is attractively furnished. Several deluxe units have a kitchen, gas fireplace and a private deck with an enchanting falls/rapids view of the river.

Black Butte Ranch   *(541)595-6211*
30 mi. NW on US 20 (Box 8000) - Black Butte Ranch 97759
  100 units   *(800)452-7455*   *Moderate-Expensive*
A small spring-fed lake in a high country meadow, surrounded by a ponderosa pine forest backed by a trio of snow-capped peaks, is the site of a superb resort. Recreation facilities include a large pool by the lake (plus three others), whirlpools, saunas, hiking and jogging trails, a recreation center, and (for a fee) two scenic 18-hole golf courses, many tennis courts, bicycles, horseback riding and canoes. The handsome wood-toned lodge has a plush dining room and lounge with spectacular views. Units range from well-furnished lodge rooms to spacious beautifully furnished condominiums and private houses. All have a private view deck. Many have a kitchen and fireplace.

Inn & Suites of Bend - Best Western   *(541)382-1515*
just E at 721 NE 3rd St. - 97701
  102 units   *(800)528-1234*   *Moderate*
A pool and whirlpool are features in a contemporary motel where each room is well furnished and has a kitchenette. More spacious suites are also available. Some have a whirlpool bath.

Inn of the Seventh Mountain   *(541)382-8711*
7 mi. SW at 18575 SW Century Dr. - 97702
  260 units   *(800)452-6810*   *Moderate-Expensive*
Bend's largest lodging is a complete contemporary resort. The wood-trimmed hotel/condominium complex in a pine forest near the Deschutes River has hiking and jogging trails, two large pools, three whirlpools, sauna, four tennis courts, and (for a fee) an adjacent 18-hole golf course, whitewater rafting, horseback riding, hay rides, bicycles, and roller skating in summer, plus ice skating, sleigh rides and snowmobiling in winter. There are also dining rooms, a deli, lounge and resort store. Each unit (up to a three-bedroom condo) is attractively furnished. Many have a full kitchen, private mountain-view balcony and/or a gas fireplace.

Lara House Bed & Breakfast   *(541)388-4064*
just W at 640 NW Congress St. - 97701
  5 units   *(800)766-4064*   *Moderate*
Bend's first and finest bed-and-breakfast is in a stately turn-of-the-century home across a street from a lovely riverfront park. There is a whirlpool. Full breakfast is complimentary. Each well-furnished room is individually decorated and has a private bath.

Bend, Oregon
Mount Bachelor Village Resort   *(541)389-5900*
3 mi. SW at 19717 Mt. Bachelor Dr. - 97702
100 units   *(800)452-9846   Moderate-Very Expensive*
On a high bluff above the Deschutes River is a well-landscaped condominium resort with a pool; whirlpool; six tennis courts; walking, biking and jogging trails; a fine restaurant (see Scanlon's) and lounge. Each spacious, one- to three-bedroom condo is beautifully furnished and has a gas fireplace and a private view balcony. Some have a romantic river view from a large whirlpool on a private deck.

Pine Ridge Inn   *(541)389-6137*
2 mi. SW at 1200 SW Century Dr. - 97702
20 units   *(800)600-4095   Moderate-Very Expensive*
This quiet country inn has a choice setting on a bench above the Deschutes River. A full buffet breakfast and afternoon regional wines, beers and treats are complimentary. Each beautifully furnished room has a gas fireplace and a large private deck. Many have an outstanding river view and a large in-bath whirlpool.

The Riverhouse   *(541)389-3111*
1 mi. N at 3075 N. Hwy. 97 - 97701
220 units   *(800)547-3928*   *Moderate-Expensive*
The picturesque Deschutes River borders this contemporary three-story hotel. Amenities include two pools, one indoors; whirlpools, saunas, two tennis courts; exercise room, fishing, an adjacent (fee) 18-hole golf course; plus a view dining room and entertainment lounge. Each well-furnished room is spacious. Some (up to two-bedroom) have a kitchen and private river-view deck, while a few have a big in-room whirlpool.

Shilo Inn Suites Hotel   *(541)389-9600*
1 mi. N at 3105 O.B. Riley Rd. - 97701
151 units   *(800)222-2244*   *Moderate-Expensive*
One of Bend's best newer lodgings is a well-landscaped all-suites hotel by the Deschutes River. Amenities include two pools (one indoors), whirlpools, sauna, steam room, exercise room, restaurant and lounge. Breakfast buffet is free. Each well-furnished room has a mini-kitchen. There are many spacious river-view suites with a private balcony and a gas fireplace. Some units have a big in-room whirlpool.

Sunriver Resort   *(541)593-1000*
16 mi. SW via US 97 at 1 Center Dr. (Box 3609) - Sunriver 97707
426 units   *(800)547-3922   Expensive-Very Expensive*
One of the West's renowned resorts is in a meadow surrounded by a vast pine forest. Units ranging from hotel rooms to private homes have panoramic views of distant snow-capped peaks. A remarkable array of facilities includes pools, whirlpools, saunas, recreation rooms, hiking trails, marina and fishing on the Deschutes River, and (a fee for) championship golf (54 holes), miniature golf, tennis courts, racquetball courts, bicycles (many miles of scenic separated bikeways), horseback riding, and canoes. Gourmet dining (see listing) includes a grand view, and there are entertainment lounges and resort shops. Each spacious, beautifully furnished unit has a private view deck and fireplace. Some condos also have a whirlpool bath.

BASIC INFORMATION
Elevation: 3,623 feet   Population (1990): 20,469
Location: 157 miles Southeast of Portland, OR
Nearest airport with commercial flights: Redmond, OR - 14 miles
Bend Area Chamber of Commerce   (541)382-3221 (800)905-2363
2 mi. N at 63085 N. Hwy. 97 - 97701   www.bendchamber.org

Cannon Beach, Oregon

Cannon Beach is an artistic haven in an extraordinary coastal setting. Whitewashed and weathered-wood cottages and shops border miles of broad "singing sands" beaches backed by low dunes and Haystack Rock, one of the world's largest coastal monoliths. Inland, a natural amphitheater of sylvan hills extends in a graceful curve to a massive seaward headland. From the beginning shortly before the turn of the century, the local economy has served vacationers, plus increasing numbers of artists and craftsmen, attracted by the grand location.

Cannon Beach is still a village in which the artistry of residents is apparent everywhere—in subtleties of human-scaled architecture; abundant flowers and meticulous gardens; memorable public sculptures; and a perfectly-attuned playhouse offering year-round live entertainment. Numerous studios and galleries display first-rate local handicrafts and artwork. Restaurants are plentiful. Lodgings include many posh ocean-view rooms in facilities loaded with romantic amenities.

WEATHER PROFILE

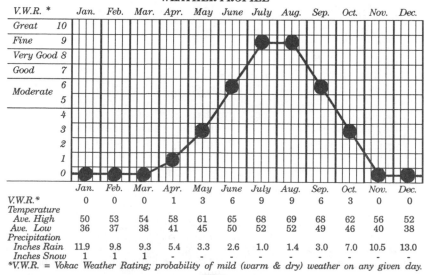

V.W.R. *		Jan.	Feb.	Mar.	Apr.	May	June	July	Aug.	Sep.	Oct.	Nov.	Dec.
Great	10												
Fine	9												
Very Good	8												
Good	7												
Moderate	6												
	5												

	Jan.	Feb.	Mar.	Apr.	May	June	July	Aug.	Sep.	Oct.	Nov.	Dec.
V.W.R.*	0	0	0	1	3	6	9	9	6	3	0	0
Temperature												
Ave. High	50	53	54	58	61	65	68	69	68	62	56	52
Ave. Low	36	37	38	41	45	50	52	52	49	46	40	38
Precipitation												
Inches Rain	11.9	9.8	9.3	5.4	3.3	2.6	1.0	1.4	3.0	7.0	10.5	13.0
Inches Snow	1	1	1	-	-	-	-	-	-	-	-	-

*V.W.R. = Vokac Weather Rating; probability of mild (warm & dry) weather on any given day.

Bicycling

Coastal highways and byways give bicyclists access to countryside that is relatively gentle and remarkably scenic. Bicycles or three-wheeled funcycles can be rented by the hour or longer at these shops.

Manzanita Fun Merchants *1 mi. S at 1160 S. Hemlock St.* *436-1880*
Mike's Bike Shop *downtown at 248 N. Spruce St.* *436-1266*

Cannon Beach
borders downtown on W side

One of the most idyllic beaches in the Northwest—or anywhere—forms the town's three-mile-long western boundary. Above the broad hard-sand beach, low dunes of dry and powdery "singing sands" provide a picturesque backdrop.

Ecola State Park *(503)436-2844*
1 mi. N via Ecola Park Rd.

This large park occupies most of the southern slopes of Tillamook Head—the massive promontory between Cannon Beach and Seaside. Several well-spaced picnic tables overlook magnificent coastline views from a pine-bordered highland meadow. Nearly six miles of protected coastline include two picturesque sandy beaches. Rock fishing, tide pool exploring, sunbathing, surfing, and kayaking are popular. Hiking trails lead to secluded coves, and to overlooks of sea lion and bird rookeries on offshore rocks.

Food Specialties

Blue Heron French Cheese Factory *(503)842-8281*
39 mi. S on US 101 - Tillamook

French-style brie cheese is produced, sold, and available for sampling here daily. A fine assortment of international cheeses is also featured, and samples are generously offered. Knudsen-Erath wines, jams, and other regional gourmet specialties are displayed, sampled and sold.

Tillamook Cheese Factory *(503)815-1300*   *(800)542-7290*
38 mi. S on US 101 - Tillamook

One of the world's largest cheese-processing plants produces the West's most renowned cheddar cheese. Visitors can watch through picture windows, and there is a video presentation. Samples of all of their cheeses are offered. An excellent regional food and gift shop, and a cafe featuring Tillamook dairy products, adjoin.

Haystack Rock
1 mi. S - just offshore

The third largest coastal monolith in the world rises 235 feet from the surf adjacent to Cannon Beach. Its natural scenic beauty is a major source of local pride. While the rookery and tidepools around the base of the rock are protected, observing the small marine life that abounds there is a favorite pastime.

Horseback Riding

Sea Ranch Stables *(503)436-2815*
just N on Beach Loop

Guided rides along the beach or into the mountains are offered daily from mid-May to mid-September.

Manzanita Area
15 mi. S on US 101 - Manzanita

Where a broad sandy beach several miles long abuts 1,800-foot Neahkahnie Mountain, the tiny village of Manzanita is developing as an artisan and recreation center. The main street includes good restaurants (see listings), galleries, a bookstore, and distinctive lodgings. Inland two miles, where US 101 crosses the tranquil Nehalem River, another appealing village caters to sportfishing. Nehalem Bay State Park, on a large sandspit between the river and the ocean, attracts fishermen and campers.

Oswald West State Park   *(800)551-6949*
   10 mi. S on US 101
This state park memorializes the farsighted governor who, in 1912, preserved all of Oregon's coastal beaches for the people. An outstanding walk-in campground one-quarter mile from the parking lot provides tent sites set in an old-growth coastal rain forest. A sheltered cove and tidepools are a short walk beyond.

RESTAURANTS

Bill's Tavern   *(503)436-2202*
   downtown at 172 S. Hemlock St.
   L-D.   *Moderate*
The village's favorite tavern reopened in late 1997 bigger and better than ever. They now serve their own premium brews (made out back) with an expanded selection of Northwestern comfort foods in a warm, fun setting.

Blue Sky Cafe   *(503)368-5712*
   15 mi. S via US 101 at 154 Laneda Av. - Manzanita
   D only.   *Expensive*
Seasonally fresh local harvest is featured in New Northwestern dishes, and desserts like cranberry ice cream. Colorful folk art, flowers and greenery enliven wood-trim dining rooms with a garden view.

Cafe de la Mer   *(503)436-1179*
   just S at 1287 S. Hemlock St.
   D only.   *Expensive*
Fresh regional seafoods are prepared simply and well, while support dishes like salmon pate and marionberry/chocolate pie suggest continuing innovative artistry in this long-established culinary haven. Full linen enhances cozy dining rooms.

Cannon Beach Bakery   *(503)436-2592*
   downtown at 144 N. Hemlock St.
   B-L.   *Moderate*
One of the Northwest's best bakeries is famous for its bread loaf in the shape of Haystack Rock, as well as outstanding cinnamon rolls and other pastries, cookies, and some unusual treats like Chinese Fruit pockets. It's all available with coffee at a few tables, or to go.

JP's at Cannon Beach   *(503)436-0908*
   just S at 1116 S. Hemlock St.
   L-D.   *Expensive*
A short well-thought-out selection of fresh fish, steaks and chicken is given creative Northwestern styling in an expo kitchen. The little dining room has the warm easy comfort of a San Francisco bistro, and the luscious desserts are all made here.

Lazy Susan Cafe   *(503)436-2816*
   downtown at 126 N. Hemlock St.
   B-L-D.   *Moderate*
The area's best breakfasts have been served here for years. Omelets featuring Tillamook cheese are expertly prepared, and there are specialties like oatmeal waffles and fresh seasonal fruit. Seating is on two levels in a handcrafted wood-toned dining room. Classical music and fresh bouquets of flowers further commend one of the most appealing restaurants on the Oregon coast.

Midtown Cafe   *(503)436-1016*
just. S at 1235 S. Hemlock St.
B-L.   *Expensive*
Imaginative contemporary fare is typified by buckwheat buttermilk
waffles with real maple syrup for breakfast, or flavorful burritos
anytime. The really casual little cafe is a local favorite.
Morris' Fireside Restaurant   *(503)436-2917*
downtown at 207 N. Hemlock St.
B-L-D.   *Expensive*
Traditional and innovative Northwestern dishes like pan-fried razor
clams with eggs, hash browns and biscuits, oat-bran pancakes and
Dungeness crab omelets have been served here for years. Warm wood
tones contribute to the charm of a hand-hewn log dining room with a
giant river-rock two-sided fireplace, lots of Northwestern art and
greenery, and an intimate downtown view.
Stephanie Inn   *(503)436-2221*
2 mi. S at 2740 S. Pacific St.
D only.   *Very Expensive*
By reservation, you can join guests at the luxurious inn for fixed-price
four-course dinners that showcase fresh seasonal ingredients with an
emphasis on the Northwest. The gourmet fare is presented in a room
that artistically conveys the nostalgic refinement of a New England
country inn.
Wayfarer Restaurant & Lounge   *(503)436-1108*
just S at 1190 Pacific Dr.
B-L-D.   *Expensive*
Contemporary American fare with an appropriate emphasis on
Northwestern dishes is served at all meals in the village's best
oceanfronting restaurant. Try to get a table near the large picture
windows for a magnificent view of Haystock Rock.

LODGING

Many romantic small resorts, inns and motels feature Northwestern
artistry and ocean views. There are also a few moderately priced non-
view motels on Hemlock St. High season is June through September.
Prices may be reduced 25% or more at other times.
Hallmark Resort   *(503)436-1566*
just S at 1400 S. Hemlock St. (Box 547) - 97110
132 units   *(800)345-5676*   *Expensive*
Hallmark Resort is one of the finest resort motels in the Northwest.
The complex, on a beachfront bluff overlooking Haystack Rock, has a
big indoor pool, whirlpool, sauna, and exercise room are housed in
contemporary woodcrafted buildings that favor the site. Stairs access
the "singing sands" beach and monolith. Each unit has beautiful
contemporary furnishings, a wood-burning fireplace, and a balcony
overlooking the ocean and Haystack Rock. Some suites also have a
large in-room whirlpool.
The Inn at Manzanita   *(503)368-6754*
15 mi. S via US 101 at 67 Laneda (Box 243) - Manzanita 97130
13 units   *Expensive*
One of the Oregon coast's most romantic inns is tucked away in a
peaceful village by the sea (see listing). The modern shingled inn is a
short stroll from miles of sandy beach. Each beautifully furnished
room has a refrigerator/wet bar and both a fireplace and an in-room
whirlpool. Some also have a skylight and view deck.

Lands End Motel   *(503)436-2264*
downtown at 263 W. 2nd St. (Box 475) - 97110
14 units   *(800)793-1477*   *Moderate-Expensive*
This contemporary beachfront motel has an outdoor whirlpool. Each well-furnished unit has a (pressed wood) fireplace and an ocean view.
Schooner's Cove   *(503)436-2300*
downtown at 188 N. Larch St. (Box 86) - 97110
30 units   *(800)843-0128*   *Moderate-Expensive*
One of Oregon's most handsome oceanfront motels is by the beach in the heart of town. There is a large surf-view whirlpool. All of the well-furnished studios and one-bedroom units have a kitchenette and gas fireplace. Most have a private deck with a grand beach and surf view.
Stephanie Inn   *(503)436-2221*
2 mi. S at 2740 S. Pacific St. (Box 219) - 97110
46 units   *(800)633-3466 Expensive-Very Expensive*
One of the Northwest's most elegant country inns opened in 1993 in a tranquil oceanfront site near Haystack Rock. A fine sandy beach stretches for miles in front of the wood-trimmed three-story building. A gourmet breakfast buffet and an afternoon wine gathering are complimentary. The plush dining room (see listing) offers four-course dinners by reservation. Each luxuriously furnished room has a gas fireplace, large in-bath whirlpool, and a private mountain- or ocean-view deck.
Surfsand Resort   *(503)436-2274*
just S at W end of Gower St. (Box 219) - 97110
82 units   *(800)547-6100 Expensive-Very Expensive*
In 1996, a three-story oceanfront building was added to this modern motor hotel. Amenities, in addition to direct access to a fine-sand beach near Haystack Rock, include a large indoor pool and whirlpool, plus an ocean-view restaurant and lounge. Each room is beautifully furnished. Eleven units on the top floor have a gas fireplace, private ocean-view deck, and two-person in-bath whirlpool.
Tolovana Inn   *(503)436-2211*
2 mi. S at 3400 S. Hemlock St. (Box 165) - Tolovana Park 97145
176 units   *(800)333-8890*   *Moderate-Expensive*
Wood-trim and shingles distinguish this large condo hotel. Amenities include a choice location on the beach, a big indoor pool, whirlpool, saunas, and a game room with table tennis and pool tables, plus an adjoining view restaurant and lounge. Each room is comfortably refurbished. Studios to two-bedroom units have a kitchen, gas fireplace, and a private deck (many with an ocean view).
The Waves   *(503)436-2205*
downtown at 188 W. 2nd St. (Box 3) - 97110
39 units   *(800)822-2468 Moderate-Very Expensive*
Artistically handcrafted newer units are especially memorable in the most romantic lodging on the beach next to the heart of town. Each room is beautifully furnished. Most have a kitchen, wood-burning fireplace, and a private ocean-view deck.

BASIC INFORMATION

Elevation: 20 feet   Population (1990): 1,221
Location: 80 miles Northwest of Portland
Nearest airport with commercial flights: Portland - 88 miles
Cannon Beach Chamber of Commerce   (503)436-2623
downtown at 207 N. Spruce (Box 64) - 97110

Florence, Oregon

Florence is the hub of the most diverse outdoor recreation wonderland in the Pacific Northwest. To the north, lush pine forests cover mountain slopes that rise precipitously from the sea. The lovely little Siuslaw River estuary adjoins the heart of town. Sand dunes along the far side of the river extend to Pacific Ocean beaches a mile to the west. Southward along the coast for more than forty miles are some of the world's most spectacular sand formations. Numerous small freshwater lakes with sandy or pine-forested shorelines are tucked into the surrounding countryside. The village grew slowly after settlement began during the 1870s.

Today, Oregon Dunes National Recreation Area, Siuslaw National Forest, and state parks protect a remarkable assortment of natural attractions, and provide unlimited recreation opportunities. Old Town is flourishing again with a large marina, river-view dining, nightlife, specialty shops, and lodgings.

WEATHER PROFILE

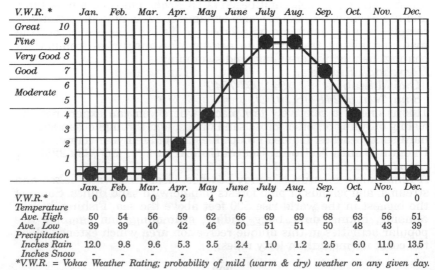

V.W.R. *		Jan.	Feb.	Mar.	Apr.	May	June	July	Aug.	Sep.	Oct.	Nov.	Dec.
Great	10												
Fine	9												
Very Good	8												
Good	7												
Moderate	6												
	5												
	4												
	3												
	2												
	1												
	0												

	Jan.	Feb.	Mar.	Apr.	May	June	July	Aug.	Sep.	Oct.	Nov.	Dec.
V.W.R.*	0	0	0	2	4	7	9	9	7	4	0	0
Temperature												
Ave. High	50	54	56	59	62	66	69	69	68	63	56	51
Ave. Low	39	39	40	42	46	50	51	51	50	48	43	39
Precipitation												
Inches Rain	12.0	9.8	9.6	5.3	3.5	2.4	1.0	1.2	2.5	6.0	11.0	13.5
Inches Snow	-	-	-	-	-	-	-	-	-	-	-	-

*V.W.R. = Vokac Weather Rating; probability of mild (warm & dry) weather on any given day.

ATTRACTIONS
Boating and Fishing Rentals
Boat rentals can be arranged for freshwater fishing and cruising near town to the south on Siltcoos and Woahink Lakes. For salmon and trout fishermen, there are marinas in Old Town and about three miles to the east with boat launch and moorage, plus boats and tackle for rent or sale year-round.
Dune Buggy Rentals
The most exhilarating way to explore the vast rolling seas of sand that border the ocean south of Florence is on an ATV dune buggy. Two nearby places rent these by the hour or longer.

Buggy Express   *4 mi. S on US 101*   *(541)997-5363*

Sandland Adventures *1 mi. S at 85366 US 101 S.* *(541)997-8087*
Dune Tours
Sand Dunes Frontier & Theme Park   *(541)997-3544*

4 mi. S at 83960 US 101

Balloon-tired open-air buses are used for approximately half-hour tours into some of the world's highest sand dunes at the heart of a vast sandy "frontier" that begins just south of Florence and continues for forty-one miles along the coast. The tour is a unique experience. Longer private tours can be arranged, or rent your own ATV. There is also a miniature golf course, trout fishing pond, game room and souvenir shop at this deservedly popular roadside attraction by the dunes.

Heceta Head Lighthouse

12 mi. N on US 101

High on a precipitous slope of a massive headland is one of the most photographed buildings in the West. The lighthouse (not open to the public) stands watch over a ruggedly beautiful section of the Oregon coast, as it has since 1894.

Honeyman State Park   *(541)997-3851*

3 mi. S at 84505 US 101

Tiny Cleawox Lake is the gem-like center of a peerless recreation wonderland. Picnic tables are well-spaced along a pine-shaded shoreline. In sharp contrast, a few hundred feet away on the other side of the small lake, enormous sand dunes plunge into crystal-clear waters. The clean, soft-sand beach is an idyllic place for sunbathing, and the fresh water lake is warm enough for swimming in summer. A complete campground in a pine forest amid the dunes is just south. A road and hiking trails lead to nearby Woahink Lake—popular for boating, fishing, water-skiing, and swimming.
Horseback Riding
C & M Stables   *(541)997-7540*

8 mi. N at 90241 US 101 N.

This is one of a relatively few places where you can experience the feeling of riding a horse across sand dunes, and through ocean surf on hard sand beaches. Guided group rides are offered year-round.

Oregon Dunes National Recreation Area   *(800)280-2267*

starts 1 mi. S on US 101

A remarkable mixture of sandy beaches, clear freshwater lakes and streams, and islands of pine forests mingle with sand dunes. Some of the biggest in the world rise 500 feet above the sea. Fishing, beach-combing, hiking, dune buggy riding, swimming, and camping are popular activities in this unique recreation area which extends along the coast for more than forty miles.

Sea Lion Caves   *(541)547-3111*
  11 mi. N at 91560 US 101
Here is the only year-round natural habitat for wild sea lions on the American mainland. A scenic walkway and an elevator take visitors down to the world's largest sea cave. The wave-carved grotto, more than three hundred feet long and one hundred feet high, is in the base of a cliff. Hundreds of sea lions can usually be seen from the viewing area, which is open during daylight hours all year. There is also a large gift shop and a dramatic life-sized bronze sculpture of the "Stellar Sea Lion Family."

Siltcoos Park   *(541)271-3611*
  8 mi. S via US 101 and park access road
This large coastal park provides trailheads for hikers, staging areas for ORVers, miles of dunes from the park northward, several campgrounds, and picnic areas in the dunes.

Siuslaw National Forest   *(541)547-3289*
  E, N and S of town
This is the only coastal national forest in the Northwest. Cape Perpetua Visitor Center (27 mi. S on US 101) offers a movie and exhibits about the Oregon Coast. Ten miles of scenic hiking trails branch out from the center into a lush rain forest, driftwood-strewn beaches, and rock-bound tidepool formations. The view from the top of Cape Perpetua (the highest point on the Oregon coast) is magnificent and accessible by car. Nearby are some fascinating rock and sea attractions—including Cook's Chasm where a natural blowhole in volcanic rock can send seawater forty feet in the air. Inland, luxuriant forests blanket Coast Range mountains that top out at nearly 4,000 feet above sea level.

South Jetty Dune and Beach   *(541)997-3426*
  1 mi. S on US 101
ORV staging areas, hiking trailheads, and sand dune and beach access parking lots are positioned along a six-mile paved road to the south jetty—where the Siuslaw River empties into the ocean. There are also shore fishing sites and a crabbing pier.

RESTAURANTS

BJ's Ice Cream   *(541)997-7286*
  Old Town at 1441 Bay St.
  L-D.   *Low*
Dozens of delicious flavors of ice creams made in a roadside parlor at 2930 Hwy. 101 N. can be enjoyed in assorted fountain treats in this cheerful shop in the heart of Old Town, or to go.

Blue Hen Cafe   *(541)997-3907*
  1 mi. N at 1675 Hwy. 101 N.
  B-L-D.   *Moderate*
The Blue Hen Cafe has the best breakfasts in town. They really know how to use a good egg. Hearty, all-American fare is served throughout the day, topped off by many tasty homemade desserts. Comfortable dining areas are also worth crowing about because of the bounty of blue chicken art objects.

Bridgewater Restaurant   *(541)997-9405*
  Old Town at 1297 Bay St.
  L-D.   *Moderate*
Seafoods star among contemporary American fare served in a restored historic building with nostalgic vintage decor and bric-a-brac.

International C-Food Market Restaurant   *(541)997-7978*
Old Town at 1498 Bay St.
L-D.   *Moderate*
Fresh regional seafoods are tastily transformed into a wealth of dishes
like popcorn shrimp, crab sandwich, pan-fried oysters, seafood pot pie
or sand dabs in white wine. The big casual dining room and sunny
deck adjoin their riverside fish-receiving station and the fishing fleet.

La Serre   *(541)547-3420*
24 mi. N on US 101 at 160 W. 2nd St. - Yachats
D only.   *Expensive*
First-rate fresh local seafood like clams baked in puff pastry, and a
creative spirit with herbs and sauces, are the hallmarks of one of the
Oregon Coast's foremost dinner houses. In the capacious atrium dining
room, a skylit jungle of healthy greenery surrounds diners at stylish
tables. A tranquil firelit lounge adjoins.

Lotus Seafood Palace   *(541)997-7168*
Old Town at 1150 Bay St.
L-D.   *Moderate*
Many Chinese and American seafoods are served in big, plain dining
rooms with a great view of a marina and sand dunes.

Mo's Restaurant   *(541)997-2185*
Old Town at 1436 Bay St.
L-D.   *Low*
The popular Oregon Coast chain is well represented locally. Fresh and
tasty, simply prepared seafood is served at long picnic tables in a big
dining room with a cannery-like setting especially appealing to
families. The bridge-and-river view is notable.

Windward Inn Restaurant   *(541)997-8243*
2 mi. N at 3757 Hwy. 101 N.
B-L-D.   *Moderate*
Windward Inn is Florence's most impressive roadside restaurant. With
a tradition going back to 1932, fresh local seafood and steaks are
carefully prepared, as are homebaked breads and desserts. One of the
comfortable wood-paneled dining rooms has a large fireplace, another
a skylight; all have fine forest views.

LODGING

There is an oceanfront hotel and several distinctive river-view
accommodations, plus standard motels along the highway. Apart from
summer high season, rates may be reduced 30% or more.

The Adobe   *(541)547-3141*
24 mi. N at 1555 Hwy. 101 (Box 219) - Yachats 97498
94 units   *(800)522-3623*   *Moderate-Expensive*
A basalt coastline borders spacious lawns of this contemporary hotel.
Facilities, in addition to shore access, include a whirlpool, sauna,
restaurant and lounge with spectacular ocean view, and a gift shop.
Most of the well-furnished rooms have fine surf views. Many have a
fireplace and/or a double whirlpool.

The Blue Heron Inn   *(541)997-4091*
3 mi. E at 6563 Hwy. 126 (Box 1122) - 97439
6 units   *(800)997-7780*   *Moderate-Expensive*
A panoramic view of the Siuslaw River is a feature of this
contemporary bed-and-breakfast. Gourmet breakfast is complimentary.
Each well-furnished room is individually themed, and has a private
bath and conveniences, except TV or phone. The "Bridal Suite" also has
a large in-room whirlpool.

Driftwood Shores   *(541)997-8263*
6 mi. NW via Rhododendron Dr. at 88416 First Av. - 97439
136 units   *(800)422-5091*   *Expensive*
Florence's only oceanfront lodging is also its largest motor hotel. The four-story complex includes a sandy beach, indoor pool, whirlpool, and an ocean-view restaurant and lounge. Each well-furnished room has a private deck with a fine oceanfront view. Many also have a kitchen.

Edwin K Bed & Breakfast   *(541)997-8360*
Old Town at 1155 Bay St. (Box 2687) - 97439
6 units   *(800)833-9465*   *Moderate-Expensive*
A handsome 1914 home across a street from the river was artistically restored. Full formal breakfast is complimentary. Each spacious, beautifully furnished room blends antiques and contemporary conveniences. Four also have a sensual bath (whirlpool, clawfoot tub, or double shower) and a view of the river and dunes, or a waterfall.

Ocean Haven   *(541)547-3583*
18 mi. N at 94770 Hwy. 101 - 97439
8 units   *Low-Moderate*
Perched by the highway in a meadow high above a rugged shoreline is an old lodge with a lot of character. Each simply furnished room has a fine sea view. Most have a kitchen. Two share a bath. The "Shag's Nest," a tiny studio cabin for lovers, has a new bath, kitchenette, fireplace, and glorious coastal views from three sides.

Overleaf Lodge   *(541)547-4880*
25 mi. N at 2055 Hwy. 101 N. (Box 291) - Yachats 97498
39 units   *(800)338-0507*   *Expensive*
One of the most sybaritic lodgings on the Oregon Coast is Overleaf Lodge. It opened in 1997 on a volcanic headland above the surf with convenient access to beaches. An extended Continental breakfast is complimentary. All rooms are beautifully furnished in contemporary Northwest style, and have a romantic surf view. Six suites also have a gas fireplace, plus a large in-room whirlpool and private deck with an ocean view.

Pier Point Inn - Best Western   *(541)997-7191*
just S at 85652 US 101 S. (Box 2235) - 97439
55 units   *(800)435-6736*   *Moderate*
This contemporary three-story motel on a bluff across the river from Old Town has two whirlpools and a sauna. Each well-furnished room has a private balcony and a river/town view.

River House Motel   *(541)997-3933*
Old Town at 1202 Bay St. - 97439
40 units   *Moderate*
Part of this 1989 motel on the Siuslaw River overlooks a nearby bridge and dunes, and there is a large view whirlpool. Each room is well furnished. Some have a private riverside balcony.

BASIC INFORMATION

Elevation: 25 feet   *Population (1990): 5,162*
Location: 160 miles Southwest of Portland
Nearest airport with commercial flights: Eugene - 60 miles
Florence Area Chamber of Commerce   (541)997-3128
   downtown at 270 US 101 (Box 26000) - 97439

Gold Beach, Oregon

Gold Beach is the Northwest's best source for freshwater and saltwater adventures in one place. It is ideally located on the flat little delta at the mouth of the famed Rogue River. The Coast Range rises abruptly to the east, while a fine sandy beach borders the Pacific Ocean to the west. With the warmest winter climate of any great town in the Pacific Northwest, freezes and snow are so scarce that a date palm flourishes in a valley near town. Gold first attracted miners to this site during the 1870s. However, it was the river that gave the remote settlement permanence. In 1895, mail boats began to provide postal service to isolated up-river settlers.

Hydro-jet boats take visitors on swift, thrilling whitewater trips into the beautiful Rogue River canyon these days. Salmon and steelhead fishing are the area's other passions. Shops and restaurants arc relatively rustic, while gracious ocean-view and riverside resorts serve multitudes drawn by the river and the sea.

WEATHER PROFILE

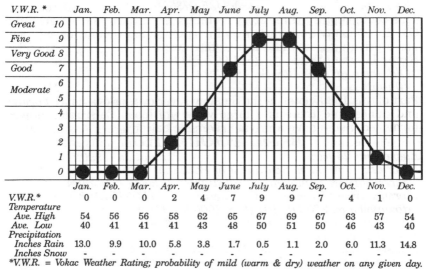

V.W.R. *		Jan.	Feb.	Mar.	Apr.	May	June	July	Aug.	Sep.	Oct.	Nov.	Dec.
Great	10												
Fine	9												
Very Good	8												
Good	7												
Moderate	6												
	5												
	4												
	3												
	2												
	1												
	0												

	Jan.	Feb.	Mar.	Apr.	May	June	July	Aug.	Sep.	Oct.	Nov.	Dec.
V.W.R.*	0	0	0	2	4	7	9	9	7	4	1	0
Temperature												
Ave. High	54	56	56	58	62	65	67	69	67	63	57	54
Ave. Low	40	41	41	41	43	48	50	51	50	46	43	40
Precipitation												
Inches Rain	13.0	9.9	10.0	5.8	3.8	1.7	0.5	1.1	2.0	6.0	11.3	14.8
Inches Snow	-	-	-	-	-	-	-	-	-	-	-	-

*V.W.R. = Vokac Weather Rating; probability of mild (warm & dry) weather on any given day.

Azalea Park
29 mi. S on US 101 - Brookings

Several kinds of mature Western azaleas grow here. The park is especially beautiful in late spring at peak bloom. You can enjoy the sight and fragrance while having a picnic at a table among the flowering bushes (many are over ten feet tall). A trail leads to a rock-lined observation structure.

Boat Rides

Whitewater jet boat rides are Gold Beach's most famous attraction. The Northwest's most exhilarating narrated cruises are offered by three companies with a choice of 64, 80, or 104-mile round trips up the magnificent Rogue River canyon daily from May through October. The shorter trip (approximately six hours) explores a scenic section of the lower Rogue and includes a meal break. Longer excursions go beyond to some thrilling whitewater. It's an all day (approximately eight hours) trip with a meal break at a wilderness lodge. Each company charges the same amount as the others, provides meals at the same up-river lodges, and leaves from near the bridge in town (their docks are well-marked).

Jerry's Rogue Jets	*(Box 1011)*	*247-4571*	*(800)451-3645*
Mail Boat Hydro Jet Trips	*(Box 1165)*	*247-7033*	*(800)458-3511*
Rogue River Reservations	*(Box 548)*	*247-6022*	*(800)525-2161*

Cape Sebastian State Park   *(541)469-2021*
6 mi. S on US 101

A steep paved road winds up to the crest of a precipitous headland more than 700 feet above the sea. From the parking lot, visitors have a panoramic view of the coast to the Rogue River and beyond. Well-marked trails lead to other spectacular overlooks along the crest of the cape. To the south is a "perfect" Northwestern scene—forested mountains tumbling down to broad sandy ocean beaches. Offshore, oddly shaped rocks and tiny islands are constantly battered by the pounding surf.

Fishing Charters   *(800)525-2334*
just N at Gold Beach Marina

Many charter boats operate daily for river and ocean salmon and steelhead fishing during summer and fall seasons. Guides are also readily available at other times for river fishing trips. You can get more information on who's available, and what's being caught, by calling the Gold Beach Chamber of Commerce.

Harris Beach State Park   *(541)469-2021*
27 mi. S on US 101 - Brookings

Here is a fine introduction to the Oregon coast—sandy beaches, rugged offshore rocks, pine forests, and luxuriant undergrowth. Beachcombing, and rock and surf fishing, are popular activities. There are nature trails, picnic areas, and a campground with all facilities in a luxuriant forest.

Horseback Riding

One hour (and longer) guided trail rides leave several times daily for horseback rides along a sandy beach near Pistol River or in mountains.

Hawk's Rest Ranch	*(541)247-6423*	*(800)525-2161*
Indian Creek Trail Rides	*(541)247-2050*	

Humbug Mountain State Park   *(541)332-6774*
21 mi. N on US 101

The state has developed a sylvan park along a creek at the base of a mountain towering 1,756 feet above the sea. Well-marked trails lead to the top of Humbug Mountain (three miles); along a scenic (two-plus miles) stretch of no-longer-used coastal highway; and for miles along a remote beach. Creek swimming and stream and ocean fishing are also popular; and there are excellent camping facilities in a sheltered little valley.

Loeb State Park   *(541)469-2021*
37 mi. S via US 101 & Northbank (Chetco River) Rd. - Brookings
One of the largest virgin stands of rare myrtle trees grows here, and a redwood grove is nearby. The clear water of the Chetco River delights swimmers and fishermen on warm summer days. Camping and picnic facilities have been provided.

Prehistoric Gardens   *(541)332-4463*
15 mi. N at 36848 US 101 - Port Orford
Here is an unusual tourist attraction that's surprisingly well done. Life-sized technically-correct replicas of prehistoric dinosaurs are situated along meandering paths in a coastal rain forest luxuriant with gigantic ferns and hanging moss. The gift shop is also notable.

Rogue River
The ruggedly beautiful Wild Rogue Wilderness lies in deep canyons upstream beyond roads and jet boats from Gold Beach. Access is only by raft from the Grants Pass side (see listing) or on foot. The Rogue River Trail is a well-marked pathway along the entire forty-mile wilderness stretch through an enchanting canyon. Spring is the quietest time—the weather is mild and wildflowers are at peak bloom. Summer is the most popular season—days are often hot, and the crystal-clear river is perfect for rafting, swimming, and fishing. As an unusual added feature, rustic riverside lodges are an easy hike a day apart along the entire trail. You can travel for days in the wilderness carrying only a light pack and enjoy hot showers, clean beds, and hearty meals by reserving these places well in advance. For more information, contact:

Half Moon Bar Lodge   *Box 455 (541)247-6968*
Paradise Lodge   *Box 456 (541)247-6022 (800)525-2161*

RESTAURANTS

Captain's Table   *(541)247-6308*
1 mi. S at 29251 S. Ellensburg Av. (US 101)
D only.   *Moderate*
All local seafood is either broiled or steamed—a nice change from the usual emphasis on frying. Steak and prime rib are also served in a relaxed setting with nautical antiques and a distant ocean view.

Grant's Pancake & Omelette House   *(541)247-7208*
1 mi. NE at 94682 Jerry's Flat Rd.
B-L.   *Moderate*
All kinds of pancakes, waffles and choose-your-own-combination omelets are served in hearty portions in a plain roadside cafe with a view (across a road) of the Rogue River valley.

Honeybear   *(541)247-2765*   *(800)822-4444*
9 mi. N via US 101 at 34161 Ophir Rd. - Ophir
D only.   *Low*
Authentic German fare, sausages, potato pancakes, sauerkraut, and more are generously served along with some American dishes. The big casual dining room in a campground achieves the warm appeal of a classic German beer hall when the talented owner, Gary Saks, provides the musical entertainment.

The Landing   *(541)247-5444*
1 mi. NE at 94749 Jerry's Flat Rd.
L-D.   *Moderate*
Contemporary American fare is offered in a long-established riverside
roadhouse. The big, recently improved dining room shares the area's
best window-wall view of the lower Rogue River with an adjoining
lounge.

Nor'Wester Seafood Restaurant   *(541)247-2333*
just N at Port of Gold Beach
D only.   *Expensive*
Fresh regional seafood stars—broiled, baked or sauteed, as well as
grilled or fried—in Gold Beach's best dinner house. Located upstairs,
the warmly contemporary split-level dining room includes a massive
raised-relief wood mural of two whales, a freestanding fireplace, and
a fine picture-window view of the mouth of the Rogue.

Rod 'n Reel   *(541)247-6823*   *(800)367-5687*
1 mi. N at 94321 Wedderburn Loop
B-L-D.   *Moderate*
A wide range of contemporary American dishes is presented on a
balanced menu. Several dining areas and a lounge have a comfortable
rusticity appropriate to Jot's Resort (see listing) by the Rogue River.

Soakers   *(541)247-6114*
downtown at 29844 Ellensburg Av. (US 101)
B-L-D.   *Moderate*
They make their own tasty pastries and light fare to go along with
gourmet coffee, teas and espresso served in a relaxed hideaway that
also features some books, regional art and distinctive gifts.

LODGING

Most of the area's best lodgings are a stroll from the ocean or river.
High season is from June through September. Prices are often reduced
30% or more at other times.

Gold Beach Resort   *(541)247-7066*
1 mi. S at 29232 Ellensburg Av. (US 101) - 97444
40 units   *(800)541-0947*   *Moderate*
Gold Beach Resort is the area's most elaborate oceanfront lodging. The
contemporary motel/condo has a private path to an unusual dark sand
beach, plus an indoor pool and whirlpool. Each spacious, well-furnished
room has a private ocean-view balcony. Condos also have a kitchen and
a fireplace in the living room.

Inn at Nesika Beach   *(541)247-6434*
6 mi. N at 33026 Nesika Rd. - 97444
4 units   *Moderate-Expensive*
One of the Southern Oregon Coast's most delightful bed-and-breakfasts
is a recently built Victorian-style home on a bluff above the Pacific
with beach access and a whirlpool. Full breakfast and afternoon treats
are complimentary. Each spacious room is beautifully furnished,
including period touches, a private bath with a two-person whirlpool
tub, an ocean view, and (in three rooms) a fireplace.

Inn of the Beachcomber - Best Western   *(541)247-6691*
1 mi. S at 29266 Ellensburg Av. (US 101) - 97444
49 units   *(800)528-1234*   *Moderate*
This contemporary motel has a paved path to a fine sandy beach, a
large indoor pool, and whirlpool. Many well-furnished rooms have an
ocean view. Two have a kitchenette, fireplace and private balcony.

Ireland's Rustic Lodges   *(541)247-7718*
1 mi. S at 29330 Ellensburg Av. (US 101) (Box 774) - 97444
40 units   Low-Moderate
Lovely pine-shaded lawns and colorful gardens surround individual log
cabins and modern motel rooms, and a trail extends to a picturesque
black-sand beach. Each room is comfortably furnished. Most have a
fireplace. Several also have a kitchenette and/or a private ocean-view
balcony.

Jot's Resort   *(541)247-6676*
1 mi. N at 94360 Wedderburn Loop (Box J) - 97444
140 units   *(800)367-5687*   Moderate
The South Coast's largest and most complete motor hotel is Jot's. The
contemporary complex sprawls along a choice site by the Rogue River
near the ocean. Amenities include two pools (one indoors), whirlpool,
sauna, dock and gift/tackle shop, restaurant (see Rod 'n Reel) and
lounge, plus rental bicycles, boats, fishing equipment and reservations
for (fee) river excursions and fishing charters. Each well-furnished
room has a private river-view balcony. Spacious one- or two-bedroom
condos also have a kitchen and fireplace.

Shore Cliff Inn   *(541)247-7091*
1 mi. S at 29346 Ellensburg Av. (US 101) - 97444
38 units   Moderate
This modern motel has easy access to a fine-grained, dark-sand beach.
Each room is comfortably furnished. Some have a private ocean-view
balcony.

Tu Tu Tun Lodge   *(541)247-6664*
7 mi. NE at 96550 North Bank Rogue Hwy. - 97444
20 units   *(800)864-6357*   Expensive
Tun Tu Tun is the most gracious lodge on the Rogue River. Beautifully
landscaped grounds surrounding the contemporary wood-trimmed
complex include a lap pool with a view, pitch and putt course, boat
dock and ramp, scenic hiking trails and fishing holes, gift shop, plus
(fee) guided salmon fishing and excursion boat trips. A gourmet river-
view restaurant and bar are available to guests (non-guests by
reservation). Each room is a study in understated elegance, with fresh
flowers instead of TV, and a private patio or balcony overlooking the
picturesque river valley. Some rooms have a large private soaking tub
on the deck.

BASIC INFORMATION

Elevation: 50 feet   *Population (1990): 1,546*
Location: 290 miles Southwest of Portland
Nearest airport with commercial flights: Coos Bay - 80 miles
Gold Beach Chamber of Commerce (541)247-7526 (800)525-2334
   1 mi. S at 29279 Ellensburg Av. #3 - 97444
   www.goldbeach.org

Grants Pass, Oregon

Grants Pass is the West's ultimate river town. The Rogue River is calm and clear as it flows past the heart of town. A few miles upstream, several small dams have created scenic lakes. Downstream, the river dashes wildly down breathtaking gorges and meanders through forested vales. After the first discovery of gold in Oregon in nearby Jacksonville in 1851, and the last major Indian battle in 1854, a settlement began to develop here with a diversified economy.

While wood products and farming are still important, residents' pride in their river is the town's binding force today. Sharing the Rogue with visitors has become a major industry. Guide and rental services now offer jet boats, inflatable kayaks and sailboards, plus old favorites like fishing boats and whitewater rafts. One of the West's finest riverside parks is near an unpretentious downtown with a notable historic district. Many restaurants and lodgings serve crowds enjoying the peerless river and mild four-season climate.

WEATHER PROFILE

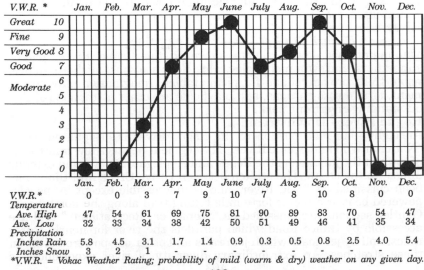

V.W.R. *		Jan.	Feb.	Mar.	Apr.	May	June	July	Aug.	Sep.	Oct.	Nov.	Dec.
Great	10												
Fine	9												
Very Good	8												
Good	7												
Moderate	6												
	5												
	4												
	3												
	2												
	1												
	0												

	Jan.	Feb.	Mar.	Apr.	May	June	July	Aug.	Sep.	Oct.	Nov.	Dec.
V.W.R.*	0	0	3	7	9	10	7	8	10	8	0	0
Temperature												
Ave. High	47	54	61	69	75	81	90	89	83	70	54	47
Ave. Low	32	33	34	38	42	50	51	49	46	41	35	34
Precipitation												
Inches Rain	5.8	4.5	3.1	1.7	1.4	0.9	0.3	0.5	0.8	2.5	4.0	5.4
Inches Snow	3	2	1	-	-	-	-	-	-	-	-	-

*V.W.R. = Vokac Weather Rating; probability of mild (warm & dry) weather on any given day.

Boat Rides

An exciting and popular way to enjoy the spectacular Rogue River in summer is via jet boat. Narrated excursions involve some whitewater and range from two to five hours for the round trip to Hellgate Canyon. Some trips include a champagne brunch or country dinner by the river. For more information and reservations, contact:

Hellgate Jetboat Excursions *966 SW 6th St. 479-7204(800)648-4874*

Crater Lake National Park   *(541)594-2511*

80 mi. NE via I-5 & OR 234 on OR 62

Oregon's only national park has as its centerpiece Crater Lake. The clear, brilliant blue waters of this magnificent mountain-rimmed lake are 1,932 feet deep—America's deepest. The renowned six-by-five-mile water body was formed when rain and snow filled what was left of volcanic Mount Mazama more than 6,000 years ago after violent eruptions collapsed the mountaintop. A breathtakingly beautiful thirty-two-mile rim drive around the lake doesn't open until approximately the 4th of July except in years of light snowfall. The highway (OR 62) is kept open to Rim Village year-round, in spite of normal winter snowfall of fifty feet. Boat tours leave daily to Wizard Island, a symmetrical cinder cone that rises about 760 feet above the lake's surface. Scenic panoramas and fields of wildflowers line spur roads and trails that extend from many points along the rim drive.

Hellgate

14 mi. NW on Galice Rd.

The Rogue River's phenomenal entrance into the Coast Range is a narrow passage with sheer volcanic rock walls more than 250 feet high. It is an especially popular section for river trips. Far above, a vertiginous viewpoint is by the road that parallels the river.

Oregon Caves National Monument   *(541)592-3400*

49 mi. SW via US 190 on US 46 - Cave Junction

Visitors can explore many dramatic and beautiful chambers in the "Marble Halls of Oregon." Guide service is required and available year-round for strenuous cave tours. Visitors should have a jacket since the average temperature is only 42°F, and non-slip walking shoes. There are hiking trails and picnic and camping facilities nearby in the lush mountain forest.

Riverside Park

just S on E. Park St.

Well-maintained lawns sloping down to the Rogue River delight sunbathers, and swimmers enjoy calm, clear pools just offshore. Above, noble trees provide shade for picnic tables. Imaginative play equipment, formal rose gardens, and playfields are other attractions of this outstanding riverfront park.

Rogue River - Downstream

An eighty-four-mile portion of the Rogue River is designated as a "National Wild and Scenic River." The segment begins a few miles west of town at the junction of the Rogue and Applegate Rivers, and extends almost to the ocean. The stretch between Grave Creek and Illahe has been classified as "Wild River" and is inaccessible except by people-powered boat or a scenic forty-mile hiking trail along the north bank. Gentler sections are classified as "Scenic" or "Recreational," and are accessible by Galice Road which parallels the river for nearly thirty miles, and by jet boats which join rafts and other oar-powered craft on these stretches. An extraordinary diversity of river experiences is available. Guided scenic, whitewater, or fishing trips varying from a half day to several days can be arranged in crafts ranging from jet boats to individual inflatable kayaks. Do-it-yourself rental kayaks or rafts, and shuttle services, are also available. Visitors bringing their own raft can easily arrange to be left off and picked up at prearranged spots. Several rustic lodges and picturesque campgrounds are scattered along the river. Excellent maps, books, and complete lists of guide services can be obtained at the Chamber of Commerce. Some of the best local outfitters are:

Briggs Rogue River Guide Service *(541)479-8058 (800)845-5091*
The Galice Resort *(541)476-3818*
Orange Torpedo Trips *(541)479-5061 (800)635-2925*
Rogue Wilderness *(541)479-9559 (800)336-1647*
Sundance Expeditions *(541)479-8508*

Rogue River - Upstream
east of town
Several small scenic reservoirs upstream from Grants Pass are popular for speed boating, waterskiing and most watercraft. Areas for picnicking, sunbathing, swimming and fishing abound. Riverside campgrounds, lodges, and motels are also numerous along the Rogue River Highway (OR 99) which parallels the river east of town.

Siskiyou National Forest *(541)471-6500*
S & W of town
This vast forest includes most of the southwestern corner of Oregon. The only redwood trees outside of California are an unusual feature. The Kalmiopsis Wilderness Area is a botanist's paradise of rare plants. Nearly half of the designated National Wild and Scenic River portion of the Rogue River is in the forest, as is Oregon Caves National Monument. A good system of roads and hundreds of miles of trails provide access for river running, swimming, fishing, hiking, backpacking, horseback riding, and camping. Information and maps can be obtained at the Forest Supervisor's office in town.

RESTAURANTS

The Bistro *(541)479-3412*
1 mi. N at 1214 NW 6th St.
L-D. Low
The Bistro has all the right stuff for the best hand-thrown pizzas in Southern Oregon. White or whole wheat dough is made fresh several times daily, and pizzas with a wide choice of fresh toppings are baked on traditional fire bricks. Comfortable booths or chairs fill a parlor decorated with old movie star posters.

The Brewery *(541)479-9850*
downtown at 509 SW G St.
L-D. Moderate
Classic American fare can be accompanied by assorted premium tap beers in the nostalgic brick-lined dining rooms and saloon of a turn-of-the-century brewery.

Hamilton House *(541)479-3938*
1 mi. E at 344 NE Terry Lane
D only. Moderate
Skillfully prepared American entrees always include seasonally fresh seafood as well as assorted steaks, chops and poultry. Delicious desserts like chocolate peanut butter pie are homemade. In this local favorite among dinner houses, handsome dining rooms have peaceful garden views.

Laughing Clam   *(541)479-1110*
downtown at 121 SW G St.
L-D.
                                                            Moderate
Beer-batter fish 'n chips (or prawns) star among first-rate pub grub
served in a restored historic building with a well-worn wood floor and
a polished wood-trim interior enhanced by a dramatic backbar.

Legrand's   *(541)471-1554*
just N at 323 NE E St.
D only.
                                                            Moderate
French and Continental dishes are given expert attention in this
sophisticated addition to the local culinary scene. Delectable baked
goods and desserts are all made here and served to go, or with
delicious entrees in intimate dining rooms with a European flair.

Pongsri's Thai Cuisine   *(541)479-1345*
1 mi. N at 1571 NE 6th St.
L-D.
                                                            Low
Thai creations prepared at Pongsri's are flavorful and authentic—so
starred items will be too hot for most palates. Don't miss their pork
satay with homemade peanut sauce (sold by the pint). Cozy, colorful
dining areas are an easy backdrop to the culinary delights of this
deservedly popular restaurant.

Powderhorn Cafe   *(541)479-9403*
downtown at 321 NE 6th St.
B-L.
                                                            Low
For hearty American-style home-cooked breakfasts, this is the place.
But, there is more. The really big cinnamon rolls are fine and desserts
on display like black bottom or peanut butter pie can be outstanding.
The cheerful, no-frills cafe has developed a loyal local following.

Wild River Brewing & Pizza Company   *(541)471-7487*
1 mi. E at 595 NE E St.
L-D.
                                                            Low
Delicious wood-fired hand-thrown pizzas and calzone star in the
flagship of a Southern Oregon chain. A wide selection of carefully made
pub grub features their fine Bohemian-style brew in several dishes.
Seasonal fruit cobbler and other luscious desserts and flavorful breads
are also made here and served in several warm relaxed dining areas.

Yankee Pot Roast   *(541)476-0551*
just N at 720 NW 6th St.
D only.
                                                            Moderate
Traditional American classics are all served with a giant biscuit freshly
made out front. Waitresses costumed in granny gowns blend smoothly
amidst nostalgic decor in several pleasant dining rooms of a turn-of-
the-century landmark house.

LODGING

Several of the best area lodgings are near the river. Moderately priced
contemporary motels are plentiful on the main roads into town. May
through September is high season. Rates may be at least 20% less at
other times.

Del Rogue Motel   *(541)479-2111*
3 mi. E at 2600 Rogue Valley Hwy. - 97526
15 units
                                                            Low-Moderate
Luxuriant rhododendrons and colorful gardens accent this beautifully
landscaped little motel in a delightfully tree-shaded location by the
river. Each well-furnished unit has a large, private screened porch.
Most overlook the tranquil Rogue. A kitchen can be added.

Morrison's Rogue River Lodge   *(541)476-3825*
17 mi. NW at 8500 Galice Rd. - Merlin 97532
13 units   *(800)826-1963*   *Expensive*

A sylvan bend of the Rogue River is an ideal site for this popular ranch-style lodge-and-cabins complex. There's boating, fishing, swimming, gold panning and rock hounding in the river, a pool, whirlpool, two tennis courts, putting green, gift shop and a family-style river-view dining room and deck. (Full breakfast and four-course dinner are included in lodging price.) Each room is comfortably furnished with all modern conveniences. Cottages also have a fireplace.

Paradise Resort   *(541)479-4333*
8 mi. NW via I-5 (Merlin exit) at 7000 Monument Dr. - 97526
17 units   *Moderate*

This resort is in a delightful ranch setting overlooking the Coast Range. Manicured grounds include a large pool and whirlpool, two tennis courts, a 9-hole golf course, boating and fishing ponds, and hiking and biking trails. The Black Swan Restaurant (D only —Moderate) serves contemporary American fare in a lovely plush dining room with tranquil pond/mountain views on three sides. Each well-furnished room (no phone or TV) has a private bath.

Riverside Inn   *(541)476-6873*
just S at 971 SE 6th St. - 97526
174 units   *(800)334-4567*   *Moderate-Expensive*

The best riverfront location in town (across from the beautiful town park) is the site for the area's largest motor hotel. Facilities include two pools (one overlooking the river), two whirlpools, jet boat trip dock, gift shop, and a big upscale river-view restaurant and lounge. Most of the well-furnished rooms have a large private balcony overlooking the river. Several units also have a gas fireplace. Best of all are two recently added suites with a large river-view whirlpool.

Weasku Inn   *(541)471-8000*
6 mi. E at 5560 Rogue River Hwy. - 97527
16 units   *(800)493-2758*   *Expensive-Very Expensive*

A historic lodgepole pine fishing lodge in the woods by the Rogue River was restored and enhanced in 1997. An expanded Continental breakfast and afternoon wine and cheese are complimentary. All of the units are beautifully furnished with knotty-pine decor and all contemporary conveniences. Some rooms in the new cabins overlook the river and have a gas fireplace, large whirlpool bath, and private deck.

Wolf Creek Inn   *(541)866-2474*
20 mi. N on I-5 at 100 Front St. - Wolf Creek 97497
8 units   *Moderate*

An authentic pre-Civil War stagecoach stop has been painstakingly restored and furnished in period pieces. Operated by the state, the large wood-frame building houses a nostalgic dining room and parlor. Upstairs, little simply furnished rooms evoke a rustic yesteryear, but they do have modern plumbing.

BASIC INFORMATION
Elevation: 950 feet   *Population (1990): 17,503*
Location: 240 miles South of Portland, OR
Nearest airport with commercial flights: Medford - 28 miles
Grants Pass Visitors & Convention Bureau (541)476-5510 (800)547-5927
* 1 mi. N at 1995 NW Vine St. (by Morgan & 6th) (Box 1787) - 97528*
www.grantspass.com/vcb

Newport, Oregon

Newport is the keystone of the Pacific Northwest coast. The town covers a favored site bordered by broad sandy Pacific beaches and a calm harbor sheltered by bluffs near the Yaquina River mouth. Seafaring activities have always been the compelling attraction of Newport, named after the Rhode Island resort in the 1880s. During the Depression, the magnificent Yaquina Bay bridge was completed, opening the entire Oregon coast to tourism.

Today, in the shadow of the bridge, the compact bayfront district known as Old Town still is the real heart of Newport. An exhilarating hodgepodge of regional arts and crafts galleries, specialty shops, restaurants and bars share refurbished Victorian buildings amidst unpretentious canneries, seafood markets, and other maritime businesses. Visitors can opt to stay at plush bay or oceanfront lodgings while exploring Old Town, the Oregon Coast Aquarium and diverse recreation on the bay, beaches, ocean and Coast Range mountains.

WEATHER PROFILE

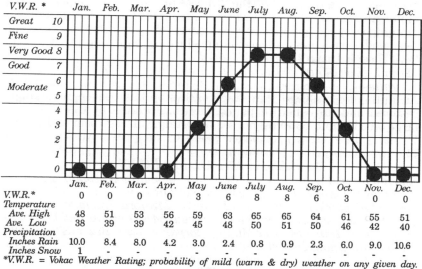

		Jan.	Feb.	Mar.	Apr.	May	June	July	Aug.	Sep.	Oct.	Nov.	Dec.
V.W.R.*		0	0	0	0	3	6	8	8	6	3	0	0
Temperature													
Ave. High		48	51	53	56	59	63	65	65	64	61	55	51
Ave. Low		38	39	39	42	45	48	50	51	50	46	42	40
Precipitation													
Inches Rain		10.0	8.4	8.0	4.2	3.0	2.4	0.8	0.9	2.3	6.0	9.0	10.6
Inches Snow		1	-	-	-	-	-	-	-	-	-	-	-

*V.W.R. = Vokac Weather Rating; probability of mild (warm & dry) weather on any given day.

Boat Rentals
Embarcadero Dock   *just E at 1000 SE Bay Blvd.* (541)265-5435
For many years, Embarcadero Dock has been the reliable place to go for boats and gear rented by the hour or day.
Depoe Bay   *(541)765-2889*
14 mi. N on US 101
An appealing village has grown up around a tiny rock-bound harbor that may be the nation's smallest. A sea wall promenade and bridge overlook sportfishing and pleasure boats negotiating the remarkably narrow channel between the harbor and the sea. Just west of the promenade are "sprouting horns"—natural rock formations throwing geyserlike sprays of surf high in the air. Various sightseeing and deep sea fishing trips depart from the north wharf.

Devil's Punch Bowl State Park
8 mi. N on US 101
A huge bowl-shaped rock formation fills from below with a roar at high tide. Scenic picnic sites, a long curve of clean sandy beach, tidepools, and ocean-carved caves are other features of this unusual day use park.

Fishing Charters
Salmon fishing is one of the major attractions off the Oregon coast. Newport is home port to several sportfishing charters. Salmon trolling, deep sea fishing, river fishing and whale watching excursions that take from a few hours to overnight can be arranged at a number of places located along the Old Town waterfront.

Hatfield Marine Science Center   *(541)867-0126*
2 mi. S at 2030 S. Marine Science Dr.
Oregon State University operates a large coastal research center on Yaquina Bay. The public wing has marine fish and invertebrates in tanks and interactive exhibits, plus displays explaining coastal geology, tides, and harbor life. Summer marine workshops, field trips, lectures, and films are also offered to the public.

Newport Marina at South Beach   *(541)867-3321*
2 mi. S via US 101 at 2301 SE Marine Science Dr.
One of the Northwest's largest and most complete marina facilities is near the outlet of Yaquina Bay. In addition to a huge moorage and complete marine services, there is a public fishing pier with fine bay and bridge views, a bait and tackle store, deep sea charters, a picnic area with barbecues, crab cooking facility, and brew pub.

Ona Beach State Park
8 mi. S on US 101
A bathhouse and boat ramp contribute to this day use park's appeal for swimming and fishing. Many scenic picnic sites on a lawn with shade trees overlook the mouth of a creek and a sandy ocean beach.

Oregon Coast Aquarium   *(541)867-3474*
2 mi. S via US 101 at 2820 SE Ferry Slip Rd.
The aquarium opened in 1992, and was soon ranked among the top ten in the country. The theme is following a drop of water from the Coast Range to the Pacific Ocean. Beyond a first-rate gift shop and cafe, indoor exhibits feature marine life in wetlands, sandy and rocky shores and in deep waters. Acres of outdoor exhibits feature an underwater cave with a giant octopus; a rocky pool with sea otters, seals and sea lions; and the largest walk-through seabird aviary in America. "Free Willy" star Keiko, the killer whale, was relocated here after that movie was made, and rehabilitated for return to the ocean.

South Beach State Park   *(541)867-4715*
2 mi. S on US 101
Campground and picnic facilities lie behind low dunes and a broad sandy ocean beach. Fishing and beachcombing are popular.

Undersea Gardens   *(541)265-2206*
Old Town at 250 SW Bay Blvd.
Thousands of marine creatures can be viewed in their natural habitat through more than 100 underwater viewing windows in this floating aquarium that rises and falls with the tides. There are scuba diving shows several times daily.

Yaquina Bay State Park   *(541)265-5679*
just SW on US 101 at N end of bridge
Dozens of scenic picnic sites are positioned on a well-landscaped blufftop with panoramic views of ocean beaches and the mouth of Yaquina Bay. Sunbathing, beachcombing, fishing, and swimming (for the hearty) are also popular. The park also features the historic Yaquina Bay Lighthouse (1871). This combined lighthouse/residence has been restored and refurnished in period style and has a gift shop.

Yaquina Head Outstanding Natural Area   *(541)574-3100*
3 mi. N via US 101 on Lighthouse Dr.
An interpretive center displays the area's human and natural history. Trails lead to a historic lighthouse, beaches, tidepools and overlooks.

RESTAURANTS

Bay House   *(541)996-3222*
20 mi. N at 5911 SW Hwy. 101 - Lincoln City
D only.   *Expensive*
Contemporary Northwest cuisine with emphasis on the freshest seasonal seafood and produce is expertly prepared. The casually elegant dining room with a fine picture-window view of adjoining Siletz Bay is a long-time culinary landmark of the Oregon Coast.

Canyon Way Bookstore & Restaurant   *(541)265-8319*
Old Town at 1216 SW Canyon Way
L-D.   *Expensive*
For more than a quarter of a century, Canyon Way has been a favorite for fine food on the Oregon coast. Delicious and unusual specialties, broiled and sauteed local seafoods, and homemade baked goods and desserts are served in several stylish dining areas and in a garden patio. Gourmet beverages of all kinds are also available. An outstanding bookstore adjoins.

Champagne Patio   *(541)265-3044*
1 mi. N at 1630 N. Coast Hwy. (US 101)
L only.   *Moderate*
Delectable fresh-baked bread and rich desserts are served with creative, flavorful dishes in a cozy, attractive dining room. Their wine list includes any selection from the expansive wine shop and outstanding Oregon specialty foods store in the next room.

Chez Jeannette   *(541)764-3434*
17 mi. N at 7150 Old Hwy. 101 - Gleneden Beach
D only.   *Expensive*
For many years, Chez Jeannette has been one of the Northwest's best gourmet hideaways. Classic and innovative French cuisine reflects the discipline and spirit of a talented chef. A cottage in the woods has the look and feel of a French country inn. Intimate rooms are outfitted with candlelit tables adorned with full linen and flowers. Classical music, forest views and two fireplaces contribute to the romantic mood.

Mo's Annex   *(541)265-7512*
Old Town at 657 SW Bay Blvd.
L-D.   *Moderate*
In addition to the touted clam chowder, this best of the little Oregon
chain features seafood stews, steamers, casseroles, bakes and sautees.
(Fans of fish and chips and deep-fried dishes shouldn't miss the
original **Mo's** across the street.) The deservedly popular Annex has a
tidy, congested bayfront dining room with close-up views of waterfront
activity.

Rogue Ales Public House   *(541)265-3188*
Old Town at 748 Bay Blvd.
L-D.   *Moderate*
Award-winning Rogue brews are showcased in a big, cheerful pub
where they are featured in ale-brewed chili, beer cheese soup, and
garlic ale bread, plus pizzas and many other pub favorites. The
premium brews served here are made at **Brewers by the Bay** in the
Marina at South Beach area, where patrons have a view of the kettles
and waterfront.

Sharks Original   *(541)574-0590*
Old Town at 852 SW Bay Blvd.
L-D.   *Moderate*
Shellfish are featured in expertly prepared cocktails, pan roasts, stews,
pastas and salads served in a spiffy little seafood bar and steamer cafe
that opened in 1995.

Tidal Raves Seafood Grill   *(541)765-2995*
14 mi. N on US 101 - Depoe Bay
L-D.   *Moderate*
Contemporary Northwestern dishes with an emphasis on regional
seafood enliven a creative American menu. Apart from the food, the
awesome window-wall view of surf breaking in a picturesque cove far
below the comfortable split-level dining room is a spell-binding crowd-
pleaser.

Whale Cove Inn   *(541)765-2255*
11 mi. N at 2345 SW Hwy. 101 - Depoe Bay
B-L-D.   *Moderate*
A cinnamon roll of truly epic proportions stars on a customary
American menu, along with bountiful breakfasts. From atop a slope
high above the ocean, the simply comfortable dining room features a
window-wall view of Whale Cove, a quintessential example of the
spectacular Oregon coast. Binoculars are available at tables by the
windows.

Whale's Tale   *(541)265-8660*
Old Town at 452 SW Bay Blvd.
B-L-D.   *Moderate*
Breakfasts have been especially notable here since 1976, including
unusual treats like poppyseed pancakes from stone-ground flour, and
hearty oyster omelets. Later, Northwest seafoods, poached or sauteed,
are featured along with homemade bread and tasty desserts. Local
artwork enlivens the handcrafted wood-toned interior of cozy dining
areas.

LODGING

Most of the area's best lodgings are near ocean beaches. Low and
moderately priced motels are inland along US 101 through town. High
season is June through September. Rates are reduced as much as 20%
at other times.

Channel House   *(541)765-2140*
14 mi. N via US 101 at 35 Ellingson St. (Box 56) - Depoe Bay 97341
12 units   *(800)447-2140*   *Expensive*
Channel House is one of America's great bed-and-breakfast inns.
Perched on rocks above the harrowing channel between Depoe Bay and
the ocean is a contemporary wood-shingled building that seems
remarkably close to the thrilling scene. "Downtown" is just across a
bridge. Full breakfast is complimentary. Each beautifully furnished
unit has some ocean view. "Ocean Front Rooms and Suites" have a
spectacular view from a private deck, gas fireplace, and a large indoor
or outdoor whirlpool.

Embarcadero Resort Hotel & Marina   *(541)265-8521*
1 mi. E at 1000 SE Bay Blvd. - 97365
85 units   *(800)547-4779*   *Expensive*
Nicely landscaped grounds along Yaquina Bay house several three-
story contemporary wood-trimmed buildings, large indoor bay-view
pool, whirlpool, sauna, fishing and crabbing piers, marina with rental
boats and charter fishing, and a stylish seafood restaurant that shares
a bay view with a lounge. Each spacious, well-furnished room has a
private balcony. Suites also have a kitchen and fireplace.

Hallmark Resort   *(541)265-2600*
just SW at 744 SW Elizabeth St. - 97365
158 units   *(888)448-4449*   *Expensive*
This recently expanded and upgraded five-story motor hotel is on a
bluff above the ocean. The contemporary complex has easy access to
miles of broad sandy beach, plus an indoor pool, whirlpool, sauna,
exercise room, surf-view restaurant (new in 1998) and lounge. Each of
the attractively furnished rooms has an ocean view. Many spacious
newer rooms also have a private deck, gas fireplace, and a two-person
in-room whirlpool.

Holiday Inn Newport   *(541)265-9411*
2 mi. N at 3019 N. Coast Hwy. - 97365
148 units   *(800)547-3310*   *Expensive*
Tucked back from picturesque Agate Beach is a newly refurbished
modern six-story hotel with a big pool; whirlpool; exercise room; ocean-
view restaurant and entertainment lounge. Each room is well
furnished. Some have a small private balcony with a fine ocean view.

The Inn at Otter Crest   *(541)765-2111*
9 mi. N at 301 Otter Crest Loop (Box 50) - Otter Rock 97369
100 units   *(800)452-2101*   *Expensive*
Dramatically located in a pine forest high above the ocean, this
contemporary condominium resort hotel offers a private sandy cove, a
large view pool, whirlpool, sauna, nature trails, a hill-climbing
funicular, tennis courts, ocean-view restaurant and entertainment
lounge. Each well-furnished room has a private deck. Some also have
a kitchen and pressed-log fireplace.

Little Creek Cove   *(541)265-8587*
2 mi. N via US 101 at 3641 NW Ocean View Dr. - 97365
31 units   *(800)294-8025*   *Expensive*
A secluded beachfront cove has been transformed with perfectly scaled
naturalistic buildings and landscaping into a delightful little
condominium complex. Each of the units is beautifully furnished and
includes a kitchen, fireplace and private deck. Some have an intimate
beach/ocean view.

Moolack Shores Motel   *(541)265-2326*
5 mi. N on US 101 at 8835 N. Coast Hwy. - 97365
14 units   Moderate-Expensive
This contemporary single-level motel is in a secluded spot on a bluff above the beach. Each well-furnished room is artistically decorated in a different theme. Some have a pressed-log fireplace and an ocean view.

Salishan Lodge   *(541)764-2371*
18 mi. N on US 101 (Box 118) - Gleneden Beach 97388
205 units   *(800)452-2300*   Expensive-Very Expensive
Salishan is an ideal blend of luxurious leisure facilities with a pristine Oregon landscape. The renowned resort's low-profile wood-trimmed buildings are sequestered into expansive manicured landscapes on a forested hillside. Amenities include a big indoor pool, whirlpool, sauna, exercise center, nature trails and (for a fee) a championship 18-hole golf course, putting green, and tennis courts, plus lavish gourmet dining and lounge facilities and a stylish complex of specialty shops. Each spacious, beautifully furnished room has a gas fireplace and private balcony. Some have a distant bay view and a whirlpool bath.

Schooner Landing   *(541)265-4293*
4 mi. N on US 101 at 201 NE 66th Dr. (Box 703) - 97365
42 units   Expensive
Amenities of this modern condominium complex on a wooded coastal bluff include private hiking paths to the beach, a long indoor pool, whirlpool, sauna, and racquetball court. Each well-furnished Cape Cod-style unit has a full kitchen, fireplace deck and whirlpool bath.

Shilo Inn Newport Oceanfront Resort   *(541)265-7701*
just SW at 536 SW Elizabeth St. - 97365
179 units   *(800)222-2244*   Expensive
Newport's largest lodging was recently remodeled. The four-story motor hotel is on a bluff with easy access to miles of broad sandy beach. There are two indoor pools, plus an oceanfront restaurant and lounge. Most well-furnished rooms have a fine surf view.

Starfish Point   *(541)265-3751*
3 mi. N on US 101 at 140 NW 48th St. - 97365
6 units   Expensive
High on the rim of a forested bluff overlooking the ocean is a superb example of post-modern Northwestern architecture intended for living with nature. Each condo is a beautifully furnished two-bedroom unit with a designer kitchen, unusual octagonal study, fireplace, and a whirlpool bath. Picture windows and a private deck provide spectacular ocean views. A secluded path winds down to a sandy beach.

Surfrider Oceanfront Resort   *(541)764-2311*
16 mi. N at 3115 NW Hwy. 101 (Box 219) - Depoe Bay 97341
52 units   *(800)662-2378*   Moderate-Expensive
Topping a bluff above the ocean by Fogarty Creek State Park is a handsome motel with a large indoor pool, whirlpool, sauna, plus an ocean-view restaurant and lounge. Each spacious, nicely furnished room has a coastline view. Some have a kitchen, gas fireplace, whirlpool, or balcony. The five "Anniversary Suites" have it all.

BASIC INFORMATION

Elevation: 140 feet   *Population (1990): 8,437*
Location: 114 miles Southwest of Portland
Nearest airport with commercial flights: in town
Greater Newport Chamber of Commerce (541)265-8801 (800)262-7844
downtown at 555 SW Coast Hwy. - 97365   www.newportnet.com

Seaside, Oregon

Seaside is the premier coastal playground of the Pacific Northwest. For more than a century, vacationers have been attracted to the broad sandy beach that links the ocean with a massive forested headland at one of the most dramatic sites on the coast. Seaside began, in 1806, as the end of the Lewis and Clark Trail. Settlement didn't really start until the 1870s, however, when the site's handsome coastal location established this as the first major coastal resort town in the Northwest.

Today, a well-landscaped little pedestrian-and-auto thoroughfare in the heart of town is lined with specialty shops, restaurants, atmospheric bars, and an upgraded old-fashioned amusement zone. A stylish landmark hotel anchors a two-mile-long pedestrian promenade at the thoroughfare's turnaround by the beach. Many other modern lodgings along the shoreline also serve summer crowds enjoying beachcombing, moped and three-wheeled "brike" riding, strolling on the Promenade, and auto driving on hard sand nearby.

WEATHER PROFILE

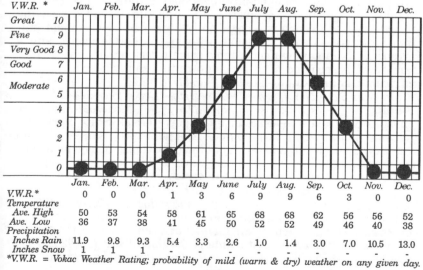

V.W.R. *		Jan.	Feb.	Mar.	Apr.	May	June	July	Aug.	Sep.	Oct.	Nov.	Dec.
V.W.R.*		0	0	0	1	3	6	9	9	6	3	0	0
Temperature													
Ave. High		50	53	54	58	61	65	68	68	62	56	56	52
Ave. Low		36	37	38	41	45	50	52	52	49	46	40	38
Precipitation													
Inches Rain		11.9	9.8	9.3	5.4	3.3	2.6	1.0	1.4	3.0	7.0	10.5	13.0
Inches Snow		1	1	1	-	-	-	-	-	-	-	-	-

*V.W.R. = Vokac Weather Rating; probability of mild (warm & dry) weather on any given day.

413

ATTRACTIONS
Astoria   *(503)325-6311   (800)875-6807*
17 mi. N on US 101
The oldest permanent American settlement in the Northwest dates back to the erection of Fort Astoria in 1811. Many examples of Victorian architecture remain. Historic events in the region are depicted in spiral murals on the Astoria Column—a 125-foot tower on Coxcomb Hill topped by an observation deck more than 700 feet above the Columbia River. The **Maritime Museum**, the most comprehensive of its kind in the Northwest, is housed in a strikingly modern building on the waterfront. Near downtown, a toll bridge more than four miles long spans the Columbia River between Oregon and Washington. This final link in US 101 (a highway from Canada to Mexico) was completed in 1966.

Bicycling
There is a lot of flat coastal terrain in the Seaside area that can be toured on miles of paved separated bikeways. Bicycles, brikes (zany three-wheelers), surreys and skates are rented downtown by the hour at:
Distinctive Outdoor Fun for All   *407 S. Holladay Dr. 738-8447*
Seaside Surrey Rentals   *622 12th Av.   738-0242*

Fishing Charters
16 mi. N off US 101 - Hammond
Numerous charter boat services feature salmon fishing over the nearby Columbia River Bar. Each provides bait and tackle and can arrange for freezing or canning your catch. Nearest to the ocean are in Hammond.

Food Specialties
Bell Buoy Crab Co.   *(503)738-2722   (800)529-2722*
1 mi. S at 1800 S. Holladay Dr.
For more than half a century, delicious fresh or canned Dungeness crab, and fresh or smoked salmon, have been specialties in an impressive line of seasonally available fresh, smoked, and canned seafoods. Custom smoking or canning can also be arranged. Various seafood cocktails are displayed to go.

Fort Clatsop National Memorial   *(503)861-2471*
17 mi. N: 12 mi. N on US 101 & 5 mi. E on marked hwy. - Astoria
A full-scale reconstructed log fort is on the site of the Lewis and Clark expedition's headquarters during the winter of 1805. An adjacent visitor center houses a museum, audio-visual programs, and store. Frontier skills are demonstrated by rangers in period costumes.

Fort Stevens State Park   *(503)861-1671*
17 mi. N via US 101
The park features remnants of military installations that protected the mouth of the Columbia River from the Civil War through World War II. There is an interpretive center and self-guided trails to batteries, guardhouses, and earthworks. Nearby are camping and picnicking facilities, ocean beaches, sand dunes, and bike paths. Swimming areas with sandy beaches are on Coffenbury Lake, which is also popular for boating and fishing.

Fun Zone   *(503)738-7361*
downtown on Broadway
Skill games, electronic amusements, and rides are still featured in a cluster of commercial entertainment places on the main street between the river and the beach. Some have gone high-tech, but the name of the game is family fun, as it has been for decades.

The Promenade
N & S from downtown

Built in 1920, this concrete walkway borders the beach for nearly two miles. It is a delightful place to stroll, skate, or ride a bicycle with sand and surf views on one side and charming beach homes on the other. Near the midpoint, "the Turnaround" at the west end of Broadway is the designated "End of the Lewis and Clark Trail."

Seaside Beach
W of downtown

Bordering the west side of town is a broad beach of hard-packed sand backed by low dunes extending to the Promenade. Lifeguard services are provided in summer. While the inviting surf is inevitably cold, sunbathing and beachcombing are popular activities. Surfing is not permitted in town, but one of the most popular "breaks" along the entire Northwest coast is just south. To the north beyond Gearhart, ten miles of hard sand beach is open to autos when the tide is low. It is an exhilarating scenic drive.

Tillamook Head
2 mi. SW via Sunset Blvd.

The area's most impressive landmark is a massive quarter-mile-high cape jutting into the sea between Seaside and Cannon Beach. Tillamook Head Trail, which is six miles each way, rewards energetic hikers with memorable coastal panoramas while attaining a height of nearly 1,200 feet above sea level. The trailhead begins at a parking lot at the end of Sunset Road.

RESTAURANTS

Dooger's Seafood & Grill   *(503)738-3773*
downtown at 505 Broadway
L-D.   *Moderate*

The original (of a small coastal chain of restaurants) has some of the Northwest's best clam chowder. Regional seafoods including (in season) Dungeness crab claws and razor clams are prepared from scratch. Homemade accompaniments range from homemade blue cheese dressing to luscious peanut butter pie. The pleasant dining room is still the area's favorite.

Harrison's Bakery   *(503)738-5331*
downtown at 608 Broadway
B-L.   *Low*

At this full-line takeout bakery, there has been a good selection of coffee cakes and Danish pastries, plus breads and assorted desserts, since 1902.

Norma's   *(503)738-6170*
downtown at 20 N. Columbia St.
L-D.   *Moderate*

Clam chowder, razor clams, and other seafood, plus homemade pies, are featured. The long-popular family-oriented restaurant is in a cheerful dining room with casual nautical decor.

Oceanside Restaurant   *(503)738-7789*
4 mi. N at 1200 N. Marion Av. - Gearhart
L-D.   *Expensive*

Seafood is appropriately featured among contemporary American dishes served in a dining room outfitted with full linen and fresh flowers. A superb 180° oceanfront view beyond sawgrass-covered low dunes contributes to the restaurant's appeal.

Pacific Way Cafe & Bakery   *(503)738-0245*

2 mi. N at 601 Pacific Way - Gearhart

B-L-D.   *Moderate*

Outstanding cinnamon rolls, croissants, and other pasties are served with all sorts of beverages for breakfast in the bakery. Spectacular fresh berry pies and cakes accompany fine designer sandwiches for lunch and pizzas for dinner in an atmospheric wood-trimmed cafe next door with a lovely garden patio.

Shilo Inn Seaside Oceanfront Resort   *(503)738-8481*

downtown at 30 N. Prom

B-L-D.   *Moderate*

Updated American dishes, with an emphasis on regional seafoods in the evening, are served amidst appealing contemporary decor in the casually elegant dining room of Seaside's landmark hotel. The wraparound window-wall view of the Promenade, beach, ocean and turnaround (shared with a snazzy entertainment lounge) is the best in town.

LODGING

Among an impressive assortment of lodgings, the best have ocean views and are an easy stroll from the heart of town. High season is May through September. Prices at other times may be as much as 20% less.

Comfort Inn Boardwalk   *(503)738-3011*

downtown at 545 Broadway - 97138

65 units   *(800)228-5150*   *Moderate-Expensive*

An indoor pool, whirlpool and sauna are features of this contemporary motel four blocks from the beach. Most of the well-furnished rooms overlook a peaceful little river and have a private patio or balcony. Some also have a gas fireplace and whirlpool bath.

Ebb Tide Motel   *(503)738-8371*

downtown at 300 N. Prom - 97138

99 units   *(800)468-6232*   *Expensive*

This modern oceanfront motel has an indoor pool, whirlpool, and saunas. Most of the beautifully furnished rooms have a mini-kitchen, gas fireplace and a surf view.

The Edgewater Inn   *(503)738-4142*

downtown at 341 S. Prom - 97138

14 units   *(800)822-3170*   *Expensive*

The beach and prom adjoin this modern motel. Each well-furnished unit has a kitchen, fireplace and large whirlpool bath. Some also have a private ocean-view deck.

Gearhart by the Sea Resort   *(503)738-8331*

3 mi. N at 1157 N. Marion Av. (Box 2700) - Gearhart 97138

83 units   *(800)547-0115*   *Expensive*

A large indoor pool, a whirlpool, and a (fee) 18-hole golf course are features of this six-story condo complex directly above the beach. The adjoining Oceanside Restaurant (see listing) shares the sea view. Each spacious, comfortably furnished one- or two-bedroom unit has a kitchen, fireplace, and a private balcony.

Hi-Tide Motel   *(503)738-8414*

downtown at 30 Av. G - 97138

64 units   *(800)621-9876*   *Moderate-Expensive*

This shingled oceanfront motel has a small indoor pool and a whirlpool. Each well-furnished unit has a mini-kitchen. Many also have a gas fireplace and an ocean view.

Inn at the Shore   *(503)738-3113*
1 mi. S at 2275 S. Prom - 97138
18 units   *(800)713-9914*   *Moderate-Expensive*
One of the nicest lodgings on the Oregon Coast opened in 1995 at the
quiet end of the prom on the beach. Rental bikes are available. All of
the beautifully furnished rooms have a gas fireplace and a private
balcony or patio. "Oceanfront king jacuzzi" rooms also have a mini-
kitchen, an in-bath whirlpool for two, and a terrific view of the surf.

Ocean View Resort - Best Western   *(503)738-3334*
downtown at 414 N. Prom - 97138
104 units   *(800)234-8439*   *Moderate-Very Expensive*
The beach and prom border this contemporary five-story motor hotel
with an indoor pool, whirlpool, restaurant and bar. Many of the well-
furnished rooms have a kitchenette, private ocean-view balcony or
patio, and a gas fireplace. Eight have a big in-room whirlpool with an
ocean view.

Sand and Sea   *(503)738-8441*
downtown at 475 S. Prom (Box 945) - 97138
24 units   *(800)628-2371*   *Moderate-Expensive*
Seaside's highest lodgings are in this modern six-level oceanfront
condominium/motel with a small round indoor pool and saunas. Each
well-furnished one- or two-bedroom suite has a floor-to-ceiling window,
a kitchen, a private view balcony, and a gas fireplace.

Sea Side Inn   *(503)738-6403*
downtown at 581 S. Prom - 97138
14 units   *(800)772-7766*   *Expensive-Very Expensive*
One of the area's newest oceanfront bed-and-breakfasts is in a four-
story building that opened in 1995 on the Promenade. Full breakfast
is complimentary. Each well-furnished room features antiques or
unique themes, and has a private bath. Some also have a gas fireplace
and a one- or two-person whirlpool bath.

Seashore Resort Motel   *(503)738-8314*
downtown at 60 N. Prom - 97138
53 units   *(888)738-6368*   *Moderate*
By the beach and prom in the heart of town, this modern motel has a
large indoor pool, whirlpool and sauna. Each room is nicely furnished.

Shilo Inn Seaside Oceanfront Resort   *(503)738-9571*
downtown at 30 N. Prom - 97138
112 units   *(800)222-2244*   *Expensive-Very Expensive*
Seaside's largest and most complete motor hotel has a choice site by
the beach and Promenade at the turnaround. Other features of the
contemporary five-story complex include an indoor pool, whirlpool,
steam room, sauna, exercise room, and gift shop, plus a view
restaurant (see listing) and lounge with live entertainment. Each room
is beautifully furnished. Ocean rooms have a kitchenette, private surf-
view balcony and a gas fireplace. A few also have an in-bath whirlpool.

BASIC INFORMATION

Elevation: 10 feet   Population (1990): 5,359
Location: 80 miles Northwest of Portland, OR
Nearest airport with commercial flights: Portland - 88 miles
Seaside Chamber of Commerce   (503)738-6391   (800)444-6740
   just E at 7 N. Roosevelt Dr. (US 101) (Box 7) - 97138
   www.clatsop.com / seaside
Seaside Visitor Bureau   (503)738-3097   (888)306-2326
   just E at 7 N. Roosevelt Dr. (mail: 989 Broadway) - 97138

Myrtle Beach, South Carolina

Myrtle Beach is the playful hub of the coastal South. It is centered on sixty miles of superb sandy shoreline by the Atlantic Ocean. The Intracoastal Waterway parallels the beach about two miles inland. Isolation deterred settlement until 1900. The town's destiny as a tourist capital was fulfilled slowly at first, and full-tilt in recent years.

Today, the aptly named "Grand Strand" displays one of America's most lavish concentrations of recreation and leisure facilities. Instead of a traditional downtown, Myrtle Beach features amusement parks, water parks and sportive attractions of all kinds. Beyond, the classic beach is fronted by a prodigious collection of skyscraper hotels and condos where more visitors can enjoy an ocean view than in any other great town. There are other superlatives. The Grand Strand claims America's greatest collection of public golf courses; more grandiose fresh seafood buffets than anywhere; and one of the nation's biggest clusters of live music/variety theaters.

WEATHER PROFILE

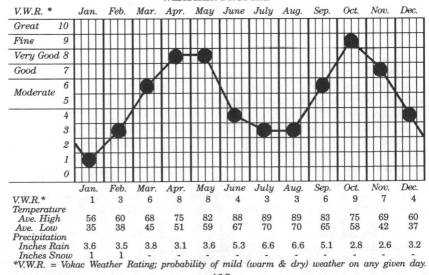

		Jan.	Feb.	Mar.	Apr.	May	June	July	Aug.	Sep.	Oct.	Nov.	Dec.
V.W.R.*		1	3	6	8	8	4	3	3	6	9	7	4
Temperature													
Ave. High		56	60	68	75	82	88	89	89	83	75	69	60
Ave. Low		35	38	45	51	59	67	70	70	65	58	42	37
Precipitation													
Inches Rain		3.6	3.5	3.8	3.1	3.6	5.3	6.6	6.6	5.1	2.8	2.6	3.2
Inches Snow		1	1	-	-	-	-	-	-	-	-	-	-

*V.W.R. = Vokac Weather Rating; probability of mild (warm & dry) weather on any given day.

The Beach
downtown off Ocean Blvd.

The heart of the "Grand Strand" is the fine sand beach that extends for twelve miles along the Atlantic Ocean in Myrtle Beach. Hotels and condo towers line most of the shoreline. They do not block access, however, and their bulk is mitigated by palms and other semitropical landscaping. A boardwalk and piers also appeal to strollers, as do occasional parks and two major seaside amusement parks.

Bicycling

Scenic bike paths and bike routes extend for many flat miles near the ocean and Intracoastal Waterway. All sorts of bicycles can be rented by the hour or longer at several shops. In town are:

Bicycles-N-Gear	*(843)626-2453*
The Bike Shop at Western Auto	*(843)448-5335*

Boat Rentals

Jet skis, pontoon boats, sailboats and other watercraft rentals, lessons, and guide services are available at several places in and near town. Cruising the scenic Intracoastal Waterway and coast are popular.

Barefoot Watersports	*(843)272-2255*	
Captain Dick's	*(843)651-3676*	*(800)344-3474*

Boat Rides

Enjoy the sights and sounds of the Intracoastal Waterway or the picturesque Waccamaw River aboard an authentic paddlewheeler, an old-fashioned riverboat, or a modern cruise ship. Narrated sightseeing, sunset or dinner cruises can be reserved.

Great American Riverboat Co.	*(843)650-6600*	*(800)685-6601*
Hurricane Fleet	*(843)249-3571*	

Brookgreen Gardens   *(843)237-4218*   *(800)849-1931*
18 mi. SW on US 17 at 1931 Brookgreen Gardens Dr.

Brookgreen Gardens is the quintessential collection of American sculpture. More than 500 sculptures by American artists from the mid-19th century to the present are showcased in magnificent gardens. Railroad heir Archer Huntington and his sculptor wife Anna created the country's first public sculpture gardens in the 1930s on the site of colonial rice plantations. Today, Live Oak draped with Spanish Moss tower over dogwood, azalea, magnolia, palmetto and colorful flowerbeds. Pools, fountains, terraces and galleries frame sculptures ranging from monumental to intimate. Nearby, the wildlife park provides close-ups of alligators, foxes, raptors and other native wildlife and plants. The Welcome Center has information about tours and programs, a cafe and museum shop.

Family Kingdom Amusement Park   *(843)626-3447*
downtown at 300 4th Av. South

The beach's only wooden roller coaster has a 62-foot freefall drop. A historic carousel, a giant Ferris wheel, plus other rides, a newly expanded waterpark, and fast food contribute to oceanfront fun.

Fishing Charters

In-shore and offshore waters all the way to the Gulf Stream offer rich sportfishing rewards. The Grand Strand is home port to numerous charters. All equipment is provided for half-day and all-day trips. For information and reservations, contact:

Captain Dick's	*(843)651-3676*	*(800)344-3474*
Hurricane Fleet	*(843)249-3571*	
Venture Charter	*(843)249-8662*	

Golf   *(800)845-4653*

Unlike other great Sunbelt golfing destinations, the Grand Strand claims to have the greatest collection of *public* golf courses in the world. Golfers here have unlimited access to nearly 100 courses, many of championship quality. Layouts range from manicured parkland by cypress marshes (complete with resident gators), to wide open courses with waterway or ocean views.

Huntington Beach State Park   *(843)237-4440*
17 mi. SW on US 17

Atalaya, a big Moorish-style castle, was built by Archer and Anna Huntington (see Brookgreen Gardens) in the 1930s as a home and studio. Today, it is a museum centerpiece of a large beachfront park. A boardwalk-nature trail and observation decks provide unique views of all sorts of native marshlife, including alligators. In addition to a saltwater marsh and freshwater lagoon, there are also beach areas, picnicking and camping.

Live Theater

Myrtle Beach is one of America's leading destinations for live theater entertainment. Since 1986, a dozen theaters have opened in and around town. Most are lavish state-of-the-art showplaces for all kinds of music from country-and-western to rock-n-roll, variety shows, comedy, ice skating, and themed dinner theater. Following are the author's top eight:

Alabama Theatre *music & comedy stars* 272-1111 *(800)342-2262*
All American Music Theatre *various musical styles*   236-9700
The Carolina Opry *musical variety & comedy*   238-8888
Dixie Stampede *dinner theater extravaganza* 497-9700 *(800)433-4401*
Gatlin Brothers Theatre *country stars* 236-8800 *(800)681-5209*
Legends in Concert *star impersonations* 238-7827 *(800)960-7469*
Medieval Times *medieval dinner/tournament* 236-4635 *(800)436-4386*
Palace Theater *name stars in music & comedy* 448-0588 *(800)905-4228*

Myrtle Beach Pavilion Amusement Park   *(843)448-6456*
downtown at 812 North Ocean Blvd.

The Pavilion by the beach in the heart of town has been the region's foremost amusement park for more than half a century. Nearly forty rides include a looping metal coaster, log flume, and hydro-river raft ride for thrills. The oceanfront boardwalk is *the* place for people-watching. Other features include a handcrafted pipe organ, antique merry-go-round, a dance hall, restaurant and dozens of snack stands, gift shops, and arcade games.

Myrtle Beach State Park   *(843)238-5325*
5 mi. S on US 17 at 4401 S. Kings Hwy.

South Carolina's premier state park has a popular oceanfront site. Features include ocean or pool swimming, a long sandy beach, nature trail and interpretive center, pier and surf fishing, picnicking and a big complete campground.

Myrtle Waves Water Park   *(843)448-1026*   *(800)524-9283*
2 mi. W at 3000 10th Av. North

The largest water park in the Carolinas has over thirty rides and attractions. For thrills, there is the world's tallest tubular slide, or a tube ride through foggy mist in a twisting black tunnel. The wave pool and lazy river offer fun for everyone, and there are food stands, video arcade, and a souvenir shop.

RESTAURANTS

Austin's at the Beach   *(843)448-9058*
2 mi. NE on US 17 at 2606 N. Kings Hwy.
L-D.   *Expensive*
Austin's is a newer restaurant that quickly won acclaim for fine dining. Contemporary American cuisine achieves gourmet status in fresh, flavorful dishes. Outstanding desserts made here, like apple crisp with walnut crumb topping, are also served amid casually elegant decor.

Bovines   *(843)651-2888*
12 mi. SW on US 17 - Murrells Inlet
D only.   *Expensive*
Wood-fired grilled and baked specialties highlight an eclectic menu (devoid of fried seafood) of American dishes ranging from Cajun oyster stew to shrimp brochette or glazed honey-crust designer pizzas. The comfortable multilevel dining room and bar share a waterfront view.

Chestnut Hill   *(843)449-3984*
8 mi. NE on US 17 at 9922 N. Kings Hwy.
D only.   *Expensive*
Prime rib tops a contemporary American menu offered in this casually elegant dinner house.

Collectors Cafe   *(843)449-9370*
6 mi. NE on US 17 at 7726 N. Kings Hwy.
D only.   *Expensive*
A wide selection of creative Mediterranean cuisine is served in stylish dining areas displaying local art. Assorted coffee drinks and distinctive baked goods are served in the European-style coffee house after noon.

Horst Gasthaus   *(843)272-3351*
8 mi. NE at 802 37th Av. South
D only.   *Moderate*
Authentic German dishes are served amid decor that is reminiscent of a Bavarian beer hall. Nightly live entertainment features traditional German and American songs, and sing-alongs.

Latif's Bakery & Cafe   *(843)449-1716*
4 mi. NE on US 17 at 503 61st Av. North
B-L.   *Moderate*
Some of the Strand's best breakfast pastries, plus cakes, cookies and other luscious desserts, are showcased in the modish bakery. They are served to go or with unusual light fare in the snazzy bistro bar or on a terrace.

The Library   *(843)448-4527*
downtown on US 17 at 1212 N. Kings Hwy.
D only.   *Very Expensive*
Classic French cuisine is given skilled contemporary preparation in one of the most critically acclaimed dinner houses in the area. Posh candlelit decor in a library mode provides an urbane backdrop.

The Original Benjamin's Calabash Seafood   *(843)449-0821*
7 mi. NE on US 17 at 9301 N. Kings Hwy.
D only.   *Expensive*
The Original Benjamin's is the premier source of the coastal lowlands' most notable culinary contribution—a prodigious seafood buffet. Dungeness crab, shrimp and crawfish in the shell with drawn butter, popcorn shrimp, clams, oysters, scallops, smoked salmon and fresh catfish typify the mind-boggling selections at several serve-yourself bars and islands. All breads and a lavish array of desserts are made

here. Several vast dining rooms overlooking the Intracoastal Waterway and a lounge are festooned with a museum-load of nautical memorabilia, including a one-third sized Mayflower replica.

Pier 14 Restaurant & Lounge   *(843)448-4314*
downtown at 1304 N. Ocean Blvd.
L-D.   *Moderate*
Contemporary American dishes like beer-battered chicken strips provide a good excuse to visit the Grand Strand's only restaurant and lounge over the waves. The casual comfortable dining room, bar and deck all have fine beach-and-surf views, and there is live entertainment nightly.

Skeeters Breakfast and Lunch   *(843)497-2781*
5 mi. NE on US 17 at 410 70th Av. North
B-L.   *Low*
All kinds of tasty crepe-style omelets with cottage fries and biscuits help explain why this cheerful coffee shop is one of the area's best deals for breakfast.

LODGING

Myrtle Beach has more oceanfront hotels and resorts than any city or town in America. It is also the "lazy river" capital of America. High season is late May through August. Fall and winter rates are usually reduced 50% or more.

Beach Colony Resort   *(843)449-4010*
3 mi. NE at 5308 N. Ocean Blvd. - 29577
221 units   *(800)222-2141*   *Expensive*
More than half of the units in this contemporary 21-story all-suites hotel face an adjoining white sand beach. Amenities include a lazy river ride, indoor and outdoor pools, two whirlpools, racquetball court, saunas, exercise room, dining room and lounge. Each unit is well furnished. The one- to four-bedroom suites have a private view balcony. Many overlook the ocean.

Captain's Quarters Resort   *(843)448-1404*
1 mi. SW at 901 S. Ocean Blvd. (P.O. Drawer 2486) - 29578
318 units   *(800)843-3561*   *Expensive*
This contemporary fourteen-story oceanfront apartment hotel has a covered lazy river ride and children's lazy river, indoor and big outdoor pools, three whirlpools, exercise equipment, (fee) bowling lanes, and a restaurant. Each well-furnished unit has a private view balcony. Most face the beach.

The Caribbean Resort & Villas   *(843)448-7181*
2 mi. NE at 3000 N. Ocean Blvd. - 29577
340 units   *(800)845-0883*   *Expensive*
A fine sand beach bounds this contemporary fourteen-story complex with a lazy river ride, big outdoor and indoor pools, and two whirlpools. Each well-furnished unit has a private balcony. Most have an oceanfront view.

Coral Beach Resort   *(843)448-8421*
1 mi. SW at 1105 S. Ocean Blvd. - 29577
301 units   *(800)843-2684*   *Expensive*
In addition to a broad sandy beach, this contemporary twelve-story apartment hotel has a lazy river ride, two outdoor and one indoor pool, four whirlpools, saunas, steam room, exercise room; plus (fee) bowling lanes. There is also a dining room, lounge and gift shop. Each well-furnished unit has a private balcony. Most overlook the ocean.

Crown Reef Resort   *(843)626-8077*
4 mi. SW at 2913 S. Ocean Blvd. - 29577
363 units   *(800)405-7333*   *Expensive*
One of the newest and largest apartment hotels is a fourteen-story complex paralleling a wide sandy beach. There is also a long lazy river ride, big outdoor and indoor pools, two whirlpools, exercise and game room, and cafe/bar. All of the beautifully furnished units have a private balcony overlooking the ocean. Some also have a whirlpool tub.

The Patricia Grand   *(843)448-8453*
2 mi. NE at 2710 N. Ocean Blvd. (Box 1855) - 29578
307 units   *(800)255-4763*   *Moderate-Expensive*
A white sand beach adjoins this contemporary eighteen-story hotel with an indoor lazy river ride, big indoor and outdoor pools, two whirlpools, sauna, plus an ocean-view restaurant and lounge. Each well-furnished unit has a private balcony. Most overlook the surf.

Sea Crest Resort   *(843)626-3515*
1 mi. SW at 803 S. Ocean Blvd. - 29577
360 units   *(800)845-1112*   *Moderate-Expensive*
This contemporary fourteen-story hotel fronts on a fine sand beach. Facilities include a small lazy river ride, big indoor and outdoor pools, two whirlpools, exercise room and 6-hole miniature golf, plus a restaurant, lounge and gift shop. Each unit is well furnished and has a private balcony. Most are efficiencies and have an ocean view.

Sea Mist Resort   *(843)448-1551*
1 mi. S at 1200 S. Ocean Blvd. (Box 2548) - 29578
827 units   *(800)732-6478*   *Moderate-Expensive*
Family-fun stars in this big contemporary complex of buildings up to twelve stories by a choice beach. Expansive, palm-shaded grounds include the region's largest on-site waterpark featuring a long lazy river ride and tubular slide, miniature golf, eleven pools (two indoors), tennis court, exercise room, restaurant, lounge, ice cream parlor, and resort shops. Each unit is comfortably furnished. Some have an ocean view.

Wyndham Myrtle Beach Resort   *(843)449-5000*
9 mi. NE via US 17 at 10000 Beach Club Dr. - 29572
392 units   *(800)248-9228*   *Expensive-Very Expensive*
An on-site championship 18-hole (fee) golf course competes with a broad sand beach as the major features of Wyndham's stylish fifteen-story resort. Other amenities include four lighted tennis courts, a pool, ocean-view dining room, entertainment lounge and resort shops. Each well-furnished room has a private balcony with an ocean view.

The Yachtsman Resort   *(843)448-1441*
downtown at 1400 N. Ocean Blvd. - 29577
142 units   *(800)868-8886*   *Expensive*
The twenty-story oceanfront glass tower is one of the region's most notable landmarks. Amenities of the all-suites complex include a small indoor and two outdoor pools, two whirlpool spas, a sauna, exercise room and miniature golf. Each attractively furnished suite has a fully equipped kitchen, private balcony with a splendid beach/surf view, and a two-person whirlpool bath.

BASIC INFORMATION

Elevation: 30 feet   Population (1990):   24,848
Location: 175 miles Southeast of Charlotte, NC
Nearest airport with commercial flights: in town
Myrtle Beach Area Chamber of Commerce (843)626-7444 (800)356-3016
* just N at 1200 N. Oak St. (Box 2115) - 29578 www.myrtlebeachlive.com*

Spearfish, South Dakota

Spearfish is the quietly beautiful gateway to the Black Hills. Three peaks surround the little valley at the mouth of spectacular Spearfish Canyon. But, the choice site and a four-season climate that was more gentle than on the Great Plains just to the east didn't cause the first settlement. It was gold. One of the world's great Mother Lodes was found in the mountains above Deadwood Gulch a few miles to the south. In 1876, settlement began here. No gold was discovered, but by 1877 (with the end of Indian hostilities) the town's growth was assured as the peaceful alternative to the lusty nearby boom towns.

Today, the legacy of quiet, steady growth is apparent in the university, opera house and fish hatchery that still contribute to the town's charm. Black Hills gold is featured here in handcrafted jewelry that is sold with other regional collectibles downtown. A renowned Passion Play, and a wealth of recreation opportunities for all seasons, further ensure an improving number and mix of restaurants and lodgings.

WEATHER PROFILE

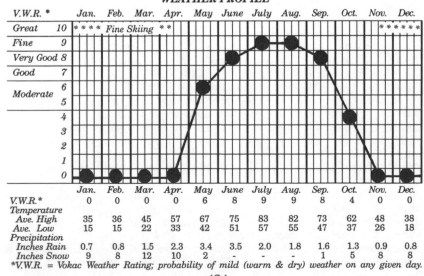

V.W.R. *		Jan.	Feb.	Mar.	Apr.	May	June	July	Aug.	Sep.	Oct.	Nov.	Dec.
Great	10	*	*	*	*	Fine Skiing	*	*				*	* * * * *
Fine	9												
Very Good	8												
Good	7												
Moderate	6												
	5												

V.W.R.*	Jan.	Feb.	Mar.	Apr.	May	June	July	Aug.	Sep.	Oct.	Nov.	Dec.
	0	0	0	0	6	8	9	9	8	4	0	0
Temperature												
Ave. High	35	36	45	57	67	75	83	82	73	62	48	38
Ave. Low	15	15	22	33	42	51	57	55	47	37	26	18
Precipitation												
Inches Rain	0.7	0.8	1.5	2.3	3.4	3.5	2.0	1.8	1.6	1.3	0.9	0.8
Inches Snow	9	8	12	10	2	-	-	-	1	5	8	8

*V.W.R. = Vokac Weather Rating; probability of mild (warm & dry) weather on any given day.

ATTRACTIONS

Black Hills National Forest   *(605)642-4622*
2 mi. S on US 14
The highest mountains in America east of the Rockies are the Black Hills, topping out at Harney Peak (elevation 7,242 feet). The huge pine forest also surrounds Mount Rushmore National Memorial, the Crazy Horse Memorial, and a major ski area (see listings); plus numerous canyons, small scenic lakes and streams. A fine system of roads and trails accesses unlimited recreation opportunities.

Black Hills Passion Play   *(605)642-2646*   *(800)457-0160*
just W on St. Joe St.
Each summer since 1939, the epic drama of the last week of Jesus Christ has been enacted in a vast amphitheater with a memorable mountain backdrop. The play unfolds for more than two hours on the world's largest stage, and involves a huge authentically-costumed cast and many animals. Reservations are recommended.

Black Hills State University   *(605)642-6539*
1 mi. N at 1200 University Av.
South Dakota's first college was founded here in 1883. The university now has an enrollment of about 3,000 students and offers a diverse curriculum on a handsome contemporary campus. A full schedule of sports and theater productions is open to the public.

Crazy Horse Memorial   *(605)673-4681*
66 mi. S via US 85 & US 385
The largest sculpture in the world is being carved from the granite of Thunderhead Mountain. When completed, the full upper body of Crazy Horse, a renowned Sioux Indian warrior, astride a horse, will be 563 feet high and 641 feet long. Only his nine-story face has been completed to date. Grounds include a large Indian Museum, sculptures, studio/home, galleries, food service, and gift shop.

D.C. Booth Historic Fish Hatchery   *(605)642-7730*
just S at 423 Hatchery Circle
One of the West's oldest fish hatcheries established a century ago led to the introduction of trout into the Black Hills. Buildings (on the National Register) contain historic displays. Lovely grounds also include the National Fish Culture Hall of Fame. Visitors also enjoy feeding big trout, and viewing them through underwater windows.

Deadwood and Lead   *(605)578-1876*
15 mi. SE on US 85
These neighboring towns began as gold rush boom towns. Since 1876, the Homestake Mine in Lead has been a major producer. Down the gulch, Deadwood became a magnet for gamblers and gunfighters, and Wild Bill Hickok was shot and killed there during a poker game in 1876. After a long hiatus, gambling was legalized again in 1989. Boom times have returned. Many major restored buildings serve as gaming halls, saloons, restaurants, and nostalgic hotels. Tours of "Boot Hill," gold mines, and the historic district are more popular than ever.

High Plains Heritage Center & Museum   *(605)642-9378*
1 mi. SE at 825 Heritage Dr.
A handsome contemporary building crowns a hill with a panoramic view. The complex includes a sod dugout, log cabin, one-room schoolhouse, and longhorn steers and buffaloes displayed outdoors. Inside, Western paintings, sculpture and artifacts are topped by a dramatic seventeen-foot-high statue of a trail driver. This is also the home of the Cowboy Song and Poetry Hall of Fame.

Matthews Opera House   *(605)642-7973*
downtown at 614½ Main St.
Built in 1906, this ornate historic theater remains a center for summer
plays, plus readings and other entertainment year-round.

Mount Rushmore National Memorial   *(605)574-2523*
60 mi. S via I-90 & US 16
The colossal sculpted heads of four great American presidents—
Washington, Jefferson, Lincoln, and Theodore Roosevelt—are as grand
and enduring as their achievements. The detailed, sixty-foot-high faces
were carved from a massive granite outcropping at the top of a
mountain by Gutzon Borglum between 1927 and 1941 when he died
with the work nearly finished. His nearby studio houses tools and scale
models. There is a new interpretive center, food service and gift gallery.
A summer evening program ends with floodlighting of the memorial.

Spearfish Canyon
2 mi. S (starts) along US 14
Limestone walls tower a thousand feet above pine and aspen forests on
both sides of US 14 (a National Scenic Byway) as it parallels Spearfish
Creek for seventeen miles deep into the Black Hills. The Cultural
Center in Latchstring Village (12 mi. south) presents area history in
exhibits and film. Many trails access picturesque waterfalls, trout
fishing, picnic areas and campsites.

Winter Sports
Terry Peak Ski Area   *(605)584-2165*   *(800)456-0524*
22 mi. S via US 85 - Lead
From the 7,076-foot elevation at the top, you're as high as you can get
on a ski slope east of the Rockies. The view is terrific. The vertical rise
is 1,052 feet and the longest run is nearly two miles. There are five
chairlifts. Related services and rentals, food and drink are available at
the base. There are plenty of lodgings in nearby Lead and Deadwood.
The skiing season is mid-November into April.

RESTAURANTS

A Little Bit of Italy   *(605)642-5701*
downtown at 447 Main St.
L-D.   *Low*
New York style pizzas are homemade from scratch and served with
Italian and American dishes in a casual dining room, on a patio or to go.

The Bay Leaf Cafe   *(605)642-5462*
downtown at 126 W. Hudson
L-D.   *Moderate*
The Bay Leaf offers Spearfish's best innovative cuisine. An eclectic
selection of light and flavorful fare ranges from choice beef and buffalo
to vegetarian, plus fresh pastries and desserts. The relaxed, intimate
setting in a historic building is enhanced by folk art and greenery.

The Bell Steakhouse   *(605)642-2848*
just W at 539 W. Jackson Blvd.
D only.   *Moderate*
Steaks, prime rib, and trout are specialties. There is also a salad bar
in the simply comfortable dining room and lounge.

Cedar House Restaurant   *(605)642-2104*
just N at 130 E. Ryan Rd.
B-L-D.   *Low*
Homemade pies and pastries are part of the appeal of this pleasant
source of American down-home cooking.

Cheyenne Crossing Cafe & Store   *(605)584-3510   (800)400-7722*
17 mi. S at jct. of US 14 & US 85 - Lead
B-L-D.   *Moderate*
All-American fare includes specialties like homemade sausage gravy,
sourdough pancakes, and buffalo sausage and burgers. Decor is casual,
warm and Western in a complex with a store, gallery and lodge.

Spearfish Canyon Resort   *(605)584-3435*
12 mi. S on US 14-A, Spearfish Canyon
B-L-D.   *Moderate*
The resort's **Latchstring Village Restaurant** is one of the Black
Hills' best. Game is featured on a contemporary American menu. A
stone fireplace lends warmth to the comfortable wood-trimmed dining
room and lounge overlooking the picturesque canyon.

LODGING

Lodgings are relatively plentiful and prosaic, with a few exceptions.
High season is late May into September. Winter rates may be 25% less.

Cottonwood Lodge   *(605)642-2234*
downtown at 506 5th St. - 57783
14 units   *Moderate*
Cottonwood Lodge is Spearfish's most charming lodging. The authentic
log lodge opened in the mid-1990s with a great room accented by a
three-story flagstone fireplace, massive log walls, a wealth of local
artifacts, and a cozy rustic pub. Out back is a covered whirlpool. Each
beautifully furnished room has a pine log bed and unexpected details.

Downtown Spearfish - Best Western   *(605)642-4676*
just W at 346 W. Kansas - 57783
35 units   *(800)528-1234*   *Moderate*
This modern motel has an indoor recreation center with a pool,
whirlpool, game room and lounge. Each room is well furnished.

Fairfield Inn by Marriott   *(605)642-3500*
1 mi. SE (near I-90) at 2720 1st Av. E. - 57783
57 units   *(800)228-2800*   *Moderate*
A small indoor pool and whirlpool are features of this modern motel.
Each room is well furnished. Some also have a whirlpool bath.

Holiday Inn Spearfish   *(605)642-4683*
1 mi. SE (at I-90) at exit 14 (Box 399) - 57783
145 units   *(800)999-3541*   *Moderate*
The town's largest lodging is a motor hotel on a hill with an indoor
recreation center, pool, two whirlpools, game room, exercise room,
coffee shop and lounge. Each room is attractively furnished.

Spearfish Canyon Resort   *(605)584-3435*
12 mi. S on US 14-A, Spearfish Canyon (Box 705) - 57783
54 units   *(800)439-8544*   *Moderate-Expensive*
The area's best full service resort is nestled deep in Spearfish Canyon.
The 1996 complex includes a trout stream, hiking trails to two nearby
waterfalls, mountain bike rentals, a fine restaurant (see listing) and
gift shop. Each room is beautifully furnished. Some spacious suites also
have a private deck, gas fireplace and whirlpool bath.

BASIC INFORMATION

Elevation: 3,650 feet   *Population (1990):   6,966*
Location: 390 miles North of Denver
Nearest airport with commercial flights: Rapid City - 55 miles
Spearfish Area Chamber of Commerce (605)642-2626   (800)626-8013
  downtown at 115 E. Hunson (Box 550) - 57783   www.spearfish.sd.us

Gatlinburg, Tennessee

Gatlinburg is a peerless blend of Southern mountain culture and recreation. Several spring-fed streams cascade through the town sequestered in a narrow valley next to Great Smoky Mountains National Park. Luxuriant woodlands blanket surrounding slopes of some of the highest peaks in eastern America. Farmers and craftsmen began settling here in the early 1800s. But it took more than a century for the village to become a renowned travel destination.

Today, the park and mountains, streams and woodlands offer unlimited four-season recreation opportunities. Gatlinburg's studios, galleries and specialty shops house the South's finest treasury of authentic mountain crafts and collectibles. Dozens of museums and attractions include some that are unique. Among abundant restaurants are many with homespun charm. The nearby area has burgeoned into one of America's top music and variety show capitals. Abundant lodgings often capture the artistry and romance of this beguiling place.

WEATHER PROFILE

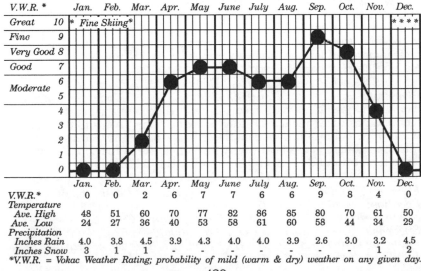

V.W.R. *		Jan.	Feb.	Mar.	Apr.	May	June	July	Aug.	Sep.	Oct.	Nov.	Dec.
Great	10	* Fine Skiing*											* * * *
Fine	9												
Very Good	8												
Good	7												
Moderate	6 / 5												
	4												
	3												
	2												
	1												
	0												

	Jan.	Feb.	Mar.	Apr.	May	June	July	Aug.	Sep.	Oct.	Nov.	Dec.
V.W.R.*	0	0	2	6	7	7	6	6	9	8	4	0
Temperature												
Ave. High	48	51	60	70	77	82	86	85	80	70	61	50
Ave. Low	24	27	36	40	53	58	61	60	58	44	34	29
Precipitation												
Inches Rain	4.0	3.8	4.5	3.9	4.3	4.0	4.0	3.9	2.6	3.0	3.2	4.5
Inches Snow	3	1	1	-	-	-	-	-	-	-	1	2

*V.W.R. = Vokac Weather Rating; probability of mild (warm & dry) weather on any given day.

428

ATTRACTIONS

Aerial Tramways
Gatlinburg Aerial Tramway   *(423)436-5423*
downtown on US 441 at 1001 Parkway
"America's largest aerial tramway" travels 2.2 miles from downtown to Ober Gatlinburg. Views of town and the mountains are breathtaking.
Gatlinburg Sky Lift   *(423)436-4307*
downtown on US 441 at 765 Parkway
For decades, a double chairlift has been transporting passengers from the heart of town to the top of Crockett Mountain for memorable panoramas of the Smokies. The round-trip is approximately one mile.
Dollywood   *(423)428-9488*
6 mi. N via US 441 at 1020 Dollywood Lane - Pigeon Forge
Dollywood lives up to its role as "the entertainment capital of the Smokies"—and then some! Thrill rides, attractions, live music shows, and crafts are brought together in a big, beautifully landscaped park that evokes the fun and traditions of the Smoky Mountains. Among numerous rousing rides, "The Slidewinder" (a free-flow water toboggan) was rated the #1 non-roller coaster ride in America. Now there is "Daredevil Falls" (a beautiful water ride with a breathtaking fall)—America's highest, longest, and fastest waterfall ride. Attractions include Dolly Parton's Museum, a water-powered grist mill, and a five-mile journey aboard a coal-fired steam train. Nearly forty live musical performances daily range from country and bluegrass to pop and gospel. Dozens of master artisans showcase crafts ranging from glass blowing to dulcimer making. Several major festivals and concerts are also held here annually. Dozens of quaint shops, snack bars, and restaurants are conveniently located throughout the colorful grounds
Downtown
centered around Parkway & Airport Rd.
Crystal-clear streams are a major part of the charm of downtown Gatlinburg. Flowery walkways and roads line their banks and extend to a remarkable concentration of shops featuring mountain handicrafts, museums, and tourist attractions (including the nation's largest concentration of scenic chairlifts and trams). Mountain style is appropriately featured among the many restaurants, lounges and nightlife possibilities, and in romantic streamside lodgings.
Flyaway   *(423)453-7777*
7 mi. N on US 441 at 3106 Parkway
The nation's premier indoor sky diving chamber simulates the feeling of flight in a vertical wind tunnel. Instructors provide a short orientation and assistance to participants who then soar, turn and swoop in the circular tunnel.
Gatlinburg's Fun Mountain   *(423)430-7275*
downtown at 130 E. Parkway
A long chairlift provides scenic views of downtown and the mountains. The amusement park has something for everyone, with rides galore, bumper boats and cars, go-carts, a waterfall, miniature golf course, lazar tag, the area's largest arcade, and food service.
Great Smoky Arts & Crafts Community
13 mi. NE via US 321 on Glades Rd.
A bonanza of traditional Smoky Mountain handicrafts and art are created, displayed and sold by talented artisans along a picturesque eight-mile loop (of Glades Road, Buckhorn Rd. and US 321). Several distinctive restaurants are on the loop, which is also served by trolleys.

Great Smoky Mountains National Park   *(423)436-1200*
just S on US 441
America's most visited national park attracts more than nine million
people annually to the heart of the largest Eastern mountain range.
Tennessee and North Carolina share the 52-by-18-mile park. Most of
the highest peaks east of the Mississippi River are found here. The
highest is Clingman's Dome, 6,642 feet above sea level, which can be
accessed by a seven-mile spur road and a half-mile path to an
observation tower with an outstanding panorama of the surrounding
mountains. Conifers crown the summits, while luxuriant broadleaf
forests blanket lower ridges and valleys with streams and waterfalls
bordered by rhododendrons and azaleas. More than 800 miles of hiking
and riding trails include a major section of the Appalachian Trail.
Sugarland Visitor Center near town has exhibits and more information
about hiking, horseback riding, trout fishing, camping and sightseeing
opportunities.
Horseback Riding
There are almost a dozen stables in the area offering guided trail rides
along streams and through flowery meadows and cool forests in the
surrounding mountains. The two places listed below feature hour (and
longer) guided rides on scenic trails inside the national park.
   McCarter's Riding Stables   *2 mi. S on US 441*   *(423)436-5354*
   Smoky Mountain Stables   *4 mi. NE on US 321*   *(423)436-5634*
Live Theater
   6 mi. N on US 441 - Pigeon Forge
Nearby Pigeon Forge boasts more than a dozen live music/variety
theaters along the main thoroughfare (Parkway). Diverse venues
showcase music ranging from the sweet sound of a single dulcimer to
star-studded performances with state-of-the-art special effects.
Following are the author's six favorites:
   Dixie Stampede *dinner theater extravaganza 453-4400(800)356-1676*
   Dollywood   *esp. Dolly Parton's signature show*   *428-9488*
   Eagle Mountain Theatre   *Grand Ole Opry stars*   *429-0009*
   Louise Mandrell Theater *L. Mandrell / state-of-the-art variety 453-3534*
   Memories Theatre   *impressions, 50s / 60s revue*   *428-7852*
   Music Mansion   *variety spectacular*   *428-7469*
Ober Gatlinburg   *(423)436-5423*
   downtown at 1001 Parkway
Gatlinburg's all-season recreation park is a delight for the young at
heart. It can be reached by a scenic aerial tramway (see listing) from
downtown. The mountaintop resort features an 1,800-foot alpine slide,
a sightseeing chairlift to spectacular views atop Mt. Harrison, an
indoor ice skating rink, bungee jumping, a velcro wall jump, water
rides, an astroturf ski slope, crafts and gift shops, cafes and live
entertainment. In winter, six hundred feet of vertical rise and ski runs
nearly a mile long can be accessed by four chairlifts. All facilities,
services, rentals and restaurants on the mountain, plus abundant
lodgings downtown at the tram base. Ski season is December through
February.
Ogle's Water Park   *(423)453-8741*
   6 mi. N on US 441 at 2530 Parkway - Pigeon Forge
The largest water fun complex in the Smokies is really popular on hot
summer days, with a wave pool, ten waterslides, and a lazy river, plus
food and gift concessions.

Pigeon Forge   *(423)453-8574   (800)251-9100*
   6 mi. N on US 441
In recent years, this village on the flatlands near the Smokies and Gatlinburg has burgeoned into a boomtown fueled by tourism. The five-mile Parkway through town is lined with live theaters (see listing); more than forty family-oriented attractions ranging from Dollywood to waterslides and indoor sky diving (see listings); dozens of modern hotels, motels and restaurants; plus more than 200 factory outlet stores.

River Running
The Big Pigeon River offers five miles of challenging scenic whitewater next to the national park. Two companies provide guided trips of various lengths, including all equipment and shuttles. Unguided rafts can be reserved for the gentle lower Pigeon River, too.
   Rafting in the Smokies   *(423)436-5008   (800)776-7238*
   The Whitewater Company   *(423)487-2030   (800)723-8426*
Space Needle   *(423)436-4303*
   just S at 115 Airport Rd.
Glass-enclosed elevators take visitors 342 feet up to an observation deck for a beautiful view of the town and mountains. At the base is a large family fun center.

Wineries
   Smoky Mountain Winery   *(423)436-7551*
   1 mi. NE via US 321 at 450 Cherry St., Suite 2
East Tennessee's oldest operating winery lets you browse among the oak barrels and tanks in the aging cellar, taste a range of grape and mountain-fruit wines, and visit The Cellar gift shop.

RESTAURANTS
Atrium Restaurant   *(423)430-3684*
   downtown on US 441 at 432 Parkway
   B-L.   *Moderate*
Contemporary American dishes like fresh trout are enhanced by breads and desserts made here. You can dine by a waterfall on the patio or in the casual comfortable dining room.
The Burning Bush Restaurant   *(423)436-4669*
   downtown on US 441 at 1151 Parkway
   B-L-D.   *Expensive*
Bountiful breakfasts stand out among skillfully prepared traditional and contemporary American fare. A view of the park, caged birds, fieldstone, polished wood, crystal and candlelight contribute to gracious rusticity each evening. There is also a lounge and gift shop.
Greenbrier Restaurant   *(423)436-6318*
   2 mi. NE via US 321 at 370 Newman Rd.
   D only.   *Moderate*
Prime rib, steaks and other American standards are served with homemade bread in a historic (1939) log cabin on a hill. There is a pleasant window-wall view of woodlands from the casual firelit dining room and lounge.
Heidelberg Restaurant   *(423)430-3094   (800)726-3094*
   1 mi. N via US 441 at 148 Parkway
   L-D.   *Moderate*
German and American dishes are served in big, family-oriented Bavarian-themed dining rooms and bar. A live show with German music and dancing contributes to the fun each evening.

Maxwell's Beef & Seafood   *(423)436-3738*
downtown on US 441 at 1103 Parkway
D only.   *Expensive*
Fresh seafood stars among contemporary American dishes that get
expert attention, as do flambé desserts. Piano entertainment is part of
the appeal of the casually elegant dining room and lounge.

The Park Grill   *(423)436-2300*
downtown on US 441 at 1110 Parkway
D only.   *Expensive*
Hickory-grilled steaks are featured among traditional American dishes,
along with housemade breads and desserts. Comfortably rustic dining
areas and lounge are in a mountain lodge of massive logs.

The Peddler Restaurant & Lounge   *(423)436-5794*
downtown at 820 River Rd.
D only.   *Expensive*
The specialty is steaks cut to the thickness you desire at your table,
then charcoal-broiled and served with a bountiful salad bar. Upscale
rusticity is part of the appeal in a big log cabin overlooking a stream.

Smoky Mountain Trout House   *(423)436-5416*
downtown on US 441 at 410 Parkway
D only.   *Moderate*
Fresh rainbow trout prepared a dozen different ways stars among
traditional American dishes served in a casual setting.

LODGING

Lodgings are superabundant. Gatlinburg is the whirlpool tub capital
of America. High season is summer and October (leaf-peeper season).
Early in the year, rates are usually reduced 30% or more.

Bent Creek Golf Resort   *(423)436-2875*
11 mi. E on US 321 at 3919 E. Parkway - 37738
108 units   *(800)251-9336*   *Moderate-Expensive*
Gary Player designed the (fee) 18-hole golf course for this resort in the
mountains, and there is a large pool and dining rooms. Each nicely
furnished room has a private balcony. Many have a fireplace.

Brookside Resort   *(423)436-5611*
1 mi. E on US 321 at 463 E. Parkway - 37738
220 units   *(800)251-9597*   *Moderate-Expensive*
A sylvan stream is next to this contemporary four-story motel, and
there is a delightful tri-level waterfall swimming pool with a slide.
Many well-furnished units have a private balcony by the stream. Some
also have a fireplace and/or whirlpool tub and steam bath.

The Colonel's Lady   *(423)436-5432*
6 mi. NE via US 321 at 1120 Tanrac Trail - 37738
8 units   *(800)515-5432*   *Expensive*
One of the area's best bed-and-breakfast inns is an English-style
country manor high atop a ridge. Full gourmet breakfast and afternoon
snacks are complimentary. Each beautifully furnished room has a
private bath, all modern conveniences, plus an indoor or outdoor
whirlpool tub. Some also have a fireplace and kitchen.

Days Inn - Glenstone Lodge   *(423)436-9361*
just S at 504 Airport Rd. (Box 330) - 37738
215 units   *(800)362-9522*   *Moderate*
This contemporary five-story hotel by a stream has a delightful split-
level indoor pool with a waterfall, a new outdoor pool with a river deck,
whirlpool, indoor putting green, and restaurant. Each well-furnished
room has a private balcony. Some also have a fireplace.

Gatlinburg Travelodge   *(423)436-7851*
just S at 610 Airport Rd. - 37738
125 units   *(800)876-6888*   *Moderate-Expensive*
A clear mountain stream borders this modern five-story motor lodge. There is also an outdoor pool, a delightful freeform indoor pool in a grotto with a waterfall and whirlpool, a sauna, and a deli. Most of the well-furnished units have a private balcony above the wooded stream. Suites also have a gas or wood fireplace and in-room whirlpool tub.

Holiday Inn Sunspree Resort   *(423)436-9201*
just S at 520 Airport Rd. - 37738
402 units   *(800)435-9201*   *Moderate-Expensive*
Holiday's best in the region is a contemporary eight-story hotel by a stream with two indoor pools, an outdoor pool, two whirlpools, sauna, dining rooms, lounge, and gift shop. Each room is well furnished. Most have a mountain or stream view.

Park Vista Resort Hotel   *(423)436-9211*
just S at 705 Cherokee Orchard Rd. (Box 30) - 37738
312 units   *(800)421-7275*   *Moderate-Expensive*
A circular fifteen-story tower is the heart of a hotel complex that includes two indoor pools, whirlpool, exercise room, restaurant, entertainment lounge and gift shop. Each well-furnished unit has a private balcony and a dramatic mountain view.

Rivermont Motor Inn   *(423)436-5047*
just N on US 441 at 293 Parkway - 37738
70 rooms (800)624-2929 (except TN); TN: (800)634-2929   Moderate
The river is next to this contemporary four-level motel with a pool. Each well-furnished unit has a private balcony overlooking the sylvan stream. Some also have a two-person whirlpool bath and/or fireplace.

Tennessee Ridge Inn   *(423)436-4068*
1 mi. N at 507 Campbell Lead - 37738
7 units   *(800)737-7369*   *Expensive*
One of the Smokies' most romantic bed-and-breakfast inns is in a stylish building perched high above Gatlinburg with a grand view of the mountains and town. An outdoor pool is available for guests. A full gourmet breakfast is complimentary. Each beautifully furnished room has no phone to take attention away from a private view balcony and an in-room two-person whirlpool tub. Most of the rooms also have a gas or wood fireplace.

Zoder's Inn - Best Western   *(423)436-5681*
downtown on US 441 at 402 Parkway (Box 708) - 37738
90 units   *(800)528-1234*   *Moderate-Expensive*
This handsome contemporary motel by a sylvan stream also features an indoor recreation center with a pool, whirlpool and waterfall, two racquetball courts and an exercise room, plus an outdoor pool. Many of the well-furnished rooms have a private balcony above the creek. Suites also have an in-room two-person whirlpool tub and a fireplace.

BASIC INFORMATION

Elevation: 1,290 feet   *Population (1990): 3,417*
Location: 220 miles East of Nashville, TN
Nearest airport with commercial flights: Knoxville - 45 miles
Gatlinburg Tourism/Convention Center   (423)436-2392
   just S at 234 Airport Rd. (Box 5) - 37738   (800)267-7088
   www.gatlinburg. com

Fredericksburg, Texas

Fredericksburg is the heart of the Texas Hill Country. It lies amid gentle oak-covered folds of ancient limestone extending more than fifty miles in every direction. German farmers settled here in 1846, attracted by fertile soil, spring water, and a mild climate.

Much of Fredericksburg's distinctive past remains. Many native limestone houses, stores, public buildings, monuments and a square contribute to "Old World" charm. The wide main street is lined with meticulous storefronts of stone, German woodwork, and Victorian gingerbread. Shops proudly featuring Texas art, crafts, antiques and culinary delights, plus numerous eating and drinking places (many with real gemutlichkeit) have made Main Street one of the state's favorite destinations. Nearby, bed-and-breakfast inns reflect the town's rich heritage. Beyond, scenic spring-fed streams, reservoirs, caves and a massive granite dome provide all sorts of recreation opportunities in surrounding hills and valleys.

WEATHER PROFILE

V.W.R. *		Jan.	Feb.	Mar.	Apr.	May	June	July	Aug.	Sep.	Oct.	Nov.	Dec.
Great	10												
Fine	9												
Very Good	8												
Good	7												
Moderate	6												
	5												

	Jan.	Feb.	Mar.	Apr.	May	June	July	Aug.	Sep.	Oct.	Nov.	Dec.
V.W.R.*	7	7	8	9	8	5	4	4	7	9	8	7
Temperature												
Ave. High	62	65	70	78	84	90	93	93	86	80	69	63
Ave. Low	36	39	46	55	61	67	69	69	64	55	45	38
Precipitation												
Inches Rain	1.0	1.7	2.0	2.6	3.3	2.7	2.4	2.0	2.8	2.8	1.6	1.3
Inches Snow	-	1	-	-	-	-	-	-	-	-	-	-

*V.W.R. = Vokac Weather Rating; probability of mild (warm & dry) weather on any given day.

434

ATTRACTIONS

Admiral Nimitz Museum State Historical Park   *(830)997-4379*
downtown at 340 E. Main St.
The restored Steamboat Hotel landmark, originally built in 1852, houses the large Museum of the Pacific War dedicated to millions who served under Admiral Nimitz. The last U.S. five-star admiral was born in Fredericksburg in 1885. Behind the hotel is the Garden of Peace—a gift from the people of Japan. One block east, the History Walk displays planes, boats, tanks, etc. from World War II. There is also a comprehensive selection of gifts and books.

Enchanted Rock State Natural Area *(915)247-3903 (800)792-1112*
18 mi. N via Route 965
Among the oldest and largest exposed rocks in North America is this 500-foot-high dome of solid granite. The massive landmark offers rock climbing, several miles of hiking trails, picnicking and primitive camping, plus outstanding star-gazing opportunities.

Food Specialties
Fredericksburg is remarkably well endowed with stores featuring tastes and sales of regional gourmet goodies. Don't miss:

Das Peach Haus   *(830)997-8969   (800)369-9257*
2 mi. S on US 87
A big picturesque roadside country store has featured peaches fresh in season and in jams, jellies, cobblers and more since 1969.

The Epicurean Shop   *(830)997-0124   (800)369-9257*
downtown at 315 E. Main St.
Fischer & Wieser stars among many Texas jams, jellies and specialty foods generously offered for tastes and sales in this cheerful shop.

Fredericksburg Herb Farm   *(830)997-8615   (800)259-4372*
1 mi. W ul 402 Whitney St.
Experience flowering, culinary and ornamental herbs used for gourmet, decorative, bath and body products, and get pampered in a day spa.

Wildseed Farms Market Center   *(830)990-1393*
7 mi. E on US 290
At the largest working wildflower farm in America, you can enjoy the displays of crops, and buy seeds, Texas specialty foods, and wines.

LBJ State & National Historical Parks *(830)644-2252 (830)868-7128*
16 mi. E on US 290 - Stonewall & Johnson City
The state park includes a visitor center, pioneer cabin, living history farmstead, nature trails, plus picnic and recreation areas. National Park buses depart from the visitor center to tour President Johnson's ranchlands, "Texas White House," birthplace and family cemetery.

Lady Bird Johnson Municipal Park   *(830)997-4202*
3 mi. SW via Texas Hwy. 16
Fredericksburg's largest park includes a wooded area by a creek with a small lake for boating and fishing, swimming pool, 18-hole golf course, sports fields and courts, plus camping and picnicking facilities.

Pioneer Museum Complex   *(830)997-2835*
downtown at 309 W. Main St.
An 1849 stone pioneer home and store is the centerpiece among several structures furnished with many relics of German colonists.

Vereins Kirche Museum   *(830)997-2835*
downtown on Market Square
This exact replica of an 1847 octagonal building that was a church, school and fort contains archives and a local history collection.

RESTAURANTS

Alfredo's Restaurant   *(830)997-8593*
downtown at 505 W. Main St.
L-D.   *Low*
Stuffed poblano chiles, chalupas, nachos and other Tex-Mex favorites
are carefully prepared and served in simply decorated little dining
rooms of a tidy cottage.

Der Lindenbaum   *(830)997-9126*
downtown at 312 E. Main St.
L-D.   *Moderate*
Authentic Rheinland-style dishes including house-baked breads and
specialty desserts are served (with gemutlichkeit) in a comfortable
dining room or biergarten.

Fredericksburg Bakery   *(830)997-3254*
downtown at 141 E. Main St.
B-L.   *Moderate*
German and American baked goods and ice cream have been featured
in this handsome bakery/coffee shop since 1917.

Fredericksburg Brewing Company   *(830)997-1646*
downtown at 245 E. Main St.
L-D.   *Moderate*
The town's first brew pub offers fresh ales and lagers brewed here in
copper kettles and served with flavorful pub grub in an atmospheric
lager room and biergarten of a historic Victorian building.

Friedhelm's Bavarian Inn   *(830)997-6300*
1 mi. W at 905 W. Main St.
L-D.   *Moderate*
Traditional Bavarian and American dishes are served in the relaxed
dining room, and there is a full service bar.

The Gallery Restaurant   *(830)997-8777*
downtown at 230 E. Main St.
B-L-D.   *Moderate*
Italian, German and American fare compete for diner's attention with
handsome turn-of-the-century decor in the main dining room, garden
room, or posh upstairs Blue Room.

Opa's Smoked Meats   *(830)997-3358*   *(800)543-6750*
just S at 410 S. Washington St. (Hwy. 87)
takeout only.   *Expensive*
The thick choice filets of peppered and hickory-smoked beef tenderloin
made here are the best in America. Get some for the ultimate snack or
picnic. Smoked ham or turkey, beef sticks or sausage, are other stellar
meat treats available to go or for shipment.

The Plateau Cafe   *(830)997-1853*
downtown at 312 W. Main St.
L-D.   *Moderate*
Traditional German and Texas dishes including homemade desserts
are served in the atmospheric dining room or patio of a historic building.

LODGING
Hotels and motels are surprisingly scarce, but there are many small
bed-and-breakfasts. There is no high season in Fredericksburg. Rates
stay the same year-round.

Country Cottage Inn - Nimitz Birthplace   *(830)997-8549*
downtown at 249 E. Main St. - 78624
11 units   *Expensive*
A complex of historic limestone homes on the National Register houses

a romantic bed-and-breakfast. Full breakfast is complimentary. Each room has a private entrance and is attractively furnished with antiques and all contemporary conveniences. Most have a fireplace and a whirlpool tub for two.

Dietzel Motel   *(830)997-3330*
1 mi. W at 909 W. Main St. (Box 266) - 78624
20 units   *Low*
This modern single-story motel has a pool. Each room has no phone, but is comfortably furnished.

Fredericksburg Bed and Brew   *(830)997-1646*
downtown at 245 E. Main St. - 78624
12 units   *Moderate*
Downstairs is the area's first brew pub (see listing). Each room is individually nicely furnished and has a private bath.

Fredericksburg Inn & Suites   *(830)997-0202*
downtown at 201 S. Washington St. (US 87) - 98624
50 units   *(800)446-0202*   *Moderate*
One of the area's newest motels has a pool and features well-furnished spacious rooms and suites with microwaves and refrigerators.

Magnolia House   *(830)997-0306*
just N at 101 E. Hackberry St. - 78624
6 units   *(800)880-4374*   *Moderate-Expensive*
A skillfully restored 1923 home now serves as a fine bed-and-breakfast. Full Southern breakfast and afternoon beverages are complimentary. Each room is beautifully furnished, and has all contemporary conveniences except phones. Two suites have a fireplace.

Old Mill Settlement   *(830)997-1610*
just NE at 508 E. Schubert St. - 78624
15 units   *Expensive*
Old Mill Settlement is Frederickburg's most romantic lodging. In 1995, a collection of antique log cabins and old-style German rock homes opened around a serene rock pond with waterfalls. Expanded Continental breakfast and treats are complimentary. Each beautifully furnished room combines period decor and a wood-burning fireplace plus all contemporary conveniences including a kitchenette, and (most have) a whirlpool.

Peach Tree Inn   *(830)997-2117*
just S at 401 S. Washington St. - 78624
24 units   *(800)843-4666*   *Low*
One of the area's original motels (built in the 1940s) has been restored and has a pool. Each room is comfortably furnished with 1940s decor, plus contemporary remote control TV and a phone.

Sunday House Inn - Best Western   *(830)997-4484*
downtown at 501 E. Main St. - 78624
97 units   *(800)528-1234*   *Moderate*
This modern motor inn has a pool and comfortably furnished rooms.

BASIC INFORMATION

Elevation: 1,743 feet   *Population (1990):   6,934*
Location: 70 miles Northwest of San Antonio
Nearest airport with commercial flights: San Antonio - 70 miles
Fredericksburg Convention & Visitors Bureau   (830)997-6523
   downtown on Market Square at 106 N. Adams St. - 78624
   www.fredericksburg-texas.com

New Braunfels, Texas

New Braunfels is the fresh-water-fun capital of America. Texas' largest springs, gushing from limestone crevices at the southern edge of the Texas hill country, have created the clear, warm Comal River exclusively within the city. German immigrants attracted by abundant water, rich soil, and mild climate began a settlement here in 1845.

Today, New Braunfels is a water wonderland. The springs and river are showcased in Landa Park, one of the nation's best, where visitors can enjoy huge swimming pools, glass-bottom boat rides, and idyllic river tubing. Also sharing the riverfront is Schlitterbahn, the biggest and best waterpark in the United States. Downtown, a plaza, fountains, and historic limestone buildings retain the community's "Old World" charm. So does the Gruene neighborhood. Shops in both areas specialize in Texas art, handicrafts and culinary delights. Some of the best restaurants and lodgings reflect the continuing German heritage and feature memorable river views.

WEATHER PROFILE

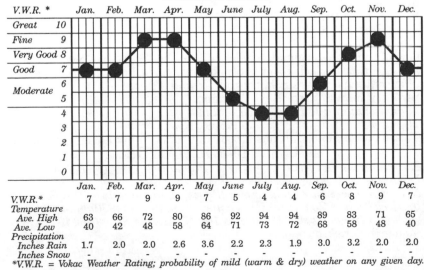

V.W.R. *		Jan.	Feb.	Mar.	Apr.	May	June	July	Aug.	Sep.	Oct.	Nov.	Dec.
Great	10												
Fine	9												
Very Good	8												
Good	7												
Moderate	6												
	5												
	4												
	3												
	2												
	1												
	0												

	Jan.	Feb.	Mar.	Apr.	May	June	July	Aug.	Sep.	Oct.	Nov.	Dec.
V.W.R.*	7	7	9	9	7	5	4	4	6	8	9	7
Temperature												
Ave. High	63	66	72	80	86	92	94	94	89	83	71	65
Ave. Low	40	42	48	58	64	71	73	72	68	58	48	40
Precipitation												
Inches Rain	1.7	2.0	2.0	2.6	3.6	2.2	2.3	1.9	3.0	3.2	2.0	2.0
Inches Snow	-	-	-	-	-	-	-	-	-	-	-	-

*V.W.R. = Vokac Weather Rating; probability of mild (warm & dry) weather on any given day.

Canyon Lake   *(830)964-3341*
12 mi. NW via Route 306
One of Texas' most scenic reservoirs extends for about ten miles among evergreen hills. Fishing is excellent for catfish and bass in the lake and trout in the Guadalupe River below. Swimming, boating, water-skiing, picnicking and camping are also popular.

Comal River   *(830)620-7600*
just N via San Antonio St.
Texas' shortest river begins at the giant springs in Landa Park and ends three miles later at its junction with the Guadalupe River—all in town. The clear, warm stream flows gently between luxuriant forest galleries and sunny greenswards bordered by peaceful riverside walkways. But, this is the supreme destination for tubing. Highlights include an exhilarating waterslide on the river, and turtle's-eye views of Schlitterbahn's (see listing) waterslides that end in the Comal River. The **Ole Mill Stream** has rentals and shuttles.

Gruene Historic District   *(830)625-2385*
4 mi. NE on Gruene Rd.
German immigrants established a village on a bluff above the Guadalupe River before 1850. Now part of New Braunfels, the site has picturesque ruins and two dozen restored buildings housing collectibles and specialty shops, charming restaurants, the state's oldest (1880) dance hall, and a romantic bed-and-breakfast inn above the river.

Hummel Museum   *(830)625-5636*   *(800)456-4866*
downtown at 199 Main Plaza
The world's largest collection (more than 300 paintings and drawings) of the art of Sister. M.I. Hummel is displayed. Her work inspired the famous porcelain figurines made in Germany. The gift shop has an extensive selection.

Landa Park   *(830)608-2160*
1 mi. NW via Landa St.
One of America's most outstanding town parks is the pride of New Braunfels. At the heart of the expansive site, Texas' largest springs form the state's shortest river—less than three miles. (See Comal River.) A spring-fed swimming pool is built into the natural streambed. Pretty little Landa Lake can be enjoyed via glass-bottom boat rides or paddleboat rentals. A miniature train ride winds through the park. The huge 300-year-old Founders Oak stars on a self-guided tour of the park's arboretum. Towering trees shade idyllic picnic and fishing sites, nature trails, a recreation-and-special-events complex, miniature golf course, and an 18-hole public golf course.

Natural Bridge Caverns   *(830)651-6101*
14 mi. W via TX 46 at 26495 Natural Bridge Caverns Rd.
The state's largest cavern extends for more than a mile and includes both exquisite and awesome formations in narrow corridors and gigantic chambers with quiet, crystal-clear pools.

Natural Bridge Wildlife Ranch   *(830)438-7400*
12 mi. W via TX 46 at 26515 Natural Bridge Caverns Rd.
In this drive-through wildlife park in the oak-brush-covered hill country, you will encounter free-roaming exotic animals. Some, like the ostrich, will put their heads into car windows for a treat from your complimentary food container. There are also protected observation areas and petting zoos.

River Running   *(830)625-2385*
4 mi. N along River Rd.
New Braunfels is the river rafting and tubing capital of Texas. Several outfitters provide guided float trips of various lengths on the Guadalupe River. Or, rent a canoe, raft or tube to float the scenic easy stretches below Canyon Dam, and reserve a shuttle back to your car.

Schlitterbahn   *(830)625-2351*
1 mi. N at 305 W. Austin St.
Schlitterbahn (Slippery Road) is America's biggest and best waterpark. The picturesque Comal River (see listing) borders the big, colorfully landscaped complex. Its spring water is circulated through some of the flumes, including a few that slide delighted riders right into the river. A German-style castle towers over more than thirty attractions. There's always something new being invented here! State-of-the-art water rides that originated here include the world's first uphill water coasters, the world's first tidal wave river, and the first ocean-sized continuous wave for body boarding. There are also more than two dozen waterslides and flumes, a wave pool, water playground, hot tubs, lazy river, and more than a mile of interconnecting tube chutes. Towering trees also shade a restaurant and refreshment center, several gift shops, picnic areas and lodgings (see listing).

RESTAURANTS

Bavarian Village   *(830)625-0815*
1 mi. N at 212 W. Austin St.
L-D.   *Low*
New Braunfels' oldest restaurant and biergarten features authentic German dishes and American foods, plus a large selection of beers in a beer garden with (weekend) live polka music. There is a gift shop.

Gristmill Restaurant & Bar   *(830)625-0684*
4 mi. NE at 1287 Gruene Rd.
L-D.   *Moderate*
Texas comfort foods, including luscious desserts, are served amid the delightfully remodeled ruins of a century-old stone cotton gin, and on a multilevel terrace nestled in the trees above the Guadalupe River.

Gruene Mansion Restaurant   *(830)620-0760*
4 mi. NE at 1275 Gruene Rd.
L-D.   *Moderate*
The area's most romantic restaurant opened in 1995 with a tantalizing array of contemporary Southern and German dishes, and homemade pastries baked fresh daily. Candles and firelight (even for lunch) contribute to the rustic elegance of the dining room. Beyond, grand covered porches overlook the tranquil Guadalupe River.

Huisache Grill   *(830)620-9001*
downtown at 303-D W. San Antonio St.
L-D.   *Low*
Traditional and innovative South Texas dishes are given careful attention, and served in a dining room that has the comfort of a recently renovated Old Texas roadhouse.

Naegelin's Bakery   *(830)625-5722*
downtown at 129 S. Seguin Av.
B-L.   *Low*
Naegelin's is one of Texas' best bakeries and the oldest, dating back to 1868. The German sweet pretzel alone would be worth a detour. The Danish butterfly roll is another star among morning delights that can be enjoyed with coffee, or to go.

New Braunfels Smokehouse   *(830)625-2416*
 3 mi. E (near I-35) at 140 Hwy. 46 S.
 B-L-D.   *Low*
This New Braunfels original has offered samples of their delicious
hickory-smoked meat for over half a century. All meals feature smoked
meats of all kinds with homemade support dishes in several
comfortable dining rooms and a patio. There is also a gourmet general
store and gift shop.

Oma's Haus Restaurant   *(830)625-3280*
 4 mi. E at 541 Hwy. 46
 L-D.   *Low*
A good selection of German dishes with a Texas accent is the highlight
at Oma's, and the desserts like apple strudel are homemade. In
addition to casual family-oriented dining rooms, there is an authentic
German biergarten, and a well-stocked gift shop.

Tree Tops Riverside Grille   *(830)606-8677*
 downtown at 444 E. San Antonio St.
 L-D.   *Moderate*
Contemporary American and European fare is greatly enhanced by
handsome indoor and outdoor dining areas with enchanting views of
the bordering Comal River.

Wolfgang's Keller Restaurant   *(830)625-9169*
 downtown at 295 E. San Antonio St.
 D only.   *Expensive*
Contemporary American and German cuisine is skillfully prepared
from fresh quality ingredients and served amidst the romantic charms
of a Texas Historic Landmark Inn.

LODGING

Accommodations are numerous and conventional along I-35. Notable
alternatives are described below. Mid-May into September is prime
time. Some places reduce rates 25% or more at other times.

Faust Hotel   *(830)625-7791*
 downtown at 240 S. Seguin St. - 78130
 62 units   *Moderate*
This local landmark hotel, opened in 1929, has been restored with
period decor blended with modern conveniences. Each refurbished room
is comfortably furnished.

Gruene Homestead Inn   *(830)606-0216*
 3 mi. NE at 832 Gruene Rd. - 78130
 21 units   *Moderate-Expensive*
Restored historic buildings are the centerpiece of this haven of
tranquility in the country with a pool, whirlpool and a restaurant and
lounge added in 1998. Attractively furnished rooms blend period decor
and all contemporary conveniences, but no phone. Some also feature a
whirlpool bath and a private porch.

Gruene Mansion Inn   *(830)629-2641*
 4 mi. NE at 1275 Gruene Rd. - 78130
 17 units   *Moderate-Expensive*
High on a bluff overlooking the Guadalupe River is one of Texas'
delightful country inns. In the heart of the historic village of Gruene,
a Victorian mansion on the National Register and historic cottages
have been skillfully restored. There is romantic dining indoors and out
(see listing) and a picturesque bar. Each room is beautifully furnished
with period antiques and all modern conveniences except phone. Many
rooms also have a gas fireplace and a private river-view balcony.

Heidelberg Lodges   *(830)625-9967*
2 mi. N at 1020 N. Houston Av. - 78130
46 units   *Moderate*
The cottages overlook springs where the Comal River begins. Guests enjoy swimming, floating or snorkeling on the crystal-clear river. The family-oriented complex also has a pool, and game room with ping pong and pool. Each cottage is nicely furnished. Most have a kitchenette.

Karbach Haus Bed & Breakfast   *(830)625-2131*
just S at 487 W. San Antonio St. - 78130
6 units   *(800)972-5941*   *Expensive*
A historic brick mansion now serves as a fine bed-and-breakfast near downtown. Trees and gardens surround a pool and whirlpool. Gourmet breakfast is complimentary. Each well-furnished room has all contemporary facilities. Two have a whirlpool bath.

The Other Place   *(830)625-5114*
1 mi. E at 385 Other Place Dr. - 78130
41 units   *Moderate*
You can swim, tube or fish in the crystal-clear Comal River next to this apartment-style complex. Each nicely furnished unit has a kitchen.

Prince Solms Inn   *(830)625-9169*
downtown at 295 E. San Antonio St. - 78130
10 units   *(800)625-9169*   *Moderate-Expensive*
The Prince Solms Inn has been in continuous operation since it was completed in 1898 by German craftsmen. Old World atmosphere lends romance to the garden courtyard and Wolfgang's Keller Restaurant (see listing). Continental-plus breakfast is included. Each room is a comfortable blend of period pieces and modern conveniences.

Riverside Haven Bed and Breakfast   *(830)625-5823*
4 mi. N at 1491 Edwards Blvd. - 78132
4 units   *Moderate*
The blue-green Guadalupe River adjoins this expansive bed-and-breakfast inn. Use of a canoe and a European breakfast are complimentary. Each comfortably furnished room has all contemporary conveniences and a river view.

Schlitterbahn Resort "at the Bahn"   *(830)625-2351 ext. 2*
1 mi. N at 305 W. Austin St. - 78130
131 units   *Moderate-Expensive*
New Braunfels' largest family vacation complex adjoins the renowned waterpark with three pools, two hot tubs, and recreation facilities. Each motel, cottage or apartment unit is comfortably furnished. Two units have both a whirlpool tub and a fireplace.

Schlitterbahn Resort "at the Rapids"   *(830)625-2351 ext. 2*
1 mi. N at 370 W. Lincoln - 78130
88 units   *Moderate-Expensive*
The crystal-clear Comal River laps gently against the lawns and walkways of this sprawling motel. Texas' best tubing can be enjoyed out your front door, and America's best waterpark adjoins (with discounts available to guests). Each spacious, nicely furnished unit has a lovely river view.

BASIC INFORMATION

Elevation: 630 feet   *Population (1990):   27,334*
Location: 37 miles Northeast of San Antonio
Nearest airport with commercial flights: San Antonio - 32 miles
New Braunfels Chamber of Commerce (830)625-2385   (800)572-2626
*   just SE at 390 S. Seguin Av. (Box 311417) - 78131 www.nbcham.org*

San Marcos, Texas

San Marcos is a gateway to the Texas hill country. It is favored by both a choice location and a rich heritage. Enormous, clear springs gush from the base of an escarpment where the hills and plains meet. The resulting Spring Lake and San Marcos River led to the town's founding in 1851. With abundant water, good soil, and a mild climate, growth was steady, enhanced after the turn of the century by a state college and major tourist attraction.

The clear spring lake, and the gentle river where people love to swim, tube, snorkel, fish and canoe, are still the town's centerpieces. A wealth of Victorian buildings, including an entire residential neighborhood, also contribute to local charm. So do the shared cultural and recreational facilities of a now-major university. Texas-made arts, crafts and culinary treats are a source of pride downtown. Restaurants and bars share the regional tilt. Lodgings are surprisingly ordinary, except for a historic lakeside inn and a bed-and-breakfast.

WEATHER PROFILE

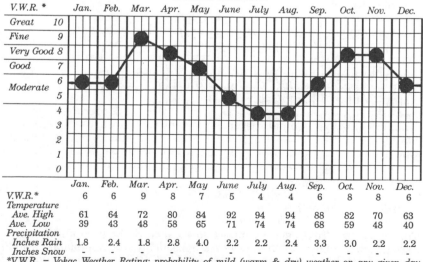

		Jan.	Feb.	Mar.	Apr.	May	June	July	Aug.	Sep.	Oct.	Nov.	Dec.
V.W.R.*		6	6	9	8	7	5	4	4	6	8	8	6
Temperature													
Ave. High		61	64	72	80	84	92	94	94	88	82	70	63
Ave. Low		39	43	48	58	65	71	74	74	68	59	48	40
Precipitation													
Inches Rain		1.8	2.4	1.8	2.8	4.0	2.2	2.2	2.4	3.3	3.0	2.2	2.2
Inches Snow		-	-	-	-	-	-	-	-	-	-	-	-

*V.W.R. = Vokac Weather Rating; probability of mild (warm & dry) weather on any given day.

ATTRACTIONS

Aquarena Springs   *(512)245-7575*   *(800)999-9767*
1 mi. NE at 1 Aquarena Springs Dr.
One of Texas' long-popular attractions is centered around Spring Lake, the beginning of the San Marcos River. Glass-bottom boats tour the spring formations, exotic plants, and rare aquatic life. Across the lake are luxuriant hillside gardens, a grist mill, historical exhibits, and aquariums showcasing endangered species.

Belvin Street Historic District
just W on Hopkins St.
This quiet neighborhood of lovingly maintained private Victorian residences amid towering oaks is on the National Historic Register.

San Marcos River
just E along C.M. Allen Pkwy.
The San Marcos River is the city's most outstanding attraction. A scenic walkway connects several parks along the bank of the warm (72° year-round) spring-fed river. Lush landscaping and towering trees shade idyllic picnic sites. The crystal-clear gentle stream beckons swimmers, snorklers, and fishermen. The best way to enjoy the river is via a leisurely float in a tube. **Tube Rental** ((512)396-5466) at City Park is open daily.

Southwest Texas State University   *(512)245-2121*
just N at 601 University Dr.
Southwest Texas State University, established in 1899, has a picturesque setting by the river and hills north of downtown. More than 20,000 students are enrolled. The public can also enjoy cultural and athletic events scheduled in impressive theater, music, art, library and sports facilities.

Wonder World   *(512)392-3760*   *(800)782-7653 ext. 2283*
1 mi. W at 1000 Prospect St.
Texas' only earthquake-formed cave open to the public offers guided tours accessible by elevator. An observation tower provides panoramic views of the area from 110 feet above the fault. Other attractions include a miniature train ride, large wildlife petting park, an "anti-gravity house," a large gift shop, an import market place, snack bar and picnic area.

RESTAURANTS

Bubha's Bar-B-Que   *(512)392-6111*
downtown at 119 E. Hutchison St.
L-D.   *Low*
Pork ribs, ham, turkey, beef or sausage are prepared using the Texas tradition of mesquite wood smoking for tender and flavorful barbeque and served in a comfortable Q parlor, or to go.

Cafe on the Square & Brew Pub   *(512)353-9289*
downtown at 126 N. LBJ Dr.
B-L-D.   *Moderate*
San Marcos' first brew pub features tap beers and a "totally Texas" menu of regional burgers, tacos, etc. in a popular coffee shop/pub with nightly live entertainment.

Grins Restaurant   *(512)396-0909*
1 mi. N at 802 N. LBJ Dr.
L-D.   *Low*
Contemporary Texas-style comfort foods include homemade desserts like peach cobbler or carrot-pecan cake. The big handsome wood-trimmed dining room, bar and deck are built into a tree-covered slope.

Palmer's Restaurant   *(512)353-3500*
just W at 218 Moore St.
L-D.   *Moderate*
Contemporary American dishes with a Texas accent are served in an
atmospheric stone restaurant and bar with four fireplaces, or in a
pleasant fountain courtyard.

Pepper's at the Falls   *(512)396-5255*
just NE at 100 Sessoms Dr.
L-D.   *Low*
Texas-style comfort foods, like big burgers or sizzling fajitas, plus
homemade desserts are served in a cheerful dining room with picture
windows overlooking a waterfall on the San Marcos River. A tree-
shaded deck above the water is delightful.

Texas Reds Steakhouse & Saloon   *(512)754-8808*
just S at 120 Grove St.
D only.   *Moderate*
The salt-cured charbroiled Windsor cut smoked pork chop may be the
best of its kind anywhere. Prime rib and steaks can be mighty fine, too,
in this rustic roadhouse and saloon in a historic cotton gin.

LODGING

Accommodations are plentiful, but plain. Most are along I-35. Summer
is prime time. Rates may be reduced 10% at other times.

AmeriHost Inn   *(512)392-6800*
3 mi. S at 4210 I-35 South
61 units   *(800)434-5800*   *Moderate*
AmeriHost's modern local motel has an indoor pool, whirlpool and
exercise room. Expanded Continental breakfast is complimentary. Each
room is well furnished. Some have a whirlpool bath.

Aquarena Springs Inn   *(512)245-7500*
1 mi. NE at 1 Aquarena Springs Dr. (Box 2330) - 78667
24 units   *(800)893-9466*   *Moderate*
The historic little inn was built at Aquarena Springs (see listing) by
Spring Lake in 1929. There is a pool and an 18-hole (fee) golf course.
Some nicely furnished units have view balconies.

Crystal River Inn   *(512)396-3739*
just W at 326 W. Hopkins St. - 78666
13 units   *Moderate-Expensive*
A handsome Victorian mansion by the city's historic residential district
is now San Marcos' finest bed-and-breakfast. A courtyard fountain and
gardens surround the inn. Full breakfast is complimentary. All units
are attractively furnished. Most have private baths, several with a
clawfoot tub, and/or a fireplace.

The Inn Above Onion Creek   *(512)268-1617*
15 mi. N at 4444 Hwy. 150 West - Kyle 78640
9 units   *Expensive*
In this romantic Hill Country hideaway, full breakfast and dinner are
complimentary. Most beautifully furnished units have a whirlpool bath,
gas or wood fireplace, and other elegant touches.

BASIC INFORMATION

Elevation: 580 feet   Population (1990):   28,743
Location: 30 miles Southwest of Austin
Nearest airport with commercial flights: Austin - 32 miles
San Marcos Conv. & Visitor Bureau / C of C (512)393-5900
* downtown at 202 N. C.M. Allen Pwy. (Box 2310)-78667 (888)200-5620*
www.centuryinter.net / smchamber

Park City, Utah

Park City is the recreation capital of the Utah Rockies. It sprawls along the gentle rim of a sage-covered basin backed by the majestic Wasatch Range. The town was settled by adventurers from around the world looking to strike it rich from the silver bonanza discovered in these hills in the 1860s. The boom lasted until the Depression. Snow in prodigious powdery abundance was discovered to be Park City's ultimate bonanza with development of ski areas in the 1960s.

Today the miners' colorful legacy is preserved in more than sixty buildings on the National Historic Register. The photogenic main street now houses one of the West's finest concentrations of art galleries, specialty shops, restaurants and saloons. Nearby, numerous historic buildings serve as upscale bed-and-breakfasts. These and a burgeoning array of condos and hotels serve winter visitors in three major ski areas and a winter sports park that will play a key role in the 2002 Winter Olympics.

WEATHER PROFILE

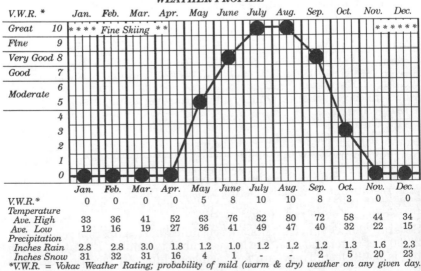

V.W.R.*	Jan.	Feb.	Mar.	Apr.	May	June	July	Aug.	Sep.	Oct.	Nov.	Dec.
V.W.R.*	0	0	0	0	5	8	10	10	8	3	0	0
Temperature												
Ave. High	33	36	41	52	63	76	82	80	72	58	44	34
Ave. Low	12	16	19	27	36	41	49	47	40	32	22	15
Precipitation												
Inches Rain	2.8	2.8	3.0	1.8	1.2	1.0	1.2	1.2	1.2	1.3	1.6	2.3
Inches Snow	31	32	31	16	4	1	-	-	2	5	20	23

*V.W.R. = Vokac Weather Rating; probability of mild (warm & dry) weather on any given day.

446

Alpine Slide
1 mi. NW at 1345 Lowell Av.

A chairlift gives passengers a good view of the basin on the way to the top of a half-mile slide. Riders guide an easily-braked toboggan-like sled down the slope at the speed of their choice.

Ballooning

Fine summer weather and spectacular alpine scenery make the Park City area ideal for hot-air balloon flights. Year-round, several companies offer a choice of sunrise or evening lights. For a half hour or hour, guests enjoy a unique vantage to area sights and sounds.

Bicycling

Scenic byways and high-country trails provide fine touring or mountain bike opportunities in and around Park City. The **Historic Union Pacific Rails-to-Trails State Park**, a gentle 28-mile-long trail between Park City and Echo built on an old railroad right-of-way, is especially popular. Several places offer bike rentals and tours.

Jordanelle State Park   *(435)649-9540*
5 mi. E via US 40 & Hwy. 319

Opened in 1995, the Jordanelle Reservoir provides nearly five square miles of water for boating, fishing and water sports. There is a marina, rental boats, a restaurant and campground. **Rockport State Park** (16 mi. NE) is a smaller reservoir with similar facilities.

Park City Museum   *(435)649-6104*
downtown at 528 Main St.

The old city hall now houses artifacts and videotapes related to the town's silver boom and its evolution into a great winter and summer destination. The Territorial Jail has been preserved in the basement. There is also a visitor information center.

Park City Silver Mine Adventure   *(435)655-7444 (800)467-3828*
1 mi. S on Hwy. 224

Visitors travel 1,500 feet underground and ride a mine train through 3,200 feet of tunnel in a silver mine. There are also interactive displays and exhibits (you can dig for pyrite in a manmade drift), a cafe with old-fashioned pasties, and a gift shop.

Wasatch-Cache National Forest   *(435)783-4338*
around town

The majestic mountains that separate Salt Lake City from Park City are part of this vast forest. So are some of Utah's loftiest peaks—in the High Uintas Wilderness, where there are also hundreds of small glacial lakes. Scenic canyons and valleys, reservoirs and rivers provide a wealth of recreation reached by a good system of roads and nearly 1,000 miles of trails. In winter, there are several major ski areas.

Winter Sports
The Canyons   *(435)649-5400 (800)754-1636*
3 mi. NW at 4000 Parkwest Dr.

Utah's snowboarding headquarters has a vertical drop of 2,580 feet and the longest run is 2.5 miles. Elevation at the top is 9,380 feet. There are nine chairlifts. All facilities, services and rentals are at the base, plus restaurants and bars. Skiing season is December into April.

Deer Valley Resort   *(435)649-1000 (800)424-3337*
4 mi. SE at 2250 Deer Valley Dr.

Several 2002 Olympic events are scheduled in this upscale resort with 2,200 feet of vertical rise. The longest run is two miles. Elevation at the top is 9,400 feet. There are fourteen chairlifts. All facilities, services and rentals are at the base for downhill skiing, plus gourmet restaurants, lounges and lodgings. Skiing season is December into April.

Park City Mountain Resort   *(435)649-8111   (800)222-7275*
1 mi. NW at 1345 Lowell Av.
Utah's largest ski area, "Home of the U.S. Ski Team," and site of alpine and snowboard events at the 2002 Winter Olympics, has a vertical rise of 3,100 feet. The longest run is 3.5 miles. Elevation at the top is 10,000 feet. There are fourteen chairlifts. All facilities, services and rentals are at the base, plus many restaurants, bars and lodges. Skiing season is mid-November to mid-April.

Utah Winter Sports Park   *(435)658-4200*
7 mi. NW at 3000 Bear Hollow Dr.
The site of the 2002 Olympic bobsled, luge and ski jumping events is a haven for elite and recreational ski jumpers. There are also bobsled and luge training track runs, and thrilling public recreational rides. The winter season is December through March.

RESTAURANTS

Chimayo   *(435)649-6222*
downtown at 368 Main St.
D only.   *Very Expensive*
For innovative brilliance, Chimayo is the best restaurant in Utah. Each dish looks like a work of art. Many succeed in capturing the zestful spirit of the Southwest in fresh and flavorful ways. Examples on the grazing menu are jalapeno-cheddar focaccia, tortilla soup, and housemade desserts like grilled banana sundae. Rough bricks, handpainted tile, carved wood, hand-hewn beams and abundant greenery blend into a perfect setting for a culinary adventure.

Gamekeepers Grille   *(435)647-0327*
downtown at 508 Main St.
D only.   *Very Expensive*
New in 1997, Gamekeeper's Grille is doing a superb job of living up to its name with innovative Western cuisine like buffalo and venison chili, pan-seared ostrich or maple-pecan-crusted trout. Housemade desserts like the nectarine and blueberry crisp are also fine. A historic brick building is decorated with polished and rough woods and a wealth of Western touches in three dining rooms, including one with a raised fireplace, expo kitchen and rotisserie.

Grappa   *(435)645-0636*
downtown at 151 Main St.
D only.   *Very Expensive*
Wood-burning ovens, grills, and rotisseries all contribute to the talented chef's ability to produce memorably creative Italian cuisine like artichoke bisque topped with artichoke crisps. Housemade tiramisu and other desserts are beautiful and delicious. A century-old building has been given the feeling of a warm country inn and the most enchanting multilevel garden patio in town.

Lakota   *(435)658-3400*
downtown at 751 Main St.
L-D.   *Expensive*
New American cuisine is carefully prepared with seasonally fresh ingredients for dishes (on a grazing menu) like shrimp and corn chowder, grilled chicken quesadillas or roasted whitefish with garlic spinach. Two big spiffy dining areas and a lounge adjoin a large umbrella-shaded deck practically under the main town chairlift.

Mercato Mediterraneo   *(435)647-0030*
downtown at 628 Park Av.
L-D.   *Expensive*
Park City's authentic European specialty food market, bakery and cafe
lives up to its billing, and then some. Deli case displays alone are a tip-
off. From spectacular designer salads to creative entrees like honey-
glazed wood-oven-roasted chicken, the Mediterranean cuisine is a
winner. So are the enchantingly colorful dining areas on several levels.
Lots of live greenery includes date palms and an olive tree. An
umbrella-shaded streetside patio provides slope and lift views.

Morning Ray Cafe & Bakery   *(435)649-5686*
downtown at 268 Main St.
B-L.   *Expensive*
Here is *the* place for breakfast. Big fluffy pan omelets, specialties like
blueberry sourdough hot cakes, or buckwheat cornmeal buttermilk
cakes, and an array of croissants and pastries, can be enjoyed with a
wealth of hot or cold beverages. Desserts are also made here and
served in a cheerfully rustic coffee house.

Riverhorse Cafe   *(435)649-3536*
downtown at 540 Main St.
D only.   *Very Expensive*
Fresh seafood is a highlight on a menu of contemporary American
cuisine in dishes like sizzling whole striped bass or macadamia-crusted
halibut. An outdoor dining deck hangs over Main Street. The simply
stylish atrium dining room offers grand ski slope views and periodic
live entertainment.

Stein Eriksen Lodge   *(435)649-3700*
4 mi. S at 7700 Stein Way
B-L-D.   *Very Expensive*
In **Glitretind**, New American cuisine is beautifully presented in dishes
like coastal greens with gorgonzola, pears and toasted pecan
vinaigrette or entrees like buffalo tenderloin with root-vegetable cake,
foie gras and truffle jus, or dry aged New York strip with horseradish
mashed potatoes. Warm wood tones enliven a formally elegant firelit
dining room overlooking a picturesque dining deck by the ski slopes.

Texas Red's   *(435)649-7337*
downtown at 440 Main St.
L-D.   *Moderate*
Authentic Texas-style pit barbecue is used to slow-cook six different
meats over applewood. From T-bone steak or rack of ribs to catfish or
two-alarm chili, here are down-home delights, complemented by easy-
going Western decor and half a dozen beers on tap.

350 Main   *(435)649-3140*
downtown at 350 Main St.
D only.   *Expensive*
Contemporary American cuisine gets some creative touches in fresh
seafood dishes ranging from smoked shrimp quesadilla to citrus-baked
trout. The big, handsome bistro opened in 1996 in a historic building
transformed into an urbane firelit dining room and oyster bar.

Wasatch Brew Pub   *(435)649-0900*
downtown at 250 Main St.
L-D.   *Moderate*
Delicious beer bread, apple beer chutney, and beer-batter shrimp
contribute to the appeal of Utah's best pub grub served with several
outstanding premium brews made here. In addition to warm wood-

toned dining areas full of greenery overlooking the kettle room, there is an umbrella-shaded deck with a town-and-mountain view.

Zoom Roadhouse Grill   *(435)649-9108*
downtown at 660 Main St.
L-D.   *Very Expensive*
Robert Redford has made Zoom an instant star among Park City's burgeoning list of contemporary gourmet restaurants. But the grazing menu is also part of the appeal with a wealth of creative American fare and specialty desserts. The dining room is stylish and relaxed, and when the weather is right, the stone-walled garden patio is delightful.

LODGING

Accommodations are plentiful and varied. High season is mid-December through March. At other times, rates may be reduced by 50% or more.

The Gables at Mountain Village   *(435)649-0800*
1 mi. NW at 1335 Lowell Av. (Box 905) - 84060
20 units   *(800)443-1045*   *Very Expensive*
Slopes and lifts are steps away from this four-story brick condo with a whirlpool. Each well-furnished one-bedroom unit has a kitchen, fireplace, in-bath whirlpool, and a private deck. There are also penthouses.

Goldener Hirsch Inn   *(435)649-7770*
4 mi. SE at 7570 Royal St. East (Box 859) - 84060
20 units   *(800)252-3373*   *Very Expensive*
This Austrian-style hotel has ski-in and ski-out convenience in Deer Valley, whirlpools, sauna, exercise equipment, gift shop and fireside lounge. The **Goldener Hirsch Restaurant** (L-D—Very Expensive) offers acclaimed European cuisine, including wild game specialties, in an elegant alpine setting. Each room is beautifully furnished. Suites have a fireplace and private mountain-view balcony.

The Lodge at Mountain Village   *(435)649-0800*
1 mi. NW at 1415 Lowell Av. (Box 3449) - 84060
120 units   *(800)443-1045*   *Moderate-Very Expensive*
This contemporary five-story hotel/condo complex is at the base of the Park City Mountain Resort. Amenities include an indoor/outdoor pool, whirlpools, steamroom, sauna, restaurant, lounge and an ice skating rink. Well-furnished units range from hotel rooms to four-bedroom condominiums. Many have a gas fireplace and view balcony.

1904 Imperial Hotel   *(435)649-1904*
downtown at 221 Main St. (Box 1628) - 84060
10 units   *(800)669-8824*   *Expensive*
A restored turn-of-the-century boarding house is now a Victorian-style bed-and-breakfast. A whirlpool, full breakfast, and afternoon treats are complimentary. Each cozy, attractively furnished room has period touches and a full bath (most with an oversized tub).

The Old Miner's Lodge   *(435)645-8068*
downtown at 615 Woodside Av. (Box 2639) - 84060
12 units   *(800)648-8068*   *Expensive*
A Victorian boarding house near the downtown ski lift has been restored as a bed-and-breakfast with a whirlpool. Full breakfast and evening refreshments are complimentary. Each antique-filled room is comfortably furnished and has a private bath.

Olympia Park Hotel   *(435)649-2900*
2 mi. NE at 1895 Sidewinder Dr. (Box 4439) - 84060
310 units   *(800)754-3279*   *Expensive-Very Expensive*
Park City's largest full-service hotel is within a mile of downtown and

skiing. The modern four-story complex has an atrium pool, whirlpool, sauna, restaurant and nightclub. Each spacious room is well furnished. Suites and condominiums are also available.

Radisson Inn Park City   *(435)649-5000*
2 mi. N at 2121 Park Av. (Box 1778) - 84060
131 units   *(800)333-3333*   *Expensive*
This three-story hotel has an indoor/outdoor pool, whirlpools, sauna, restaurant, nightclub and gift shop. All rooms are well furnished.

Shadow Ridge Hotel   *(435)649-4300*
1 mi. NW at 50 Shadow St. (Box 1820) - 84060
150 units   *(800)451-3031   Expensive-Very Expensive*
Park City Mountain Resort adjoins this five-story condo hotel and conference center. Amenities include a pool, whirlpool, sauna, fitness center and lounge. Well-furnished units (up to three-bedroom) have a kitchen, private balcony, and fireplace. Some also have a whirlpool.

Silver King Hotel   *(435)649-5500*
1 mi. NW at 1485 Empire Av. (Box 2818) - 84060
58 units   *(800)331-8652*   *Very Expensive*
One of the area's finest condominium hotels is a five-story complex steps from the Park City Mountain Resort. In addition to (fee) downhill skiing, there is an indoor/outdoor pool, whirlpool and sauna. Each beautifully furnished, spacious (up to three-bedroom) unit has a kitchen, fireplace, and whirlpool (many have a big in-room whirlpool).

Stein Eriksen Lodge   *(435)649-3700*
4 mi. S at 7700 Stein Way (Box 3177) - 84060
131 units   *(800)453-1302*   *Very Expensive*
One of the West's most elegant mountain resorts is in an idyllic setting by ski slopes at Deer Valley Resort. The Norwegian-style five-story condo hotel has a view pool, whirlpool, sauna, exercise room, and resort shops, plus (fee) downhill skiing. There is also an outstanding gourmet dining room (see listing) and lounge. Each spacious unit is luxuriously furnished. Many suites (up to four bedrooms) have a kitchen, fireplace, big view balcony, and a large whirlpool bath.

Washington School Inn   *(435)649-3800*
downtown at 543 Park Av. (Box 536) - 84060
15 units   *(800)824-1672   Expensive-Very Expensive*
An 1889 limestone schoolhouse listed on the National Register has been transformed into a handsome bed-and-breakfast with a whirlpool and sauna. Full breakfast and après-ski refreshments are free. Each well-furnished room combines period decor with modern conveniences like a private bathroom. Two also have a fireplace.

Yarrow Resort Hotel   *(435)649-7000*
2 mi. N at 1800 Park Av. (Box 1840) - 84060
181 units   *(800)927-7694   Expensive-Very Expensive*
The Yarrow is a modern full-service hotel with a pool, whirlpool, sauna, restaurant, and lounge. Skiing is nearby. Some well-furnished rooms have a private balcony and a kitchenette and/or fireplace.

BASIC INFORMATION

Elevation: 6,910 feet   Population (1990):   4,468
Location: 32 miles East of Salt Lake City
Nearest airport with commercial flights: Salt Lake City - 36 miles
Park City Ch. of Com. / Convention & Visitors Bureau (435)649-6100
*   2 mi. N at 1910 Prospector Av. (Box 1630) - 84060   (800)453-1360*
*   www.parkcityinfo.com*
Visitor Information Center is 2 mi. N at junction of Hwys. 224 & 248

St. George, Utah

St. George is a peaceful, picturesque link between the Southwest and the Rocky Mountains. It sprawls across a small desert basin surrounded by towering forested peaks, multicolored domes and precipices, and enormous red sandstone cliffs. In this unique site, St. George has the distinction of being the only town in the Rocky Mountain area where hard freezes and snowfalls are scarce enough that palm trees grow outdoors year-round. Mormon colonizer Brigham Young brought settlement and cotton farming to this area during the Civil War. The town grew slowly until the 1950s when modern air conditioning began to make the deserts of the Southwest livable.

Today, St. George is a major destination with a rich diversity of mountain and desert parks, a burgeoning array of golf courses, an aquatic complex, and a large college. Downtown has been refurbished, but cafes, restaurants and lodgings remain among the most prosaic of any great town.

WEATHER PROFILE

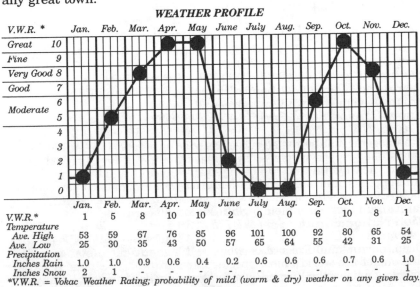

V.W.R.*	Jan.	Feb.	Mar.	Apr.	May	June	July	Aug.	Sep.	Oct.	Nov.	Dec.
V.W.R.*	1	5	8	10	10	2	0	0	6	10	8	1
Temperature												
Ave. High	53	59	67	76	85	96	101	100	92	80	65	54
Ave. Low	25	30	35	43	50	57	65	64	55	42	31	25
Precipitation												
Inches Rain	1.0	1.0	0.9	0.6	0.4	0.2	0.6	0.6	0.6	0.7	0.6	1.0
Inches Snow	2	1	-	-	-	-	-	-	-	-	-	1

*V.W.R. = Vokac Weather Rating; probability of mild (warm & dry) weather on any given day.

452

Bicycling

Bicycle Warehouse *1 mi. E at 1060 E. Tabernacle (435)673-0878*
The gentle basin around town offers fine bicycling on paved and off-road byways to nearby dramatic rock formations, sand dunes, hot springs, and ghost towns. Bike rentals, accessories, and maps are available.

Brigham Young's Winter Home *(435)673-2517*
downtown at 67 W. 200 N.
The second President of the Mormon Church used this as his winter residence for several years. Its spacious, modified colonial style set it apart from the rough pioneer dwellings of the time (1870s). Both the grounds and building have been meticulously restored and outfitted with authentic period furnishings. Guided tours are offered daily.

Dixie National Forest *(435)628-4491*
approximately 30 mi. N via UT 18
The Pine Valley Mountains that loom over St. George are thought to be the world's largest intrusion of igneous lava. A paved road provides access to the mountain village of Pine Valley and beyond to forested campgrounds near the Santa Clara River and picnic sites at Pine Valley Reservoir. In addition, hiking, biking, horseback riding, and fishing are popular summer activities.

Golf *(435)652-4653*
Numerous public golf courses have been constructed around town in recent years. Each has distinctive landscaping, grand "color country" backdrops, a clubhouse, pro shop, carts, and equipment rentals. Contact St. George Leisure Services for locations and details.

Gunlock State Park *(435)586-4497*
19 mi. NW off UT 18
A small scenic reservoir has been created on the Santa Clara River. Boating, fishing, and primitive camping are enjoyed, along with swimming and water-skiing from spring to fall. In the spring, picturesque waterfalls are created by heavy runoff overflowing red sandstone cliffs near the southern shore.

St. George Temple *(435)673-5181*
just S at 250 E. 400 S.
St. George's most impressive manmade landmark is a 175-foot-high Latter Day Saints (Mormon) Temple constructed of red sandstone covered with gleaming white plaster. Its size and condition belie the fact that it was dedicated in 1877. The Temple Visitors Center, open year-round, offers guided tours of the center and beautifully landscaped grounds—complete with palm trees.

Snow Canyon State Park *(435)628-2255*
10 mi. NW via UT 18
A photogenic, flat-bottomed gorge has been cut deeply into multicolored sandstone, capped in places by a black mantle of lava spewed from extinct nearby volcanoes. Hiking trails abound amid massive rock outcroppings and sand dunes featured in numerous major motion pictures. Tree-shaded picnic sites are thoughtfully located, and a campground with complete facilities is used year-round.

Zion National Park *(435)772-3256*
41 mi. E on UT 9
Deep, narrow multicolored canyons and gigantic stone masses make this one of the world's most spectacular natural attractions. A paved roadway follows the Virgin River for several miles along Zion Canyon.

Sheer cliffs and awesome rock formations soar to great heights above the gentle floor of the narrow chasm where the river beckons with swimming and tubing opportunities. Scenic trails lead climbers, hikers, and horseback riders into a silent realm of secluded canyons with emerald pools and veiled waterfalls. The Zion Visitor Center has a museum and shop. Large campgrounds are open all year.

RESTAURANTS

Andelin's Gable House   *(435)673-6796*
just E at 290 E. St. George Blvd.
L-D.   *Moderate*
Traditional American fare like prime rib or fresh fish with homemade rolls and desserts is served amid relaxed yesteryear atmosphere.

Basila's Greek & Italian Cafe   *(435)673-7671*
downtown at 2 W. St. George Blvd.
L-D.   *Moderate*
Creative American cuisine with Greek and Italian accents has made this the area's best fine dining venue. In addition to a comfortably relaxed dining room with greenery, there is a covered dining porch.

Nielsen Frozen Custard   *(435)628-5579*
just E at 445 E. St. George Blvd.
L-D.   *Moderate*
Their original fresh frozen custard is made here in assorted creations to go or with light fare at red padded booths in a spiffy little diner.

San Francisco Bakery Cafe   *(435)674-2800*
1 mi. E at 968 E. St. George Blvd.
B-L-D.   *Moderate*
Homemade pastries and breads are displayed and sold to go or at a congestion of little tables in a cafe or on a covered patio. Italian sodas, pizzas, sandwiches and light fare are served later in the day.

Scaldoni's   *(435)674-1300*
2 mi. NW at 929 W. Sunset Blvd. in Phoenix Plaza
L-D.   *Moderate*
Rustic Italian fare and signature homemade dill rolls distinguish this casual grill room with a covered courtyard by a little gourmet Italian grocery.

Sullivan's Rococo Steak House   *(435)628-3671*
2 mi. SW at 511 S. Airport Rd.
L-D.   *Moderate*
T-bones and other steaks and American standards, and the big neo-rococo dining room, are incidental to a memorable panoramic town-and-mountain view beyond the window wall of this blufftop restaurant.

LODGING

Accommodations are plentiful and surprisingly prosaic with a few exceptions. High season is April through October. Rates are often reduced 10% or more in winter apart from weekends.

Abbey Inn - Best Western   *(435)652-1234*
2 mi. S (near I-15) at 1129 S. Bluff St. - 84770
130 units   *(888)222-3946*   *Moderate*
The handsome three-story complex opened in 1996 with a pool, whirlpool and exercise room. Full breakfast is complimentary. Each unit is well furnished (including kitchenette) in a neo-Victorian mode.

Comfort Suites   *(435)673-7000*
2 mi. S (near I-15) at 1239 S. Main St. - 84770
123 units   *(800)245-8602*   *Moderate*
A pool and whirlpool are features of this contemporary all-suites motel.

Each well-furnished unit has a sitting area and kitchenette. Two dozen also have a two-person whirlpool bath.

Coral Hills Motel - Best Western   *(435)673-4844*
downtown at 125 E. St. George Blvd. - 84770
98 units   *(800)542-7733*   *Moderate*
This contemporary motel has a palm-lined outdoor and a large indoor pool, two whirlpools, putting green, and an exercise room. Compact rooms are comfortably furnished. A few rooms have a small private balcony. Three also have an in-room whirlpool tub.

Greene Gate Village Bed & Breakfast Inn   *(435)628-6999*
downtown at 76 W. Tabernacle St. - 84770
18 units   *(800)350-6999*   *Moderate-Expensive*
Several pioneer houses (circa 1870) were relocated to adjoin two existing homes across from the tabernacle. They have been carefully transformed into a large bed-and-breakfast inn with period furnishings and all modern conveniences. The atmospheric site includes a pool and whirlpool. Full breakfast is complimentary. Each room is well furnished. Some also have a fireplace, and a two-person whirlpool tub in a separate room.

Hilton Inn of St. George   *(435)628-0463*
2 mi. S (near I-15) at 1450 S. Hilton Dr. - 84770
100 units   *(800)662-2525*   *Moderate*
A large palm-lined courtyard pool enhances this contemporary hotel, along with a whirlpool, sauna, three lighted tennis courts, restaurant, bar and gift shop. Each room is well furnished.

Holiday Inn Resort Hotel & Convention Center   *(435)628-4235*
2 mi. S at 850 S. Bluff St. - 84770
172 units   *(800)457-9800*   *Moderate-Expensive*
St. George's largest lodging is a well-equipped hotel with a large indoor/outdoor pool, whirlpool, tennis court, putting green, mini-gym, billiards and table tennis, plus restaurant, lounge, and gift shop. Three of the well-furnished rooms have an in-room large whirlpool.

Ramada Inn   *(435)628-2828*
2 mi. E (near I-15) at 1440 E. St. George Blvd. - 84770
136 units   *(800)713-9435*   *Moderate*
One of the area's newest motels has a pool and whirlpool in a palm-shaded courtyard adjacent to a volcanic bluff. Full breakfast is complimentary. All of the units are spacious and well furnished. A few also have a whirlpool tub.

Seven Wives Inn   *(435)628-3737*
downtown at 217 N. 100 West - 84770
13 units   *(800)600-3737*   *Moderate-Expensive*
For Southern Utah's premier bed-and-breakfast inn, two large adjacent homes on the National Register have been lovingly restored and outfitted with period decor. Well-tended grounds have a small pool. Full gourmet breakfast is complimentary. Each well-furnished room has a private bath. Some also have a fireplace and whirlpool.

BASIC INFORMATION

Elevation: 2,880 feet   *Population (1990): 28,572*
Location: 300 miles Southwest of Salt Lake City
Nearest airport with commercial flights: in town
Washington County Travel & Convention Bureau   *(435)634-5747*
   just E at 425 S. 700 E. - 84770   *(800)869-6635*
St. George Area Chamber of Commerce   *(435)628-1658*
   downtown at 97 E. St. George Blvd. - 84770 www.stgeorgechamber.com

Manchester, Vermont

Manchester continues a long run as the urbane heart of a splendid mountain realm. A fabled fly fishing stream meanders through a gentle valley surrounded by some of Vermont's highest mountains. From the beginning in Victorian times, the villages of Manchester have primarily served visitors seeking the area's increasing abundance of recreation and leisure opportunities.

Towering elm and maple trees, and marble sidewalks, border curving streets in little business districts. Beautifully restored Victorians mix easily with compatible contemporary buildings. Many house an unusual mix of upscale factory outlet stores, and shops displaying fine regional arts and crafts, antiques, recreation and gourmet specialties. Excellent restaurants are plentiful. So are lodgings, including a world class historic hotel, gracious bed-and-breakfast inns, and charming contemporary resorts serving travelers drawn by the area's natural beauty, cultural charms and serenity.

WEATHER PROFILE

V.W.R. *		Jan.	Feb.	Mar.	Apr.	May	June	July	Aug.	Sep.	Oct.	Nov.	Dec.
Great	10	* * * * Fine Skiing * *										* * * * * *
Fine	9												
Very Good	8												
Good	7												
Moderate	6												
	5												
	4												
	3												
	2												
	1												
	0												

	Jan.	Feb.	Mar.	Apr.	May	June	July	Aug.	Sep.	Oct.	Nov.	Dec.
V.W.R.*	0	0	0	0	6	8	8	8	7	4	0	0
Temperature												
Ave. High	27	28	38	52	67	74	79	77	70	60	43	30
Ave. Low	10	10	18	33	40	49	53	52	49	37	27	16
Precipitation												
Inches Rain	3.2	2.8	3.5	3.0	3.1	3.0	3.5	3.3	3.1	3.0	3.3	3.0
Inches Snow	23	26	17	11	-	-	-	-	-	-	10	20

*V.W.R. = Vokac Weather Rating; probability of mild (warm & dry) weather on any given day.

Boat Rentals

Batten Kill Canoe Ltd.   *(802)362-2800*   *(800)421-5268*
9 mi. SW on VT 7A- Arlington
The Batten Kill is one of the clearest and prettiest rivers in New England with enough gentle and faster water to please anyone. They will arrange a trip of two hours or longer with pick-up provided.

Bromley Mountain   *(802)824-5522*   *(800)865-4786*
6 mi. NE on VT 11 - Peru
Summer can be as much fun as winter at this ski area (see listing). You control the speed of a plastic sled down a choice of slow, medium, or fast tracks that were the first and may be the longest alpine slides in the country—nearly a mile. A scenic chairlift goes to the summit, observation tower and trails. Since 1995, America's first Deval Karts from France (plastic four-wheeled go-carts) let you steer and brake as gravity lets you cruise down a mountain trail with ease.

Emerald Lake State Park   *(802)362-1655*
9 mi. N on US 7 - North Dorset
Scenic limestone bedrock and lush foliage contribute to the appeal of this big park. A swimming beach, fishing, boat rentals (no motors on the lake), nature trail, picnic sites and campground are provided.

Green Mountain National Forest   *(802)362-2307*
just E on VT 11
Luxuriant stands of pine and broadleaf trees (magnificent in fall) blanket the picturesque backbone of the Green Mountains in this large forest. Several major ski areas are a winter highlight. In summer, hiking, swimming, fishing, boating, and camping are popular.

Hildenc   *(802)362-1788*
2 mi. S via VT 7A
Robert Todd Lincoln's 24-room Georgian Revival manor house was the home of Abraham Lincoln's son and his heirs until 1975. Original furnishings and family effects are displayed throughout. Nearby are a carriage barn/visitors center, formal gardens, and nature trails.

Mount Equinox Skyline Drive   *(802)362-1114*
5 mi. SW on VT 7A
A sinuous five-mile paved toll road rises to the mountain's summit, 3,816 feet above sea level. The highest peak in the Taconic Range offers a magnificent view of four states and Canada on a clear day.

Norman Rockwell Exhibition   *(802)375-6423*
9 mi. SW on VT 7A - Arlington
Picture this. The artist's former models are tour guides. The display, in a Victorian church in Rockwell's hometown, includes hundreds of *Saturday Evening Post* covers, drawings, and ads. There is a gift shop.

Southern Vermont Art Center   *(802)362-1405*
1 mi. N on West Rd.
Ten galleries display contemporary paintings and prints in the state's oldest cultural organization. Grounds include a sculpture garden, botany trail, cafe and gift shop, plus performances and workshops.

Winter Sports

Bromley Mountain   *(802)824-5522*   *(800)865-4786*
6 mi. NE on VT 11 - Peru
Vermont's only mountain with a (warmer) southern exposure has a vertical rise of 1,334 feet. The longest run is 2.5 miles. There are seven chairlifts. All facilities, services, rentals, restaurants, and lodgings are at the base. Ski season is mid-November into April.

Stratton Mountain   *(802)297-2200   (800)787-2886*
16 mi. SE via VT 11 & VT 30
Southern Vermont's highest peak (3,875 feet) provides a vertical rise
of 2,003 feet. The longest run is more than three miles. There are
twelve chairlifts and a gondola. All facilities, services and rentals, plus
restaurants, bars, and lodgings, are in a nifty neo-Tyrolean village near
the base. Ski season is mid-November to mid-April.

RESTAURANTS

Al Ducci's Italian Pantry   *(802)362-4449   (800)579-4449*
downtown on Elm St.
B-L.   *Moderate*
Homemade mozzarella, sausage, bread, fresh pastas and ravioli are
among authentic Italian specialties served in the cozy cafe, or to go.

Barrows House   *(802)867-4455*
6 mi. NW on Main St. (VT 30) - Dorset
B-D.   *Expensive*
Contemporary Northeastern cuisine has real appeal, and delicious
homemade desserts also contribute to the appeal of this country inn's
pleasant greenhouse dining room or cozy tavern.

The Black Swan   *(802)362-3807*
just S on VT 7A
D only.   *Expensive*
Continental cuisine is prepared with a creative flair in flavorful
seasonal specialties and homemade desserts, and served in plush
candlelit dining rooms and a lounge of an 1834 brick house.

Chantecleer   *(802)362-1616*
3 mi. NE on VT 7A - East Dorset
D only.   *Very Expensive*
For years, Chantecleer has been one of the region's most distinguished
dinner houses for classic Continental cuisine. Luscious housemade
desserts round out the sophisticated fare served in an elegantly
remodeled old dairy barn with a big fieldstone fireplace and intimate
dining nooks.

The Dorset Inn   *(802)867-5500   (800)835-5284*
6 mi. NW on VT 30 at Church St. - Dorset
L-D.   *Expensive*
Yam fritters with maple syrup, bread pudding with whiskey sauce, or
(in fall) cider sorbet typify the creative New England dishes now
featured in Vermont's oldest continuously operating country inn. Warm
Colonial decor distinguishes the venerable dining room and tavern.

The Equinox   *(802)362-4700*
1 mi. S on Main St. (VT 7A)
L-D.   *Expensive-Very Expensive*
The resort hotel's main restaurant is **The Colonnade** (D only—Very
Expensive). Contemporary American cuisine with a creative regional
flair has earned critical acclaim for the large, luxurious dining room
where jackets are required. **The Marsh Tavern** (L-D—Expensive)
offers traditional Yankee dishes amid warm New England tavern decor.

The Little Rooster Cafe   *(802)362-3496*
downtown on VT 7A
B-L.   *Expensive*
Sauteed herbal mushrooms open-faced on seven-grain bread with
smoked bacon and melted Swiss cheese might be one of the eclectic
European cafe delights offered in a cheerful little coffee shop where
some of the region's best breakfasts and lunches are served.

Mark Anthony's Ye Olde Tavern   *(802)362-0611*   *(800)450-1790*
just NE on VT 7A
L-D.   *Expensive*
The chef/owner starts each meal with his delicious specialty, cranberry corn fritters with maple butter, as a prelude to seasonally fresh creative cuisine with a Yankee flair. Candles flicker on tables set with full linen and fresh flowers in several romantic dining rooms in a historic tavern that was built in 1790.

Mother Myrick's Confectionery & Ice Cream Parlor *(802)362-1560*
downtown on VT 7A
L-D.   *Moderate*
Mother Myrick's is Vermont's best ice cream parlor and confectionery. Homemade hot fudge sundaes are irresistible. So are the award-winning chocolates and all the other decadent delights, and desserts like Vermont maple cheesecake and fresh fruit pies. The stylish art deco setting is a delightful backdrop to gourmet goodies.

The Reluctant Panther   *(802)362-2568*
1 mi. S on VT 7A at West Road - Manchester Village
D only.   *Very Expensive*
Expertly prepared contemporary American specialties, reflecting their flavorful European roots, are served in the inn's romantic and refined restaurant and lounge.

LODGING

Accommodations are plentiful and distinctive. Many are quaint inns in historic buildings, or small contemporary resorts with fine views of the scenic countryside. Weekends and early fall are prime time. Weekday rates in late spring are often reduced at least 20%.

Barrows House   *(802)867-4455*
6 mi. NW on Main St. (VT 30) - Dorset 05251
28 units   *(800)639-1620*   *Expensive*
A two-hundred-year-old main house and other historic buildings are nestled in a parklike setting. Amenities include a pool, sauna, two tennis courts and bicycles, plus a restaurant (see listing) and tavern. A full breakfast is included (plus dinner with Modified American Plan). Each room is comfortably furnished with antiques and has a private bath. Six units also have a gas or woodburning fireplace.

Cornucopia of Dorset   *(802)867-5751*
6 mi. NW on Main St. (VT 30)(Box 307) - Dorset 05251
5 units   *(800)566-5751*   *Expensive*
A handsome turn-of-the-century Colonial-style home has been transformed into a well-landscaped bed-and-breakfast with firelit common rooms. Full gourmet breakfast, champagne welcome and evening treats are complimentary. Each spacious room is individually beautifully furnished with a blend of period and contemporary conveniences except phone. Two also have a fireplace.

The 1811 House   *(802)362-1811*
1 mi. S on Route 7A (Box 39) - Manchester Village 05254
14 units   *(800)432-1811*   *Expensive*
Built in the 1770s, this house has operated as an inn since 1811 except when it was the residence of President Lincoln's granddaughter. The landmark now serves as a bed-and-breakfast surrounded by lawns and gardens by a golf course. Full breakfast is complimentary. Period antiques blend with contemporary amenities including private bath in each well-furnished room. Six rooms also have a fireplace.

The Equinox   *(802)362-4700*
1 mi. S on Main St. (VT 7A) (Box 46) - Manchester Village 05254
172 units   *(800)362-4747   Expensive-Very Expensive*
The Equinox is the heart of Manchester as it has been since Vermont
was part of the British Empire. Recently it was restored to its original
splendor and enhanced with every contemporary convenience. The
luxurious four-story complex includes a (fee) 18-hole championship golf
course, plus a putting green, two pools (one indoors), three tennis
courts, whirlpool, sauna, steam room, exercise room, plus (fee) massage,
bicycles, horseback riding, cross-country skiing, and ice skating in
winter, gourmet restaurant (see listing) and tavern, and village shops.
Each beautifully furnished room combines nostalgic touches with all
contemporary conveniences. The property's posh **Charles Orvis Inn**
reopened in 1995 as a Vermont-style showplace. Each luxuriously
furnished suite has a kitchen, gas fireplace and whirlpool bath.

The Inn at Manchester   *(802)362-1793*
1 mi. S on VT 7A (Box 41) - Manchester Village 05254
18 units   *(800)273-1793*   *Expensive*
A classic 1880 white clapboard building on the National Historic
Register is now a picturesque bed-and-breakfast with a pool. Full
breakfast, afternoon tea and treats are complimentary. Each room is
well furnished with antiques and contemporary conveniences except TV
and phone. Two rooms also have a fireplace.

Manchester View Motel   *(802)362-2739*
2 mi. N on VT 7A (Box 1268) - Manchester Center 05255
35 units   *(800)548-4141*   *Moderate-Expensive*
The best motel in Southern Vermont is the Manchester View Motel.
Expansive lawns surround a complex on a hill with delightful
mountain and valley views. Amenities include a view pool, exercise
room, and complimentary light breakfast. Half of the well-furnished
rooms have a gas or woodburning fireplace, while several also have a
two-person whirlpool bath.

Palmer House Resort Motel   *(802)362-3600*
just N on VT 7A (Box 657) - Manchester Center 05255
40 units   *(800)917-6245*   *Moderate-Expensive*
The Palmer House has more on-site amenities than any other motel in
the region. A 9-hole pitch-and-putt golf course, two tennis courts, view
pool, whirlpool, sauna, and trout pond occupy well-landscaped grounds.
Light breakfast is complimentary. Rooms are well furnished.

The Reluctant Panther   *(802)362-2568*
1 mi. S on VT 7A at West Rd. (Box 678) - Manchester Village 05254
16 units   *(800)822-2331   Expensive-Very Expensive*
Lovely gardens and shade trees surround an 1850s mansion that has
been transformed and expanded into a romantic village inn with an
intimate gourmet dining room (see listing) and cozy firelit bar. Full
breakfast and dinner are included. Each individually decorated room
is beautifully furnished, including all contemporary conveniences. Four
newer suites also have a fireplace and whirlpool bath.

BASIC INFORMATION

Elevation: 750 feet   Population (1990):   5,341
Location: 180 miles Northwest of Boston
Nearest airport with commercial flights: Albany, NY - 60 miles
Manchester-and-the-Mountains Chamber of Commerce (802)362-2100
   downtown at 2 Main St. (RR 2, Box 3451) - Manchester Center 05255
www.manchesterandmtns.com

Stowe, Vermont

Stowe is the renowned ski capital of New England. Skiers on Mt. Mansfield (Vermont's highest peak) have a grand view of the village far below in a broad valley surrounded by gentle mountains blanketed by hardwood forests. The town was founded in 1794, and became a vacation destination before the Civil War. A century later, the Trapp Family of "Sound of Music" fame settled here and provided a major boost to the coincident development of winter sports areas.

Today, Stowe is a world class winter, summer and fall destination. The heart of the village is tiny but rich in New England charm with whitewashed church steeples, a lovely park, trim Victorian buildings, a covered bridge, and an award-winning recreation path. Some of Vermont's best gourmet food and craft specialty shops are here and nearby. So are numerous cosmopolitan restaurants. Romantic inns and small resorts also celebrate the area's abundance of recreational and cultural attractions.

WEATHER PROFILE

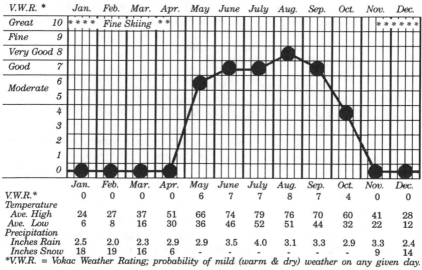

V.W.R. *		Jan.	Feb.	Mar.	Apr.	May	June	July	Aug.	Sep.	Oct.	Nov.	Dec.
Great	10												
Fine	9												
Very Good	8												
Good	7												
Moderate	6												
	5												
	4												
	3												
	2												
	1												
	0												

	Jan.	Feb.	Mar.	Apr.	May	June	July	Aug.	Sep.	Oct.	Nov.	Dec.
V.W.R.*	0	0	0	0	6	7	7	8	7	4	0	0
Temperature												
Ave. High	24	27	37	51	66	74	79	76	70	60	41	28
Ave. Low	6	8	16	30	36	46	52	51	44	32	22	12
Precipitation												
Inches Rain	2.5	2.0	2.3	2.9	2.9	3.5	4.0	3.1	3.3	2.9	3.3	2.4
Inches Snow	18	19	16	6	-	-	-	-	-	-	9	14

*V.W.R. = Vokac Weather Rating; probability of mild (warm & dry) weather on any given day.

461

ATTRACTIONS
Alpine Slide   (802)253-3000
8 mi. NW on VT 108
A scenic chairlift takes you up Spruce Peak to the top of the slide. Gravity brings you back down. But, you control the speed of your sled on the 2,100-foot slide track.

Bicycling
For thrill-seekers, Stowe Mountain Resort's **Mountain Biking Center** (at Spruce Peak Base Area) offers rentals for lift-served mountain biking on Mt. Mansfield and Spruce Peak. For tamer but still memorable cycling, unspoiled rural countryside is accessible by the famed recreation path and many miles of byways and trails along the gentle valley floor and up into the mountains. Bikes and more can be rented by the hour and longer in town at:
AJ's Mountain Bike   (802)253-4593
Action Outfitters   (802)253-7975
Mountain Bike Shop   (802)253-7919

Food Specialties
Ben & Jerry's Ice Cream Factory   (802)244-8687
8 mi. S on VT 100 - Waterbury
Ben & Jerry's is Vermont's most popular family attraction. The ingratiating complex features a guided thirty-minute tour that displays each step in the ice cream making process, and includes a free sample. There is also a multimedia show, expansive gift shop, ice cream scoop shop, and colorful, whimsical places to enjoy ice cream and picnics.
Cabot Creamery Annex   (802)244-6334
8 mi. S on VT 100 - Waterbury Center
Acclaimed Vermont cheddar cheese and others can be sampled at generous tasting tables and purchased along with other regional gourmet products and gifts. The big friendly store also offers a video tour of the cheese-making plant.
Cold Hollow Cider Mill   (802)244-8771   (800)327-7537
7 mi. S on VT 100 - Waterbury Center
New England's most appealing cider mill is also the biggest. All aspects of apple cider production can be observed on a free self-guided tour, and video. There are free cider samples. Other exhibits depict maple sugaring. These and other Vermont foods, crafts and gifts are also sold in a big complex that captures the feeling of yesteryear.
Elmore State Park   (802)888-2982
15 mi. NE via VT 100 & VT 12
The centerpiece of this park is tranquil little Lake Elmore. There is a swimming beach and bathhouse, fishing, boat rentals and a concession, plus hiking trails, picnic sites and a campground.
In-Line Skate Park   (802)253-3000
8 mi. NW on VT 108
Radical ramps, pipes, a lift-served downhill slalom course, roller hockey rink, speed track and training loop are open to everyone from experts to beginners for all-day or shorter sessions. All necessary protective gear can also be rented at this premier in-line skate park.
River Running
Umiak Outdoor Outfitters   (802)253-2317
just S on VT 100
In the summer, canoe and kayak rentals (half day or longer) tours and instruction are offered, along with shuttles to a nearby river and lake. In winter, snowshoes, cross-country skis and sleds are rented.

Stowe Gondola   *(802)253-3000*
8 mi. NW on VT 108

An eight-passenger enclosed gondola goes to the top of Vermont's highest peak. Mt. Mansfield is 4,393 feet above sea level. The spectacular view is shared by a dinner house restaurant and gift shop. The scenic five-mile **Auto Toll Road** is another way to get to the top.

Stowe Recreation Path   *(802)253-7321*
downtown and NW

A five-mile paved path follows a gentle stream past fishing and swimming holes, forests, and meadows. Sensitivity to the bucolic beauty has won international acclaim for the route. It is free, and open day and night only to pedestrians, bicyclists and roller skaters.

Winter Sports

Smuggler's Notch Ski Resort   *(802)644-8851*
9 mi. NW on VT 108

Northern Vermont's biggest vertical (2,600 feet) is here. The longest run is 3.5 miles. There are four chairlifts. All facilities, services, and rentals are within a short walk. So are restaurants, bars, and modern lodgings. The ski season is late November to early April.

Stowe Mountain Resort   *(802)253-3000*
8 mi. NW on VT 108

One of the East's premier ski resorts has been upgraded. Slopes on Mt. Mansfield (Vermont's highest at 4,393 feet) have a vertical rise of 2,360 feet. The longest run is nearly four miles. There are nine chairlifts. All facilities, services and rentals, plus restaurants, bars and lodgings, are at the base. Ski season is mid-November to mid-April.

RESTAURANTS

Blue Moon Cafe   *(802)253-7006*
downtown at 35 School St.
D only.   *Expensive*

The Blue Moon Cafe is one of New England's great sources of New American cuisine. Fresh, first-rate regional ingredients, skill, and creative flair make dishes like pan-roasted Atlantic salmon with pine nut crust and golden tomato sauce outstanding. So are housemade desserts like blueberry crunch tart. The intimate dining room and bar, enclosed porches and summer patio are simply charming.

Edson Hill Manor   *(802)253-7371*
5 mi. NW via VT 108 at 1500 Edson Hill Rd.
B-D.   *Expensive*

Creative American fare with a Northeastern accent is delightfully presented. The informally elegant dining room with a garden-like setting overlooks a dining terrace and lovely Vermont country views.

The Gables Inn   *(802)253-7730*
1 mi. NW at 1457 Mountain Rd. (Route 108)
B-D.   *Moderate*

Breakfast has starred here for more than twenty years, partly because they offer both traditional and unusual dishes supported by pure Vermont maple syrup and other local products. The country inn's comfortable dining room, front porch and lawn share bucolic views.

Gracie's   *(802)253-8741*
downtown at 20 Main St.
L-D.   *Moderate*

Half-pound burgers top an eclectic selection of all-American comfort foods. They're proud of their homemade buns and desserts, too, in this friendly family eatery. There is also a gourmet shop.

Green Mountain Inn   *(802)253-7301*
downtown at intersection of VT 100 & VT 108 on Main St.
L-D.   *Moderate*
The inn's **Whip Bar & Grill** has been a popular gathering place for many years. Contemporary American fare featuring regional ingredients and homemade desserts contribute to the appeal of a stylish dining room with an antique buggy whip collection. There is also a bar, deck, and a handsome seasonal dining room.

Restaurant Swisspot   *(802)253-4622*
downtown at Main & School Sts.
L-D.   *Expensive*
Authentic cheese, beef and chocolate fondues highlight a varied menu with numerous Swiss specialties. The restaurant in the Swiss Pavilion at Expo '67 in Montreal has continued to please fondue fans ever since it was relocated here in 1968.

The Shed Restaurant & Brewery   *(802)253-4364*
2 mi. NW on VT 108
L-D.   *Moderate*
Stowe's first brew pub opened in 1994. Their handcrafted ales are served with a wide selection of fine pub grub in the bar, by a see-through natural stone fireplace, and in the garden room or sunny greenhouse.

Stoweflake Inn & Resort   *(802)253-7355*
2 mi. NW at 1746 Mountain Rd. (VT 108) at Cape Cod Rd.
B-L-D.   *Expensive*
Prime ribs and charbroiled steaks top a well-rounded selection of contemporary American dishes served in the resort's popular, warmly elegant **Winfield's** (B-D). More casual pub fare can be enjoyed with all kinds of wine by the glass or tap beers in **Charlie B's** (L-D).

Stowehof Inn   *(802)253-9722*
4 mi. NW via VT 108 at 434 Edson Hill Rd.
B-D.   *Expensive*
Innovative international cuisine reflects skilled use of Vermont products in the **Seasons Restaurant**. The inn's casually elegant dining room has a spectacular view of the mountains, and a classical pianist entertains at dinner. The **Tap Room** offers flavorful, diverse pub fare in a cozy firelit setting.

Ten Acres Lodge   *(802)253-7638*
3 mi. NW via VT 108 & Luce Hill Rd. at 14 Barrows Rd.
D only.   *Expensive*
New American cuisine features top-quality seasonally fresh ingredients skillfully prepared with a creative flair. The style is beautifully represented in everything from appetizers to housemade sorbets. The inn's informally elegant restaurant continues a tradition of restaurant excellence going back more than forty years.

Topnotch at Stowe Resort & Spa   *(802)253-8585*
4 mi. NW at 4000 Mountain Rd.
B-L-D.   *Expensive*
Acclaimed spa cuisine stars in **Maxwell's** (B-D). Seasonal and regional ingredients are showcased, while freshness and flavor distinguish every expertly prepared, creative dish presented in the resort's comfortably upscale dining room. **The Buttertub** (L-D) offers appealing favorites like six-onion soup, and ribs with Vermont maple syrup BBQ sauce, served in a casual American bistro setting. There is also a popular lounge with live entertainment.

Ye Olde England Inne   *(802)253-7558*
just NW at 433 Mountain Rd. (Route 108)
B-L-D.   *Moderate*
Merrie New England is delightfully displayed in the authentic English
inn's **Mr. Pickwick's Pub and Restaurant.** Beef Wellington and
seasonal game like boar, antelope, or venison are gourmet specialties,
along with steak and kidney pie and other British favorites. Innovative
American dishes are also accompanied by fresh baked goods, rich
desserts (don't miss the Crowning Glory), and a peerless selection of
wines, rare cognacs, fine ales and tap beers. The convivial dining
rooms, pub, and (in season) alfresco canopied garden decks are as
memorable as the cuisine.

LODGING

Lodgings are abundant. Most are related to the famed ski area or the
Vermont village inn tradition. Early fall (leaf-peeper season) and
winter are high seasons. Rates in early spring may be reduced 30% or
more.

Edson Hill Manor   *(802)253-7371*
5 mi. NW via VT 108 at 1500 Edson Hill Rd. - 05672
25 units   *(800)621-0284*   *Expensive*
A secluded estate in the rolling countryside now serves as one of
Stowe's best bed-and-breakfasts. The mansion and carriage houses
share forested grounds with a fishing pond, spring-fed pool, stables
with (fee) horseback riding and carriage rides; cross-country ski center
and (fee) sleigh rides in winter, and gourmet dining (see listing) and
lounge. Gourmet buffet breakfast is complimentary. Each cozy view
room in the manor and spacious room in the carriage houses is
beautifully furnished. Many have a fireplace.

Golden Eagle Resort   *(802)253-4811*
just NW on Mountain Rd. (Route 108) (Box 1090) - 05672
92 units   *(800)626-1010*   *Moderate-Expensive*
This handsome resort motel includes a tennis court, three pools (one
indoors), whirlpool, sauna, and exercise room on landscaped and
wooded grounds. Each unit (up to two bedrooms) is attractively
furnished. Some have a private balcony, gas or woodburning fireplace,
and large in-room whirlpool.

Green Mountain Inn   *(802)253-7301*
downtown at intersection VT 108/VT 100 (Main St.) (Box 60) - 05672
67 units   *(800)253-7302*   *Expensive*
The red brick inn in the center of town has been a landmark since
1833. The three-story complex has been restored and expanded to
retain the charm of a village inn while offering a landscaped courtyard
pool and health club with whirlpool, sauna, steam room and exercise
equipment, plus restaurants (see listing) and a lounge. Each well-
furnished room has period touches and all modern conveniences.
Several also have a gas fireplace and large whirlpool bath.

The Mountain Road Resort   *(802)253-4566*
1 mi. NW at 1007 Mountain Rd. (VT 108) (Box 8) - 05672
30 units   *(800)367-6873*   *Expensive*
Set back from the highway is one of Vermont's most complete newer
resort motels. Well-landscaped grounds include (fee) tennis, plus indoor
and outdoor pools, whirlpools, sauna, exercise room and bicycles. All of
the rooms (up to two bedrooms) are beautifully furnished. Many have
a private deck, gas fireplace, and a large whirlpool in-room or on the
terrace.

Stowe Inn at Little River   *(802)253-4836*
downtown at 123 Mountain Rd. (VT 108) - 05672
43 units   *(800)227-1108*   Moderate-Expensive
An 1825 village inn has been restored and expanded to include a pool, whirlpool, and a window-walled restaurant by a garden terrace and river. Each comfortably furnished room combines nostalgic touches and modern conveniences. One bedroom condos have a kitchen, gas fireplace and whirlpool bath.

Stowe Mountain Resort   *(802)253-3000*
6 mi. NW at 5781 Mountain Rd. (VT 108) - 05672
34 units   *(800)253-4754   Expensive-Very Expensive*
This contemporary resort at the base of Vermont's highest peak has (fee) an 18-hole championship golf course, eight tennis courts, an in-line skate park and gondola rides in summer and downhill skiing in winter, plus a pool, whirlpool, sauna, exercise room, restaurants (including a dining room with a panoramic view from the top of a gondola lift) and a lounge. Each of the beautifully furnished rooms has a private deck overlooking the mountain and reflects the inn's comfortably posh style.

Stoweflake Inn & Resort   *(802)253-7355*
2 mi. NW at 1746 Mountain Rd. (VT 108) (Box 369) - 05672
94 units   *(800)253-2232   Expensive-Very Expensive*
One of Stowe's most complete resorts is a posh contemporary small hotel on spacious landscaped grounds. Amenities include a (fee) golf practice facility adjacent to a scenic public 18-hole golf course, two tennis courts, two pools (one indoor), whirlpool, saunas, exercise room, gourmet restaurants (see listing) and lounge, and a resort shop. Each unit (up to three bedrooms) is attractively furnished. Many have a fireplace.

Stowehof Inn   *(802)253-9722*
4 mi. NW via VT 108 at 434 Edson Hill Rd. (Box 1108) - 05672
47 units   *(800)932-7136   Expensive-Very Expensive*
A soaring alpine design distinguishes this contemporary country inn on a hilltop with exceptional mountain views. Luxuriant gardens and stands of birch trees surround the peaceful three-story complex that includes a trout pond, four tennis courts, a large view pool, whirlpool, saunas, fine view restaurant (see listing) and lounge; plus (fee) buggy and horseback rides in summer and sleigh rides in winter. Gourmet breakfast and afternoon treats are complimentary. Each beautifully furnished room combines antique nostalgic touches with modern conveniences and has a private mountain-view balcony or patio. Some also have a fireplace.

Ten Acres Lodge   *(802)253-7638*
3 mi. NW via VT 108 & Luce Hill Rd. at 14 Barrows Rd. - 05672
18 units   *(800)327-7357*   *Expensive*
An authentic Vermont farmhouse circa 1830 on a quiet hillside was restored and expanded into a gracious bed-and-breakfast. Surrounding woods and pastures give way to well-tended lawns and gardens surrounding several buildings, a pool, whirlpool, tennis court, renowned dining room (see listing) and lounge. Gourmet breakfast is complimentary. Most spacious, beautifully furnished rooms are individually decorated with antiques and all contemporary conveniences. Newer suites also have a fireplace and mountain-view balcony.

Topnotch at Stowe Resort & Spa   *(802)253-8585*
4 mi. NW at 4000 Mountain Rd. (Box 1458) - 05672
110 units   *(800)451-8686*   *Very Expensive*
Topnotch is one of New England's most complete four-season resorts. The contemporary three-story wood-and-stone complex overlooks Mt. Mansfield. Expansive forested grounds house two large pools (one indoors), a big whirlpool with hydromassage waterfalls, saunas, steam room, exercise room; plus (for a fee) fourteen tennis courts, horseback riding, bicycles, and (in winter) cross-country ski center, and ice skating. There are also gourmet and casual dining rooms (see listing), a lounge, beauty salon, and resort shops. Each individually decorated room is beautifully furnished. Some condominiums (up to three bedrooms) also have a fireplace, sauna or whirlpool bath.

Trapp Family Lodge   *(802)253-8511*
4 mi. NW via VT 108 & Luce Hill Rd. at 42 Trapp Hill Rd. - 05672
93 units   *(800)826-7000   Expensive-Very Expensive*
The legacy of the "Sound of Music" von Trapp family is an Austrian-style lodge high on a hill. Amenities of the four-story complex include mountain views, three pools (one indoors), sauna, exercise room, four tennis courts, plus (fee) cross-country skiing and sleigh rides in winter, as well as a restaurant, Austrian Tea Room, entertainment lounge, and gift shop. Each unit is well furnished.

Ye Olde England Inne   *(802)253-7558*
just NW at 433 Mountain Rd. (VT 108) - 05672
30 units   *(800)477-3771   Expensive-Very Expensive*
Stowe is exactly right for New England's most authentic English bed-and-breakfast inn. The colorful four-story complex crowns a granite bluff overlooking the valley and mountains. Amenities include a large courtyard pool, whirlpool, merry pub and gourmet dining room (see listing). Full English breakfast and afternoon tea are complimentary. Each room is luxuriously furnished to convey the feeling of a posh romantic getaway. Spacious "Bluff House Suites" have spectacular view decks, gas fireplace, and oversized whirlpool baths.

BASIC INFORMATION

Elevation: *720 feet*   *Population (1990): 3,433*
Location: *190 miles Northwest of Boston*
Nearest airport with commercial flights: Montpelier, VT - 60 miles
Stowe Area Association   *(802)253-7321   (800)247-8693*
  downtown on Main St. (Box 1320) - 05672
  www.stoweinfo.com

Woodstock, Vermont

Woodstock is the perfect embodiment of a New England village. A clear stream meanders through this urbane enclave at the heart of a pastoral valley surrounded by rolling hills. The town was settled in 1768 by farmers, merchants and millers. It wasn't until 1934 that America's first ski-tow was built nearby, and the village began to fulfill its destiny as a summer, fall, and winter resort.

Today, Woodstock is a serene world class destination. Leafy green hills and clear streams remain unspoiled. So do white-steepled churches, covered bridges, tree-lined rows of 200-year-old homes and trim human-scaled businesses, and a landmark wayside inn on a picture-perfect green. Vermont specialty shops abound downtown, along with fine restaurants. Numerous historic inns and resorts in and around town reflect the wealth, cosmopolitan spirit and endless concern for conservation of the best of man's works and nature's grandeur that has distinguished villagers here for more than six generations.

WEATHER PROFILE

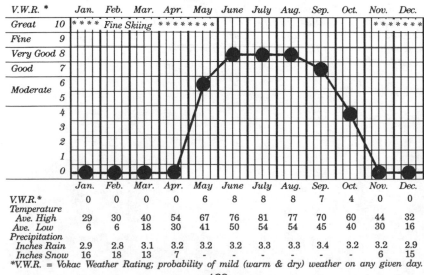

		Jan.	Feb.	Mar.	Apr.	May	June	July	Aug.	Sep.	Oct.	Nov.	Dec.
V.W.R.*		0	0	0	0	6	8	8	8	7	4	0	0
Temperature													
Ave. High		29	30	40	54	67	76	81	77	70	60	44	32
Ave. Low		6	6	18	30	41	50	54	54	45	40	30	16
Precipitation													
Inches Rain		2.9	2.8	3.1	3.2	3.2	3.2	3.3	3.3	3.4	3.2	3.2	2.9
Inches Snow		16	18	13	7	-	-	-	-	-	-	6	15

*V.W.R. = Vokac Weather Rating; probability of mild (warm & dry) weather on any given day.

Bicycling
Woodstock Sports   *(802)457-1568*
downtown at 30 Central St.
Miles of byways and trails tunnel through hardwood forests in a picturesque landscape of woodlands and meadows, farms and villages tucked amid rolling green hills. Hourly bike rentals, information and maps are available.

Billings Farm & Museum   *(802)457-2355*
just N on VT 12 at River Rd.
One of America's premier agricultural museums combines a modern working dairy farm with extensive exhibits of 19th century Vermont farm life. The meticulously restored and furnished 1890 Farm House amid gardens and orchards is a living-history center with hands-on demonstrations of traditional rural activities from butter churning to milking.

Downtown
around Central & Elm Streets
The heart of Woodstock evokes the charm of Norman Rockwell's paintings. There are white-steepled churches, and trim buildings of whitewashed wood and brick on streets lined by towering maple and other hardwoods. A world class historic hotel fronts on a shady village green near a picture-postcard covered bridge over a stream. Vermont arts and crafts and gourmet foods abound in quaint shops interspersed with fine restaurants and there is a thriving performing arts complex.

Grafton   *(802)843-2231*
39 mi. S via VTs 106,11, & 35
One of the prettiest villages in New England is tucked away amid gentle forested hills. Two-hundred-year-old buildings have been lovingly restored by the Windham Foundation and proud residents. Photogenic churches; stores featuring regional art, crafts and antiques; and a cheese company surround **The Old Tavern** ((800)843-1801). The remarkably preserved landmark inn has provided gracious hospitality since 1801. Rooms are beautifully furnished and decorated with antiques throughout. The firelit pub and dining rooms exude rustic elegance. Guests still enjoy a swim in the pond in a meadow out back.

Horseback Riding
Kedron Valley Stables   *(802)457-1480*
6 mi. S on VT 106 - South Woodstock
Hardwood forests, babbling brooks and beaver ponds enhance trail rides. For a unique adventure, take a Weekend Riding Vacation (with your horse or theirs) that includes two nights' lodging, all meals, and one and a half days riding through scenic countryside.

Plymouth   *(802)672-3773*
16 mi. SW via US 4 on VT 100A
The Plymouth Historic District features the birthplace and boyhood home of Calvin Coolidge. Nearby is a visitor center and museum devoted to the president. The Plymouth Cheese Factory and General Store are also worth a visit in a bucolic village that hasn't changed much in well over a century.

Silver Lake State Park   *(802)234-9451*
10 mi. N on VT 12 - Barnard
The centerpiece of this park is a small lake with a swimming beach and bathhouse, fishing and boat rentals. A campground and picnicking are also popular.

Specialty Foods

Sugarbush Farm   *(802)457-1757   (800)281-1757*
6 mi. NE via US 4 on Hillside Rd.

This picturesque working farm tucked away on a scenic country road ages and smokes several cheeses, and produces maple syrup. Samples are generously offered in the well-stocked shop. Free exhibits, a tour, opportunities to get up close to farm animals, and demonstrations of the sugarhouse are other highlights.

Winter Sports

Killington Ski Area   *(802)422-3261   (800)343-0762*
22 mi. W via US 4 on Killington Rd.

One of the East's biggest ski areas touts 3,150 feet of vertical rise, and runs several miles long. There are sixteen chairlifts and a high-speed gondola. All facilities, services and rentals are at the base of mountains that top out at 4,241 feet above sea level. A number of restaurants, bars and lodgings are nearby. Ski season is early November to June.

Suicide Six Ski Area   *(802)457-1666*
4 mi. N on VT 12

In 1934, the world's first rope tow started taking skiers up a hill near here. The vertical rise is only 650 feet and the longest run is about a mile. The nation's oldest continuously-operating rope tow now is supplemented by two chairlifts. All facilities, services and rentals are available at the base for downhill and cross-country skiing. The Woodstock Inn (see listing) offers fine dining and lodgings nearby. Ski season is mid-December through March.

Woodstock Historical Society   *(802)457-1822*
downtown at 26 Elm St.

The Society's Dana House Museum occupies a Federal-style building that dates from 1807. Several rooms provide a glimpse into Woodstock's early days with exhibits of decorative arts, toys, tools, costumes and furnishings. There is also a research library and store.

RESTAURANTS

Barnard Inn Restaurant   *(802)234-9961*
9 mi. N on VT 12 - Barnard
D only.   *Very Expensive*

Some of the region's finest New American cuisine reflects classic training and a creative spirit in preparing top quality regional ingredients. Attention to details is apparent in everything from the house-smoked salmon to the homemade sorbets and cakes. Intimate, informally elegant dining rooms in a candlelit Colonial inn are a charming backdrop for leisurely gourmet dining.

Bentleys Restaurant   *(802)457-3232*
downtown at 3 Elm St.
L-D.   *Expensive*

Broiled pecan-coated chicken breast with a maple-mustard sauce is a star among innovative American dishes with a New England accent. The bustling dining room has several levels and areas with an eclectic atmosphere that is as appealing as the Victorian sofas are relaxing.

Kedron Valley Inn   *(802)457-1473*
5 mi. S on VT 106 - South Woodstock
B-D.   *Very Expensive*

New Vermont cuisine is skillfully prepared from fresh regional ingredients paired with flavorful herbs and spices and light sauces. The inn's stylish dining rooms offer a choice of fireside seating or a garden room with view windows.

The Lincoln Inn   *(802)457-3312*
3 mi. W on US 4
D only.   *Expensive*
Fine contemporary Continental and American dishes like Vermont
maple shrimp with housemade biscuits are served in a country-elegant
candlelit setting of the inn's picturesque historic farmhouse.

Mountain Creamery   *(802)457-1715*
downtown at 33 Central St.
B-L.   *Moderate*
Mile-high apple pie and all-natural homemade ice creams and candies
are good reasons to check out the pastry and espresso shop downstairs.
Hearty country breakfasts are featured in the coffee shop upstairs.

Parker House Inn   *(802)295-6077*
6 mi. E via US 4 at 16 Main St. - Quechee
D only.   *Expensive*
Innovative American cuisine is carefully prepared and well regarded,
including the housemade desserts. There are two gracious dining rooms
and a lounge with a river-view balcony.

The Prince and the Pauper   *(802)457-1818*
downtown at 34 Elm St.
D only.   *Very Expensive*
Creative Continental and French cuisine on a three-course prix fixe
menu has won critical acclaim. So have delicious homemade bread,
baked desserts and sorbets. The laid-back intimate dining room has
cozy wooden booths attractively outfitted with linens, lamp and flowers.
A moderately priced bistro menu is offered in the tavern.

The Quechee Inn at Marshland Farm   *(802)295-3133*
6 mi. E via US 4 on Clubhouse Rd. - Quechee
D only.   *Expensive*
New American cuisine gets an appealing regional accent in dishes like
house-smoked Eastern brook trout with maple-horseradish mustard.
Luscious desserts are made here, too. The classic country inn's inviting
dining room (**The Meadows**) is outfitted with nostalgic antiques.

Simon Pearce Restaurant   *(802)295-1470*
6 mi. E on US 4 at The Mill - Quechee
L-D.   *Very Expensive*
The Simon Pearce Restaurant is one of the most enchanting in
America. Top-quality seasonal ingredients are prepared with expert,
creative attention for dishes that celebrate New England and the
owner's Irish roots. Housemade breads and a wealth of desserts are
also splendid. Simon Pearce's lovely handblown glassware and pottery
adorn crisp white linen at tables in a large dining room with arched
picture windows overlooking a river millpond and waterfall. A
(seasonal) deck is right by the falls. Elsewhere in the transformed mill,
you can watch glass blowing and pottery demonstrations. An excellent
retail shop features their glass, pottery and other sophisticated arts
and crafts.

Woodstock Inn & Resort   *(802)457-1100*
downtown at 14 The Green
B-L-D.   *Expensive-Very Expensive*
Creative contemporary cuisine reflects fresh seasonal ingredients from
the region in the landmark inn's two-level **Dining Room**. Jackets are
appropriate for gentlemen in the glamorous, curved room overlooking
luxuriant grounds. The **Eagle Cafe** (B-L-D—Expensive) is stylish and
casual, while **Richardson's Tavern** is a quiet, cozy place for a drink.

LODGING
Lodgings are plentiful in the area, with an emphasis on historic inns, resorts and bed-and-breakfast inns. Even the motels are delightfully small and individualistic. Early fall is high (leaf-peeper) season. Non-weekends in winter, rates may be reduced 30% or more.

The Andrie Rose Inn   *(802)228-4846*
26 mi. SW on VT 100 at 13 Pleasant St. - Ludlow 05149
20 units   *(800)223-4846   Moderate-Very Expensive*
One of America's great bed-and-breakfast inns is the Andrie Rose. Tucked away on a side street in Ludlow is a stately 1829 Federal-style building. Full New England country breakfast and evening favors are complimentary. Epicurean dinner is offered on selected Saturday nights. Each room is individually luxuriously furnished and full of romantic antique accents. All rooms have private baths. Most have a fireplace. Numerous suites also have a large in-room whirlpool.

Ascutney Mountain Resort   *(802)484-7711*
18 mi. S via VT 106, on VT 44 (Box 699) - Brownsville 05037
214 units   *(800)243-0011   Moderate-Expensive*
Mount Ascutney looms over this self-contained four-season resort. A contemporary cluster of four-story clapboard buildings includes seven tennis courts, indoor and outdoor pools, sauna, fitness center, racquetball courts, rental bikes, restaurant, tavern and gift shop. In winter, there is (fee) on-site skiing—both downhill and cross-country. Each room is well furnished. Suites (up to three-bedroom) have a kitchen and fireplace. Some also have a view balcony.

The Charlestown House   *(802)457-3843*
downtown at 21 Pleasant St. - 05091
9 units   *(888)475-3800*   *Expensive*
This 1835 Greek revival house, listed on the National Historic Register, is now a gracious bed-and-breakfast. Full gourmet breakfast is complimentary. Each room has a private bath and is attractively furnished with period antiques and Oriental rugs, and a queen four-poster bed, but no phone. Some of the rooms have a gas fireplace and a whirlpool bath.

Hawk Inn and Mountain Resort   *(802)672-3811*
16 mi. SW via US 4 (Rt. 100 HCR 70, Box 64) - Plymouth 05056
50 units   *(800)685-4295   Expensive-Very Expensive*
The Green Mountains surround the area's most complete four-season resort. Summer amenities include a small, spring-fed lake and beach; a nearby lake and dock with rental boats; plus (for a fee) three tennis courts, horseback riding, wagon rides and rental bicycles; as well as indoor pool and outdoor whirlpool, sauna, exercise room, restaurant, lounge and gift shop. On-site winter activities include (fee) sleigh rides, cross-country skiing, and ice skating. Each lodge room is beautifully furnished. Some nearby townhouses also have a kitchen, private deck, fireplace and whirlpool bath.

Kedron Valley Inn   *(802)457-1473*
5 mi. S on VT 106 - South Woodstock 05091
27 units   *(800)836-1193   Expensive-Very Expensive*
A natural swimming pond with sand beaches distinguishes the picturesque grounds of this historic country inn (circa 1822). There is also a fine restaurant (see listing). Each room is beautifully furnished with period decor and a private bath, but no phone. Some rooms have a fireplace and private view deck.

The Maple Leaf Inn   *(802)234-5342*
9 mi. N on VT 12 (Box 273) - Barnard 05031
7 units   *(800)516-2753*   *Expensive*
This Victorian-style country inn nestled in a maple and birch forest opened in 1994. Full breakfast and afternoon beverages and treats are complimentary. Each beautifully furnished, spacious room blends nostalgic decor touches with all contemporary conveniences. Most also have a fireplace and a large whirlpool bath.

The Quechee Inn at Marshland Farm   *(802)295-3133*
6 mi. E via US 4 on Clubhouse Rd. (Box 747) - Quechee 05059
24 units   *(800)235-3133*   *Expensive*
A Colonial homestead (circa 1793) has been transformed into a classic bed-and-breakfast country inn overlooking a river and green mountains. Amenities include a famed (fee) fly-fishing school, rental bicycles and canoes; and cross-country skiing school, plus fine dining (see listing). Full breakfast buffet and afternoon refreshments are complimentary. Each beautifully furnished room has all contemporary conveniences, plus many nostalgic touches.

Twin Farms   *(802)234-9999*
10 mi. N via VT 12 on Stagecoach Rd. (Box 115) - Barnard 05031
14 units   *(800)894-6327*   *Very Expensive*
Twin Farms is one of America's acclaimed small country resorts. A secluded farm once owned by Sinclair Lewis was meticulously transformed into an opulent inn in 1993. Good taste is reflected in elegant rusticity of the decor; comfort of understated furnishings; and museum-quality art objects. Amenities include a pond for fishing; creekside pub; Japanese soaking tubs; mountain bikes; a fitness center; winter ice skating and cross-country skiing, and ski area with a poma lift; and a baronial dining hall with a fieldstone fireplace at either end. Full breakfast, lunch and dinner, drinks and all recreation are complimentary. Each spacious room is luxuriously furnished with fine art, nostalgic and contemporary conveniences and special touches, and a fireplace. Some have a whirlpool bath. Enchanting cottages also have a screened porch or deck.

Woodstock Inn & Resort   *(802)457-1100*
downtown at 14 The Green - 05091
144 units   *(800)448-7900*   *Expensive-Very Expensive*
There's been an inn on Woodstock's lovely village green for two centuries. The landmark Woodstock Inn & Resort is the quietly elegant heart of town today. The classic three-story red-brick complex surrounded by colorful gardens has a large pool, putting green, bike rentals, gourmet restaurant (see listing) and resort shop. Nearby are the inn's country club and (fee) 18-hole golf course; sports center with indoor pool, whirlpool, sauna, steam room, exercise room, squash, racquetball and twelve (fee) tennis courts; plus (in winter) complete (fee) alpine and cross-country ski centers. Each room is beautifully furnished with nostalgic and all contemporary conveniences. Many also have a fireplace.

BASIC INFORMATION

Elevation: 700 feet   Population (1990):   3,212
Location: 145 miles Northwest of Boston
Nearest airport with commercial flights: Lebanon, NH - 15 miles
Woodstock Area Chamber of Commerce (802)457-3555 (888)496-6378
   downtown at 18 Central St. (Box 486) - 05091 www.woodstockvt.com
Information Booth (June-Oct.)   (802)457-1042

Charlottesville, Virginia

Charlottesville is a continuing celebration of a brilliant legacy. It is located where gentle, forested foothills of the Blue Ridge Mountains meet the relatively flat Piedmont Plateau. In 1672, the town (named after the wife of King George III) was established as a county seat. Thomas Jefferson, Charlottesville's most famous son, single-handedly provided a magnificent architectural and horticultural endowment.

Today, most of Jefferson's great works are meticulously maintained. Travelers from all over the world come here to explore his home and gardens and his University of Virginia. Tree-shaded streets, and parks with dramatic statues and fountains, dignify downtown, where historic and compatible newer buildings line a pedestrian mall with a wealth of stylish galleries and regional specialty shops. Cosmopolitan restaurants, plus nostalgic and contemporary inns and hotels, reflect the sophistication and civility that have made Charlottesville special for more than two centuries.

WEATHER PROFILE

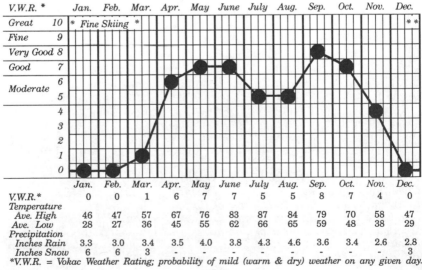

V.W.R.*	Jan.	Feb.	Mar.	Apr.	May	June	July	Aug.	Sep.	Oct.	Nov.	Dec.
V.W.R.*	0	0	1	6	7	7	5	5	8	7	4	0
Temperature												
Ave. High	46	47	57	67	76	83	87	84	79	70	58	47
Ave. Low	28	27	36	45	55	62	66	65	59	48	38	29
Precipitation												
Inches Rain	3.3	3.0	3.4	3.5	4.0	3.8	4.3	4.6	3.6	3.4	2.6	2.8
Inches Snow	6	6	3	-	-	-	-	-	-	-	-	3

*V.W.R. = Vokac Weather Rating; probability of mild (warm & dry) weather on any given day.

Ash Lawn - Highland   *(804)293-9539*
6 mi. SE via VA 20 & VA 53 on County Road 795
James Monroe, fifth president of the United States, moved into this estate (on a site selected by his friend Thomas Jefferson) in 1799. Guided tours include original rooms displaying many Monroe possessions, the overseer's cottage, smokehouse and slave quarters. Demonstrations of cooking and spinning, herb and vegetable gardens, grazing livestock, and peacocks roaming in boxwood gardens evoke the quiet dignity of this plantation in the early 1800s.

Bicycling
Many miles of bike paths and byways access the forested hills, vineyards, orchards and bucolic countryside surrounding Charlottesville. Rental bicycles, plus accessories, are available in town.

Boat Rentals
The scenic James River is less than twenty miles south of town. The best way to enjoy its tranquil appeal is aboard a canoe, raft or inner tube. Rentals, equipment and transportation can be arranged at:

James River Reeling & Rafting   *(804)286-4386*
James River Runners   *(804)286-2338*

Downtown
centered around 3rd St. & Main St.
An eight-block-long mall distinguishes the heart of Charlottesville. Shade trees and whimsical sculptures enhance this pedestrian zone between the city's largest hotel and the city hall park. Also by the park is the **Virginia Discovery Museum**, where visitors explore arts and sciences through interactive exhibits. Solid buildings as much as 200 years old house a wealth of restaurants and shops featuring Virginia cuisine, art and handicrafts. Few cities of any size have downtown parks with monuments as stately as those dedicated to Lewis and Clark, Robert E. Lee, and Stonewall Jackson.

Historic Michie Tavern   *(804)977-1234*
3 mi. S on VA 20
An authentically restored 1784 tavern was relocated near Monticello to serve as a showcase of 18th century tavern life. Rooms contain extensive Colonial furnishings, and the old wine cellar houses the **Virginia Wine Museum**. A re-created general store and related buildings are also here, including a 1797 grist mill and a converted log cabin restaurant (see listing).

Monticello   *(804)984-9822*
4 mi. SE via VA 20 & VA 53
Monticello is the quintessential manifestation of the most complex mind ever produced in America—or anywhere. Thomas Jefferson started building an estate atop his "little mountain" in 1769, and made additions and alterations until 1809. He continued living in his architectural masterpiece until his death on July 4, 1826 (exactly half a century after the signing of his Declaration of Independence). He is buried here in the family graveyard, which is still in use. Virginia's first mountaintop plantation (earlier ones were all river-oriented) has been restored to its appearance during his retirement. Most of the furnishings were owned by Jefferson or his family. The house and grounds display many of his ingenious inventions and original contributions to American architecture, interior design and horticulture. Guided and specialized tours of most of the principal

rooms on the main floor, plus (except in winter) the restored orchard, vineyard and 1,000-foot-long vegetable garden, are offered daily. The Monticello Visitors Center (2 mi. W on VA 20 near I-64) features personal and family memorabilia, and a related film.

Shenandoah National Park   *(540)999-3500*
18 mi. W via I-64

Many of the highest portions of the Blue Ridge Mountains are included. The whole park is a wildlife sanctuary amid luxuriant hardwoods which produce spectacular color each fall, while azaleas, redbud and dogwood are lovely in spring. Hiking trails and picnic facilities are plentiful, and there are complete campgrounds. The main attraction is **Skyline Drive**. One of the most scenic drives in the East winds for 105 miles along the ridgetops cresting at 3,680 feet. There are dozens of parking overlooks and trailheads along the pristine two-lane road.

University of Virginia   *(804)924-7969*
1 mi. W on Main St. & University Av.

The University of Virginia, founded in 1819 by Thomas Jefferson and built according to his plans, is an architectural masterwork. About 18,000 students attend classes in classical Colonial red brick pavilions with white trim, surrounded by spacious greenswards, ancient trees, gardens, and Jefferson's ingenious one-brick-thick serpentine walls. Tours begin daily from the Pantheon-inspired Rotunda. In 1976, the American Institute of Architects voted Jefferson's University the most outstanding achievement in American architecture.

Wineries   *(804)977-1783*
around town

Thomas Jefferson began the development of European-style vineyards near Monticello more than two centuries ago. The "wine capital of Virginia" now has several picturesque wineries within fifteen miles of town. Most have tours, tastes, and a gift shop. The Visitors Bureau has more information and maps.

Winter Sports
Wintergreen Resort   *(804)325-2200*   *(800)325-2200*
42 mi. SW via I-64 & VA 151 on Route 664

High in the Blue Ridge Mountains, Virginia's biggest ski area has 1,000 feet of vertical rise. The longest run is nearly one mile. There are five chairlifts. All facilities, services and rentals are at the summit including restaurants, bars and lodgings. Skiing season is mid-December to mid-March.

RESTAURANTS

Aberdeen Barn   *(804)296-4630*
2 mi. NW at 2018 Holiday Dr.
D only.   *Very Expensive*

For charcoal-broiled steaks and prime rib of beef, this has been the place since 1965. Candlelit intimacy and an open hearth contribute to upscale rusticity, and there is live entertainment in the lounge.

Blue Ridge Brewing Company   *(804)977-0017*
just W at 709 W. Main St.
L-D.   *Moderate*

Virginia's first combination restaurant/brewery features homemade meals (some with Caribbean accents) and handmade beers created on the premises. Good times reign amid the casual setting in a turn-of-the-century building.

Boar's Head Inn   *(804)296-2181*
3 mi. W on Route 250 W
B-L-D.   *Very Expensive*
The Inn's **Old Mill Room** is acclaimed for New American cuisine with a Virginia accent. Refined meals are perfectly complemented by Early American decor in a restored 1834 grist mill. The **Terrace Lounge** offers light fare and drinks indoors or on the veranda.

C & O Restaurant   *(804)971-7044*
downtown at 515 E. Water St.
L-D.   *Expensive*
Creative American cuisine with Southwest and Pacific Rim influences is given expert attention, including housemade breads and desserts. Upstairs is a formal dining room with a dress code, while downstairs is a relaxed bistro.

The Hardware Store Restaurant   *(804)977-1518*   *(800)426-6001*
downtown at 316 E. Main St.
L-D.   *Moderate*
A really wide menu of American fare features traditional Virginia dishes, old-fashioned ice cream and soda fountain treats and their bakery goodies and drinks in dining areas festooned with antique rolling ladders, bins and memorabilia.

Historic Michie Tavern   *(804)977-1234*
2 mi. S at 683 Thomas Jefferson Pkwy.
L only.   *Moderate*
A buffet of hearty Southern dishes typical of the Colonial period is complemented by Virginia wines and ales served by a costumed staff amid period tavern decor in a 200-year-old converted log house. The historic complex also houses a restored grist mill, museum, and general store.

Ivy Inn   *(804)977-1222*
3 mi. W at 2244 Old Ivy Rd.
D only.   *Expensive*
Creative American cuisine is enhanced by quality fresh regional ingredients, including vegetables from their own garden. A transformed two-century-old house now offers casually elegant firelit dining rooms, an intimate bar and a garden patio.

Keswick Hall   *(804)979-3440*
8 mi. E at 701 Club Dr. - Keswick
B-L-D.   *Very Expensive*
By reservation, guests can partake of classically derived contemporary European cuisine (including five-course prix-fixe dinners) amid the opulence of Sir Bernard Ashley's Country House Hotel.

Silver Thatch Inn   *(804)978-4686*
6 mi. N via US 29 at 3001 Hollymead Dr.
D only.   *Very Expensive*
Contemporary American cuisine features grilled meats and fresh fish, unusual sauces and vegetarian specials, Virginia wines, and gourmet homemade desserts. Charlottesville's oldest country inn (circa 1780) is an informally elegant setting for a candlelit culinary experience.

Southern Culture   *(804)979-1990*
just W at 633 W. Main St.
D only.   *Moderate*
Their Gulf Coast cuisine is an eclectic blend of Southern, Cajun, Caribbean, and Tex-Mex specialties served in a festive yet relaxing Florida Keys setting.

Tastings *(804)293-3663*
downtown at 502 E. Market St.
L-D. *Expensive*
Eclectic contemporary dishes (especially wood-grilled entrees) can be enjoyed with your selection of over 100 wines by the half or full glass. They also serve housemade desserts in the casual wood-trimmed dining room overlooking a wine bar and wine shop.

LODGING

Accommodations are plentiful, ranging from modern motels at the freeway exits to luxurious country inns and resorts in and around town. Rates remain the same year-round in most places.

The Boar's Head Inn *(804)296-2181*
3 mi. W on US 250 W (Box 5307) - 22903
175 units *(800)476-1988* *Expensive-Very Expensive*
Foothills of the Blue Ridge Mountains frame the manicured grounds and tranquil ponds of this sprawling resort with the look and feel of a posh country inn. Amenities include an adjacent (fee) 18-hole golf course, plus three pools, tennis and squash courts, and rental bicycles, saunas, exercise room, plus fine dining (see listing) and lounge. Each room is beautifully furnished.

Clifton Country Inn *(804)971-1800*
4 mi. SE at 1296 Clifton Dr. - 22911
14 units *(888)971-1800* *Expensive-Very Expensive*
A historic country inn (circa 1799) is the romantic centerpiece of spacious, landscaped grounds that include a pool, whirlpool, tennis court, and a private lake. Gourmet dinners are available by reservation. Full breakfast and afternoon tea are complimentary. Each room is beautifully furnished and has a private bath and fireplace.

Doubletree Hotel Charlottesville *(804)973-2121*
5 mi. N on US 29 at 2350 Seminole Trail - 22901
235 units *(800)222-8733* *Expensive*
Charlottesville's largest lodging is a conference-oriented contemporary seven-story hotel that was recently completely renovated. Amenities include an indoor and outdoor pool, whirlpools, tennis court, exercise room, dining room, lounge and nightclub. Each room is well furnished. There are also suites with a whirlpool bath.

The Inn at Montecello *(804)979-3593*
2 mi. S on VA 20 at 1188 Scottsville Rd. (Route 19, Box 112) - 22902
5 units *Expensive*
An antebellum manor, circa 1850, on expansive grounds in rolling hill country has been transformed into a handsome bed-and-breakfast. Full country breakfast is complimentary. Each room is well-furnished with period antiques and modern conveniences like a private bath. There are no phones or TVs. Some rooms also have a fireplace or private patio.

Keswick Hall *(804)979-3440*
8 mi. E at 701 Country Club Dr. - Keswick 22947
48 units *(800)274-5391* *Very Expensive*
The luxurious Country House Hotel is a haven of tranquility. Gourmet breakfast and traditional afternoon tea are complimentary. Amenities include fine restaurants (see listing), pub, and access through the Club to a (fee) Arnold Palmer signature golf course, plus indoor/outdoor pool, whirlpool, tennis courts, sauna and steam room. Each room is an opulent reflection of the Laura Ashley style.

Omni Charlottesville Hotel   *(804)971-5500*
downtown at 235 W. Main St. - 22902
204 units   *(800)843-6664*   *Moderate-Expensive*
This modernistic seven-story hotel is a handsome brick-and-glass landmark on the Downtown Mall. Amenities include indoor and outdoor pools, whirlpool, saunas, exercise room, and a well-regarded restaurant. Each room is well furnished.

Palmer Country Manor   *(804)589-1300*
19 mi. SW via VA 53 at VA 640 (Rt. 2, Box 1390) - Palmyra 22963
13 units   *(800)253-4306*   *Expensive*
An 1830 manor house on expansive grounds is now a fine country inn with a restaurant, pool, bicycles, a fishing pond, hiking trails, and (fee) hot air ballooning. Each room is attractively furnished. The ten contemporary cottage suites have a gas or wood fireplace. Some also have a large in-room whirlpool.

Prospect Hill Inn   *(804)967-0844*
18 mi. E via I-64 (Rt. 3, Box 430) - 23093
13 units   *(800)277-0844*   *Very Expensive*
One of Virginia's most romantic lodgings is a plantation dating from 1732 that has been transformed into a refined bed-and-breakfast. Manicured, tree-shaded grounds feature a gazebo and pool. Full breakfast and afternoon refreshments, and dinner in the elegant dining room, are complimentary. There is no phone, but each room is beautifully furnished, including a fireplace. Most also have a large whirlpool tub.

Silver Thatch Inn   *(804)978-4686*
6 mi. N via US 29 at 3001 Hollymead Dr. - 22911
7 units   *Expensive*
A historic building dating to 1780 is now a stylish country inn with a pool and gourmet restaurant (see listing). Continental-plus breakfast is complimentary. There are private baths, but no phone. Each room is beautifully furnished with antiques and reproductions. Some rooms also have a fireplace.

200 South Street Inn   *(804)979-0200*
downtown at 200 South St. - 22902
20 units   *Expensive*
This four-story inn in an 1850s building in the heart of town has complimentary light breakfast and afternoon beverages. Each room is attractively furnished. Some of the rooms also have a fireplace and whirlpool tub.

BASIC INFORMATION

Elevation: 480 feet   *Population (1990):* 40,341
Location: 110 miles Southwest of Washington, D.C.
Nearest airport with commercial flights: in town
Charlottesville/Albemarle Convention & Visitors Bureau (804)977-1783
2 mi. S at jct. I-64 & US 20 (Box 178) - 22902
Charlottesville/Albemarle Chamber of Commerce   (804)295-3141
downtown at Fifth & E. Market St. (Box 1564) - 22902
www.charlottesvilletourism.org

Fredericksburg, Virginia

Fredericksburg is America's matchless treasury of the spoils of war and peace. The town was founded among low rolling hills by the tidewaters of the Rappahannock River in 1728 as a river port for oceangoing ships. Trade flourished. George Washington grew up on a farm across the river, and was heavily involved with family here until 1789, when he became president. Peace and prosperity were shattered abruptly in 1862. For two years, this was the most fought-over land in the history of the Western hemisphere. After the Civil War, shattered buildings of the exceptional legacy were restored.

Today, Fredericksburg is a peerless showcase of more than two centuries of urbane development, and two years of epic savagery. Travelers are inevitably subdued at the battlements, monuments and cemeteries. But, they marvel at the scope and historical integrity of the National Historic District downtown where hundreds of buildings are occupied by charming restaurants and shops featuring local specialties.

WEATHER PROFILE

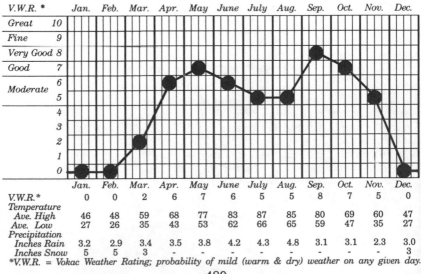

V.W.R. *		Jan.	Feb.	Mar.	Apr.	May	June	July	Aug.	Sep.	Oct.	Nov.	Dec.
Great	10												
Fine	9												
Very Good	8												
Good	7												
Moderate	6 5												
	4												
	3												
	2												
	1												
	0												

	Jan.	Feb.	Mar.	Apr.	May	June	July	Aug.	Sep.	Oct.	Nov.	Dec.
V.W.R.*	0	0	2	6	7	6	5	5	8	7	5	0
Temperature												
Ave. High	46	48	59	68	77	83	87	85	80	69	60	47
Ave. Low	27	26	35	43	53	62	66	65	59	47	35	27
Precipitation												
Inches Rain	3.2	2.9	3.4	3.5	3.8	4.2	4.3	4.8	3.1	3.1	2.3	3.0
Inches Snow	5	5	3	-	-	-	-	-	-	-	-	3

*V.W.R. = Vokac Weather Rating; probability of mild (warm & dry) weather on any given day.

480

ATTRACTIONS
Belmont   *(540)654-1015*
2 mi. N via US 1 at 224 Washington St.
The **Gari Melchers Estate and Memorial Gallery,** topping a hill above the Rappahannock River, began as an 18th century farmhouse. The expanded manor house and studio are a memorial to the artist who painted here until his death in 1932. Buildings are tastefully furnished with heirlooms, antiques, and art. There is a museum shop.
Boat Ride
Fredericksburg Cruises   *(540)453-2628*
just S on Sophia St. at City Dock
Cruise the scenic Rappahannock River aboard "the City of Fredericksburg," a two-deck 100-foot paddle-wheeler. Lunch, dinner or narrated cruises with entertainment can be reserved.
Downtown   *(540)373-1776*
centered around William and Princess Anne Sts.
Downtown Fredericksburg is America's preeminent showcase of the monumental flow of war and peace during the nation's first century. Original buildings, authentic furnishings and hallowed grounds distinguish a forty-block National Historic District. More than 350 buildings from the 18th and 19th century line tree-shaded streets above the riverfront. The 1852 **Court House** was designed by James Ronwich, who later designed the Smithsonian "Castle" in Washington, D.C. In the tower hangs the only known bell in Virginia cast in the Paul Revere foundry in Boston. **St. George's Episcopal Church** (1849), with three signed Tiffany windows, was hit dozens of times during the 1862 bombardment, and served as a hospital. So did the 1833 **Presbyterian Church**, where Clara Barton (later founder of the American Red Cross) is said to have nursed Union wounded. Damage done by cannonballs is still evident. The **Rising Sun Tavern** (circa 1760) was originally George Washington's younger brother Charles' home. It is restored to its 1792 appearance as a tavern, outfitted with a splendid pewter collection and costumed tavern wenches offering living history tours and spiced tea. At **Hugh Mercer Apothecary Shop** (late 1700s), costumed tour guides present Colonial medical instruments and discuss surgical techniques. A medicinal herb garden adjoins. These and other attractions plus notable monuments and mini-parks all share the picturesque district with a wealth of restaurants, handicrafts, antique and specialty shops, plus quaint inns with period touches. In addition to walking tours, narrated trolley and horse-drawn carriage tours are popular.
Fredericksburg Area Museum & Cultural Center   *(540)371-3037*
downtown at 907 Princess Anne St.
The former town hall and market building (circa 1816) is the second oldest continually used town hall in America. Exhibits in the three-story brick structure interpret the town's history from its first settlers to modern times.
Fredericksburg/Spotsylvania National Military Park   *(540)373-6122*
1 mi. SW at Lafayette Blvd. & Sunken Rd.
Fredericksburg is the epicenter of the bloodiest battles ever seen on the continent. During the Civil War, this location halfway between the Union and Confederate capitals at Washington, D.C. and Richmond was militarily critical to both sides. Four epic conflicts took place

beginning with the Battle of Fredericksburg in December 1862, where fighting raged from building-to-building downtown. During the Battle of Chancellorsville (May 1863) "Stonewall" Jackson was mistakenly shot by his own men, and died days later. The Battle of the Wilderness (May 1864) was the first-ever meeting of Gen. Robert E. Lee and Gen. Ulysses S. Grant. Their armies fought soon after at the Battle of Spotsylvania Court House (May 1864) to no clear-cut victory. But, enormous losses finally destroyed Lee's offensive capability, allowing Grant to move inexorably to Richmond. The four battlefields are all within a seventeen-mile radius of town. Miles of interpretive trails lead to battlegrounds with their original trenches, gun pits, stone walls and historic buildings. There are also many narrative markers, monuments, museum exhibits, and cemeteries.

James Monroe Museum   *(540)654-1043*
downtown at 908 Charles St.
The premier collection of Monroe-related material is located where he first practiced law in the 1780s. Exhibits include the Louis XVI desk on which President Monroe signed what became known as the Monroe Doctrine in 1823, formal attire the Monroes wore at the Court of Napoleon, and items he carried into battle as a Revolutionary War soldier. There is also a major library and an old-fashioned walled garden.

Kenmore   *(540)373-3381*
just W at 1201 Washington Av.
Fielding Lewis and his wife Betty (George Washington's only sister) rose to prominence while living in this classic example of Tidewater Virginia Colonial architecture. The meticulously restored brick manor includes exquisite original plasterwork and woodwork, plus elaborate, authentic period furnishings. Tours end in the kitchen with spiced tea and ginger cookies.

Lake Anna State Park   *(540)854-5503*
25 mi. SW via VA 208 on Route 601
A swimming beach, pontoon boat rides, boating and fishing are featured on this big popular reservoir. There are also lakefront picnic sites and nature trails. A modern visitor center exhibits local wildlife and traces the history of the area, including gold mining that occurred here in the 1730s.

Mary Washington College   *(540)654-1000*
1 mi. W via William St. at College Av.
In 1972, this became an independent liberal arts college. Founded in 1908 as a school for women, men have been part of a student body of 3,700 since 1970. Visitors can enjoy galleries, concerts, theater, and festivals at the photogenic, highly regarded campus where stately brick buildings are accented by towering hardwood trees, luxuriant lawns and fountains. The college's Center for Historic Preservation plays a role in securing Fredericksburg's legacy.

Mary Washington House   *(540)373-1569*
downtown at 1200 Charles St.
George Washington's mother lived in the house he bought for her (in 1772) until her death in 1789. It was from here that he left for New York to be inaugurated as first president of the United States after receiving his mother's blessing. Several of Mary Washington's personal possessions are on display, and some of her original boxwood trees still shade a lovely garden.

Carl's Creme Shakes & Sundaes
just N at 2200 Princess Anne St.
L-D.   *Low*
Since 1947, they've used the same old ice cream machine to make soft frozen custard (only enough for that day) that is silky smooth, truly delicious, and looks so good that people don't mind standing in line at this beloved, one-of-a-kind takeout.

Goolrick's   *(540)373-3411*
downtown at 901 Caroline St.
B-L-D.   *Low*
Fresh-squeezed lemonade, milk shakes and ice cream sodas are served with light meals in Fredericksburg's classic old-time soda fountain.

Kenmore Inn   *(540)371-7622*
downtown at 1200 Princess Anne St.
L-D.   *Expensive*
Creative and traditional Virginia recipes like roasted quail with country ham and cornbread stuffing are given careful attention. The refined parlors of an 18th century brick house are just right for upscale candlelit dining. There is also pub and patio dining.

Le Lafayette Restaurant   *(540)373-6895*
downtown at 623 Caroline St.
L-D.   *Expensive*
Fresh Virginia ingredients of the season lend distinction to the French and American cuisine presented amid casual elegance in a Colonial Georgian-style landmark on the National Register.

Merriman's   *(540)371-7723*
downtown at 715 Caroline St.
L-D.   *Expensive*
Fresh fish, crabcakes and conch fritters are some highlights on a creative menu where freshness and quality matter. Vegetarian dishes are also taken seriously in this snazzy contemporary restaurant.

Olde Towne Steak and Seafood   *(540)371-8020*
just N at 1612 Caroline St.
D only.   *Expensive*
Quality steaks, prime rib and seafood attract a loyal following of natives and visitors to this large comfortable dinner house.

Ristorante Renato   *(540)371-8228*
downtown at 422 William St.
L-D.   *Expensive*
Authentic Northern Italian cuisine includes an appealing selection of fresh pastas, veal, seafood, poultry and steaks. A classical guitarist on weekends contributes to the upscale firelit ambiance.

The Riverview Room   *(540)373-6500*
downtown at 1101 Sophia St.
L-D.   *Expensive*
A diverse menu of contemporary American fare is served in a casually elegant firelit dining room with a window-wall view by the riverfront. There is also a river-view patio and lounge.

Sammy T's   *(540)371-2008*
downtown at 801 Caroline St.
L-D.   *Low*
Many skillfully prepared vegetarian dishes, plus homemade soups and breads, highlight a health-conscious menu served in a casual wood-trimmed setting.

LODGING

Contemporary motels and motor lodges are numerous along nearby I-95. Historic inns are surprisingly scarce. Spring through early fall is high season. Rates in winter may be reduced by about 10%.

Comfort Inn Southpoint　　*(540)898-5550*
5 mi. S (near I-95) at 5422 Jefferson Davis Hwy. - 22407
125 units　　　　　　　*(800)228-5150*　　　　　　*Moderate*
The chain's contemporary five-story motel by an outlet center has an indoor pool, whirlpool, sauna and exercise room. Each room is well furnished. Several also have a whirlpool tub.

Fredericksburg Colonial Inn　　*(540)371-5666*
just N at 1707 Princess Anne St. - 22401
32 units　　　　　　　　　　　　　　　　　*Moderate*
The only motel within walking distance of downtown is modern, with some period decorations. Each unit is comfortably furnished.

Holiday Inn South　　*(540)898-1102*
5 mi. S (near I-95) at 5324 Jefferson Davis Hwy. - 22408
200 units　　　　　　*(800)465-4329*　　　　　　*Moderate*
This conventional, modern motor hotel has an indoor pool, whirlpool, sauna, exercise room and game room, plus a restaurant and entertainment lounge. Each room is attractively furnished.

Kenmore Inn　　*(540)371-7622*
downtown at 1200 Princess Anne St. - 22401
12 units　　　　　　　　　　　　　　　　　*Expensive*
A stately Colonial brick home was painstakingly transformed into a lovely bed-and-breakfast inn, with an elegant restaurant (see listing) and pub. Continental breakfast is complimentary. Each room is beautifully furnished with period and contemporary amenities, except TV. Some have a working fireplace.

Richard Johnson Inn　　*(540)899-7606*
downtown at 711 Caroline St. - 22401
9 units　　　　　　　　　　　　*Moderate-Expensive*
A late 18th century brick home now serves as a pleasant bed-and-breakfast inn. Breakfast and afternoon tea is complimentary. Each well-furnished room combines antiques and reproductions with modern conveniences, except phones or (in some) TVs.

Selby House Bed & Breakfast　　*(540)373-7037*
downtown at 226 Princess Anne St. - 22401
4 units　　　　　　　　　　　　　　　　　*Moderate*
A Victorian home and annex now serve as a bed-and-breakfast. Full breakfast is complimentary. Each room is comfortably furnished with period pieces, and has a private bath, but no phone or TV.

Sheraton Inn Fredericksburg　　*(540)786-8321*
4 mi. W (at I-95) on Rt. 3 at 2801 Plank Rd. (Box 618) - 22404
193 units　　　　　　*(800)682-1049*　　　　　　*Moderate*
The area's most complete motor hotel is a contemporary three-story complex with a large pool, three lighted tennis courts, exercise room, restaurant, entertainment lounge and gift shop. Each well-furnished room has a private patio or balcony. Some also have a whirlpool bath.

BASIC INFORMATION

Elevation:　60 feet　　　　　Population (1990):　19,027
Location:　52 miles Southwest of Washington, D.C.
Nearest airport with commercial flights:　Washington, D. C - 48 miles
Fredericksburg Department of Tourism　(540)373-1776　(800)678-4748
downtown at 706 Caroline St. - 22401　www.fredericksburgva.com

Williamsburg, Virginia

Williamsburg is the preeminent showcase of Colonial Americana. Rolling woodlands surround the choice site on a peninsula between tidewater reaches of the James and York Rivers. Settlement began in 1633. In 1699, the newly planned and renamed village of Williamsburg served (for eighty years) as the capital of the Virginia Colony. It continued as a quiet little college town until 1926, when John D. Rockefeller began restoration of the central area.

Today the Historic Area is a peerless treasury of original and authentic re-creations of stately Colonial public buildings, homes, shops and taverns. Many are outfitted with period artifacts, costumed interpreters, and craftsmen plying their trades. Compatible modern shops feature Virginia specialties near the College of William and Mary—still vital after more than 300 years. Nearby are historic Jamestown and Yorktown; Busch Gardens Williamsburg and Water Country USA theme parks, and abundant distinctive lodgings.

WEATHER PROFILE

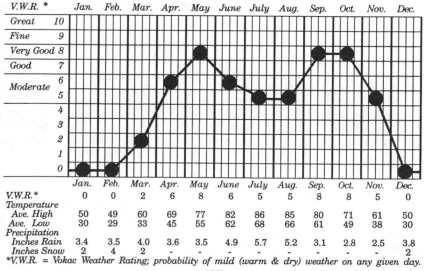

V.W.R. *	Jan.	Feb.	Mar.	Apr.	May	June	July	Aug.	Sep.	Oct.	Nov.	Dec.
V.W.R.*	0	0	2	6	8	6	5	5	8	8	5	0
Temperature												
Ave. High	50	49	60	69	77	82	86	85	80	71	61	50
Ave. Low	30	29	33	45	55	62	68	66	61	49	38	30
Precipitation												
Inches Rain	3.4	3.5	4.0	3.6	3.5	4.9	5.7	5.2	3.1	2.8	2.5	3.8
Inches Snow	2	4	2	-	-	-	-	-	-	-	-	2

*V.W.R. = Vokac Weather Rating; probability of mild (warm & dry) weather on any given day.

ATTRACTIONS
Busch Gardens Williamsburg   *(757)253-3350   (800)343-7946*
3 mi. SE via US 60 at Busch Gardens Blvd.
One of America's most beautiful entertainment theme parks occupies
rolling woodland where 17th century Europe is artfully replicated in
several detailed Old World hamlets. Among more than thirty thrill
rides are several roller coasters (including one of the world's largest)
and an exciting water ride. The Old Country theme is coordinated in
dozens of gift shops, restaurants and stage shows. Transportation
options include a skyride or steam train. A monorail runs to the
Anheuser Busch Hospitality Center, where visitors can enjoy free
samples and a self-guided brewery tour.
Carter's Grove   *(757)220-7645*
6 mi. SE via US 60
An imposing Georgian mansion built in 1754 by the grandson of
Virginia's wealthiest planter crowns a bluff above the James River. The
restored building is furnished in Colonial revival style. Grounds also
house reconstructed slave quarters, and the site of a village destroyed
by Indians in 1622. Artifacts are displayed at the nearby Winthrop
Rockefeller Archeology Museum.
College of William & Mary   *(757)221-4000*
just W at Jamestown & Richmond Rds.
America's second oldest college (after Harvard) was chartered by the
British monarchy in 1693. Presidents Jefferson, Monroe and Tyler were
alumni. Almost 8,000 students attend classes in classical brick
buildings amid expansive, tree-shaded greenswards. Phi Beta Kappa
Society was founded here. The Wren Building (1695) is the oldest
academic building still in use in America.
Colonial Williamsburg   *(757)229-1000   (800)447-8679*
downtown around Duke of Gloucester St. (Historic Area)
The 173-acre Historic Area is a meticulous 20th century restoration of
18th century Williamsburg when it was the political and cultural capital
of Britain's largest colony in the Americas. The mile-long living
museum has hundreds of houses, stores, taverns and public buildings
(including nearly one hundred Colonial-era originals) amid lovely
gardens and greens. Visitors stroll tree-shaded streets, mingle with
historical interpreters in Colonial attire, observe costumed tradesmen
plying artistic crafts and historic trades, and tour the Capitol,
Governor's Palace, and others furnished with authentic Colonial pieces.
The nearby visitor center has complete information.
Jamestown   *(757)898-3400*
7 mi. SW on Jamestown Rd.
An island in the James River was the site of America's first permanent
English settlement in 1607. The National Park Service Visitor Center
offers an orientation film, exhibits, shop, and tours of the site that
includes foundations of houses and public buildings. A five-mile loop
drive through natural woodlands and marshes, with stops at
interpretive markers and large paintings of Colonial life, is a must.
Jamestown Settlement   *(757)253-4838   (888)593-4682*
6 mi. SW on Jamestown Rd.
The story of America's first permanent English settlement is presented
through a docudrama film, museum exhibits and outdoor living history
areas. Costumed interpreters portray life in the early 1600s in re-
creations of James Fort, a Powhatan Indian village, and full-scale
reproductions of the three ships that transported the first settler.

Water Country USA   *(757)253-3350   (800)343-7946*
3 mi. E on VA 199
Virginia's largest water-themed park has a wave pool; giant inner tube
river ride; two-person tube ride; flumes, slides and pools; plus water
shows and children's play areas. There are also lockers, bathhouse
facilities, shops and food service.
Yorktown Battlefield   *(757)898-3400*
13 mi. E via Colonial National Historical Pkwy.
American independence was won here with the surrender of Lord
Cornwallis to General George Washington after the last battle of the
Revolutionary War in 1781. The visitor center has a film, museum,
shop and battlefield overlook. Ranger or self-guided walking or auto
tours pass earthworks; surrender site; Washington's headquarters; plus
historic buildings and monuments in Yorktown.
Yorktown Victory Center   *(757)253-4838   (888)593-4682*
12 mi. E by the Colonial National Historical Pkwy.
The American Revolution is chronicled through an evocative film, a
timeline walkway with dramatic exhibits themed to the period from
1750 to 1776, and innovative living history. Costumed interpreters re-
create life in a Continental army camp and on a Colonial farm.
RESTAURANTS
Aberdeen Barn   *(757)229-6661*
2 mi. NW at 1601 Richmond Rd.
D only.   *Very Expensive*
Slow-roasted prime rib of beef and tender steaks are outstanding
crowd-pleasers in this comfortably rustic candlelit dinner house.
Berret's Seafood Restaurant   *(757)253-1847*
downtown at 199 S. Boundary St. (Merchants Square)
L-D.   *Expensive*
Contemporary Virginia specialties like she-crab soup with sherry or
Virginia ham with cheese grits souffle are some of the best in town. So
are housemade desserts like coconut cream pie with chocolate graham
cracker crust. A working fireplace, fresh flowers and greenery, candles,
and linen contribute to an urbane feeling in intimate dining areas.
The Cheese Shop   *(757)220-0298*
downtown at 424 Prince George St. (Merchants Square)
L only.   *Moderate*
Freshly baked bread and a vast array of domestic and imported
cheeses and other gourmet deli items make great sandwiches. Top it
off with a premium regional wine for a memorable meal to go or in the
cheerful shop. Next door, the **Peanut Shop** (229-3908) glorifies
Virginia's peanuts, and offers free tastes of great goobers.
Chowning's Tavern   *(757)229-2141*
downtown at 109 E. Duke of Gloucester St. (Historic Area)
L-D.   *Expensive*
Regional dishes like Brunswick stew and homemade black walnut ice
cream are served amid the raucous good cheer of a genuine Colonial
alehouse. After dinner, do not miss period drinks and light fare with
gambols—18th century games and strolling costumed musicians.
The Jefferson Restaurant   *(757)229-2296*
2 mi. NW at 1453 Richmond Rd.
D only.   *Moderate*
Virginia hams and Virginia peanut soup have starred among Southern
dishes including local seafood and char-broiled steaks since 1956.
Simply comfortable decor reflects the restaurant's easy-going appeal.

King's Arms Tavern   *(757)229-2141*
downtown at 416 E. Duke of Gloucester St. (Historic Area)
L-D.   *Expensive*
Colonial dishes like peanut soup, Virginia ham, and hearty game pie
are served by staff in 18th century costumes. Genteel candlelit Colonial
decor is enhanced by authentically dressed balladeers.

Le Yaca Restaurant Français   *(757)220-3616*
4 mi. SE on US 60 at 1915 Pocahantas Trail
L-D.   *Very Expensive*
Innovative French cuisine including leg of lamb prepared over an open
hearth and their own desserts have won critical and popular acclaim.
Plush French country decor is part of the charm.

Shields Tavern   *(757)229-2141*
downtown at 422 E. Duke of Gloucester St. (Historic Area)
B-L-D.   *Expensive*
Spit-roasted meats, fowl and fish are accompanied by apple fritters and
other dishes prepared from Colonial recipes of the season. The
authentically restored rustic tavern is complete with balladeers.

The Trellis Restaurant   *(757)229-8610*
downtown at 403 W. Duke of Gloucester St. (Merchants Square)
L-D.   *Expensive*
A seasonal menu of creative American cuisine features mesquite-grilled
meats ranging from catfish to venison, plus housemade ice cream and
other delicious desserts, in a stylish contemporary setting.

Williamsburg Inn   *(757)229-1000 ext. 3201*
downtown at 136 E. Francis St. (Historic Area)
B-L-D.   *Very Expensive*
The Inn's **Regency Room** presents New American cuisine with a
classic French flair. Fresh seasonal ingredients and expert preparation
are apparent in all dishes. Housemade desserts include a splendid
pecan pie with bourbon custard sauce. Coat and tie are appropriate.
Formally attired staff and a well-played grand piano contribute to the
gracious opulence of the expansive dining room.

LODGING

Accommodations are abundant and varied—from motels and hotels
along US 60 through town and bed-and-breakfasts around the historic
area to charming resorts. Summer is high season. In winter, many
lodgings reduce their rates 40% or more.

Applewood Colonial Bed & Breakfast   *(757)229-0205*
just NW at 605 Richmond Rd. - 23185
4 units   *(800)899-2753*   *Moderate-Expensive*
A 1929 home built in detailed 18th century style by the construction
manager for the Colonial Williamsburg restoration now serves as a
charming bed-and-breakfast inn. A full breakfast by candlelight and
afternoon refreshments are complimentary. Each beautifully furnished
room has a private bath and romantic Colonial decor. The spacious
suite also has a fireplace.

Fort Magruder Inn & Conference Center   *(757)220-2250*
2 mi. SE on US 60 at 6945 Pocahontas Trail (Box 3050) - 23187
303 units   *(800)331-5204*   *Moderate-Expensive*
Embankments from a Civil War fort can still be seen on tree-shaded
grounds of the contemporary four-story hotel. Amenities include tennis
courts, large outdoor and indoor pools, whirlpool, saunas, exercise
room, gift shop, restaurant and entertainment lounge. Each room is
well furnished. Most have a private deck.

Williamsburg, Virginia

Kingsmill Resort   *(757)253-1703*
5 mi. SE via US 60 at 1010 Kingsmill Rd. - 23185
405 units   *(800)832-5665   Expensive-Very Expensive*
One of Virginia's most complete resorts is a handsome contemporary complex sprawled among three (fee) 18-hole championship golf courses in lush woodlands by the James River. Other amenities include a beach, 9-hole par-3 golf course, fifteen tennis courts, racquetball courts, big indoor and outdoor view pools, whirlpool, saunas and steam room, plus (fee) full-service spa, boats, bicycles, fine view dining and entertainment lounges. Each beautifully furnished unit has a private deck. Spacious suites also have a living room, kitchen and fireplace.

Legacy of Williamsburg Bed & Breakfast Inn   *(757)220-0524*
1 mi. SW at 930 Jamestown Rd. - 23185
4 units   *(800)962-4722*   *Moderate-Expensive*
Fireplaces and handsome period furnishings convey romance in this Colonial-style bed-and-breakfast by a forest. Full breakfast is complimentary. Beautifully furnished suites also have a fireplace.

Primrose Cottage   *(757)229-6421*
just NW at 706 Richmond Rd. - 23185
4 units   *(800)522-1901*   *Moderate*
In spring, primroses line the walkway to this delightful bed-and-breakfast inn decorated with quality antiques and family treasures. A full gourmet breakfast is complimentary. Each spacious room has a private bath and is individually beautifully furnished.

Williamsburg Inn   *(757)229-1000*
downtown at 136 E. Francis St. (Historic Area) (Box 1776) - 23187
143 units   *(800)447-8679*   *Very Expensive*
One of America's best historic sanctuaries opened in 1937 next to the heart of Colonial Williamsburg. The resort continues to offer the opulence of a grand manor house surrounded by luxuriant grounds and world class facilities, including two (fee) championship golf courses and related club facilities, ten tennis courts, outdoor and indoor pools, whirlpool, sauna, steam room, exercise room and resort shop, plus gourmet dining (see listing) and lounge. Each room is luxuriously furnished including antiques and fresh flowers.

Williamsburg Lodge   *(757)229-1000*
downtown at 310 South England St. (Historic Area) (Box 1776) - 23187
315 units   *(800)447-8679*   *Expensive*
Manicured grounds surround a handsome four-story resort with tennis courts, indoor and outdoor pools, whirlpools, saunas, steam rooms, exercise room, bicycle rentals, gift shop, fine dining, and entertainment lounge. Each spacious room is beautifully furnished.

Williamsburg Woodlands   *(757)229-1000*
just N at 102 Visitor Center Dr. (Box 1776) - 23187
315 units   *(800)447-8679*   *Moderate-Expensive*
Woodlands and gardens surround this family-oriented modern hotel with tennis courts, indoor and outdoor pools, (fee) miniature golf, rental bicycles, dining rooms and shops. Each room is well furnished.

BASIC INFORMATION

Elevation: 80 feet   Population (1990):   11,409
Location: 50 miles East of Richmond, VA
Nearest airport with commercial flights: Newport News, VA - 14 miles
Williamsburg Area Convention & Visitors Bureau   (757)253-0192
1 mi. SE at 201 Penniman Rd. (Box 3585) - 23185   (800)368-6511
www.visitwilliamsburg.com

Chelan, Washington

Chelan is the gateway to America's most extraordinary big lake. The little town is situated among apple orchards along the sunny eastern end of Lake Chelan, the largest lake in Washington, and one of the world's deepest. Remarkably, the western end of the long, narrow lake is surrounded by glacier-clad peaks, lush pine forests, streams and waterfalls in the magnificent North Cascades. Mining and lumber brought settlers here in the 1880s, but apple growing and tourism became the economic mainstays.

Today, the lake's great reach gives Chelan a special closeness to an enormous complex of national forests, parks and recreation areas beyond the towering mountain backdrop. In town, every imaginable water activity can be enjoyed during warm dry summer days, thanks to well-maintained shoreline parks with sandy beaches, marinas, and a major waterslide park. Downtown still has a limited assortment of shops, restaurants, and nightlife, but there are fine lakefront lodgings.

WEATHER PROFILE

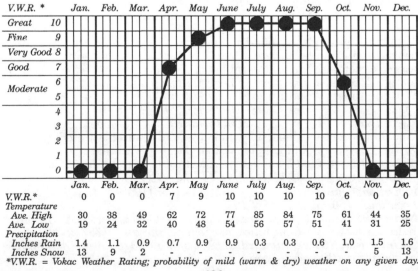

V.W.R. *	Jan.	Feb.	Mar.	Apr.	May	June	July	Aug.	Sep.	Oct.	Nov.	Dec.
V.W.R.*	0	0	0	7	9	10	10	10	10	6	0	0
Temperature												
Ave. High	30	38	49	62	72	77	85	84	75	61	44	35
Ave. Low	19	24	32	40	48	54	56	57	51	41	31	25
Precipitation												
Inches Rain	1.4	1.1	0.9	0.7	0.9	0.9	0.3	0.3	0.6	1.0	1.5	1.6
Inches Snow	13	9	2	-	-	-	-	-	-	-	5	13

*V.W.R. = Vokac Weather Rating; probability of mild (warm & dry) weather on any given day.

490

Boat Rentals

Pleasure, sail, skiing, pontoon, and fishing boats can be rented at these small marinas just west of town:

Chelan Boat Rentals, Inc.   *1210 W. Woodin Av.* *(509)682-4444*
Ship-n-Shore Boat Rental   *1230 W. Woodin Av.* *(509)682-5125*

Boat Rides

Lake Chelan Boat Co.   *(509)682-4584*
1 mi. SW at 1418 W. Woodin Av.

"The Lady of the Lake" is a large excursion boat that takes passengers the entire fifty-five-mile length of Lake Chelan. After cruising past miles of orchard-covered slopes, the boat enters a narrow fiord-like canyon in the Cascade Range. Glacier-clad peaks, lush pine forests, waterfalls, and occasional big game seem near because the lake is never more than two miles wide. At the north end, passengers can have lunch or explore tiny Stehekin before returning.

Lake Chelan

downtown

One of the world's most extraordinary lakes is also the largest, longest, and deepest in the State of Washington. Well over fifty miles long and less than two miles wide, it was formed by a gigantic glacier. The trough is now filled with water 1,500 feet deep—actually below sea level. The town of Chelan occupies a small portion of an enormous natural dam created by the ancient glacier. No other lake on the continent has the variety of topography and climate found here, from fruit orchards and rangeland in a near-desert setting to dense pine forests and glacier-shrouded peaks. All kinds of outdoor activities are available on and near the crystal-clear lake, yet the area's awesome recreation potential has only been lightly tapped.

Lake Chelan National Recreation Area   *(509)682-2549*

access by Lake Chelan

Majestic peaks of the North Cascade Range that enclose the northern end of Lake Chelan are the highlight of a large sylvan preserve with wilderness hiking, backpacking, and rock climbing opportunities. The gateway is tiny, scenic Stehekin. One of America's most isolated communities has all necessary supplies, food, lodging and camping facilities. Access to the area is only by boat, seaplane, or hiking trails.

Lake Chelan State Park   *(509)687-3710*

9 mi. SW via US 97 & S. Lakeshore Rd.

This large lakeshore park has spectacular up-lake views, a sandy beach and a protected swimming area, docking, picnicking, and a complete campground by the water.

Lakeshore Park

downtown on WA 150

Chelan's civic keystone is a delightful park with superb lake views. Grassy slopes extend to a sandy beach, a popular swimming area, picnic tables, imaginative play equipment, marina with seaplane flights, and a full-service campground. Nearby, Chelan Riverfront Park has a mile of night-lighted sidewalks along the scenic shore.

North Cascades National Park   *(360)856-5700*

90 mi. NW via US 97, WA 153 & WA 20

Some of the most rugged mountains in the West are within this park. Many miles of trails are threaded throughout a wilderness of jagged peaks with more than three hundred active glaciers, jewel lakes hidden in dense forests, and deep canyons with clear streams and waterfalls.

Warm Water Feature
Slidewaters at Lake Chelan   *(509)682-5751*
1 mi. SW via US 97 at 102 Waterslides Dr.
With a splendid view from a slope near the lake, this state-of-the-art
waterslide complex offers slides ranging from slow and tame to fast
and scary. The inner tube river ride is especially exhilarating.
Whirlpools, picnic areas, a viewing deck, fast food and a gift shop are
available.
Wenatchee National Forest   *(509)682-2576*
W of town
This vast forested area includes most of Lake Chelan and the majestic
Glacier Peak Wilderness. An excellent trail system (including part of
the Pacific Crest National Scenic Trail) accesses a myriad of glaciers,
peaks, streams, waterfalls, and lakes. Hiking, backpacking, climbing,
boating, fishing, hunting and camping are popular.

RESTAURANTS

Campbell's Lake Chelan Resort   *(509)682-4250*
downtown at 104 W. Woodin Av.
B-L-D.   *Moderate*
Contemporary American fare served in the **Campbell's House** is the
best for many miles. Fine regional specialties include apple-oatmeal
buttermilk pancakes with homemade syrup, and seasonal treats like
baked Copper River salmon. A sunny veranda adjoins stylish dining
rooms, and there is a friendly pub.
Goochi's Restaurant   *(509)682-2436*
downtown at 104 E. Woodin Av.
L-D.   *Moderate*
American fare includes some creative seasonal dishes and dozens of tap
beers served amid warm wood surroundings.
Judy-Jane Bakery   *(509)682-2151*
downtown at 216 W. Manson Rd.
B-L-D.   *Low*
Yummy pastries, rolls and desserts are baked from scratch daily,
including unusual morning delights like peanut butter savannahs or
cinnamon pecan snuggles. Enjoy them with assorted beverages, and
(later) light fare and chicken inside, at patio tables, or to go.
Lakeview Drive-In   *(509)682-5322*
just NW at 323 Manson Rd.
L-D.   *Low*
Burgers, foot-long hot dogs and popcorn shrimp are among many
family favorites enjoyed with assorted hard or soft ice cream treats at
this long-popular takeout by the main lakeside park.

LODGING

Lakefront resorts and motels are scarce but distinctive. High season is
from June into September. Winter rates may be at least 40% lower.
Campbell's Lake Chelan Resort   *(509)682-2561*
downtown at 104 W. Woodin Av. (Box 278) - 98816
170 units (800)553-8225 (in Northwest only)   Expensive-Very Expensive
Campbell's is the premier resort on Lake Chelan. The original four-
story hotel has been the downtown landmark by the lake since 1901.
Nicely landscaped contemporary facilities include a quarter-mile of
sandy beach, boat moorage and lakefront boardwalk, two lakeview
pools, two whirlpools, landmark restaurant (see listing) and lounge. All
beautifully furnished rooms offer grand lake views and a big private
deck. Some also have a kitchenette and gas fireplace.

Captain's Quarters   *(509)682-5886*
5 mi. SW at 283 Minneapolis Beach Rd. - 98816
3 units   *(888)977-1748*   *Expensive*
Chelan's only lakefront bed-and-breakfast has panoramic lake views
from public areas and access for lake swimming. Bountiful gourmet
breakfast is complimentary. Each spacious suite is individually well
furnished and has a refrigerator and private bath (no phone or TV).
Two also have a private sunroom with a two-person whirlpool.

Caravel Resort   *(509)682-2582*
just W at 322 W. Woodin Av. (Box 1509) - 98816
92 units   *(800)962-8723*   *Moderate-Expensive*
Downtown Chelan is across a bridge from this contemporary four-story
lakefront motel with lake swimming, a large view pool, whirlpool and
boat dock. All well-furnished rooms have a private waterfront terrace
with a fine up-lake view. Some also have a kitchen and fireplace.
Spacious fourth floor suites also have a big in-room whirlpool.

Darnell's Resort Motel   *(509)682-2015*
1 mi. NW at 901 Spader Bay Rd. (Box 506) - 98816
40 units   *(800)967-8149*   *Moderate-Expensive*
A private sandy beach is a feature of this secluded three-story resort
motel. The family-oriented complex also has docks, a 9-hole putting
green, tennis courts, a large view pool and whirlpool, sauna, exercise
room, and bicycles. Each well-furnished room has a lake view. Most
one- and two-bedroom units have a full kitchen.

The Inn Above the Lake   *(509)682-3184*
just SW at 914 Cone Rd. - 98816
3 units   *(888)444-6352 pin # 0240*   Expensive
This bed-and-breakfast opened on a hill near the lake in 1996 with a
pool, whirlpool, and sauna. Full breakfast is compli-mentary. Each
room is well furnished with all contemporary conveniences. Two have
fine lake views. One has a big in-room whirlpool.

Mary Kay's Romantic Whaley Mansion   *(509)682-5735*
just SW at 415 3rd St. - 98816
6 units   *(800)729-2408*   *Expensive*
The 1911 Whaley Mansion on a hill near the lake is now an ornate
bed-and-breakfast. Full gourmet breakfast is complimentary. Each
room is well furnished with all contemporary conveniences (except a
phone) blended with elaborate touches and period antiques.

Midtowner Motel   *(509)682-4051*
just E at 721 E. Woodin Av. (Box 1722) - 98816
45 units   *Moderate*
Chelan's best off-lake motel is a modern facility with an indoor pool,
whirlpool and sauna. Each spacious room is comfortably furnished.

Westview Resort Motel   *(509)682-4396*
2 mi. SW at 2312 W. Woodin Av. (Rt. 1, Box 14) - 98816
25 units   *(800)468-2781*   *Expensive*
This 1992 motel by a lakefront park has a large view pool and
whirlpool. Each well-furnished room has a mini-kitchen. Most also
have a private lake-view balcony. Three suites have a gas fireplace.

BASIC INFORMATION

Elevation: 1,200 feet   *Population (1990): 2,969*
Location: 180 miles East of Seattle
Nearest airport with commercial flights: Wenatchee - 48 miles
Lake Chelan Chamber of Commerce (509)682-3503 (800)424-3526
    downtown at 102 E. Johnson Av. (Box 216) - 98816 www.lakechelan.com

La Conner, Washington

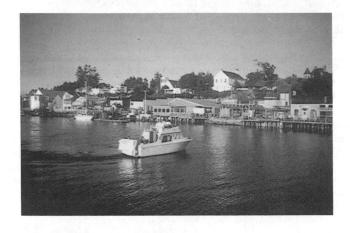

La Conner is the hidden gem of the Pacific Northwest. The village is sequestered along the mainland side of a natural channel of Puget Sound. Rich, unfenced farmlands to the east are framed by the Cascade Range and the glacial crest of majestic Mt. Baker. Farmers and traders began settling here in the 1870s. But, La Conner remained a backwater until a century later when the area's beauty began to attract artists and craftsmen.

Today, La Conner has one of the most charming business districts in the West. Flowery landscaping and waterfront miniparks intersperse historic buildings filled with first-rate studios, galleries, antique stores, and shops emphasizing Northwestern collectibles. Good restaurants are numerous. Nightlife is confined to a few atmospheric taverns—some with waterfront view decks. Lodgings are all unconventional and artistic, with special appeal to romantics attracted by the vibrant village, pastoral countryside, and scenic waterways.

WEATHER PROFILE

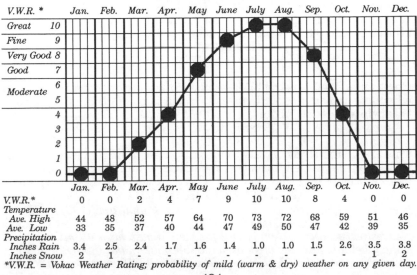

V.W.R.*	Jan.	Feb.	Mar.	Apr.	May	June	July	Aug.	Sep.	Oct.	Nov.	Dec.
V.W.R.*	0	0	2	4	7	9	10	10	8	4	0	0
Temperature												
Ave. High	44	48	52	57	64	70	73	72	68	59	51	46
Ave. Low	33	35	37	40	44	47	49	50	47	42	39	35
Precipitation												
Inches Rain	3.4	2.5	2.4	1.7	1.6	1.4	1.0	1.0	1.5	2.6	3.5	3.8
Inches Snow	2	1	-	-	-	-	-	-	-	-	1	2

*V.W.R. = Vokac Weather Rating; probability of mild (warm & dry) weather on any given day.

494

ATTRACTIONS

Boat Rides
Mystic Sea Charters	*Box 1443*	*(800)308-9387*
Viking Cruises	*Box 327*	*(360)466-2639*

Scenic lunch or dinner cruises to Deception Pass and the San Juan Islands can be arranged any day from April through October aboard the 100-foot "Mystic Sea." From November through March the 58-foot "Viking Star" offers exciting whale-watch/nature cruises of various lengths. Both depart from La Conner.

Chuckanut Drive   *(360)676-2093*
starts 16 mi. N on WA 11

Fairhaven Park with its pretty rose gardens is at the far end of one of the Northwest's most beautiful maritime drives. A narrow paved road clings to lush forested hillsides above Puget Sound for a distance of about ten miles. Along the way are turnouts overlooking island-dotted waterways and the distant Olympic Mountains, several restaurants, and Larrabee State Park, a picturesque rocky cove on Puget Island with a forested picnic area and campground.

Fairhaven Historic District   *(800)487-2032*
23 mi. N via WA 11 - Bellingham

An assortment of surprisingly large brick buildings, clustered on a slope above Puget Sound, was the heart of a town that competed with nearby Bellingham a century ago for dominance of the area. It lost. Fairhaven is now a suburb, but the remnants of the Victorian business district, on the National Register, now house many specialty shops, restaurants, saloons and the charming Fairhaven Bed & Breakfast.

Gaches Mansion   *(360)466-4288*
downtown at 703 S. Second St.

La Conner's most imposing historic residence has been skillfully restored to its 1890s' elegance, and filled with period furnishings.

Lynden   *(360)354-5995*
42 mi. N via WA 11 & WA 539

In an area that is the tulip capital of the West, what can be more appropriate than a Dutch village? Lynden is a delightful getaway with authentic Dutch food and architecture, tidy flower-adorned shops and homes on tree-lined streets, and immaculate parks. Downtown, the **Dutch Village Inn** offers three unique hotel rooms in a 72-foot windmill that anchors a mall with specialty shops, cafe and theater along an indoor canal.

Mount Baker - Snoqualmie National Forest   *(360)599-2714*
E of town

Much of the Cascade Range is encompassed in this forest. Features include majestic Mount Baker, the glistening high point (10,775 feet) of La Conner's backdrop. It is an all-year recreation destination with a large, well-developed ski area—one of seven in the forest. Glacier Peak and the surrounding wilderness area are part of the reason why this forest contains more than one-third of the glacier-covered area in the United States outside of Alaska. Farther south, the Alpine Lakes Wilderness Area has hundreds of crystal-clear lakes. A good network of peripheral roads and more than 1,000 miles of hiking trails (including part of the Pacific Crest National Scenic Trail) provide access to these and several newer wilderness areas. Recreation opportunities abound in this wonderland of peaks and glaciers, waterfalls and cascades, streams and lakes, emerald forests, and fields of flowers.

La Conner, Washington

The Museum of Northwest Art   *(360)466-4446*
downtown at 121 S. First St.
The only museum devoted exclusively to Northwest art opened in 1995. In addition to the handsome gallery, there is a well-stocked museum store full of fine art, crafts, jewelry and books of the region.

Rainbow Bridge
just S on Reservation Rd.
This award-winning span across the Swinomish Channel is the epitome of graceful simplicity. The russet-hued bridge is both an elegant landmark and a perfect prospect for viewing the seaway, La Conner, and farmlands extending toward distant Mt. Baker.

Roozengaarde   *(360)424-8531*   *(800)732-3266*
6 mi. E at 1587 Beaver Marsh Rd.- Mt. Vernon
Tulips, dahlias, and other bulb plants are showcased and identified in a tranquil exhibition garden by a windmill, and there is a gift shop.

Skagit County Historical Museum   *(360)466-3365*
just E at 501 S. Fourth St.
Pioneer memorabilia is showcased in a contemporary building on the brow of a hill. As an added feature, picture windows frame flower bulb farms and mountains east of town.

RESTAURANTS

Andiamo Ristorante Italiano   *(360)466-9111*
downtown at 505 S. First St.
L-D.   *Expensive*
Northern Italian cuisine is skillfully prepared from fresh, quality ingredients. The fine channel view from the stylish upstairs dining room is another reason why this is a local favorite.

Calico Cupboard   *(360)466-4451*
downtown at 720 S. First St.
B-L.   *Moderate*
The Calico Cupboard is one of the Northwest's best bakery cafes. Bear claws, cinnamon rolls, scones, coffee cakes, muffins and other morning delights are made here from scratch with quality natural ingredients. So are breads and a luscious assortment of cakes, cookies and pies. It's all served by calico-clad waitresses in a country-cute dining room with hearty American fare, or to go.

Farmhouse Inn Restaurant   *(360)466-4411*
4 mi. N on WA 20 at 1376 La Conner-Whitney Rd.
B-L-D.   *Moderate*
Homestyle cooking including a fine selection of pies on display is part of the appeal of the oak-furnished dining room with warm country decor.

Georgia's Bakery   *(360)466-2149*
downtown at 109 N. First St.
B-L.   *Moderate*
Innovative baked goods include pochettes (croissants in a pocket form stuffed with turkey and Jarlsburg cheese, etc.), buttery rich scones with orange peel, or raspberry/almond Danish. All are delicious, and perfect with coffee on a nearby bench by the water.

La Conner Brewing Company   *(360)466-1415*
downtown at 117 S. First St.
L-D.   *Moderate*
Wood-fired traditional and designer pizzas are featured along with their premium beers and ales in a spiffy young brew pub.

La Conner Seafood & Prime Rib House   *(360)466-4014*
downtown at 614 S. First St.
L-D.   *Expensive*
Sure enough, fresh seafood and prime rib are given careful attention
in this big popular restaurant and bar where diners on two levels and
on the waterfront deck have fine channel views.

La Conner Tavern   *(360)466-9932*
downtown at 702 S. First St.
L-D.   *Moderate*
Family comfort foods are served with all sorts of brews and other
beverages in a big friendly tavern with pool, darts, and a nifty dining
deck by the channel with a fine view of the bridge.

Lighthouse Inn   *(360)466-3147*
downtown at 512 S. First St.
L-D.   *Moderate*
Barbecued salmon (an alderwood smoker is out front) stars among
contemporary American fare. The big, informal dining room and lounge
have waterfront views. There is also a streetside deli.

Palmers Restaurant & Pub   *(360)466-4261*
downtown at 205 E. Washington St.
L-D.   *Expensive*
European-inspired innovative Northwestern cuisine distinguishes one
of the region's most sophisticated restaurants. Upstairs, casually
elegant dining rooms are enhanced by a wood stove. There is also a
dining deck. Downstairs is a cozy wood-trimmed pub.

Wildflowers   *(360)424-9724*
13 mi. E at 2001 E. College Way - Mt. Vernon
L-D.   *Expensive*
Wildflowers is the region's best dinner house. Innovative cuisine
showcases top-quality, seasonal ingredients typified by Northwestern
dishes like roast chicken breast stuffed with sausage, almonds and
dried apricots served with a port-orange-ginger sauce. Housemade
breads and desserts can be wonderful, too, served in an elegant firelit
dining room of an older home amid gardens.

LODGING

Lodgings are all distinctive, small, and romantic in La Conner. High
season is April through September. At other times, prices may be
reduced 25% or more.

The Heron in La Conner   *(360)466-4626*
just E at 117 Maple St. (Box 716) - 98257
12 units   *Moderate-Expensive*
The Heron is one of Washington's most sybaritic adult getaways.
Opened in 1986, the stylish inn captures the spirit of Victorian La
Conner on a lovely site at the edge of farmlands. Guests can enjoy the
scene from a porch or hot tub. Breakfast is complimentary. Each
beautifully furnished room is entirely modern, yet conveys nostalgic
charm. Spacious corner rooms have a gas fireplace and/or in-room
whirlpool, and a fine view of Mt. Baker.

Hotel Planter   *(360)466-4710*
downtown at 715 First St. (Box 702) - 98257
12 units   *(800)488-5409*   *Moderate-Expensive*
La Conner's historic little hotel, built in 1907, was completely restored
in 1989. The building now encloses a garden court with a gazebo and
whirlpool. Each well-furnished room balances a romantic past with all
modern comforts. One also has a large in-room whirlpool.

La Conner Channel Lodge   *(360)466-1500*
downtown at 205 N. First St. (Box 573) - 98257
41 units   *Expensive-Very Expensive*
La Conner's only waterfront lodging is a delightful contemporary craftsman-style inn in a garden by the channel. The romantic wood-trimmed complex on the quiet side of downtown includes a boat dock and pier. An expanded Continental breakfast is complimentary. Each luxuriously furnished room showcases present-day Northwestern art and detailed craftsmanship, and has a gas fireplace. Many also have a private balcony by the peaceful little waterway, and a large whirlpool bath.

La Conner Country Inn   *(360)466-3101*
downtown at 107 S. Second St. (Box 573) - 98257
28 units   *Moderate-Expensive*
The tranquil feeling of the area is reflected in this artistic little wood-crafted inn. An expanded Continental breakfast is complimentary. Each spacious, well-furnished room has a gas fireplace and nostalgic decor blended with all contemporary conveniences.

Rainbow Inn   *(360)466-4578*
1 mi. E at 1075 Chilberg Rd. (Box 15) - 98257
8 units   *(888)266-8879*   *Moderate*
A turn-of-the-century farmhouse has been lovingly converted into a stylish pastoral retreat amid flat Skagit Valley tulip fields. There is a whirlpool on the back deck. Full breakfast is complimentary. Most of the well-furnished rooms have a private bath. One room has a whirlpool bath. Another has a pot-bellied stove.

Ridgeway Bed & Breakfast   *(340)428-8068*
4 mi. E at 14914 McLean Rd. (Box 475) - 98257
7 units   *(800)428-8068*   *Moderate-Expensive*
A Dutch Colonial brick farmhouse surrounded by flower fields now serves as a stylish bed-and-breakfast. Full breakfast, evening dessert, and use of a hot tub are complimentary. Each well-furnished room overlooks peaceful gardens and fields.

The Wild Iris   *(360)466-1400*
just E at 121 Maple Av. (Box 696) - 98257
20 units   *(800)477-1400 (Northwest)*   *Expensive*
One of Puget Sound's most romantic bed-and-breakfast inns has a serene view of rich farmlands and Mt. Baker. The Victorian-style 1990s building has a posh dining room offering dinner (open to the public by reservation). Bountiful buffet breakfast is complimentary. All rooms are beautifully furnished. Smaller standard rooms face the parking lots. Spacious view suites have a gas fireplace, two-person in-room whirlpool, and bucolic view deck.

BASIC INFORMATION

Elevation: 30 feet   *Population (1990): 1,000*
Location: 68 miles North of Seattle
Nearest airport with commercial flights: Bellingham - 30 miles
La Conner Chamber of Commerce (360)466-4778 (888)642-9284
just E at 315 E. Morris St. (Box 1610) - 98257
www.laconner-chamber.com

Langley, Washington

Langley is a romantic getaway by the sea. Off the beaten path on Whidbey Island, it is perched on a bluff overlooking the tranquil waters of Saratoga Passage in Puget Sound. Spectacular Cascade Mountains punctuate the horizon. Settlement began during the 1880s. Growth was slow but steady for a century.

Village atmosphere still prevails. There are no stoplights or chain stores. But, the picturesque little business district displays its vitality in miniparks with whimsical sculptures; specialty shops and galleries featuring regional arts, crafts and antiques; and in splendid new public buildings like the library and Center for the Arts. A burgeoning concentration of notable restaurants and taverns includes several that celebrate the lovely waterfront view. Lodgings are also personalized, ranging from plush seaside inns to historic bed-and-breakfasts. All reflect the town's commitment to a human scale in harmony with the peaceful intimate setting.

WEATHER PROFILE

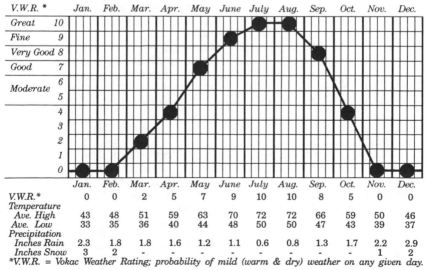

V.W.R. *		Jan.	Feb.	Mar.	Apr.	May	June	July	Aug.	Sep.	Oct.	Nov.	Dec.
V.W.R.*		0	0	2	5	7	9	10	10	8	5	0	0
Temperature													
Ave. High		43	48	51	59	63	70	72	72	66	59	50	46
Ave. Low		33	35	36	40	44	48	50	50	47	43	39	37
Precipitation													
Inches Rain		2.3	1.8	1.8	1.6	1.2	1.1	0.6	0.8	1.3	1.7	2.2	2.9
Inches Snow		3	2	-	-	-	-	-	-	-	-	1	2

*V.W.R. = Vokac Weather Rating; probability of mild (warm & dry) weather on any given day.

ATTRACTIONS

Bicycling
Velocity Bikes Inc.   *(360)321-5040*
3 mi. SW at 5603½ Bayview Rd.
Many miles of paved byways pass through bucolic countryside and luxuriant forests on the way to scenic beaches, coves and parks. This place has provided rentals and related maps and supplies since 1978.

Boat Rides   *(800)843-3779 (in WA)*
Clinton-Mukilteo Ferry
6 mi. SE via Langley Rd. & WA 525
Keystone-Port Townsend Ferry
20 mi. NW via WA 525 at Keystone Ferry Dock
Large passenger/car ferry boats sail every thirty minutes from Clinton and every forty-five minutes from Keystone. Either way, views of Puget Sound, islands, and glacier-covered peaks on the horizon are delightful. From May into October, arrive at the terminal an hour prior to departure on weekdays, and two hours early on weekends.

Coupeville   *(360)678-5434*
25 mi. NW via WA 525 & WA 20
A long, colorful history is carefully preserved in this seaside village. Concentrated along the waterfront are a picturesque wharf, historic block houses and buildings on the National Historic Register and a museum, plus specialty and souvenir shops and some eating and drinking places. Among several quaint lodgings, the best is nearby overlooking Penn Cove. The Captain Whidbey Inn (see listings) is one of the island's most romantic restaurants and lodgings.

Deception Pass State Park   *(360)675-2417*
42 mi. NW on WA 20
Washington's most popular state park has many miles of beaches and quiet coves, freshwater swimming and a sandy beach at Cranberry Lake, almost thirty miles of forested hiking trails, and a big full-service campground. A lofty highway bridge connecting two islands offers memorable views of swirling waters in narrow rock-bound Deception Pass far below. There is a marina with boat rentals. Boating and fishing are popular. So are scuba diving in an underwater park and clear, cold-water swimming. Four other state parks on the island's coastline to the south have more limited facilities.

Greenbank Farm   *(360)678-7700*
14 mi. NW at 765 E. Wonn Rd. - Greenbank
A historic loganberry farm (once the world's largest) now houses a large, well-organized visitor center with tastes of loganberry liqueur and distilling information. Other features include wine tasting, sales, gourmet gifts, picnic grounds, and pick-your-own loganberries in July and August.

Whidbey Island
around town
Whidbey Island, the largest island in Puget Sound, is 45 miles long. Gentle forested hills and bucolic valleys are surrounded by more than one hundred miles of scenic shoreline with numerous public beaches, parks, and marinas. Most water sports are enjoyed around the island, but the best swimming and scuba diving areas are on the northern half. Scenic drives and bike routes connect all areas. Wild free-for-the-picking blackberries can be found along most roads. Access is by highway bridge from the north, and ferries from Port Townsend or Mukilteo.

Winery

Whidbey Island Winery   *(360)221-2040*
1 mi. S at 5237 S. Langley Rd.
Estate-grown grapes and island rhubarb are featured in this family winery with tasting and sales.

RESTAURANTS

Cafe Langley   *(360)221-3090*
downtown at 113 First St.
L-D.   *Expensive*
Mediterranean cuisine has earned renown for dishes like lamb shish-ka-bob or seafood stew—and for fresh flavorful treatment of Northwest salmon, halibut, mussels and other seafood. The cozy, wood-trimmed dining room provides a relaxing backdrop to fine dining.

The Captain Whidbey Inn   *(360)678-4097*
27 mi. NW at 2072 W. Captain Whidbey Inn Rd. - Coupeville
L-D.   *Expensive*
Creative Northwestern cuisine is prepared with an emphasis on freshness, featuring ingredients from their garden and the region. A beach-stone fireplace and an intimate cove view lend appeal to the romantic madrona-wood-trimmed dining room of the venerable inn.

The Dog House   *(360)221-9825*
downtown at 230 First St.
L-D.   *Moderate*
The Dog House is Whidbey Island's most captivating tavern. All kinds of tasty pub grub, from fish and chips to pasties, can be enjoyed with a wide choice of premium and regional tap beers. The decor is classic Northwest—a handsome wood backbar, hardwood floors, wooden chairs, and a spectacular channel view from the back room.

Five 10 Bar & Grill   *(360)221-6959*
just E at 510 Cascade Av.
L-D.   *Moderate*
Contemporary Northwest dishes include specialties like Dungeness crabcakes. Patrons have a choice of armchair comfort in a tri-level dining room with a wrap-around channel-and-mountain view, or umbrella-shaded tables on a patio high above the water.

Inn at Langley   *(360)221-3033*
downtown at 400 First St.
D only.   *Very Expensive*
The heart of the inn is the Country Kitchen. On weekends by reservation, guests can indulge in a prix fixe five-course dinner. The gourmet celebration of the region's rich seasonal bounty is presented in casually elegant surroundings.

Langley Village Bakery   *(360)221-3525*
downtown at 221 Second St. #1
B-L.   *Moderate*
A wide assortment of baked goods is made fresh daily. Distinctive specialties like delectable peach bear claws or stuffed foccacia can be enjoyed with other light fare at tables inside or outdoors, or to go.

Star Bistro Cafe & Bar   *(360)221-2627*
downtown at 201 First St.
L-D.   *Moderate*
Contemporary Northwest bistro fare ranging from salmon pasta to shepherd's pie is given light and careful attention in this local favorite above the landmark Star Store. The sunny deck with an excellent town-and-water view is especially popular.

Village Pizzeria   *(360)221-3363*
downtown at 108 First St.
L-D.   *Moderate*
The best pizza in town is featured with an added bonus—al fresco
dining on a grassy tree-shaded terrace topping a bluff with a
panoramic view of the scenic waterway.

LODGING

Langley is one of a few great towns with no motels. Instead, there are
numerous small inns and romantic bed-and-breakfasts. There is no high
season. But, a few places reduce rates 10% or more on winter weekdays.

Boat Yard Inn   *(360)221-5120*
just E at 200 Wharf St. (Box 866) - 98260
9 units   *Expensive*
This contemporary all-suites motor inn is located right on the water by
a marina and fishing pier. Each spacious, beautifully furnished suite
has a kitchen with microwave, a living and dining area with a gas fireplace, and a terrific view of Puget Sound and the Cascade Mountains
from bed and from a private deck.

The Captain Whidbey Inn   *(360)678-4097*
27 mi. NW at 2072 W. Captain Whidbey Inn Rd. - Coupeville 98239
32 units   *(800)366-4097*   *Moderate-Expensive*
The Captain Whidbey Inn is the island's most historic lodging. The
charming turn-of-the-century inn, made entirely of distinctive madrona
logs, is surrounded by gardens overlooking Penn Cove. At a dock is the
classy Cutty Sark, available for day sail cruises. The dining room (see
listing) reflects the inn's romantic appeal. Full gourmet breakfast is
complimentary. Historic inn rooms (shared baths) and newer lagoon
rooms, cabins, and cottages are all well furnished with antiques and
modern conveniences. Some have a fireplace.

Country Cottage of Langley   *(360)221-8709*
just S at 215 Sixth St. - 98260
5 units   *(800)713-3860*   *Expensive*
On a knoll above the village is a serene bed-and-breakfast inn with a
whirlpool and gazebo in a garden. Full breakfast is complimentary.
Each room is beautifully furnished with a blend of period pieces and
all contemporary conveniences. Two rooms also have a private deck,
fireplace and two-person whirlpool.

Galittoire   *(360)221-0548*
2 mi. S at 5444 S. Coles Rd. - 98260
3 units   *Expensive-Very Expensive*
Serene woodlands surround this luxurious contemporary bed-and-
breakfast. Lavish use of wood and oak trim; lots of windows, glass
doors and skylights; and whimsical details make the building seem a
sensual extension of the surrounding glade. Amenities include
whirlpools, sauna, exercise room and bicycles. Gourmet breakfast and
evening treats are complimentary. Each room is luxuriously furnished.

Guest House Cottages   *(360)678-3115*
12 mi. NW at 3366 S. WA 525 - Greenbank 98253
7 units   *Expensive-Very Expensive*
One of the Northwest's most romantic hideaways is a complex of
storybook cottages and a log lodge nestled in a forest. Lush natural
grounds also include a picturesque pond, pool, whirlpool, and exercise
room. A generous "country Continental" breakfast in the cottage is
complimentary. Each spacious, luxuriously furnished cottage has every
convenience (except phone), including a kitchen, fireplace, and a large

whirlpool bath. The lodge has all this plus a large in-room whirlpool beneath a glass ceiling that is perfect for star-gazers.

Inn at Langley   *(360)221-3033*
downtown at 400 First St. (Box 835) - 98260
24 units   *Expensive-Very Expensive*
The Inn at Langley is the island's most romantic landmark. The four-story contemporary complex was built into a gentle bluff next to the waterfront. Rough wood-cedar shingles; spare, appealing detail; and lots of water-view windows reflect the tranquil beauty of the Northwest. So do epicurean weekend dinners (see listing) and the complimentary expanded Continental breakfast. Each room is luxuriously furnished and features a private waterfront view deck, fireplace, and a large in-room whirlpool.

Island Tyme Bed & Breakfast   *(360)221-5078*
2 mi. SW at 4940 S. Bayview Rd. - 98260
5 units   *(800)898-8963*   *Moderate-Expensive*
This contemporary three-story bed-and-breakfast with a delightful Victorian flair is surrounded by peaceful woods and meadows. Full country breakfast is complimentary. Each spacious room is a beautifully furnished blend of old and new. Three rooms feature an antique oak-mantled fireplace and/or an in-room two-person whirlpool.

Saratoga Inn   *(360)221-5801*
downtown at 201 Cascade Av. (Box 428) - 98260
15 units   *(800)698-2910*   *Expensive-Very Expensive*
One of Langley's newer landmarks is a handsome shake-shingle building at the eastern edge of downtown overlooking Puget Sound. Continental breakfast and afternoon teas are complimentary. Each spacious, beautifully furnished room has a gas fireplace. Many overlook the water. The "Carriage House" also has a kitchen, private view deck, and double cast-iron antique tub.

Villa Isola   *(360)221-5052*
2 mi. S at 5489 S. Coles Rd. - 98260
6 units   *(800)246-7323*   *Moderate-Expensive*
An Italian (surprise!) country villa surrounded by gardens in tall pines opened in 1994 and has become one of the island's most appealing bed-and-breakfasts. Gourmet breakfast, Italian desserts, and mountain bikes are complimentary. Each spacious, beautifully furnished room conveys sleek contemporary Mediterranean charm. Most feature an in-room whirlpool.

The Whidbey Inn   *(360)221-7115*
downtown at 106 First St. (Box 156) - 98260
6 units   *Moderate-Expensive*
The Whidbey Inn is a romantic getaway in the heart of Langley. It is perched on a bluff overlooking the waterway and Cascade Mountains. Full breakfast and afternoon refreshments are complimentary. Each beautifully furnished room includes a private bath and water view. The three suites feature more private views and a fireplace.

BASIC INFORMATION

Elevation: 30 feet   Population (1990):   1,022
Location: 40 miles (plus ferry) North of Seattle
Nearest airport with commercial flights: Seattle - 50 miles (plus ferry)
Langley Chamber of Commerce   (360)221-6765
downtown at 208 Anthes St. (Box 403) - 98260
Island County Tourism   (888)747-7777
Box 1641 - Coupeville 98239   www.whitney.net/islandco

Leavenworth, Washington

Leavenworth is "the Bavarian village" in an alpine wonderland. The village is ensconsed in a flat little valley by the lovely Wenatchee River. Pine forests carpet mountains of the Cascade Range that loom abruptly on all sides, while fruit orchards attuned to an idyllic four-season climate mantle slopes downstream. Settlement began in the 1890s with a railroad and logging, but the town barely survived the Depression. In 1965, the citizenry adopted a Bavarian theme.

Today, a manicured park faces solid blocks of colorful alpine chalets. Ornate wall paintings, old-fashioned street lamps, hand-carved signs and multicolored flowers are everywhere. The theme-identity is close to reality. Specialty shops, galleries, restaurants, beer halls and bakeries are staffed in part by European craftsmen, chefs and shopkeepers attracted here in response to the village's fame and prosperity. Richly varied lodgings also reflect gemütlichkeit in town, and alpine grandeur beyond.

WEATHER PROFILE

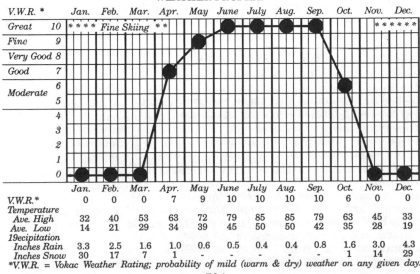

V.W.R. *		Jan.	Feb.	Mar.	Apr.	May	June	July	Aug.	Sep.	Oct.	Nov.	Dec.
V.W.R.*		0	0	0	7	9	10	10	10	10	6	0	0
Temperature													
Ave. High		32	40	53	63	72	79	85	85	79	63	45	33
Ave. Low		14	21	29	34	39	45	50	50	42	35	28	19
19ecipitation													
Inches Rain		3.3	2.5	1.6	1.0	0.6	0.5	0.4	0.4	0.8	1.6	3.0	4.3
Inches Snow		30	17	7	1	-	-	-	-	-	1	14	29

V.W.R. = Vokac Weather Rating; probability of mild (warm & dry) weather on any given day.

ATTRACTIONS

Chelan County Museum *(509)782-3230*
11 mi. E via US 2 at 600 Cottage Av. - Cashmere
More than a dozen century-old buildings are outfitted with pioneer memorabilia in a landscaped park. An adjacent museum houses one of the Northwest's largest collections of American Indian artifacts.

Food Specialties
Liberty Orchards Candies *(509)782-4088*
11 mi. E via US 2 at 117 Mission St. - Cashmere
Washington's most famous confection was first made here more than seventy years ago. Aplets (from apples and walnuts) and cotlets (apricots and walnuts) are as luscious as ever. Visitors are invited to sample these and other fruit candies, and to tour the spotless factory. The **Country Store**, in the same complex, is well-stocked with locally oriented gifts and gourmet foods.

Prey's Orchard & Fruit Bar *(509)548-5771*
2 mi. E on US 2
All of the area's best fruits and vegetables, plus selected local cider and juices, preserves, sauces, and candies, are displayed and sold here in season. Many are generously offered for sampling in one of the state's largest and friendliest roadside markets.

Horseback Riding
In the valley above Leavenworth, trails ascend through sylvan forests to flower-filled meadows backed by snow-capped peaks of the Cascade Range. Hourly and longer guided horseback rides to the high country, plus wilderness pack trips, can be arranged at these stables:

Eagle Creek Ranch   *8 mi. NE via WA 209*   *(800)221-7433*
Icicle Outfitters   *19 mi. NW via WA 209*   *(800)497-3912*
Lake Wenatchee State Park   *(509)763-3101*
20 mi. NW via US 2 on WA 207
A crystal-clear five-mile-long alpine lake is the centerpiece of a superb state-operated recreation facility. A long pebbly beach has been set aside for sunbathers, and the lake is much used in summer by swimmers, canoeists, wind surfers, and fishermen. The up-lake view of a pine-rimmed shoreline and towering peaks of the Cascades on all sides is magnificent. A bathhouse and boat ramp are available, and a large campground adjoins in a forest near the lake.

Ohme Gardens   *(509)662-5785*
19 mi. E via US 2 at 3327 Ohme Rd. - Wenatchee
On a promontory overlooking the Wenatchee valley, nine acres of nationally acclaimed mountain greenery crown a basalt bluff. Pathways meander past fern grottoes and trickling waterfalls to a lookout point with a sweeping view of the Columbia River valley. The gardens have been evolving for more than sixty years.

River Running
From April into July, whitewater rafting on the upper reaches of the Wenatchee River is very popular through a spectacular deep canyon west of Leavenworth. Calmer sections east of town are popular through summer. All equipment, meals, shuttle vans, and professional guides can be arranged for two hour or longer floats. Outfitters also provide support for unguided trips, and rent canoes.

All Rivers Adventures   *(509)782-2254*   *(800)743-5628*
11 mi. E on US 2 - Cashmere
Leavenworth Outfitters   *(509)763-3733*   *(800)347-7934*
16 mi. W at junction WA 207/WA 209 at 21312 Hwy. 207

Rocky Reach Dam   *(509)663-7522*
27 mi. E on US 2 - Wenatchee
A visitors information center in this massive dam on the Columbia River has an underwater fish-viewing gallery linked to a mile-long "fish ladder" for spawning salmon to go around the dam. Equally impressive are free interpretive museums within the power house related to electricity and the area's evolution. Colorful gardens and shady lawns by the dam provide inviting picnic sites.

Waterfront Park   *(509)548-5807*
downtown at W end of Commercial St.
A lovely one-half-mile-long town park borders the scenic Wenatchee River. Well-lit paths wind along a forested shoreline connected by a bridge to Blackbird Island. Benches, lawns, and tiny sandy beaches by calm natural pools are pleasant places to cool off on hot summer days.

Winter Sports
Stevens Pass Ski Area   *(509)973-2441*
36 mi. W on US 2
One of Washington's biggest ski areas boasts a large variety of lighted terrain. The vertical rise is 1,800 feet, and the longest run is well over one mile. Elevation at the top is 5,800 feet. There are eleven chairlifts. All facilities, services, and rentals for downhill skiing are available at the base, along with a restaurant, cafe and lounge, but no lodgings. The skiing season is mid-November to mid-April.

RESTAURANTS

Andreas Keller Restaurant   *(509)548-6000*
downtown at 829 Front St.
L-D.   *Moderate*
Rotisserie-broiled pork hocks and chicken, schnitzels and other authentic Middle European dishes are served with a wide assortment of Bavarian beers. Communal tables, warm wood-toned cellar decor, and frequent live music all contribute to the gemütlichkeit.

Big Y Cafe   *(509)548-5012*
5 mi. E on US 2 at US 97
B-L-D.   *Low*
Homemade biscuits and gravy, and pies are featured in a big roadside coffee shop where everything is all-American, plain and plentiful.

Cafe Crista   *(509)548-5074*
downtown at 801 Front St.
L-D.   *Moderate*
German dishes, beers and wines, and American specialties can be topped off with homemade desserts. The upstairs dining room has comfortable Old World atmosphere. There is also a delightful dining balcony bordered by flowers overlooking the square and mountains.

Cafe Mozart Restaurant   *(509)548-0600*
downtown at 829 Front St.
L-D.   *Expensive*
Cafe Mozart is Leavenworth's best setting for Old World charm. Traditional Viennese-style cuisine is skillfully and authentically prepared and served in a casually elegant upstairs dining room that reflects European good taste and charm.

Gustav's   *(509)548-4509*
downtown at 617 US 2
L-D.   *Moderate*
Casual German and American pub grub can be washed down with two dozen tap beers in a wood-trim tavern or a rooftop mountain-view deck.

Home Fires Bakery   *(509)548-7362*
3 mi. SW via Icicle Rd. at 13013 Bayne Rd. (off Icicle Rd.)
B-L.   *Moderate*
Tucked away in a picturesque alpine setting is the region's best bakery. Authentic Old Country breads are carefully prepared with a sourdough starter from organic flour, and baked in a German wood-fired masonry oven. Delicious cinnamon rolls, specialty pastries and mini-pies (like luscious strawberry-rhubarb) are also displayed to go.

Katzenjammer's   *(509)548-5826*
downtown at 221 8th St.   (800)330-5826
D only.   *Expensive*
Steak and seafood are served in a congested half-timbered dining room and lounge with a large hooded fireplace to lend warmth in winter.

King Ludwig's Gasthaus   *(509)548-6625*
downtown at 921 Front St.
L-D.   *Moderate*
Authentic German and Hungarian dishes include specialties like sausage platters, and apple strudel or crepes. Casual Old World atmosphere, frequent live music and a covered outdoor dance floor contribute to the gemütlichkeit.

The Leavenworth Brewery Restaurant & Pub   *(509)548-4545*
downtown at 636 Front St.
L-D.   *Moderate*
Handcrafted beers and root beer from their brew house are served with pub treats like beer-batter fish, soft pretzels, and brewery cheese bread. The big, popular pub is friendly and relaxed.

Lorraine's Edel House   *(509)548-4412*
downtown at 320 9th St.   (800)487-3335
D only.   *Expensive*
The Edel House is Leavenworth's best restaurant. Innovative Northwestern cuisine is expertly prepared from top-quality, seasonally fresh herbs, vegetables and meats. Game dishes like venison tenderloin with grapefruit and apple demi-glace are superb. So are housemade desserts like apple strudel with a light filo crust. The stylish dining room overlooks a tranquil dining patio and garden.

Restaurant Osterreich   *(509)548-4031*
downtown at 633 A Front St.
L-D.   *Expensive*
Middle European cuisine is skillfully, authentically prepared and served in a casually elegant setting. Outdoor dining is also seasonally available in this well-liked young restaurant.

LODGING

There are many European-style pensions, country inns, and modern lodgings overlooking the river or mountains. There is no high season. A few places reduce prices by about 10% in early spring.

All Seasons River Inn   *(509)548-1425*
1 mi. SW at 8751 Icicle Rd. (Box 788) - 98826
6 units   (800)254-0555   Moderate-Expensive
All Seasons is one of the Northwest's most appealing bed-and-breakfast inns. A handsome contemporary building is on a forested bench by the scenic Wenatchee River. Hiking, bicycling, and fishing are popular. Full gourmet breakfast is complimentary. Each spacious room is luxuriously furnished with modern conveniences (except phone or TV) blended with stylish antiques, and has a private riverfront deck. Most also have a large in-room whirlpool tub and gas fireplace.

AlpenRose Inn   *(509)548-3000*
just W via Hwy. 2 at 500 Alpine Place - 98826
   15 units   *(800)582-2474*   *Moderate-Expensive*
In 1994, this romantic bed-and-breakfast with a contemporary Bavarian style opened with a pool and whirlpool in a quiet garden setting. Full breakfast and evening dessert are complimentary. Each room is attractively furnished. Some have a large in-room whirlpool and a gas fireplace.

Bayern on the River   *(509)548-5875*
just E on Hwy. 2 (Box 288) - 98826
   26 units   *(800)873-3960*   *Moderate*
The Wenatchee River adjoins this modern motel in a quiet forest. There is an outdoor pool and whirlpool. Each spacious, attractively furnished room has a fine view of river rapids from a private balcony. Kitchenettes are available.

Blackbird Lodge   *(509)548-5800*
downtown at 305 8th St. - 98826
   15 units   *(800)446-0240*   *Moderate*
This 1993 motel is delightfully located on the quiet side of downtown above the tranquil riverside park. A light room-service breakfast is complimentary and there is a mountain-view whirlpool. Several of the spacious attractively furnished rooms have a private deck with spectacular river/mountain views. Some also have a gas fireplace.

Enzian Motor Inn   *(509)548-5269*
downtown at 590 Hwy. 2 - 98826
   104 units   *(800)223-8511*   *Moderate-Expensive*
The Enzian is Leavenworth's biggest and best motor inn. Its Bavarian design captures the village's spirit. There are large indoor and outdoor pools, two whirlpools, a racquetball court, exercise equipment, and a ping pong room on nicely landscaped grounds. A fine European buffet breakfast in a cheerful mountain-view room is complimentary, as is a (daily) memorable Alpenhorn concert. Each spacious room is well furnished. Eight suites also have a pressed-wood fireplace and large in-room whirlpool.

Haus Lorelei   *(509)548-5726*
just E at 347 Division St. - 98826
   8 units   *(800)514-8868*   *Moderate-Expensive*
Perched in a luxuriant forest above the river is a 1903 landmark that now serves as a bed-and-breakfast in the European tradition. Amenities include hiking trails, a tennis court, a whirlpool overlooking the river, and a gift shop. Full breakfast in the alpine-view dining room is complimentary. Each spacious room is beautifully furnished with charming period decor and has a private bath and alpine views.

Haus Rohrbach Pension   *(509)548-7024*
1 mi. NW via Ski Hill Dr. at 12882 Ranger Rd. - 98826
   10 units   *(800)548-4477*   *Moderate-Expensive*
This European-style bed-and-breakfast high on the valley rim has hiking trails up a mountain, a pool and whirlpool, plus snowshoeing and sledding in winter. Gourmet breakfast and evening desserts are complimentary. There are no phones or TVs, but each well-furnished room has a fine view, and all but two have a private bath. Three spacious luxury suites also have a gas fireplace, large in-room whirlpool, and a private view deck.

Leavenworth Village Inn   *(509)548-6620*
downtown at 1016 Commercial St. - 98826
18 units   *(800)343-8198*   *Moderate-Expensive*
One of the area's newest lodgings is a handsome little motel near the heart of town. All of the rooms are well furnished, and have a contemporary European flavor. Spacious suites also have a fireplace and/or whirlpool.

Lorraine's Edel House   *(509)548-4412*
downtown at 320 9th St. - 98826
4 units   *(800)487-3335*   *Moderate*
An older home has been transformed into a stylish little inn with a whirlpool and a fine restaurant (see listing) where guests receive a 50% discount. Each beautifully furnished room has all conveniences except a phone. The cottage has a large whirlpool and a gas fireplace.

River's Edge Lodge   *(509)548-7612*
4 mi. E at 8401 Hwy. 2 - Peshastin 98826
23 units   *(800)451-5285*   *Moderate*
The scenic Wenatchee River borders this modern motel. You can fish in the backyard, and there is a pool and whirlpool. Each comfortably furnished room has a river view. Some also have a kitchenette.

Rodeway Inn   *(509)548-7992*
just W at 185 Hwy. 2 - 98826
33 units   *(800)693-1225*   *Moderate-Expensive*
The chain is represented locally by a contemporary motel with an indoor pool and whirlpool. Each room is well furnished. Two suites have a gas fireplace and big whirlpool.

Run of the River   *(509)548-7171*
2 mi. SE at 9308 E. Leavenworth Rd. (Box 285) - 98826
6 units   *(800)288-6491*   *Moderate-Expensive*
Run of the River is the perfect embodiment of a Northwest bed-and-breakfast inn. It is also a nonpareil luxurious getaway for adults. Natural log buildings surrounded by colorful gardens are ideally sited by Icicle Creek to maximize a superb view of the stream, forest and snow-capped mountains. A bountiful country breakfast served by the view, afternoon treats, bicycles and a whirlpool are complimentary. Each room is luxuriously furnished with all contemporary conveniences (except a phone), and features hand-hewn log and rock craftsmanship and tranquil views. Most also have a wood stove and/or two-person whirlpool bath.

BASIC INFORMATION

Elevation: 1,160 feet   *Population (1990): 1,692*
Location: 130 miles East of Seattle
Nearest airport with commercial flights: Wenatchee - 30 miles
Leavenworth Chamber of Commerce & Visitor Center   (509)548-5807
  downtown at 894 Hwy. 2 (the Clocktower Bldg.) (Box 327) - 98826
  www.leavenworth.org

Port Townsend, Washington

Port Townsend is a showcase for the arts in a town that time forgot. Here on the remote northeastern tip of the Olympic Peninsula is one of America's finest collections of Victorian architecture. Nearby to the southwest are the glacier-covered peaks of Olympic National Park. To the east, open water, natural canals, and tiny hidden harbors distinguish Puget Sound. Port Townsend flourished in the 1880s with logging and maritime activity. During the 1890s, however, the boom collapsed as the town and port lost preeminence to Seattle.

Today, Port Townsend is a designated National Historic District. Solid rows of substantial 19th century brick buildings still line the downtown waterfront. Many house studios and shops displaying fine local arts and crafts, or atmospheric restaurants and bars. Even the adjoining fort site is a major cultural and recreational asset. Dozens of splendid century-old homes and mansions now comprise one of the nation's greatest collections of bed-and-breakfast inns.

WEATHER PROFILE

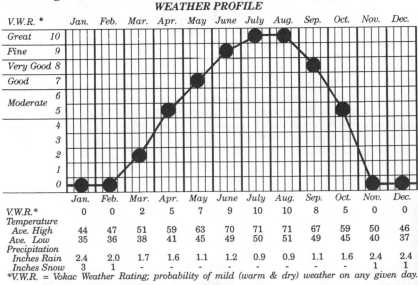

V.W.R.*		Jan.	Feb.	Mar.	Apr.	May	June	July	Aug.	Sep.	Oct.	Nov.	Dec.
V.W.R.*		0	0	2	5	7	9	10	10	8	5	0	0
Temperature													
Ave. High		44	47	51	59	63	70	71	71	67	59	50	46
Ave. Low		35	36	38	41	45	49	50	51	49	45	40	37
Precipitation													
Inches Rain		2.4	2.0	1.7	1.6	1.1	1.2	0.9	0.9	1.1	1.6	2.4	2.4
Inches Snow		3	1	-	-	-	-	-	-	-	-	1	1

*V.W.R. = Vokac Weather Rating; probability of mild (warm & dry) weather on any given day.

Bicycling
PT Cyclery   *(360)385-6470*
downtown at 100 Tyler St.

An excellent system of relatively flat, tree-shaded byways provides access to picturesque hidden harbors, sandy beaches, and tiny coastal villages. For leisurely explorations, bicycles can be rented here by the hour or day.

Chetzemoka Park
just N at Blaine/Jackson Sts.

On a bluff overlooking Admiralty Inlet is a large town park named after a friendly chief of a local Indian tribe. It features panoramic marine views with snow-capped Mt. Baker in the distance; access to a long rocky beach; well-spaced picnic facilities; and beautifully landscaped grounds with meandering streams, ponds, flower gardens, and a gazebo.

Courthouse
just SW at 1820 Jefferson St.

Built in 1891, this monumental brick building with a 124-foot-tall clock tower is a masterwork of Victorian overstatement. One of the two oldest courthouses in the state, the building still serves as it always did. Visitors marvel at the expansive interior and museum-like quality of the Victorian craftsmanship.

Customs House
downtown at Washington/Van Buren Sts.

Public areas in this imposing stone building (circa 1893) remain untouched by time—with polished redwood trim, inlaid marble floors, curved glass windows, and elaborate wrought-iron staircases.

Fishing Charters

Salmon fishing in season, and year-round bottom fishing with all necessary equipment, can be arranged in the area. Charter boat services featuring whale-watching and scenic tours are available seasonally.

Fort Worden State Park   *(360)385-4730*
2 mi. N via Walker & Cherry Sts.

The state now operates the 1880s fort as a cultural center. The Centrum Foundation presents concerts, workshops, and summer festivals. Carefully maintained structures lining the parade ground include imposing Victorian houses (some furnished with period pieces) that were officers' quarters. Lawns and gardens extend to dense forests bordered by long expanses of beach. A rhododendron garden contains more than 1,000 plants. Gun emplacements and the Point Wilson Lighthouse (built in 1870 and operated by the Coast Guard) are highlights of shore hikes. The Marine Science Center (housed on the dock) has "wet tables" where local sea creatures may be viewed and touched, plus many glass tanks. A popular campground has been provided near the beach.

Haller Fountain
downtown at Washington/Taylor Sts.

At the bottom of a long scenic stairway that connects downtown with the blufftop is a tiny garden park with a wonderfully old-fashioned fountain sculpture. The bronze sea nymph "Innocence" has been a proud symbol of local artistry since 1906.

Olympic National Forest   *(360)956-2400*
20 mi. SW via WA 20 & US 101

Surrounding Olympic National Park are lush temperate rain forests; one of the world's heaviest stands of Douglas fir; abundant wildlife—including Roosevelt elk; and sparkling lakes, streams and rivers in picturesque canyons far below glacier-capped peaks. Hundreds of miles of hiking trails and self-guided nature trails lead to camping, hiking, hunting, fishing, river running, and swimming sites.

Olympic National Park   *(360)452-0330*
55 mi. SW via WA 20 & US 101

More than 1,400 square miles of wilderness extends from glacier-clad peaks to primordial ocean shores. The wettest climate in the coterminous United States (averaging 140 inches of precipitation a year) has created luxuriant coniferous rain forests in the western river valleys. From Hurricane Ridge Highway, there are breathtaking panoramas of Mt. Olympus (the highest peak at 7,965 feet) and dozens of glaciers that lend a shimmering brilliance to the extremely rugged mountains at the top of the peninsula. Wildlife is abundant, including elk, bear, deer, and bald eagles. Seals are common on the rocky fifty-seven-mile strip of primitive Pacific coastline. Hundreds of miles of trails (including many self-guided nature trails) provide access to scores of lakes, streams, waterfalls and peaks. Hiking, backpacking, mountain climbing, horseback and pack trips, fishing, and camping are popular, as is swimming at Sol Duc Hot Springs.

Port Gamble   *(360)297-8074*
28 mi. SE via WA 20 & WA 104

Founded in 1853, this tiny 19th century town was built by a logging company that still owns it. What may be the oldest continuously operating sawmill in America is here. On a picturesque site overlooking Puget Sound, the company has restored/preserved more than thirty Victorian homes, churches, and commercial buildings that are part of a National Historic District lighted by gas lamp replicas. There is a historical museum, and a sea-and-shore museum with an outstanding shell collection.

Whitney Gardens & Nursery   *(360)796-4411*
35 mi. S on US 101 - Brinnon

In spring when giant rhododendrons are in fullest bloom, this display garden/nursery is a floral wonderland.

RESTAURANTS

The Bayview   *(360)385-1461*
just SW at 1539 Water St.

B-L-D.   *Moderate*

Homestyle breakfasts and old-fashioned American dishes contribute to the enduring popularity of this unassuming cafe. So does the fact that it was built over the water with a beguiling maritime panorama.

The Belmont   *(360)385-3007*
downtown at 925 Water St.

L-D.   *Moderate*

The Belmont is the best restaurant in Port Townsend. Fresh local seafood is superb in dishes like Dungeness crabcakes with lemon cucumber sauce, and steamed Northwest salmon with tomato-basil cream sauce. Seasonal desserts like apple-blueberry cobbler are delicious. The fully restored and upgraded 1880s restaurant and saloon include a dining level and deck in back by the bay.

Bread and Roses Bakery   *(360)385-1044*
downtown at 230 Quincy St.
B-L.   *Moderate*
Bread and Roses is one of the finest full-line bakeries in the West. The
beauty of the roses out front is matched by the quality of the breads
and pastries made from scratch. Scones, galettes, cinnamon rolls,
croissants, muffins and other morning delights, plus gourmet pizza,
soups and sandwiches, can by enjoyed here or to go.

Elevated Ice Cream Co.   *(360)385-1156*
downtown at 627 Water St.
B-L-D.   *Moderate*
Elevated Ice Cream is a major contender for "the best ice cream parlor
in the West." Homemade ice creams, fresh fruit Italian ices, plus
delicious hand-dipped chocolates made here, are served in a cheerful
parlor and on a sundeck overlooking the bay.

Fountain Cafe   *(360)385-1364*
downtown at 920 Washington St.
L-D.   *Moderate*
An eclectic selection of fresh seafood, international dishes and desserts
is given careful creative attention. The charming little dining room is
distinguished by colorful wall art and extra touches that reflect the
owners' concern for details.

Lanza's Ristorante & Pizzeria   *(360)379-1900*
just NW at 1020 Lawrence St.
D only.   *Moderate*
Gourmet pizzas, calzones and other Southern Italian dishes featuring
local seasonal vegetables are first-rate. The modish dining room is a
local favorite where live music is periodically offered on weekends.

Manresa Castle   *(360)385-5750*
2 mi. S at Sheridan / 7th Sts.
B-D.   *Expensive*
Expertly prepared contemporary Northwest cuisine accompanied by
freshly baked bread and homemade desserts is presented amid
informal elegance. The hotel's Edwardian lounge also has a town and
bay view.

Nancy's Place   *(360)385-5285*
8 mi. SE at 10893 Rhody Dr. - Hadlock
B-L-D.   *Moderate*
Homemade breakfast pastries and desserts are part of the appeal of an
all-American roadside coffee shop where "from scratch" still means
something. There is also a gift shop.

Salal Cafe   *(360)385-6532*
downtown at 634 Water St.
B-L-D.   *Moderate*
The Salal Cafe serves some of the best breakfasts in the Northwest.
Omelets are featured. Everything is skillfully prepared with a light
touch using fresh local ingredients. A cheerful solarium-style back room
decorated with local wall art is especially popular.

Silverwater Cafe   *(360)385-6448*
downtown at 237 Taylor St.
L-D.   *Moderate*
Fresh Northwest seafood stars in simply-but-carefully prepared dishes
like salmon salad or shrimp burgers for lunch or steamed shellfish at
night. Desserts are homemade. The relaxed, comfortable cafe is in a
historic building.

Port Townsend is one of America's bed-and-breakfast capitals. Resorts and motels are surprisingly scarce. High season is May into October. Prices at other times are reduced as much as 15%.

Ann Starrett Mansion   *(360)385-3205*
just N at 744 Clay St. - 98368
11 units   *(800)321-0644*   *Moderate-Expensive*
The Ann Starrett Mansion is the crown jewel in a town full of grand Victorian buildings. On the National Register, the ornate 1889 home with a sixty-foot octagonal tower has been fully restored to serve as a bed-and-breakfast. The interior includes a free-hung three-tiered spiral staircase and an arresting ceiling fresco, plus a wealth of antiques and rococo touches. Full breakfast is complimentary. Beautifully furnished rooms all have private baths. Many have splendid views of Puget Sound and Mount Baker. Some also have a private balcony and a big soaking tub or whirlpool.

Bishop Victorian Guest Suites   *(360)385-6122*
downtown at 714 Washington St. - 98368
13 units   *(800)824-4738*   *Moderate-Expensive*
Recent remodeling and upgrading enhanced this small all-suites hotel with a pleasant Victorian style. Each suite has a kitchen and private bath. Some have town/water views and a soaking tub.

Chanticleer Inn Bed & Breakfast   *(360)385-6239*
just W at 1208 Franklin St. - 98368
5 units   *(800)858-9421*   *Moderate-Expensive*
A historic Victorian home is now a gracious bed-and-breakfast with quality art and antique accents. Full breakfast is complimentary. Each well-furnished room has modern conveniences (except TV or phone) and a private bath.

The English Inn   *(360)385-5302*
1 mi. NW at 718 F St. - 98368
5 units   *(800)254-5302*   *Moderate*
Tranquility reigns in this bed-and-breakfast on a hill overlooking gentle countryside backed by the Olympic Mountains. The lovingly transformed 1885 home has a colorful garden with a gazebo and hot tub. Full breakfast is complimentary. Each attractively furnished room has some antiques (no phone or TV) and a private bath.

F.W. Hastings House Old Consulate Inn   *(360)385-6753*
just SW at 313 Walker St. - 98368
8 units   *(800)300-6753*   *Moderate-Expensive*
On a high bluff above the bay, a photogenic 1889 mansion now serves as a fashionable bed-and-breakfast. A grand multicourse breakfast, afternoon tea, game room and gazebo whirlpool are complimentary. Each beautifully furnished room features period decor (no phone or TV). Some also have a fine bay view and clawfooted bathtub.

The Inn at Ludlow Bay   *(360)437-0411*
18 mi. SE at One Heron Rd. (Box 65460) - Port Ludlow 98365
37 units   *Expensive-Very Expensive*
A tranquil spit jutting into Ludlow Bay recently became the site for a luxurious adult getaway. The small New England-style hotel is adjacent to a full service marina (with all sorts of rental boats and bicycles), and has a gourmet dining room with a view, wine nook, and fireplace lounge. Expanded Continental breakfast is complimentary. Each luxuriously furnished room has a mountain or water view, fireplace and oversized whirlpool.

The James House   *(360)385-1238*
just W at 1238 Washington St. - 98368
13 units   *(800)385-1238*   *Moderate-Expensive*
The first bed-and-breakfast in the Northwest opened in 1973 in a substantial Victorian mansion on the bluff above downtown. Full breakfast and evening refreshments are complimentary. Each beautifully furnished room has period antiques (no phone or TV). Most have a private bath. Some have a bay view and/or fireplace.

Manresa Castle   *(360)385-5750*
2 mi. S at Sheridan / 7th Sts. (Box 564) - 98368
40 units   *(800)732-1281*   *Moderate-Expensive*
Port Townsend's largest lodging landmark was built in 1892 atop a hill overlooking town. Since 1968, the National Register property has served as a hotel with a popular restaurant (see listing) and lounge. Each comfortably furnished room has some period touches and all modern conveniences. Two suites have a grand bay/town view.

Palace Hotel   *(360)385-0773*
downtown at 1004 Water St. - 98368
15 units   *(800)962-0741*   *Moderate-Expensive*
A handsome century-old brick building in the heart of town is now a small Victorian-style hotel with a cafe off the lobby. Most of the nicely furnished rooms have a private bath, some antiques, (no phone), and downtown views. Marie's Suite (she was a madam when this was a bordello) is spacious, and has the original working fireplace.

Port Ludlow Resort & Conference Center   *(360)437-2222*
18 mi. SE at 9483 Oak Bay Rd. - Port Ludlow 98365
183 units   *(800)732-1239*   *Moderate-Expensive*
Naturalistic contemporary architecture and decor distinguish the area's largest bayfront resort. Amenities include a beach, marina, nearby (fee) 27-hole championship golf course, tennis courts, indoor and outdoor pools, whirlpool, sauna, rental boats and bicycles, and a handsome bay-view restaurant and lounge. All rooms are well furnished, but the suites (one- to four-bedroom) are the way to go for a fine water view from a private deck, kitchen and fireplace.

Ravenscroft Inn   *(360)385-2784*
just N at 533 Quincy St. - 98368
8 units   *(800)782-2691*   *Moderate-Expensive*
This imposing Colonial-style bed-and-breakfast (circa 1987) is an appealing blend of Southern charm and modern amenities (except phone or TV). Bountiful gourmet breakfast is complimentary. Each room is beautifully furnished. Many have bay views. Three rooms also have a gas or wood-burning fireplace and/or soaking tub.

The Tides Inn   *(360)385-0595*
just SW at 1807 Water St. - 98368
21 units   *(800)822-8696*   *Moderate-Expensive*
The Tides Inn is the peninsula's best-situated modern motel. It is right on the water. Most of the nicely furnished rooms have a fine bay view. Several also have a big romantic whirlpool on a private view deck.

BASIC INFORMATION

Elevation: 100 feet   *Population (1990): 7,001*
Location: 50 miles Northwest of Seattle (via ferry)
Nearest airport with commercial flights: Port Angeles - 50 miles
Port Townsend Visitor Center   (360)385-2722
1 mi. SW at 2437 E. Sims Way - 98368   www.visitpt.com

Green Lake, Wisconsin

Green Lake is the epitome of a peaceful, scenic village in the rural American heartland. Luxuriant farmlands and forests surround this little town by the spring-fed waters of Wisconsin's deepest inland lake. Settlement began in 1840, but took off after 1867 with the opening of the first summer resort west of Niagara Falls.

The area's pastoral beauty, the lake's recreational appeal, and the town's heritage of hospitality remain as it was in "the good old days." Visitors enjoy swimming off a sandy beach by a tree-shaded town park just as they did more than a century ago. The trim little downtown, nearly surrounded by water, includes a growing number of specialty shops and restaurants in carefully maintained historic and newer buildings. Beyond, individual stores feature regional art, collectibles, and gourmet treats. A fine lakefront resort and several stylish lodgings reflect the serenity of the locale and the prospect of fine fishing, boating, swimming and sailing on a clear deep lake.

WEATHER PROFILE

V.W.R. *		Jan.	Feb.	Mar.	Apr.	May	June	July	Aug.	Sep.	Oct.	Nov.	Dec.
Great	10	* Fine Skiing *											* * * *
Fine	9												
Very Good	8						●	●	●	●			
Good	7					●							
Moderate	6												
	5										●		
	4												
	3												
	2												
	1												
	0	●	●	●	●							●	●

	Jan.	Feb.	Mar.	Apr.	May	June	July	Aug.	Sep.	Oct.	Nov.	Dec.
V.W.R.*	0	0	0	0	7	8	8	8	8	5	0	0
Temperature												
Ave. High	24	29	38	54	69	77	81	80	71	60	43	30
Ave. Low	8	11	22	35	45	55	61	59	51	40	28	15
Precipitation												
Inches Rain	1.1	1.2	2.0	3.1	3.3	3.8	3.6	3.2	3.5	2.1	1.8	1.6
Inches Snow	10	9	11	2	-	-	-	-	-	-	4	10

*V.W.R. = Vokac Weather Rating; probability of mild (warm & dry) weather on any given day.

Boat Rentals
Personal water craft, pontoon boats, canoes, fishing or sailboats can be rented by the hour or longer.

Bay View Motel & Resort *downtown at 439 Lake St.* *(920)294-6504*
Shoreline, Inc. Water Sports *1 mi. SE on Illinois Av.* *(920)294-3145*

Boat Rides
The Heidel House   *(920)294-3344*
1 mi. SE at 643 Illinois Av.

In summer, public sightseeing cruises, cocktail and dinner cruises can be reserved aboard a sixty-foot twin-engined catamaran.

Food Specialties
Wallenfang's of Green Lake   *(920)294-3386*   *(800)523-4657*
just N at 540 North St.

This delightfully eclectic complex features their own delectable creations like cherry creamed honey, along with an abundance of Wisconsin cheese and sausages, ice cream and candy treats, antiques, art and unique gifts.

Green Lake Conference Center   *(920)294-3323*   *(800)558-8898*
2 mi. SW at W 2511 WI 23

The American Baptist Assembly now owns and operates a famed century-old 1,000-acre estate with two miles of lakefront. The general public can benefit from two championship 18-hole golf courses with a handsome clubhouse and restaurant, plus swimming off a sandy beach, tennis, hiking, biking, bookstore, gift shop and country store. In winter, there is nordic skiing, tobogganning and ice skating.

Hattie Sherwood Park
just SW on S. Lawson Dr.

A fine sandy beach with bathhouses, restrooms and lifeguards in summer make this a popular swimming site. There are also fishing spots, shady picnic tables and a campground.

Larson's Famous Clydesdales   *(920)748-5466*
18 mi. SE at W. 12654 Reeds Corner Rd. - Ripon

From May through October, by reservation, you can enjoy a 90-minute guided tour and performances at the home of more than a dozen huge Clydesdales. There are also exhibits of antique wagons and gear and a gift shop.

Playground Park
downtown by Mill & Water Sts.

A scenic mill pond and waterfall have been features next to downtown since 1845, when the Puckyan River near its outlet from Green Lake was dammed. The mill is gone, replaced by a lovely park.

Sunset Park
just SE on Lake St.

This long-popular lakefront park has a sand-bottomed swimming beach (no lifeguards), pier, four-season fishing and restrooms.

Winter Sports
Nordic Mountain   *(920)787-3324*   *(800)253-7266*
29 mi. NW via WI 23

There is plenty of snow for cross-country skiing and snowmobiling around Green Lake, but this is the nearest alpine ski area. Vertical rise is a tiny 270 feet, but the longest run is close to a mile. There are two chairlifts, rentals and food service.

RESTAURANTS

Alfred's Supper Club   *(920)294-3631   (800)664-3631*
downtown at 506 Hill St.
D only.   *Moderate*
Aged steaks and Italian dishes are accompanied by a big salad bar and homemade desserts amid pleasant decor in the dining room and lounge.

Carvers on the Lake   *(920)294-6931*
just SE at N. 5529 County Road A
D only.   *Expensive*
New American and traditional Midwestern cuisine are given expert attention in the area's best dinner house. Fresh seafood and house-baked goods are highlights served amid fine antiques in an old English-style country inn overlooking the lake. There is also a firelit bar and a lakeside patio lounge.

The Goose Blind   *(920)294-6363*
downtown at 512 Gold St.
L-D.   *Moderate*
The eclectic menu ranges from burgers to stir-fries, and from broiled pike to chili or pizza, and there is a full bar. You can top it off with homemade fruit pie in this fun place that also has patio dining.

The Heidel House   *(920)294-3344*
1 mi. SE at 643 Illinois Av.
B-L-D.   *Moderate-Expensive*
The venerable resort's culinary landmark is the **Grey Rock Mansion Restaurant** (D only—Expensive). The award-winning dinner house features contemporary American fare in an elegant lakefront setting. The **Sunroom** (B-L—Moderate) has casual dining with a peaceful lake view. **Boathouse Lounge and Eatery** (L-D—Moderate) offers relaxed indoor and outdoor dining, and live entertainment.

The Little Corporal Restaurant   *(920)294-6772*
downtown at 499 Hill St.
B-L-D.   *Moderate*
Fresh-baked breads, pastries, pies and ice cream treats distinguish traditional American fare served in a casual family-oriented setting.

Nordic Hill Restaurant   *(920)294-0230*
1 mi. W at W 1917 WI 23
B-L-D.   *Moderate*
Friday night seafood buffet smorgasbords and homemade desserts are specialties. Relaxed, comfortable dining rooms provide a panoramic view of Green Lake. A new nightclub has frequent music and dancing, and there are several specialty shops and a bakery.

Norton's Marine Dining Room   *(920)294-6577*
just SW at 380 S. Lawson Dr.
L-D.   *Moderate*
Seafood and steak are featured, along with homemade desserts, in a big casual restaurant with a lake view shared by a bar and dining patio.

LODGING
There are more than a dozen lodgings ranging from a first class resort to motels and lakeside inns. May through October is high season. Rates may be reduced 40% or more at other times.

Bay View Motel & Resort   *(920)294-6504*
downtown at 439 Lake St. - 54941
17 units   *Moderate*
You can fish from their private pier or rent a boat at this modern motel. Comfortably furnished rooms have pleasant lakeside views.

Carvers on the Lake   *(920)294-6931*
just SE at N. 5529 County Rd. A - 54941
9 units   *Moderate-Expensive*
Amenities of this gracious country inn include a private pier for
swimming or fishing, and a sophisticated dining room (see listing) and
fireside or lakeside lounge. Each individually decorated room is well
furnished in the style of an English country home, and has all
contemporary conveniences. Most have a view of the lake. Some also
have a kitchen, or a fireplace, whirlpool bath, and private deck.

Greenway Log Cottages   *(920)294-6222*
just S at 401 Strauss Av. - 54941
7 units   *Moderate*
This little cabin complex is on well-maintained, tree-shaded grounds by
the lake. There is a pier and fishing boat rentals. Each spacious two-
bedroom cottage has a screened porch.

The Heidel House   *(920)294-3344*
1 mi. SE at 643 Illinois Av. - 54941
200 units   *(800)444-2812   Expensive-Very Expensive*
The Heidel House is one of the finest four-season resort and conference
centers in the Midwest. Amenities of the contemporary four-story
complex include a quarter-mile of lake shore with a sandy beach and
piers. An 18-hole (fee) golf course is adjacent. There are all sorts of
watercraft rentals, and boat rides (see listing), plus two tennis courts,
indoor and outdoor pools, two whirlpools, sauna, exercise and game
rooms, rental bicycles, fine restaurants (see listing) and entertainment
lounge, plus gift and resort shops. Many of the beautifully furnished
rooms and suites have a serene lake view. Some also have a whirlpool
bath and a private balcony.

Lakeside Motel   *(920)294-3318*
downtown at 488 South St. - 54941
15 units   *Moderate*
The lake is across a street from this single-level downtown motel. Each
room is nicely furnished.

McConnell Inn   *(920)294-6430*
just W at 497 S. Lawson Dr. - 54941
5 units   *Moderate-Expensive*
A handsome turn-of-the-century home has been skillfully transformed
into a bed-and-breakfast inn. Full gourmet breakfast is complimentary.
Each well-furnished room is individually decorated, and features
antiques and a private bath with a clawfoot tub and shower. The
spacious suite has a fireplace and large whirlpool bath.

Oakwood Lodge   *(920)294-6580*
just S at 365 Lake St. - 54941
12 units   *Moderate-Expensive*
One of Wisconsin's best bed-and-breakfast inns is Oakwood Lodge. The
historic, Civil War-era inn on a knoll by the lake has a private pier and
raft for swimming and fishing. Full breakfast served with a lake view
is complimentary. Most of the well-furnished rooms have a private
bath and some antique decor, but no phone or TV.

BASIC INFORMATION

Elevation: 830 feet   Population (1990):   1,064
Location: 90 miles Northwest of Milwaukee
Nearest airport with commercial flights: Oshkosh - 24 miles
Green Lake Area Chamber of Commerce (920)294-3231 (800)253-7354
  just N on Mill St. (Box 386) - 54941   www.greenlakecc.com

Sturgeon Bay, Wisconsin

Sturgeon Bay is the gateway to one of America's freshwater wonderlands—Door County. Midway on an eighty-mile-long peninsula, the town straddles a scenic little bay and canals that connect the surrounding waters of Green Bay and Lake Michigan. Hundreds of miles of shoreline include towering limestone bluffs and sandy beaches backed by lush woodlands. Settlement began in the 1850s with lumber mills. After the canal opened in 1881, shipbuilding and freighter traffic contributed to growth, along with fishing, pleasure boating, cherry and apple orchards, and dairy farms.

While all are still important a century later, the town's key role as a travel destination is finally apparent. Many buildings from the prosperous past now serve as galleries, specialty shops, restaurants and inns in the charming, compact downtown. Nearby, intimate resorts are bases for enjoying all sorts of water recreation in town and in quaint villages along the shoreline.

WEATHER PROFILE

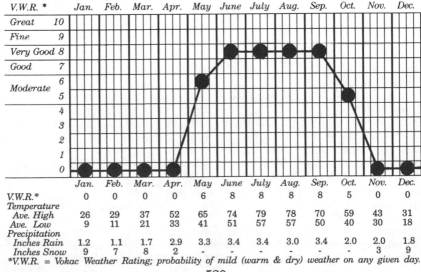

V.W.R.*		Jan.	Feb.	Mar.	Apr.	May	June	July	Aug.	Sep.	Oct.	Nov.	Dec.
Great	10												
Fine	9												
Very Good	8												
Good	7												
Moderate	6 5												
	4												
	3												
	2												
	1												
	0												

	Jan.	Feb.	Mar.	Apr.	May	June	July	Aug.	Sep.	Oct.	Nov.	Dec.
V.W.R.*	0	0	0	0	6	8	8	8	8	5	0	0
Temperature												
Ave. High	26	29	37	52	65	74	79	78	70	59	43	31
Ave. Low	9	11	21	33	41	51	57	57	50	40	30	18
Precipitation												
Inches Rain	1.2	1.1	1.7	2.9	3.3	3.4	3.4	3.0	3.4	2.0	2.0	1.8
Inches Snow	9	7	8	2	-	-	-	-	-	-	3	9

*V.W.R. = Vokac Weather Rating; probability of mild (warm & dry) weather on any given day.

Bicycling
Door County Bicycle Works   *(920)743-4434*
downtown at 20 N. 3rd Av.
Scenic rural landscapes in all directions from town can be visited via relatively level byways and trails on a regular or mountain bike rented by the hour or longer. They also have maps.

Boat Rentals
Snug Harbor Marina   *(920)743-2337   (800)231-5767*
1 mi. SE at 1627 Memorial Dr.
You can rent a boat by the hour or longer, reserve a harbor tour, or arrange for guide service at these docks.

Collector Showcase   *(920)743-6788*
3 mi. N at 3910 WI 42-57
One of the largest Barbie doll collections anywhere, hundreds of old Marshall Fields' animated Christmas window displays, and many vintage autos are showcased.

Door County Maritime Museum   *(920)743-5958*
just S at 120 N. Madison Av.
A large building on the bay showcases Door County's long history of shipbuilding. Exhibits include boats dating back to 1900, an actual pilot house of a Great Lake ore carrier, marine artifacts, and carved ship models. There are also interactive displays and a gift shop.

Door County Museum   *(920)743-5809*
downtown at 18 N. 4th Av.
A turn-of-the-century street scene, general store, fire station and log cabin, plus historic photos and memorabilia are artistically displayed, along with a native wildlife exhibit. There is a gift shop.

Downtown
downtown is centered around 3rd Av. & Louisiana St.
More than one hundred buildings in the heart of town and nearby along Louisiana Street are on the National Historic Register. A variety of Victorian structures of brick, stone or wood share the compact district near the waterfront with similarly human-scaled newer buildings. A growing number house distinctive specialty shops, restaurants and nostalgic inns. Landmarks include a working bell tower, the Door County Museum (see listing), the library and Miller Art Center with an impressive local art collection.

The Farm   *(920)743-6666*
4 mi. N on WI 57
Rural America is showcased in a living museum. Pioneer homestead and farm buildings amid natural surroundings house all sorts of exhibits of farm implements and animals. You can pick up a piglet, bottle-feed a lamb, or watch a chick hatch or a milking demonstration. There are also nature trails, lush flowers, herb and vegetable gardens, and a gift shop.

Fishing Charters
Sturgeon Bay is a major destination for anglers. It is possible to fish for salmon and trout in Lake Michigan in the morning, and bass, perch, or pike in the afternoon without leaving your boat. Charter boats for fishing trips can be arranged at several places, notably:

J.E. Fishing Enterprise   *(920)743-7877*
Leathem Smith Lodge & Marina   *(920)743-5555*
Snug Harbor Inn   *(920)743-2337   (800)231-5767*
Wacky Wally's Guide Service   *(920)743-5731*

Otumba Park   *(920)746-2914*
just W on Joliet Av. & Juniper St.
The feature here is a nice view of downtown from a swimming beach and picnic area. Play equipment and tennis courts are also available.
Potawatomi State Park   *(920)746-2890*
3 mi. NW via WI 42 at 3740 Park Rd.
In summer, fishing and boating, hiking and biking and a campground are popular in this 1,178-acre park along the bay. Winter activities include snowmobiling, Nordic and chairlift-served downhill skiing.
Sunset Park   *(920)746-2914*
just N off 3rd Av.
This fine sand beach is the largest in town. The large, popular park also has picnic facilities, tennis courts and more.
Whitefish Dunes State Park   *(920)823-2400*
10 mi. NE on WI T at 3701 Clark Lake Rd.
The highest sand dunes in Wisconsin are here. Miles of hiking trails access more than two miles of rugged, forested shoreline. Some of the most photogenic sea caves anywhere are in the Cave Point County Park area of the park.

RESTAURANTS

The Cookery   *(920)868-3634*
21 mi. NE on WI 42 (Main St.) - Fish Creek
B-L-D.   *Moderate*
The Cookery offers contemporary regional cuisine at its best. Consider cherry pancakes for breakfast, or whitefish chowder later. Everything is made from scratch, including luscious desserts from their bakery. Near the warm wood-trimmed dining room is a gift shop brimming with local jams, salsas, dressing and much more.
The Inn at Cedar Crossing   *(920)743-4249*
downtown at 336 Louisiana St.
B-L-D.   *Moderate*
Breakfasts in the Inn at Cedar Crossing are among America's finest. From hearty omelets to assorted scones or cherry coffee cake, here is outstanding cuisine from the nation's heartland. So are the fresh fish and other dishes and homemade desserts served later. The innovative fare is complemented by antiques, fireplaces, and country-elegant decor in a Victorian building.
Leathem Smith Lodge & Marina   *(920)743-5555*
1 mi. SE at 1640 Memorial Dr.
B-L-D.   *Moderate*
Traditional fish boils (in season) are a highlight. Contemporary American dishes and bountiful desserts are served in the lodge's expansive candlelit dining room with a marina view.
The Nautical Inn   *(920)743-3399*
downtown at 234 Kentucky St.
L-D.   *Moderate*
Homestyle cooking is featured in prime rib and seafood served amid the nostalgic atmosphere of a Victorian inn with hardwood floors, stained glass, and a stone fireplace.
Paulson's Old Orchard Inn   *(920)854-5717*
26 mi. NE at 10341 Hwy. 42 - Ephraim
B-L-D.   *Low*
Fish boils star from May through October in a separate building with traditional atmosphere. Midwestern fare and homemade desserts also distinguish this casual family restaurant with a gift shop.

Perry's Cherry Diner   *(920)743-9910*
downtown at 230 Michigan St.
B-L-D.   *Low*
Old-fashioned malts and shakes and other classic diner fare, plus homemade pies, contribute to Perry's popularity, along with casual comfortable 1950s diner decor.

Scaturo's   *(920)746-8727*
1 mi. S on WI 42 at 19 Green Bay Rd.
B-L-D.   *Low*
Cherry-filled treats like turnover and streusel, and a fine selection of baked goods, can accompany a wide range of American fare in the coffee shop, or to go.

Summer Kitchen   *(920)854-2131*
26 mi. NE on N. WI 42 - Ephraim
B-L-D.   *Moderate*
Creative American cuisine ranges from cherry buttermilk pancakes for breakfast to broiled whitefish for dinner, topped off with delicious homemade pies and other desserts. The dining room is relaxed and comfortable, and there is a garden patio.

Village Cafe   *(920)868-3342*
16 mi. NE on WI 42 at 7918 Egg Harbor Rd. - Egg Harbor
B-L.   *Low*
Healthy oatmeal or spicy crab and cream cheese omelet typify popular breakfasts served amid casual decor and local art or on a screened porch. Fish boils (using fresh whitefish) are the specialty on weekends.

White Gull Inn   *(920)868-3517*
21 mi. NE on WI 42 at 4225 Main St. - Fish Creek
B-L-D.   *Moderate*
Traditional fish boils, local maple syrup for pancakes, and housemade desserts suggest their commitment to fresh regional cuisine. The comfortable firelit dining room exudes the warmth and antique charm of a century-old country inn.

LODGING

Lodgings in and north of town on the peninsula are varied, with many fine, romantically-oriented historic bed-and-breakfast inns, lakefront lodges and resorts. Summer is high season. Rates are often at least 40% less in winter in those places that remain open.

The Barbican   *(920)743-4854*
downtown at 132 N. 2nd Av. - 54235
18 units   *Expensive*
The Barbican is one of the Midwest's most romantic inns. Three turn-of-the-century homes in the historic district have been lovingly converted. Homemade light breakfast delivered to your room is complimentary. Each individually decorated, beautifully furnished two-room suite combines period antiques with all modern conveniences, plus a gas fireplace and an in-room double whirlpool.

Bay Shore Inn   *(920)743-4551*
3 mi. N at 4205 N. Bay Shore Dr. - 54235
30 units   *(800)556-4551 Expensive-Very Expensive*
A sandy swimming beach is one of the amenities of this stylish contemporary all-suites lodge. Well-landscaped grounds also have indoor and outdoor pools, a tennis court, game room, gym, bikes, and rowboats. Each beautifully furnished one- or two-bedroom suite has a kitchen, waterview balcony, and a whirlpool bath.

Bridgeport Resort   *(920)746-9919*
just S at 50 W. Larch St. - 54235
59 units   *(800)671-9190*   *Expensive*
In 1997 this handsome waterfront resort opened on well-landscaped grounds with an indoor pool, outdoor pool with a waterfall play area, and a sauna. Each room is well furnished. Many one- to three-bedroom suites have a kitchen, electric fireplace, double whirlpool, and/or private balcony with water views.

The Chadwick Inn   *(920)743-2771*
just E at 25 N. 8th Av. - 54235
3 units   *Expensive*
A century-old home has become a romantic bed-and-breakfast inn. Homemade Continental breakfast delivered to your room is complimentary. Each room combines period antiques and all contemporary amenities, including a gas fireplace, balcony, and large whirlpool.

The Chanticleer   *(920)746-0334*
1 mi. N at 4072 Cherry Rd. - 54235
8 units   *Expensive*
A renovated farmhouse and barn (circa 1915) in a bucolic setting are now a romantic country bed-and-breakfast inn with groomed nature trails through woods and fields of wildflowers, plus a sauna and pool. Homemade light breakfast delivered to the room is complimentary. Each beautifully furnished room blends quality antiques with all modern conveniences, plus a private terrace and a gas fireplace in view of a double whirlpool.

Cherry Hills Lodge & Golf Course   *(920)743-4222*
5 mi. N at 5905 Dunn Rd. - 54235
30 units   *(800)545-2307*   *Moderate-Expensive*
One of the area's newer resorts overlooks a (fee) 18-hole golf course. There is also a view pool and whirlpool, and a popular, upscale restaurant. Each spacious, well-furnished room has a private view deck. Two rooms also have a large whirlpool bath.

Glidden Lodge Beach Resort   *(920)746-3900*
9 mi. NE at 4676 Glidden Dr. - 54235
31 units   *(888)281-1127   Expensive-Very Expensive*
A sandy beach on Lake Michigan borders this contemporary three-story condominium resort. There is also an indoor pool, whirlpool, sauna, and exercise room. Each of the one- to three-bedroom units is beautifully furnished, including a kitchen, private deck with a fine lake view, gas fireplace, and double whirlpool.

The Inn at Cedar Crossing   *(920)743-4200*
downtown at 336 Louisiana St. - 54235
9 units   *Moderate-Expensive*
Nestled in the downtown historic district is one of the Midwest's most delightful bed-and-breakfast inns. A two-story 1884 brick building has been carefully restored, and is now on the National Historic Register. There is a gourmet restaurant (see listing) and pub. Homemade hearty Continental breakfast and afternoon treats are complimentary. Each room is beautifully furnished in fine antiques and a private bath. Most have a double whirlpool bath and/or a gas fireplace.

Leathem Smith Lodge & Marina   *(920)743-5555*
1 mi. SE at 1640 Memorial Dr. - 54235
63 units   *(800)366-7947*   *Moderate-Expensive*
Sturgeon Bay's most complete resort is on well-landscaped grounds overlooking the bay and their marina. Amenities of the low-rise

contemporary complex include (fee) par-3 golf and putting green, plus two tennis courts, a pool, gift shop, restaurant (see listing) and entertainment lounge. Each well-furnished room has a private patio or balcony. Spacious two-room suites also have a gas fireplace and whirlpool tub for two.

The Scofield House Bed & Breakfast   *(920)743-7727*
just E at 908 Michigan St. (Box 761) - 54235
6 units   *(888)463-0204*   *Moderate-Expensive*
Original carved and inlaid woodwork, and stained and beveled glass-work contribute to the charm of a 1902 mansion that is now one of the Midwest's most romantic bed-and-breakfast inns. Full gourmet breakfast and evening sweet treats are complimentary. Each distinctively different room is luxuriously furnished with Victorian antiques and all contemporary comforts except phones. Most also have a gas fireplace and a double whirlpool. "The Room at the Top" is one of America's ultimate rooms for romance.

Westwood Shores   *(920)746-4057*
3 mi. N at 4303 N. Bay Shore Dr. - 54235
38 units   *(800)440-4057*   *Expensive*
One of the region's best all-suites resorts opened on a scenic shoreline in 1996. Amenities on the manicured grounds include a large indoor pool, an outdoor view pool, whirlpool, sauna and exercise room. Each of the beautifully furnished one- or two-bedroom suites has a kitchen, a gas fireplace, an in-bath two-person whirlpool and a lovely bay view from a private balcony.

White Lace Inn   *(920)743-1105*
downtown at 16 N. 5th Av. - 54235
18 units   *Moderate-Expensive*
This complex of four historic homes now serves as a delightful bed-and-breakfast inn. Homemade Continental breakfast is complimentary. Each room is beautifully furnished with a mix of fine antiques and contemporary amenities except phone or TV. Many rooms have a gas fireplace or a double whirlpool. Several rooms have both.

BASIC INFORMATION

Elevation: 590 feet   Population (1990): 9,176
Location: 140 miles North of Milwaukee, WI
Nearest airport with commercial flights: Green Bay - 48 miles
Door County Chamber of Commerce (920)743-4456   (800)527-3529
* just SW at 1015 Green Bay Rd. (Box 406) - 54235*
www.doorcountyvacations.com

Wisconsin Dells, Wisconsin

Wisconsin Dells is the peerless playground of the Upper Midwest. The village is located by a picturesque gorge of the Wisconsin River. All around are lush woodlands and farms punctuated by sylvan hills. Founded in 1856 as Kilbourn, the community's name was changed in 1931 to capitalize on its preeminent natural attraction.

Today, the town is a top spot for fun-for-all-ages. Wisconsin Dells is to water what Las Vegas is to glitz. The dramatic gorge is more popular than ever. Downtown teems with family-oriented amusements, souvenir shops, and food outlets. Continuing on the other side of the river for four miles south, the Wisconsin Dells Parkway is lined on both sides by a bonanza of water attractions, playful diversions, dining and drinking places, shops, and lodgings. Abundant accommodations showcase America's greatest assortment of playful water features for ever-increasing numbers of romantic adults as well as families here to experience the town's rambunctious spirit.

WEATHER PROFILE

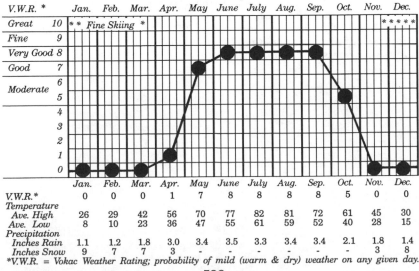

	Jan.	Feb.	Mar.	Apr.	May	June	July	Aug.	Sep.	Oct.	Nov.	Dec.
V.W.R.*	0	0	0	1	7	8	8	8	8	5	0	0
Temperature												
Ave. High	26	29	42	56	70	77	82	81	72	61	45	30
Ave. Low	8	10	23	36	47	55	61	59	52	40	28	15
Precipitation												
Inches Rain	1.1	1.2	1.8	3.0	3.4	3.5	3.3	3.4	3.4	2.1	1.8	1.4
Inches Snow	9	7	7	3	-	-	-	-	-	-	3	8

*V.W.R. = Vokac Weather Rating; probability of mild (warm & dry) weather on any given day.

526

ATTRACTIONS

Amusements
downtown and south for 4 mi. along US 12

A mind-boggling array of tourist attractions is concentrated downtown and south for four miles along US 12, apart from those described below. In addition to hundreds of holes of mini-golf, and dozens of go-cart circuits, there are biblical and storybook gardens; a deer park; museums featuring autos and railroads; Norman Rockwell's art and H.H. Bennett's photography; a haunted mansion and dungeon of horrors; helicopter rides; thrill rides ranging from a roller coaster to bungee jumping; and music theaters.

Boat Rentals
Several places in and near town rent assorted watercraft by the hour or longer to enjoy the Wisconsin River or Lake Delton. To reserve a ski boat, waverunner, pontoon, paddle boat, canoe, or tube, contact:

Lake Delton Water Sports	*(608)254-8702*
Point Bluff Resort	*(608)253-6181*
Water Sports Rentals	*(608)254-2878*

Boat Rides
Dells Boat Tours   *(608)254-8555*
downtown at 11 Broadway

Guided sightseeing cruises through the upper and lower dells of the Wisconsin River have been the state's top attraction for decades. Tours (up to two-plus hours) wind along a calm narrow waterway between high sandstone cliffs and unusual rock formations, and make two stops for walks through lush fern grottoes and to long-renowned Stand Rock.

Circus World Museum   *(608)356-0800*
14 mi. S on US 12 at 426 Water St. - Baraboo

At the original winter operators of the Ringling Brothers Circus, every day is still circus day. The expansive complex includes a wealth of buildings full of colorful exhibits like the premier collection of circus vehicles. During the summer, there are daily circus parades, live big-top performances, demonstrations of circus operations, magic shows, and organ concerts, plus picnic areas, food service and a gift shop.

Horseback Riding
Several stables near town offer one-hour guided horseback rides through natural woodlands. For reservations, contact:

Beaver Springs Riding Stable	*(608)254-2735*	
Canyon Creek Riding Stables	*(608)253-6942*	
OK Corral	*(608)254-2811*	*(800)254-2811*
The Ranch Riding Stable	*(608)254-3935*	

Original Wisconsin Ducks   *(608)254-8751*
1 mi. S via US 12 at 1890 Wisconsin Dells Pkwy.

Restored World War II amphibious vehicles travel 8.5 miles in hour-long journeys over land and water. Highlights showcase an exotic fern dell, precipitous gorges, and a roller coaster hill, plus splash-downs in scenic Lake Delton and the Wisconsin River dells.

Timber Falls Adventure Golf   *(608)254-8414*
just W on WI 13

In a town with an overwhelming number of miniature golf courses, the only one by the scenic Wisconsin River has five challenging 18-hole courses amid sandstone cliffs, waterfalls, gardens and woodlands. Nearby, one of the best log flume rides in America is a quarter mile of scenery and thrills involving waterfalls, caves, an "active volcano," and two big drops. There are also shops and food service.

Tommy Bartlett's Robot World & Exploratory   *(608)254-2525*
2 mi. S via US 12 at 560 Wisconsin Dells Pkwy.
Interactive virtual reality is here in a tour of the original Russian MIR
Space Station, and one hundred hands-on activities ranging from
computerized touch-screen games to hair-raising electric energy
exhibits.
Tommy Bartlett Thrill Show   *(608)254-2525*
2 mi. S via US 12 at 560 Wisconsin Dells Pkwy.
A big outdoor theater by the river is the location for a two-hour
extravaganza. Evolving for more than forty years, the show features
professional water skiers, stunt boats, helicopter trapeze daredevils and
stage acts, plus an evening laser/water spectacle and fireworks finale.
Warm Water Features
Wisconsin Dells has one of America's finest collections of water parks.
The three best each have a wave pool, slides, whitewater tube rides,
and bumper boats, plus shops and food service. **Noah's Ark** ((608)254-
6351) claims to be America's largest waterpark. It is enormous, and the
most complete in the Midwest, with two wave pools, two endless rivers
(including a half-mile-long adventure river), giant inner tube rapids,
and more than thirty slides, plus go-carts, mini-golf, restaurant and
five gift and clothing stores. **Family Land** ((608)254-7766) claims the
region's largest wave pool, longest continuous tube slide, and first
family interactive water-play area, plus skeeter boats, mini-golf,
bumper cars, and kiddie rides. **Riverview Park & Waterworld**
((608)254-2608) also has assorted racing vehicles, a petting zoo, and
kiddie rides.
Winter Sports
Cascade Mountain   *(608)742-5588*
19 mi. SE via I-90 on Cascade Mt. Rd.
One of Wisconsin's biggest ski areas has fine views and a vertical rise
of 460 feet. The longest run is one mile. There are seven chairlifts.
Related services and rentals, food and drinks are available at the base.
Christmas Mountain   *(608)253-1000*   *(800)289-1066*
4 mi. W at S944 Christmas Mt. Rd.
The family-oriented little area has a vertical rise of 250 feet, and the
longest run is one-half mile. There are two chairlifts. Related services
and rentals, food and drinks are available at the base. Golf, riding
stables and a hotel complex are nearby.
RESTAURANTS
The Cheese Factory Restaurant   *(608)253-6065*
4 mi. S on US 12 at 521 Wisconsin Dells Pkwy. S
B-L-D.   *Moderate*
A creative array of vegetarian dishes, soda fountain specialties, and
housemade desserts are served by a costumed staff amid 1950s decor.
The Del-Bar Steakhouse   *(608)253-1861*
3 mi. S on US 12 at 800 Wisconsin Dells Pkwy. S
D only.   *Expensive*
Custom-aged Angus steaks and slow-roasted prime rib have been
specialties since 1943. Informally posh dining rooms are enhanced by
a baby grand piano and fireplaces in the spacious dinner house.
Field's Steak & Stein   *(608)254-4841*
2 mi. N on WI 13
D only.   *Expensive*
Roast prime rib (regular, blackened, or barbecued), steaks, seafood and
other traditional American dishes and homemade desserts have been

presented in this casually elegant dinner house for over forty years.

Fischer's Supper Club   *(608)253-7531*
4 mi. S on US 12 at 441 Wisconsin Dells Pkwy.S - Lake Delton
D only.   *Expensive*
Prime rib and fresh seafood are specialties among American standards served in this traditional supper club for half a century.

The Ishnala Supper Club   *(608)253-1771*
4 mi. S via US 12 & Gasser Rd. on Ishnala Rd. - Lake Delton
D only.   *Expensive*
Contemporary American cuisine is typified by roast duckling with orange sauce or barbecued baby pork back ribs. In the delightfully rustic dining room, Norway Pines grow through the floor and ceiling, and every seat has a romantic view of Mirror Lake.

Monk's Bar & Grill   *(608)254-2955*
downtown at 220 Broadway
L-D.   *Low*
One of the state's favorite burger joints has been featuring all kinds of burgers, plus half-pound Polish or bratwurst sausage sandwiches, amid relaxed, family-friendly atmosphere for half a century.

Thunder Valley Inn   *(608)254-4145*
1 mi. N on WI 13 at W 15344 Waubeek Rd.
B-L-D.   *Moderate*
Everything is homemade from scratch, including hearty family-style breakfasts and assorted desserts. Both traditional American and Scandinavian dishes are popular in the pleasant dining room of a picturesque country inn with Scandinavian hospitality.

Wally's House of Embers   *(608)253-6411*
3 mi. S on US 12 at 935 Wisconsin Dells Pkwy. S - Lake Delton
D only.   *Expensive*
Hickory-smoked barbecued ribs star, while steaks, prime rib, and fresh seafood are also carefully prepared. A pianist plays a baby grand piano in casually elegant, romantic rooms of a dinner house that has been a family tradition since 1959.

LODGING

Accommodations are superabundant. Most are oriented to water—either the river and lakes, or manmade waterfalls, pools, slides, or in-room romantic whirlpools. Late June to late August is high season. From fall through spring, rates may be reduced as much as 50%.

Aloha Beach Resort & Suites   *(608)253-4741*
3 mi. S at 1370 E. Hiawatha Dr. - 53965
60 units   *Moderate-Expensive*
This four-story contemporary motel among the pines by Lake Delton has a sandy beach, dock, canoes, indoor and outdoor pools, whirlpools, and sauna. Each well-furnished room has a private view balcony. Suites also have a large whirlpool.

The Atlantis Hotel   *(608)253-6606*
3 mi. S on US 12 at 1570 Wisconsin Dells Pkwy. (Box 75) - 53965
72 units   *(800)800-6179   Moderate-Very Expensive*
The Atlantis is a water park within a contemporary four-story motel. Amenities include an outdoor lagoon pool by an erupting geyser with swim-under waterfalls and waterslides; kiddie water park; and two indoor pool areas, whirlpool, sauna, and game room. Most well-furnished rooms have a private balcony. Fantasy-theme rooms have a gas fireplace and a big in-room whirlpool.

Black Wolf Lodge   *(608)253-2222*
5 mi. SW (near I-94) at 1400 Black Wolf Dr. (Box 50) - 53965
206 units   *(800)559-9653   Expensive-Very Expensive*
One of the Midwest's most spectacular resort hotels (opened in 1997) captures the spirit of the North Woods in massive logs and whimsical decor. America's largest indoor water park includes the longest lazy river. Outdoors are more pools, slides, and two four-story tube rides. Other amenities include game and fitness rooms, a restaurant, bar and gift shop. Every beautifully furnished room has a kitchenette and private balcony. There are many spacious suites with a gas fireplace and a big in-room whirlpool.

Carousel Inn & Suites   *(608)254-6554*
3 mi. S at 1011 Wisconsin Dells Pkwy.(Box 296) - 53965
102 units   *(800)648-4765*   *Expensive*
"Lollipop Lagoon" is a new outdoor water activity center with a big pool, waterslides, waterfalls, net bridges and a whirlpool. There is also an indoor pool and gift shop. All well-furnished rooms have a deck and refrigerator/microwave. Suites also have a big in-room whirlpool.

Chula Vista   *(608)254-8366*
2 mi. N at 4031 N. River Rd. (Box 30) - 53965
200 units   *(800)388-4782   Moderate-Very Expensive*
The Upper Dells of the Wisconsin River adjoin this full-service six-story resort. The outstanding Southwestern-themed complex features a vast indoor activity center with pools and waterfalls, whirlpools, steambath and sauna, ping pong and exercise room. Outdoor pools with waterslides, kiddie water park, two tennis courts, miniature golf, restaurant and entertainment lounge, and a gift shop are other amenities. Each room is well furnished. Many have a private river-view balcony. Five exotic fantasy suites also have a two-person in-room whirlpool.

Holiday Inn Aqua Dome   *(608)254-8306*
1 mi. W on WI 13 (by I-94) at 655 Frontage Rd. (Box 236) - 53965
230 units   *(800)543-3557*   *Expensive*
Holiday Inn's most water-fun-oriented motor hotel has an outdoor lagoon pool with waterslides; kiddie water park; indoor water park with whirlpools; pool; sauna; game room; restaurant; lounge and gift shop. Each room is attractively furnished.

The Polynesian Resort Hotel & Suites   *(608)254-2883*
1 mi. W on WI 13 (by I-94) at 857 Frontage Rd. (Box 570) - 53965
230 units   *(800)272-5642   Expensive-Very Expensive*
The Polynesian really lives up to its water-wonderland theme. Sheltered by the contemporary three-story complex are palm-accented lagoon pools with rock waterfalls, whirlpools, a long lazy river, adventure water works, long waterslides, geysers, a cave; and two kiddie activity pools. Indoors are two water parks with pools, slides, whirlpools and a sauna, plus a bar, grill and gift shop. Each well-furnished room has a kitchenette. Spacious suites also offer a two-person in-room whirlpool and a private balcony.

Raintree Resort   *(608)253-4386*
3 mi. S on US 12 at 1435 Wisconsin Dells Pkwy. - 53965
158 units   *(888)253-4386   Expensive-Very Expensive*
A rain forest theme enhances this fun-filled 1997 resort. A big fanciful indoor water park has pools, slides, waterfalls and an adventure water walk. So does the outdoor water park. A fitness center, pizza pub, lounge, nightclub and gift shop are also available. Each well-furnished room has a kitchenette. Suites have a large in-room whirlpool.

River Inn   *(608)253-1231*
downtown at 1015 River Rd. (Box 329) - 53965
54 units   *(800)659-5395*   *Expensive*
The Wisconsin River and downtown adjoin this modern five-story hotel with indoor and outdoor pools, whirlpool, sauna, exercise equipment, and a riverside restaurant and lounge. Many of the comfortably furnished rooms have a private river-view deck. Some also have a whirlpool/steam bath.

Treasure Island Resort Hotel & Suites   *(608)254-8560*
3 mi. S on US 12 at 1701 Wisconsin Dells Pkwy. - 53965
94 units   *(800)800-4997   Expensive-Very Expensive*
Wisconsin's only indoor wave pool tops the hotel's water features which include slides and a whirlpool inside, and an on-site outdoor water-play area with a big pool and waterslide, waterfall, geysers and a kiddie pool. These and other amenities like a game room and gift shop, and complimentary use of the adjoining **Family Land Waterpark**, explain the real appeal of this 1995 motel. Each attractively furnished room has a microwave/refrigerator, and there are suites with a large in-room whirlpool.

The Wilderness Hotel & Golf Resort   *(608)253-9729*
4 mi. S via US 12 at 501 E. Adams St. (Box 75) - 53965
222 units   *(800)867-9453   Expensive-Very Expensive*
One of America's most spectacular themed resorts opened in 1995. An 18-hole championship golf course adjoins the three-story wilderness-themed hotel. In addition to (fee) golf, guests have free use of an outstanding water activity complex. Outdoors, lagoon pools carry out the theme with swim-under waterfalls, waterslides tumbling from dramatic rock outcroppings, a 400-foot tunnel slide, a 600-foot lazy river, and a huge whirlpool, plus imaginative kiddie water play areas. Indoors, the "Wilderness Fort Exploratory" complex has dozens of interactive hands-on splash-and-spray features, plus underwater tunnels, and hollow-log waterslides that empty into a large pool. A sauna, game room, bar and grill, and gift shop are also available. All rooms are well furnished and have a mini-kitchen, and a view patio or balcony. Suites have a big in-room whirlpool.

Wintergreen Resort   *(608)254-2285*
5 mi. S via US 12 at 60 Gasser Rd. (Box 296) - 53965
111 units   *(800)648-4765   Expensive-Very Expensive*
New in 1996 was this major addition to the area's "pool" of themed water park resorts. "Glacier Mountain" has a 100-foot waterslide, and there are waterfalls, imaginative ice castles, snow forts and ice flows by a lagoon pool. There is also a major indoor water park with chilly-themed slides, and much more. Other features include a sauna, game room, restaurant and gift shop. Many of the well-furnished rooms have a mini-kitchen and a private patio or balcony. Some also have a large in-room whirlpool.

BASIC INFORMATION

Elevation: 910 feet   *Population (1990):   2,393*
Location: 120 miles Northwest of Milwaukee, WI
Nearest airport with commercial flights: Madison - 46 miles
Wisconsin Dells Visitor & Convention Bureau   *(608)254-8088*
  downtown at 701 Superior St. (Box 390) - 53965   *(800)223-3557*
  www.dells.com

Cody, Wyoming

Cody is the eastern gateway to a Rocky Mountain recreation wonderland. The town is located a mile high near the edge of a vast sagebrush-covered basin. Nearby mountains along the western skyline are within one of the nation's largest wildernesses next to Yellowstone National Park. Colonel William F. "Buffalo Bill" Cody and several friends came here in the 1890s to build a community. The town was named Cody at the insistence of his fellow developers in 1895. In 1902, he opened his landmark hotel and a railroad was built into town.

Today, Cody prospers as a classic New Western town. The world's foremost museum/gallery complex dedicated to Western lore is the major attraction. This incomparable tribute to Buffalo Bill and the unspoiled grandeur of the "Cody Country" are attracting renowned artists and fine art galleries, just as a famed nightly rodeo has attracted real cowboys for many years. West of town, historic mountain lodges retain the spirit and decor of their thoroughly Western settings.

WEATHER PROFILE

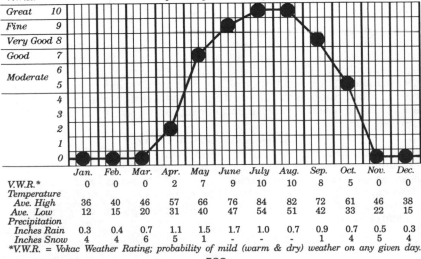

V.W.R. *	Jan.	Feb.	Mar.	Apr.	May	June	July	Aug.	Sep.	Oct.	Nov.	Dec.
V.W.R.*	0	0	0	2	7	9	10	10	8	5	0	0
Temperature												
Ave. High	36	40	46	57	66	76	84	82	72	61	46	38
Ave. Low	12	15	20	31	40	47	54	51	42	33	22	15
Precipitation												
Inches Rain	0.3	0.4	0.7	1.1	1.5	1.7	1.0	0.7	0.9	0.7	0.5	0.3
Inches Snow	4	4	6	5	1	-	-	-	1	4	5	4

*V.W.R. = Vokac Weather Rating; probability of mild (warm & dry) weather on any given day.

ATTRACTIONS

Buffalo Bill Dam and State Park   *(307)527-6076*
6 mi. W on US 20

When this dam was completed in 1910, it was the world's highest. The concrete-arch structure (recently raised 25 feet) is 350 feet high, with a crest length of only 200 feet. The canyon view from the crest is spectacular—and unsettling. There is a visitor center and gift shop. Beyond, on the several-mile-long reservoir is Buffalo Bill State Park with day-use facilities and a campground. Boating and trout fishing are popular.

Buffalo Bill Historical Center   *(307)587-4771*
just W at 720 Sheridan Av.

The Buffalo Bill Historical Center is America's preeminent Western museum. From a small museum started in memory of Col. William Cody, it has grown into a vast four-part complex housing the finest collection of Western art and memorabilia ever assembled. Included are the Whitney Gallery of Western Art, the world's most inclusive collection of nineteenth century Western art (highlighted by superb exhibits of works by both Charles M. Russell and Frederic Remington). In the Buffalo Bill Museum, thousands of his personal belongings provide a feeling for the life and times of the legendary frontiersman and showman. Cody Firearms Museum houses the world's most prestigious and comprehensive collection of American arms, plus European arms dating to the sixteenth century. In the Plains Indian Museum, personal belongings of some of the 19th century's most renowned Indians are showcased among notable exhibits of tribal artifacts. Other facilities include a research library, special exhibitions, food service and a large gift shop.

Buffalo Bill Monument
just W at Sheridan Av./8th St.

Photogenically positioned at the western end of the main street is one of the largest bronze equestrian statues in the world. This monument to Buffalo Bill and the adjoining acreage occupied by the Historical Center were donated to Cody by Gertrude Vanderbilt Whitney in 1924.

Cody Nite Rodeo   *(307)587-5155*
2 mi. W on US 20

Mountains frame the horizon around the substantial grandstands and arena of the "Rodeo Capital of the World." Performances are nightly under lights in summer, and daily July 1-4 for the Stampede.

Horseback Riding   *(307)587-2777*

Several area guest ranches and lodges in the mountains west of town offer trail rides. There are also stables in town offering hour or longer guided rides. The Chamber has details.

River Running

The excitement of whitewater is coupled with the peace of a scenic river during two-hour to half-day float trips through a picturesque red rock canyon near town. Reservations can be made daily in summer at:

River Runners   *(307)527-7238 (800)535-7238*
Wyoming River Trips   *(307)587-6661 (800)586-6661*
Shoshone National Forest   *(307)527-6241*
18 mi. W

The nation's oldest national forest (1891) frames the entire eastern side of Yellowstone National Park and extends for another hundred miles to the south. Major attractions include the scenic Southfork, Northfork, and Sunlight valleys; Buffalo Bill's Wapiti hunting lodge; Wapiti

Ranger Station, the first built with government funds; four wilderness areas; most of Dinwoody Glacier (the largest in the American Rockies) and Wyoming's highest, Gannett Peak (13,804 feet). Innumerable trails give hikers, backpackers, and fishermen access to a myriad of peaks, canyons, lakes, rivers, and streams throughout the forest. An outstanding variety of wilderness pack trips is another way for visitors to experience the vastness and unspoiled grandeur of this high country in summer. Big game attracts sportsmen in the fall, and cross-country skiing and snowmobiling are popular in winter.

Southfork Valley
for approximately 40 mi. SW on WY 291

The unspoiled little valley carved by the South Fork of the Shoshone River fulfills everyone's fantasy of what the Old West looked like at its best. Deer and antelope still graze sagebrush-covered rangelands beneath majestic snow-capped peaks. A mostly-paved highway provides easy access to long-established guest ranches and to well-situated campgrounds, picnic areas, and hiking trails.

Sunlight Country
approximately 40 mi. NW via WY 120 & WY 296

A graded dirt road over a high pass is the shortest route between Cody and the natural grandeur of a remote mountain-rimmed realm of rivers, forests, and meadows with an abundance of scenic campgrounds, picnic areas, hiking trails, and fishing sites.

Trail Town   *(307)587-5302*
3 mi. W via US 20 at 1831 Demaris Dr.

Historic buildings and relics of the Wyoming frontier have been painstakingly relocated here, and authentically displayed by a wagon trail through the original Cody townsite. An outlaw cabin from the "Hole-in-the-Wall" Country used by Butch Cassidy and the Sundance Kid, and the grave of Jeremiah "Liver Eating" Johnson, are highlights. The memorable complex is the continuing life's work of Bob Edgar, an eminent local historian and artist.

Wapiti Valley
for approximately 50 mi. W on US 20

Snow-capped peaks provide a dramatic backdrop for Buffalo Bill Reservoir, the "Chinese Wall," "Holy City," and other strange lava formations; the nation's first ranger station; and an outstanding assortment of lodges, guest ranches, campgrounds, picnic areas, hiking and horseback trails, and fishing sites along the valley of the North Fork of the Shoshone River. An unforgettably scenic paved highway parallels the river between Buffalo Bill Dam and the eastern entrance of Yellowstone Park. President Theodore Roosevelt called it the most scenic fifty miles in America.

Warm Water Feature
Thermopolis Hot Springs State Park *(307)864-3192 (800)786-6772*
84 mi. SE on WY 120 - Thermopolis

The world's largest single mineral hot springs is located on the banks of the Big Horn River at the north edge of Thermopolis. Millions of gallons pour forth daily at a constant 135°F. This and other springs result in a fanciful area of mineral deposits, pools and waterfalls. **Star Plunge** has big indoor and outdoor pools, a hot soaking pool, a delightful steam grotto hollowed into a cliff, and a warm water slide. Nearby are giant mineral deposit cones, a herd of bison, shady picnic facilities, a motor lodge, and campground.

Yellowstone National Park   *(307)344-7381*
52 mi. W on US 20
The world's first (1872) national park is a 3,472-square-mile preserve symbolized by "Old Faithful," the famous relatively predictable geyser. Thousands of other thermal spectacles are scattered throughout the enormous park, including clear hot geothermal pools; boiling, bubbling mud pots; beautiful hot springs terraces; and a river made warm and swimmable by the many hot springs pouring into it. A scenic loop drive provides panoramic views of snow-capped peaks, pine forests recovering from recent massive burns, meadows with a remarkable variety of wild animals, crystal-clear rivers, spectacular waterfalls, and one of the world's largest and clearest high mountain lakes. Just beyond the heavily-trafficked loop highway, the largest continuous wilderness south of Canada awaits the adventurous. Park roads are usually open from late May into October.

RESTAURANTS

Cassie's Supper Club   *(307)527-5500*
2 mi. W on US 20 at 214 Yellowstone Av.
L-D.   *Expensive*
Good steaks and hearty portions still distinguish this roadhouse. The original building opened in the 1920s and through colorful expansions also served as a speakeasy and brothel. Dining rooms with rustic decor, a saloon with Western music for dancing, and a bar with pool tables continue the tradition of good food, fun and games.

Franca's Italian Dining   *(307)587-5354*
downtown at 1421 Rumsey Av.
D only.   *Expensive*
Franca's Italian Dining is the best restaurant in the Cody country. Northern Italian cuisine is given skilled personalized attention in fixed price four-course dinners that change nightly to take advantage of fresh seasonal ingredients and the chef/owner's herbs and vegetables. A historic house in a quiet neighborhood has been artistically transformed into several handsome dining areas.

Granny's   *(307)587-4829*
downtown at 1550 Sheridan Av.
B-L-D.   *Low*
Homestyle Western fare is served in hearty helpings in a big, cheerful coffee shop with an attitude as warm as a real Western welcome.

The Irma Hotel   *(307)527-4221*
downtown at 1192 Sheridan Av.
B-L-D.   *Moderate*
Traditional Western fare is served in generous portions, and there are appropriate specialties like buffalo in burgers or steaks. Colonel Cody's great hardwood backbar distinguishes the large casual dining room, along with period photos, Western art objects and trophy game heads. Next door is a rowdy updated lounge.

La Comida   *(307)587-9556*
downtown at 1385 Sheridan Av.
L-D.   *Moderate*
Dishes like chicken bites baked in cream with green chiles and swiss cheese, and margarita mud pie, suggest the creative spirit of the best Mexican restaurant in the state. Expertly prepared traditional and innovative south-of-the-border dishes have earned a loyal following for the casual colorful cantina and tree-shaded sidewalk patio.

Maxwell's *(307)527-7749*
downtown at 937 Sheridan Av.
L-D.   *Moderate*
Traditional American and Italian dishes are served with breads and
other baked goods made here. Well-liked dining rooms are simply,
attractively decorated in a landmark building that has housed a
restaurant for many years.

Proud Cut Saloon *(307)527-6905*
downtown at 1227 Sheridan Av.
L-D.   *Moderate*
"Kickass Cowboy Cuisine" is an apt description of classic Western fare
that features a variety of steaks and some unusual treats like Rocky
Mountain oysters, along with all sorts of hearty helpings. The
unabashedly Old West-themed dining room/saloon is a good choice for
adults.

LODGING

Motels are plentiful along the main highway through town. Several
young bed-and-breakfast inns, historic lodges, and guest ranches
toward Yellowstone showcase the authentic charm of the Old West.
High season is June into September. At other times, rates may be 40%
less.

Absaroka Mountain Lodge *(307)587-3963*
39 mi. W on US 20 at 1231 E. Yellowstone Hwy. - Wapiti 82450
16 units   *Moderate*
A historic (1910) lodge and log cabins are nestled deep in an alpine
forest by a stream near the picturesque North Fork River. Hiking, (fee)
horseback riding, and fishing are featured. An atmospheric firelit
restaurant (B-D—Moderate) has generous mountain fare, and there is
a saloon. Each cabin is comfortably furnished in rustic pine wood style,
and has a private bath.

Buffalo Bill Village Resort *(307)587-5544*
just E at 1701 Sheridan Av. - 82414
348 units   *(800)527-5544*   *Moderate-Expensive*
Cody's largest lodging complex includes a modern convention-oriented
Holiday Inn, plus a newer **Comfort Inn**, and a historic log cabin
cluster. Grounds include a pool, restaurants, lounges, and a block of
Old-West-style shops. Hotel and motel rooms are well furnished. The
rustic little cabins have modern conveniences, yet convey a feeling of
"roughing it" as early-day motorists did in the West.

Burl Inn *(307)587-2084*
just E at 1213 17th St. - 82414
40 units   *(800)388-2084*   *Moderate*
In this 1995 motel, each well-furnished room features individually
handcrafted furniture designed and built to showcase burls. Bizarre,
naturally twisted wood is used for unique headboards, lamps, clothes
hangers and more. The Honeymoon Suite also has a large whirlpool.

Goff Creek Lodge *(307)587-3753*
40 mi. W on US 20 at 995 E. Yellowstone Hwy. (Box 155) - 82414
17 units   *(800)859-3985*   *Moderate*
Since 1909, this little mountain lodge with cabins by a pine-shaded
stream near the highway has featured (fee) guided horseback riding,
plus hiking, and fishing in the nearby river. The rustic wood-trimmed
dining room (B-D—Moderate) offers traditional Western fare. Each
cabin is simply furnished in knotty pine style, and has a private bath.

The Irma Hotel   *(307)587-4221*
downtown at 1192 Sheridan Av. - 82414
40 units   *(800)745-4762*   *Moderate*
Buffalo Bill's turn-of-the-century hotel is still the most illustrious
landmark downtown. On the first floor are a large family-oriented
dining room/coffee shop (see listing) with a splendid cherrywood
backbar, and a lounge. Simply comfortable rooms blend all modern
conveniences with some period details.

Pahaska Tepee Resort   *(307)527-7701*
49 mi. W on US 20 at 183 Yellowstone Hwy. - 82414
50 units   *(800)628-7791*   *Moderate*
Yellowstone Park is just beyond this cottage/motel complex in the pines
by the highway. Grounds include Buffalo Bill's original hunting lodge
(now a picturesque small museum), hiking trails, a restaurant (B-L-
D—Expensive), lounge, and gift shop. Each room is simply furnished
and there are large log cabins.

Parson's Pillow Bed & Breakfast   *(307)587-2382*
downtown at 1202 14th St. - 82414
4 units   *(800)377-2348*   *Moderate*
A 1902 church was skillfully transformed into a bed-and-breakfast with
Western hospitality. Full homestyle breakfast is complimentary. Each
cozy, well-furnished room has all contemporary conveniences, including
a private bath, plus delightful touches.

Shoshone Lodge   *(307)587-4044*
47 mi. W on US 20 at 349 Yellowstone Hwy. (Box 790) - 82414
16 units   *Moderate*
Tucked away off the highway is a historic 1920s mountain lodge
delightfully unchanged with a roaring fire in a parlor by the native log
pine dining room (B-D—Moderate). Hiking, (fee) horseback riding, and
fishing in the nearby river are features. Each cabin in the forest is
comfortably furnished with rustic knotty pine decor, and has a private
bath.

Sunset Motor Inn - Best Western   *(307)587-4265*
just SW on US 20 at 1601 8th St. (Box 1720) - 82414
120 units   *(800)624-2727*   *Moderate-Expensive*
The Buffalo Bill Historic Center is only two blocks from Cody's most
complete contemporary motor inn. Spacious grounds include an indoor
and an outdoor pool, whirlpool, exercise room, family restaurant and
a lounge. Each room is well furnished.

Wind Chimes Cottage Bed & Breakfast   *(307)527-5310*
downtown at 1501 Beck Av. - 82414
4 units   *(800)241-5310*   *Moderate*
A Victorian-style home now serves as a tranquil bed-and-breakfast.
Hearty country breakfast and afternoon treats are free to guests. Each
well-furnished room has many nostalgic touches, plus a private bath
and most modern amenities.

BASIC INFORMATION

Elevation: 5,018 feet   *Population (1990): 7,897*
Location: 480 miles Northwest of Denver
Nearest airport with commercial flights: in town
Cody Country Chamber of Commerce (307)587-2297
just W at 836 Sheridan Av. - 82414
www.codychamber.org
Cody Area Central Reservations   *(888)468-6996*

Jackson, Wyoming

Jackson is a year-round rendezvous for leisure pursuits in the heart of the Rocky Mountains. The little town is at the edge of a broad grass-and-sage-covered valley between the two highest mountain ranges in Wyoming. Fur trappers eventually gave way to permanent settlers, and a townsite was laid out in 1897. After Grand Teton National Park was created in 1929, and skiing facilities were built in town, Jackson's role as a year-round visitor destination was assured. It was also becoming an internationally known artists' colony.

Downtown Jackson still reflects the town's original frontier appearance. Elkhorn arches, board sidewalks, and clapboard and log buildings surround the well-landscaped town square. A phenomenal assortment of fine art galleries, Western ware shops, live theaters, atmospheric bars and gourmet restaurants are all within an easy stroll. In town and nearby, several of the West's most luxurious lodgings feature amenities appropriate to the majestic alpine setting.

WEATHER PROFILE

V.W.R. *		Jan.	Feb.	Mar.	Apr.	May	June	July	Aug.	Sep.	Oct.	Nov.	Dec.
Great	10	* * * *	Fine Skiing	* *								* * * * *	
Fine	9												
Very Good	8												
Good	7												
Moderate	6												
	5												
	4												
	3												
	2												
	1												
	0												

	Jan.	Feb.	Mar.	Apr.	May	June	July	Aug.	Sep.	Oct.	Nov.	Dec.
V.W.R.*	0	0	0	0	5	8	10	9	7	4	0	0
Temperature												
Ave. High	26	31	40	51	62	71	82	79	69	59	40	29
Ave. Low	2	5	13	24	31	36	41	39	31	26	14	7
Precipitation												
Inches Rain	1.4	1.4	1.2	1.2	1.6	1.4	1.0	1.2	1.3	1.2	1.1	1.5
Inches Snow	17	16	16	5	2	-	-	-	1	3	10	15

*V.W.R. = Vokac Weather Rating; probability of mild (warm & dry) weather on any given day.

Aerial Tramways
Jackson Hole Aerial Tram   *(307)733-2292*
12 mi. NW via WY 390 in Teton Village
Large gondolas carry passengers 2.4 miles from the valley floor to the
top of 10,450-foot Rendezvous Mountain. The view of the Teton Range
and Jackson Hole is breathtaking. The summit is also a trailhead for
backpackers. The tram operates daily summer and winter.
Snow King Scenic Chairlift   *(800)522-5464*
just S at King St./Snow King Av.
During the summer, a double chairlift takes passengers up Snow King
Mountain to splendid panoramic views of town and the Tetons.
Alpine Slide   *(307)733-5200*
just SE at 400 E. Snow King Av.
A chairlift on Snow King Mountain offers a fine view of the Tetons and
Jackson Hole. From the top, riders guide an easily-braked, toboggan-
like sled down either of two half-mile-long fiberglass paths at the speed
of their choice for an exhilarating or leisurely ride.
Bicycling
Bicycling is very popular in summer. Some roads in Jackson Hole have
wide shoulders, and all provide sensational views of mountain scenery.
So do mountain bike trails. Bicycle rentals are available at:
Hoback Sports *downtown at 40 S. Millward St.*   *(307)733-5335*
Teton Cyclery *downtown at 175 N. Glenwood St.* *(307)733-4386*
Boat Rides & Rentals
Scenic cruises or guided fishing trips on lakes and rivers are offered.
Motorboat and canoe rentals are also available at:
Colter Bay Marina   *38 mi. N on US 8*   *(307)543-2811*
Signal Mountain Lodge   *30 mi. N via US 89*   *(307)543-2831*
Teton Boating Co.   *20 mi. NW via US 89* *(307)733-2703*
Bridger-Teton National Forest   *(307)739-5500*
surrounding town
The nation's largest forest outside of Alaska includes the vast unspoiled
Teton Wilderness between Grand Teton and Yellowstone National
Parks. The Bridger Wilderness includes part of the Wind River Range,
with nearly 1,000 lakes scattered beneath the state's highest mountain
(Gannett Peak) and the Rocky Mountain's largest system of glaciers
outside of Canada accessed by hundreds of miles of scenic trails.
Camping, hiking, backpacking, mountain climbing, pack trips, hunting,
fishing, and winter sports are seasonally popular.
Grand Teton National Park   *(307)733-3399*
begins 6 mi. N on US 89
Founded in 1929 and greatly expanded in 1950, this has become one
of the nation's most beloved parks. The renowned centerpiece—the
Grand Teton (13,770 feet)—is the highest peak this far north in the
Rocky Mountains, and one of the world's most photographed
mountains. The first panoramic view of the Tetons (as the highway
crests a hill three miles north of Jackson) is unforgettable. For about
fifty additional miles, the Rockefeller Parkway provides continuous
panoramas of the rugged Tetons and glimpses of the Snake River
etched into sagebrush-covered rangeland. Returning by the Teton Park
Road offers more intimate close-ups of majestic peaks, dazzling
glaciers, waterfalls, streams, lakes, forests, and wildlife. Hundreds of
miles of alpine trails entice hearty backpackers, hikers, rock climbers,

horseback riders, campers, and fishermen to leave their cares, and cars, behind. Far below, the Snake River accommodates a remarkable number of scenic float trips as it meanders throughout the park. Boating, fishing, and cruises are enjoyed on twenty-mile-long Jackson Lake, and swimming is popular in mid-summer near Colter Bay and in String Lake.

Horseback Riding   (307)733-3316
In addition to guided scenic trail rides, there are breakfast rides, evening campfire rides, steak fry rides, pack trips and hunting trips. Contact the Chamber regarding area corrals and outfitters.

National Museum of Wildlife Art   (307)733-5771
2 mi. N on US 89
An expansive stone building (circa 1994) that blends into a hillside overlooking the National Elk Refuge is home to America's premier public collection of fine art devoted to North American animals. More than 2,000 paintings, sculptures and other images are beautifully showcased in fourteen galleries. There is also a cafe and museum store.

River Running   (307)733-3316
Jackson is the base for one of the world's most popular rivers for both whitewater and scenic float trips. The Snake River is fairly gentle throughout Jackson Hole—perfect for easygoing floats beneath the magnificent Grand Teton. South of town, an eight-mile stretch through the spectacular Snake River Canyon offers thrilling whitewater. In between, guided trout fishing boat trips are popular. Nearly twenty professional companies offer half day, full day, and overnight river trips, and they provide all equipment, food, and connections. The Chamber of Commerce has details.

Warm Water Features
Astoria Hot Springs   (307)733-2659
15 mi. S at 12500 S. US 89
Warm mineral water is used to fill a large outdoor pool located by the Snake River. A well-maintained picnic area and a private campground are nearby. The pool is open June through August.

Granite Hot Springs
35 mi. SE via US 191 & S. Granite Creek Rd.
A concrete dam across a hot springs creek has created a memorable pool backed by giant granite boulders in a pine forest. A campground, picnic areas, and a big waterfall are nearby. This is also a favorite cross-country skiing and snowmobile destination in winter.

Winter Sports
Jackson Hole Mountain Resort   (307)733-2292
12 mi. NW in Teton village
The greatest continuous vertical rise in America is 4,139 feet, and the longest run is 4.5 miles. Elevation at the top is 10,450 feet. There is an aerial tramway, a gondola, and seven chairlifts. All facilities, services, rentals, restaurants, bars and lodges are available at the base. Downhill and cross-country skiing season is December into April.

Sleigh Rides   (307)733-9212
5 mi. NE via E. Broadway
A horsedrawn sleigh takes passengers into an expansive snowy meadow that is the winter home of the largest elk herd in North America. Rides can be reserved daily from Christmas through March.

Snow King Ski Resort   (307)733-5200
just S via Cache St. on Snow King Av.
Wyoming's oldest downhill skiing complex has a vertical rise of 1,570

feet. The longest run is about one mile. Elevation at the top is 7,800 feet. The panorama of Jackson and the Teton Range is superb. There are three chairlifts. All facilities, services and rentals are at the base and downtown for downhill and cross-country skiing. Many restaurants, bars and lodges are located within five blocks of the base. The skiing season is late November through March.

Snowmobile Rentals

From December to May, Jackson Hole, Granite Hot Springs, and Yellowstone Park are among the West's most popular destinations for guided or self-guided tours by snowmobile. More than a dozen places offer rentals and/or guided tours and all gear, including:

Cache Creek Snowmobile Tours *(307)733-4743*		*(800)522-0035*
Flagg Ranch Resort	*(307)543-2861*	*(800)443-2311*
High Country	*(307)733-5017*	*(800)524-0130*
Yellowstone National Park	*(307)344-7381*	

57 mi. N on US 89

In the nation's first national park, "Old Faithful" is only the most predictable among many geysers. Collectively, there are thousands of geothermal pools, bubbling mud pots, and hot springs terrace formations are unforgettable. The photogenic Grand Canyon of the Yellowstone is highlighted by two spectacular waterfalls, one twice as high as Niagara. Yellowstone Lake is the highest big lake on the continent. Wildlife is abundant, and includes some of the nation's largest herds of buffalo, elk, and moose, as well as endangered species like grizzly bear, wolves, and trumpeter swan. Just beyond the Park's famed loop drive to the southeast lies the nation's largest continuous wilderness area outside of Alaska.

RESTAURANTS

Anthony's Italian Restaurant   *(307)733-3717*
downtown at 62 S. Glenwood St.
D only.   *Moderate*
Traditional Southern Italian dishes are served in abundance in a big casual dining room that has welcomed hungry families for many years.

The Blue Lion   *(307)733-3912*
downtown at 160 N. Millward St.
D only.   *Expensive*
Creative New American cuisine includes game dishes like pheasant cakes with chipotle mayo, and luscious homemade desserts. For more than twenty years, locals and visitors have enjoyed this plush, intimate bistro in a converted house, and a shaded view deck.

The Bunnery   *(307)733-5474*
downtown at 130 N. Cache St.
B-L-D.   *Moderate*
One of Jackson's two best breakfast places is the Bunnery. Splendid homemade pastries like sticky buns and almond sticks, breads and desserts are made here daily, and temptingly displayed. They serve as a delicious accompaniment to fine omelets and other traditional Western fare in a pleasant coffee shop with distinctive wall art.

Cadillac Grille   *(307)733-3279*
downtown at 55 N. Cache St.
L-D.   *Expensive*
Creative Western cuisine is featured in fresh seafood, game and homemade desserts served amid loud and lively art nouveau decor in the dining room and lounge. A 1950s diner-style cafe adjoins.

Dornan's   *(307)733-2415*
12 mi. N via US 89 - Moose
B-L-D.   *Moderate*
Since 1948, chuckwagon dinners with all-you-can-eat barbecue short
ribs and dutch-oven-style beef stew have been enjoyed at picnic tables
overlooking the Grand Teton, or in a tepee. Nearby, pizzas and pastas
are served in a Western-style dining room/saloon with a great Teton
view. A deli/cheese shop and the best wine shop in Wyoming adjoin.

Granary at Spring Creek Resort   *(307)733-8833*
4 mi. NW on Spring Gulch Rd.
B-L-D.   *Expensive*
Innovative American cuisine includes seasonal exotic game. The classic
Western elegance of the Spring Creek Resort is made even more
memorable by magnificent views of the Tetons.

Jackson Hole Racquet Club Resort   *(307)733-1071*
9 mi. NW via WY 22 on WY 390 - Teton Village
D only.   *Expensive*
In **Stiegler's**, traditional and innovative Continental cuisine with an
Austrian accent is served in a formally elegant firelit setting. A
sundeck and bar share the tranquil alpine view.

Jedediah's House of Sourdough   *(307)733-5671*
downtown at 135 E. Broadway
B-L-D.   *Moderate*
In one of Jackson's two best breakfast spots, sourdough cookery is the
specialty, and the jam is homemade. Hearty breakfasts all come with
silver-dollar-sized sourdough pancakes or biscuits and gravy. The ever-
popular eatery is housed in a nostalgic pioneer log cabin.

Jenny Lake Lodge   *(307)733-4647*
25 mi. N via US 89 on Jenny Lake Loop Rd. - Moran
B-L-D.   *Very Expensive*
Traditional and New American cuisine is expertly prepared from fine
seasonal ingredients. Dishes range from prime rib to wild game on a
changing fixed-price menu. Delicious baked goods and desserts made
here are also served in a posh pine lodge with a Teton view.

The Range   *(307)733-5481*
just N at 225 N. Cache St.
D only.   *Expensive*
The talented chef invites your attention to an open-style kitchen as he
prepares creative Western cuisine like fresh Rocky Mountain trout or
elk medallions. Presentation and flavor are outstanding for each dish
from soups to luscious housemade desserts. Boisterous, upscale dining
areas are a sophisticated complement to the contemporary Western
style of this deservedly popular gourmet haven.

Snake River Grill   *(307)733-0557*
downtown at 84 E. Broadway
D only.   *Very Expensive*
New American cuisine is presented on an ever-changing grazing menu
in a young upstairs restaurant with relaxed upscale decor.

Strutting Grouse   *(307)733-7788*
8 mi. N via US 89
L-D.   *Expensive*
Bison medallion and venison sausage are appropriately featured among
contemporary Western dishes served in the Jackson Hole Golf and
Tennis Club. The casually elegant dining room, decorated with local art
and artifacts, overlooks the Tetons beyond a golf course.

Lodgings of every kind are plentiful. High season is May into September. Late spring and fall rates may be as much as 50% less.

The Alpenhof Lodge   *(307)733-3242*
12 mi. NW via WY 22 on WY 390 (Box 288) - Teton Village 83025
42 units   *(800)732-3244*   *Moderate-Very Expensive*
The four-story Bavarian-chalet-style lodge at the base of the Tetons includes a large pool, whirlpool, sauna, game room, and resort shop. Ski lifts are steps away in winter. There is also a plush popular dining room, casual bistro and lounge. Some of the spacious well-furnished rooms have a private view balcony and a fireplace.

The Inn at Jackson Hole - Best Western   *(307)733-2311*
12 mi. NW via WY 22 on WY 390 (Box 328) - Teton Village 83025
80 units   *(800)842-7666*   *Expensive-Very Expensive*
Ski slopes rise abruptly by the four-story Western-style complex. Amenities include a fishing pond, view pool, three whirlpools, sauna, restaurant and the Beaver Dick Lounge. Each spacious room is well furnished. Some have a fireplace and private view balcony.

Jackson Hole Racquet Club Resort   *(307)733-3990*
9 mi. NW via WY 22 on WY 390 (Box 387) - Teton Village 83025
120 units   *(800)443-8616*   *Expensive-Very Expensive*
Upscale Western-style condominiums share well-tended grounds with a pool, whirlpools, sauna, tennis and racquetball courts, plus a (fee) adjacent 18-hole championship golf course, fine restaurant (see listing) and lounge. Each spacious, beautifully furnished one- to four-bedroom unit has a kitchen, wood-burning fireplace, and private deck.

Jackson Lake Lodge   *(307)543-3100*
35 mi. N on US 89 (Box 240) - Moran 83013
385 units   *(800)628-9988*   *Expensive-Very Expensive*
From a bluff overlooking Jackson Lake, this famed resort hotel complex has an awesome view of the Teton Range. Expansive landscaped grounds include a large pool and nature trails, plus (fee) horseback riding, bicycles, and (nearby) guided fishing, float trips, boat tours and resort shops. The capacious **Mural Room** (B-L-D—Expensive) offers contemporary American fare and a panoramic view. Nearby are a coffee shop and an entertainment/view lounge. While all rooms are well furnished, visitors should request one with a Teton view.

Jenny Lake Lodge   *(307)733-4647*
25 mi. N via US 89 on Jenny Lake Loop Rd. (Box 240) - Moran 83013
37 units   *Very Expensive*
A solid wood lodge and historic log cabins are sequestered in a pine-shaded meadow at the base of the Grand Teton. Horseback riding, bicycles, river swimming, fishing, hiking, and a renowned dining room (see listing) are amenities. Each beautifully furnished cabin has a private porch, Western charm and most modern conveniences. Some also have a fireplace and/or whirlpool bath. Modified American plan rates include breakfast and dinner.

The Lodge at Jackson Hole - Best Western   *(307)739-9703*
just SW at 80 S. Scott Lane (Box 7478) - 83002
154 units   *(800)458-3866*   *Expensive*
Lodgepole style and whimsical wood carvings distinguish this modern four-story motor lodge with a large indoor/outdoor pool, whirlpools, sauna, restaurant, bar, and gift shop. Many of the well-furnished rooms have a kitchenette, fireplace, and/or a large whirlpool bath.

Ranch Inn   *(307)733-6363*
downtown at 45 E. Pearl Av. (Box 596) - 83001
57 units   *(800)348-5599*   *Moderate-Expensive*
The Ranch Inn is the closest motel to Jackson Town Square. While all
rooms are well furnished, tower rooms (newest) have a kitchenette and
private balcony with a fine view of Snow King Mountain. Suites have
a kitchenette, fireplace and private town-view balcony.

Rusty Parrot Lodge   *(307)733-2000*
just NW at 175 N. Jackson St.(Box 1657) - 83001
32 units   *(800)458-2004   Expensive-Very Expensive*
Wyoming's finest bed-and-breakfast inn is a paragon of Western charm
near a tranquil stream a short stroll from the town square. Amenities
include a whirlpool on a view deck, and (fee) spa services. Full gourmet
breakfast is complimentary. Each room is a seamless blend of elegant
contemporary amenities and rustic touches like a pine-pole bed frame,
cowboy lamps, and whimsical Western art. Four also have an in-room
double whirlpool bath and fireplace.

Signal Mountain Lodge   *(307)543-2831*
30 mi. N via US 89 on Teton Park Rd. (Box 50) - Moran 83013
80 units   *Moderate-Expensive*
This older motel-and-cabin complex by a marina has a beach for
swimming and fishing, (fee) guided fishing or float trips, rental boats,
a restaurant, view lounge, store, and gift shop. There are clean rustic
wood cabins, or comfortable motel or kitchenette units by the lake.

Snow King Resort   *(307)733-5200*
just. SE at 400 Snow King Av. (Box SKI) - 83001
254 units   *(800)522-5464*   *Expensive-Very Expensive*
Jackson Hole's largest year-round resort hotel is a seven-story lodge at
the base of Snow King Mountain. Amenities include trails, a pool,
whirlpools, saunas, gift shop, restaurants, and entertainment lounge;
plus (fee) alpine slide, miniature golf, stables and bicycles. In winter,
there are (fee) ski lifts and ice skating. Hotel rooms are nicely furnished.
Well-furnished condos have a kitchen and fireplace.

Spring Creek Resort   *(307)733-8833*
4 mi. NW via Spring Gulch Rd. (Box 3154) - 83001
86 units   *(800)443-6139*   *Very Expensive*
Crowning an isolated butte is a plush contemporary Western resort with
a Teton panorama. Amenities include a pool, whirlpool, tennis courts,
trails, (fee) horseback riding, and ice skating in winter; gourmet
restaurant (see Granary) and lounge, and resort shop. All spacious,
beautifully furnished rooms have a private view deck and fireplace.

Wort Hotel   *(307)733-2190*
downtown at 50 N. Glenwood St. (Box 69) - 83001
60 units   *(800)322-2727*   *Expensive*
Jackson's landmark hotel is a charming blend of Old Western artistry
and upscale facilities. Amenities include whirlpools, exercise equipment,
a dining room, a renowned bar (with more than 2,000 inlaid silver
dollars) and an entertainment lounge. Each spacious, beautifully
furnished room has delightful Western touches.

BASIC INFORMATION

Elevation: 6,230 feet   *Population (1990): 4,472*
Location: 270 miles Northeast of Salt Lake City, UT
Nearest airport with commercial flights: Jackson Hole - 6 miles
Jackson Hole Chamber of Commerce (307)733-3316 (800)443-6931
*   just E at 555 E. Broadway (Box E) - 83001 www.jacksonhole.com / ski*

Livability

The preceding pages have all of the information you need to translate your ideas and dreams into fun-filled travel adventures and vacations. But, suppose you fall in love with one of the great towns of America after a memorable visit. What if you decide you want to live there?

The following table will help anyone considering relocation to a great town. In earlier chapters, each town is described in detail regarding weather, attractions, restaurants, lodgings, and in terms of its population as well as distance from a metropolis and commercial airport. Now, with livability data, each town can be directly compared with every other great town, with the nation as a whole, and with America's largest cities.

The extent to which each town is favored or problematic is presented for seven key indicators. Each indicator reveals an aspect of livability that is a concern of most of us in our day-to-day lives. Most Americans would agree that mild weather; high levels of education, health services, and individual income, plus low levels of housing costs and crime each impact every community's quality of life. So does politics. The prevailing political attitude is especially important in a great town, where you will get to know your neighbors and the political movers and shakers more intimately than you usually would in any city. Several sources are available for obtaining statistics about these indicators, including: U.S. Department of Commerce, Comparative Climatic Data for the U.S.; 1994 County and City Data Book, plus the 1997 Extra; and Federal Bureau of Investigation Uniform Crime Reports.

All data for each town except for weather were derived for the locale from the latest available countywide information because some statistics are not available for small towns. To support easy consistent comparisons, numbers shown in each of the seven categories are a percentage of the national norm. All data for towns that are in relatively better shape than the United States as a whole in any category are displayed in bold type.

•**Weather** Visitors and residents alike talk about the weather—a lot. To make all great towns comparable, the U.S. "center of population" in 1990 (near Steelville, Missouri) was used as the national norm. Steelville's Vokac Weather Rating (see page 10 for details) point total for all twelve months (45) was then divided into each great town's total. Most (sixty) of the great towns have more mild weather than Steelville, while Ojai, Solvang and San Luis Obispo, California have more than twice as much warm and dry weather each year.

•**Education** Contrary to popular mythology, residents of rural communities (at least great towns) are better educated than in our biggest cities or in the nation as a whole. Seventy-nine towns had a higher percentage of high school graduates (among adult residents 25 years or older) in 1990 than the U. S. In some Western towns (Aspen, Telluride, Breckenridge and Steamboat Springs, Colorado; Jackson, Wyoming; Ketchum, Idaho; and Park City, Utah) more than 90% of adults are graduates.

•**Health** Only twenty-five great towns had more resident doctors (per 100,000 people) in 1993 than the country as a whole. While a few towns have far more, including Charlottesville, Virginia; Petoskey, Michigan; Cooperstown, New York; Aspen, Colorado; St. Michaels, Maryland; and Freeport, Maine, most have relatively fewer medical professionals and facilities than are available in cities.

•**Income** This is the other major quality-of-life category, along with health services, where residents of rural areas (and 72% of great towns) are less well off than in cities and the nation. The range of per capita income in 1994 in great towns does, however, include some of America's wealthiest enclaves, including Aspen and Vail, Colorado; Jackson, Wyoming; Naples and Vero Beach, Florida; St. Michaels, Maryland; and Ketchum, Idaho.

•**Housing** Everyone is concerned about housing—its value if you are a resident owner; its cost if you are a relocating buyer. Slightly more than half of all great towns had housing values above the national average in 1990 to the benefit of everyone already owning a home there. All sixteen California towns; Aspen, Breckenridge, Telluride and Vail, Colorado; Key West and Naples, Florida; Ketchum, Idaho; Chatham, Massachusetts; North Conway and Wolfeboro, New Hampshire; Williamsburg, Virginia; and Jackson, Wyoming had housing values at least half again as high as the national average. Happily for anyone contemplating a move to a great town, 47% have housing costs lower than the national average. Towns as diverse as Natchez, Mississippi; Red Lodge, Montana; New Ulm, Minnesota; Eureka Springs, Arkansas; Galena, Illinois; Bandon, Oregon; and Spearfish, South Dakota have housing bargains.

•**Crime** Great towns are notably safer than the country as a whole. This is apparent in the latest (1995) data about violent crime against people (murder, rape, robberies and aggravated assault per 100,000 residents). (A word of caution—crime data are gathered more frequently but less systematically/reliably than in other categories.) Only twelve towns exceeded the national average, while six towns had less than one-tenth the national rate. Sturgeon Bay, Wisconsin; New Ulm, Minnesota; Red Lodge, Bigfork and Whitefish, Montana; and Stowe, Vermont have been remarkably peaceful.

•**Politics** While politics impact all of us, the only way to determine whether a community is oriented toward the right or the left is in their vote for President (plus Vice-President) of the United States. This is because it is the only vote that every American can make. In the 1996 election, residents in four-fifths of the great towns voted right, continuing a long tradition. Clinton received less than one-third of all votes cast in St. George, Utah; Fredericksburg and New Braunfels, Texas; Cody, Wyoming; Holland, Michigan; Naples, Florida; Bigfork and Whitefish, Montana; Covington, Louisiana; and Gatlinburg, Tennessee. He received a higher percentage of votes than the national average in only one-fifth of the great towns, including a few left-leaning outposts like Taos, New Mexico; Natchez, Mississippi; Aspen and Telluride, Colorado; Sonoma and Healdsburg, California; Stowe and Woodstock, Vermont.

While indicators in the table are not all-inclusive, they do suggest strengths and weaknesses in each great town's livability. No town is in better shape than the nation as a whole in every indicator. But, the great town you are interested in may be especially well off in livability indicators that are important to you. If it is, the Basic Information section at the end of each chapter identifies the organization that will have detailed relocation materials.

Livability Table*

State Great Town	Weather	Education		Health	Income	Housing	Crime	Politics
	1.	2.	3.	4.	5.	6.	7.	
Arizona								
Prescott	**149**	**105**	50	76	107	**82**	**74**	
Sedona	**169**	**105**	79	73	105	**58**	108	
Arkansas								
Eureka Springs	**116**	91	42	73	**61**	**39**	**85**	
California								
Calistoga	**171**	**107**	135	120	233	**66**	103	
Cambria	**180**	**111**	97	88	272	107	**82**	
Carmel	**193**	97	68	**104**	251	129	108	
Healdsburg	**176**	**112**	108	**112**	254	**74**	113	
Mendocino	**120**	**105**	88	87	157	124	**93**	
Monterey	**193**	97	68	**104**	251	129	108	
Nevada City	**129**	**115**	78	91	196	**61**	**72**	
Ojai	**207**	**105**	82	**104**	310	**67**	**90**	
Pacific Grove	**193**	97	68	**104**	251	129	108	
Palm Desert	**149**	99	54	85	176	147	**87**	
St. Helena	**173**	**107**	135	120	233	**66**	103	
San Luis Obispo	**204**	**111**	97	88	272	107	**82**	
Solvang	**220**	**109**	**110**	**113**	316	**73**	**95**	
Sonoma	**178**	**112**	108	**112**	254	**74**	113	
Sonora	**149**	**106**	74	81	152	137	**83**	
South Lake Tahoe	98	88	55	98	196	**56**	**74**	
Colorado								
Aspen	89	**126**	164	**193**	573	**92**	115	
Breckenridge	67	**127**	44	**124**	154	**43**	**96**	
Crested Butte	76	**120**	47	78	100	**12**	**95**	
Durango	**122**	**114**	111	92	108	**34**	**76**	
Estes Park	89	**118**	**75**	93	106	**47**	**85**	
Glenwood Springs	**122**	**113**	65	91	115	**18**	**82**	
Steamboat Springs	84	**122**	63	**118**	120	**18**	**95**	
Telluride	78	**124**	49	**102**	192	**41**	114	
Vail	84	**119**	74	**126**	172	**77**	**91**	
Florida								
Key West	**189**	**106**	63	**116**	191	105	**95**	
Mt. Dora	**164**	94	56	84	**86**	**93**	**81**	
Naples	**171**	**105**	92	**142**	153	113	**65**	
St. Augustine	**169**	**106**	82	**118**	109	**92**	**70**	
Vero Beach	**164**	**102**	105	**134**	100	**90**	**76**	
Georgia								
St. Simons Island	**158**	99	88	96	**85**	144	**76**	
Idaho								
Coeur d'Alene	**122**	**108**	67	87	**82**	**79**	**71**	
Ketchum	100	**122**	122	**128**	161	**35**	**95**	
McCall	98	**111**	67	93	**90**	**54**	**74**	
Sandpoint	**109**	**104**	47	77	**77**	**51**	**74**	
Illinois								
Galena	100	99	8	96	**62**	**26**	**92**	
Louisiana								
Covington	**131**	**102**	85	92	**95**	**82**	**66**	

* All numbers are percentage of United States norm.
Number in Bold=Great Town relatively better in this category than the U.S. as a whole.

Livability Table*

State Great Town	Weather	Education		Income	Housing	Crime	Politics
			Health				
	1.	2.	3.	4.	5.	6.	7.
Maine							
Bar Harbor	87	**111**	79	93	108	**19**	**94**
Boothbay Harbor	87	**108**	71	98	130	**13**	**91**
Camden	87	**107**	99	95	118	**11**	**95**
Freeport	87	**113**	**150**	**111**	149	**40**	109
Kennebunkport	87	**106**	49	91	146	**15**	104
Maryland							
St. Michaels	**111**	**102**	**151**	**137**	149	**92**	76
Massachusetts							
Chatham	93	**118**	88	**115**	205	110	109
Michigan							
Charlevoix	96	**106**	40	90	**68**	**21**	87
Holland	96	**106**	41	**103**	95	**15**	58
Petoskey	96	**108**	**191**	**102**	82	**28**	79
Traverse City	100	**113**	**123**	98	85	**37**	79
Minnesota							
New Ulm	96	95	41	91	**62**	**8**	**80**
Red Wing	93	**104**	54	94	**80**	**23**	**99**
Mississippi							
Natchez	**136**	90	81	73	**56**	200	116
Vicksburg	**133**	90	63	87	**65**	225	92
Missouri							
Branson	**120**	94	27	87	**70**	**42**	71
Montana							
Bigfork	**109**	**109**	92	85	**81**	**8**	**66**
Red Lodge	80	**101**	21	79	**58**	**5**	**79**
Whitefish	**109**	**109**	92	85	**81**	**8**	**66**
New Hampshire							
North Conway	91	**111**	62	**111**	151	**14**	87
Wolfeboro	91	**111**	62	**111**	151	**14**	87
New Mexico							
Taos	**127**	95	60	63	**91**	78	134
New York							
Cooperstown	87	**103**	**171**	79	**86**	**28**	**97**
Lake Placid	71	99	35	82	**78**	**32**	**95**
Saratoga Springs	91	**110**	54	100	137	**42**	**95**
North Carolina							
Beaufort	**129**	100	50	79	**92**	55	74
Blowing Rock	87	96	76	74	**92**	35	87
Manteo	**127**	**108**	31	86	137	**42**	85
Waynesville	**120**	90	62	78	**76**	46	**95**
Ohio							
Marietta	**102**	**103**	42	80	**66**	**37**	86
Oregon							
Ashland	**149**	**107**	84	87	**95**	73	81
Bandon	91	100	79	79	**63**	**30**	89
Bend	**133**	**111**	88	94	**95**	**33**	77
Cannon Beach	82	**109**	50	89	**80**	44	102
Florence	93	**110**	81	88	**84**	63	101
Gold Beach	96	**104**	39	85	105	**21**	78
Grants Pass	**138**	100	56	75	**95**	**33**	70
Newport	82	**107**	49	82	**87**	44	104
Seaside	82	**109**	50	89	**80**	44	102

* All numbers are percentage of United States norm.
Numbers in Bold=Great Town relatively better in this category than the U.S. as a whole.

548

Livability Table*

State / Great Town	Weather 1.	Education 2.	Health 3.	Income 4.	Housing 5.	Crime 6.	Politics 7.
South Carolina							
Myrtle Beach	**138**	99	57	82	**96**	177	**88**
South Dakota							
Spearfish	98	**109**	51	81	**66**	**30**	**77**
Tennessee							
Gatlinburg	**122**	84	23	80	**89**	**14**	**69**
Texas							
Fredericksburg	**184**	91	77	95	**81**	**29**	**41**
New Braunfels	**182**	**101**	47	87	**97**	**86**	**56**
San Marcos	**171**	**102**	44	75	103	**55**	**88**
Utah							
Park City	98	**122**	90	**122**	137	**28**	**91**
St. George	**136**	**112**	50	67	**99**	**13**	**39**
Vermont							
Manchester	91	**103**	**108**	98	123	**22**	102
Stowe	87	**107**	**104**	90	114	**7**	111
Woodstock	91	**108**	**106**	**102**	123	**11**	110
Virginia							
Charlottesville	**111**	**108**	**455**	**114**	141	**25**	**92**
Fredericksburg	**113**	**102**	80	97	132	**15**	**80**
Williamsburg	**118**	**110**	**141**	**109**	152	**34**	**79**
Washington							
Chelan	**138**	99	**121**	98	**91**	**49**	**73**
Langley	**124**	**117**	42	85	130	**21**	**87**
La Conner	**120**	**108**	89	93	104	**24**	**90**
Leavenworth	**138**	99	**121**	98	**91**	**49**	**73**
Port Townsend	**124**	**115**	63	89	113	**64**	**98**
Wisconsin							
Green Lake	98	99	38	88	**69**	**21**	**81**
Sturgeon Bay	96	**106**	38	89	**85**	**2**	**93**
Wisconsin Dells	100	**104**	38	87	**71**	**26**	**98**
Wyoming							
Cody	**113**	**110**	63	91	**84**	**36**	**54**
Jackson	96	**122**	**125**	**172**	168	**15**	**91**
MAJOR CITIES							
New York City	100	93	**186**	**133**	240	244	148
Chicago	96	98	**142**	**115**	129	214	136
Los Angeles	**233**	93	**118**	100	286	224	121
UNITED STATES	100	100	100	100	100	100	100

* All numbers are percentage of United States norm.
Number in Bold=Great Town relatively better in this category than the U.S. as a whole.

1. Weather = VWR for 12 months ÷ VWR for 12 months for national population center in Steelville MO (45)
2. Education = % residents 25+ yrs. old with high school diploma (1990) ÷ US (1990) % (75.2)
3. Health = Physicians per 100,000 (1993) ÷ U.S. (1993) physicians per 100,000 (224)
4. Income = Per capita income (1994) ÷ U.S. (1994) per capita income average ($21,696)
5. Housing = Median value of owner-occupied housing (1990) ÷ U.S. (1990) median value ($79,100)
6. Crime = Violent crime rate (1995) ÷ U.S. (1995) violent crime rate average (639)
7. Politics = % voted for Clinton (1996) ÷ U.S. % voted (1996) for Clinton (49.2)

Index

Index

Index

Index

Westside Bakery 384
Westview Resort Motel 493
Westwood Shores 525
Whale Cove Inn 410
Whale Watching 40,92,247,259,408,511
Whale's Tale 410
Whaling Station 61
Wharf Master's House 289
Wheatfields 344
Wheelhouse 378
Whidbey Inn 503
Whidbey Island WA 500
Whidbey Island Winery 501
Whip Bar & Grill 464
Whiskey Row 14
White Barn Inn 250, 252
White Doe Inn 360
White Gull Inn 523
White Lace Inn 525
White Mtn. Hotel 318,321
White Mountain National Forest 317
White River 24
White River National Forest 148,163
White Water 297
Whiteface Mountain 337
Whiteface Mountain Ski Area 338
Whitefish Area Chamber of Com. 314
Whitefish Dunes State Park 522
Whitefish Lake 311
Whitefish Lake Lodge 314
Whitefish Lake Restaurant 313
Whitefish MT 310-314,546,548
Whitefish State Park 311
Whitehall Inn 240, 241
Whitewater Co. 431
Whitewater Rafting 148
Whitman's Bakery 364
Whitney Gardens & Nursery 512
Wilbur's Ice Cream Parlour 244
Wild Iris 498
Wild River Brewing Co. 405
Wild Rose Bakery 150
Wild Waters 199
Wildcat Inn 319
Wilderness Hotel & Golf Resort 531
Wildflowers 497
Wildsee Farms Market Center 435
Wildwater Ltd. 363
Wildwood on the Lake 340
Williamsburg Area CONVIS 489
Williamsburg Inn 488,489
Williamsburg Lodge 489
Williamsburg VA 485-489,546,549
Williamsburg Woodlands 489
Williamstown WV 367
Willows Historic Palm Springs Inn 84
Willows Inn 309
Wilma's 112
Wilmington NY 337,338
Wilson Frank's Restaurant 201
Winchester Country Inn 374,375
Wind Chimes Cottage B & B 537
Windemere 93
ill Island 268
Point Restaurant 359
s Ashland Hills Inn 375
278
Rose English Tea Room 177
ard Inn Restaurant 395
Cellar 201

Wine Country Inn 90
Wineries 29,40,46-47,52,59,65,86,93,
  99,104,110,276,372,431,476,501
Winfield's 464
Winnipesaukee Belle 323
Winslow Memorial Park 243
Winter Sports 64,110,116,117,122,
  123,128-129,133,134,138,148,149,153,
  154,158,163,164,199,204,210,211,214,
  218,239,263,271,276,281,284,285,302,
  307,311,316,317,323-324,,328,337-338,
  353,363,371,372,381,382,426,430,447-
  448,457-458,462,463,470,476,495,506,
  517,522,528,533-534,539,540-541
Wintergreen Resort 476,531
Wisconsin Dells Visit/Conv. Bureau 531
Wisconsin Dells WI 526-531,549
Wolf Creek Inn 406
Wolfeboro NH 322-325,546,548
Wolfeboro Inn 325
Wolfeboro Chamber of Commerce 325
Wolfeboro Marina 323
Wolfe's Neck Woods State Park 243
Wolfgang's Keller Restaurant 441
Wonder World 444
Wooden Nickel 134
Wooden Shoe Factory 267
Woodlands BBQ 354
Woods Resort 300
Woodshed Restaurant 339
Woodstock Area Chamber of Com. 473
Woodstock Historical Society 470
Woodstock Inn & Resort 471,473
Woodstock Sports 469
Woodstock VT 468-473,546,549
Woodstock's Pizza 95
Woodwind 115
Wooten's 180
Wort Hotel 544
Wrecker's Museum 171
Wright Bros. National Memorial 358
Wright Museum 324
Wyman Hotel 138
Wyndham Myrtle Beach 423
Wyndham Resort 131
Wyoming River Trips 533

Yachats OR 395,396
Yachtsman Resort 423
Yakov Smirnoff 296
Yampah Spa & Vaper Caves 148
Yankee Pot Roast 405
Yaquina Bay State Park 409
Yarrow Resort Hotel 451
Yavapai Dining Room 19
Ye Olde England Inne 465,467
Yellowstone National Park 307,541,535
Yesterdays 319
York Harbor ME 250,252
Yorktown Battlefield/Victory 487
Yosemite Natl. Park 111
Yountville CA 86-90

Zazoo Cafe 225
Zephyr Cove Stables 116
Zion National Park 453-454
Zoder's Inn 433
Zoom Roadhouse Grill 450
Zoos 24,176,180,187,275,353,377,439,444

About the Author

David Vokac was born in Chicago and grew up on a ranch near Cody, Wyoming. During summers while an undergraduate, he served as the first airborne fire-spotter for the Shoshone National Forest next to Yellowstone National Park. Later, he taught courses in land economics while completing a Master's degree in geography at the University of Arizona. In Denver, Colorado, Vokac was in charge of economic base analysis for the city's first community renewal program, and later became Chief of Neighborhood Planning. He moved to Southern California in 1974 to prepare San Diego County's first local parks plan, and stayed to act as Park Development Director.

Mr. Vokac is now a full-time travel writer living in Southern California. He is the author of seven guidebooks, including *Destinations of Southern California* and the acclaimed *Great Towns* series. During the past two-plus years, he logged nearly sixty thousand miles criss-crossing forty-eight states while identifying and field-checking all of the great towns of America. When he's not researching, writing, or speaking, you might pass him on a road he's traveling for the sheer joy of it somewhere in America.

The "Great Towns" Series

The "Great Towns" series of travel guidebooks offers accurate, concise information about scenic, civilized outlands throughout America. All notable attractions, restaurants, lodgings and more (like the weather) are described and rated for a wealth of exciting locales. Each feature was personally evaluated by the author.

Over the years since 1985, David Vokac's guides have delighted travelers nationwide and earned critical acclaim.